Joyce's *Ulysses* Notesheets

in the British Museum

Edited by Phillip F. Herring

Joyce's *Ulysses* Notesheets

in the British Museum

Published for the Bibliographical Society of

the University of Virginia

By the University Press of Virginia

Charlottesville

THE UNIVERSITY PRESS OF VIRGINIA
Copyright © 1972 by the Rector and Visitors
of the University of Virginia
Rights to all manuscript
material reserved to
the Trustees of the James Joyce Estate

First published 1972

Frontispiece: Statue of Joyce at his grave
in Zurich. (Foto Frugoni, Firenze)

ISBN: 0–8139–0296–7
Library of Congress
Catalog Card Number: 70–109222
Printed in the United States of America

Para Lydia

de los ojos bonitos

Acknowledgments

THIS book could be described as the collaborative effort of literally hundreds of people who in the last eight years have allowed me to pick their brains. Nearly every time I suspected anyone, during the course of a conversation, of having specialized information on some subject, I was sure to attempt to enlist their aid. I have embarrassed a nice Italian lady with questions on a word I could find in no Italian dictionary (for a very good reason); I have inadvertently sent a martini down the windpipe of a biologist by asking him if he had any knowledge of a "fleadislodging bug"; and I am sure that I bored many unselfish people who must have felt they could spend their time more wisely than in answering my questions.

Obviously I cannot begin to name everyone who has helped, but I would especially like to express my gratitude to Professors David Hayman of the University of Iowa and Richard Kain of the University of Louisville, and to the late Mr. Eoin O'Mahony of Dublin for many valuable suggestions. I am also indebted to Professors Robert Kellogg and Marvin Colker of the University of Virginia, Helmut Rehder and Oscar Maurer of the University of Texas, Edmund Epstein of Southern Illinois University, Bernard Benstock of Kent State University, Robert Montgomery of the University of California at Irvine, Walton Litz of Princeton, Richard Madtes of Allegheny College, James Card of Old Dominion University, Norman Silverstein of Queens College, and Robert Janusko of Ashland College; to the poet Thomas Kinsella; and to Mrs. Vivien Igoe of Dublin, Mr. Patrick McCarthy of the University of Wisconsin at Milwaukee, Mr. Ottocaro Weiss of New York, and Mr. John E. Vaughan of Madison.

I wish also to thank the library staffs of the British Museum, the University of Virginia, the University of Wisconsin, the University of Texas, the University of Pittsburgh, the State University of New York at Buffalo (especially Messrs. K. C. Gay and Oscar Silverman), and Harvard University. The Society of Authors, representing the James Joyce Estate, was kind enough to grant me permission to publish the *Ulysses* notesheets, and I am indeed grateful for it. I was aided financially by the Faculty Research Committee of the University of Virginia and by an Andrew Mellon Postdoctoral Fellowship at the University of Pittsburgh, where I was in residence during the 1968/69 academic session.

For permission to include quotations of copyrighted material I am indebted to Random House, Inc. (James Joyce's *Ulysses*, copyright 1942, 1946, by Nora Joseph Joyce; Stuart Gilbert's *James Joyce's* Ulysses, copyright 1930, 1952, by Stuart Gilbert); Oxford University Press (Richard Ellmann's *James Joyce*; Robert M. Adams's *Surface and Symbol: The Consistency of James Joyce's* Ulysses; A. Walton Litz's *The Art of James Joyce*); Indiana University Press (Frank Budgen's *James Joyce and the Making of* Ulysses); St. Martin's Press (*Chambers's Biographical Dictionary*); The McGraw-Hill Book Company (Bradley M. Patten's *Human Embryology*, copyright 1946 by the Blakiston Company); *Modern Fiction Studies*, © 1969 by Purdue Research Foundation, Lafayette, Indiana, for permission to include material from my article entitled "The Bedsteadfastness of Molly Bloom"; The Macmillan Company, New York (S. H. Butcher and Andrew Lang's translation of Homer's *Odyssey*; Eric Partridge's *Dictionary of Slang and Unconventional English*, copyright © 1961 by Eric Partridge); The Viking Press, Inc. (James Joyce's *Portrait of the Artist as a Young Man; The Letters of James Joyce*, ed. Stuart Gilbert and Richard Ellmann); The Houghton Mifflin Company (Jonathan Swift, *Gulliver's Travels*, ed. Louis A. Landa); and to Professors James Card, Robert Janusko, and Richard Madtes for permission to quote from their doctoral dissertations. Definitions from *Webster's Third New International Dictionary*, copyright © 1966, and *Webster's Seventh New Collegiate Dictionary*, copyright © 1969, are used by permission of the copyright owner, G. & C. Merriam Company, publishers of Merriam-Webster dictionaries.

Madison, Wisconsin
1971

Contents

Illustrations

Joyce's *Ulysses* Notesheets

in the British Museum

I   General Introduction

THE difficulties encountered in reading *Ulysses* and *Finnegans Wake* are the direct result of Joyce's creative process, which Joyceans, and Joyce himself, have described as that of a mosaic craftsman. *Ulysses* was not written from first to last in a logical, sequential fashion; each of the eighteen episodes was continually revised and expanded (almost never condensed) from early sketches right up to a few days before the date of publication, February 2, 1922. The novel was literally an organically evolving book. Joyce's method was meticulous and exacting; he could never be completely satisfied with anything he wrote. The piecing together of ideas and phrases through the various drafts of *Ulysses*, though his goal was always to give both unity and depth to his mosaic design, resulted from an almost psychotic compulsion. To paraphrase my predecessors, Joyce never really finished *Ulysses*; the printers took it out of his hands.

The *Ulysses* notesheets in the British Museum (Add. MS. 49975) comprise one of the most important sources of information on Joyce's creative techniques. Together with the Buffalo notebooks, they served as a repository of information on diverse subjects, a repository which Joyce exploited from the early stages of *Ulysses* until *Finnegans Wake* was well begun. These sheets have been examined, quoted, and sometimes misquoted, ever since they were made available to scholars by Harriet Weaver, but prior to the publication in the spring of 1965 of one "Circe" notesheet only brief excerpts had appeared in print.[1] The present printing of the *Ulysses* note-

---

[1] Phillip F. Herring and Norman Silverstein, "Some Corrections and Additions to Norman Silverstein's 'Magic on the Notesheets of the *Circe* Episode,'" *James Joyce Quarterly*, II (Spring 1965), 217–226. See also A. Walton Litz, "Joyce's Notes for the Last Episodes of *Ulysses*," *Modern Fiction Studies*, IV (Spring 1958), 3–20; and his *Art of James Joyce: Method and Design in* Ulysses *and* Finnegans Wake (London and New York, 1961), *passim* (hereafter any reference to "Litz" is to this work); Robert M. Adams, *Surface and Symbol: The Consistency of James Joyce's* Ulysses (New York, 1962), p. 259 (all refer-

sheets should prove valuable to the student of Joyce. It contains thousands of germinal ideas out of which Joyce, through his process of accretion, expansion, and exploration of germane parallels, wove the tapestry of the last seven, and most complex, episodes of his novel. Here is a happy hunting ground for professional and amateur alike. Here is also a rare opportunity to observe a literary genius in his workshop. Occasionally the notesheets will show the reader Joyce's intent in an obscure passage. They also provide the means for discovering what *Ulysses* could have become had Joyce seen fit to include portions of the rejected material.

This volume is also a reflection of the growing awareness on the part of scholars that the ultimate solution to many textual and critical problems is to be found in the manuscripts. The recent publication of *A First-Draft Version of* Finnegans Wake, *The Art of James Joyce*, *Scribbledehobble*, and *The Workshop of Daedalus*,[2] to speak of Joyce studies alone, is evidence of this. The study of an author's creative process can supplement many of the critical approaches to literature currently espoused by our graduate schools, since it forces one to look beyond the text, as it were, to discover how it arrived in its published form. This is well documented by the publishing trends of university presses today and requires no further substantiation. If textual criticism of this sort teaches us much about the works of fairly conventional authors, it reveals proportionately more about an author like Joyce, who covered his typescripts and galleys with thousands of emendations.[3] Through all this we seek to discover what Joyce meant to write, and the study of the notesheets may lead us to a deeper understanding of the author's intention.

I DESCRIPTION OF THE NOTESHEETS

The publication by A. Walton Litz of *The Art of James Joyce* makes unnecessary a long introduction to the notesheets and Joyce's process of composition in *Ulysses*. I

---

ences to "Adams" hereafter are to this work); Norman Silverstein, "Magic on the Notesheets of the *Circe* Episode," *James Joyce Quarterly*, I (Summer 1964), 19–26; and Richard E. Madtes, "Joyce and the Building of 'Ithaca,' " *ELH*, XXXI (Dec. 1964), 443–459.

[2] David Hayman, ed., *A First-Draft Version of* Finnegans Wake (Austin, Tex., 1963); Thomas E. Connolly, ed., *James Joyce's* Scribbledehobble: *The Ur-Workbook for* Finnegans Wake (Evanston, Ill., 1961); and Robert Scholes and Richard M. Kain, eds., *The Workshop of Daedalus: James Joyce and the Raw Materials for* A Portrait of the Artist as a Young Man (Evanston, Ill., 1965).

[3] Eventually it may instruct us as to the best means of convincing publishers that corrected texts of such works as *Ulysses* and *Finnegans Wake* would be in their interest as well as ours.

am much indebted to him, and although he is wrong in some particulars, or so it seems to me, his analysis of the role played by the notesheets in the creation of this novel is sound and enlightening. In his first Appendix he describes the notesheets as follows:

In 1938 Paul Léon, who was acting as Joyce's secretary, sent a number of note-sheets for the last seven episodes of *Ulysses* to Harriet Shaw Weaver. These have since been deposited in the British Museum. On the envelope containing the sheets Joyce wrote: 'Some sheets of notes for certain episodes in *Ulysses*'. There are twenty-nine separate sheets: eighteen of these are double (folded) and eleven are single. Joyce usually wrote on both sides of a sheet; allowing for the few blank pages, there are approximately ninety sides of notes. The double sheets are approximately 12 × 8 inches in size when folded; the single sheets vary widely, some being 9 × 7½ inch sheets of graph paper. The handwriting is extremely difficult, and some of the entries are completely illegible. The following is a census of the note-sheets by episode:

	Double Sheets	Single Sheets	Total
Cyclops	3	0	3
Nausicaa	2	0	2
Oxen of the Sun	6	0	6
Circe	2	5	7
Eumaeus	1	2	3
Ithaca	2	4	6
Penelope	2	0	2
	—	—	—
	18	11	29

With a red, green, blue, or slate pencil, depending on the draft or particular section of the draft he happened to be working on, Joyce carefully crossed through the words or phrases he decided to use in that draft. Uncanceled notes almost never appear in these drafts, though Joyce was at times fallible. Reading of the notesheets is further complicated by the cluttered appearance of many of them. Words, phrases, and occasionally complete sentences were crowded helter-skelter onto each sheet in columns or blocks, in lines straight or slanted, in the margins, and sometimes even upside down. Although the material on a given sheet is usually restricted to one episode of *Ulysses*, there is rarely any sense of progression. Clusters of ideas, phrases, or words for a particular scene appear occasionally, but generally the sequence is a random one.

All that survive in the British Museum are the notesheets for the last seven episodes listed by Litz, but it is possible, in fact likely, that there were notesheets for the earlier episodes of *Ulysses* and, perhaps, even a few additional ones for the last seven. One can easily imagine Joyce's making lists of literary allusions for "Telemachus" or giving Stuart Gilbert[4] a notesheet containing the table of rhetorical forms that served him in the construction of "Aeolus" as the embryological chart did for "Oxen of the Sun."

It is curious that Joyce's admittedly "desperate need for principles of order and authority"[5] is not reflected in an orderly set of notes; what order there was derived from his mind. He knew at the time he made these entries the probable destination of each note; then in the subsequent mental sorting processes and in the drafts he apparently decided against the use of some of them. For the student this means chaos: to trace the provenance of each note he must depend on Miles L. Hanley's sometimes unreliable *Word Index to James Joyce's* Ulysses[6] for the words which appear in the text, his memory of *Ulysses* for those not used, and his imagination for the various diagrammatical oddities.

In the eighteenth century such a repository of data would have been called a commonplace book, one difference being, however, that Joyce's would not have been comprehensible to any of his contemporaries. The contents of the notesheets will be discussed at length later, but perhaps it might be said here that the material ranges from "plot indicators," as Richard Madtes called them, to words and phrases of stylistic interest, to Homeric parallels, and to notes and word lists on such specialized topics as embryology.

II CRITICAL BACKGROUND

The background of criticism relevant to the *Ulysses* notesheets is not difficult to sketch in because surprisingly little has been written about them. Probably the first to give serious consideration to the critical implications of Joyce's manuscripts was Joseph Prescott, whose unpublished doctoral dissertation at Harvard University (1944) dealt

---

[4] *James Joyce's* Ulysses (1930; 2d ed. rev., 1952; rpt. New York, 1960), pp. 194–198.

[5] Litz, p. 24.

[6] 1937; rpt. Madison, Wis., 1951 (a mimeographed edition with corrections entered by hand). See Appendix A for my corrections.

with the textual growth of the novel as seen in the proof sheets.[7] Then came Litz, the first to make a careful examination of the notesheets. His 1954 doctoral dissertation at Oxford University was eventually published as *The Art of James Joyce*.[8] Since then there have been at least five dissertations on the textual development of individual episodes of *Ulysses*. These, in chronological order, have been studies by Norman Silverstein of "Circe," by Richard E. Madtes of "Ithaca," by Robert E. Hurley of "Proteus," by James V. D. Card of "Penelope," and by Robert Janusko of "Oxen of the Sun."[9] All except Janusko were students of William York Tindall at Columbia University. Concurrently there appeared articles and a book or two in which the notesheets were described or cited in passing. More recently I have exploited them in gauging Molly's symmetry in "The Bedsteadfastness of Molly Bloom" and in the introduction to "*Ulysses* Notebook VIII.A.5 at Buffalo,"[10] which publishes a manuscript that Joyce made use of in his compilation of the notesheets. As the reader will probably discover for himself, the exploration of this promising territory has scarcely begun.

III   THE ORDER OF COMPOSITION

Although the idea for *Ulysses* as a short story "to portray, evidently with irony similar to that of 'Grace' and 'The Last Supper,' a dark-complexioned Dublin Jew named Hunter"[11] occurred to Joyce as early as 1906, the actual years of composition were 1914 through early 1922. The creative process apparently began with a primitive

---

[7] It was called "James Joyce's *Ulysses* as a Work in Progress."

[8] The dissertation title is "Evolution of James Joyce's Style and Technique from 1918–1932."

[9] Silverstein, "Joyce's 'Circe' Episode: Approaches to *Ulysses* through a Textual and Interpretative Study of Joyce's Fifteenth Chapter" (Columbia University, 1960); Madtes, "A Textual and Critical Study of the 'Ithaca' Episode of James Joyce's *Ulysses*" (Columbia University, 1961) (hereafter, any reference to "Madtes" is to this dissertation); Hurley, "The 'Proteus' Episode of James Joyce's *Ulysses*" (Columbia University, 1963); Card, "A Textual and Critical Study of the 'Penelope' Episode of James Joyce's *Ulysses*" (Columbia University, 1964) (hereafter any reference to "Card" is to this dissertation); and Janusko, "The Sources and Structure of the 'Oxen of the Sun' Episode…" (Kent State University, 1967).

[10] *Modern Fiction Studies*, XV (Spring 1969), 49–61; *Studies in Bibliography*, XXII (1969), 287–310. Readers unfamiliar with the Joyce collection at Buffalo may wish to consult Peter Spielberg, *James Joyce's Manuscripts and Letters at the University of Buffalo: A Catalogue* (Buffalo, 1962).

[11] Richard Ellmann, *James Joyce* (New York, 1959), pp. 238–239. Subsequent references to this standard biography will be simply to "Ellmann."

draft of the entire book, probably not much more than a skeleton plot outline and "quite plain"[12] stylistically. In the years to come this draft took on flesh and substance in much the same way as candles are made: each episode was repeatedly "dipped" into the storehouse of material contained in Joyce's notes and supplemented by his memory. Each episode was expanded along preconceived stylistic and thematic lines, though always in the direction of the more complex, the more parodic and ironic, and, sometimes, the more fantastic. As the epiphanies and other manuscript materials published in Scholes and Kain or even *Giacomo Joyce*[13] can illustrate, Joyce from an early period was given to taking notes which were either self-contained acts of literary creation or destined to be reworked for inclusion in later prose passages.

IV   THE ROUGH NOTES

One can speculate that Joyce made rough notes for the first, or primitive, draft of *Ulysses* and that those for which he found no place were entered on the British Museum notesheets. This would be characteristic of Joyce's compositional economy. Certainly thousands of them were amassed between 1914 and 1922. At this time they were jotted down on scraps of paper, tablets, shirt cuffs, napkins, and other items just when and where they presented themselves to Joyce's imagination. There is no better description of this procedure than Frank Budgen's:

Joyce's method of composition always seemed to me to be that of a poet rather than that of a prose writer. The words he wrote were far advanced in his mind before they found shape on paper . . . he was a great believer in his luck. What he needed would come to him. That which he collected would prove useful in its time and place. And as, in a sense, the theme of *Ulysses* is the whole of life, there was no end to the variety of material that went to its building. Of the time detail of 1904 there was none around him, but what he saw and heard in 1918 or 1919 would do just as well, for the shapes of life remain constant: only the dress and manners change. I have seen him collect in the space of a few hours the oddest assortment of material: a parody on the *House that Jack Built*, the name and action of a poison, the method of caning boys on training ships, the wobbly cessation of a tired unfinished sentence, the nervous trick of a convive turning his glass in inward-turning circles, a Swiss music-hall joke turning on a pun in Swiss dialect, a description of the Fitzsimmons shift.

In one of the richest pages of *Ulysses* Stephen, on the seashore, communing with himself and tentatively building with words, calls for his tablets. . . . As far as concerns the need

---

[12] *The Letters of James Joyce*, ed. Stuart Gilbert and Richard Ellmann (New York, 1957–66), I, 143.
[13] Ed. by Richard Ellmann (New York, 1968).

for tablets, the self-portrait was still like, only in Zürich Joyce was never without them. And they were not library slips, but little writing blocks specially made for the waistcoat pocket. At intervals, alone or in conversation, seated or walking, one of these tablets was produced, and a word or two scribbled on it at lightning speed as ear or memory served his turn. No one knew how all this material was given place in the completed pattern of his work, but from time to time in Joyce's flat one caught glimpses of a few of those big orange-coloured envelopes that are one of the glories of Switzerland, and these I always took to be storehouses of building material. The method of making a multitude of criss-cross notes in pencil was a strange one for a man whose sight was never good. A necessary adjunct to the method was a huge oblong magnifying glass.[14]

One day in Locarno, Joyce apparently teased Budgen by asking him to read something from a slip of paper torn from one of these pocketbooks. When Budgen failed to make out one complete word, Joyce handed him a magnifying glass, but this merely "magnified the pencil smudges and made the labyrinth of pencilled lines bigger but not clearer."[15]

In February 1923 Joyce proudly told Myron Nutting (a painter living in Paris) that the "unused notes weighed twelve kilos."[16] Nearly every stage of composition involved a great deal of sorting and ordering of material. Those notes Joyce found promising were transferred to large sheets of paper generally referred to as "notesheets" (I prefer to drop the hyphen). The question then becomes one of dating: we cannot say with any degree of certainty either *when* the rough notes were compiled or what notesheet material originated in rough notes and what did not. On occasion we can, however, date a particular notesheet on the basis of internal evidence (see Appendix B on dating). If one has time, patience, and access to the manuscripts—and is willing to exert a maximum of effort for a minimal return—he may trace each canceled word or phrase through the various drafts, galleys, and proof sheets of the last seven episodes of *Ulysses* to see at what stage it entered the text.[17] Some notes were apparently entered on one draft and then, like unwelcome guests, were rudely ejected on the next. Although no rough notes survive, at least one manuscript Joyce cribbed

---

[14] *James Joyce and the Making of* Ulysses (1934; rpt., with new appendix, Bloomington, Ind., 1960), pp. 171–172.

[15] *Ibid.*, p. 173.

[16] Ellmann, p. 558. Another early reference to Joyce's sequence of composition is in Silvio Benco's "James Joyce in Trieste," *The Bookman*, LXXII (Dec. 1930), 380 (also cited in Litz, p. 9).

[17] Samples of this tracing may be seen in the five dissertations previously mentioned. It is beyond the scope or aspiration of this volume.

from in the notesheets does, the "Zurich notebook," VIII.A.5 in the Buffalo collection, noted above. It dates from the early months of 1918.

Once this repository of "proto-odyssean" matter was accumulated, Joyce took what he found useful and left the rest, carefully deleting the selected items with ordinary coloring pencils. No one has yet produced a rationale for Joyce's color scheme in the manuscripts, though several rather unconvincing attempts have been made with individual episodes. It is probable that he used a different color at each harvesting of material, and Joyce's system may not have been any more complicated than this. Only a painstakingly thorough study will reveal the answer, and this is more ground than Appendix C, "The Coloring Pencils," is designed to cover.

Thus, though the procedure varied with the specific episode, scholars seem generally to agree that *Ulysses* was composed in the following stages:

1. primitive draft or rough notes (chicken or egg)
2. notesheets
3. more rough drafts
4. Rosenbach MS (fair copy)
5. typescripts
6. galley proofs
7. page proofs
8. bound page proofs

V   THE HANDWRITING

The first obstacle one must overcome when working with a holograph manuscript is, of course, the handwriting. Madtes divides Joyce's into three categories: the personal, the epistolary, and the publication hands. The first has already been described by Budgen as being frequently illegible. This is, with few exceptions, the style of the notesheets. At times it seems determined more by Joyce's writing speed, the material, his mood, and perhaps even his sobriety than by any conscious awareness of his penmanship. The two illustrations which face pages 162 and 278 are good examples of this style. The second style is, of course, that of the letters; I am not qualified to comment on the variations in his handwriting in them. A sample of the third style, the clearest and most beautiful, can be found in *Giacomo Joyce*, which includes a facsimile reproduction of the manuscript. Joyce had plenty of opportunity to acquire a beautifully legible hand (which he did with more success, apparently, than Farrington of

"Counterparts") when he worked as a clerk in a Roman bank in 1906, writing "between two hundred and two hundred and fifty letters a day."[18]

It is hoped that this short general introduction will serve to illustrate the place the British Museum notesheets occupy in the creative evolution of Joyce's *Ulysses*. The following "Descriptive Essays" take up individual episodes of the manuscript for a look at the disorderly laboratory that was the birthplace of one of this century's greatest novels.

[18] Ellmann, p. 234.

II   Descriptive Essays

Scene	The Tavern
Hour	5 p.m.
Organ	Muscle
Art	Politics
Symbol	Fenian
Technic	Gigantism[1]

Cyclops

PROBABLY nowhere in *Ulysses* did Joyce have a better opportunity to strike a blow against bigotry than in the "Cyclops" episode, but for reasons which are central to an understanding of Joyce the artist and the man he was careful not to do so. Given the ignorant chauvinism, the pugnaciousness, the anti-Semitic views of Joyce's "Citizen," most readers of *Ulysses* no doubt instinctively desire to see this latter-day Polyphemus soundly trounced, at least verbally, by Leopold Bloom. But if we consider for a moment the Homeric equivalent of this chapter, we realize that however disgusting cannibalism may have been to the Greeks, Homer did not allow Odysseus a decisive victory. The "Citizen" and Polyphemus violate the sacred laws of hospitality; but Odysseus, and perhaps Bloom to some extent, are guilty of *hubris* in taunting their enemies when out of reach. In some respects, the situations are dissimilar. It is Odysseus's curiosity which tempts him to lead his men into danger; it is he who, in fact, is the invader; and despite the horrible scenes that follow, he rather enjoys pitting his superior intellect against the might of the Cyclops. Joyce put Bloom at a disadvantage, intellectually, because Bloom does not know that the basis of the "Citizen's" hostility is not just anti-Semitism. His animosity springs also from the erroneous belief that Bloom has won money on the race horse Throwaway and refuses to honor the occasion with a round of drinks. Further, in a verbal battle such as this intellect, or rather logical reasoning, is no real advantage when the opposition (including the narrator) disparages it in favor of bluster and rude wit. Thus the match could hardly have been more uneven, and Bloom's final taunt "Your God was a jew. Christ was a jew like me" merely gives the "Citizen" a defensible reason to

---

[1] This subject outline and those which follow are taken from the chapter headings of Stuart Gilbert's *James Joyce's* Ulysses.

react in the violent way which, as *lanceur des roches* ("Cyclops" 6:27; *U* 311),[2] is his trademark.

It is clear that Joyce abhorred the "Citizen's" political stance and recognized the nobility of the liberal humanitarian sentiments of Bloom. But all sociopolitical positions are indiscriminately undercut by Joyce's use of exaggeration ("gigantism" is the technique here) and irony. Serious statements and events become mythopoeic; they are magnified to such absurd dimensions that it is impossible in this episode to take anything seriously. Joyce wants us to laugh, not to sympathize, and his characteristic aversion to didacticism gives him a further reason to avoid anything resembling a moralistic stand against provinciality. As the "Citizen" hurls the Jacob's Biscuit tin at Bloom, "the observatory at Dunsink registered in all eleven shocks, all of the fifth grade of Mercalli's scale, and there is no record extant of a similar seismic disturbance in our island since the earthquake of 1534" (*U* 337). Bloom, having made good his escape from the Cyclops's den, ascends into heaven in a chariot: "And there came a voice out of heaven, calling: *Elijah! Elijah!* And he answered with a main cry: *Abba! Adonai!* And they beheld Him even Him, ben Bloom Elijah, amid clouds of angels ascend to the glory of the brightness at an angle of forty-five degrees over Donohoe's in Little Green Street like a shot off a shovel" (*U* 339).

Although we can only speculate about the first draft of "Cyclops," it is likely that Joyce began with the idea of exposing the ugliness of racism and chauvinism, using a straightforward approach which, in later drafts, was submerged as his more natural predilection for satire took over. Once again in his creative method Joyce characteristically moved in the direction of the more exaggerated, comic, and ironic. One needs but compare *Stephen Hero* with *A Portrait* or the *Finnegans Wake*[3] drafts with the final text to see that this tendency was not unique in *Ulysses*. If he was con-

---

[2] All references to *Ulysses* are to the 1934 Random House edition. See Appendix D for a conversion table to other editions. My reasons for citing only the 1934 edition are: (1) Miles L. Hanley's *Word Index to James Joyce's* Ulysses is based on that edition, and I have had to use it continually in deciphering Joyce's handwriting and in locating words and phrases in the text. (2) The 1961 Random House edition, though somewhat more free of errors than the 1934 edition, will not for long be the standard American edition since another is in preparation which will have yet another pagination. (3) The latest Random House printing of *Ulysses* gives references to the 1934 edition in the margins of each page. (4) Joyce scholars will own the 1934 edition because it was the standard edition for Joyce criticism between 1934 and 1961.

[3] *Stephen Hero* (1944; rev. ed., New York, 1963); *A Portrait of the Artist as a Young Man* (1916; corrected ed., New York, 1964); *Finnegans Wake* (New York, 1939).

sistent in "Cyclops," then this technique might well have been the most important factor in determining his tendency to undercut Bloom's liberal humanitarianism.

Few, if any, persons would want to exchange the humor of the "Cyclops" episode for a sermon on ecumenism, and in terms of his art Joyce was right to maintain a consistent moral neutrality in his novel. But it is also important to remember that by temperament Joyce was incapable of any sort of altruistic political commitment.[4] Indeed, his political position was no less egocentric than that of Homer's Cyclops, as Ellmann makes implicitly clear in his biography.[5] Joyce regarded all bureaucracy with horror, all organizations with distrust, and war as something like a massive conspiracy to kidnap his reading public. As early as 1904, ironically enough, Joyce claimed to be a socialist, and he reiterated his claim for at least the next fifteen years, but as Ellmann rightly sees,[6] his motives were entirely selfish. He hoped that in a socialist state he might be entitled to a lucrative pension.

Joyce endorsed the politics of self-interest for a number of reasons. At an early age he had learned the price of political involvement from the fall of Charles Stewart Parnell, and he half-expected to meet the same betrayal at the hands of his friends. He even longed for it as proof of his messianic role in the world of letters. A second reason is that although he kept his British passport and although his fiction deals solely with Ireland, Joyce for thirty-seven years was a man without a country. And, more specifically, the year 1919, when "Cyclops" was written, was especially noteworthy in Joyce's stagnant political consciousness because of his litigation with a British consular official, Henry Carr, in Zurich. More than any previous single event, this battle aroused his hostility toward the British—British bureaucracy. The effects of his fury can be seen in *Ulysses* in such characters as Rumbold the hangman barber (Sir Horace Rumbold was the British minister to Bern from 1916 to 1919) and Private Carr, who knocks Stephen Dedalus down in "Circe." Joyce was probably in a bitterly satirical mood by the time he finished "Cyclops," and though, like Bloom, he may have been a pacifist in daily life, he was not above demonstrating that the pen was a mighty weapon. All that checked his sweet vengeance at this time were the context and the symmetry of the book he had resolved to finish.

---

[4] This has been amplified in my paper entitled "Joyce's Politics," read at the Second International James Joyce Symposium. The paper will be published in Fritz Senn, ed., *Spotlight on Joyce: The Dublin Symposium* (Bloomington, Ind.: Indiana University Press, 1972).

[5] Pp. 113–114, 147, 204, 394, 460.

[6] P. 204.

15

It is not, therefore, surprising to find that the tone of the "Cyclops" notes is sour, negative, and anarchistic. The sentiments point more directly to Joyce than to any specific character. Through all the humorous conceits emerges a consistent political viewpoint that expresses Joyce's lifelong distrust of the authority of ecclesiastical and secular institutions, a distrust intensified, perhaps, by the events of daily life.

One curious aspect of the "Cyclops" notes is that many of the ideas Joyce chose not to use made their way into the "Eumaeus" notesheets (especially "Eumaeus" 5). Spielberg mentions that the earliest existing draft of "Cyclops" (notebook V.A.6 at Buffalo) puts Stephen Dedalus in Barney Kiernan's pub. In preparation for an exhibition of Stephen's cynicism, Joyce apparently wrote out all the clever slogans he could think of relating to the law, Jews, the Church, English rule, and Fenianism. When he decided to cut Stephen from the scene, he was left with material too promising to abandon. At some time before the end of 1920, when Joyce was ready to begin "Eumaeus," he must have transferred the unused "Cyclops" notes to the notesheets of later episodes (especially "Eumaeus"), anticipating an occasion for Stephen to open his bag of aphorisms. Several notes were selected for an early draft of the confrontation scene with Private Carr (notebook V.A.19 at Buffalo), but they must have sounded too much like a stump speech, and Joyce deleted them. By the time of the "Eumaeus" episode Stephen was too fatigued to bother with polemics. Some of the material was suitable for Bloom, however, and Joyce gave him a few lines in "Eumaeus" which, if they had been delivered to the pub patrons in "Cyclops," would doubtless have necessitated a serious political battle. Thus it seems that Joyce had the makings of a really lively verbal exchange in "Cyclops," but he decided instead to emphasize the inherent comedy of the episode through exaggeration and parody.

Some ammunition for the Fenians is to be found here (anti-Semitic and anti-British statements), but most of the notes for "Cyclops" ridicule Fenianism, Ireland, Catholicism, and, above all, the Establishment. Here are some examples (spacing and line divisions do not follow the manuscript):

"Cyclops"

1:23   Rule: dead rule living: 1 enslaved by many

1:25   Anarchists: who accuse them? Kriegshetzer

1:32–35 Law: effective when consecrated by custom = useless. Communists also men? Some evil needed in doing good. Altruism makes survive race, egoism individ. ½ and ½.

1:71   Minority privilege to disappear not physically but socially

1:72   Neither with violence suppressed nor achieved (Anarchy)   [*U* 627]

2:23   State: 12 soldiers shoot, none is bloodguilty. Jury.

2:29–30 Property could be collective, wages individual (according to needs?, deeds?)
        [*U* 603]

5:62   Solitudinem faciunt et pacem appellant

10:36–37 State: monster fed with our blood, must be starved. sceptics of ?Gods doubt here
        too! [Cf. 628]

10:41   Election: 20 fools to elect 1 genius.

10:42–43 Govt: why add govt to moral & material forces existing. police provoke crimes
        or disappear, armies war.

On the subject of English rule:

"Cyclops"

1:61   empire on which sun never rises   [Cf. *U* 323]

1:66   Eng. work well ∴ so bored by Sunday

2:57   Eng. afraid to commit themselves

4:80   Irel: European fights Englands wars. Why? [*U* 626]

5:39–40 Engl: a noble race, rulers of the waves, who sit on thrones of alabaster, silent as
        the deathless gods.   [*U* 319]

5:63   Eng. Not so spoiled by success as others ?romans

On the Roman Catholic Church:

"Cyclops"

1:44   R.C. = sacrificing mother to child secures baptism & funeral

5:50   Church: iron girders to Irel.

10:40   R.C. money on false pretences.   [*U* 628]

From Victor Bérard's *Phéniciens et l'Odyssée* Joyce learned of the Semitic background of the *Odyssey*, and this no doubt whetted his already keen interest in racial parallels between Jew, Greek, and Irishman.[7] Perhaps he saw himself as an avatar of the Wandering Jew. Little sympathy is manifested, however, in his exploitation of Bloom's situation for humorous incongruities. The Fenian bigots have their day.

"Cyclops"

1:53   Jews & Irish remember past

1:54–55 Jew = cuckoo = profiteer: the cuckoo's a fine bird / He sings as he flies

1:57   Jews fouled wells of thought

1:58   Circumcised coins

---

[7] 2 vols. (Paris, 1902); see Ellmann, pp. 383–385. For Joyce's theory of Jewish men as effeminate, see Gilbert, p. 184; Ellmann, p. 477; "Oxen" 14:51; "Circe" 16:52; and "Ithaca" 10:70 and 14:20.

4:84–86 Irel: centripetal ambition (Zionism) / —fugal ambition (Columb) / her ?unmade captivities

5:42   never let jews in   [*U* 37]

5:76   Jew: love his country when sure which it is.   [*U* 331]

5:79–80   Cromwell: curse, [*U* 335], jews England rich: . . . so long as we control the money bags.

8:66   commend me to a jew   [*U* 308]

8:78   Zionism retrograde

10:8–9   Noman: unnameless & unrestless in Israel, attempters of many enterprises

10:11   the jew hates the jew in the jew.

10:69   Israel. 'sons of the law' no law, a tongue, Israel's god.

10:77   chosen people, God on our side

10:88   Lousy jews fox & fleas, last flea LB

10:104   Torquemada banished Jews, England let 'em in.   [*U* 628]

The technique of the "Cyclops" episode is gigantism, and the notesheets provide interesting insights into some germinal matter which grew to maturity in *Finnegans Wake*.[8]

"Cyclops"

1:39   Irish pantomime Brian Boru & Finn MacCool.

5:33   Compare: Giant: giant :: giant: dwarf

5:44   Feefawfum

8:36   Dwarf? Leprechaun, fairey [*sic*]

8:37   Gods not gigantic

8:38   Buckley & Russian general (bloody boy)

8:40   buttons—shields

8:41   Difficulty of painting giant

8:42   Timanthes, satyr with thyrsus measure his thumb

8:43   Dwarf—Marcella, the midget queen   [*U* 620]

Yet another salient aspect of the "Cyclops" notes is that, as elsewhere, Joyce molded style to fit content. Thus we have exaggeration (another form of gigantism) in character, dialogue, and description.[9]

"Cyclops"

1:45   Polypheme: ?tuns, exaggeration, polysyllable,

---

[8] See also Hayman, ed., *First-Draft Version*, p. 17.

[9] If Joyce had not been reading Swift's *Gulliver's Travels* while drafting "Cyclops," he was at least in conscious competition with Swift: "Golbasto Momaren Evlame Gurdilo Shefin Mully Ully Gue, most

5:17   Ossian. Jewish rhetoric. Ulysses. Kolossal!

5:18   Cycl. Exaggeration of things previously given: Superlatives

5:20   Style. Longwinded simile.

5:29–30 Technique: Sudden vituperation follows depression (ferocity Iliad)

5:36–38 Style: ?and like a wheatfield under the ~~strong~~ wind and like the mountain ash
        / hazel grove under the whirlwind. / ″10: like a sunbeam at 7.48

8:57   Exaggeration (Rhet. SD's lies, Molly's romancing)

8:76   Fenian tells secret—shouts

8:77   Gestures of fenian cause tornado.

At the bottom of "Cyclops" 1 is a cryptic dialogue that has been identified by Hugh Staples as characteristic of a nationalist group known as the Ribbonmen. So called because they wore green ribbons, the Ribbonmen organized in 1808 in opposition to the landlord class, or Protestant Orangemen. Both Orangemen and Ribbonmen apparently had secret oaths and passwords, and many on each side swore to help exterminate the opposition. Although the term *Ribbonmen* is not mentioned in the text of *Ulysses*, it does appear at "Cyclops" 1:77 together with *password*. Staples found that parts of the dialogue as given on "Cyclops" 1 were copied from Alexander M. Sullivan's *New Ireland*.[11] In the following dialogue from the text of "Cyclops" (*U* 290) the italicized portions appear on "Cyclops" 1 and were taken from Sullivan:

---

mighty Emperor of Lilliput, delight and terror of the universe, whose dominions extend five thousand blustrugs (about twelve miles in circumference) to the extremities of the globe; monarch of all monarchs, taller than the sons of men; whose feet press down to the center, and whose head strikes against the sun: at whose nod the princes of the earth shake their knees; pleasant as the spring, comfortable as the summer, fruitful as autumn, dreadful as winter. His most sublime Majesty proposeth to the Man-Mountain, lately arrived at our celestial dominions, the following articles . . ." (ed. Louis A. Landa, Boston, 1960, p. 35).

Here is a description of Joyce's "Citizen": "From shoulder to shoulder he measured several ells and his rocklike mountainous knees were covered, as was likewise the rest of his body wherever visible, with a strong growth of tawny prickly hair in hue and toughness similar to the mountain gorse (Ulex Europeus). The widewinged nostrils, from which bristles of the same tawny hue projected, were of such capaciousness that within their cavernous obscurity the fieldlark might easily have lodged her nest. The eyes in which a tear and a smile strove ever for the mastery were of the dimensions of a good-sized cauliflower" (*U* 291).

But see also Philip L. Marcus, "Three Irish Allusions in *Ulysses*," *James Joyce Quarterly*, VI (Summer 1969), 299–305.

[10] The ditto marks here refer to "Style" above.

[11] See Staples, " 'Ribbonmen' Signs and Passwords in *Ulysses*," *Notes and Queries*, XIII (March 1966), 95–96, and Sullivan, *New Ireland: Political Sketches* (Glasgow, 1877), p. 40.

– Stand and deliver, says he.

– That's all right, citizen, says Joe. Friends here.

– Pass, friends, says he.

Then he rubs his hand in his eye and says he:

– *What's your opinion of the times?*

Doing the rapparee and Rory of the hill. But, begob, Joe was equal to the occasion.

– *I think the markets are on a rise*, says he, sliding his hand down his fork.

So begob the citizen claps his paw on his knee and he says:

– *Foreign wars is the cause of it.*

And says Joe, sticking his thumb in his pocket:

– *It's the Russians wish to tyrannize.*

At this point in *Ulysses* the dialogue, accompanied by secret gestures, is broken off in favor of a round of drinks, but in Sullivan the conclusion is "May sons the of Erin wherever they be continue ever in loyalty." The notesheet omits this sentence but follows with another dialogue (slightly changed) out of Sullivan (p. 40):

Q. What is the age of the moon?

A. Really I don't know.

Q. R. Hand rubbed over brow.

Left hand down the pocket.

R. Hand to knee.

L. thumb in breeches' pocket

This is only one of several examples of Joyce's utilization of secret gestures in *Ulysses*. Joyce's interest in sign language is particularly apparent in "Circe" (*U* 425–426) and is discussed in the chapter on that episode.

Scene	The Rocks
Hour	8 p.m.
Organ	Eye, nose
Art	Painting
Symbol	Virgin
Technic	Tumescence: detumescence

Nausicaa

THROUGH the centuries Nausicaa has probably excited more interest and speculation than any figure in the *Odyssey* other than Odysseus himself. If he exemplifies wisdom and cunning, elements in a heroic ideal which such imperfect examples as bellicose Ajax and the vain Achilles would do well to emulate, then Nausicaa embodies those qualities of beauty and modesty which make her (in the idiom of Gerty MacDowell) a pearl of Greek maidenhood. After Odysseus has lain in the captive embrace of Calypso and Circe, one might expect him to respond to Nausicaa's solicitous attentions; she is young, beautiful, and obviously willing. She tells her maids, "Would that such an one might be called my husband, dwelling here, and that it might please him here to abide!"[1] Her father, Alcinous, offers Odysseus her hand on apparently no better credentials than Odysseus's royal appearance[2]—though this may just be a narrator's tribute to the epic stature of his hero. Odysseus apparently enchants Nausicaa with his stories (as Othello does Desdemona), thus producing a potentially romantic setting which the alert reader might expect a poet to exploit. Why, indeed, should he go beyond the narrative convention which prescribes coincidental meetings of royal personages (Odysseus immediately encounters Princess Antiphates in the Laestrygonian episode, for example) to paint such an enticing portrait of Nausicaa only to ignore the dramatic possibilities of such a meeting? Readers (or listeners) have frequently been disappointed that, as in the Circe and Calypso affairs, our hero remains true to his Aeneas-like vision of the homeland and merely uses

---

[1] *The Odyssey*, trans. S. H. Butcher and Andrew Lang (London and New York, 1879 and subsequent printings), p. 100. Joyce used one of the printings of this edition. All subsequent page references are to this edition.

[2] *Ibid.*, p. 112.

21

Nausicaa as wind for his sails.[3] But one must not confuse narrative goals and human nature.

The Nausicaa interlude troubled Samuel Butler, as Joyce well knew. Indeed Butler was so suspicious of the narrator's motives that he seriously proposed Nausicaa herself as the "authoress" of the *Odyssey*. This would explain, he believed, the intimate detail of Nausicaa's characterization, the relative prominence of the episode, and the "whitewashing" of Penelope (who was surely unfaithful, and what reason other than loyalty to her sex could deter the narrator from exposing this adultery?). It is Nausicaa's seafaring people, the Phaeacians, who finally manage to land Odysseus in Ithaca and who are punished for their meddling by the sea-god Poseidon.[4]

Joyce must have read Butler's *Authoress of the* Odyssey,[5] and he probably had the book in mind when he wrote his "Nausicaa" episode. In fact, he may well have endeavored to show us what a latter-day *Odyssey* would sound like if it were written in the "namby-pamby jammy marmalady drawersy"[6] style of a love-struck young maid. Here again we see how Joyce employs the *reductio ad absurdum* to satirize that stillborn romance which remains, like the lovers on Keats's Grecian urn, transfixed in time and unconsummated.

In *Ulysses* the style of "Nausicaa" resembles the interior monologues of Stephen in "Proteus" and Molly in "Penelope"—but with a difference. Gerty's heart throbs (which comprise approximately the first two-thirds of the episode) are revealed to us by an omniscient narrator in the consciously literary manner noted by Budgen:

She [Gerty] is described in the familiar novelette style of the period, and we must remember that *Poppy's Paper* and *Florrie's Paper*, with their yarns about typists and factory hands who get off with the young governor in his sports Bentley, had not yet, in 1904, supplanted the *Bow Bells* and *Heartsease* novelettes, where the young governess makes the crowded ballroom floor gasp with her beauty, dressed in a simple white frock and wearing a single white

---

[3] W. B. Stanford, *The Ulysses Theme* (1954; rev. ed., Oxford, 1963), pp. 51–55, gives a number of convincing reasons why Homer could not have permitted such a romantic liaison, but the important question here is what Joyce did with the idea.

[4] *Odyssey*, p. 212. With regard to the "whitewashing" of Penelope, see my "Bedsteadfastness of Molly Bloom," pp. 54–55.

[5] 1897; rpt. Chicago, 1967. It is listed in Thomas E. Connolly's *The Personal Library of James Joyce: A Descriptive Bibliography*, University of Buffalo Studies, XXII, no. 1 (Buffalo, 1955), though this in itself is no guarantee that Joyce read it.

[6] Quoted in Ellmann, p. 487. I must credit Professor Edmund Epstein for this idea, though I wish it had been my own.

rose. Carefully listening we can hear undertones of Gerty's own Sandymount outlook and dialect in the rich prose of the *Heartsease* library. [Pp. 203–204]

During the remainder of the episode we are in the practical mind of Leopold Bloom familiar to us from earlier episodes.

He and Gerty in "Nausicaa" are such shabby counterparts of their epic ancestors that one is more tempted here than elsewhere in *Ulysses* to concur in the frequent judgment that Joyce employs epic scaffolding for no other reason than to expose the degeneracy of the modern wasteland, a temptation which nags more persistently if the reader forgets his sense of humor. As in the *Odyssey*, the "Nausicaa" episode is for Bloom but an interlude in his journey to Ithaca. On the surface it is a rather uneventful diversion. Children play on the beach at sunset, Gerty obligingly lifts her skirts as the enticing (but prudent) stranger finds the solution to a nagging problem, and there is a fireworks display.[7] We are given a great deal of absurd information on the mental fantasies of an adolescent girl, but this does little more than reveal her place in the social fabric of Dublin in 1904. Although she returns to haunt Bloom in "Circe," her part in the novel is insignificant. This lends credit to the idea that for Joyce she is an interesting digression prompted by Butler and the romantic enthusiasts. What is important awaits revelation in the episode which follows as we learn that Bloom's "crime against fecundity" is equated with the slaughter of the sacred oxen in the *Odyssey*.

All this suggests a number of things about Joyce and the preoccupations that thicken the texture of *Ulysses* and entertain the author (sometimes at the expense of the reader). "Nausicaa," like the "Oxen" episode, is a stylistic tour de force, but apart from this there are structural and symbolic correspondences which only in the most general sense relate to Gerty, Bloom, or the developing plot of the novel. The more private the satirical concerns of the author, the more gratuitous they seem to the reader no matter how he may laugh at them. There is, then, as I see it, an implicit invitation here to turn the tables on Joyce by the introduction of external or biographical evidence to solve his riddles.

On the symbolic level Gerty is clearly to be equated with the Virgin Mary. Her color is blue; she reclines near "the quiet church whence there streamed forth at

---

[7] For an examination of the fireworks scene and interesting literary analogues, see Erich Köhler's "Nausicaa, Danae und Gerty MacDowell: Zur Literaturgeschichte des Feuerwerks," in *Lebende Antike: Symposion für Rudolf Sühnel*, ed. Horst Meller and Hans-Joachim Zimmermann (Berlin, 1967), pp. 451–472.

times upon the stillness the voice of prayer to her who is in her pure radiance a beacon ever to the stormtossed heart of man, Mary, star of the sea.''[8] Her father sings to her *Tell me, Mary, how to woo thee* (U 348), an innocent enough song until one remembers Bloom's fixation on Milly's sexual maturing (U 66–67, 373, and elsewhere) and the incest motif in *Finnegans Wake*. On the religious level, adoration becomes voyeurism,[9] and Mary, "refuge of sinners" and "comfortess of the afflicted," has degenerated into a cliché-ridden adolescent who momentarily fixes on an admiring stranger all the romantic aspirations of her frustrated youth and allows him in her imagination the liberties which she would not have the courage to grant him in bed. This is, of course, as much "comfort" as the "prudent member" requires.

This frustration-of-the-ends-of-nature motif pervades the "Nausicaa" episode. A temperance retreat is conducted in a nearby church (a bit ludicrous for Dublin, as Joyce well knew). It is a benediction service in which the Host is exposed for the adoration of the congregation, though communion is withheld.[10] Perhaps the Benediction is suggested in Gerty's departing wave of her perfumed handkerchief. Gerty herself has been frustrated in the loss of a sweetheart (here the adoration appears to be exclusively on her side) who once "snatched a half kiss (the first!) but it was only the end of her nose" (U 345). As Bloom rightly suspects, her menstrual period has arrived to negate the possibility of fruition (immaculate conception?), thus providing a curious parallel to the Molly-Blazes affair since Molly too is plagued with the onset of her "monthlies" after a sexual engagement (U 754). Then, too, Bloom's watch has stopped, and that, apparently, at just the moment when Molly and Blazes finish copulation in *coitus interruptus*. Our cuckold traces in the sand "I. AM. A." (U 375), but the limited space prevents him from finishing the sentence. What Joyce is signaling through all of this, beyond his own ingenuity, is open to speculation.

In writing "Nausicaa," Joyce must have had in mind not only Butler and Homer but his own literary past. I doubt that he could have completed one draft without remembering the scene in *A Portrait* where Stephen casts admiring eyes on the wading girl with uplifted skirts, a crucial scene in Stephen's developing aesthetic consciousness. There too the style is impassioned and fervent, but perfectly straightforward. After his vision Stephen reflects:

---

[8] *U* 340; cf. "Nausicaa" 1:22—"virgo parathalassia (Star of the Sea)."

[9] It is interesting that Joyce was so enamoured of ladies' panties that he carried a miniature pair in his pocket (Budgen, pp. 319–320).

[10] Harry Blamires, in *The Bloomsday Book: A Guide through Joyce's* Ulysses (London, 1966), p. 143, notes the "double act of adoration" here.

Her image had passed into his soul for ever and no word had broken the holy silence of his ecstasy. Her eyes had called him and his soul had leaped at the call. To live, to err, to fall, to triumph, to recreate life out of life! A wild angel had appeared to him, the angel of mortal youth and beauty, an envoy from the fair courts of life, to throw open before him in an instant of ecstasy the gates of all the ways of error and glory. On and on and on and on!
[*A Portrait*, p. 172]

If Joyce consciously used this scene as a model for "Nausicaa," then the episode must surely be judged on one level as self-parody. Note the religious imagery in the adoration: "soul," "holy," "angel," and the like.[11] Immediately following their encounters both Stephen and Bloom fall asleep, their emotional reservoirs spent. The similarities are too obtrusive to be accidental. If Joyce's fetishism was fair grist for the mill of *Ulysses*, so was his previous literary work.[12]

The "Nausicaa" notesheets are less interesting than those for "Cyclops": they contain mostly material for the stylistic embellishment of the chapter. There are, however, occasional bits that enlighten us as to potentialities and analogues which Joyce considered at the time, and these are definitely worth surveying.

Leopold Bloom's cuckoldry is central to any interpretation of his role in *Ulysses* for a number of reasons: it was for Joyce an inseparable part of Bloom's Jewishness[13] (what there is of it) and therefore serves to emphasize his isolation from his fellow Dubliners. It is through Molly, ironically, that he experiences all the brotherly love he is likely to know. The consequent loneliness manifests itself (after his forcible banishment in "Cyclops") in masturbation in "Nausicaa"; this in turn brings castigation in "Oxen" and in "Circe" protects him, like Odysseus's moly, from the wiles of the temptresses. At the end of "Nausicaa" this cuckoldry is proclaimed by the clock in the priests' house, which sounds "cuckoo" nine times in announcing the hour, and is synchronized by the priests themselves in their discussion of marital infidelity. Even Gerty appears to recognize Bloom for what he is though it is a mystery how she could:

[11] This seems to be an established pattern. Previously, in the *Dubliners* (1914; corrected ed., New York, 1967) story "Araby," Joyce couched the young boy's love for Mangan's sister, a madonna figure, in the vocabulary and context of Mariolatry. See also the letters of 1909 to Nora.

[12] "Nausicaa" could be an early sign of Joyce's increasingly pronounced taste for fetishism. In the 1930's Budgen remarked to Joyce, " 'As I remember you in other days you always fell back upon the fact that the woman's body was desirable and provoking, whatever else was objectionable about her.' This produced an impatient '*Ma che*!' and the further comment: 'Perhaps I did. But now I don't care a damn about their bodies. I am only interested in their clothes' " (Budgen, p. 319). Cf. "Circe" 3:34—"Woman's character depends on things they wear."

[13] See the "Cyclops" essay above and Ellmann, pp. 383–385.

Because it was a little canarybird bird that came out of its little house to tell the time that Gerty MacDowell noticed the time she was there because she was as quick [as] anything about a thing like that, was Gerty MacDowell, and she noticed at once that that foreign gentleman that was sitting on the rocks looking was

> *Cuckoo.*
>
> *Cuckoo.*
>
> *Cuckoo.* [*U* 376].

This clock is heard again in "Circe" (*U* 461) as "the brass quoits of a bed are heard to jingle."

Joyce's interest in the cuckoo as a symbol for Bloom goes deeper than this. At "Cyclops" 1:54–55 is the following: "Jew = cuckoo = profiteer: the cuckoo's a fine bird / He sings as he flies." The first part of the riddle is easy: the cuckoo is a profiteer since the female lays her eggs in the nests of other birds for them to hatch. So does Israel, the anti-Semite might say. The last part is one version of a folk song widely known in the English-speaking world.[14] This string of equations was put to use in "Cyclops" in the following way: Bloom has momentarily stepped out of the pub, and Lenehan erroneously suggests that Bloom has gone out to collect on a racing bet which he does not intend to share. As the narrator urinates in the WC, he reflects with envy on this cuckolded Jewish profiteer who has "flown the coop":

flabbyarse of a wife speaking down the tube *she's better* or *she's* (ow!) all a plan so he could vamoose with the pool if he won or (Jesus, full up I was) trading without a licence (ow!) Ireland my nation says he (hoik! phthook!) never be up to those bloody (there's the last of it) Jerusalem (ah!) cuckoos. [*U* 329]

At "Nausicaa" 3:64–65 are more obscure references to cuckoos: "Kuckoo: peewit (Galliphone: maneater) how sing flying / (major & minor third) perhaps air goes other way." The cuckoo is not a gallinaceous bird and is certainly no maneater. "Kuckoo" is neither English nor German; "galliphone" sounds like a Bérardian term to suggest the bird's tonal qualities. But the equation remains obscure. "Nausicaa" 3 does reveal the title of one source of information on both cuckoo and peewit: "B.

---

[14] A version given in G. L. Kittredge, "Ballads and Songs," *Journal of American Folklore*, XXX (1917), 350–351, which contains also a discussion and a bibliography, reads:

> "Oh the cuckoo is a pretty bird, he sings as he flies;
> He brings us glad tidings and tells us no lies;
> He feeds on young birds to make him sing clear,
> And when he sings cuckoo the summer draws near."

Hoffmann: Kunst u. Vogelgesang" (line 50),[15] a work which has six pages (pp. 175–181) devoted to the musicological aspects of the cuckoo's song and numerous other references besides. The peewit, *der Kiebitz*, is mentioned twice, but the bat, an anthropomorphic character in "Nausicaa," does not appear. I can find no evidence that Joyce consulted Hoffmann, however, so it may be that he either never got around to it or rejected some contemplated allusion because it might have distracted the reader.[16] Or perhaps he had not recovered from the musicological saturation of the "Sirens" episode. It is interesting, though, that Joyce found in the cuckoo a symbol which united at once Bloom's Jewishness, his cuckoldry, and his bourgeois mentality with the avian imagery of "Nausicaa."

There is a curious nexus of allusion at "Nausicaa" 1:10–12 which deserves special mention because it points to an Irish comic tradition of which Joyce apparently saw himself the linear descendant:

onanism: Sterne, Swift, Wilde
    (pruriency: misanthropy—satire
    ?prolongation—cloacism—hatred of action)

At first glance one might conclude that Joyce is associating all these characteristics with Sterne, Swift, and Wilde (there is just enough truth here to invite credulity), but he was too keen a student of literature to put forth such a sophomoric theory. In what way could Wilde's writing be called prurient, cloacal, or misanthropic? The inference, apparently, is that their literary careers and/or works were strongly influenced by their sexual frustrations, a somewhat surprising idea coming from a man who professed contempt for Freud.

As we see in "Oxen" and "Circe," Bloom, like Onan, is condemned, not for the act of masturbation itself, but for the wasting of his seed: "Has he not nearer home a seedfield that lies fallow for the want of a ploughshare? A habit reprehensible at puberty is second nature and an opprobium [*sic*] in middle life" (*U* 402–403). Each of the writers in this equation may be condemned on this ground. Wilde's problem brought him a prison sentence, Sterne's marital infidelities and abortive romances are well known, and much has been made of Swift's unrequited love for young Esther Johnson.

---

[15] Bernhard Hoffmann, *Kunst und Vogelgesang* (Leipzig, 1908).

[16] It would fit my purpose to have Joyce reluctant to call attention to Stephen's "bird girl" on the beach or the prevalent bird imagery in *A Portrait*, but I cannot justify such speculation. See "Circe" 4:14 and 17:98 for other references to cuckoos in the notesheets.

The peculiarities of each are listed beneath each name (more or less), and Joyce associated them with the one author only. Thus pruriency and prolongation of plot are characteristic of Sterne, misanthropy and cloacism of Swift, and so on. Of Sterne, George Sherburn writes:

Sterne's grossness is not subtly psychological; it derives from the sort of stimulus that moves the urchin to scrawl with chalk upon a sidewalk—the desire to be bold and shocking, to evoke a snigger. His prurience is, however, by intention and in effect comic rather than corrupting.[17]

The same cannot be said of Swift, whose satirical objective was reform and not a snigger. Nevertheless, Swift did, no doubt, derive great pleasure from his "cloacal" descriptions, and anyone who doubts that his satire was basically misanthropic need only examine his description of the Yahoos.

Perhaps Joyce associated "satire" with all three, and not just with Wilde. Wilde enjoyed shocking the bourgeoisie as much as the other two, but he did not employ pruriency to this end: he merely turned conventional values upside down. His hatred of action was the primary cause of both his legal trials and his imprisonment: the British government would have welcomed relief from the responsibility of imprisoning him for his homosexuality. All he had to do was flee the country. But Wilde merely sat about in disbelief. He is in this respect an important model for Stephen Dedalus as esthete (as well as for Buck Mulligan), and Wilde's inertia during a time of crisis was probably in Joyce's mind when he created Stephen's confrontation scene in "Circe":

PRIVATE CARR

(*His cap awry, advancing to Stephen.*) Say, how would it be, governor, if I was to bash in your jaw?

STEPHEN

(*Looks up in the sky.*) How? Very unpleasant. Noble art of self-pretence. Personally, I detest action. (*He waves his hand.*) Hand hurts me slightly. *Enfin, ce sont vos oignons.* (*To Cissy Caffrey.*) Some trouble is on here. What is it, precisely?   [*U* 573]

It is likely that Joyce's interest in the Sterne-Swift-Wilde association was initially prompted by a statement of H. G. Wells that "Joyce, like Swift, had a cloacal obsession." Joyce replied to Budgen, "Why, it's Wells's countrymen who build waterclosets wherever they go."[18] In *Ulysses* the English are "a race of mighty valorous

---

[17] In Albert C. Baugh *et al.*, *A Literary History of England* (New York, 1948), p. 1025.
[18] Ellmann, pp. 427–428.

heroes, rulers of the waves, who sit on thrones of alabaster silent as the deathless gods" (*U* 319).

Other phrases in the "Nausicaa" notesheets reveal the humorous contradictions of man as sexual animal. I list them here for others to piece together as they like:

"Nausicaa"

2:74	love marriage is a sacrilege
4:80–81	Love ?excuses all: Coition without love in & out of wedlock not desired
5:18	N. puts key in door with LB
6:82	Friggers live by themselves.
6:84	Frigging, girls little paps.
6:107	Martha gives virility to man
8:49	false lover: daddy

Scene	The Hospital
Hour	10 p.m.
Organ	Womb
Art	Medicine
Colour	White
Symbol	Mothers
Technic	Embryonic Development

Oxen of the Sun

IN LEAVING "Nausicaa," the tenth episode in the "Odyssey" section of *Ulysses*, we move from the twilight ambience of parodied sexual infertility to the nocturnal world of the Holles Street Hospital, where we witness the birth of a child, the rebirth of English prose, and both the assertion and mockery of moral values.[1] Joyce's interest in evolution and cyclical movements, an interest which later helped determine the form of *Finnegans Wake*, manifests itself in his notes for "Oxen of the Sun," which may conveniently be divided into three rather distinct groups: stylistic parody, the recapitulation of previous episodes, and embryology. These categories provided Joyce with a tripartite structure and a wealth of thematic correspondences which function in the chapter in roughly the same way that Homer's *Odyssey* does in the novel. Once the framework and pattern were clear, Joyce required little more than a gestation chart, a book such as George Saintsbury's *History of English Prose Rhythm*,[2] and his natural comic genius.

It has always been obvious that, in "Oxen," Joyce was parodying many of the prominent figures in English literature, more or less in chronological order and without any apparent satirical malevolence. What has not been clearly understood is the relevance of his parody to the gestation cycle or the plot of *Ulysses*. Harry Levin, for example, asks, "For what organic reason, if any, must Lyly represent the foetus in the third month, and Goldsmith in the sixth? And what's Bunyan to Mrs. Purefoy, or Mrs. Purefoy to Junius?"[3] The answer is none or nothing. Joyce fabricated a system,

---

[1] Eleven is a curiously appropriate symbolic number for the "Oxen of the Sun" in that it suggests the beginning again of a cycle or evolution, while ten, ironically enough, suggests completion, fulfillment. Cf. Janusko, pp. 24, 127; Joseph Campbell and Henry Morton Robinson, *A Skeleton Key to* Finnegans Wake (1944; rpt. New York, 1961), pp. 193–196.

[2] London, 1912.

[3] *James Joyce: A Critical Introduction* (1941; rev. ed., New York, 1960), p. 106.

and not always a consistent one, which finds its only justification in its humorous effect. The "Oxen of the Sun" episode is, like "Nausicaa," a tour de force where sterility, gestation, and birth are *dramatized* stylistically, and any resemblance to other labyrinthine systems (whether living or dead) is purely coincidental. Although the writing of this chapter was doubtless great fun for Joyce, it must be admitted that it is an ostentatious display of literary finesse calculated to mystify as much as to entertain. This is apparent in the frequently quoted letter of March 1920 to Budgen:

Am working hard at *Oxen of the Sun*, the idea being the crime committed against fecundity by sterilizing the act of coition. Scene, lying-in hospital. Technique: a nineparted episode without divisions introduced by a Sallustian-Tacitean prelude (the unfertilized ovum), then by way of earliest English alliterative and monosyllabic and Anglo-Saxon ("Before born the babe had bliss. Within the womb he won worship" [*U* 378]. "Bloom dull dreamy heard: in held hat stony staring") [*U* 379] then by way of Mandeville ("there came forth a scholar of medicine that men clepen etc") [*U* 382] then Malory's *Morte d'Arthur* ("but that franklin Lenehan was prompt ever to pour them so that at the least way mirth should not lack") [*U* 383], then the Elizabethan chronicle style ("about that present time young Stephen filled all cups") [*U* 384], then a passage solemn, as of Milton, Taylor, Hooker, followed by a choppy Latin-gossipy bit, style of Burton-Browne, then a passage Bunyanesque ("the reason was that in the way he fell in with a certain whore whose name she said is Bird in the hand") [*U* 389] after a diarystyle bit Pepys-Evelyn ("Bloom sitting snug with a party of wags, among them Dixon jun., Ja. Lynch, Doc. Madden and Stephen D. for a languor he had before and was now better, he having dreamed tonight a strange fancy and Mistress Purefoy there to be delivered, poor body, two days past her time and the midwives hard put to it, God send her quick issue") [*U* 391] and so on through Defoe-Swift and Steele-Addison-Sterne and Landor-Pater-Newman until it ends in a frightful jumble of Pidgin English, nigger English, Cockney, Irish, Bowery slang and broken doggerel. This progression is also linked back at each part subtly with some foregoing episode of the day and, besides this, with the natural stages of development in the embryo and the periods of faunal evolution in general. The double-thudding Anglo-Saxon motive recurs from time to time ("Loth to move from Horne's house") [*U* 382] to give the sense of the hoofs of oxen. Bloom is the spermatozoon, the hospital the womb, the nurse the ovum, Stephen the embryo. How's that for high?[4]

It is indeed "high" enough to impress Budgen and us besides with Joyce's ingenuity, but the letter was not intended to be a study guide to the episode.

A. M. Klein, in an imaginative excursion worthy of the master, has employed

[4] *Letters*, I, 139–140.

Joyce's epistolary commentary on "Oxen" in the creation of a carefully detailed set of correspondences for gestation, embryology, recapitulation of previous episodes, historical evolution, and stylistic parody.[5] Hugh Kenner, Ellsworth Mason, and Janusko rightly object that Klein's chart is overly schematic and its originator too credulous in using Joyce's comments on his own work.[6] Joyce was demonstrably anachronistic and arbitrary in working out the details of his correspondences in "Oxen," as an artist has a right to be, and it is naïve of the scholar to attempt to piece the puzzle together word by word and image by image. To finish the puzzle honestly is to expose Joyce's mathematical inconsistencies at the expense of his art.

Janusko has successfully used the "Oxen" notesheets to trace the elements of Joyce's parody back to the original sources. Joyce probably began with Saintsbury, a scholar whom he genuinely admired, studied the brief quotations Saintsbury gives to illustrate the historical development of English prose, and then went to the original works to be parodied for a greater variety of stylistic and thematic idiosyncrasies. I will not reap Janusko's harvest by quoting him in detail before he publishes his findings, but he has consented to my giving the reader an idea of the works parodied and the extent of Joyce's borrowings from them in the notesheets. (But see p. 165.)

"Oxen"

1:9–46   (*passim*)   Daniel Defoe, *The History and Remarkable Life of the Truly Honourable Col. Jacque, Commonly Call'd Col. Jack*

2:1–20   Defoe, *Col. Jack*

2:55–100   (*passim*)   Sir Thomas Malory, *Le Morte d'Arthur*

3:8–9   Jonathan Swift, *Polite Conversation*

3:36–64   *Froissart's Chronicles* (Lord Berners's translation)

3:56–66   George Saintsbury, *A History of English Prose Rhythm* (on Froissart and Fisher; some lines appear both in Saintsbury and in the originals)

7:11–15, 19–56   Malory (7:53–56 also in Saintsbury)

7:96–101, 116, 122–129, 142   *The Travels of Sir John Mandeville*

7:111–114, 119–121, 144 ("shoon")   Saintsbury (Wyclif)

8:19–33, 104–106   Swift, *Polite Conversation*

11:46, 100–102   Sir Thomas Browne, *Religio Medici and Other Writings*

---

[5] "The Oxen of the Sun," *Here and Now*, I (Jan. 1949), 22–48.

[6] Kenner, *Dublin's Joyce* (1956; rpt. Boston, 1962), p. 259; Mason, "The 'Oxen of the Sun,'" *The Analyst*, no. 10 (March 1956), p. 10; and Janusko, pp. 6ff. Janusko's dissertation is the most complete study that has been done of "Oxen." I have occasionally relied upon both its critical judgment and its data on Joyce's source materials.

11:56–60, 62–64, 107–111   Saintsbury (Sir Thomas Browne)

13:15–19, 36–37   Saintsbury (Aelfric, Ethelbald)

14:3–35, 69–102 *passim*   Laurence Sterne, *A Sentimental Journey through France and Italy*

14:49–68 *passim*   Oliver Goldsmith, *Citizen of the World; A Reverie at the Boar's Head Tavern in Eastcheap* (1 ref.)

14:116–119, 120, 121–122, 124, 125, 126–127, 128   Saintsbury (Cowley, Dryden, South, Halifax, Temple, Swift, Bolingbroke)

15:72   Goldsmith, *Citizen*

15:114   Thomas De Quincey, *Suspiria de Profundis*

16:1–57   (*passim*)   *The Letters of Junius*

19:52–53, 57–58, 130–133   Saintsbury (Macaulay)

19:84–92   Thomas Carlyle, *Sartor Resartus*

19:91–92, 127–128   Saintsbury (Carlyle)

20:11, 15, 20, 30–32   Charles Dickens, *David Copperfield*

20:60–65, 66–69   Saintsbury (Ruskin, Carlyle)

The second level of correspondence in the "Oxen of the Sun," that of recapitulation of previous episodes, is really nothing more than the leitmotiv technique by means of which we see the *idées fixes* of Stephen and Bloom recur in different episodes throughout the day. Neither Stephen nor his companions can be aware of any relationship between the slaughter of Hyperion's sacred oxen and a crime against fecundity, yet Joyce infused into the episode appropriate references to Garrett Deasy's letter concerning hoof-and-mouth disease (*U* 33–34) which, thanks to Stephen, has appeared in the evening paper. The recapitulation of thoughts concerning gestation and childbirth is less contrived given the scene, the circumstances, and the characters' predilections for associative thought patterns, but throughout the episode we are continually aware that the artist is not as "invisible, refined out of existence, indifferent, paring his fingernails"[7] as he is elsewhere.

Whereas Homer and the history of English prose style enabled Joyce to form the skeleton of "Oxen," the recapitulation of relevant motifs from other episodes helped him put meat on the bones. The following lists, though not complete, give blocks of "Oxen" notesheet material which were both relevant to the thematic concerns of the episode and useful in the maintenance of continuity in the novel. (Where I could find no later reference, I put an *x* in the right column. A question mark there means that I can find no specific reference in "Oxen of the Sun.")

[7] *Portrait*, p. 215.

"Oxen" 4:40–54	"Nestor"	"Oxen"
pier—bridge	*U* 25	x
Sargent	28	x
foot & mouth disease	33	*U* 392
Dixon warns SD	x	x
European conflagration	33	x
pluterperfect imperturbability	34	412
Rinderpest in Habsburgs	34	393
Bull by the horns	34	393
thanking you for hospitality	34	393
fruitful mothers,	35?	?
Austr. doctors	34	?
sinned v the light	34	387; 420
who not?	34	?
Bullockbefriending bard	36	408
God shout in street	35	388
Helen, O'Rourke of Breffni	35	x
Field, M.P. = hero	36	x

"Oxen" 4:61–73	"Proteus"	"Oxen"
Womb -oomb-tomb	*U* 48	*U* 386
Melon dream SD	47	x
changeling	46	x
Ineluctable	38	x
Flor. MacCabe	38	x
creation from nothing	38	383?
navelcord not by death severed	38	385
omphalos	39	396
mystic monks	39	x
God: couples	39	?
Kidneys of wheat	41	381
fichue position	42	385
seeds of brightness, wind	45	383
bulrushes	46	387
saved from water	46	387
dwarfs	46	Cf. 380
blubber of turlehide whales	46	x

"Oxen" 4:59–60	"Calypso"	"Oxen"
Model farm Kinnereth	*U* 59	*U* 396?
dead sea barren	61	407

The following phrases from "Scylla and Charybdis," though marked through on the "Oxen" notesheet, were apparently not used in "Oxen of the Sun."

"Oxen" 19:59–65	"Scylla and Charybdis"
mole on breast	194
what way?	x
6 medicals	182
quaker	Twelve times in "Scylla"
female catheter	182
telegram	Six times in "Scylla." Cf. *U* 419:8–11
M. MacLir	187

Embryology, the third level of correspondence in "Oxen," was a somewhat alien subject to Joyce and one which therefore required homework. Apparently his medical studies in 1902 taught him little about it. Indeed, two years later, when Nora was pregnant with Giorgio, Joyce revealed his ignorance by asking his brother to read "books on midwifery and embryology and to send him the results."[8] As he warmed to his subject, however, the idea occurred to him to relate the growth of artistic sensibility to that of the foetus, so that, as Ellmann tells us:

His brother records that in the first draft of *A Portrait*, Joyce thought of a man's character as developing 'from an embryo' with constant traits. . . . For *A Portrait of the Artist as a Young Man* is in fact the gestation of a soul, and in the metaphor Joyce found his new principle of order. [P. 307]

If the metaphor provided Joyce with his new principle of order, it is also responsible for serious structural and thematic flaws in "Oxen" which have confused well-intentioned readers such as Klein. If the reader accepts Joyce's statement in the letter to Budgen that Stephen is the embryo, Bloom the sperm, Nurse Callan the ovum, and the hospital the womb, then he may easily be led up the garden into a maze of speculations about possible symbolic links between Nurse Callan and Molly and Stephen's mother. Do we see any dynamic artistic growth in Stephen in "Oxen"? And in nine successive stages? Is he any maturer when he leaves the hospital? He is a

[8] Ellmann, p. 196.

35

good deal drunker, but hardly changed in any other measurable way. And how do Mina Purefoy and her long-awaited issue fit into the picture? Has Joyce carefully relegated them to another symbolic level so that he can allow Mina to give birth in (as far as I can make out) the seventh month?[9] Since the stylistic gestation continues, he must have had another foetus in mind. All these irreconcilable factors lead one to question whether or not Joyce, usually careful in meticulous details, has not fallen victim to his own ingenuity in the "Oxen of the Sun." But all this depends, of course, on whether Joyce himself believed his own explanation to Budgen. There is a good deal of evidence to show that he could not have been ignorant of the inconsistencies involved in the scheme he outlined.

Embryology figures importantly as a structural parallel to the developing prose style and as a reservoir of metaphor from which Joyce could draw in reproducing the blasphemous chatter of a group of drunken medical students. During the writing of the "Oxen" episode, Joyce had an ever-present reminder in the form of "a diagram showing the ontogeny of the foetus during nine months."[10] This diagram contains nine concentric ovoid rings in each of which are the characteristics of the foetus for a given month. A copy of this chart is on "Oxen" 1; another, quite similar to the first but with some variations, appears as item 58 in Robert E. Scholes's *The Cornell Joyce Collection*.[11] Embryological information and terminology are concentrated not only on "Oxen" 1 but also on "Oxen" 2, 6, 9, 10, 11, 12, 17, 18, and 19.

At least one of Joyce's source books on embryology appears to have been Italian, as seen in the lists on "Oxen" 17 and 18, which are concerned with such matters as birth control and the various positions which a foetus may assume during gestation (see also "Oxen" 12). These lists could, perhaps, have been reproduced from memory, but Joyce moved back to Trieste in October 1919 during the composition of "Nausicaa," and there Italian embryology books would have been more readily available than they were in Zurich.

Meticulous in stylistic matters if not always in structural ones, Joyce made sure that he had at least a superficially impressive knowledge of medical history to lend authenticity to the terminology he employed. Along with diverse gynecological information one encounters the names of such great physicians as Hippocrates, Empedocles of Sicily, Galen, the Arab Averroës, and Francesco Redi. There are the anatomist and embryologist Geronimo Fabrizio (Fabricius), William Harvey (discoverer

---

[9] "Though it had poured seven showers" (*U* 398); "any time these seven months" (*U* 399).

[10] Ellmann, p. 489. See color illustration below, opposite p. 162.

[11] Ithaca, N.Y., 1961. See notes to "Oxen" 1 for variations.

of the circulatory system of the blood), and the anatomists Albrecht von Haller, Kaspar Wolff, and Friedrich Henle. All appear on "Oxen" 18. The names of such modern physiologists and biologists as Jacques Loeb ("Oxen" 10:61), August Weismann ("Oxen" 6:104), and Graham Lusk ("Oxen" 6:5) are also to be found.

In looking through the "Oxen" notesheets, one is continually reminded of Joyce's interest in the strange, the monstrous, and the ludicrous. Although this sometimes verges on morbidity (see, for example, his notes on foetal monstrosities; mostly on "Oxen" 12), his interest seems basically motivated by a desire to mine each subject for material conducive to ridicule or irony. Joyce, like the caricaturist, can stretch any matter into a humorous shape by exaggerating, as we have seen in "Cyclops," or by distorting so as to illuminate incongruities. Thus he was quick to catalogue the absurdities and strange phenomena he found while browsing through embryology books. At "Oxen" 18:46 we see Hippocrates' name associated with the theory that the fertilization of right ovaries produce male children. Galen, according to the next line, apparently believed the right ovaries to be warmer than the left. On "Oxen" 10 are amusing theories by Livy and Virgil (lines 50–51), and in line 56 and at "Oxen" 11:3 notes tell us that worms fertilize each other by means of their urine. The raw material on the notesheets appears to be an accumulation of trivia, but transformation of the trivial into the sublime is one of the salient characteristics of Joyce's art.

Scene	The Brothel
Hour	12 Midnight
Organ	Locomotor Apparatus
Art	Magic
Symbol	Whore
Technic	Hallucination

Circe

JOYCE'S notesheets for the "Circe" episode are perhaps the richest and most fascinating in the entire collection. In earlier episodes he had been limited, more or less, by the confines of structure, theme, and parallel; in the night world of "Circe" he could give free rein to his imagination, break down the barriers between conscious and subconscious, and dredge up from the spiritus mundi visions that might have made cautious one such as William Butler Yeats, lest in his studies of magic he open some Pandora's box of the psychic realms.

Joyce grew to maturity during an age when a Dubliner with education and curiosity could hardly have been ignorant of the widespread interest in occultism. Madame Blavatsky had published her influential *Isis Unveiled* in 1877; two years earlier she and others had formed a Theosophical Society in London to rival the already flourishing Society for Psychical Research. In 1885 Yeats, George Russell (Æ), and others founded their Dublin Hermetic Society to propagate the faith in Ireland.[1] Ellmann says Joyce

joined the rest of intellectual Dublin in taking an interest in occultism; his copy of H. S. Olcott's *A Buddhist Catechism* is dated May 7, 1901. His brother Stanislaus thought James was looking for a substitute religion, but it is probable that he, like Yeats and unlike George Russell, was attracted more by the symbology than by the pious generalizations of Theosophy.[2]

The symbolism of occultism, together with Catholic ritual, never ceased to interest Joyce, but it is in the digestion and application of these subjects that one sees the unique quality of Joyce's mind. His contemporaries D. H. Lawrence, T. S. Eliot, Yeats, and Æ were innately religious and sought, in various ways, ritualistic and philosophical (or theosophical) symbol systems which would reconcile mystic vision

---

[1] Richard Ellmann, *Yeats: The Man and the Masks* (New York, 1948), pp. 61–62.
[2] *James Joyce*, p. 79.

with external structure and at the same time provide metaphors with which they could recreate or translate into artistic-didactic terms their various inner visions. Joyce expresses a minimal interest in mankind beyond its more ludicrous characteristics, habits, and situations; and though profoundly superstitious himself, he sees man not in any religious or cosmological framework but rather in a historical one. Joyce's mind might be said to have been all dressed up in systems, cycles, categories of knowledge, rituals, and similar paraphernalia, but with nowhere to go beyond a literary creation that is anything but didactic. If this is a true assessment, then the *Ulysses* notesheets (especially those for "Circe") are a curiously appropriate documentation of the artist's mind, and one which would probably have dismayed such serious practitioners of applied occultism as the poet Æ. But then "Who reads Æ?" Joyce would have countered.

Among the exotic species and subspecies of occultic-scientific information one encounters in the "Circe" notesheets are jottings on such diverse subjects as palmistry, fortune-telling by cards, astrology, the language of gesture (fan, parasol, umbrella, handkerchief), botany, pharmacology (and home remedies), common superstitions, Egyptology, the symbolism of jewelry, the Black Mass, demonology, bestialogy, sinistrism (my word), fetishism, and psychophysics.

To see the relevance of all this to the sorceress in the *Odyssey*, the reader must understand Joyce's somewhat idiosyncratic (but in no way whimsical) interpretation of this episode. His most important scholarly authority here is Victor Bérard's *Phéniciens et l'*Odyssée. His notes on Circe, which may be found on pages 302–304 of *Ulysses* Notebook VIII.A.5 at Buffalo (pagination here and elsewhere follows that of *Studies in Bibliography*, XXII [1966]), are taken from Bérard's chapter entitled "L'Épervière," or "The Sparrow-Hawk" (II, 261–310). Joyce later transferred most of this material to the British Museum notesheets, especially "Circe" 1, 3, 6, 17, and 18. Bérard's bestialogical identification, plus the more important fact that Circe transforms men into swine and is the "déesse des fauves," was sufficient reason for Joyce to assemble a large collection of notes on the lore of wild beasts. In addition, Joyce's experience had probably taught him that men were at their most bestial when intoxicated while visiting prostitutes. Dublin's women of the night probably encouraged such metamorphoses in the interest of good business. Thus Circe, who seems to have invited Odysseus to bed as much out of fear as from desire, becomes a madam in modern Dublin.

The fact that Homer's Circe is a sorceress accounts for much of the occultism in the notes. Some knowledge of the rudiments of palmistry, fortune-telling, and astrology might well have been common among Dublin prostitutes in 1904. Even Molly reads the playing cards (*U* 760). In notebook VIII.A.5 Joyce has notes on Egyptology out of Bérard as well as some on Feronia, the Italian counterpart of Circe. It is her magic wand which probably suggested the notes on the language of gesture. Similarly, those on demonology, the Black Mass, and similar topics were probably compiled as a plausible bridge between the world of Homer's (or Bérard's) Circe and the haunted psyches of Bloom and Dedalus.

Gilbert (p. 317), Litz (pp. 25–26), and Ellmann (pp. 510–511) have already discussed Joyce's notes on moly, the herb that Hermes gives Odysseus for use as an antidote to the potion Circe will give him to drink. Joyce assigned Molly the role of antidote (in a sense) for Bloom against the wiles of Bella Cohen and her temptresses. But this was not sufficient. His imagination was obviously titillated with the prospect of modern equivalents for moly. In notebook VIII.A.5 (p. 304), Joyce's notes are restricted to his source book (Bérard, II, 288).

Moly—mlh (Heb) = Sel
atriplex halimus
pourpier de mer
salad with vinegar   milky yellow flower

In the "Circe" notesheets, however, his imagination suggested further possibilities:

"Circe"

2:3	Moly—circumcis.
2:4	Circe—pox
2:49	Moly hard to dig. [*Odyssey*, p. 163]
3:110	Homebrew. Moly.
3:121	Moly (met—salt) [Cf. "mlh (Heb) = Sel" above.]
7:110	charm = Moly (narrow ?shawl)
10:26–30	Moly—indifference
	Moly—beauty
	Moly—laughter
	Moly—satire
	Moly—pessimism
12:32	Moly = escape from prison
12:36	Moly = conscience
21:35	Moly = absinthe, mercury,
21:50	Moly = chastity[3]

[3] Gilbert seems to have thought moly symbolized chance, or luck (p. 325).

If one keeps in mind the antidotal quality of moly, most of these notes are fairly clear, though as potential plot indicators for the "Circe" episode they appear to be puzzle pieces that Joyce never quite worked into the episode. In the *Odyssey* Hermes warns Odysseus that he must accept Circe's invitation to her bed, but first he must make her "swear a mighty oath by the blessed gods, that she will plan nought else of mischief to thine own hurt, lest she make thee a dastard and unmanned, when she hath thee naked" (p. 163). This castration threat has its counterpart in Bloom's sex transformation, though in more realistic terms the "Circe—pox" note above would seem to be a more appropriate rendering for the atmosphere of Nighttown. And indeed in these notes on moly Joyce appears to be considering plausible circumstances that would dampen the ardor of a visitor to Nighttown and thus spare him the painful consequences.

It may be that moly loomed so large in Joyce's thinking here that he decided to explore the possibilities of other herbs and their medicinal applications, though it is also true that by this stage of the novel Bloom's grasp (sometimes muddled) of similar kinds of quasi-scientific knowledge has already been established. Even if Bloom's mind were not such a rag bag of information, the recollection of his father's suicide would probably have set him to thinking about poisons, antidotes, home remedies, and by association, herbs, drugs, aphrodisiacs, and the effects of more common nutriments. Then, too, appropriateness may have been balanced by convenience, since in writing "Oxen of the Sun" Joyce obviously dipped into several medical handbooks. Here is a selection of the more interesting notes on these subjects:

Home Remedies

"Circe"

3:61–63	Starve warts, caustic prevents rebirth, wartblood spreads blood snip off ?with horsehair no denned neck
4:92	lip pomade—swinefat rendered with rosewater
4:100–101	v hiccup tie a knot on y^r· shift & stick it back in y^r· breeches
4:121	oxygenated water gold hair
4:133–134	stye cure (wheatenmeal honey, nutmeg, salve, smear, bath)
4:140	Paolini's eyewash
4:145	goldring v stye [As above, v = versus.]
8:93–94	lick of dog good—on old sore
9:33	?Ringpissen v impotence

Botany, Pharmacology, and Foods

"Circe"

1:7	parsley for corpse (Greek)
2:1	garlic
2:44	cheese, barley, wine ?seed honey
2:70	Camel's hump pot still., ferns datejuice
2:148 & 3:110	truffles
3:8	rosemary
3:15	gum benjamin
3:16	kohol [See Gilbert, p. 320n.]
3:39	new taste of chocolate
3:40–41	gilt off gingerbread unripe fruit
3:64	Tansy, pennyroyal spanish fly
3:122	Rings candies [Cf. notebook VIII.A.5, p. 305.]
3:143	sicksweet weed
4:129	rhubarb
4:142	fennel & bee
4:146	Bitter almonds = amethyst
4:154	tobacco an aphrodisiac
4:155	pinch of t in wine makes drunk
4:159	potato came 130 yrs after.
6:9–14	hawthorn, ?shaking grass, bad
	4 leaved shamrock
	loves me, loves me not
	fairies eat daisyroot
	rosemary strengthens memory
	applepeels Hallow eve
6:105–106	allium redyellow flower
	allium niger aphros.
7:20	rhododendrons
7:26–28	Mercury, lavender, valerian, mandrake
	liquorice, fennel, parsley, horehound
	elecampane
9:66	LB & the spinach with hemlock
11:75	thistledown refracts
12:30	ant milks aphis
14:49	gravel cabbagestumps
14:56	porksteaks

14:85–87	musk
	chive (civet)
	mandrake
16:31	eat roast heretic
17:47	scent & roseleaves
17:75	rosewater
18:23	Cat sleeps on cocaine
19:30	cornjuice
19:31	cow eats yewtree dies
19:35	quinine
19:37–38	knuckle of veal
	saddle of mutton
19:60	Manna white pearly pea melt in sun on twigs
	of tamarisk tree by bite of ?cacos insect

Equally important are lists of notes on animal characteristics and the dance, but space does not permit the exploration of all the curiosities of the "Circe" note-sheets.[4] One subject will, however, be examined in some detail to show how the notes illuminate the text of *Ulysses*. Any of several subjects would serve this purpose, but palmistry seems most manageable.

Not the least impressive aspect of Joyce's study of palmistry is his meticulousness in seemingly minor details. Palmistry provided Zoe Higgins with no more than a dozen lines (*U* 547–549), but it was important enough for Joyce to ask Budgen to bring him a handbook on the subject.[5] Just as he studied handbooks on embryology for "Oxen of the Sun" and others on Gibraltar for "Penelope," Joyce researched palmistry with great care or at least closely supervised the research which others did for him. The bulk of his notes on palmistry may be found on "Circe" 1 and 5, but Joyce probably learned a good deal more than this before he was through. Such a passion for authority does Joyce exhibit in the notesheets that one can almost see him preparing himself to justify in scholarly terms the inclusion of every detail in *Ulysses*.

In the left margin of "Circe" 1 (lines 8ff.) is a list of phrases beginning with "Hold out hand" (*U* 547), a command which begins the section on palm reading in

[4] For a detailed treatment of certain other aspects of the "Circe" notesheets, see Norman Silverstein's "Magic on the Notesheets"; my corrections and additions (with Silverstein); and Silverstein's doctoral dissertation. See also Ulrich Schneider, "Freemasonic Signs and Passwords in the *Circe* Episode," *James Joyce Quarterly*, V (Summer 1968), 303–311.

[5] *Letters*, III, 54.

the text also. All that Joyce tells us about Stephen's hand is that it is long, but a brief glance through any book of palmistry would have been enough to convince Joyce that Stephen could only have long fingers. Joyce was, of course, practicing palmistry in reverse here: he knew Stephen's personality and picked the type of hand to suit it, or merely used his own. Cheiro, whose book Joyce could have used but didn't, describes the "philosophic hand" in terms which Joyce would have immediately recognized as appropriate for both Stephen's character and his own:

This shape of hand is easily recognized: it is generally long and angular, with bony fingers, developed joints, and long nails. As far as success in the form of wealth is concerned, it is not a favorable type to have; it gleans wisdom, rarely, if ever, gold. People with such a type are, as a rule, students, but of peculiar subjects. They study mankind; they know every chord and tone in the harp of life. They play upon it, and are gratified with its responsive melody more than with the clink of coin. . . . They like to be distinct from other people. . . . Such people love mystery in all things.[6]

Although he denies it, Zoe sees that Stephen has courage (*U* 547), a feature attributable to the prominence of the Mount of Mars (see illus.). This characteristic later emerges as a kind of Wildean stoicism in Stephen's drunken encounter with Private Carr. At "Circe" 5:47 is the phrase "Mount of Mars (at side) domination," perhaps too forceful a phrase to describe Stephen's personality. Lynch sees the irony of Zoe's pronouncement and mocks Stephen for his earlier cowardice at the hospital: "Sheet lightning courage. The youth who could not shiver and shake."

To further undermine our faith in Zoe's accuracy in reading palms, Joyce conjures up a vision from *A Portrait* (evoked by the word *pandybat*) where the sadistic Father Dolan paddles Stephen for having broken his glasses: "Any boy want flogging? Broke his glasses? Lazy idle little schemer. See it in your eye" (*U* 547). Stephen's recollection is appropriate since Father Dolan was practicing a method of character analysis similar to palmistry.

Zoe also sees that Stephen has a "woman's hand," which could also describe Cheiro's "philosophic hand." She "traces lines on his hand" and concludes "Line of Fate. Influential friends" (*U* 548). This is identical with a note at "Circe" 5:55. Near this phrase ("Circe" 5:48) is "Mount of the Moon, imagination," which is what Zoe sees next in Stephen's hand. This is followed in the text by "You'll meet with a . . . (*She peers at his hands abruptly.*) I won't tell you what's not good for you. Or do you want to know?" Here Zoe seems about to tell Stephen that he is to meet with a

---

6 [Louis Hamon], *Cheiro's Language of the Hand* (1894; 7th ed., New York, 1897), p. 34.

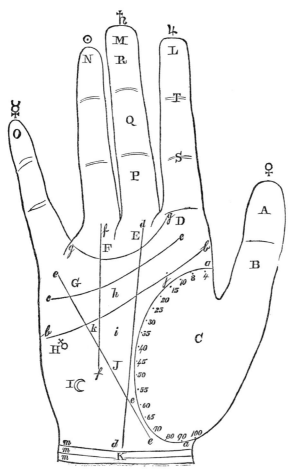

A. Will.
B. Logic.
C. The Mount of Venus.
D. The Mount of Jupiter.
E. The Mount of Saturn.
F. The Mount of the Sun.
G. The Mount of Mercury ⎫
H. The Mount of Mars ⎬ The Percussion.
I. The Mount of the Moon ⎭
J. The Plain of Mars.
aa. Line of Life.
bb. Line of Head.
cc. Line of Heart.
dd. Line of Saturn or Fate.
ee. Line of Liver.
ff. Line of the Sun or Fortune.
gg. Belt of Venus.

K. The Rascette.
L. Square finger.
M. Spatulate finger.
N. Conic finger.
O. Pointed finger.
P. The 1st Phalange.
Q. The 2nd Phalange.
R. The 3rd Phalange.
S. The 1st Joint (Order).
T. The 2nd Joint (Philosophy).
h. The Quadrangle.
i. The Triangle.
j. The Upper Angle.
k. The Inner Angle.
l. The Lower Angle.
mmm. The Bracelets of Life.

Diagram of the hand. From Henry Frith, *The Language of the Hand* (New York, 1899?)

45

stranger, and the stranger is, of course, Bloom, who at this point nervously interrupts Zoe on the pretext of wishing to have his palm read.

Bella takes Bloom's hand and makes an obscene allusion to his knobby knuckles. Zoe sees a gridiron (*U* 549) and from his short little finger believes him to be a "henpecked husband." In the margin of "Circe" 1 (lines 10ff.), Joyce tells us more about Bloom's hand: in relation to Stephen's hand, Bloom's is "shorter, all fingers equal & round tips," certainly an appropriate hand for his personality since it indicates pragmatic materialism. Joyce notes that if the subject's third and fourth fingers are far apart, he is "impulsive"; presumably, if the first and second are far apart, he is "self-willed." If they bend back easily, he is "shy." The remainder of the phrases do not appear to pertain directly either to Stephen or to Bloom, but like the material on "Circe" 5 provide Joyce with additional information for possible later use.

The most complete and scholarly book on palmistry of the eight or ten I have seen in my unsuccessful search for Joyce's source is a 600-page book by Adolphe Desbarrolles entitled *Les Mystères de la main*.[7] With such a reference work at hand the job of deciphering these often bewildering phrases becomes relatively simple. It has already been mentioned that Zoe connects Mars with courage (*U* 547) while examining Stephen's hand, but it is obvious that while she knows enough of the terminology to impress Lynch, her analysis lacks any real authority. "(She counts.) Two, three, Mars, that's courage." Zoe attributes the right quality to Mars,[8] but she appears to be counting fingers, and the domain of the Mount of Mars is the side cushion of the palm. That this is Joyce's mistake is highly doubtful since, as quoted earlier, he places the Mount of Mars "at side." This, together with Zoe's obvious uncertainty, shows that she has only a superficial knowledge of palmistry.

The fleshy part of the palm connected to the side cushion is the Mount of the Moon (the next item, "Circe" 5:48), and its prominence is an indication of imagination (*U* 548). The lines of heart, head, and life (see diagram 1) reveal one's fortune in obvious ways. The phrase at "Circe" 5:50—"If L of L broken on *both* accident"— means that if the line of life is broken on both palms, one will die a sudden death.[9] The lines may differ from left hand to right. For instance, a broken line of life on one palm and a feeble line on the other indicate a grave illness to come. In general, inherited

---

[7] Paris, 1880.

[8] Desbarrolles says "Mars donne le courage, le calme, le sang-froid dans le danger, la résignation, la domination de soi-même" (p. 205).

[9] *Ibid.*, p. 230.

characteristics are most visible on the hand one uses least; acquired ones are seen on the other.

Lines 51–52 on "Circe" 5 are self-explanatory. Desbarrolles confirms line 53, "double L of L luck"; he says, "Si la ligne de vie est double, c'est luxe d'existence" (p. 230). Three phrases down the notesheet (line 56) is the "Girdle of Venus," a half-ring which runs between Jupiter and Saturn and a very bad sign indeed: "L'anneau de Vénus enferme, comme dans une île, Saturne et Apollon, la fatalité et la lumière, et laisse sans guides et sans conseils les instincts de l'ambition démesurée, du mensonge, du libertinage et du caprice" (p. 247).

A triangle "annonce l'aptitude aux sciènces" (p. 258). The number of children and marriages is also determinable from the lines of the hand. That the first joint of the thumb indicates the force of one's will is likewise confirmed by Desbarrolles. Still on "Circe" 5 we move from a study of palmistry to that of the significance of facial characterisics, which may have suggested to Joyce the pandybat sequence in "Circe." Desbarrolles argues that like the palm, the face and head are reflections of all that one is and is to become.

Lines 68–71 contain the four "humors" well known in medieval physiology: "sanguine, lymphatic, melancholic, and bilious." Except for the third, these adjectives denote personalities whose fates are dominated by two stars rather than one. Although Desbarrolles does not use these four terms, he nevertheless describes them:

1. "Sanguine (Mars & Jupiter): red: curly hair" ("Circe" 5:68). "L'union de Jupiter avec Mars donne une certaine rougeur à la peau, des yeux grands" (p. 487). (Desbarrolles goes on to explain that if the planets are in accord, such people are energetic seekers of glory; if they are not, the person tends to be rebellious and quarrelsome.)

2. "lymphatic (moon & Venus): pale: ash hair: fairness" ("Circe" 5:69). "L'union de la Lune et de Vénus donne un teint blanc légèrment coloré, mais un peu mat; de beaux sourcils, des yeux noirs" (p. 492).

3. "melancholic Saturn: velvety skin: heavy hair" ("Circe" 5:70). "Les saturniens sont maigres, pâles, grands, *leur peau est très-brune*, souvent terreuse, rude et sèche; elle se ride facilement; leurs cheveux, d'abord épais, noirs, et souvent d'un noir dur, tombent de bonne heure, et sont plats et gros" (p. 442).

4. "bilious (sun & Mercury): sallow: lank black hair" ("Circe" 5:71). "L'union du Soleil et de Mercure donne le teint couleur de miel jaune, la barbe belle sans être épaisse ni longue, les yeux de médiocre grandeur" (p. 489).

As we move on down "Circe" 5 we see how to read the nose, teeth, throat, feet, such idiosyncrasies of facial features as wrinkles, and the manner in which one laughs and walks. It seems safe to say, in conclusion, that a person of Joyce's superstitious disposition and half-serious interest in hermetic science would have been fascinated by these studies even if innocent of an ulterior motive such as art. They also enabled Joyce to add depth and a certain strange authenticity to "Circe," while at the same time tweaking the noses of Yeats, Æ, and their fellow hermeticists by working their science into a scene at a brothel. It is my guess that in fathoming the depths of occult influence on this episode, we have scarcely got our feet wet.

Scene	The Shelter
Hour	After Midnight
Organ	Nerves
Art	Navigation
Symbol	Sailors
Technic	Narrative (old)

Eumaeus

and the Homeric Parallels in the Notesheets

E UMAEUS" is an anticlimactic episode for one primary reason—it is a way station in which the author and his characters attempt to recuperate, after the excesses of "Circe," so that they may continue the voyage to "Ithaca." (Conversely, the corresponding episode in the *Odyssey* allowed the narrator to build suspense while father and son meet and plot the downfall of the suitors.) This sobering interlude represents a stylistic plunge, as it were, from zenith to nadir, from hallucinatory and orgiastic drama to the impoverished prose of the commercial entrepreneur. The transition can be justified in terms of function, since the ugly reality of the Dublin streets in the early morning hours provides a sharp contrast to the psychodrama of Nighttown; and we are once again outside the now-exhausted consciences of Bloom and Dedalus. If one looks closer, however, one can see the bloodshot eyes and frayed nerves of Joyce as he attempts to recover, with his characters, for a new assault on Nostos.

Gilbert, under Joyce's direction, described the numbness of "Eumaeus" solely in terms of function:

The style seems to be paralysed by that sort of aphasia which the Germans aptly name *Hexenschuss* [*sic*], an after-effect of Circe's bane. The silent monologue, utterly disintegrated, ramifies into the structure of an equally decrepit narrative, so that not only the meditations of Mr Bloom but descriptive passages, too, are clouded o'er with the dark cast of fatigue.[1]

There is, however, a distinct possibility that Joyce's own fatigue played a dominant role, for in the "Eumaeus" notesheets one sees Joyce more dependent than usual on repetitious notes, external structure, and mythological allusion. It is as if his creative imagination were momentarily bankrupt, thus compelling him to work exclusively within the previously erected framework. In the "Oxen" and "Circe" note-

[1] Pp. 360–361. See also Litz, p. 20.

49

sheets there are allusions to previous episodes which provide thematic unity, but nowhere do they predominate as here.[2] In "Eumaeus" Joyce plods methodically along, like a horse with blinders.

Rather than emulate the tediousness of the "Eumaeus" notesheets by examining phrases intended for stylistic padding, it would seem fitting to exceed the confines of the single episode and explore an important aspect of the collection as a whole—Joyce's notes on Homeric and mythological parallels. It is apparent that Joyce knew the *Odyssey* thoroughly, in translation at least, and that he went beyond the text to Homeric scholarship in his search for fresh ideas. In notebook VIII.A.5 at Buffalo there are numerous entries based on his reading of Bérard's *Phéniciens et l'*Odyssée, W. H. Roscher's *Ausführliches Lexikon der griechischen und römischen Mythologie*,[3] and the Butcher-Lang translation of the *Odyssey*. The notebook was probably compiled early in 1918, and a few of the notes made their way into the *Ulysses* notesheets. To call attention to these in the following survey I have labeled them "VIII.A.5," followed by the page number in *Studies in Bibliography*, XXII (1969).

Allusions to the Homeric world in the notesheets for "Cyclops," "Nausicaa," and "Oxen of the Sun" are neither plentiful nor very influential, and the reason for this may well lie in the fact that these episodes have self-contained structural rationales that propel them forward along clearly defined lines. In part "Cyclops," like "Ivy Day in the Committee Room," exposes the hypocrisy and provincialism of Irish political thinking, and Joyce required no reservoir of classical allusions to support an Irish cyclops. He knew Dublin pub life too well. "Nausicaa" may have sent him to Butler and the penny novelettes, but it placed no strain on his imagination. "Oxen" necessitated such a reservoir more than the other two, since a structural and thematic evolution was constructed, but Joyce had the entire range of English literature counterbalanced by a textbook on embryology to draw from there, and the classical world, as with the two earlier episodes, served more as a departure point than a Baedeker. Then came "Circe," a free-for-all in which Joyce apparently taxed his imagination to the limit to create the most fantastic episode in *Ulysses*. It is there as he labors under the spell of Circe's witchcraft that we first encounter significant numbers of classical allusions.

Of the twenty-odd classical references in the "Cyclops" notesheets, it is significant that none point to the corresponding episode in the *Odyssey*. Most are concerned with the *Iliad*, Herodotus, and Greek history generally, and three reflect

---

[2] See also "Cyclops" chapter, p. 16.
[3] 6 vols., with 2 supp. vols. (Leipzig, 1884–1937).

Joyce's impression of Penelope. There are scarcely a quarter as many in "Nausicaa," two of the most interesting being "λευκόλενος"[4] (2:43), an epithet for Nausicaa, and "Odyssey—struggles [against the] unknown" (6:100). In the "Oxen" section there are only a few more, and all but two of the notes appear on "Oxen" 6. Here we see the first important borrowing from notebook VIII.A.5, the only previous instance being "Nausicaa" 6:103 (VIII.A.5, p. 296).

"Oxen"

6:31 Taormina

6:32 neir Elohim: le gerre: phalli:

6:33 Lampetie. Phaethusa

6:34 Ul. goes alone in . . . . :sleep(?)

6:36 Ireland: pontine marsh

The first four came from page 300 of notebook VIII.A.5, the fifth from page 303. The ultimate origin of the first four is volume II of Bérard (pp. 375–384). This is appropriate for "Oxen" since Bérard refers to the etymological and historical origins of Taormina, a Sicilian seacoast town, to show that it was there that Odysseus and his men must have encountered Hyperion's sacred oxen.

A partial summary of Homer's equivalent episode appears on one "Circe" notesheet (2:31–37, 44–49, 52). Though Joyce certainly did not need to be reminded of the action there, correspondences, like algebra problems, seem to have been easier for him to work out when one-half of the equation was down on paper. He borrowed extensively from notebook VIII.A.5 in compiling "Circe" 3. Among other things he relates the treachery of Eriphyle (VIII.A.5, p. 310), notes the opposition of Eurylochus to Odysseus's authority, and in lines 100–129 he incorporates almost all of his notes on Bérard's Circe chapter (VIII.A.5, mostly pp. 302–305). Further down on "Circe" 3 Joyce gives Circe's family tree (lines 166–168) and at "Circe" 7:29–33 makes reference to the witch's deeds as related in Apollonius Rhodius's *Argonautica* and elsewhere. Since it is really Hermes who saves Odysseus from making a pig of himself, Joyce decided to search for interesting details in Hermes' mythological past, and the results appear at "Circe" 7:73–87. In his imagination Bloom does not of course fare as well as Odysseus: among other things he suffers a sex transformation. It is clear from several notes scattered through various episodes ("Circe" 3:123–124, 10:19, 16:43, and elsewhere) that Joyce was thinking here more of the ordeals of Tiresias than of those of Odysseus. Through it all one senses that Joyce is carting bones from

[4] The word is misspelled; the middle omicron should have been an omega. Cf. Gilbert, p. 289.

one end of the graveyard to the other in the hope of finding a skeleton intact enough to bear the journey through time.

He found such a figure in Alcmene, the mother of Hercules by Zeus, whose story is recounted at "Circe" 3:125–129 (from VIII.A.5, p. 309). When she died, Zeus ordered Hermes to rob the coffin of her body, which Hermes cleverly did by filling the coffin with stones, thus deceiving Alcmene's pallbearers. This idea recurs at "Eumaeus" 7:67 as "coffin full of stones (C.S.P.)." A glance at pages 111 and 633 of *Ulysses* reveals the ultimate use to which Joyce put this phrase. First Jack Power in "Hades" and then Fitzharris (alias "Skin-the-Goat"), the proprietor of the cabmen's shelter, subscribe to a renovated myth popular in the 1890's that Charles Stewart Parnell did not die and that he would one day return as Ireland's savior. (This is precisely the theory that Eumaeus holds concerning Odysseus.) Fitzharris says:

One morning you would open the paper . . . and read, *Return of Parnell.* He bet them what they liked. A Dublin fusilier was in that shelter one night and said he saw him in South Africa. . . . Dead he wasn't. Simply absconded somewhere. The coffin they brought over was full of stones. He changed his name to De Wet, the Boer general. [*U* 633]

It is difficult to say whether the Alcmene story or the deep Irish longing for a messianic leader (or perhaps both) is responsible for this idea, but it is entirely appropriate for the "Eumaeus" episode, where deception and disguise form a primary motif. In thinking through the ramifications of this, Joyce obviously had in mind the exploits of Hermes (cf. "Circe" 7:73–87) and probably Autolycus's legacy to his grandson Odysseus ("Cyclops" 10:52). So powerful is the deceptive impulse in Odysseus that he exceeds situational requirements a number of times, especially when he spins a beggar's yarn for Eumaeus, toys with Penelope's emotions, and cruelly tricks his father Laertes.

As indicated earlier, there is an extensive amount of plot summary in the "Eumaeus" notesheets, especially on "Eumaeus" 6, where Joyce made notes on the action surrounding the separate arrivals of Odysseus and Telemachus in Ithaca, the meeting with Eumaeus, and the reunion and alliance of father and son. Among the most interesting phrases here are "Ul. doublemeaning," "Eum. laments Telemachus off to Paris," and "Ul. upbraids Pallas sending off Telem. (didn't want son go to sea)" ("Eumaeus" 6:107–111). Here the two epics merge and identities become confused, but the results are interesting. Stephen is undisputably Telemachus, Bloom is Odysseus, and "Skin-the-Goat" is Eumaeus, the faithful swineherd of Odysseus. But a fourth character climbs onstage in the notesheets—"Ps.Ul." (pseudo-Ulysses) or ψευδαγγελος. Gilbert describes the salty sailor in "Eumaeus" as a "marine Munchausen, an Odysseus Pseudangelos" (p. 361), and his yarn is indeed reminiscent of the one Odysseus tells while disguised as a beggar.

This leaves us with several problems of character identity and suggests that Joyce may have been performing with characters the same sleight-of-hand tricks he pulled with plot in "Wandering Rocks." If Stephen is still Telemachus, what relationship does he have to the sailor? Is Bloom still Odysseus if the sailor is Pseudangelos? If the answer is yes, we have the complicated situation of a false Odysseus attempting to take in a real one. If no, then the wanderers' identities merge somehow, and the sailor becomes a kind of ironic projection of the adventurer our Dublin "stick-in-the-mud" would like to become (cf. U 712). And it is the sailor (U 615) who complains that his son Danny has run off to sea, while Bloom's son Rudy is lost through death (*sea* would work nicely as a death symbol here). Bloom, in turn, has found a son in Stephen/Telemachus who is forever lost to his mother. The similarity is remarkable, but the waters are still murky.

Other instances in which identities merge are the following:

1. "Tel wants to start for Sandycove" ("Eumaeus" 6:611; U 641). The imprudence of such an idea occurs to Bloom in deciding what to do with Stephen. If there is a Homeric parallel, it is Telemachus's impatience to start for town at the beginning of Book 17 of the *Odyssey*.

2. "Sailor's tale resembles SD's / Ps Ul's tale resembles Ul's" ("Eumaeus" 6:125–126). Stephen's voyage in *Ulysses* is probably more mental than physical, just as the sailor's tale of strange sights and narrow escapes is no doubt more imaginary than real, but there must be more to it than this. Since Stephen tells no tale here (he can barely speak, in fact), this may be an idea for expanding "Eumaeus" rather than a comment on the episode as it stands. Stephen's break with his family resembles that of Murphy's son Danny, but this is hardly a satisfying explanation. The yarn Pseudangelos spins to Eumaeus is, of course, like Homer's account of the voyage of Odysseus in many ways. He claims to have been disinherited (by suitors?), to have commanded a fleet of ships, and to have fought against Troy, and he asserts that his present poverty is attributable to the treachery of the gods.

3. "Ps Ul, hates roaming, place as vallet [*sic*]" ("Eumaeus" 6:131; U 615). Pseudangelos tells Eumaeus, "no mortal may vie with me in the business of a serving-man, in piling well a fire, in cleaving dry faggots, and in carving and roasting flesh and in pouring of wine, those offices wherein meaner men serve their betters."[5] The

[5] *Odyssey*, p. 250.

sailor in *Ulysses* says he has a friend who is a valet, one who has given him clothes. (Eumaeus gives his guest a cloak at the end of Book 14.) "I'm game for that job, shaving and brushup. I hate roaming about."

4. "Theo[clymenus] asks if Si[mon] D[edalus] can get [him a] job   Tel[emachus] refers him to Eurym[achus]" ("Eumaeus" 6:149). This occurs near the end of Book 15, where the seer Theoclymenus, a companion of Telemachus on board ship, asks on their arrival in Ithaca "And whither shall I go, dear child?" Telemachus declines to play host because of the suitors in his house and refers him to Eurymachus: "For he is far the best man of them all, and is most eager to wed my mother and to have the sovereignty of Odysseus."[6] Although Gilbert (pp. 172–173) associates Theoclymenus with the mysterious M'Intosh of the "Hades" episode, the job seeker who approaches Stephen in "Eumaeus" is less than mysterious. He is Lord John Corley (*U* 600), of "Two Gallants" fame, and Stephen refers him to Deasy's school. Corley's introduction is followed by a typical Homeric genealogy.

Two of the most curious references in the "Ithaca" notesheets are evidence of Joyce's persistent concern with character equivalents in *Ulysses* and the *Odyssey*, and if he never quite made them work in places, he never gave up on them. At "Ithaca" 8:30 is "Mrs Thornton = Euryclée," with a recurrence at "Ithaca" 11:82. Euryclea, the ancient nursemaid of Odysseus, sees through his disguise when she discovers a familiar scar while bathing him.[7] Robert M. Adams tells us that Mrs Thornton was a "midwife, a very real person, of 19A Denzille Street, who delivered Margaret, Charles, Eileen and Florence Joyce" (p. 235). In *Ulysses* Bloom remembers having summoned her to deliver Milly (*U* 66).

The second curiosity is "Victoria = Penelope" ("Ithaca" 8:34). Previously Joyce had noted "108 MP's = suitors" ("Eumaeus" 4:112), and as if he were seriously considering making the parallel visible for once, he notes that the date of Prince Albert's death was 1861 ("Ithaca" 8:25). What prompts this is, of course, the similarity between Victoria's long widowhood and the ordeal of Penelope, but Joyce does not indicate whether this would make Prince Albert a Pseudangelos, a Jewish cuckold, or a legitimate son of Laertes.

Almost all but the left margin of "Ithaca" 11 consists of plot summary of the action subsequent to Odysseus's arrival at the palace. Among the more glimmering

---

[6] *Ibid.*, p. 256. Eurymachus, like Melanthius (see below, p. 55), later offers the disguised Odysseus a job as a farm laborer (p. 306).

[7] *Ibid.*, p. 325. At "Ithaca" 11:79 Joyce noted "footbath water spilled" and two lines later "Offers to wash SD."

nuggets is a reference to his skill in archery: "Ul. = W. Tell." There is a nice pun in "Irus a bounder (Iris)." Iris is a messenger of the gods in the *Iliad*. Irus literally "bounds" as lackey for the suitors and is a "bounder" for abusing Odysseus. His name (really a nickname) means "errand boy" and is derived from Iris. To Joyce it may also have suggested the relationship of the Irish to the English.

In line 95 of "Ithaca" 11 is a pun on Antinous, who as the obnoxious ring-leader of the suitors is (from where Odysseus stands) strictly "anti-nous." In disguise, Odysseus tests the suitors by begging table scraps, and when Antinous loudly refuses, Odysseus says, "Lo, now I see thou hast not wisdom with thy beauty!" (Note the Italian phrase two lines down the notesheet: " 'Sei bello ma non savio,' Antinuo.") This insolence causes Antinous to strike Odysseus with a stool.[8]

Yet another equation, indicative of just how far Joyce was willing to carry his joke, is "Melanthius = Joe Cuffe" ("Ithaca" 11:108). The former is the goatherd who insults Odysseus on the road to town (while at the same time offering him a job) and swears allegiance to the suitors. During the great battle he is captured and tied up; later he is mutilated. Joe Cuffe is a former employer of Bloom "in the adjacent Dublin Cattle market on the North Circular road" (*U* 664).

An even more ludicrous connection which Joyce apparently worked into *Ulysses* is "the cat = Argos" ("Ithaca" 1:23). Argos was the vermin-infested hound who mourned the absent Odysseus for nineteen years and died in a spasm of content-ment the moment he set eyes on his master.[9] At the opening of the "Calypso" epi-sode, Bloom descends to the kitchen and gives his cat a saucer of milk. Gilbert says of Bloom, "There is much of the *ewig weiblich* about the hero of *Ulysses*; he is no servile replica of his Homeric prototype, for he has a cat instead of a dog, and a daughter in-stead of a son" (p. 134). (This *Weiblichkeit*, as Ellmann notes (p. 477), is an integral part of Bloom's Jewishness.) Cats were rather mysterious animals for Joyce, as we see at "Ithaca" 15:27: "Cats at night, cries of suitors murdered."

Other tantalizing Homeric allusions in the "Ithaca" notesheets are these:

"Ithaca"

1:48	Laertes & Ul. only kings by marriage, Penelope right
9:100	Homer saw same stars
12:77–78	calculus = sacrifice = slaughter of wooers
12:81	family of curves (Pen) = slayer & slain
13:52	LB dislikes meet Ithacans

---

[8] *Odyssey*, pp. 289–290.

[9] *Ibid.*, pp. 284–285.

Joyce's cribbings from the *Odyssey* continue into "Penelope," where they are especially numerous on "Penelope" 2. A couple of interesting phrases Joyce found a use for are "Pen. upbraids impure servant" ("Penelope" 2:6; repeated at "Penelope" 7:47) and "Rather die than marry another" ("Penelope" 2:74). In the *Odyssey* it is Odysseus who upbraids Melantho, the mistress of Eurymachus, for her insolence (pp. 305–306). In *Ulysses* Molly is likewise "no servile replica" of Penelope, for with similar moral indignation she chastises a female servant on whom she suspects Bloom of having amorous designs (*U* 724). (The circumstantial evidence is Molly's discovery of a pair of sexy garters.) In addition, there is perhaps an autobiographical element here if, as Ellmann suggests (p. 48), Joyce's first sexual encounter was with the family slavey, though he could have had in mind George Moore's *Esther Waters* (1894) or simply the obvious catalysis which a young girl in service would have produced in a household such as the Blooms'.

There is also an ironic reversal in "Rather die than marry another" if we examine the parallels. The faithful Penelope says she would rather die than marry one of the suitors; this is a measure of her love for Odysseus, though she uses the promise of her hand to keep the suitors at bay. When Molly says it (*U* 729), it is a measure of her detestation of her husband and all his sex: "Id rather die 20 times over than marry another of their sex of course hed never find another woman like me to put up with him the way I do."

This brings us ultimately to the question of the purpose and effect of Joyce's use of mythological, historical, and literary parallels. As is strikingly obvious in the notesheets, Joyce made no attempt to limit these associations even when they became hopelessly obscure and private. Does this really serve to enrich and universalize his characters and subject matter, or does the significance of the parallels decrease as the metaphorical strata accumulate?

At this point one should make a careful distinction between the *function* of mythic and literary parallels in Joyce's creative process, together with their intended symbolic overtones, and their *effect*, or the extent to which the meaning of *Ulysses* is dependent upon them. We have seen that in terms of function they provide in some cases a convenient superstructure and in others the material for stylistic expansion. In still others they serve merely as an imaginative outlet or give comic relief from the drudgery of writing. This is the way *Ulysses* evolved from its nucleus. It made the evolution fun for Joyce, and attempts by critics to force the entire allusive context into the symbolic realm reveal their misunderstanding of its function in the creative process. Of course, Joyce invited such fertile speculation because he enjoyed mystifying his audience with the enigmatic, and he was under no obligation to reveal his method. In this way the total allusive context of *Ulysses* differs from the poetry of, say, Yeats or Eliot, where the strength and richness of the metaphorical level generally depends on its calculated effect on the ideal reader.

In *Ulysses* Joyce is his own ideal reader, and though he cared greatly what others thought of his work, he is his own best critic and most enthusiastic appreciator. A difficult problem emerges here, because in calling his novel *Ulysses* Joyce is beckoning the reader to follow him along mythic pathways; and when the initiate finds himself lost in a labyrinth, he often feels that Joyce is secretly smiling at him. In one sense, therefore, the title is a tease rather than an injunction to measure the circumference of an iceberg, for, though beckoned, the reader need not follow. The mythic superstructure has been effectively sublimated in *Ulysses* (which could hardly have succeeded as a novel if it had not been), the Homeric chapter headings have been struck out, and the average attentive reader is intended to enjoy the novel without map and guidebooks. If on subsequent readings the enthusiast with a taste for acrostics wishes to unveil the mythic level, he may puzzle it out as he pleases. Perhaps Joyce misjudged his audience. For him this body of allusion, after serving its functional purpose and adding joy to his creation, was no longer essential; on the surface of the novel it has to a great extent been refined out of existence. As the future author of *Finnegans Wake*, he was probably not terribly concerned about effect (as long as it produced admiration) or the precise pinpointing of symbols, allusions, or parallels.

This publication of the *Ulysses* notesheets constitutes a kind of invasion of privacy, a forbidden view revealing the secret manipulations of the on-stage magician, but it is hoped that it will lead to clarification of Joyce's method and intent rather than to ridicule of a practice we were never meant to see. Gilbert, writing ex cathedra, first drew attention to the extensive metaphorical detail, thus counteracting Joyce's sublimation and opening the door to endless speculation. Scholars everywhere have joined in the quest, and the worst of them have given to Joycean scholarship a reputation for unrestrained speculation that more informed scholars must counteract when inviting credulity. Limits must be set, not by the imagination, but by concrete evidence of Joyce's intent in a given passage of his work and of the allusive context, if any, which he envisioned. If this printing of the notesheets has merit, it will add impetus to an already noticeable movement back to Joyce's texts and their origins.

Scene	The House
Hour	After Midnight
Organ	Skeleton
Art	Science
Symbol	Comets
Technic	Catechism (impersonal)

Ithaca

THE "Ithaca" episode was the last chapter to be completed, and for Joyce it was one of the most difficult.[1] Although unique in that it was created from a mass of scientific data and molded into a catechetical form, Joyce's artistic technique here closely resembles that of several previous episodes in that he fed into his notesheets a great quantity of extraneous information which was then distilled through his creative imagination to form another highly idiosyncratic tour de force. As in "Nausicaa," the style is parodic, the target this time being post-Darwinian scientific method, but here the complexities were far greater because he was not merely parodying style and sentiment, where source books and imagination would suffice, but the ideas, methods, and vocabularies of several academic subjects which he only vaguely understood. He could not just parody; he had to go back and study basic handbooks so that he could recreate theory and terminology with some measure of verisimilitude.

Once he felt comfortable in this new milieu, he could exaggerate and parody in his characteristic ways. We see the results in the answers to catechetical questions in "Ithaca," which sound as though they come out "of a computer which has not been programmed to distinguish between what is important and what is not," as Clive Hart says.[2] The scientist as computer as robot (insofar as a caricature may be inferred) is thus perhaps intended to remind us of another monster, the Cyclops, whose vision is similarly limited and whose position with regard to humanitarian principles is

---

[1] Joyce interrupted "Ithaca" to write "Penelope." See *Letters*, I, 172–173. Additional information on the "Ithaca" notesheets may be found in Madtes's dissertation and in his article "Joyce and the Building of 'Ithaca.'" I am much indebted to Professor Madtes for reading my transcription of the "Ithaca" notesheets and for making numerous helpful corrections and suggestions.

[2] *James Joyce's* Ulysses (Sydney, 1968), p. 74.

58

equally estranged. Or, to shift the legs of our compass slightly, by coupling catechetical style and scientific principles, Joyce may be reminding us of the post-Darwinian conflict between religion and science, both of which rather awkwardly straddle the circumference of humanitarian interests. If there is a satirical thrust to the episode, it is in this direction.

If one considers for a moment the movement of *Ulysses* in a historical context, it becomes apparent that science is so appropriate a subject for the penultimate chapter that one is tempted to impose a historical schema on the entire novel. It works only for the beginning and ending, however. We begin in the round tower of Ireland's past, proceed through the medieval period of superstition and witchcraft ("Circe"), see the rise of commercial interests and scientism ("Eumaeus"; "Ithaca"), and are finally engulfed in the stream of consciousness of a Jungian archetype. *Finnegans Wake*, where all the "floors of memory" are dissolved, was but the inevitable extension of this process. Seen in this rather McLuhanesque context, the turgid scientism of "Ithaca" is the appropriate herald of its own negation, an age of psychic (and psychedelic) exploration in which time, space, and the physical laws governing them are meaningless. In *Ulysses* Joyce had no such scheme in mind, of course, though in *Finnegans Wake* (as McLuhan would agree) he seems to be moving closer to historical prophecy.

As seen in his notes on embryology for "Oxen," Joyce was navigating in unfamiliar waters when the subject was science. His approach therefore required a considerable amount of cribbing from handbooks on mathematics, astronomy, and physical geography. In the "Ithaca" notesheets one finds algebraic equations, calculations for interest on loans, geometric doodling, curious statistics, ciphers, and above all lists of impressive scientific words. Although almost none of these are above the high-school level, many of them are calculated to amuse and confound. As with the notes on embryology, Joyce's mind is continually drawn to the curious and exotic; and where distortion is not inherent in the material, he exaggerates for comic effect. When Joyce exaggerates here, it is usually in one of two ways: either he produces ludicrous results by a *reductio ad absurdum* of scientific method or he parodies scientific prose by the exaggerated use of jargon. The result in both cases is monstrous, but absurdly humorous. (*Absurd* is one of the most prominent words in the "Ithaca" notesheets.)

Many of Joyce's experiments fall into a category Madtes calls "mathematical doodling." He tries several experiments with numbers, and one of his major interests is infinity. In the four examples below I have converted symbols into words for greater clarity.

"Ithaca"

8:62	circle = infinity of isosceles triangles
8:67	$1 = \frac{1}{2} + \frac{1}{4} + \frac{1}{8} + \frac{1}{16}$ —— infinity
9:96	infinity = escape from hypothesis
9:97	zero produces infinity

Other examples of mathematical doodling are these:

"Ithaca"

5:8	every power of 9 = 9
5:9	abc = bac = cab
5:12	JC = $\sqrt[3]{God}$
5:17	ax^3 = 4 dimensions
5:24	x = 10 A.D. –3x = 30 BC
11:30	9th. power of 9th. power of 9 [*U* 684]
16:18	square ○ [*U* 684, 703]
16:24	$\frac{0}{0}$ = indeterminate [*U* 686?]

In an example cited by Madtes, "Ithaca" 1:1–4, the joke is on Joyce. (He did not use italics for the second *H*.)[3]

ABCDEFGHIJK*H*LMNOPQRSTUVWXYZ
YXWVUTSRQPONMLKJIHGFEDCBA

Madtes says:

The story is clear. Joyce was transposing the alphabet to work out Bloom's "reversed alphabetic" cipher concealing Martha Clifford's name and address (the same notesheet contains the entry, "LB etwas in cipher"). Working quickly, he set down the alphabet in regular order, but failed to see that he had included an extra "H." [P. 50]

When Joyce had assimilated the jargon lists and refreshed his memory with mathematical problem solving, he was ready to turn his attention to the expansion of plot. There are numerous "plot indicators," as Madtes calls them, which served to re-

---

[3] Other examples of Joyce's slips include spelling errors, which can provide an editor with more headaches than chuckles. Much has been said of Joyce's facility with languages, but in spite of this (or because of it) he makes errors in spelling which are sometimes surprising. It is difficult to believe an Irishman could misspell *Tipperary*, but at "Cyclops" 2:62 Joyce does. In the "Ithaca" notesheets he consistently misspells *isosceles*. At "Ithaca" 7:65 is "acqueduct," and on line 152 of the same page he has "acquacity." Joyce apparently confused these words with the Italian *acqua* and *acquadotto*. At "Ithaca" 10:64 is "Nurves transmit pain 28 m per sec." With editors the transmission sometimes seems a bit more rapid.

mind Joyce of previously envisioned ideas for thematic development. With all this at the tips of his fingers, he was ready to produce such typically "Ithacan" linguistic monstrosities as the one which emanated from "Ithaca" 13:110: "See star by day from bottom of gully." In the text this is prompted, as usual, by a question.

With what meditations did Bloom accompany his demonstration to his companion of various constellations?

Meditations of evolution increasingly vaster: of the moon invisible in incipient lunation, approaching perigee: of the infinite lattiginous scintillating uncondensed milky way, discernible by daylight by an observer placed at the lower end of a cylindrical shaft 5000 ft deep sunk from the surface towards the centre of the earth. [U 683]

This passage illustrates several characteristics of Joyce's creative process and his mind. The language of science fascinates him, and he responds more dynamically to auditory and linguistic phenomena than to, say, theoretical and structural ones. Here he has left the original idea basically intact; yet the language has become quite stilted and the astronomical problem is absurdly magnified. A simple idea in simple form has thus been made grotesque. However, quite a number of ideas in the "Ithaca" notesheets are humorous or curious enough to require only the appropriate catechetical setting, ideas which show how inventive Joyce could be while rummaging through material as abstract as that to be found in a technical handbook.

"Ithaca"

1:63–64	Tooth & Mouth Starlings feed on worms dislodged by feet of cattle.
3:10	gynecocracy coming
4:77	35,000 birds killed for ladies' hats
4:81	Earth knows which side her bread is buttered.
5:80	Woman fucked: cries fill space
6:13	all point— S[outh]— Jutland
6:19	to what S of Eq[uator] corresponds Dublin?
6:82	Woman's arse honest
7:136–137	boiling water in Quito will not cook potatoes
11:8	1 rook in 1 yr eats 52 lbs
12:28	lunatics work by mathematics
13:48	men less longlived after flood (damp = death) [U 663]
13:67	wipe mouth & arse paper, 1st. dirtier.
14:71	Fear base of life
15:61	If Earth got drunk!

15:99	LB when elderly son & old mother fight looked at sky [LB evidently expected an eclipse.]
16:25	milky way points to our lady of Walsingham, holy land,
16:42	papering a trench[4]
16:122	reduce $\dfrac{SD}{LB}$

In the "Cyclops" chapter it was mentioned that Joyce made copious notes of a number of parallels between Irishman and Jew and that he also collected anti-Semitic slogans as ammunition for the "Citizen." The "Ithaca" notesheets also contain references to Jews, but these are of a different sort. The subject has risen to prominence again for several reasons. After "Eumaeus," Bloom and Stephen are probably more acutely aware of their racial differences than their other dissimilarities. This is especially true of Bloom, who is envious of Stephen (see "Ithaca" 1:49—"SD what LB like to be"), defensive about his Jewishness, and overly solicitous in his hospitality. Stephen's attitude is reflected in his slight feeling of revulsion when he and Bloom become linked in "Eumaeus." (Note the intentional ambiguity in this passage.)

> — It will (the air) do you good, Bloom said, meaning also the walk, in a moment. The only thing is to walk then you'll feel a different man. It's not far. Lean on me.
> Accordingly he passed his left arm in Stephen's right and led him on accordingly.
> — Yes, Stephen said uncertainly, because he thought he felt a strange kind of flesh of a different man approach him, sinewless and wobbly and all that. [*U* 644]

In the *Odyssey* the hero's arrival in Ithaca climaxes ten years of wandering and frustration following his departure from Troy.[5] The role of the returning exile becomes threefold in Joyce's version, as seen in "Ithaca" 10:73: "comet wandering jew." The idea of equating Bloom with the Wandering Jew will occur readily to most readers who are aware that Joyce's Odysseus is a Jew, even if they have never heard of Bérard. Joyce evokes this identification through Bloom's preoccupation with the Agendath Netaim land scheme, advertised in a prospectus in the butcher's shop in "Calypso" (*U* 60). It is a promised land full of melon fields and orange groves, and it beckons the afflicted wanderer to the racial homeland. In "Ithaca" the distances he must travel are magnified to stellar proportions, for here the Wandering Jew becomes a comet, the primary symbol of the episode.

---

[4] See David Hayman's review of Scholes and Kain's *Workshop of Daedalus* in *James Joyce Quarterly*, III (Fall 1965), p. 88.

[5] Robert Graves, *Greek Myths*, 2 vols. (Baltimore, 1955), II, 354.

Would the departed never nowhere nohow reappear?

Ever he would wander, selfcompelled, to the extreme limit of his cometary orbit, beyond the fixed stars and variable suns and telescopic planets, astronomical waifs and strays, to the extreme boundary of space, passing from land to land, among peoples, amid events. Somewhere imperceptibly he would hear and somehow reluctantly, suncompelled, obey the summons of recall. Whence, disappearing from the constellation of the Northern Crown he would somehow reappear reborn above delta in the constellation of Cassiopeia and after incalculable eons of peregrination return an estranged avenger, a wreaker of justice on malefactors, a dark crusader, a sleeper awakened, with financial resources (by supposition) surpassing those of Rothschild or of the silver king. [*U* 712]

Although Odysseus reaches his promised land and slays Penelope's suitors, he is fated to "fare to many cities of men, carrying a shapen oar in [his] hands, till [he] should come to such men as know not the sea."[6] But for Leopold Bloom the victory is his attainment of equanimity, and the promised land is the fleshy posterior of his overripe Penelope ("Ithaca" 11:29: "her rump = promised land"). In celebration of his arrival at Agendath Netaim he kisses "the plump mellow yellow smellow melons of her rump" in true pilgrim fashion and feels

satisfaction at the ubiquity in eastern and western terrestrial hemispheres, in all habitable lands and islands explored or unexplored (the land of the midnight sun, the islands of the blessed, the isles of Greece, the land of promise) of adipose posterior female hemispheres, redolent of milk and honey. [*U* 719]

---

[6] *Odyssey*, p. 384.

Scene	The Bed
Hour	. . .
Organ	Flesh
Art	. . .
Symbol	Earth
Technic	Monologue (female)

Penelope

AT FIRST glance one is struck with the obvious irony of Joyce's using Penelope as one of the models for Molly Bloom.[1] Penelope is a paragon of wifely fidelity; Molly seems to have an insatiable appetite for adultery. The irony takes a peculiar turn, however. A look at post-Homeric commentary on the Ulysses myth will show that Joyce had abundant precedent for the portrayal of a wanton Penelope. Graves says:

Some deny that Penelope remained faithful to Odysseus. They accuse her of companying with Amphinomus of Dulichium, or with all the suitors in turn, and say that the fruit of this union was the monstrous god Pan—at sight of whom Odysseus fled for shame to Aetolia, after sending Penelope away in disgrace to her father Icarius at Mantinea, where her tomb is still shown. [II, 373–374]

The theory that Joyce was using this post-Homeric variant is not a new one,[2] but it would perhaps be useful to examine specific accounts of Penelope's infidelity.

Herodotus says that "Pan the son of Penelope (for according to the Greeks Penelope and Hermes were the parents of Pan) was about eight hundred years before me, and thus of a later date than the Trojan war."[3] Cicero mentions a number of variant theories as to the origin of Mercury (Hermes): "A third, of whom, and of

---

[1] A portion of the following chapter appeared in slightly altered form in "The Bedsteadfastness of Molly Bloom," *Modern Fiction Studies*, XV (Spring 1969), 49–61, © 1969 by Purdue Research Foundation, Lafayette, Indiana. For additional information on the "Penelope" notesheets, see Card's dissertation and his "A Gibralter Sourcebook for 'Penelope,' " *James Joyce Quarterly*, VIII (Winter 1971), 163–175.

[2] See Gilbert, p. 395, and Stanford, p. 217.

[3] *Herodotus*, trans. A. D. Godley (London and New York, 1921), i.453.

Penelope, Pan was the offspring, is the son of the third Jupiter and Maia."[4] Pausanias gives a more detailed account:

[By] a sanctuary of Artemis . . . is a high mound of earth. It is said to be the grave of Penelope, but the account of her in the poem called *Thesprotis* is not in agreement with this saying. For in it the poet says that when Odysseus returned from Troy he had a son Ptoliporthes by Penelope. But the Mantinean story about Penelope says that Odysseus convicted her of bringing paramours to his home, and being cast out by him she went away at first to Lacedaemon, but afterwards she removed from Sparta to Mantineia, where she died.[5]

Another commentator, much discussed as an influence on *Finnegans Wake*, is Giambattista Vico, who in *La scienza nuova* says:

In other versions Penelope prostitutes herself to the suitors (signifying the extension of *connubium* to the plebs) and gives birth to Pan, a monster of two discordant natures, human and bestial. This is precisely the creature *secum ipse discors* of Livy, for the Roman patricians told the plebeians that, if they were to share with them the *connubium* of the nobles, the resulting offspring would be like Pan, a monster of two discordant natures brought forth by Penelope who had prostituted herself to the plebeians.[6]

But Joyce did not have to search through Pausanias, Vico, or Herodotus to learn variants to the story of Penelope: he merely went down to the Zurich library (the Zentralbibliothek), probably in the spring of 1918, and found all he needed in Roscher's enormous *Lexikon der griechischen und römischen Mythologie*.[7] The notations he made can be found in notebook VIII.A.5 at Buffalo (p. 299):

Pen = Freier / banished by U to Sparta[8] ["von Odysseus verbannt, gelangt nach Sparta . . ." (Roscher, III, 1909).]

Pan   Antinous ["Von einem Umgang Penelopes mit Antinoos, ihrer Heimsendung zum Vater Ikarios und ihrem Aufenthalt in Mantineia, wo sie von Hermes den Pan gebiert" (*ibid.*).]

---

[4] "On the Nature of the Gods," in *The Treatises of M. T. Cicero*, trans. C. D. Yonge (London, 1892), p. 125.

[5] *Description of Greece*, trans. W. H. S. Jones (London and New York, 1918), III, 407.

[6] *The New Science*, trans. T. G. Bergin and M. H. Fisch (Ithaca, N.Y., 1948), par. 654.

[7] For further evidence of Joyce's interest in Homeric scholarship, see notebook VIII.A.5 at Buffalo and Connolly's *Personal Library of James Joyce*, items 22, 40, 47, 178, and 310.

[8] Cf. "Eumaeus" 5:9—"Pen & Freier=Pan (monster) banished."

Pen = Amphinomos killed by U ["nach anderen sei Penelope wegen Ehebruchs mit Amphinomos von Odysseus getötet worden . . ." (*ibid.*).]

LB what kind of child can much fucked whore have [cf. "Die höchst phantastische Anekdote, Penelope habe sich mit allen Freiern eingelassen und den bocksfüssigen Pan geboren, berichtet schon Duris von Samos" (*ibid.*). Above this Joyce noted "Duris v. Samos."]

Pen = Apollo, Pan ["es sei Pan aus einem Liebesverhältnis zwischen ihr und Apollon hervorgegangen . . ." (*ibid.*, p. 1910).]

Priapea   Pen (vetula) sits smutty talking amg the Freier ["Aber auch in einem der Priapea betitelten Gedichte ergeht sie sich, obwohl schon bejahrt (*vetula*), unter den Freiern in schmutzigen Reden, wie sie nur einer Buhlerin zukommen" (*ibid.*).]

Butler's *Authoress of the* Odyssey, which Joyce almost surely read, also takes a critical view of Penelope. Chapter Five of this work is entitled "On the Question Whether or No Penelope Is Being Whitewashed." The following list containing the essential points in Butler's case against her would have fascinated Joyce.[9]

1. Why would one hundred young men all at once fall hopelessly in love with a forty-year-old woman and decide not to cease their courting until she chooses one of them?

2. Why does Penelope not lock them out when they go home for the night and refuse to let them in again? They never sleep there.

3. Why does Penelope not dismiss her wanton female servants?

4. Why is there never a breath of scandal concerning her?

5. Why do the suitors never quarrel among themselves?

6. Ardent lovers are not spongers.

7. Penelope obviously has courage, for she upbraids them at times; why doesn't she tell them to leave her alone?

8. She never snubs them, bores them, sends them on silly errands, or forces them to go to family worship services.

9. Laertes went to the country because he could not bear to witness the wantonness in the house of his son.

10. Telemachus says his mother will neither choose nor state decisively that she will not marry.

[9] It was probably Joyce who told Gilbert about Butler's book (cf. *James Joyce's* Ulysses, pp. 395–397). The list is my outline of Butler's chapter.

For these reasons Butler argued that the handling of Penelope's character in the *Odyssey* was strong evidence that the author was a woman. A man, he says, would have taken delight in describing the orgies which must have taken place.

There is, indeed, some basis in the *Odyssey* for this suspicion of Penelope. Although there is no evidence that Odysseus suffers from a "deep wound of doubt," as does Richard Rowan in *Exiles*,[10] he can never know for sure whether she has remained faithful during his long absence. If Penelope had been a goddess, her promiscuity would seem natural; likewise if she had been a male, either human or divine. Her husband does not hesitate to sleep with Calypso or Circe, though decorum perhaps requires that he rise to the occasion. But Odysseus seems to have a dual standard of morality, since he is indignant at the wantonness of Penelope's female servants.[11] Taking example, perhaps, from Penelope's reluctance to make up her mind, they have shown the noble suitors the hospitality of their beds.

Then there is the cunning of Penelope, which makes her a worthy match for the wily Odysseus. She will neither promise to remarry nor accept widowhood; she weaves a shroud for her father-in-law, Laertes, and unravels it at night in order to stall for time. She teases the suitors with her beauty and attempts to extort presents in order to recover some of the financial losses their lengthy banquet has caused. If she can fool 108 suitors for three years, she is capable of deceiving her husband. Agamemnon, having been murdered by his wife, warns Odysseus in Hades that women are no longer to be trusted.[12]

The composite portrait of Penelope that comes down to us is a tantalizingly ambiguous one, and for Joyce this ambiguity was the essence of *Weiblichkeit*. It is also Penelope's most important bequest to Molly Bloom. Unlike Penelope, however, the principal problem with respect to Molly's infidelity is that of separating her imaginary lovers from her real ones (*U* 716). She is more complex than her classic ancestor and fickle in many more ways. Her most salient characteristic is her sexuality; yet she is at once repulsed, amused, and attracted by her lover Blazes Boylan. Her husband affects her in a like manner. At "Penelope" 3:5 Joyce wrote, "MB jealous of men, hates women" [comma mine]. In *Ulysses* Molly says of men: "Id rather die 20 times

---

[10] 1918; rpt. New York, 1961, p. 112. In subsequent adaptations of the *Odyssey* Odysseus is such a tormented man. See Dougald McMillan, "Influence of Gerhardt [*sic*] Hauptmann in Joyce's *Ulysses*," *James Joyce Quarterly*, IV (Winter 1967), 116, for an account of Hauptmann's "Der Bogen des Odysseus" (1914), in which Penelope is portrayed as wanton.

[11] *Odyssey*, p. 330.

[12] *Ibid.*, p. 186.

over than marry another of their sex of course hed never find another woman like me" (*U* 729). Women are likewise irritating: "no wonder they treat us the way they do we are a dreadful lot of bitches" (*U* 764). This essential ambiguity, like the circular imagery in the episode, contributes to the universality of Molly as the female principle in *Ulysses*.

Other notesheet references to Molly and her Homeric predecessor enable us to see some of the ramifications of Joyce's concept of *das Ewig-Weibliche*. They are a mixed batch of notes. Those which pertain to Molly are not necessarily applicable to Penelope (and vice versa), and a couple are relevant only by implication, but each contributes to the composite view something that is typically Joycean.

"Cyclops"
  2:76   Penelope—?her body possessed
  8:57   Exaggeration (Rhet. SD's lies, Molly's romancing)
10:63   scrivened (Penelope)
"Nausicaa"
  6:81   Molly lustful only when well dressed.
"Circe"
  1:86   son of a whore (Pan)
"Eumaeus"
  4:18   Pen brother & father advise her
  4:112 108 MP's=suitors [Cf. "Ithaca" 8:34, below]
  5:9   Pen & Freier=Pan (monster) banished
  6:245 Pen shillyshally
"Ithaca"
  1:39   Put Molly in dairy—what to do with our wives
  1:42   All MB's judgments wrong if W or R., S. And of LB?
  1:48   Laertes & Ul. only kings by marriage, Penelope right
  2:26   MB believed alias was somebody in the scriptures
  8:34   Victoria=Penelope
12:81   family of curves (Pen)=slayer & slain
14:12   LB resembles MB
"Penelope"
  1:30   1st. passion loves lover   after loves love
  2:9   her cunt, darkest Africa
  3:52   MB peneloped before marriage   Ul. overcirces her
  4:25   MB decants LB
  4:26   odyss of Pen

4:65 female spider devours male after

4:71 Pen—stupid

4:72 Pen—genitophilia

4:92 incestuous MB

7:41 MB=spinning Earth [Cf. *Letters*, I, 169–170]

Not content with anchoring Molly to the post-Homeric tradition of the unfaithful Penelope, Joyce also found it necessary to authenticate her background by reading histories and guidebooks of Gibraltar. Adams (pp. 231–233) discusses Joyce's use of several issues of the *Gibraltar Directory and Guidebook*, an annual publication similar to *Thom's Directory* (Joyce used this for the Dublin milieu) which yielded him interesting facts on the history, places of interest, and the inhabitants of Gibraltar. Evidence of Joyce's use of at least three or four additional source books is scattered through his notes.

At this time my investigation of Joyce's use of source books on Gibraltar in *Ulysses* notebook V.A.2 at Buffalo is incomplete, but I can summarize the more salient points. Whether or not Adams consulted notebook V.A.2, the evidence he uncovered on Joyce's use of the *Gibraltar Directory* in *Ulysses* was mostly filtered through this notebook. Such references as those to "Café Universal" and "Alfonso XIII b. 17/5/86" and to such common Gibraltarian surnames as "Abrines" and "Opisso" (*U* 764) could have come from any of a number of issues of the *Gibraltar Directory*, but the one for 1902 is specifically mentioned in notebook V.A.2: "Boyle Gibr. / Br. Emp. Serv –02." Cavendish Boyle was editor at the time.

The *Gibraltar Directory* and two other books on Gibraltar are noted on page 1 of notebook V.A.2, and other titles appear on pages 6 and 29. With one possible exception (Drinkwater: see below), there is evidence that Joyce consulted them. An influential work not mentioned in notebook V.A.2 is *Gibraltar and Its Sieges*, of uncertain authorship, published by Thomas Nelson and Sons.[13] On the first page of notebook V.A.2 is "undersea passa[ge] of Af. apes," which becomes in Molly's words

---

[13] In a letter of August 16, 1921 (*Letters*, I, 169–170), Joyce asked Budgen to send him two books: *Sieges of Gibraltar* and Arthur Conan Doyle's *History of [the] South African War*. Joyce had both titles wrong. Since he specifically mentions the Nelson edition, the first should be *Gibraltar and Its Sieges* (London, 1879). Reissues appeared in 1884, 1900 and 1911 (with different plates), but I find no author listed. The second book is probably Doyle's *The Great Boer War* (London, 1900). Doyle was a graduate of Clongowes Wood. On an "Ithaca" page of notebook V.A.2 Joyce listed yet another book on Gibraltar: "Drinkwater Hist of Siege," which is John Drinkwater's *History of the Siege of Gibraltar* (1785; later ed., London, 1844). As yet I cannot say with certainty whether or not Joyce used Doyle or Drinkwater.

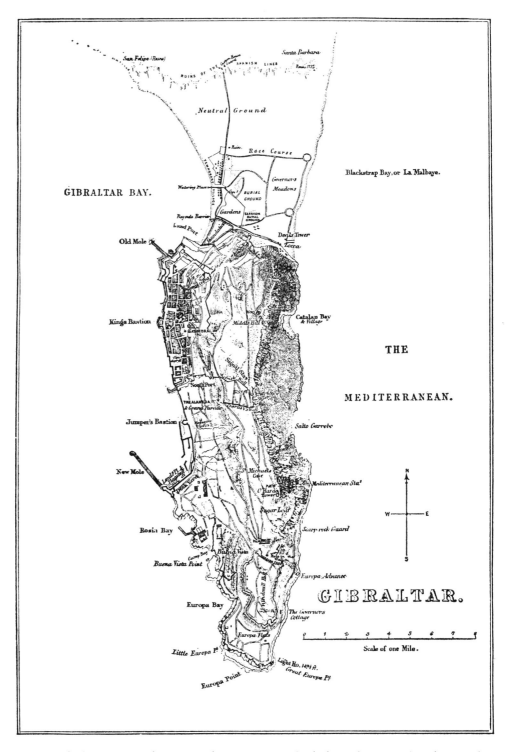

Map of Gibraltar. From Frederic G. Stephens, *A History of Gibraltar and Its Sieges* (London, 1870)

70

"the monkeys go under the sea to Africa when they die" (*U* 745). In the Nelson edition it is as follows:

The actual extent of the subterranean passages has never been ascertained, and exaggeration and popular fancy find in it a fertile subject; the vulgar believing that it is the mouth of a communication beneath the Strait with Mount Abyla, and that by this sub-oceanic passage the apes upon the Rock found their way from Africa. [P. 35]

Each author has a spelling error in one phrase. In *Gibraltar and Its Sieges* (p. 132) it is "los di*a*ntes de la vieja" and on page 5 of the notebook "los dientes de la vie*i*a." Perhaps more persuasive an example than the other two is an item on page 2 of the notebook: "S Michael's cave stalactites, rain percolates floor muddy, lower cave reached by ladders, jews' burial ground" (cf. *U* 745). The anonymous writer describes the cave in these words:

The roof is encrusted with pendent stalactites, and supported by stalactitic pillars. . . . In the deepest recesses, a still pool of water, formed by the constant percolation through the rocky vault, vividly reflects the fantastic objects above and around it. [P. 138]

As Card has demonstrated in his recent article on the "Penelope" episode, Joyce made extensive use of a third source book, Henry M. Field's *Gibraltar*.[14] Field was a rather pompous American doctor who, in 1888, published an account of his visit to Gibraltar and the hospitality of the British defenders there. His dedication sets the tone of the book: "To My Friend and Neighbor in the Berkshire Hills, Joseph H. Choate, who finds it a relief now and then to turn from the hard labors of the law to the romance of travel: I send as a Christmas present a story of fortress and siege that may beguile a vacant hour as he sits before his winter evening fire."

Most of one "Penelope" sheet of notebook V.A.2 (p. 2) was copied from Field. Here is an excerpt:

Royal hotel, Waterport, De Saŭty, manager G. Tel. Co, sir James Anderson com. Great Eastern '66, in all creation, 1 Am in G consul, Horatio J Sprague . . .

Field stayed at the Royal Hotel on Waterport Street. He met De Sauty, the manager of the Gibraltar Telephone Company—"He has a hearty grip, which speaks for the true Englishman that he is" (p. 6). An old friend of Field's was Sir James Anderson, who had commanded the *Great Eastern*, a ship which laid the transatlantic cable in 1866. Anderson was now manager of the Eastern Telegraph Company. He had given Field a license by which he could send telegrams at no cost whenever he liked:

14 New York, 1888. Card, "Gibraltar Sourcebook."

71

"It contained a sort of general direction to make myself at home in all creation!" (p. 6; cf. *U* 756:32–33). Horatio J. Sprague was the American consul, and as the only American on Gibraltar gave Field a "hearty welcome." There is more evidence of Joyce's cribbing from Field, but the foregoing should be enough to establish beyond a doubt that Joyce used the book.

In the British Museum notesheets, "Penelope" 6 is derived almost entirely from Field's *Gibraltar*. The reader can easily gauge the amount of material from Field that eventually went into the novel by comparing the list of Field page references at the beginning of the notes to "Penelope" 6 with the *Ulysses* references given on the notesheet. It is also interesting to see that Joyce did not go through Field's book from first to last but apparently skipped around at his leisure.

Another book, one which Card did not discover, is given on page 6 of notebook V.A.2 as the "O'Shea guidebook." This is Henry G. O'Shea's *Guide to Spain and Portugal*.[15] Two lines below the title Joyce noted "10,000 jews burned alive in Pamplona"; on page 249 of O'Shea's *Guide*, in reference to the coronations of the kings of Navarre at Pamplona, is: "To complete the festivities, and offer a novel spectacle pleasant to the princes, no less than 10,000 Jews, it is said, were assembled and burnt alive in the square."

Finally, Joyce appears to have looked into Frederic G. Stephens, *A History of Gibraltar and Its Sieges*, the authorship of which he mistakenly attributes to the photographer J. H. Mann on the first page of notebook V.A.2.[16] On page 1 of Stephens is "*Mare Tenebrosum*," which also appears in the notesheets at "Ithaca" 3:65.

Joyce's research on the subject of Gibraltar reveals nothing about his art that has not already become obvious. To explore the backgrounds of *Ulysses* is to be impressed with Joyce's consistent dedication to factual authenticity,[17] even where the labor is obviously great and the reward no more than a few apparently trivial references in his text. It is almost as if Joyce subscribed to an aesthetic tenet allowing him unlimited freedom in creating amalgamations of character and plot out of authentic people and events while restricting the incorporation of details where only a microscope could prove fraudulence. It seems odd to suggest that Joyce feared such a charge. Perhaps it is only that he could not settle for anything less than a demonstrably accurate Hogarthian portrait of Dublin in 1904. If Joyce had an ulterior motive, and

---

[15] 1865; rev. ed., Edinburgh and London, 1869.

[16] 1870; 2d ed., London, 1873.

[17] Except, of course, in instances where he introduces obvious errors, whether inadvertently or not. See Adams, *passim*, especially the section entitled "Bloom's Bloopers" (pp. 168–174).

there is no reason why high artistic standards should preclude one, then he may have been consciously preparing to defend his controversial novel against critics who might judge it to be a degrading and inaccurate picture of Dublin life. It is possible that he remembered the famous attacks of Arthur Griffith on John Synge's *In the Shadow of the Glen*[18] and wished to anticipate similar objections to authenticity from the Irish nationalist quarter.

So concerned with minute details was Joyce that he wrote to his Aunt Josephine on November 2, 1921, to ask:

Is it possible for an ordinary person to climb over the area railings of no 7 Eccles street, either from the path or the steps, lower himself from the lowest part of the railings till his feet are within 2 feet or 3 of the ground and drop unhurt. . . . I require this information in detail in order to determine the wording of a paragraph.[19] [Cf. *U* 652]

Yet Joyce could, when he found it expedient, bend historical facts to suit his purpose, as Adams (p. 233) points out with regard to the unlikelihood of Molly's remembering the 1877 visit of Ulysses S. Grant to Gibraltar when she was only seven (*U* 742).[20] Joyce had a realistic grasp of priorities, however, and minor inconsistencies could be tolerated when the historical occasion was as momentous as the meeting of a Ulysses and a Penelope on the Rock of Gibraltar.

---

[18] See David H. Greene and Edward M. Stephens, *J. M. Synge: 1871–1909* (1959; rpt. New York, 1961), pp. 153–155.

[19] *Letters*, I, 175.

[20] But see also Weldon Thornton, *Allusions in* Ulysses (Chapel Hill, N.C., 1968), p. 492.

III   The *Ulysses* Notesheets

Editorial Note

IN THE arrangement of the format for the printing of the *Ulysses* notesheets my primary aim has been simplicity and accuracy. This means, however, that I have had to choose between faithful adherence to Joyce in all matters of reproduction and spacing and the ease and convenience of the reader. My loyalties, when loyalties conflicted, have been squarely with the reader.

There were several alternatives to the format I have chosen, but for various reasons they have proved to be impractical. One possibility would have been an enlarged photographic reproduction of the manuscript, but the average reader would have found it frequently both illegible and incomprehensible. Another possibility would have been the reproduction of each notesheet in type, following the original in placement of lines and spacing and preceded by an acetate leaf giving the colors of deletion and page and line numbers in *Ulysses*. Textual purists would have their page, and those using the edition as a research tool would have pertinent information for each entry on the overlay. Either method, unfortunately, would have been extremely expensive and voluminous. A third possibility would have been to relegate to notes all page references and color indicators, but this would have meant thousands of additional notes to plague the reader. My system, like those of Hayman and Connolly in their printings of Joyce manuscripts, imposes a standardized arrangement on the page transcribed. Although it is the most sensible one I could devise, it may take some adjustment on the reader's part.

Each notesheet is unique in appearance, but Joyce's note-taking process is much the same on every page. He would start at the top left (hardly surprising) and continue on down the page. If the entries were brief phrases or words, he found extra room at the right and would start a new column on that side. If the entries were long, he filled in the available space at the right and then continued on to the margins, frequently writing in every space, even if it meant making notes upside down or vertically on the page. In presenting the various sections of each notesheet, I move from left to right across the page. The reader must beware of assuming that entries in the left margin, for example, were the first notations Joyce made on a notesheet merely because they appear first here. The left margin was nearly always among the last areas to be filled in, and there is seldom a thematic connection between it and, say, the first phrases in the section entitled "left column horizontal."

ANGLE PARENTHESES, preceded by COLOR INDICATORS (*B*=blue, *R*= red, *G*=green, *S*=slate), contain the portion of a phrase Joyce marked out by a coloring pencil. One cannot always assume that because only a portion is deleted Joyce meant to delete it all. This is true only part of the time. On other occasions he used two colors to delete a phrase, which indicates that one part was harvested later than the other (see "Cyclops" 10:29, "Circe" 1:106–107, "Ithaca" 1:16, and "Penelope" 5:40). Letters, words, and phrases that Joyce scratched out in order to correct or revise his wording are reproduced with a solidus through each letter (see, for example, "Cyclops" 5:36). PARENTHESES are Joyce's own.

PAGE REFERENCES are to the 1934 Random House edition of *Ulysses*. See page 14, note 2, for the reasons I have preferred this edition. A conversion table for the three editions most widely used appears in Appendix D. Where deleted phrases are not followed by references, either they did not make the final text or I have been unable to locate them. When Joyce used a word or phrase many times, references are usually restricted to the episode with which the notesheet is concerned.

QUESTION MARKS preceding a word indicate doubtful readings or guesses. Those which follow are Joyce's except, of course, in page references. Unless otherwise noted, ELLIPSES indicate the omission of an illegible word, and usually its length. Run-together words and phrases are separated when confusion could otherwise occur.

SPELLING AND PUNCTUATION: Joyce seldom capitalized titles or such things as the *s* in *street* and the *r* in *road* in an address. He often used colons or dashes, sometimes in an unconventional manner, to indicate relationships or ideas in series. At times he made spelling errors and was guilty of inconsistencies, but these notes were, of course, for his own private use.

CROSS REFERENCING is nearly an endless task in a manuscript of this size, but I have pointed out in the notes most of the instances of duplication in the notesheets and related manuscripts.

MARGINAL LINE NUMBERS aid in the location of entries on a notesheet. When "Circe" 5:87 is mentioned in an introductory chapter, for example, the reader can turn to "Circe" notesheet 5, line 87, and consider the item, the context and notes (when there are any), and usually (if the item was deleted) the page reference to the text.

Notesheet enumeration begins anew with each episode. Joyce generally identified the episode to which each notesheet belonged by an initial (C=Circe) or an abbreviation (Pen=Penelope), or he wrote the full name in the upper left-hand corner. Beyond this there is no inherent sequential order to the notesheets, and the one I have imposed on the collection is in some ways arbitrary. Where a large double notesheet has been folded, it is possible to establish the sequence of as many as four sides, but there is no visible order of precedence for sheets separated from each other unless they were literally torn apart at the crease. Litz had previously set up sequences for "Oxen," "Circe," and "Ithaca," and these have been kept intact for those episodes.

There is an ambiguity in my use of the term *notesheet* of which the reader should be aware. In the British Museum collection each individual sheet is called a notesheet. For this printing I have given a separate number to each side of a notesheet rather than to the sheet as a whole. Thus here "Circe" notesheets 1 through 4 are the four sides of a single sheet of folded foolscap paper.

Abbreviations: The following initials were frequently used by Joyce in the notesheets:

LB—Leopold Bloom

SD—Stephen Dedalus

MB—Molly Bloom (never Milly)

BB—Blazes Boylan

RB—Rudolph Bloom (never Rudy)

CSP—Charles Stewart Parnell

JHP—John Howard Parnell

CK—Corny Kelleher

Ul—Ulysses (Homer's)

PsUl—Pseudangelos (Ulysses in disguise)

Pen—Penelope

SiD—Simon Dedalus

PD—Paddy Dignam

ABS—Able Bodied Seaman (W. B. Murphy in "Eumaeus")

BM—Buck Mulligan

WS—William Shakespeare

DMP—Dublin Municipal Police

Other initials are identified in the notes.

Annotations: Thornton's *Allusions in* Ulysses is a valuable companion to the notesheets and makes unnecessary extensive identification of names. Most of the notes are therefore of a textual or interpretive nature.

"Cyclops" 1

CENTER COLUMN HORIZONTAL

All rules ought ?v Nature
B ⟨?why not ?leave between nos in ?same street⟩
B ⟨Intellectuals debtors of society⟩
B ⟨Dead govern living.⟩ *Cf. 89:19, 299:25*
5   Fear of morrow great push
run (smuggle) sike up
R ⟨John asks is that a good God to take Willie Dignam⟩ *297:21–22 & 26–27*
B ⟨History: daughters of memory. Hume. Edw. II⟩ *25:7*
B ⟨L.B.   4 pm Span. patio. provost. peartree⟩ *271:13*
10   R ⟨2nd city of empire⟩ *319:7*
R ⟨rump & dozen (sir John Beresford)⟩ *323:14*
clerkly hand
B ⟨enter a demurrer⟩ *618:11*   R ⟨wampum⟩ *300:34*
R ⟨arraign⟩   R ⟨harangue   loiter loafers⟩ *336:10?*
15   R ⟨tall talk⟩
B ⟨Heredity: few secured at cost of all.⟩ *323:25?*   money no
     warrant for after death.
B ⟨Dilly's kitchen: oatmeal water, cat devours charred
     fishheads and eggshells heaped on square of brown
20   paper, shell cocoa in kettle, sootcoated⟩ *604:23–28*
Tyrants: men lend them power,   B ⟨cut nose to please face,⟩
     bow head to yoke, custom stronger than nature
B ⟨Rule: dead rule living: 1 enslaved by many⟩ *299:25?, 323:25–27?*
B ⟨Judgment of ?God absurd between two ∴ right between many!⟩
25   Anarchists: who accuse them? Kriegshetzer
Duns Scotus: Roger O'Laughlin S.J. sent out too stupid to

see the trick of game

Memory: whim: locupletavit esurientes

B ⟨Lady Hamilton⟩

30 R ⟨LB. talks of (Dignam's) wife's admirers⟩ *307:37–38*

B ⟨Troy: liege bailiff's   LB got in wooden horse⟩

Law: effective when consecrated by custom = useless.

Communists also men? Some evil needed in doing good.

B ⟨Altruism makes survive race, egoism individ. ½

35 and ½.⟩

R ⟨Pseudonyms: "P" a very good initial too.⟩ *328:40–42*

R ⟨Heblon⟩ *669:34*

R ⟨under auspices ?most favourable⟩ *311:21?*

R ⟨Irish pantomime   Brian Boru & Finn MacCool.⟩

40 B ⟨Luck: every chap gets his ration   500 yrs⟩ *603:27*

R ⟨viands,⟩ *334:21*   R ⟨replenish⟩ *304:2–3?*

R ⟨U.P. = up.⟩ *315:4 & 17, and elsewhere*   forewent

R ⟨lopsided God.⟩ *319:21?*

R ⟨R.C. = sacrificing mother to child secures baptism & funeral⟩ *384:9–10*

45 R ⟨Polypheme: ?tuns, exaggeration, polysyllable,⟩   B ⟨?magnify

?kitten⟩

Galatea = milkmaid

R ⟨Victoria = the widow woman⟩ *328:35*

R ⟨Mead = fermented spit⟩

50 R ⟨change the venue⟩ *364:24, 503:29*

golden calf

B ⟨Suffering proof of sin (David)⟩

Jews & Irish remember past

Jew =   R ⟨cuckoo⟩ = profiteer   B ⟨: the cuckoo's a fine bird

55 He sings as he flies⟩ *329:36–37?*

B ⟨L.B.'s ?soon   Messiah⟩ *331:40?, 485:2?*

Jews fouled wells of thought

B ⟨Circumcised coins⟩

LB: ex quibus Christus *Cf. 627:19–20*

60 Family: ?Stoer, Kubler, Virag(o)

R ⟨empire on which sun never rises⟩ *323:29*   R ⟨password⟩ *418:15, 429:11*

B ⟨head is addled⟩ *308:5*

R ⟨royal Stuarts⟩ *324:19*

B ⟨jail delivery⟩ *620:10*

65 R ⟨without bail or mainprise⟩ *317:40–41*

Eng. work well ∴ so bored by Sunday

Burglar: no attack on 'property' (?abs)

Violence begets habit to lord habit to serve

B ⟨Justice: hard to establish principle but work for better

70   lot⟩ *627:24*

Minority privilege to disappear not physically but socially

B ⟨Neither with violence suppressed nor achieved (Anarchy)⟩ *627:29–30*

R ⟨Q. what is your opinion of the times

    A. I think the markets are on a rise

75   Q. Foreign war is the cause of it.

    A. It's the Russians wish to tyrannize

    Q. What is the age of the moon?   R ⟨Ribbonmen⟩

    A. Really I don't know.

    Q. R. Hand rubbed over brow

    A. Left hand down the pocket   R ⟨Kilts, scratch arse

        R. Hand to knee   quicker⟩

        L. thumb in breeches' pocket⟩ *290:24ff.*

NOTES

The following lines or phrases on "Cyclops" 1 are repeated verbatim or approximately on "Eumaeus" 5 and elsewhere:

"Cyclops" 1	*"Eumaeus" 5*	*"Cyclops" 1*	*"Eumaeus" 5*
Line 2	Line 48	Line 29	Line 59 and "Eumaeus" 7:58
3	49	34–35	61
4	50	40	58
8	51; cf. "Circe" 13:27	52	62
16	52	58	63 and "Cyclops" 5:75
18–20	55–57	64	67
21	54 and "Nausicaa" 5:90	69–70	65–66
23	53	72	64
24	60		

Line 7   In the "Hades" episode Bloom, Simon Dedalus, and others attend the funeral of Paddy Dignam. It is Bob Doran who asks this question.

8   *Daughters of memory*: see Thornton, pp. 27–28. This phrase is originally from John Milton's *The Reason of Church Government*. See James Holly Hanford, ed., *A Milton Handbook* (1926; 4th ed., rpt. New York, 1961), p. 376. The phrase is repeated at "Circe" 13:27 and "Eumaeus" 5:51. See also Joyce's *Critical Writings*, p. 81.

11   Eric Partridge says "a rump of beef and a dozen of claret" is an Irish wager (*A Dictionary of Slang and Unconventional English* [1937; rev. ed., New York, 1961]). The reference is probably to John Beresford (1738–1805), a rather infamous Irish politician and revenue commissioner who built the Customs House in Dublin. There was also an English novelist named John Davys Beresford (1873–1947).

13   *Enter a demurrer*: "a pleading by a party to a legal action that assumes the truth of the matter alleged by the opposite party and sets up that it is insufficient in law to sustain his claim or that there is some other defect on the face of the pleadings constituting a legal reason why the opposing party should not be allowed to proceed further" (*Webster's 7th*). *Wampum*: originally American Indian, now American slang for money.

23   *Dead rule living*: cf. U 89:19.

24   This may be *Gov* instead of *God*.

25   *Kriegshetzer*: warmonger(s).

26   *Duns Scotus*: looks very much like *Dung Scotus*. A Thomas O'Nowlan was on the staff of University College, Dublin (1898–1901), when Joyce was there, and this appears to be a pseudonym for him. It is repeated at "Oxen" 8:65.

28   *Locupletavit esurientes*: he has satisfied those who were hungry.

29   *Lady Hamilton* (1765–1815), Lord Nelson's mistress, born Emma Lyon, rendered "eminent services" to the British fleet during 1796–98 in furnishing information and procuring supplies. *Chambers's Biographical Dictionary* (1897; new ed., New York, 1962) calls these services "overrated but not imaginary." The name is repeated at "Circe" 14:126 and "Eumaeus" 5:59 and 7:58. Cf. "Penelope" 3:18 and 7:26.

37   *Heblon*: pseudonym of Joseph K. O'Connor, author of *Studies in Blue* (Dublin, 1903), a series of sketches of Dublin slum life.

39   *Brian Boru* and *Finn MacCool*: Boru was the hero of the Battle of Clontarf (1014 A.D.); Finn was a great legendary hero in early Irish history. They are important in *FW*. *Finn MacCool* is repeated at "Cyclops" 5:47.

44   *R.C.*: Roman Catholic Church. It is repeated at "Oxen" 6:88 and 8:66. Cf. "Eumaeus" 5:76.

47   *Galatea*: a nymph who loved Acis. Polyphemus killed Acis because he was jealous. Cf. "Cyclops" 8:39.

48   See "Ithaca" 8:25 and 8:34 and notes.

54–55   See the essay on "Nausicaa" (pp. 25–27), for a discussion of the cuckoo; cf. "Nausicaa" 3:64 and note.

58   *Circumcised coins*: suggests Jews and profiteering, but it may also refer to the time-honored practice of clipping coins around the edges in order to get the valuable metal. It is repeated at "Cyclops" 5:75 and "Eumaeus" 5:63.

59   *Ex quibus Christus*: see Thornton, p. 445.

60   *Stoer* appears in *Ulysses* (247:2, 247:22), but *Kubler* does not. *Virag* was formerly the Bloom family name. *Virago* (U 423:23) is repeated at "Cyclops" 4:51 and means "a woman of great

stature." *Stoer* is repeated at "Circe" 21:31; *Virag* at "Ithaca" 14:5.

77   See "Cyclops" essay (pp. 19–20).

80   *Kilts . . . quicker*: in pencil.

"Cyclops" 2

CENTER COLUMN HORIZONTAL

R ⟨LB. Sexual impulse only the root of tree⟩ *Cf. 289:7*
    Marriage: physical difference,   spiritual likeness
Woman Ireland: Slave no sense of honour, genius of beast
    Charakter = losigkeit. Love what is above.
5   *B* ⟨Names. Buonaparte (Goodbody) Cicero (Podmore) Christ (Doyle)
    Racine (Root)⟩ *607:2–3*   *B* ⟨Gilt off the gingerbread.⟩
B ⟨Bob Doran: French urinals, souls of dead Chinese, lord
    Abercrombie's book, "om" men.⟩   Rome will abnegate ?prov.
    divine *R* ⟨barboy ignores him,⟩ *322:33*   *B* ⟨chummies & skivvies,⟩ *626:1*
10   *B* ⟨R.C. peasant backbone of empire⟩ *625:19–20*
B ⟨Tom ?Rochford . . . . ⟩ *294:11 and elsewhere*
T. ?F. Meagher. Sword speech
L.B hates class hate (Weavers. Jacobs)
R ⟨S.D. for sake of addressing letter 'Paris'⟩
15   *R* ⟨Publican: off his head, his own drink (whiskey usquebaugh)⟩
    328:28?
B ⟨Swift: 1 man in armour will beat 10 in their shirts⟩ *573:14–15*
R ⟨Leopold. Hungarian name (cf. Stephen)⟩ *331:28–34*
R ⟨Pope: Vicar of Christ (Bray)⟩ *384:36–37*
20   *B* ⟨Nannetti: the mimber⟩ *309:21*
R ⟨Caraway seed to carry away (Lenehan)⟩ *418:24–25*
R ⟨Kaffir (Cusack re Leop)⟩ *329:14*
B ⟨State: 12 soldiers shoot, none is bloodguilty. Jury⟩
B ⟨Queen's evidence⟩ *80:23, 626:16*
25   *B* ⟨Hounslow Heath. Dick Turpin hero—law⟩ *292:10?*
R ⟨espoused the negative⟩ *311:38*

86

B ⟨Private property conceded only by all ∴ property of
    all⟩ *317:14ff.?*

B ⟨Property could be collective, wages individual (according to
30   needs?, deeds?)⟩ *603:35–36*

R ⟨gave all sorts.⟩   *R* ⟨gamehogs (Eng)⟩ *323:26*

R ⟨under all the circs⟩ *599:32*

R ⟨corruption of minors⟩ *386:19, 718:3*

R ⟨barbarous⟩ *298:28*

35 *R* ⟨Ausrüstung. 2nd ?hand clo' Greek Street⟩ *292:32?*

R ⟨L.B. plays bezique with Dante⟩ *300:33*

. . . . . . rain

R ⟨garnishee motion,⟩ *314:38*   *R* ⟨unsound mind.⟩ *317:17*

emergency planters   perches of land

40 King's Bench division courts not sit (King's birthday)
        Friday 24/6

B ⟨Irish missile troops⟩ *580:29–581:1*

R ⟨for reasons which have not transpired⟩ *410:3–4?*

R ⟨attendance was of large dimensions⟩ *311:25–26*

45 *R* ⟨proceedings then terminated⟩ *312:11*

B ⟨Danes and Romans conquered England⟩

R ⟨Take that in yr right hand & repeat after me ?etc.⟩ *326:1–2*

B ⟨policeman's helmet sweat⟩ *160:7–8*   *R* ⟨⟨LB smells jew⟩⟩ *299:14?*

R ⟨Timothy of the battered naggin (cricket)⟩ *417:7–8*

50 ? Sea   dog & dog   petty fogging

B ⟨residue⟩

B ⟨Kudos⟩ *629:6, 639:12*

R ⟨hobnob⟩ *314:37*   *R* ⟨cornerboys ?arguing outside pub⟩

R ⟨porter was up⟩ *295:19*

55 unsittuponable

R ⟨Irish   lies penal days⟩   evasion

Eng. afraid to commit themselves

R ⟨in the force DMP⟩ *287:10*

R ⟨Custom more honoured in breech than observance⟩ *323:18–19*

60 *R* ⟨aid & abet⟩ *339:2*

R ⟨Geoff. Keating wrote Hist. of Irel. in ?fortresses
        of Galtees (Tiperrary)⟩

87

B ⟨Pietro il Pittore—la lege z'e per tuti⟩

no name, number him

65   *R* ⟨by the ?mossy diamonds⟩

B ⟨evince surprise⟩ *610:21*

B ⟨speaking likeness⟩ *637:8* *B* ⟨(Emmet:)⟩ *300:25* *R* ⟨I.N.F.⟩ *321:14*

B ⟨quondam,⟩ *600:4*   erstwhile

R ⟨Gelatine lozenges on window (LB.)⟩ *238:7*

70   crossexamine, *R* ⟨roasted him⟩ *300:40?*

R ⟨pony of stout⟩ *294:20*

B ⟨every land govt. it merits⟩ *627:26*

R ⟨H.M. counsel learned in the law⟩ *314:20–21*

R ⟨LB asked for definition⟩ *325:24ff.?*

75   *R* ⟨Ulysses—?projects his envy at each chapter⟩

R ⟨Penelope—?her body possessed⟩

B ⟨Smthg of day before⟩

B ⟨I.N.R.I. & I.H.S.⟩ *80:16*

NOTES

The following lines or phrases of "Cyclops" 2 are repeated on "Eumaeus" 5 and elsewhere:

"Cyclops" 2	"Eumaeus" 5		"Cyclops" 2	"Eumaeus" 5
Line 7	Line 47		Lines 29–30	Line 41
9–10	45–46, "Oxen" 16:33, and "Circe" 1:44		48	43
24	38		63	42
25	39		72	44
27	40			

Line 4 *Charakter = losigkeit*: literally, "characterlessness." This sounds as awkward in German as it does in English.

5–6 "A muzzy but deliberate name-puzzle set by Stephen on p. 607 can be worked out fairly easily. Cicero as a name comes from Latin *cicera*, chickpea, and might well be something like Podmore in English; Napoleon = Buonaparte = Goodbody; and Jesus = Christ = Anointed = oiled = Doyle" (Adams, p. 223). Adams neglects to mention that Doyle's initials are "J. C." (see *U* 63:24). *Racine* is "root" in French. Some of the names are repeated at "Oxen" 5:20–21 and "Circe" 3:40.

6 *Gilt off the gingerbread*: appears in Ellmann, p. 425. The phrase is repeated at "Oxen" 5:21 and "Circe" 3:40–41.

7–10   The meaning in this sequence is not clear. There was a Sir Ralph Abercromby who led the British forces in Ireland during the rebellion of 1798. One of his sons, Lord Dunfermline, published his father's memoirs in 1861—*Sir Ralph Abercromby K.B. 1793–1801*. The Hindu sacred word *om* seems to be combined with *amen* to form a pun. A chummy is a chimney-sweep's assistant; a skivvy is the lowest kind of female servant. Some of these words are repeated at "Oxen" 16:33, "Circe" 1:44, and "Eumaeus" 5:45.

10   Cf. *Stephen Hero*, p. 244.

11   *Tom Rochford*: a jockey in *Ulysses*. See 175ff., 228ff., 294, and elsewhere. The name is repeated at "Oxen" 9:71.

12   *T[homas] F[rancis] Meagher* (1823–67) appears in *FW* as Wally Meagher (211:11). "One of the leaders of the Young Ireland movement, who made his famous speech 'Be it for the defense or be it for the assertion, of a nation's liberty, I look upon the sword as a sacred weapon.' The entire beautiful speech is famous in Ireland. Twice convicted by the British, the last time he was sent to Van Dieman's Land for life, convicted of treason. This was in the year 1848" (Frances Boldereff, *Reading* Finnegans Wake [Woodward, Pa., 1959], p. 171). Meagher escaped to the United States, where he served as a general in the Civil War and secretary of Montana Territory.

13   Many Huguenots driven out of France settled in Ireland, and some of them became *weavers*. The *Jacobs* Biscuit Company, a famous Dublin firm, was founded by a Huguenot family. Joyce was familiar with Hauptmann's *Die Weber* (1892). The name is repeated at "Cyclops" 4:12 and "Circe" 11:32.

14   Cf. "Oxen" 6:13 and "Circe" 3:86.

17   Joyce's (or Stephen's) memory is faulty here. The sentence is in Jonathan Swift's *Drapier's Letters*, fourth letter "To the Whole People of Ireland": "eleven men well armed will certainly subdue one single man in his shirt" (*Prose Works*, ed. Temple Scott [London, 1903], VI, 115). The sentence is repeated at "Circe" 3:43. See also *FW* 23:8–9.

20   *Nannetti*, an actual person, was a local Dublin politician and a *mimber* (a dialectal pronunciation) of the Dublin City Council.

21   *Lenehan*: racing editor on *Sport*. See also "Cyclops" 5:54 and "Oxen" 6:14.

22   Michael *Cusack*, the "Citizen" of the "Cyclops" episode, was a famous Fenian. His name is repeated at "Cyclops" 5:51 and 7:42. *Kaffir*, an Arabic word meaning "infidel," is repeated at "Cyclops" 10:114.

23   This appears in "Circe" notebook V.A.19 at Buffalo as: "In a firing party each man believes his neighbor killed the victim." Cf. "Circe" 3:44.

25   *Hounslow Heath* was long notorious as a resort of highwaymen. *Dick Turpin*: an English highwayman (1706–1739) famous for a supposed ride from London to York. The name would have been familiar to Joyce since he used to sing a ballad called "Turpin Hero" (see Ellmann, pp. 161–162).

35   *Ausrüstung*: preparation, outfit, equipment, armament.

36   *Bezique*: a card game for two or four. The word is repeated at "Cyclops" 7:11. *Dante* is Mrs. Dante Hearn Conway from Cork (see Ellmann, p. 24). She is Stephen's aunt in *A Portrait* and *Ulysses* and is also known as Mrs. Riordan. The name is repeated at "Cyclops" 5:78; see also "Nausicaa" 1:45 and note.

40   Edward VII was king in 1904 and his birthday was November 9. Presumably it could have been celebrated on the 24th of June since the British often celebrate the king's or queen's birthday in June.

42 Repeated at "Circe" 3:45.

53 *Cornerboy*: a loafer (Partridge). The word is repeated at "Oxen" 6:85.

61–62 "The first history of the whole country was the *Forus Feasa ar Erinn*, or *History of Ireland*
—from the most ancient times to the Anglo-Norman invasion, written by Dr. Geoffrey Keating, a
learned Roman Catholic priest of Tubrid in Tipperary, who died in 1644" (P. W. Joyce, *A Short
History of Gaelic Ireland* [1893; rpt. Dublin & Cork, 1924], p. 32). Keating, sought by the authorities,
hid in the Glen of Aherlow in the Galtee Mountains of Tipperary. Note that Joyce misspelled
Tipperary here.

63 *Pietro il Pittore*: Peter the Painter—Irish revolutionary slang for "mauser." *La lege z'e per tuti*:
colloquial Italian for "the law is the same for everyone." The implication here is that justice is
administered at gunpoint.

67 "Needless to say, the Irish National Foresters had nothing to do with the project of
reforesting Ireland; they were chiefly notable for the fancy Robert Emmet costumes in which they
decked themselves on ceremonial occasions" (Adams, p. 227). Cf. "Cyclops" 10:107. For *Emmet*
see "Cyclops" 5:12–14.

75 Repeated at "Oxen" 6:86.

78 *I.N.R.I.*: *Iesus Nazarenus Rex Iudaeorum* ("Jesus of Nazareth, King of the Jews"). *I.H.S.*: a
monogram for the Greek contraction of Jesus.

"Cyclops" 3

LEFT COLUMN HORIZONTAL

Titania,　*R* ⟨Seaforth Highlanders (col. Jameson & officers)⟩
R ⟨Richmond Asylum⟩ *522:12*　*R* ⟨T. W. Hamlet⟩ (----oh)
B ⟨col. Everard, Cavan, grows tobacco⟩ *624:33*
R ⟨Barclay & Cook's candles　104 Talbot Street, guess when

5　　　burns out 5 ft high⟩ *668:1–4*

pin stripe, crash linen & holland, overslip

　　　　　　　　　　　　B ⟨under⟩ *321:29*

hopsack, basket cloth.
R ⟨Egan's Hop bitters⟩ *80:35?*　　　*B* ⟨salves⟩ & simples

10　*R* ⟨James Wought alias Saphiro alias Richards alias Price,

　　　Spiro⟩ *316:22*　　　　　　　　　　Spark
R ⟨Benj. Zaretskey £1⟩ *316:27*　　*R* ⟨ancient Hebrew⟩ *316:27*
R ⟨charge preferred against him⟩ *317:41*
R ⟨a bear's hug,⟩　*R* ⟨the weight of my tongue⟩ *287:4*

15　*B* ⟨Heeltapping the case⟩ *560:12?*
R ⟨Memory of LB⟩—*R* ⟨a very long time I was going to bed some-

　　　where and there was a squareshaped or was it when I

　　　was where was that.⟩
R ⟨Weiss' sister-in-law: death of infant,　putting on an

20　　　inside vest⟩
B ⟨lay low,⟩ *633:10?*　*R* ⟨stiff ?jab⟩ *313:17?*　*R* ⟨clean knockout,⟩

　　　313:34　*R* ⟨battle⟩ *313:7*
R ⟨clave to,⟩ *335:33*　*R* ⟨hails from⟩ *608:24*　*B* ⟨butting match⟩ *322:39*
R ⟨lively claret⟩ *313:12*

25　*B* ⟨tansy pills,⟩ *331:7*　*B* ⟨pennyroyal⟩
R ⟨putting the stone⟩ *311:11*

RIGHT COLUMN HORIZONTAL

R ⟨gurnard, pollock, ling⟩ *288:40?*

R ⟨mercerized silk⟩ *321:29*

R ⟨?Chas & Co, Leeds⟩

30   B ⟨in close order⟩

Mendoza

R ⟨marquess of Q—⟩ *313:5?*

laid low   R ⟨bout of fireworks⟩ *313:10–11*

clave to   B ⟨hails from⟩ *608:24*

35   R ⟨Queensberry rules⟩ *313:5*

R ⟨O, Ireland! my sireland!

   Thou fireland! thou direland!

   No liar land shall buy our land!

   A higher land is Ireland!⟩

NOTES

(Cycl) appears in the left margin vertically.

Line 1   *Titania*: the wife of Oberon and queen of the fairies in Shakespeare's *Midsummer Night's Dream. Seaforth Highlanders*: a Scottish regiment which fought in South Africa (1899–1902) in the Boer War. Sir Leander Starr *Jameson*, 1st Bart. (1853–1917), was a South African statesman, medical doctor, and famous military leader in the Boer War.

2   *T. W. Hamlet*: suggests T. W. Lyster, the Quaker librarian in "Scylla and Charybdis." The name is repeated at "Oxen" 6:17; see also "Oxen" 6:16.

3   Repeated at "Eumaeus" 5:35.

4–5   Repeated at "Ithaca" 12:33.

7   I.e., "underslip."

8   *Hopsack, basket cloth*, and the materials in line 6 are rough fabrics.

9   A *simple* is a vegetable drug having only one ingredient.

10–12   "In the course of the 'Aeolus' and 'Cyclops' chapters, mention is made of a 'Canada swindle case' ([*U*] 126, 316); the accused was a man named Saphrio, Saphiro, or Wought, who had swindled (among others) a man named Zaretsky or Zireski by offering to procure him transportation to Canada for twenty shillings. . . . Joyce drew his details of the trial from the Dublin papers, all of which carried reports" (Adams, p. 228).

19–20   "Once [Ottocaro] Weiss told him of the grief of a young mother of his acquaintance over the death of her child; she was concerned that the pillow on which his head rested in the casket might not be soft enough. Joyce at once made a note in his notebook and said 'I'll use that' " (Ellmann, p. 478). Perhaps this is the note Joyce copied down. Joyce attributes similar motherly sentiments to Molly Bloom (*U* 763:36ff.), who has lost her son. Cf. "Oxen" 6:90.

21   *Lay low*: repeated at "Eumaeus" 1:96 and 5:36.

23   *Hails from*: repeated at line 34 and at "Eumaeus" 5:37.

25   *Tansy*: an herb with an aromatic odor and a very bitter taste. As a medication, it was thought by the Greeks to prolong human life. *Pennyroyal*: also an aromatic herb. It yields an essential oil sometimes used in folk medicine to increase perspiration, to stimulate menstrual discharge, or to repel mosquitoes. Herbs are mentioned most frequently in the "Circe" episode; these two are repeated at "Circe" 3:64.

26   *Putting the stone*: the shotput; also a term used in curling, "a game developed in Scotland in which two teams of four men each send stones spinning over a stretch of ice . . . toward a target circle in an attempt to place a stone nearest the center" (*Webster's 3rd*). See also "Cyclops" 6:27 and note.

27   All are fish. *Pollock* appears at *U* 391:22 and *ling* at *U* 657:22.

28   To mercerize is to give a cloth luster, strength, and receptiveness to dyes by treatment under tension with caustic soda.

29   There is (or was) a soap-manufacturing company named *Cha[rle]s & Co.*, Marshall Mills, Marshall Street, Holbeck, Leeds (*Kelly's Directory of Merchants, Manufacturers and Shippers of the World* [London, 1938]).

31   Daniel *Mendoza* (1763–1836), an English Jew, is known as the first scientific boxer in the history of pugilism. Although a middleweight, he beat some of the biggest and best fighters in England and won the British boxing championship. The name is repeated at "Ithaca" 12:36.

32   "Sir John Sholto Douglas, 8th *Marquess of* Q[*ueensbury*] (1844–1900), an enthusiastic supporter of Bradlaugh and a keen patron of boxing, supervised the formulation in 1867 of new rules to govern that sport, since known as the 'Queensbury rules.' In 1895 he was tried and acquitted for publishing a defamatory libel on Oscar Wilde of whose friendship with his son, Lord Alfred Douglas, he disapproved" (*Chambers's*).

"Cyclops" 4

LEFT COLUMN HORIZONTAL

kegs
roan
gelding
You bet
5   B ⟨pizzle⟩ *394:16*
     R ⟨bailiff's daughter⟩ *297:36*
amicus curiae
     R ⟨ensue⟩ *302:24?, 311:29?, and elsewhere*
     B ⟨grandson of Dan O'⟩ *103:30–31?*
10   B ⟨1ª facie case⟩ *404:22–23*
     R ⟨racy of the soil⟩ *311:12*
     R ⟨Jacob's biscuitbox⟩ *300:20*
     R ⟨Bros Guiness. 2 noble peers (Castor & Pollux)⟩ *326:21, 294:27*
     R ⟨Wolf in sheep's clothing⟩ *332:21*
15   the false scent
     R ⟨the hard word⟩
     R ⟨the soul of war replied⟩
     B ⟨the main⟩ *339:20?*
     R ⟨a main noise⟩ *339:20*
20   R ⟨streamy vale⟩ *290:2*
     R ⟨?dost darken the welkin⟩ *337:11?*
     R ⟨who comes?   it is⟩
     R ⟨pay debt of nature⟩ *296:1*
     B ⟨transient beam⟩ *298:2*
25   R ⟨red is thy rolling eye⟩ *325:21?*
     R ⟨excelled himself⟩ *312:3*

94

R ⟨extinction of the beam of heaven⟩ *298:1–2*

joy of grief

R ⟨daughter of skies (moon)⟩ *317:8*

30 *R* ⟨friend in court⟩ *308:8*

B ⟨princely (Irish?) ?hands⟩

beauteous as the moon in Donnybrook

B ⟨red eyes.⟩ *325:21?*

R ⟨by the mortal frost⟩

35 *R* ⟨wine of the country⟩ *290:36*

deponent ?with not

R ⟨every moment be his next⟩ *331:42*

R ⟨entertainment for man & beast⟩ *307:24*

R ⟨impervious to all fear⟩ *292:35*

40 Scoff

B ⟨wafted (wafty)⟩ *289:3*

B ⟨Bloody wars! says the queen of France⟩ *324:22?*

R ⟨Tell that to a fool⟩ *325:2*

put me in mind

45 *R* ⟨to cool his courage⟩ *307:14*

R ⟨not worth a roasted fart⟩ *324:27*

R ⟨assault & battery⟩ *339:2*

R ⟨quartering knife⟩ *303:36*

G ⟨little ease⟩

50 voucher

R ⟨virago⟩ *423:23*

R ⟨milk in cocoanut & absence of hair on animal's chest⟩ *314:6–7*

R ⟨when all fruit fails welcome haws⟩

?pubs   *R* ⟨not brook⟩ *294:37*

55 whilom   traversen

B ⟨impeach a nation⟩ *319:17*

B ⟨a bill of attainder⟩ *319:17*

felonsetting *Cf. 626:14*

leading question

60 bait

R ⟨cruelty to animals (J.H.P.)⟩ *315:36*

B ⟨a hat is suited for a wedding⟩

R ⟨strengthy⟩ *319:34*

B ⟨and it not in the corner⟩

65   *R* ⟨French landed at Killala⟩ *324:17–18*

R ⟨what's on you?⟩ *306:10*

B ⟨he died on me⟩

B ⟨a mitred abbot⟩ *332:35*

R ⟨Mine, as devil said to dead policeman⟩ *326:35–36*

70   *R* ⟨without a stitch on her⟩ *297:39*

R ⟨Lanty MacHale's dog.⟩ *Cf. 330:10*

RIGHT COLUMN HORIZONTAL

R ⟨Master Courtenay sitting in own chamber⟩ *317:10–11*

R ⟨1st chargeant on property⟩ *317:13–14*

evidence by commission

75   counterclaimed & traversed sale & delivery

R ⟨Mr Justice Andrews sitting without a jury in the probate.⟩ *317:12*

R ⟨V. Livingstone and another⟩ *317:17*

? 'compo' in bootsoles

ex parte

80   *B* ⟨Irel: European fights Englands wars. Why?⟩ *626:2–4*

B ⟨Beran v. officer = two impostors⟩

overseas empire.

wooden heads of Downing Street

Irel: centripetal ambition (Zionism)

85   —   fugal   ″   (Columb)

     her ?unmade captivities

Germany: steelshod syntaxes of syllogisms

Chair in middle Irish: stool in Manx

R ⟨a roasted fart⟩ *324:27*

90   *B* ⟨acquitted himself⟩

B ⟨Bartle the Basket⟩ *420:7–8?*

B ⟨we did ample justice⟩ *231:4*

R ⟨boiled owl⟩ *300:38*

Longbow from Irel. Strongbow Tweed

95   Blazes Boyl. 6 sisters: Armagh camp

96

R ⟨Kelleher: 2nd hand coffins⟩ *316:18*

B ⟨Circumstantial evidence⟩ *98:39–40, 618:24, 691:3*

B ⟨Contracts invalidated by violence done to 1 party ∴ social
contract no validity for individual constraint by
violence of birth to enter the society of the living on
their terms.⟩

R ⟨Prophecy: when 1st Irish gunboat is seen breasting the waves
with the green flag at her helm⟩ *322:18–19*

All comparisons proportionate

Shorthorn bullock = ?EUV

gusty swells

LB. SD.   smart fellow.

R ⟨Invincibles⟩ *300:2*

R ⟨Here's to us! Sinn Fein⟩ *301:10*

R ⟨commit his ideas to paper⟩

B ⟨Connemara ?simpleton—fire in the west⟩ *422?*

R ⟨Sinhedrim⟩ *317:22*

old Hooper's owl

speech from dock: oracle

Godstruck holy fool, ?frig

    epipelsy

R ⟨Dairy arse   darius⟩

R ⟨Black '47⟩ *324:3*

B ⟨⎰Haines = ear of the world⟩

B ⟨⎱S.D. = Horace's deaf donkey⟩

R ⟨hotfoot⟩ *293:38*

R ⟨?erin ex ?lectularius⟩

B ⟨Lombard = why pay feed of maniacs⟩

R ⟨Signo P: a very good initial too⟩ *328:42*

R ⟨?P I wouldn't sell for ½ crown⟩ *290:34*

R ⟨Killybegs = 3rd harbour in world (other two bray & bullock)⟩ *337:7?, 391:20?*

B ⟨Dunleary⟩

R ⟨specific performance⟩

R ⟨nefarious designs⟩ *386:17*

R ⟨corporation meeting (Irish)⟩ *305:25*

NOTES

A long vertical line separates the left column from the right. Phrases in the following lines are repeated on "Eumaeus" 5 and elsewhere:

"Cyclops" 4	*"Eumaeus"* 5		*"Cyclops"* 4	*"Eumaeus"* 5
Line 58	Line 68		Lines 98–101	Line 107
80	104		119–120	110
81	105		123	111
96	108 and "Cyclops" 8:52		128	112 and "Circe" 1:86
97	106			

Line 12   See "Cyclops" 2:13 and note.

13   *Bros Guiness*: Arthur and Edward Guinness (later Baron Ardilaun and Baron Iveagh respectively) were the sons of Benjamin Lee Guinness, who founded the Guinness Brewery in the eighteenth century. The sons carried on the family business and their father's philanthropies.

37   Cf. "Oxen" 7:79 and 8:78.

51   See "Cyclops" 1:60 and note.

53   *Haws*: fruits of the hawthorn; they were eaten by early Celts.

61   *J.H.P.*: John Howard Parnell, Dublin city marshal and brother of the Irish hero Charles Stewart Parnell. Cf. "Circe" 16:36 and 19:6.

65   *Killala*: city on the northwest coast of Ireland where Wolfe Tone landed on August 22, 1798, with General Humbert, a soldier of fortune, and 1,000 men he had assembled at La Rochelle. They quickly took two towns and then moved on to defeat General Lake at Castlebar before they were surrounded and forced to surrender by the British.

71   See *Stephen Hero*, p. 112.

72   *Master Courtenay*: unidentified. He was probably a master in the Four Courts in Dublin.

76   *Mr Justice Andrews*: probably the Rt. Hon. William Drennan Andrews (1832–1924) of Lower Regent St., Dublin; a member of King's Inn, Dublin, 1855; Bencher, 1882; and Judge of Exchequer Division of the High Court of Justice in Ireland (later merged with the King's Bench Division), 1882–1910.

78   *'Compo'*: "a monthly advance of wages: nautical colloquialism from around 1850. Probably *ex compo*, jargon for a composition paid by a debtor" (Partridge).

79   *Ex parte*: "(1) on or from one side only—used of legal proceedings; (2) from a one-sided or partisan point of view" (*Webster's 7th*).

81   *Beran*: probably the Swiss poet Félix Beran (1868–1937). See *Letters*, III, 255. Cf. "Eumaeus" 5:105 .

84–85   *Zionism* may be described as a *centripetal* force since Jews around the world look toward Israel as the center of Jewish religion and culture. Saint Columba, Colum-cille, or Colm (521–597), when excommunicated from Ireland, set out to convert the Northern Picts and "founded monasteries on the Pictish mainland, the Western Islands and the Orkneys. The parent house of Iona [his headquarters] exercised supremacy over all these, as well as over the Columban churches in Ireland and those afterwards established in the North of England" (*Chambers's*). *Centrifugal* is appropriate since the evangelism of Columba and his followers proceeded in all directions away from their headquarters on Iona.

94 *Strongbow*: the name by which Richard FitzGilbert (not Fitzherbert, as *Chambers's* has it), the 2nd Earl of Pembroke (c. 1130–1176), was known. In 1170 he invaded Ireland with the permission of Henry II. He married the daughter of Dermot MacMurrough, King of Leinster, and offered his conquests to Henry to appease the latter's jealousy. His place of burial may still be seen in Christ Church, Dublin. During this invasion Strongbow used Welsh longbowmen and some crossbowmen. The *Tweed* is a river in Scotland, but Strongbow was from Clare in Wales. This may be a reference to Molly Bloom's father, Major Tweedy.

95 *Armagh*: a county in Northern Ireland. *6 sisters*: possibly a reference to the six counties of Ulster.

96 Corny *Kelleher*: an undertaker's assistant in *Ulysses*. See also "Cyclops" 8:52 and note and "Eumaeus" 5:108.

102 *Gunboat*: this looks very much like *bumboat* (cf. *U* 395:2).

108 *Invincibles*: the notorious murderers of Thomas H. Burke and Sir Frederick Cavendish in Phoenix Park, Dublin, on May 6, 1882. Myles Crawford has the date wrong (*U* 134:17–18). "The Invincibles were not identified, and the story of their conspiracy [was not] made public, till a year later" (Adams, pp. 161–162).

109 *Here's to us*: repeated at "Oxen" 7:80. *Sinn Fein*: repeated at "Cyclops" 5:55.

110 Repeated at "Oxen" 7:81.

112 *Sinhedrim*: a spelling variant of the Hebrew *sanhedrin* or *sanhedrim*. The Greek word is *synedrion*. This was "the supreme council and tribunal of the ancient Jewish nation consisting of 70–72 members and having jurisdiction over religious matters and important civil and criminal cases" (*Webster's 3rd*).

113 "Alderman John Hooper . . . gave the Blooms a stuffed owl as a wedding present (p. 692)." He had "previously been an Alderman in Cork" and was the father of Paddy Hooper (Adams, p. 40).

116 *Epipelsy*: Joyce's misspelling.

117 Repeated at "Oxen" 7:82

118 *Black '47*: 1847 was the worst year of the Great Famine in Ireland. The potato crop failed for the third time, and more than half a million people died of famine and plague. See Seumas MacManus, *The Story of the Irish Race* (1921; rev. ed., New York, 1944), pp. 606–607.

119–120 This is an allusion to Horace, *Epistles* ii.1.199—"He would think those who take the trouble to write plays fools for their pains." In *asello surdo*, Lambinus says, "Horace has put together two proverbial expressions for wasted labour, 'to speak to the deaf' . . . and 'to speak to an ass'" (Horace, *Works*, trans. E. C. Wickham [Oxford, 1891]).

122 This phrase is almost illegible. It is repeated at "Oxen" 8:36.

123 The cold practicality of this idea suggests the Lombard Bank of Ireland or H. P. Lombard, Ltd., financiers, both at 30 Nassau Street in Dublin.

126 *Killybegs*: an important fishing center in Donegal. With its natural harbor it "has all the potentialities of a first-class port" (*Ireland Guide* [Dublin, n.d.], p. 447).

128 *Dunleary*: *Dun Laoghaire* in Gaelic. It is famous for its harbor and is the Irish terminus of the chief mail-steamer service between Ireland and Great Britain. It was also known as Kingstown (*U* 7:8, 25:40, and elsewhere). The name is repeated at "Circe" 1:86 and "Eumaeus" 5:112.

130 Repeated at "Oxen" 7:83.

"Cyclops" 5

CENTER COLUMN HORIZONTAL

R ⟨LB made up to mother-in-law.⟩

B ⟨L.B excited wants to say many things.⟩ *326:38ff.*

B ⟨L.B "I'll give him a lottery ticket" (Cycl)⟩

R ⟨Nannetti is leaving Ireland⟩ *310:8–9*

5 Pinkerton, ..., G.P.O., glaze scrape away (Budgen?)
  S.Martin's le Grand

R ⟨LB. She clasped him to her bosoms⟩ (intellects) *304:16–17?*

LB. At a cursing duel.

LB. Present at unpleasant scene: ?leave bloke on the hip

10 *R* ⟨LB. Woman oughtn't make rows unless she can win them⟩ *Cf. 364:6*

R ⟨Cycl. I must have notice of that question (J.J.O'M)⟩ *310:37*

B ⟨Tiser. Rob. Emmet's prophecy. Longer delayed the
  better (LB)⟩ *286:3?, 300:25?*

B ⟨S.Michan's: Rob. Emmet buried there. Glasnevin. ?etc.⟩ *237:8–12*

15 *B* ⟨L.B. Whom God has joined let no man put asunder⟩ *405:7–8?*
  (pleasure reserved)

Ossian.   Jewish rhetoric.   Ulysses. Kolossal!

Cycl. Exaggeration of things previously given: *B* ⟨Super-
  latives⟩ *312:3ff., 313:10?*

20 *R* ⟨Style. Longwinded simile.⟩

R ⟨Geneology: Leopold, son of Rudolph, son of Leopold Peter,
  son of P.R.⟩ *Cf. 302:10*

Objects: tram (crystal sliding ark)   *B* ⟨?noserag (Irish history)
  shout⟩ *326:4*   *B* ⟨(welsh mariner, Cambrian bear)⟩ *337:12–13?*   *R* ⟨market
25 (crystal palace)⟩ *289:16*

R ⟨Names: O'Bloom, O'Kiernan⟩ *292:35*

B ⟨Clanspirit.⟩ *314:19*

R ⟨Brehons Laws.⟩ *317:20*

B ⟨Technique: Sudden vituperation follows depression⟩   (ferocity

30   Iliad)

B ⟨Archimedes: Sun flashing roof.⟩   herd in Leitrim   scratches

nape

Compare: Giant: giant :: giant: dwarf

L.B. sharpens pencil   *B* ⟨⟨writes word⟩⟩

35   Fenian & his grandfather.

R ⟨Style: ?and like a wheatfield under the ~~strong~~ wind and like

the mountain ash / hazel grove under the whirlwind.⟩

″   : like a sunbeam at 7.48

R ⟨Engl: a noble race, rulers of the waves, who sit on thrones

40   of alabaster, silent as the deathless gods.⟩ *319:37–38*

B ⟨It seems history is to blame.⟩ *22:19, 31:28, 405:16–17, 572:7*

nightmare.   *B* ⟨God noise in street, never let jews in, O'Rourke,

?1ˢᵗ goal, Pyrrhus, Helen⟩ *184:14–15, 388:14ff., 494:17, 559:12*

Feefawfum

45   Justice.

Pretenders

R ⟨Giant's Causeway⟩ *338:17*   *B* ⟨Finn McCool.⟩ *311:34*

Wit. read Freud: (are you shitting, honey?)

R ⟨Art: Colleen Bawn⟩ *292:10*

50   Church: iron girders to Irel.

B ⟨Cycl. Cusack bespatten.⟩ *325:37ff.*

R ⟨Miracles. Jesus cut off by clouds, multiply fish.⟩ ?Story

11.a.m.   —   4p.m.   *334:5ff.*

R ⟨Lenehan: Rose of Castile⟩ *133:3–4*

55   *R* ⟨Sinn Fein.⟩ *301:10*   *B* ⟨?Eng. no music⟩

R ⟨adultery: a mensa et a thalamo (from bed & breakfast)⟩ *201:24*

R ⟨L.B. sleeps at other end of bed⟩ *756:34–35*

R ⟨S.D. tempted to drink⟩ *298:34?*

Maxim: in gov. office leave dignity with umbrella. always keep

60   a good one for the last (trot for the avenue) *Cf. 270:15–16*

R ⟨L.B. Walk into my parlour,⟩   regrets death of fly

Solitudinem faciunt et pacem appellant

Eng. Not so spoiled by success as others ?romans

R ⟨L.B. soft hand under a hen⟩ *310:2, 382:4?*

65   R ⟨Hist. who got away J. Stephen's⟩ *311:1–2,* shot Buckley,   *B* ⟨bore

        Wellington (horse & stable cf. Eng. law)⟩

R ⟨Lie: S.D. receives 5£⟩

?Imitation. ?Smone doing someone purposely & not

R ⟨L.B. lives on samples⟩ *301:1–5*

70   B ⟨Derwan builder's story   bucket full of porter.⟩ *442:18–19*

B ⟨Patriots: ?geese to save capitol⟩

R ⟨Irel: winebark on the winedark waterway⟩ *322:7–8*

R ⟨Molly: Police Gazette.⟩ *318:27–28*

?allarm: fleadislodging bug.   ins 1^{ae}. ?nectis

75   B ⟨Coins: circumcised⟩

R ⟨Jew: love his country when sure which it is. (SD. P.

       ?M'H)⟩ *331:15–17*

R ⟨?Bliz: . . . . : 2 women (Molly ?Dante ?about neck of him)⟩

B ⟨Cromwell: curse,⟩ *335:36*   jews England rich: ?idem Erin:

80   protest. parliament so long as we control the money bags.

NOTES

(*Cycl*) appears in the upper right-hand corner. Phrases in the following lines are repeated on "Eumaeus" 5 and elsewhere:

"Cyclops" 5	"Eumaeus" 5
Lines 12–14	Lines 113–114
65	87, "Cyclops" 8:38, and "Oxen" 5:31
66	115
70	116

Line 5   The significance of this association is undetermined. *Pinkerton* is a clear reading, but there is no such name in *Ulysses*. Lieutenant Pinkerton, the hero of Puccini's *Madam Butterfly*, is mentioned in *FW* (184:23). The name is also that of a detective agency. G.P.O.: General Post Office. *Budgen*: a close friend of Joyce's and the author of *James Joyce and the Making of* Ulysses; see also "Ithaca" 5:30 and note. *S. Martin's le Grand* (St. Martin's-le-Grand): a common name for the General Post Office in London.

12–14   *Rob[ert] Emmet*: an Irish patriot (1778–1803). *Chambers's* says: "With a few confederates he plotted to seize Dublin Castle and secure the viceroy, but the rising resulted only in a few ruffianly murders. Emmet escaped to the Wicklow mountains, but returning for a last interview with his sweetheart, Sarah Curran, daughter of the orator, was arrested, tried on September 19, 1803 and hanged the following day." His burial place—whether S[t]. *Michan's* churchyard or *Glasnevin* Cemetery—has been in dispute ever since. His prophecy is cited at the close of the "Sirens" episode (*U* 286). These lines are partially repeated at "Eumaeus" 5:113–114; the name *Emmet* is repeated at "Cyclops" 2:67 and "Circe" 17:5.

17   *Ossian*: "heroic poet of the Gael, and son of the 3rd-century hero Fingal . . . whose poems James Macpherson professed to have collected and translated" (*Chambers's*).

23–25   In each of these instances the commonplace has been blown up to be chauvinistically fantastic.

28   *Brehons Laws*: the great body of laws of ancient Ireland. They were first translated and published by a commission of Irish noblemen in the middle of the nineteenth century.

31   The connection between the individual elements escapes me. *Archimedes*: the most famous of ancient mathematicians (287–212 B.C.). *Leitrim*: a county in Connacht. There is an echo of the Archimedes phrase in "Nausicaa" (*U* 371:35). His name is repeated at "Nausicaa" 6:52.

37   Joyce wrote *ash* directly above *hazel*.

42–43   *O'Rourke* of Breffni was an eleventh-century Irish chieftain (his name is repeated at "Oxen" 4:53 and "Circe" 10:74). *Pyrrhus*, King of Epirus (318–272 B.C.), with the aid of 25,000 men and elephants defeated the Romans on the river Siris. He waged war continually until 272 B.C., when he was killed by a woman who hurled a tile at him from a roof. Stephen asks his class a question about Pyrrhus (*U* 25). O'Rourke, Pyrrhus, and *Helen* are associated with the thesis that history is a nightmare from which we seek to awaken.

44   *Feefawfum*: from "Jack the Giant Killer" or similar fairy tales (cf. *U* 45:39). It also occurs in *King Lear* III.iv.188.

47   *Giant's Causeway*: the most famous tourist attraction in Northern Ireland. *Finn M[a]cCool*: see "Cyclops" 1:39 and note.

49   *Colleen Bawn*: literally "Fair Girl," was Eily O'Connor, the heroine of Dion Boucicault's play of the same name (Adaline Glasheen, *A Second Census of Finnegans Wake* [Evanston, Ill., 1963]).

51   *Cusack*: see "Cyclops" 2:22 and note.

54   See "Cyclops" 2:21 and note. *Rose of Castil[l]e*: Lenehan's pun is a prominent motif in *Ulysses*.

55   *Sinn Fein*: repeated at "Cyclops" 4:109.

56   *A mensa et a thalamo*: from the table and from the bedchamber. This relates to a legal separation in which the parties remain husband and wife but without cohabitation. See also "Cyclops" 10:14 and Ellmann, pp. 238–239n.

57   Joyce and Nora also slept in this position. See Ellmann, p. 237, and *Letters*, II, 202. The line is repeated at "Ithaca" 12:24.

62   *Solitudinem faciunt et pacem appellant*: they make a wilderness and call it peace. This is a famous line from the *Agricola* of Tacitus: "ubi solitudinem faciunt pacem appellant."

65   *J. Stephen's*: this would be James Stephens the Fenian, not the author and Joyce's contemporary (*U* 68:16, 311:1–2, 474:27). He was born in 1825 and died in 1901. Stephens spent most of his life agitating for Irish independence. For a discussion of his escape from the Richmond jail, see MacManus, pp. 616–617. The story of *Buckley* is of major importance in *FW*. According to

the barroom story told by Joyce's father, Buckley was an Irish soldier in the Crimean War who could not bring himself to shoot a Russian general caught in the act of defecating. For repetitions, see "Cyclops" 8:38, "Oxen" 5:31, and "Eumaeus" 5:87.

66   *Horse & stable*: the significance of this phrase is undetermined.

67   Cf. "Oxen" 7:136.

68   *Imitation*: perhaps this is *Irritation*.

70   *Derwan*: probably James Derwin, a builder and alderman in 1904 for Drumcondra Ward (Adams, p. 240).

71   In *A Portrait* Stephen calls patriots "geese" (pp. 181 and 201).

72   See also *oinopa ponton* (*U* 48:31).

74   *Fleadislodging bug*: not identified. I doubt that it exists.

75   See "Cyclops" 1:58 and note.

78   The second word here looks like *cacciatore*, Italian for "hunter." *Dante*: see "Cyclops" 2:36 and note.

79   See "Cyclops" 10:104, "Eumaeus" 5:81, and *U* 628:11–15.

"Cyclops" 6

LEFT COLUMN HORIZONTAL

?Pardon Maynooth all put to the sword, Drogheda
    S. Mary's Abbey, summer day 1534
R ⟨of stature full & personable white face & withal somewhat
    ruddy⟩ *314:20*
B ⟨Sir Anthony MacDonnell left Euston (?16) for undersecre-
    tary's lodge⟩ *643:18*
B ⟨Decree nisi:⟩ *318:20, 638:20–21*   King's   *B* ⟨proctor shows
    cause⟩ *638:20*
B ⟨Gordon Bennett Race⟩ *96:5–6, 97:18–19, 631:25–26*
Hughes & Young. Patent Agents, 50 Chancery Lane ?wear that
    have brought fortunes.
R ⟨Roy. Hung. Lottery. LB rogue & vagabond⟩ *308:7–10*
R ⟨Alaki of Abeakuta⟩ *328:14*
R ⟨Navy Regulations⟩
R ⟨Gold Stick in Waiting, lord Walkup of Walkup on Eggs,⟩ *328:15*
R ⟨met to do honour to rule of Africa⟩
R ⟨her bloomers (M.B.)⟩ *318:34*   *R* ⟨the same only more so.⟩ *328:37*
B ⟨Casement on Congo Free State⟩ *329:4–6*
R ⟨horsejobber, bought horses in U.S.A. for British in Boer
    War⟩ *314:9–10*
                                    R ⟨(?George)⟩
R ⟨Span. ale, Span. wine, Galway⟩ *322:7*
Black Maria   *R* ⟨Ir. ?700 years captive⟩
                                    Vic & prince consort
R ⟨after you with the push⟩ *325:40*
R ⟨LB. w. eat meat on Friday⟩   (dispens. from pope) *300:34?*

105

B ⟨Cycl = lanceur des roches⟩ *311:2–3* bushy eyebrows, anger
    burst

Moses saved from waves

30 Milesians (Argos) exp. Euxine, America

Herodotus opens hist with Phen. version of rape of Helen

B ⟨Jenkin's ear⟩   (?sordid ?comm war)   Alex to revive Troy
    Baltic amber   Augustus. Horace mocks

Russian ?waterway   trebizond jade   *R* ⟨volley of
35   oaths⟩ *339:4*

RIGHT COLUMN HORIZONTAL

B ⟨natheless⟩ *381:7*

R ⟨propound a will⟩ *317:14*

R ⟨oppose probate⟩ *317:12?*

R ⟨Hugh Hyacinth
40   the Mac D, prince of Coolavin⟩

R ⟨?Bung⟩ *294:27?*

R ⟨great unwashed⟩

R ⟨?uphander⟩

R ⟨?the ?pigeons⟩ *160:1?*

45 *B* ⟨trumpery insanity⟩ *420:7*

NOTES

Phrases in the following lines are repeated on "Eumaeus" 5:

"Cyclops" 6	*"Eumaeus"* 5
Lines 5–6	Lines 90–91
7–8	97 & 99
9	98, "Oxen" 11:93, and "Eumaeus" 6:194
31–32	92

Line 1   See *U* 227:8ff. The rebel Lord Thomas Fitzgerald (called Silken Thomas) owned
Maynooth Castle. He threw off allegiance to England and in the next year (1535) was captured. The

survivors of his garrison in Maynooth Castle were immediately executed; Thomas was sent to London and, after two years in the Tower, was likewise executed. The slaughter of these prisoners by Sir William Skeffington is called the "Pardon of Maynooth." See Edmund Curtis, *A History of Ireland* (1936; 6th ed., 1950; rpt. London, 1961), pp. 162–164. *Drogheda*: an ancient town on the coast 20 miles north of Dublin which had nothing to do with the slaughter at Maynooth, though both were scenes of infamous events in Irish history. In 1649 Cromwell attacked Drogheda, massacred 2,000 of the defenders, and put everyone to the sword when the town was captured.

5–6 *Sir Anthony MacDonnell*: Antony Patrick MacDonnell, Baron MacDonnell of Swinford (1844–1925). "His sympathies throughout his public life were with the peasants who live on and by the land" (*DNB, 1922–1930*). He was an Irish statesman, M.P., and supporter of the Irish Reform Association. "As for the note about Sir Antony MacDonnell having left Euston yesterday for the under-secretary's lodge in Phoenix Park, it seems to have been copied from the *London Times* of Friday, June 17 [1904], p. 6" (Adams, p. 231).

7 *Decree nisi*: "the decree first made upon a petition for a divorce which is made absolute at such time thereafter as may be directed unless cause to the contrary is shown" (*Webster's 3rd*).

9 [James] *Gordon Bennett*: American newspaper editor (1841–1918), who "sent Stanley in 1870 to find Livingstone and with *The Daily Telegraph* financed Livingstone's Congo journey (1874–78)" (*Chambers's*). He also promoted polar exploration, storm warnings, motoring, and yachting. The name is repeated at "Oxen" 11:93, "Eumaeus" 5:98, and "Eumaeus" 6:194.

10 A recent London telephone directory listed *Hughes & Young*, Ltd., Registered *Patent Agents*, 7 Stone Bldgs., London, WC2.

12 *Roy. Hung. Lottery*: " 'The Royal Hungarian Lottery' which is said to have got Bloom in so much trouble till the freemasons got him out of it, was picked out of a single paragraph in the *Irish Independent* of June 16, 1904, p. 4. The episode in question took place in London; a printer was summoned into court by the Treasury, on charges of having published announcements describing the 'Privileged Royal Hungarian Lottery' " (Adams, pp. 100–101).

13 "On p. 328 of the novel, the Citizen reads from the *United Irishman* a skit about a 'Zulu chief that's visiting England.' In fact, the Alaki of Abeakuta was visiting England during the summer of 1904 and did discuss with King Edward a Bible given him by Queen Victoria. (*Irish Independent*, Tuesday, May 31, 1904, p. 6.)" (Adams, p. 202).

18 Sir Roger David *Casement* "(1864–1916), British consular official, born in Kingstown (now Dun Laoghaire) near Dublin, denounced Congo and Putumayo rubber atrocities. Knighted in 1911, he was degraded, and executed for high treason, having been arrested on landing in Ireland from a German submarine to head the Sinn Fein rebellion" (*Chambers's*).

19 Cf. "Cyclops" 8:54.

23 *Black Maria*: patrol wagon. See *U* 474:1.

24 *Vic & prince consort*: Victoria and Albert. See "Ithaca" 8:25 and 8:34 and notes.

27 *Lanceur des roches*: putter of stones. See "putting the stone" at "Cyclops" 3:26 and the note there. Homer's Cyclops hurled stones at Odysseus and his men.

30 Joyce seems to be comparing the voyages of the *Milesians* with the quest of the Argonauts for the Golden Fleece. Both were pioneers in exploring the *Euxine*, or the coast of the Black Sea. The Milesians also came to Ireland and supposedly colonized it. Perhaps Joyce read somewhere that they journeyed as far as America. *Euxine*: repeated at "Cyclops" 8:47.

31 The Phoenician version of the *rape of Helen* in Herodotus is as follows: The Greeks "carried off the king's daughter Medea. When the Colchian king sent a herald to demand reparation for the

robbery, and restitution of his daughter, the Greeks replied that as they had been refused reparation for the abduction of the Argive Io, neither would they make any to the Colchians. . . . Then (so the story runs) in the second generation after this Alexandrus son of Priam, having heard this tale, was minded to win himself a wife out of Hellas by ravishment; for he was well persuaded that, as the Greeks had made no reparation, so neither would he. So he carried off Helen" (*Herodotus*, tr. Godley, i.2–3).

32   Robert *Jenkin*[*s*]: "an English merchant captain, trading from Jamaica, who alleged that in 1731 his sloop had been boarded by a Spanish *guarda costa*, and that, though no proof of smuggling had been found, he had been tortured, and his ear torn off. The said ear—some said he had lost it in the pillory—he produced in 1738 in the House of Commons and so helped to force Walpole into the 'War of Jenkins' Ear' against Spain in 1739. Jenkins was later appointed governor of St. Helena" (*Chambers's*). See also *FW* 485:21. It would seem appropriate to describe it as a *sordid comm*[*ercial*] *war*. Perhaps Joyce was also thinking of the Trojan Wars. "[Alexander] commanded that Ilion [Troy] should rise again from its ruins, as a favoured city enjoying the rights of self-government and immunity from taxation" (J. B. Bury, *A History of Greece to the Death of Alexander the Great* [1900; 2d ed., New York, 1913], p. 750).

33–34   *Baltic amber* and *Russian waterway* seem to be connected. Joyce probably remembered a passage from one of his favorite books, Bérard's *Phéniciens et l'Odyssée* (I, 451): "Si les Phéniciens ont connu la route de l'ambre baltique, ils n'ont fait que précéder de vingt siècles leurs cousins d'Arabie. Car, entre la Baltique et la Caspienne, le long du Volga, les cachettes de monnaies arabes jalonnent une route de caravanes, qui monte aux côtes suédoises et aux îles baltiques." The peninsula of Samtland, formerly in East Prussia and now in the U.S.S.R., is famous for its amber. The primary technique of "Cyclops" is exaggeration. In *Epistle* ii.1, Horace so exaggerates his praise of the Emperor *Augustus* as to verge on mockery. He was probably serious, however, for the most part.

34   *Trebizond jade* is connected to *Baltic amber*, *Russian waterway*, and probably line 30. Trebizond (now Trabzon) was a city in the Greek empire of 1204–1461 on the southern coast of the Black Sea.

39–40   *Hugh Hyacinth* O'Rorke MacDermot, called The MacDermot (1834–1904), was born in *Coolavin*, County Sligo, eldest of twelve children. His father was Charles Joseph MacDermot, titular Prince of Coolavin. His mother was the last descendant of the Breffni family. A great liberal politician, in 1892 he became Attorney General of Ireland. His name is repeated at "Oxen" 5:2.

41   See *U* 294:27 and 78:21ff. *Bung* may refer to Bungiveagh and Bungardilaun, Irish towns, or it may mean the stopper in the bunghole of a cask. The Guinness brothers were Lords Iveagh and Ardilaun.

43   *Uphander*: military slang for a soldier surrendering (Partridge).

"Cyclops" 7

LEFT COLUMN HORIZONTAL

B ⟨Secured verdict by 1 length⟩ *632:35*

R ⟨Come home by weeping cross⟩ *315:1*

R ⟨whitehaired boy⟩

R ⟨Did I say to him or he to me?⟩

5   bloodgleam in eye of bronze dog.

R ⟨Honest injun⟩ *295:15, 419:19*

LB won't let bone go with that dog.

LB   stare him, best way out.

LB (?Mooney, jaw the wife when people by) worst thing you

10   ever did. *Cf. 636:3–4*

R ⟨bezique⟩ *300:33 and elsewhere*

R ⟨business proposition⟩ *421:6*

R ⟨English—orate pro me!⟩ *203:6?, 352:12?*

B ⟨Queen v Child⟩ *448:17–18*   mistaken identity

15 *R* ⟨LB meets people from Eccles Street⟩

R ⟨Show us entrance out⟩ *329:22*

B ⟨X.Y. heard these tidings undismayed⟩ *625:9*

B ⟨a tartan beard⟩ *643:28*

R ⟨molly coddle⟩ *300:33*   *R* ⟨fishful sea⟩ *288:40*

20 *B* ⟨noble art of self-pretence⟩ *573:25–26*

R ⟨to the manner born⟩   sown dragon's teeth

R ⟨cast nasturtiums⟩ *315:13*

R ⟨SD forgets to pay⟩   *R* ⟨Penelope keeps room for days⟩

R ⟨shrieks of silence⟩ *418:25*   *B* ⟨marvelled at the huguenot⟩

25 Tullamore plug

B ⟨Lottery—insurance swindle: one chap thinks next fellow

is going to lose   (hell (R) for the other
    fellow)⟩ *614:34–36*
R ⟨City Arms,   chewing the fat⟩ *300:42*
30   R ⟨Molly hair to her middle⟩ *736:20?*
Motley tie show no stains
Chr. Science. Well. Grief secretes tears   R ⟨Wool Sales 50
    Prussia ?st. Gavin Low⟩ *392:38–41*   R ⟨greasy hog & wether
    & down⟩ *392:37–38*
35   Dwarf oaks starved
R ⟨Nannetti asks Chief see polo played in 9 acres but comm.
    of police forbid games of the Sluagh na h-
    Eireann⟩ *310:15–18*

RIGHT COLUMN HORIZONTAL

R ⟨yahoo⟩ *323:31*
40   R ⟨bludgeon⟩ *462:31*
B ⟨bear with sore paw (Lestryg)⟩ *180:18*
R ⟨Cusack⟩
carcinoma of face
cyclostome
45   B ⟨elephantiasis.⟩ *483:12*
R ⟨in his glory hole⟩ *290:13*
R ⟨the curse of a lopsided God light sideways on the
    bloody thicklugged son of whores' gets.⟩ *319:21–22*
R ⟨a deputation of the most worthy burgesses of the most
50   obedient city waited on him.⟩ *469:28–29?*
B ⟨grilse⟩ *288:41*
trout
haddock
R ⟨halibut⟩ *288:41*
55   whiting
B ⟨duck egg⟩ *170:41–171:1*
B ⟨whirlwind on 1/5/904⟩ *297:8?*
R ⟨hearty plaudits⟩ *311:39–40*

Nisi Prius. Judge Wright & Tony ?O'M

60 ?chap v GNR

R ⟨the attendance was of large dimensions⟩ *311:25–26*

R ⟨high class vocalism⟩ *312:6*

B ⟨Do you know where Pappie is?⟩ *Cf. 604:6*

NOTES

"Cyclops" 7 is at the bottom of "Cyclops" 6 on a folded page and may be a continuation of it.
Phrases in the following lines appear on "Oxen" 7:

"Cyclops" 7	*"Oxen"* 7	*"Cyclops"* 7	*"Oxen"* 7
Line 12	Line 73	Line 23	Line 76
13	74	24	77
15	75	32–34	78 & 134–135

Phrases in the following lines appear on "Eumaeus" 5 and elsewhere:

"Cyclops" 7	*"Eumaeus"* 5	*"Cyclops"* 7	*"Eumaeus"* 5
Line 1	Line 94	Line 24	Line 101
17	100 and "Cyclops" 10:13	26–28	103
18	102		

Phrases in the following lines appear in *Ulysses* notebook VIII.A.5 at Buffalo (as paginated in
Studies in Bibliography, XXII [1969]):

"Cyclops" 7	*VIII.A.5*	*"Cyclops"* 7	*VIII.A.5*
Line 19	Page 294	Line 24	Page 310
21	296	40	297
23	297		

Line 9 *Mooney*: a doubtful reading. Bob Doran's wife (see Joyce's *Dubliners* story "The Boarding
House") was Polly Mooney before her marriage.

11 See "Cyclops" 2:36 and note.

14 The Childs murder case is discussed on pages 98–99, 448, and elsewhere in *Ulysses*. It was
publicized in the *Irish Independent*, Monday, October 23, 1899, p. 6 (Adams, p. 174). The final *s* in the
name seems to be missing in this line.

20 Repeated at "Circe" 3:49.

21 *Sown dragon's teeth*: last two words of the phrase appear in *U* 583:12. Though Joyce took it
from Bérard, the phrase probably has its ultimate source in the *Argonautica*, by Apollonius Rhodius.
It occurs rather often in classical literature, however.

25 *Tullamore*: a fertile agricultural district in County Offaly; also a kind of chewing tobacco. In

A Portrait (p. 36) Mr Casey says he had "a quid of Tullamore in my mouth and sure I couldn't say a word in any case because my mouth was full of tobacco juice."

27   *Hell (R) for the other fellow*: in pencil.

37-38   *Sluagh na h-Eireann*: the title of a contemporary chauvinistic group mentioned in the *Irish Daily Independent* of June 16, 1904 (Thornton, p. 274).

41   *Lestryg*: the "Lestrygonians" episode of *Ulysses*.

42   *Cusack*: see "Cyclops" 2:22 and note.

57   Compare this manner of writing dates with "Oxen" 5:2 and see Ellmann, p. 468. It is commonly found in the *Letters* as well.

59   The Honourable George *Wright* is listed in *Thom's Directory for 1904* as "Judge of High Court of Justice, King's Bench Division, 1 Fitzwilliam sq. east and Ryecroft, Bray."

60   *GNR*: The Great Northern Railway. The station is in Amiens Street, and the train operates between Dublin and Belfast (*U* 598:12, 714:35, 715:3).

63   *Pappie*: refers to Simon Dedalus (cf. "Eumaeus" 5:95). Joyce also called his father "Pappie" (Adams, pp. 74-75).

"Cyclops" 8

LEFT MARGIN HORIZONTAL

R ⟨burly barboy⟩
R ⟨deepen beds of Barrow & Shannon ½m. acres
    marsh⟩ *320:42–321:1*
R ⟨K. wool, textiles & potteries⟩ *320:25–26*
5   B ⟨Talismans⟩ *239:17, 467:20, 517:7*
Danish butter in Limerick
refresher

CENTER COLUMN HORIZONTAL

R ⟨Jesus did not speak Hebrew⟩
120,000 settlers   B ⟨Hebrew gymnasium in Jaffa. 200 ?scholars⟩
10   Haifa, polytechnical
Ech! ?yes! ?shield
Nestor's cup?   morning
Spider (cf. Fabre)   afternoon—ill-luck
B ⟨Grace O'Malley⟩   R ⟨Granuaile⟩ *324:13*
15   Daddy longlegs.   R ⟨oldest insects⟩
Can fly escape?
Because sp. can't fly.
B ⟨crab—cancer—get all colours grey. yellow⟩ *628:37*
B ⟨ants, bugs, lice, fleas⟩
20   8 legs, insects 3
conquest of air. John Mitchel cable £ 13/1/—2/6d
R ⟨take notice to be holden in and for the county of the

113

city of D.⟩

B ⟨licensed for the sale of beer, wine, & spirits for cons⟩

25   in Ireland— *B* ⟨consumption on the premises⟩ *171:20–21*

Mountjoy ?street

B ⟨D.M.P. (D.) (Sarah ?Ul. Isl. Bridge) (A. In Bridge

    ⋯⋯⋯

   Street) (C. Cat & Cage)

30   (A. In Camden Street) (B. Denzille Street)

   ↑A. Earl—   Charlotte—

   (E. Harold's Cross)   (Killiney 7)

   (Ringsend)⟩

Amulets & Zodiacal Gems (W.T. & K. Pavitt)

35 Wm. ?River & Son, Ltd, 8 Paternoster Row London E.C.4

Dwarf? *B* ⟨Leprechaun,⟩ *335:38* fairey

Gods not gigantic

B ⟨Buckley & Russian general (bloody boy)⟩

Galatea—little niece

40 *B* ⟨buttons—shields⟩

Difficulty of painting giant

B ⟨Timanthes, satyr with thyrsus measure his thumb⟩

B ⟨Dwarf—Marcella, the midget queen⟩ *620:31*

R ⟨cows in Connacht have long horns⟩ *322:23*

45 Gulliver, Café Gulliver

thalassocrat

B ⟨lie between Helen's thigh. silvermines of Euxine⟩

When icesheet retreated Scot & Scandinavia same race

Irish sea highway from Mittelmeer to Orkneys

50 *R* ⟨Chambered cairn at Maeshowe⟩ in = tomb at Mycene

   treasure chamber of Atreus—Ireland taught

   them to make tombs (Corny Kelleher)—long

   narrow heads, on east side roundheads (cyclops)

 R ⟨During Crimean bought horses for Br. army.⟩ *314:9–10*

55 Names (Pseudonyms, Shean Vean Vocht, *R* ⟨L.B. loss of maiden

   name⟩   Kiernan's other proprietor)

Exaggeration (Rhet. SD's lies, Molly's romancing)

non-jealous (jews, ?brothels)

B ⟨SD perhaps it is because "I" change that I am I.⟩ *Cf. 187:31*

60 *R* ⟨LB bob against man (2 types smile & scowl)⟩ *369:40*

R ⟨puissant chieftain⟩ *319:5*

B ⟨couch spear.⟩ *292:17*   apple & pear leaves

R ⟨patriot of solar system⟩

LB sees girl is that she?   skimander

65 *B* ⟨Castiglioni cardsharping⟩ *237:28?*

R ⟨commend me to a jew⟩ *308:9–10*

B ⟨to have or not to have⟩

R ⟨Inisfail the fair⟩ *288:36*

R ⟨yank to glory⟩ *421:3*

70 *R* ⟨wine-fizzling, ginsizzling booseguzzling existence

Come on, you bullnecked, bettlebrowed, hogjowled,

peanutbrained weaseleyed fourflushers, false

alarms & excess baggage⟩ *420:41–421:2*

sir James Daugherty, Castle ?funds (Orange party Ulster)

75 Parnell, Jim Macdermot, (Davitt ?'02)

B ⟨Fenian tells secret—shouts⟩

B ⟨Gestures of fenian cause tornado.⟩

Zionism retrograde

B ⟨¾ globe is sea⟩ *614:17–18*

80 Derby Rocksand (1904?)   Danny Maher

Cicero (Rosebery) 1905

maymooth ?anglicism   (Maria P.......

Irish, diversified vocabulary   of T.......)

Douglas Hyde   Canon O'Leary

85 Rothschild—got wind of Waterloo from Dutch ?navy

baron Lionel   18 gov. loans. founded the U.S. debt

financer of Austria

French railways, paid French war indem (1870)

lent 4 m. to G.B. to buy Suez Canal shares

NOTES

Phrases in the following lines are repeated on "Oxen" 7:

"Cyclops" 8	*"Oxen"* 7		*"Cyclops"* 8	*"Oxen"* 7
Line 1	Line 138		Line 63	Line 88 and "Circe" 6:76
22	139		69	89
61	cf. 25		70–73	90–93

Phrases in the following lines are repeated on "Eumaeus" 5 and elsewhere:

"Cyclops" 8	*"Eumaeus"* 5		*"Cyclops"* 8	*"Eumaeus"* 5
Line 5	Line 84		Line 43	Line 88
9	82		46	93
18	83		52	108 and "Cyclops" 4:96
27–33	85–86		79	89 and "Ithaca" 6:9
38	87, "Cyclops" 5:65, and "Oxen" 5:31			

Line 2   *Barrow & Shannon*: rivers in Ireland.

8   Cf. "Eumaeus" 6:183 and "Ithaca" 10:60–61.

9   This may have been intended for the Agendath Netaim land scheme ad which interests Bloom.

13   Jean Henri *Fabre*: a French entomologist (1823–1915).

14   *Grace O'Malley, Granuaile*: a pirate during the reign of Elizabeth I. Her Irish name was Granu Wail. She is the "Prankquean" in *FW* (pp. 21–23).

21   *John Mitchel*: an Irish patriot and founder of the *United Irishmen* (1815–1875). See also *U* 701:25.

27–33   These are divisions of the Dublin Municipal Police (cf. *U* 598:17, 599:9, 600:28–29). See also Ellmann, p. 218, and "Eumaeus" 5:85–86. Each division is designated by a letter, and the locations are easily identifiable on a map of Dublin except for *Cat & Cage*, which is a pub at 74 Upper Drumcondra Road. *Killiney* is south of Dublin, between Dun Laoghaire and Bray.

34   This is a book by William Thomas Pavitt and Kate Pavitt, entitled *The Book of Talismans, Amulets and Zodiacal Gems* (London, 1914).

35   Unidentified.

38   See "Cyclops" 5:65 and note.

39   See "Cyclops" 1:47 and note.

42   *Timanthes*: a Greek painter of the fourth century B.C., best known for his painting called the "Sacrifice of Iphigenia." "Pliny mentions his picture of a sleeping Cyclops, of a very small size (*parvula tabula*), in which the magnitude of the figure was indicated by the insertion of some satyrs, measuring his thumb with a thyrsus" (William Smith, ed., *Dictionary of Greek and Roman Biography and Mythology* [London, 1849]).

46   *Thalassocrat*: one who has maritime supremacy. Perhaps Joyce remembered the word from Bérard (I, 15 *et passim*) or the *Odyssey*.

47   See "Cyclops" 6:30 and note.

50–52   *Maeshowe*: the site of interesting tumuli in the Orkneys. Some important tombs of classical civilization are the Treasuries at Mycenæ, the chief one being the "Treasure-House of Atreus" (Oskar Seyffert, *Dictionary of Classical Antiquities* [1882; rev. ed., New York, 1956], p. 50). As an undertaker's assistant, *Corny Kelleher* would perhaps be interested in such things. Cf. "Cyclops" 4:96 and "Eumaeus" 5:108.

54   Cf. "Cyclops" 6:19.

55   *Shean Vean Vocht* (or Shan Van Vocht): literally the "old woman" in Irish, a personification symbolic of Ireland. Stephen calls her "Old Gummy Granny" (*U* 579, 584).

56   Barney *Kiernan's* pub was a famous one in Dublin and, being situated near the Four Courts, was frequented by solicitors and their clients. It is the setting for the "Cyclops" episode.

62   *Apple & pear leaves*: in pencil.

63   Cf. Scholes and Kain, p. 98.

64   *Skimander*: in pencil.

65   *Castiglioni*: Count Baldassare Castiglione (1478–1529), author of *Il Cortegiano*.

68   *Inisfail*: "isle of destiny," another name for Ireland. See also *Letters*, III, 55.

74   *James Daugherty*: a former Presbyterian minister, who was an Assistant Undersecretary in the government in Dublin (1906–1916), having succeeded Lord MacDonnell (see "Cyclops" 6:5 and note). *Castle funds*: probably refers to secret service money used for bribery and to combat Irish nationalism.

75   Desmond Ryan describes Red *Jim Macdermot* as "the infamous spy and evil genius of the Fenian organization for many years" (Thornton, p. 260). His name is repeated at "Cyclops" 9:4. Charles Stewart *Parnell* (1846–1891) needs no identification. Michael *Davitt* (1846–1906) was the founder of the Irish Land League.

80–81   Sir J. Miller's Rock Sand, with Danny Maher as jockey, won the Derby at Epsom Downs in 1903. K. Cannon rode Sir Leopold de Rothschild's St. Amant to victory in 1904. In 1905 Lord Rosebery's Cicero won with Danny Maher again riding the winner (*Ruff's Guide to the Turf* [London, 1923], p. 227).

82   This is not spelled "Maynooth."

84   *Douglas Hyde*: Irish author, philologist, and first president of the Gaelic League (1860–1949). He wrote *A Literary History of Ireland* (1899), poems and plays, and from 1938 until 1945 he was president of Ireland. *Canon* Peter *O'Leary*: a pioneer in the search for a modern Gaelic style in writing. He died in 1920. See MacManus, p. 676.

85   Meyer Amschel *Rothschild*: German financier (1743–1812). "His son Lionel (1808–1879) did much for the civil and political emancipation of the Jews in Great Britain" (*Chambers's*). In 1815 a Rothschild agent brought news of Napoleon's defeat at Waterloo to Nathan Rothschild (1777–1836) in England. Nathan made huge profits on the stock market from this advance information. The Rothschilds underwrote France's five-million-franc war indemnity to Prussia in 1870 and in 1875 financed Britain's purchase of Suez Canal stock.

"Cyclops" 9

CENTER COLUMN HORIZONTAL

B ⟨Pady Kelly's Budget⟩ *137:19*
R ⟨Conifer family⟩ *321:5*
B ⟨mountains & molehills⟩
B ⟨red Jim MacDermot⟩ *291:35*

NOTE

Line 4   See "Cyclops" 8:75 and note.

"Cyclops" 10

R ⟨Wooden horse (Hungary):⟩ *331:28–30*   R ⟨Peter the packer⟩ *292:6*
    R ⟨taxation swindle,⟩ *329:41–42*   R ⟨Irish consuls,⟩ *329:42*
    R ⟨Irish Amer capitalists, Germ—Irish boycott (USA)
    Germans studied   Semitic question in ?I (sub.
5   A.O.?H)⟩
B ⟨Skin the Goat⟩ *134:26, 605:39, and elsewhere*
R ⟨Molly Maguires⟩ *322:26*
Noman: B ⟨unnameless⟩ & unrestless in Israel, attempters of
    many enterprises
10 B ⟨John Eglinton, tried criminal assault, 2 years 2 sec⟩ *718:8?*
B ⟨the jew hates the jew in the jew.⟩
R ⟨Topical History: places remember events⟩ *163:17?*
undismayed
R ⟨a mensa et a thoro (thalamo).⟩
15 Volenti non fit iniuria
thrall, thraldom
B ⟨spider pitches her web⟩ *405:39–40*
benefit of clergy
R ⟨over all his troubles⟩ *297:23–24*
20 R ⟨sick and indignant roomkeepers⟩ *304:13*
Go yʳ· ways
B ⟨paraphernalia⟩ *328:11*
B ⟨coverture of wife⟩
R ⟨Recorder: bamboozle up to 2 eyes, heart as big as lion
25   jewman or landlord safe if not in dock, weep or blush,
    Ned Lambert no ~~respect~~ ?mercy. Understands a poor

bugger who had arrears or rent or stuck a jewman

Most natural thing in world⟩ *316:31–42*

R ⟨Market:⟩   B ⟨sales master, roaring mares,⟩ *289:35*   B ⟨sheep dip

30   scab,⟩ *309:30*   R ⟨timber tongue,⟩ *309:31*   springer, cutter,

R ⟨grazier.⟩ *309:35*

B ⟨Freedom of money⟩   of credit (mutualism), markets, land

(mint)   implead

interest

35   R ⟨Irish Land League⟩ *756:21?*

B ⟨State: monster fed with our blood, must be starved.⟩

sceptics of ?Gods doubt here too!   Cf. *628:20–22*

B ⟨Heaven: when quite sure of none men will make it on

earth⟩ Cf. *628:20–22*

40   B ⟨R.C. money on false pretences.⟩ *628:18–23*

B ⟨Election: 20 fools to elect 1 genius.⟩

Govt: why add govt to moral & material forces existing.

police provoke crimes or disappear, armies war.

R ⟨Ulysses Maximilian Browne of Camus, & Mountany⟩ *324:23–24*

45   S. ?A. bar. Browne, b.1705, f. marshal. M. Teresa

comm. Austria batt. Piacenza, carried Aust army

into France, comm. Lobositz (7 years' war). Killed

leading bayonet charge at Prague v Prussians 1757

u. prince Chas Lorraine

50   οδόν / Zeus

1 man of wrath or godless?

Grandfather Autolycus

R ⟨eye as good as a process:⟩ *294:14*   R ⟨I'm saying⟩

B ⟨H.M. ?as fireman, a DMP⟩ Cf. *72:4*   crowbar

55   R ⟨boosiness is boosiness⟩   R ⟨batten ram⟩

R ⟨Hanging (erection?)⟩ *299:38–42*

B ⟨Bantam Lyons buys flowers for girl: drunk⟩ fall about

puny (puisne)

R ⟨belabour⟩

60   R ⟨LB in knacker's yard⟩ *309:32*

R ⟨congering in church⟩   B ⟨(Mercadante)⟩ *336:17?*

R ⟨purling ale⟩ *393:8*

120

scrivened (Penelope)

R ⟨give credit bad ∴ they stay away⟩ *369:12–15*

65 shoelaces loose (? Cycl)

cycle (tour?)

Pox: great p. 15th century

   R ⟨1888 = 50% of all diseases in B. army due to it⟩ *72:1?*

R ⟨Israel. 'sons of the law'⟩ no law, a tongue, Israel's god.

70 B ⟨Cattle exp. £15m. 6m. pork, 5⅕ m. butter, 5 m. eggs.⟩ *624:25–27*
   ?fruit

B ⟨History: for schoolboys = algebra, hokuspokus: . . . . &
   evidence⟩ *183:19–20, 627:38–39*

R ⟨what is truth? truth, whole truth, nothing but truth s'elp

75   me Jimmy Johnson⟩ *315:11–12*

   LB thinks what he says about me?

   chosen people, God on our side

   doubting Thomas, past sausagemeat present.

   learn—unlearn, built—destroy, Penelope,

80 R ⟨Introit in Epiphania Domini, lectio Isaiae.

   Surge, illuminare, multitudo maris⟩ : inundatio camelorum

   operiet te, Dromedarii Madian et Epha.

   ?Gradual   R ⟨Omnes de Saba venient: aurum et thus

   deferentes⟩ *334:1–4*

85 R ⟨spoiling for a fight⟩

R ⟨martyrs long for it (Some girl in window look with

   ?pity)⟩ *281:21ff.?*

Lousy jews fox & fleas, last flea LB

B ⟨New York is new Jerusalem—new Dublin⟩ *327:3?*

RIGHT COLUMN HORIZONTAL

90 R ⟨bloodthirsty entities on astral⟩ *296:15–16*

R ⟨?thus didst thou, Eumaeus⟩

Some laugh out, some snigger

LB angry when ?man does not ?haunt Molly

R ⟨menstruates (1 day per mensa)⟩

95   R ⟨bought Neaves Food for son⟩ *332:3*

right hand up (solve)

left   — down (coagula)

R ⟨on eastern angle where the ram has rule. M & J out for

     mischief⟩ *296:30–31*

100   B ⟨gent of the jury⟩

R ⟨risk life to save life⟩ *384:4*

Golem, 33 years

let loose electic of race

B ⟨Torquemada banished Jews, England let 'em in. Jews with

105   . . . . . ⟩ *Cf. 628:11–15*

R ⟨in conseq. of information recd.⟩ *317:38*

R ⟨I.N.F. (Grand High Chief Ranger)⟩ *321:14*

B ⟨hope he won't keep us all night⟩

?bound to place

110   R ⟨conspuez les anglais⟩ *319:33*

R ⟨crim. diversion of a letter⟩ *419:11*   R ⟨come where the

G ⟨man age of arteries⟩   booze is

                                  cheaper⟩ *324:41–42*

                     R ⟨Kaffir⟩ *329:14, 436:13*

115   fuit Ilium   *142:33*

NOTES

Phrases in the following lines are repeated on "Oxen" 7:

"Cyclops" 10	"Oxen" 7		"Cyclops" 10	"Oxen" 7
Line 12	Line 84		Line 61	Line 87
55	86		101	85

Phrases in the following lines are repeated on "Eumaeus" 5:

"Cyclops" 10	"Eumaeus" 5		"Cyclops" 10	"Eumaeus" 5
Line 6	Line 69		Line 41	Line 75
10	70		70	79
32	72		72–73	78
36	73		89	80
38–39	77		104	81 and "Cyclops" 5:79
40	76; cf. "Cyclops" 1:44 note			

Line 1   *Peter the packer*: Lord Peter O'Brien, Lord Chief Justice of Ireland (Thornton, p. 263).

4   There may be a comma after *studied*.

6   *Skin the Goat*: supposedly one of the notorious Invincibles. See "Cyclops" 4:108 and note.

7   *Molly Maguires*: members of a nineteenth-century Irish secret society in America.

8   *Noman*: the fictitious name by which Odysseus identifies himself to the Cyclops.

10   *John Eglinton*: local littérateur who appears in "Scylla and Charybdis" (*U* 182ff.). This was the nom de plume of William K. Magee.

13   See "Cyclops" 7:17.

14   See "Cyclops" 5:56 and note. *Thoro*: "bed" in Latin.

15   *Volenti non fit iniuria*: To one who wills it an injury does not occur. It could also mean "to one not wishing it an injury *occurs*."

20   In the text it is "indigent roomkeepers." See also *FW* 6:4—"his ville's indigenous rome-keepers." This is mentioned in a note by Philip L. Graham in *A Wake Newslitter*, III (Oct. 1966), 117—"In a building off Dame Street, Dublin, is a sign in large letters: 'SICK AND INDIGENT ROOMKEEPERS SOCIETY—FOUNDED A.D. 1790.'" Cf. Scholes and Kain, p. 90.

26   *Lambert* was present at Dignam's funeral (*U* 89ff.), at the news office (*U* 122ff.), and at other times. His name is repeated at "Nausicaa" 2:84.

28   *Most natural thing in world*: repeated at "Ithaca" 1:54; see *U* 88:40.

44   Count *Ulysses Maximilian Browne* (1705–1757), "born at Basel, of an Irish Jacobite family, became one of the foremost fieldmarshals in Maria Theresa's army and commanded the Austrians at Lobositz (1756) in the Seven Years' War. He was mortally wounded at the battle of Prague" (*Chambers's*). See also *A Portrait* (Viking Critical ed.), pp. 19, 491.

50   The Greek word is an epithet for Zeus, meaning "farsighted."

52   *Autolycus*: grandfather of Odysseus.

57   *Bantam Lyons*: see *U* 73, 84, 175, 230, 297, 329, and elsewhere.

58   *Puisne*: an inferior or junior judge in superior courts of common law.

61   Saverio *Mercadante*: an Italian composer of music (1795–1870). Bloom mistakenly believes he was a Jew. See Adams, pp. 197–198. The name is repeated at "Eumaeus" 6:188; see also note there.

65   The question mark before *Cycl* is Joyce's.

67   *P*: pox or plague.

68   *B*: British.

72   The illegible word looks like *sombroso*.

79   This is probably a reference to the shroud which Penelope weaves for Laertes.

80–84   This is from the Mass of the Feast of the Epiphany (also in the Book of Isaiah 60: 1–6). Joyce skips from the opening "*Surge, illuminare*, Jerusalem" to "quando conversa fuerit ad te *multitudo Maris*" to "*Inundatio camelorum* venient, *aurum et thus deferentes*."

90–99   This section of the notesheet is separated by lines on three sides.

98   *M & J*: Mars and Jupiter.

102–105   This section of the manuscript is separated by lines on two sides.

102   *Golem*: "in Jewish folklore an image endowed with life. In the Bible the word signifies an unformed substance, and hence an unmarried woman may be called a *golem*. Medieval legends applied it to wooden images given life by the saints, and with the oppression of the Jews arose stories, such as that of Rabbi Low, of *golems* that protected their masters" (*Encyclopædia Britannica*).

104   Cf. "Cyclops" 5:79 and "Eumaeus" 5:81. Tomás de *Torquemada*: the first inquisitor-general of Spain (1420–98).

107 See "Cyclops" 2:67 and note.

112 Cf. "Oxen" 8:73.

114 See "Cyclops" 2:22 and note.

115 *Fuit Ilium*: see Virgil, *Aeneid*, ii.325. These are the words of the High Priest at the moment of the fall of Troy (Campbell and Robinson, p. 49).

"Nausicaa" I

LEFT MARGIN HORIZONTAL

R ⟨begin to be sensitive.   Is mine? Yes.⟩ *373:21*
childbig woman passes

LEFT COLUMN HORIZONTAL

R ⟨blown in from the bay (D.B.)⟩ *369:16*   ~~steel wire~~ v
                                                snoring   *534:2-3*

5   *R* ⟨are you at it again?⟩ *360:37*
     B ⟨child & cruelty ad.⟩ *717:37*   *R* ⟨?leaser was enough⟩
     B ⟨Change of furniture. LB foresees.⟩ *Cf. 690:14ff.*
     B ⟨golden syrup.⟩ *340:38*
     R ⟨car pass to maternity hospital.⟩   ~~luminous dials~~
10   onanism: Sterne, Swift, Wilde
          (pruriency: misanthropy—satire
          R ⟨?prolongation⟩ *403:42?*   —cloacism—hatred of action)
     R ⟨Milly sleep with Molly: her pulse⟩ *373:15-17*   *R*⟨⟨Swedenborg
          ?sense of love in ?poem of ?bauds⟩⟩
15   *R* ⟨paps (girl)⟩ *373:20*   *R* ⟨hand now big⟩ *373:18*
     R ⟨Menstruate Molly: things ton weight,⟩ *363:1*   molehills small
     R ⟨things ?monetary⟩   *R* ⟨:nestle:⟩ *343:8*
     R ⟨photographs⟩ *359:39*   ?laggenet
     R ⟨tarred with same brush (painting)⟩ *366:20-21*
20   *B* ⟨Poem to man's socks⟩   *R*: ⟨cut of his jib.⟩ *361:28*
     R ⟨My native land, goodnight.⟩ *370:5-6*
     R ⟨virgo parathalassia (Star of Sea)⟩ *340:9*

LB chocolate present   B ⟨Marcus Tertius Moses⟩ *229:41, 442:2*

B ⟨?chacone (?Durard)⟩

25   R ⟨Blumenlied⟩ *274:16*   (   )

boys' handkerch. High School cf Milly Nausikaa

R ⟨wonderful if the (?clitoris) answers "Good evening"⟩ *364:8–9*

R ⟨Kids at 2nd visit unruly.⟩ *370:32*

R ⟨l^d. for y^r. thoughts⟩ *354:27*   R ⟨winsome,⟩ *342:7*   yoke of dress

30   R ⟨pent up feelings⟩ *345:9*

ice lighter than water (poles)

B ⟨billing   (B.B. ?Jews Dillon)⟩

R ⟨Sailor, wife in every port (Ul.)⟩ *372:6–7*

R ⟨Nuns pass. Nausikaa, cool coifs, whitewashed faces⟩ *362:30–31*

35   R ⟨Phocas—no ends of the earth⟩ *333:8?, 372:5–6*

R ⟨Her chaplet⟩

R ⟨cigarsmelly gloves of BB⟩ *368:36–37*

R ⟨Smthg she told me to ?Luhan: too much: ?I loved.⟩

Mrs Sinico.

40   R ⟨O'Connor, mussel poisoning.⟩ *374:16–17*   Greek

Jews no bells.   R ⟨ram's horns.⟩ *366:24*

R ⟨LB remembers dream / 5.p.m.⟩ *364:23?*

nymphs, symphs.

German band spies.

45   ?Telgms.   ?Mr Riordan.

R ⟨Lust: stick out underjaw (Molly)⟩ *367:37*

woman (45), Men (35)

Prick ?strong morning.

R ⟨Leo Dillon (16) Goddess Venus with all her belongings.

50   Innocence⟩ *365:18*

R ⟨François Jammes.⟩

R ⟨le long des tremblements de pluie des eglantiers⟩

proud sinful throb, well in throat,

R ⟨neat way she carried that parcel⟩ *365:32–33*

55   R ⟨Women know birds' speech⟩ *365:10*

R ⟨LB. attend to appearance love⟩ *363:15–16*

R ⟨Women pleased at death because birth troubles them (Sirens:

      obituary)⟩ *86:16–17?*

R ⟨Man looks s̶t̶ mangled out after good tuck in⟩ *369:18*

60 R ⟨always at home at dinner time.⟩ *369:17*

R ⟨Buried the poor husband,⟩ *374:13* cut up.

R ⟨(Milly) Carried home change in shoe: sly little minx⟩ *365:31–32*

R ⟨Molly in pyjamas. Do I like? Difficult. Awfully⟩ *374:27*

R ⟨drawers little kick. byby.⟩ *368:22–23*

65 R ⟨heart pitapat⟩ *351:18–19*

M. sleeps.   face billygoat in twilight.

R ⟨Cat sits beyond dog's jump.⟩ *365:16*

R ⟨LB sees cat turfbrown on stairs⟩ *371:27*

RIGHT COLUMN HORIZONTAL

R ⟨baby: cocoanut skull fontanelle.⟩ *366:29–30*

70 R ⟨birds? killed in storm⟩ *371:42*

R ⟨Watch stops 4:40⟩ *363:29*

R ⟨billy winks: Sandman⟩ *356:38–39*

R ⟨Rumpled stockings⟩ *366:1, 163:35*

R ⟨(AE's ?mob) deprive him if ?born⟩ *366:1?*

75 Prick: kidney citron.

B ⟨LB wish to be ?mean⟩

R ⟨characters ?.imed together⟩

R ⟨Woman lose charm with every pin⟩ *362:20–23*

kneading

80 R ⟨Vamps (stock) warm⟩ *368:21*

R ⟨(Motto. Never begin conversation if you can't finish it)⟩ *364:6*

R ⟨whole hog⟩ *364:28*

R ⟨:Masked children:⟩ *373:10*

R ⟨Veil: under her full carnose lips.⟩ *365:3ff.*

85 R ⟨bears grease⟩ *363:14*

R ⟨eyes, full of strange shining⟩ *361:15–16*

R ⟨the man bowed his head⟩ *360:35–36*

R ⟨adamant⟩ *359:9*

R ⟨LB throws ball crooked as a ram's horn⟩ *366:23–24*

90 R ⟨Women Kraftlos?⟩

R ⟨his for the asking⟩ *362:5?*

Jew → West

East ← Zion

R ⟨Urinal before Nausikaa visits, Sings coming out⟩ *Cf. 364:4*

95 *R* ⟨Molly hand up & shake   to let blood flow back⟩ *365:34*

B ⟨painter⟩ *367:39*

NOTES

Nausikaa appears in Joyce's hand in the upper left-hand corner.

Line 1   Refers to "paps" in line 15.

2   To be inserted after "Nuns pass" in line 34.

3   *D.B.*: Dublin Bay.

7   Cf. "Nausicaa" 2:98 and "Circe" 3:69.

10–12   These lines are thematically connected. See the essay on "Nausicaa," pp. 27–29; Ellmann, p. 241; *U* 130:6–10 and 132:12–13; cf. "Circe" 11:76.

22   *Virgo parathalassia*: "Virgin by / over the sea." There may also be a play here on "Mary" / *mare* (*U* 340:9).

23   *Marcus Tertius Moses*: a tea merchant (*U* 442:2).

24   Repeated at "Circe" 3:68. A dubious reading. *Chacone* (usu. *chaconne*): a Spanish dance or musical composition therefore.

25   Joyce inserted parentheses after *Blumenlied* and may have momentarily forgotten the composer's name, Gustav Lange. Lange was the author of a book on Beethoven and Wagner entitled *Musikgeschichtliches* (Berlin, 1900), as well as *Transcriptions and Variations* (Chicago and New York, 1901), probably a translation. The word is repeated at "Nausicaa" 4:27 and "Circe" 3:59.

29   *1ᵈ· for yʳ· thoughts* is repeated at "Nausicaa" 5:64–65.

32   *Dillon*: this may be the Leo Dillon in line 49 or Val Dillon, lord mayor of Dublin (*U* 153: 17–18 and elsewhere).

35   *Phocas*: there are several possibilities here. "S. Phocas of Sinope" is mentioned in *Ulysses* (333:8). Joyce had a Greek friend in Zurich named Pavlos Phocas (Scholes, ed., *Cornell Joyce Collection*, items 963, 964). A sanguinary emperor of Constantinople named Phocas died in A.D. 610. Other men by this name were prominent in the Byzantine period.

39   *Mrs Sinico*: a character in the *Dubliners* story "A Painful Case." She was killed by a train, and Bloom attended her funeral. (See *U* 113, 680, 695.)

45   *Mr Riordan*: see "Cyclops" 2:36 and note for Dante Riordan. Perhaps this is the husband who deserted her (Ellmann, p. 24).

49   *Leo Dillon*: perhaps an acquaintance of Joyce's youth.

51   Francis (not *François*) *Jammes*: a French writer of poems on nature and religion (1868–1938).

Line 52 may be from one of his poems. It may be translated "along the shimmerings of rain on the briars."

70 Joyce's question mark.

74 These two phrases may not be connected. *AE*: George Russell, Irish poet (1867–1935). Bloom meets him in the "Lestrygonians" episode (*U* 163).

90 *Kraftlos*: without strength.

94 Cf. "Nausicaa" 5:17.

"Nausicaa" 2

LEFT MARGIN HORIZONTAL

R ⟨Get a group taken ?E.M.   7 m.⟩ *348:36*
R ⟨same teeth as mother identical⟩ *373:15*
R ⟨Seaside girls.⟩ *365:14*
B ⟨perfectly appointed⟩ *346:13?*
5   B ⟨redolent⟩ *600:26 and elsewhere*
up to some mischief
there was appeal in her voice
R ⟨cut silence icily⟩ *356:20*
R ⟨Knock spots off⟩ *367:3*
10   she sensed the—
high in heavens (sun)
R ⟨her every gesture⟩
R ⟨what doing with yourself⟩ *362:36*
R ⟨every line of her⟩
15   R ⟨conventions⟩ *358:24*
R ⟨Years slipped by⟩ *358:3–4*
R ⟨will it make very much difference?⟩ *358:16*
R ⟨lump rose in her throat⟩ *356:8?*
R ⟨head just reached his heart⟩ *361:15?*
20   B ⟨Yester eve⟩ *361:13*
R ⟨broke pitiously (voice)⟩ *345:23?*
R ⟨it hurts.⟩ *356:4*
R ⟨land of song⟩
R ⟨her slender arms⟩ *360:22*
25   R ⟨on the rocks⟩ *363:22*
R ⟨worship at her shrine⟩ *355:29*

R ⟨exquisite contours⟩ *355:28?*

R ⟨a little apart,—aloof⟩ *356:32*

R ⟨Society with a big ess⟩ *358:24*

30 R ⟨flawless⟩ *356:8*

considerably to her surprise

R ⟨lips parted swiftly⟩ *356:7*

straight youngster

displaces part of earth's mass and modifies course of moon

35 R ⟨If 1 atom stopped the whole x x ghesabo would⟩ *367:26–27*

R ⟨magnet never err, little piece of iron⟩ *367:28–29*

?swallows also.

R ⟨little needle in . . . .   jump when Sol explodes⟩ *367:28?*

LEFT COLUMN HORIZONTAL

R ⟨Milly "Me have a nice pace"⟩ *365:38*

40 R ⟨Girls ask "what is your name" "Butter & cream"⟩ *341:32*

R ⟨Only ?Mrs Paddy knows.⟩

B ⟨Pavement artist (Nausikaa)⟩ *351:14*

R ⟨λευκόλενος⟩ *Cf. 349:20–22*

R ⟨Insects: reason flight? that bee was playing with shadow

45   on ceiling⟩ *371:37–39*

the spider . . . . ?   Eunuchs drones?

R ⟨Photo Bits   "Dream of wellfilled hose" lingerie⟩ *362:9–12*

        "spanking sound comes up breeze" "spanking breeze comes

        up sound"

50 R ⟨Lamplighter's lintstock.⟩ *372:29*

R ⟨LB writes in sand. what?⟩ *375:1*

R ⟨Mice comes out   why only night,   light or noise?⟩ *371:18–20*

R ⟨All impossible till you try.⟩   R ⟨(somnambula)⟩

R ⟨Children waiting for somethg to occur.⟩ *365:1*

55 R ⟨Baby possing wet.⟩ *351:1*

R ⟨Cook: stir pudding in same direction⟩ *346:6–9*   (migration jews)

B ⟨Sippets of toast:⟩ *Cf. 167:19*   R ⟨creaming milk & sugar.⟩ *346:9*

        pattypans.

131

R ⟨Time to spray flowers.⟩ *369:41*

60 R ⟨finestretched close mail,   swell of her calf.⟩ *365:40–41*

R ⟨LB interrogat se re altro (for Titbits)⟩ *454:21?, 369:24?*

R ⟨Naus: straight on her pins.⟩ *365:39*

R ⟨Eire: land of setting sun.⟩ *370:5, 340:2*

R ⟨Women never remember verse⟩

65 Boys' toys: pegtop, whiptop.

R ⟨LB, good plan, talk to self.⟩ *Cf. 364:6*

R ⟨Hyacinth perfume,   oil of ether.⟩ *368:27–28*

R ⟨LB: her legs: goodbye, uncle.   (she can't see herself)⟩ *361:11?*

R ⟨Milly: dry handker. on mirror, save ironing. (bred in the

70   bone)⟩ *365:27–29*

R ⟨Woman in hurry—off to a fellow⟩ *362:25*

R ⟨Small woman = small man, made & matched⟩ *367:11–12*

R ⟨I know but I was told not to let on⟩ *342:23–24?*

B ⟨lilypots (tobacco)⟩ *83:9* —love marriage is a sacrilege

75 R ⟨trip on Guinness's barge.⟩ *375:14*

fuchsia (women & flowers)

R ⟨(Naus) somethg wrong with her.⟩ *361:28*

R ⟨Moon after bad weather: not my fault, old cock⟩ *372:20–21*

R ⟨Eyes clear   whites not pupils⟩ *365:14–15*

80 B ⟨Servant sings   well treated⟩

R ⟨lovelock ?over dexter optics (poet)⟩ *363:14–15*

R ⟨Bacon & Essex. (pretend you ?want smthg. then cry off

Elizabeth)⟩ *364:29–30*

R ⟨Ned Lambert: pictures of girls in jakes.⟩ *362:10?*

85 Infant LB ?pokes, little eyes dark & ?burned like sick fruits

B ⟨Merchants Arch: conjugial love⟩ *Cf. 232*

Weeds, sponges, trees of coral, they detach if not firm

animals   (thinking cabbages)

R ⟨Flowers know ?how⟩

90 B ⟨quick as lightning (? how)⟩ *356:16*

Young earth. no seasons, world of shells.

age weight of earth (?) who made world?

America no deluge: ocean will again.

R ⟨Time formed by periodic movements of bodies⟩ *367:25–26*

95 Crocodiles: eye 1 ft long.

Mask (Jap. Greek) Schrecken ?wollens

(bark, leather, voicebox) Totems

B ⟨Molly will change furniture⟩ *Cf. 690:14ff.*

R ⟨ ″ noticed man had false arm (LB said goodlooking)⟩ *365:23–24*

100 B ⟨timbrel⟩ *414:27* surf, skiffs

R ⟨are corns healthy: rain coming⟩ *369:27* R ⟨old Betty's
joints⟩ *369:30*

R ⟨O'Connor widower⟩ *374:15–16*

R ⟨Simone Brustlein's hat hides face (?or flower)⟩ *363:19–20*

105 R ⟨seasickness, ears, sharks, nose⟩ *372:17–18*

R ⟨Baby does ah ah, Fuller's earth.⟩ *366:26–27*

clap clap hands. *476:28ff.*

R ⟨There are (no lights) or colours⟩ *371:24?*

Libyan floods Mars 1882, 1888 *685:15*

110 R ⟨Love, feel funny, mushylike, smthg inside goes pop, tell by
the look in her eye, on the sly⟩ *364:33–34*

RIGHT COLUMN HORIZONTAL

Tide, waters, wind, clouds

S ⟨a nobody⟩ *365:35*

R ⟨whisk⟩ *346:9*

115 scarp.

R ⟨loi des isthmes⟩ R ⟨(Liverpool)⟩ *375:20?*

R ⟨off colour.⟩

NOTES

Line 25 *The*: inserted above a caret.

35 The *x x* stands for "blankety blank."

43 This Greek word is another of Joyce's errors: the accented omicron should be an omega.

The word means "white-armed" and is an epithet of goddesses and of Nausicaa in the *Odyssey*. See Gilbert, p. 289.

44   There is an ink blot after *reason*.

46   The ellipses are Joyce's.

55   *Possing*: suggests "sopping."

61   *LB interrogat se re altro*: LB interrogates himself about something.

82–83   It is not clear what this phrase has to do with *Bacon*, *Essex*, and Queen *Elizabeth*. Francis Bacon was a protégé of Robert Devereux, 2nd Earl of Essex, during the years 1594–98, but he later denied this. After Essex's childish rebellion Bacon was one of the prosecutors who condemned Essex to death in 1601.

84   See "Cyclops" 10:26 and note.

85   Cf. "Nausicaa" 3:18–24 and "Circe" 16:80–81.

86   Cf. *U* 401:41. "Conjugal" was corrected in the 1961 Random House edition to "conjugial" (408:33).

90   The question mark preceding *how* is Joyce's.

92   *Age . . . earth*: as written *weight* is below the line to the right of a caret inserted between *age* and *of*.

96   Joyce's German is strange here. Probably the masks are meant to terrify.

98   Repeated at "Circe" 3:69; cf. "Nausicaa" 1:7.

104   *Simone Brustlein*: probably a pseudonym.

116   Bérard (I, 69) says: "Cette loi régit plus strictement encore les navigations primitives: si l'on n'en tient pas compte, l'établissement du phénicien Kadmos à Thèbes peut sembler à bon droit légendaire. Nous invoquerons souvent cette loi; il faut donc une fois pour toutes la bien établir sur des exemples typiques. Ces exemples bien expliqués montreront ensuite dans le voyage terrestre de Télémaque, non plus le roman géographique que certains imaginent, mais un itinéraire réel, familier aux marchands de ces temps anciens: la route terrestre de la 'Télémakheia' est d'une description aussi matériellement exacte que la traversée maritime."

"Nausicaa" 3

LEFT MARGIN HORIZONTAL

?Turns nitrate to silver
?rocea (hand)
ziplenka (match)
atrog (child)
5   pivo (wine)
rutsch (smoke)
kalch (pen)
leva (left)   ura (watch)
desno (right) chrog (bread)
10   hischach (house)
morie (sea)
spat (sleep)
girla (to drink)

CENTER COLUMN HORIZONTAL

R ⟨Under cloudy sky thought dull,⟩ *Cf. 164:1–2*   *R* ⟨oysters⟩ *172:22 and elsewhere*
15   *R* ⟨If earth alone is space immovable⟩ *367:24–25?*
LB   autoscopics   (vesical dreams, prodromics)
R ⟨LB's favourite dream.⟩ *374:25ff.?*   disease foretold
B ⟨LB poked infant gently with plump protruded forefinger in
         armpit. Inf. surprised & calmed turned round eyes blue
20   as cornflower toward LB's grave face. It hiccupped:
         and a noiseless trickle of curdled milk came out of the
         corner of mouth. It gazed upward out of blue glass

135

eyes (iris no pigment everchanging) observant & unseeing.
& suddenly smiled at LB.⟩ *Cf. 476:30–33*

25 *R* ⟨In time of drought bird to get water from jar throw in
pebbles   cf⟩   (mice & ?orb) *371:21–22*

R ⟨Dialogue of signs, good as any other⟩ *366:14–15?*

R ⟨Honey of dew.⟩ *370:7?*

Lizard dragons

30 Sun in south enemy: night, coolness of rain
                                                                    friends

Aphrodite, poised hips unveiled for judgment

B ⟨In mirror left hand is right⟩   *B* ⟨optical illusion⟩ *370:4*

B ⟨Divining rod: outsiders important in science   why⟩

35 *B* ⟨auf Wasser ?seasirens Women feel storms, earthquakes.⟩ *369:29ff.*

Hot body throws off heat till it equalizes temperature of
ambiente.   *B* ⟨Cavities? ore? Coal? Water because of its
heat?⟩   the consumptive.

40 *R* ⟨They have no G.C.M. of magnitude. think a paper has reached
earth which is still in air. Air thin: don't feel
distance. Giddiness → Entfernung. Kinder haben es nicht.
so they clutch at moon⟩ *Cf. 367:24ff.*

B ⟨Warts: hanging or tight. Snip off ?w a horsehair, stops
45 blood supply, starves wart. Caustic prevents rebirth.
Warts with no denned neck, wartblood spreads warts⟩
503:11 & 27–28

B ⟨Sickness good way out of difficulty: people must⟩ *Cf. 723*
look after you & you think what you like.

50 *B.* Hoffmann: Kunst u. Vogelgesang.

R ⟨Bat little man with entomorphic head⟩ *371:22*

R ⟨Belfry: hanging head down whistling. hands⟩ *371:10*

velvety paws, ?hookers, spades, rudder, fin,

thumb separate, before sundown (eine ?Art)

55 bird with no head, mammals, torpor, migratory also

?drucklose. Hauch,   *R* ⟨take me for a tree,⟩ *371:6–7*   I see their
R ⟨phosphoresant little bones.⟩ *371:23–24*   *R* ⟨harvest⟩ *391:23*

R ⟨?Fliers: periodic & wavelike: leaves, ¢ø¢ý rut, birth,⟩

> *R* ⟨sleep & unfolding of flower & leaf, reaction of climbing sap,⟩
> 60 *R* ⟨seabeasts to tide, blood temperature,⟩
> *R* ⟨growing pains, (Milly),⟩ *373:22–23* *R* ⟨worked by stars⟩
> *R* ⟨23 (M): 28 (W): female substance: usual sex mixed:⟩
> *R* ⟨know hour of death ticketed: sickness dates 7 years period.⟩
> Kuckoo: peewit: (Galliphone: maneater) how sing flying
> 65 (major & minor third) perhaps air goes other way.
> Right = S. Left = N. J.C.
> Right hand, pledge troth
>   L (Peter)E   R(Paul)
> swear, oiled, *B* ⟨ring on left.⟩   W
> 70 *B* ⟨Devil & witches lefthanded⟩
> Right—sow,
> *B* ⟨Insects (male) follow smell of female.⟩, *504:11–12*
> *R* ⟨smell ?gauze on which she lay⟩
> *R* ⟨Jewish tablets on doorpost: good idea ∴ going ?to meet
> 75   dangers⟩

LOWER RIGHT COLUMN HORIZONTAL

B ⟨left for rings not to spoil them⟩ & to appease demons
centre of gravity of world
R ⟨drawers (cf. bed linen)⟩ *368:22–24?*

NOTES

Lines 2ff. Joyce may have been listing his entire Slovene vocabulary here. The words are phonetic approximations, and some of them are unmistakable errors. *Pivo*, for instance, is "beer" in every Slavic language; in no case could it mean *wine*. A letter of September ?8, 1920 (*Letters*, III, 19), shows that Joyce knew enough about Slovene to imitate this accent in Italian. The following is a list of correctly written equivalents for the English words in these lines:

hand = roka	to smoke = kaditi	right = desen	sea = morje
match = enak	pen = pero, pisec	bread = kruh	to sleep = spati
child = otrok	left = leva	house = hiša	to drink = piti
wine = vino	watch = ura		

Ziplenka, rutsch, girla, and *kalch* apparently have no meaning in Slovene.

17   *LB's favourite dream*: cf. "Nausicaa" 5:62.

18–24   Cf. "Nausicaa" 2:85 and "Circe" 16:80–81.

42   Joyce decided to switch to German in this line. *Entfernung*: distance. *Kinder haben es nicht* means that children do not have an adequately developed sense of distance; they clutch at the moon thinking it to be quite close.

44–46   Repeated at "Circe" 3:61–63.

50   Bernhard *Hoffmann's* book is *Kunst und Vogelgesang in ihren wechselseitigen Beziehungen vom naturwissenschaftlich-musikalischen Standpunkte* (Leipzig, 1908).

56   *Drucklos*: without pressure. *Hauch*: breath.

58–63   Repeated at "Oxen" 7:69–72.

64   More spelling variants: *Kuckoo* is neither German nor English; the German word is *Kuckuck*. Galliformes constitute an order of birds which includes turkeys, quails, partridges, and domestic fowls, but not *cuckoos* or *peewits* (pewits). But Joyce wrote *galliphone* (note "Slavophone" in *Ulysses* notebook VIII.A.5 at Buffalo, p. 295), which should refer to their speech (?) or whatever noises galliformes make. None of these birds is, of course, a *maneater*. *How sing flying* may have been suggested by a folk song entitled "The Cuckoo's a pretty bird, / She sings as she flies." See the "Nausicaa" essay, pp. 25–27; cf. "Cyclops" 1:54–55 and "Circe" 17:98.

70   Repeated at "Circe" 3:66. The commentary on the hands in lines 66–71 was doubtless meant for the "Circe" episode.

"Nausicaa" 4

LEFT MARGIN HORIZONTAL

R ⟨(Bad women Dodder bank ?beds)⟩ *358:18–20*
R ⟨Menses ?breasts it's ?nose bleed⟩
B ⟨?Gretch⟩
B ⟨do you believe?⟩
5   *R* ⟨Suitors⟩ *342:33*
R ⟨There is S and there is P. L. too.⟩
R ⟨Art thou real?   My ideal!⟩ *357:41–42*
R ⟨innate refinement⟩ *342:26*
R ⟨the lovely lips pouted⟩ *343:17*
10   *R* ⟨smthg off the common⟩ *343:37*
?lurteen jail   ?Capets ?lash
swinging

LEFT COLUMN HORIZONTAL

R ⟨eggblue, nigger, to tone⟩ *344:11–12*
hatter's plush   *B* ⟨that's not for you to say.⟩
15   *R* ⟨undies⟩ *344:28*
R ⟨slotted with rosepink ribbon⟩ *344:33*
?tomato   *R* ⟨chenille, underbrim⟩ *344:11–12*
R ⟨butterfly bow,⟩ *344:12*   pretty
R ⟨Molly—hat on top of waterjug⟩ *344:19*
20   *R* ⟨Night prayers, kiddies⟩ *363:38*
R ⟨wide garter top⟩ *344:27–28*   *R* ⟨lattice⟩ *349:17 and elsewhere*
R ⟨high spliced heels⟩ *344:27*

R ⟨(LB) French letter in pocket⟩ *364:21–22*

R ⟨answer by asking (if stuck)⟩ *364:7–8*

25   R ⟨½ past kissing time⟩ *354:34*   lavish

R ⟨anything for a quiet life⟩ *347:3*   / lave / nder

B ⟨Blumenlied (Gustav Lange)⟩ *274:16*

R ⟨made his appearance⟩

B ⟨where you know⟩ *347:10–11?*

30   R ⟨what I won't say⟩ *347:10–11?*   R ⟨a frank smile⟩

R ⟨a certain place⟩   R ⟨flushed a deep rosy red⟩ *347:15*

B ⟨hook & ?tackles⟩   R ⟨coloured like a girl⟩ *360:34*

R ⟨familiar chamber⟩ *345:7–8*   R ⟨a strong quiet face⟩ *345:31–32*

R ⟨two chubby arms⟩ *340:24?*   R ⟨pronounced beautiful⟩ *342:8*

35   R ⟨turn off gas at the main⟩ *349:10–11*   R ⟨have a good cry⟩ *345:8*

R ⟨for shame!⟩ *341:17*

R ⟨the hot tears that would well up⟩ *341:25–26*

R ⟨nasty,⟩ *341:29*   R ⟨naughty⟩ *346:39*   R ⟨O, my!⟩   R ⟨lost in
      thought⟩ *342:5–6*

40   R ⟨beeoteetom b.o.t.tom⟩ *347:12*   dislike ?Latin,

R ⟨comfort her with a hearty kiss⟩ *345:35*

R ⟨high instep showed its proportions⟩ *344:24–25*

R ⟨more a Giltrap than a MacDowell⟩ *342:9–10*

B ⟨crossest (?abty) ?on 2 sticks⟩ *347:7*

45   R ⟨don't tell Ciss I told you.⟩

R ⟨1st. God, 2nd. B.V.M., 3rd. Joe. 4th. you⟩ *343:32–33*

R ⟨smell of man⟩ *368:36*   R ⟨good as gold⟩ *340:39*

R ⟨sweet girlish shyness:⟩ *343:12*   B ⟨half offered⟩ *360:19*

R ⟨those things that⟩

50   R ⟨nestling,⟩ *493:8, 343:8*   R ⟨baby hands⟩   R ⟨Miss White (pat)⟩

R ⟨cuckoo clock,⟩ *375:39*   R ⟨fireworks⟩ *359:3 and elsewhere*

R ⟨boys will be boys,⟩ *341:5*   R ⟨eyes rather sad.⟩ *343:14*

R ⟨the love that might have been⟩ *342:34–35*

R ⟨I loved you better etc.⟩ *356:9–10*

55   R ⟨teeth under gold moustache⟩ *346:19–20*

B ⟨kissed my hand only⟩ *364:14?*

R ⟨Milly first . . . . . .⟩

R ⟨joyous little laugh which had in it all the freshness of

a May morning,⟩ *343:18–19*

60 R ⟨reform rakes⟩ *352:2–3*

R ⟨MB ate blotting paper, paraffin oil⟩

R ⟨and then he left her⟩

R ⟨that his face was strangely drawn⟩ *350:13*

R ⟨what a brute I have been⟩ *360:36–37*

65 R ⟨his & his only⟩ *345:37*   R ⟨coarse man⟩ *358:20*

R ⟨rouse the devil in him⟩ *354:18*

B ⟨I hate you,   bored to tears,⟩   R ⟨dear old ?Seth⟩

R ⟨icy⟩ *356:20?*   manners.   B ⟨she knew it was him⟩ *351:42*

R ⟨confounded. fool that he was⟩ *Cf. 356:6*

70 R ⟨he breathed hoarsely⟩ *359:24*

R ⟨endearing little ways.⟩ *340:20*   R ⟨impetuous fellow⟩ *345:25–26*

R ⟨lovers ?arms meeting ∴ not alone⟩

R ⟨all lunatics work by mathematics⟩

smile enchanting ⟨for him⟩

75 R ⟨nuns vindictive (Tranquilla)⟩ *361:35*

xi ?bijoux: pouxi ?biboux

R ⟨girls drew ?carafes like themselves⟩

Hallucinations of smell lead to sense of bodiliness

R ⟨not that: be good friends⟩ *358:22*

80 R ⟨Love ?excuses all: Coition without love in & out of wedlock
      not desired⟩

R ⟨profusion of luxuriant clusters⟩ *343:9*

   R ⟨wealth of hair⟩ *343:6–7*

R ⟨Martha & B.B. ?synchronism⟩ *363:30–31*

85 R ⟨?Hollerbusch & ?N (culo e camiza)⟩ *Cf. 394:36*   R ⟨— ?pui O⟩

RIGHT COLUMN HORIZONTAL

R ⟨Dublin bar silted up so ?that ships of big draught can't
      get in⟩ *375:14–15*

R ⟨recked⟩ *343:29*

R ⟨Little ?coud he⟩

90 R ⟨wet with contrition⟩ *350:21*

bread, leaven   R ⟨daily bread,⟩ *350:20*   mazzoth   *Cf. 79:41–42*

R ⟨LB ?writes⟩ *375:1–2*

Hair, ?seaweed, grass, ?pubert.

R ⟨No stop. (Naus. episode)⟩

95 R ⟨thorough aristocrat⟩ *349:20*

R ⟨the lamplight falls upon a face:⟩ *345:11*   R ⟨hung en-
      raptured⟩ *361:16*

R ⟨Inclination prompted her to . . .⟩ *343:16*

R ⟨dignity told her to . . .⟩ *343:16–17*

100 R ⟨Time had ?been ?when⟩ *342:40?*

R ⟨joy that ?reached his heart⟩

R ⟨paid his devoirs⟩ *342:34*

R ⟨(hug)⟩ *346:26*

R ⟨smiled assent⟩ *350:2*

105 R ⟨he knew: no-one better⟩ *343:19–20*

R ⟨lady love⟩ *349:16*

lake

R ⟨lamp⟩

R ⟨for the love of God!⟩ *362:35*

110 R ⟨gazing far away into the distance⟩ *342:6*

R ⟨downcast eyes⟩ *343:14*

R ⟨I'm dying to know⟩ *358:12*

R ⟨I'd give world to—⟩ *351:31–32, 345:6–7*

R ⟨LB dislikes to be seen in profile⟩ *363:16*

115 R ⟨little one⟩ *345:23*

R ⟨tense with suppressed meaning⟩ *342:36*

R ⟨far off look⟩ *342:6?*   R ⟨white discharges⟩ *342:13*

R ⟨queenly⟩ *342:26*

R ⟨gent to his fingertips⟩ *359:17–18*

120 R ⟨rang out | —— | voice clear—⟩ *356:19*

R ⟨drew herself up to full height⟩ *361:13–14*

R ⟨& if perchance⟩ *343:30–31*

R ⟨Herbert ?Ruthven stands silent before the . . . .⟩

R ⟨(coarse man)⟩ *358:20*   R ⟨languid⟩ *342:26*

125 R ⟨Grace before meals⟩ *Cf. 369:19*

R ⟨never see 17 again⟩ *344:29–30*

R ⟨those incenses⟩ *351:17*

NOTES

My arrangement in the right column is rather arbitrary.

Line 5   Repeated at "Nausicaa" 5:22.

27   See "Nausicaa" 1:25 and note.

31   The word *rosy* is written above *red*. A vertical purple mark runs from *flushed* through *have a good cry* in line 35.

44   (*?abty*): perhaps this should be (Edy), but it is not.

47   *Good as gold*: repeated at "Nausicaa" 6:11.

76   This looks like babytalk.

85   *Hollerbusch & N*: unidentified. *Culo e camiza*: arse and shirt.

94   Joyce may have been thinking of using the *no stop* interior monologue technique of "Penelope" in the Gerty MacDowell section of "Nausicaa."

98–99   The ellipses are Joyce's.

123   *Herbert Ruthven*: unidentified. The ellipses are Joyce's.

"Nausicaa" 5

LEFT MARGIN HORIZONTAL

gropingly
twitching
R ⟨that sort of woman⟩ *358:18*
R ⟨G. winced sharply⟩ *356:2–3*
5   *R* ⟨piteous protest⟩ *360:33*
R ⟨little girl⟩
R ⟨weeping willow⟩ *371:8–9*
R ⟨laid his lips on her white brow⟩ *360:23*

LEFT COLUMN HORIZONTAL

R ⟨pouncet box⟩ *357:35*
10   *B* ⟨twinge⟩ *516:25*
R ⟨Molly: sweat of her armpits⟩ *368:26?*
R ⟨LB: magnet: tipped: fucked⟩ *367:28–34*
R ⟨ ″ : rut: ache root of tongue⟩ *366:12*
B ⟨Mat Kane to make journey long sea⟩ *689:21–22*
15   *R* ⟨mutoscope⟩ *362:10*
R ⟨Nausikaa: slight moustache⟩ *347:29?*
R ⟨LB sings after.⟩ *364:4*
B ⟨N. puts key in door with LB⟩
R ⟨children dress up in ma's dress.⟩ *365:2*
20   fauteuil: *R* ⟨nook:⟩ *340:13*
R ⟨women ought not to have such lovely eyes.⟩ *342:38?*
R ⟨hauteur:⟩ *342:26*   *R* ⟨suitors:⟩ *342:33*   *B* ⟨sweet crushed bloom⟩

144

R ⟨Would he believe in love?⟩ *345:19*

R ⟨a swift slight telltale flush delicate as the faintest

     rosebloom⟩ *343:11*

R ⟨God's fair land of Ireland did not hold her equal⟩ *343:13*

                        R ⟨You know it⟩

R ⟨more musical than the cooing of the ringdove⟩ *356:19–20*

R ⟨learn to love me.⟩ *343:31*   R ⟨Naus: lame.⟩ *361:25, 370:23*

R ⟨hold nose: take drugs.⟩ *340:37*   R ⟨cherry ripe.⟩ *341:1*

R ⟨little wife-to-be.⟩ *345:42* R ⟨Molly: strawberry smell.⟩ *368:25*

R ⟨Jerusalem artichokes⟩ *370:17*   R ⟨nightstock (cf. woman)⟩

                         370:18

R ⟨N. thinks LB in deep sorrow⟩ *351:31*   R ⟨what you mean to me⟩

                         356:11–12

R ⟨light: factor of perfume.⟩ *368:10–11*

R ⟨smell of chaste priest (concupiscence)⟩ *368:38–42*

R ⟨turpentine (new paint) gives smell of violets to piss.⟩ *367:41*

R ⟨Water of Molly's bath.⟩ *368:24*

R ⟨Wadding with scent.⟩ *361:9, 344:7* R ⟨odour of sanctity.⟩ *371:11*

R ⟨queen of puddings.⟩ *346:6?*

shock: rubbing = smell.

B ⟨ozone⟩ *611:6*

E.C.   W.C.   R ⟨stink like polecat⟩ *366:38*

R ⟨India:⟩ *368:17* R ⟨smell: miles⟩ R ⟨5 leagues off⟩ *368:17–18*

B ⟨camphor: lavender,⟩   volatile, smelling ?salts

R ⟨heliotrope: ether: violet⟩ *367:41–368:28*

vultures: gulls: R ⟨You utter cur!⟩ *360:38*

R ⟨LB: Molly gnashed her teeth in sleep (B.B.)⟩ *364:39*

R ⟨ringdoves⟩ *356:20*   / gulls

R ⟨hold nose to take medicine⟩ *340:37*

R ⟨little wife-to-be:⟩ *345:42* R ⟨learn to love me⟩ *343:31*

R ⟨Naus: thinks LB in grief,⟩ *351:31* ⟨/ lame?⟩ *361:25, 370:23*

R ⟨LB went out—necktie⟩ *363:27*

R ⟨Muskrat (male) = navel.⟩ *368:28*

masonry of mosque musk

amber on waves

R ⟨Dolly dyes⟩—coral *344:4*

sweating whiskey casks

60   R ⟨offend woman   then make it up.⟩ *364:29*

R ⟨My thoughts (rose-coral) Naus.⟩ *357:30–31*

R ⟨L's dream⟩ *374:25ff.* — N's dream.

R ⟨Molly going to beat Milly with umbrella⟩ *373:16–17*

R ⟨She's thinking of someone else⟩ *364:30–31* R ⟨/ 1d. for yr.

65   thoughts⟩ *354:27*

R ⟨Never admit other husband wrongs / (?Row City Arms re

food)⟩ *366:37–367:2*

R ⟨Metamorphosis—transformation scene. petrified grief

stonecold⟩ *538:3ff.*

70   R ⟨LB Irish mots no class   Molly spanished⟩

R ⟨in very truth a specimen of I. womanhood⟩ *342:6–7*

R ⟨carefully trimmed sweeping moustache⟩ *346:20*

R ⟨benefit of a good education⟩ *342:30*   scum

R ⟨drunk / P.D. in bed whiff of stale booze on lips⟩ *366:39*

75   R ⟨went white to the very lips⟩ *345:22*

duly accepted

R ⟨aquiline nose: saw at 1ˢᵗ glance he was a foreigner⟩ *351:23–29*

RIGHT COLUMN HORIZONTAL

(brisket?)   B ⟨Your-love-for-me.⟩

R ⟨cat smells Molly's shift.⟩ *368:23–24*

80   Kernan—tea smeller.

R ⟨smell: touch particles of her body: :Gert.⟩ *368:14–16*

R ⟨sewage.⟩ *374:17*

R ⟨hair smells in rut.⟩ *363:21*

R ⟨cut time of moon⟩ *343:7–8, 355:27*

85   R ⟨rainbow.⟩ *368:20* (snout of dog)

caressing   snuffbox

R ⟨Milly liked my buttons.⟩ *373:19*

bug juice

R ⟨nose out of joint⟩ *343:22*

90   B ⟨cutting   " to please face⟩

blow through 1 nostril

B ⟨picking nose   ?worry⟩ *51:32–34?*

B ⟨scents hide in ?places⟩ *368:25–27?*

R ⟨heat produces scent   ⟨ballroom⟩⟩ *368:9–10*

95 R ⟨black   6⟩ *Cf. 370:1*

R ⟨blue   5⟩

R ⟨green   4⟩

R ⟨red   3⟩

R ⟨yellow 2⟩

100 R ⟨white   1⟩

x would

R ⟨not a man to be trifled with⟩ *356:21–22*

B ⟨ticktactwo would you set a shoe   yes sir. yes sir and a
        nail too.⟩ *477:4*

105 R ⟨jaspberry ram⟩ *347:23*

congratulations poured in upon them

R ⟨had the desired effect⟩ *355:34*

B ⟨the door had opened⟩

110 B ⟨passionwhite⟩ *359:14*   R ⟨draw attention⟩ *350:7*

elicited her whereabouts

R ⟨the proud head flashed up⟩ *356:17*

R ⟨potwalloping⟩ *366:25*

medusa: jellyfish

115 R ⟨whitehot passion⟩ *359:14*

(SD for her ?oh   B.B.)

NOTES

Line 14   See Adams, pp. 62–64.

17   Cf. "Nausicaa" 1:94.

22   *Suitors*: repeated at "Nausicaa" 4:5.

24   *Telltale* is written directly above *slight flush*.

26   *Land of* is written directly above *fair Ireland*.

28   *Ringdove*: appears in the plural at line 50.

29   *Lame*: repeated at line 53.

30   *Hold nose*: repeated at line 51.

31   *Little wife-to-be*: repeated in line 52.

34   See line 53.

62   Cf. "Nausicaa" 3:17.

64–65   *1d. for yr. thoughts*: repeated at "Nausicaa" 1:29.

80   See the *Dubliners* story "Grace." Cf. *U* 235–238.

90   The ditto mark refers to *nose* in the line above. The phrase is repeated at "Cyclops" 1:21 and "Eumaeus" 5:54.

110   Cf. line 115.

"Nausicaa" 6

LEFT MARGIN HORIZONTAL

R ⟨Look at that!⟩

R ⟨Looking round she smelt an onion.⟩ *366:6–7*

Bridal pair whom do they look at first?

R ⟨Were nightclouds there all time?⟩ *370:2–3*

5   R ⟨Birds hopping mice.⟩ *371:19*

R ⟨Bare teat fill baby with wind.⟩ *366:31–32*

R ⟨puffpuff⟩ *351:7*

pram   R ⟨peep!⟩ *350:30*

R ⟨birds in parliament⟩

10   B ⟨bold as brass⟩ *349:27*

R ⟨good ″ gold⟩ *340:39*

R ⟨spray⟩ *369:41*

R ⟨Puddeny pie⟩ *357:3*

R ⟨Prunes & prisms 20 times cure for fat lips⟩ *365:8–9*

15   R ⟨Nice way his hair is cut behind⟩ *343:35–36?*

firm planted instep

R ⟨bib⟩ *340:40 and elsewhere*

R ⟨bride in tight boots⟩ *361:25?*

R ⟨Lightning?⟩ *356:16, 358:41, and elsewhere*

20   R ⟨Woman never ?ashamed with men⟩ *Cf. 367:35–36*

B ⟨hole & taw⟩

R ⟨ship pursued by fate⟩ *370:3?*

R ⟨Always look at other way round: Not so bad.⟩ *374:1*

LB sees woman cook

25   R ⟨tainted curds⟩ *366:30*

R ⟨calomel purge to nettlerash⟩ *373:14*

149

R ⟨iron on a brick⟩ *344:36*

CENTER COLUMN HORIZONTAL

R ⟨He stole an arm round her waist⟩ *345:21–22*

R ⟨His eyes burned into her as though to read her through &

30   through⟩ *351:20–21*

R ⟨Contact with menstruous woman brings also ?pain.⟩ *368:32–33?*

B ⟨Anybody here for there?⟩ *560:12–13*

R ⟨Lustful woman meets ditto man⟩ *367:12?*

B ⟨Child chokes. Look up!⟩ *346:41?*

35 *R* ⟨Always know chap courting: collars & cuffs. Same time might

       prefer chap with tie loose, breeches undone? No. Don't

       like things too open. Maul in dark. Kiss & never

       tell.⟩ *363:8–12*

R ⟨Sore on mouth sticks. Summer cold also.⟩ *370:9–10*

40 *R* ⟨Walk behind man, make him awkward.⟩ *369:20–21*

Joke in govt. office.

R ⟨corns on my kismet⟩ *369:27*   violent burns.

R ⟨LB. vexes sand.⟩ *375:1*   *R* ⟨go deedaw.⟩ *356:40*   *B* ⟨burning

       glass⟩ *371:32 & 35*

45 *R* ⟨children smell of sour milk⟩ *366:30*

R ⟨Woman looks out of window⟩ *348:8?*

       cat   ?idler   — --

R ⟨parents hide from ?bairn.⟩

Totem ?angers   *B* ⟨: stare sun: yellow blotch, fatigue

50   image.⟩ *371:24–25*

R ⟨Woods on burning hills not sparks but friction of twigs in

       wind: Archimedes.⟩ *371:32–35*

R ⟨pretty girl & ugly man (beauty & beast)⟩ *363:17–18*

R ⟨birds' speech (says she and says I)⟩ *365:10*   *R* ⟨ships

55   lowing⟩ *372:1–2*

R ⟨whistle brings rain.⟩ *369:28*

R ⟨Smell you could hang your hat on.⟩ *368:33–34*

R ⟨Girl on stone: white fluxions.⟩ *370:7–8*

unhappy marriages. More damn fool he.

60   *R* ⟨1904: leap year.⟩ *356:18, 767:20*

Gulls: sinking sun lights up their fat bellies & dark wings.

Suicide (LB) must ask eternity first.

R ⟨Repetition ridiculous, circle. circus horse⟩ *370:41*

Gravitation, sign of gracelessness.

65   *B* ⟨Mary & Martha, picture.⟩ *362:23–24*   *R* ⟨letter?⟩ *364:21*

R ⟨Did I forget to write address on card.   Bold hand⟩ *363:24–26*

cottage, browsing like sheep

S. Army band.

R ⟨white stockings he hates /   LB⟩ *366:1–2*

70   *R* ⟨First thoughts best⟩ *364:34–35*

Ass knows in whose face he brays.

Woman lilts: suddenly pulls up stockings (?)

R ⟨10/– for Molly's hair combings.⟩ *363:21*

B ⟨Moustache & beards carry germs⟩ *348:27?*

75   *R* ⟨Wrinkles of sucking babe.⟩

R ⟨Milly dislikes old Goodwin for father.⟩

R ⟨Time of Barmecides.⟩ *326:17–18*   *R* ⟨Stead of pardon runs him

      through guts.⟩ *369:39–40*   *R* ⟨Two types = Scowl & Excuse⟩ *369:40*

R ⟨Woman laugh at man's fall ?bar ?one.   Yet Molly first to prop

80   me up (LB)⟩

R ⟨Molly lustful only when well dressed.⟩ *362:22ff.?*

R ⟨Friggers live by themselves.⟩

Eunuchs—youth = old age.

R ⟨Frigging, girls little paps.⟩ *373:20?*   ?nuns:

85   *R* ⟨Dolphin's Barn: saw Molly first old love is the new.

      Circle.⟩ *370:33ff.*

R ⟨1st. kiss does the trick.⟩ *364:32–33*

B ⟨Cigarettebutts   perversion.⟩ *347:30?*

Grey & violet: ?array twilight of her youth

90   thyme & sage & sprouts & onions: for an altar

Pity ?f̶o̶t̶ that's all. Hall in ballad & rest fell out.

LB keeps picked up stones

LB weeps

B ⟨shooting the taw with a cunnythumb⟩ *76:20*

95   *R* ⟨Kish—stone cruiser.⟩ *372:39?*

151

R ⟨(2 ?year) Kalypso   birds homing nesting on rocks⟩

R ⟨Molly in Gibraltar.⟩ *373:25ff.*

sticks,   wrecks.

W.   kingdom of souls: R ⟨Poseidon, Nicolo (della ?Ma . .)⟩

100 Odyssey—struggles v unknown

?Sail, night: ?faro.

Curse of war   on velvet   B ⟨turn turtle.⟩ *521:8*

Taphians.   searobbers

Clothesline in distance

105 R ⟨Girls in Nat. Lib.—Happy chairs⟩ *370:15*

R ⟨ladylike⟩ *357:9* *and elsewhere*

R ⟨Martha gives virility to man⟩

R ⟨LB turns up piece of paper.⟩ *374:32*

R ⟨Lame! O!⟩ *361:25*

110 Sposi throw. bread

red oars in sunset.

B ⟨children throw things in sea⟩ *374:37–38*   bread cast on waters

R ⟨certain positions of knife now if you tried you couldn't.

    Chance⟩ *375:16–18*

NOTES

Line 11   Repeated at "Nausicaa" 4:47.

52 *Archimedes*: see "Cyclops" 5:31 and note.

54 *Birds' speech*: repeated in *Ulysses* notebook VIII.A.5 at Buffalo (p. 308) as "understood bird speech," an apparent reference to Tiresias.

77 *Barmecides*: "a Persian family descended from Barmak, a physician and priest of Balkh. . . . Yáhyá, was in 786 made vizier by Haroun-al-Raschid, who, fearful of their power, in 803 exterminated the family" (*Chambers's*). See also U 47:40, 528:14, 570:30.

91 *For*: written below *Pity* and then scratched out.

99 *Nicolo della . . . .*: the end of the phrase is illegible. The Italian spelling is Niccolò.

103   Repeated in notebook VIII.A.5 (p. 296); cf. "Eumaeus" 5:123. The *Taphians* were notorious pirates. In Book 15 of the *Odyssey*, Eumaeus tells how they kidnaped him from his home as a boy.

104   Notebook VIII.A.5 has "Nausicaa & clothesline" (p. 296).

105   Repeated in notebook VIII.A.5 (p. 308).

110 *Sposi*: Italian for "newlyweds."

"Nausicaa" 7

LEFT COLUMN HORIZONTAL

    R ⟨Milly's little first stays⟩ *373:20*
    R ⟨homeyness⟩ *346:5*
    R ⟨voice had a cultured ring⟩ *355:9–10*
    R ⟨flecked with grey⟩ *345:33*
5   R ⟨saddest face she ever saw.⟩ *350:13–14*
    R ⟨All too soon⟩
    R ⟨his eyes misty with unshed tears.⟩ *341:19*
    R ⟨undeniably handsome⟩ *343:34*
    R ⟨wonderful eyes, but could you trust him⟩ *351:21–22*
10 Houses upside down in water
    R ⟨Stocking penwiper⟩ *366:21*
    R ⟨a jink a jink a jawbo⟩ *340:33*
    R ⟨cad⟩ *360:38*
    R ⟨won golden opinions⟩ *346:6–7*
15 R ⟨little sufferers⟩ *340:35*
    R ⟨surging into her face⟩ *350:9–10*
    R ⟨1 lingering pressure of her hand   1 loving glance at her
        sweet flowerlike face & they parted⟩ *361:14–16*
    R ⟨stole a look at him⟩
20 R ⟨blushed divinely⟩ *360:9–10*
    R ⟨delicate pink crept into P's pretty cheek⟩ *350:2–3*
    R ⟨blue lucky colour for girls to wear⟩ *344:38–39*
    R ⟨blue somewhere in bride's clothes.⟩ *344:39*
    R ⟨eyebrowleine, produce that fascinating expression of eyes
25   so becoming, used by leaders of fashion⟩ *343:1–2*
    R ⟨ashamed of her life⟩ *347:15*

153

B ⟨God made food, devil the cooks⟩ *169:35–36*

R ⟨exquisitely gowned⟩ *342:32*

R ⟨silkily lustrous⟩ *Cf. 342:39–40*

30   unlucky bride   look at herself fulldressed, glove after

B ⟨hook in wrong tache   ill luck⟩ *518:10–11*

B ⟨mount of thumb⟩

R ⟨drawers on inside out = luck⟩ *345:2*

R ⟨bib: dribbles⟩ *350:40*

35   R ⟨crimsoned up to roots of her hair⟩ *352:26*

R ⟨danger flag flamed⟩ *350:8–9*

R ⟨sheltering embrace⟩ *345:34*

R ⟨No-one heard what they said but little lark stout fluttered
      near. never tell.⟩ *361:1–3*

40   R ⟨soul in her eyes,⟩ *345:6*   Estelle,

mercy on me.

B ⟨weatherwise.⟩ *390:21*

R ⟨lovable in the extreme.⟩ *341:2*

puzzlement   R ⟨smiled wanly⟩ *361:17*

45   R ⟨"No" she laughed⟩ *356:16*

R ⟨face black as thunder⟩ *356:29*

R ⟨Next moment it was the quiet gravefaced manager resolution
      (reserve) expressed in every line of his full upright
      figure⟩ *355:2–4*

50   R ⟨Woman scrapes slipper when pissing⟩ *368:1*

R ⟨none too amiably⟩ *341:38*

R ⟨as per usual⟩ *343:22*

R ⟨to the core⟩ *343:30*

R ⟨discussed things feminine⟩ *340:14*

55   R ⟨to lay a great, a wondrous love at her feet⟩ *345:30–31*

R ⟨match some silks⟩ *344:13?*

R ⟨waxen pallor almost spiritual in its ivorylike
      purity⟩ *342:14–15*

R ⟨Honour where honour is due⟩ *342:25*

60   R ⟨burning scarlet swept from brow to throat⟩ *354:19*

R ⟨fallen woman⟩ *358:18–19*

R ⟨catching her breath⟩ *354:16*

    R ⟨the old love was waiting—waiting with little white hands
        stretched out, with blue appealing eyes.⟩ *358:27–28*

65   faltered, cheek plumper

    R ⟨end of her nose benefited⟩ *345:24?*

    R ⟨crush her soft body⟩ *352:10*

    R ⟨she said chokingly⟩ *360:22?*

    R ⟨wounds that wanted healing⟩ *352:4*

70   *R* ⟨with all the heart of her⟩ *345:37*

    R ⟨strength of character had never been ?O' W' —⟩ *345:26*

    R ⟨piquant tilt of nose⟩ *347:18–19*

    R ⟨she was glad when he left the room with a remark about
        refreshments⟩ *345:25*

75   *R* ⟨strong passionate nature,   strain her to him⟩ *345:34–35*

    R ⟨admired tall men⟩ *346:19*

    R ⟨smthg   checked words on her lips⟩ *343:15*

RIGHT COLUMN HORIZONTAL

    R ⟨bib,⟩ *340:40 and elsewhere*   *B* ⟨pinny,⟩ *346:36*   *B* ⟨overall,⟩ *469:6*
        R ⟨knicks⟩ *346:29, 360:11*

80   *R* ⟨as kind as kind could be⟩

    B ⟨little mittens⟩

    R ⟨ducky little⟩ *441:16–17, 356:41*

    R ⟨creature comforts⟩ *346:3*

    R ⟨aired⟩ *344:34,*   *R* ⟨chintz covers⟩ *346:16*

85   *R* ⟨caresses for onlookers⟩ *365:9*

    R ⟨(sees most of game) LB⟩ *365:9–10*

    R ⟨?fall in love⟩ *367:9*

    R ⟨spitfire⟩ *346:2*

    R ⟨woman beautiful⟩ *342:41*

90   *R* ⟨eyes on dying embers⟩ *348:6*

    tough guy

    ?amazes

    lumberjack

    pal

95   *R* ⟨fight back sobs that rose to her lips⟩ *356:7–8*
more than a little ?hush!
R ⟨spoilt beauty⟩ *340:40–41*

"Nausicaa" 8

LEFT MARGIN HORIZONTAL

R ⟨probed mercilessly⟩ *356:13*
B ⟨radiant reflection mirror gave back to her⟩ *344:17–18*
very gently he
B ⟨smile that verged on tears⟩ *361:17–18*
5   ?Masking words, G.M'D. —
R ⟨Scorn immeasurable⟩ *356:4*
as sure as there's a heaven (God above us)
R ⟨and if—what then,⟩ *358:16*
R ⟨feel of long hair⟩ *353:12?*
10   *R* ⟨recoiled⟩ *358:18*
knife him where he stands
R ⟨that's a lie, J.J. & you know it⟩
R ⟨scrupulously clean⟩ *357:32–33*
R ⟨end is very near⟩ *348:38*
15   *R* ⟨frugal meal⟩ *371:15*
R ⟨Quick stinging of pain⟩ *356:13*
R ⟨met his glance⟩ *359:13*
R ⟨laid to rest⟩ *348:38*
B ⟨Strained look in her face⟩ *345:5*
20   *R* ⟨Catch it while it's flying⟩ *357:9*
pittance
R ⟨oldtime chivalry⟩ *349:16*
impart knowledge
put in appearance
25   *R* ⟨I —think I understand⟩ *358:25–26*

157

LEFT COLUMN HORIZONTAL

R ⟨in most approved fashion⟩ *349:26–27*

R ⟨brown study⟩ *348:7*

R ⟨come to the rescue⟩ *349:32*

R ⟨soft job⟩ *366:27*　　R ⟨: dreamy⟩ *359:37 & 38*

30　G ⟨at a loose end⟩

R ⟨geegee⟩ *351:7*

R ⟨scathing politeness⟩ *356:1*

prompted ?Mama

B ⟨sparkling waves⟩ *340:13*

35　R ⟨lost my husband⟩

R ⟨exchanged casual glances⟩ *350:10–11*

thrilling at the new . . . . . ?in's voice

shrank

R ⟨twinkled back in sympathy⟩ *372:39–40?*

40　R ⟨steadfast look⟩ *359:17*　R ⟨(Deceiver)⟩ *356:10*

R ⟨ready for you, Mr Stephen Hartly⟩

R ⟨nondescript⟩ *367:7*　: jolly kids

R ⟨brief cold blaze from her eyes⟩ *356:3*

R ⟨countenance fell⟩ *356:28*

45　R ⟨shaft strike home⟩ *356:31*

R ⟨slightly jealous⟩ *350:6?*

R ⟨rockaby⟩ *340:24?*

B ⟨who's hindering you⟩ *327:21*

false lover:　daddy

50　R ⟨jolly good mind to ——.⟩ *350:5?*

R ⟨silent as the grave⟩ *359:14*

R ⟨there was meaning in his tone⟩ *351:19–20*

R ⟨heartbroken⟩ *356:2*

heart of Essex:　R ⟨love her for herself⟩ *352:10–11*

55　R ⟨soft, clinging white⟩ *349:18–19*

R ⟨smiled back at her own reflection⟩ *344:17–18*

R ⟨dearer than the whole world⟩ *358:10*

R ⟨"W. Tell"/dislike⟩

R ⟨as a snake looks at his prey⟩ *354:17*

158

60   R ⟨one of bravest truest hearts heaven ever made⟩ *347:31–32*

       R ⟨gild her days with happiness⟩ *358:11*

       R ⟨from the very first⟩ *345:12–13*

       R ⟨her heart went out to meet him⟩ *351:40–41*

       R ⟨Cissycums etc⟩ *347:27*

65   R ⟨the demon drink⟩ *348:3*

       R ⟨after supper walk a mile⟩ *369:19*

       R ⟨for the intentions of the sov. pontiff⟩ *384:35–36*

       R ⟨every bullet has its billet.⟩ *366:22*

       B ⟨respect yourself! (Circe)⟩ *492:14*

70   — and she smiled at him

       R ⟨love laughs at locksmiths,⟩ *358:8–9*

       R ⟨full of sympathy⟩ *356:14?*

       R ⟨servants always within beck and call⟩ *359:10*

       R ⟨nothing else mattered⟩ *358:31–32*

75   R ⟨there was no holding back⟩ *358:8*

       R ⟨of no slight description⟩ *356:28?*

       R ⟨all & sundry⟩

       in very grim earnest

       B ⟨lent to it a charm which few could resist⟩ *342:37–38*

80   R ⟨Poor though the light was⟩

       R ⟨revealed graceful beautifully shaped legs⟩ *359:22*

       R ⟨supply soft & delicately rounded⟩ *359:23*

       R ⟨throat slim & beautifully modelled⟩ *356:8–9*

       R ⟨face was one an artist might have dreamed of⟩ *356:9*

85   every feature exquisite in outline

       R ⟨lovely with a loveliness that made him gaze⟩ *355:2*

       R ⟨maddening in its sweetness⟩ *354:10–11*

       R ⟨there was that in her young voice that ---⟩ *356:20–21*

       B ⟨if you value yʳ· safety⟩

90   R ⟨set her tingling⟩ *354:13–14*

       B ⟨lily in the mire⟩ *386:18?*

       R ⟨she was not of them & never would be⟩ *356:33*

       wedlock

       keep body & soul together

95   R ⟨wild untrammelled, free⟩ *358:32–33*

159

R ⟨a different sphere⟩ *356:32*
R ⟨knew it instinctively⟩ *351:40?*

CENTER HORIZONTAL

R ⟨I wonder why⟩
R ⟨suspicion of a quiver in his mellow tones⟩ *355:11*
100   R ⟨:mack⟨intosh⟩⟩ *369:27*
kitbag   rash act
B ⟨scheduled time⟩
entry into houses
R ⟨old flame⟩ *358:24–25*
105   natural aperient
:scud
R ⟨radiant little vision⟩ *354:10*
peachlike
R ⟨claim our attention⟩ *357:5*
110   R ⟨make the great sacrifice⟩ *358:9*
R ⟨—oh yes, you have!⟩
?longruler
perfect dears
R ⟨Just too ducky⟩ *356:40–41*
115   R ⟨in your own right⟩ *342:29*
good talking to
R ⟨like the young coward he was⟩ *345:26?*
R ⟨all important question⟩ *358:12*
R ⟨cruel to be kind⟩ *358:15*
120   R ⟨with jewels on her brow⟩ *342:32–33*
R ⟨passion seething⟩ *359:14*
R ⟨did not err on the side of luxury⟩ *357:32*
wooden struts ⟨pillars⟩
R ⟨have her own way⟩
125   R ⟨light broke in upon him⟩ *359:13*
R ⟨towering rage⟩ *356:30*
B ⟨for keeps⟩

undesirable

R ⟨child of Mary⟩ *340:9?*

130   B ⟨patrician⟩ *342:33*

R ⟨magic lure in lips else⟩ *358:7*

B ⟨perfectly served lunch⟩ *346:24*

R ⟨colour became a glorious rose⟩ *354:20*

R ⟨pulses tingling⟩ *359:12*

135   R ⟨make her his⟩ *359:15*

RIGHT COLUMN HORIZONTAL

aware of occasional glances of admiration

B ⟨Mrs Reggy Wylie (not Mrs W—)⟩ *345:14–16*

R ⟨misted with tears⟩ *358:3*

thickly carpeted   *Cf. 343:6*

140   R ⟨wealth of rich tresses⟩ *354:9?*

R ⟨conceal what shortcomings there might be in the way of
    marrying beneath him⟩ *358:4–7*

R ⟨it was understood thing⟩ *358:26?*

R ⟨deportment⟩ *357:9*

145   glowing reports

R ⟨quick hot touch of his lips⟩ *359:33–34*

R ⟨smothered exclaim.⟩ *357:7*

R ⟨she drew his face down to hers⟩ *359:33*

future Mrs X—

NOTES

Line 73   *Within . . . call*: the words *beck and* are written above the line over a caret.

81   *Beautifully shaped*: written above and in part to the right of the word *legs*.

"Oxen of the Sun" 1

UPPER LEFT HORIZONTAL

R ⟨3 mile or thereabout⟩ *390:10*
I kept it in good order, being
?was a growing low
he made nothing needless (=-)
5   *R* ⟨all the world are⟩ *390:16–17*
R ⟨poring at the clouds⟩ *390:20–21*
R ⟨coffins carrying to be buried⟩ *Cf. 378:23*
everyone (their).   *R* ⟨:skip⟩ *390:26*
to the life,   *R* ⟨Welsh⟩ *392:25*
10   *R* ⟨wander ?thro' the world etc.⟩ *420:1*
R ⟨merryandrew⟩ *391:36–37*   (:tester) *392:4*
R ⟨honest pickle⟩ *391:37*
R ⟨open the design of his embassy⟩ *392:15–16*
R ⟨Burst his sides⟩ *392:7*
15   *R* ⟨every mother's son⟩ *392:6–7*
R ⟨itenerary: viz⟩
foodstuff
R ⟨pleaded her belly⟩ *391:10*
R ⟨son of shame⟩ *406:31*
20   *R* ⟨can't, won't⟩
R ⟨ignorant from a child⟩ *392:19*
nealing

UPPER RIGHT HORIZONTAL

R ⟨brought himself off with his tongue⟩ *392:5*

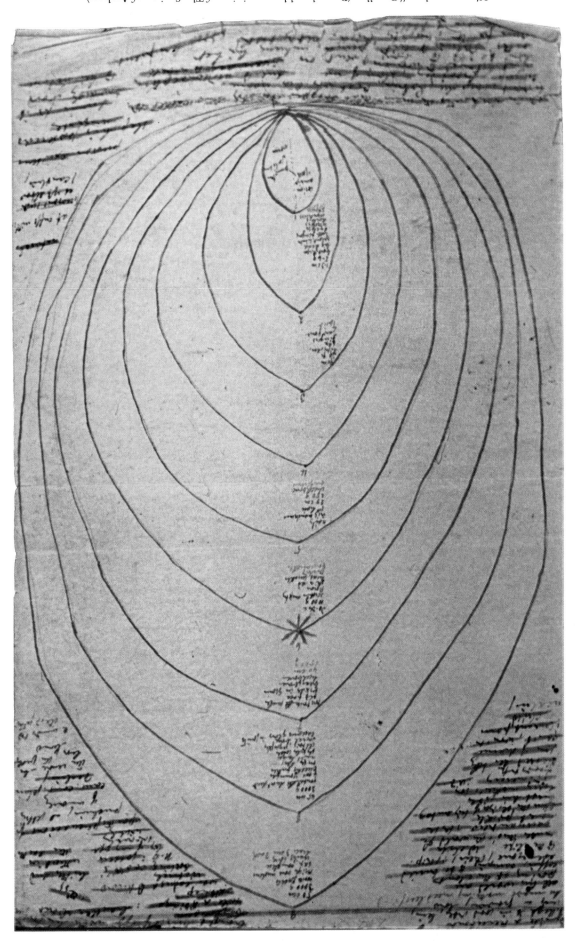

G ⟨buglehorn⟩

25   B ⟨tale or tidings⟩ *392:8*   R ⟨: hanker about⟩ *391:39*

B ⟨kidnap⟩ *392:28*

R ⟨was earnest to know⟩ *392:33–34*   R ⟨mess⟩ *392:3*

R ⟨victuals⟩ *392:4*

R ⟨boiling cook's⟩ *392:3*   R ⟨bitter end⟩

30   N.B: R ⟨gotten⟩ *392:3*   R ⟨what in the earth⟩ *390:39*

R ⟨big of my age⟩ *390:41*

savourly

R ⟨wishly⟩ *392:14*

R ⟨upon the persuasions of⟩ *391:34*

35   pushing at getting of money

R ⟨come, come, plain dealing⟩ *393:5–6*

the more he has, the . . . . lord

?e understood this, who

LOW ꓱR LEFT HORIZONTAL

R ⟨with the clerk who the man that stopped the boy had called to.⟩

40   R ⟨Indeed says he, Robin, that was his name.⟩

R ⟨crimp⟩ *391:40*   R ⟨broad day,⟩ *392:1*   R ⟨along of me⟩ *392:10*

R ⟨what belonged to women⟩ *391:37*

how he did to how I went on

R ⟨oaths,⟩ *391:33*   R ⟨offered to hit,⟩ *392:13?*   R ⟨punk⟩ *392:6*

45   R ⟨run for it,⟩   R ⟨mighty brisk,⟩ *391:35–36*   R ⟨pretty talk⟩

R ⟨gentlemen of gallows⟩

LOWER RIGHT HORIZONTAL

R ⟨naturals⟩

at cuffs with

(reason) just at yr. elbow

50   scantling

R ⟨previous existence⟩ *409:25*

R ⟨slap his posteriors⟩ *393:23*

R ⟨ingrates⟩ *394:38*

R ⟨swim for it⟩

55 *R* ⟨towardly word⟩

R ⟨to his mind⟩

R ⟨due to misconception⟩ *409:33*

B ⟨green rag to a bull⟩ *576:29*

unhung his hat

60 *R* ⟨stood his friend⟩ *393:24*

NOTES

In Janusko's dissertation (pp. 206–209) is a list of page references to Joyce's source book for most of the phrases on "Oxen" 1, Daniel Defoe's *Col. Jack*.

The major part of "Oxen" 1 is taken up with a drawing of nine concentric rings representing the nine months of foetal growth. The smallest ring is numbered "1"; the largest is "9." The first ring is divided from top to bottom by a dotted line. At the apex of the sixth month is a large asterisk.

Under the apexes of each ring on "Oxen" 1 is a notation as follows (the punctuation is mine; cm = centimeters; g = grams):

Ring 1: corion; amnion; yolk; ?puncture; ?solitary; worm.

2: 1–3 cm; 2–6 g; boatshape; big head; sprout limbs; web fingers; eyeless; noseless; earless; mouthless; sexless; 1st bone.

3: 9cm; 30 g; lips; ears; sex; fingers; jawbone; tail.

4: No notations in this month.

5: nails; iris membrane; 1st hair; 25 cm; 250 g; cheekbone; fingerbone.

6: 30–34 c [*sic*] 1000 g; scrotom empty; down; skin red; head smaller; pubis; fontanelles.

7: fore fontanelle smaller; old face; testicles in groin; breastbone; heelbone; 40 cm; 1500 g.

8: 45 cm; 2000 g; fontanelles almost shut; face younger; cheeks fuller; outer ears; nails longer; testicles lower; clitoris; ?nymphs; sacral bone; caseous gloss in joints.

9: 50 cm; 3000 g; tooth sockets; thigh bone nucleus; sex complete; nails long; hair 3 cm dark.

In the Cornell University Library is what appears to be a copy of this diagram (see Scholes, ed., *Cornell Joyce Collection*, item 58). Janusko, in a letter to me, has noted a number of differences between the two diagrams. On the Cornell chart there is no entry for the first month; "3rd month: no reference to tail; 6th month: 'head smaller' reads 'smaller head'; 7th month reads 40cm 1500 grs heelbone breastbone old face testicles in groin fore fontanelle smaller (same items, different order); [8th month:] 45cm 2000 gr face younger cheeks fuller outer ears nails longer testicles lower clitoris, nymphs sacral bones fontanelles almost shut caseous gloss in joints (same items, different order); 9th month: 50cm 3500 gr tooth sockets sex full nails long hair 3 cm dark thigh bone nucleus (different order, some difference in entries)." See also Gilbert (p. 309), and a letter of August 16, 1920 (*Letters*, III, 15–16).

Shortly before this edition of the *Ulysses* notesheets was ready to enter the galley stage, James S. Atherton published a note entitled "The Peacock in the Oxen" in *A Wake Newslitter*, VII (Oct. 1970), 77–78. (See my reply in *AWN*, VIII [August 1971], 51–53.) Working with the final text instead of the notesheets, Atherton presented evidence showing that Joyce took some fifteen words and phrases from William Peacock's *English Prose from Mandeville to Ruskin* (London, 1903). This is indeed an important find, one which enabled me to discover several hundred additional borrowings from Peacock in the "Oxen" notesheets. The following words and phrases on "Oxen" 1 are from Peacock:

"*Oxen*" 1	Peacock	"*Oxen*" 1	Peacock
Lines 6–7	Page 130	Line 12	Page 132
8 "everyone"	Cf. 130	13–14	133
8 "skip"	132	15	134
11 "merryandrew"	132	16 "itenerary"	Cf. 135
11 "tester"	133	16 "viz"	135

Line 58   Repeated at "Circe" 3:90.

165

"Oxen of the Sun" 2

LEFT MARGIN HORIZONTAL

R ⟨headborough⟩ *392:20 & 32*
was or no
(im) peached me
slept little or none
5   *R* ⟨watchman⟩
R ⟨(a) cross⟩
Mr Constable
at once or twice showing
R ⟨to buy a colour⟩
10   *R* ⟨refreshed⟩ *391:23*
Said I,
R ⟨moonshiny⟩ *392:28–29?*
Same — with
a sneaker of punch
15   *R* ⟨pushed it about apace⟩
Cap. Jack was the same man
is he in being
(en) *R* ⟨listed⟩
better than ordinary
20   upon a foot of
R ⟨pockets (naked)⟩ *392:31*
R ⟨cordial waters⟩ *397:31–32*
R ⟨husbandman⟩ *394:7*
R ⟨but of this hereafter⟩
25   (convulsions) ?way
very uneasy to ?me

166

cow with the crumbly horn
R ⟨Deine Kuh trubsal etc⟩ *416:38*
no, not to himself
30 R ⟨with their hands across⟩
though the man may be, the prayer is not, in proper
R ⟨skittish⟩ *390:41*
R ⟨confinement⟩ *401:28*
R ⟨brave dry⟩ *389:25?*
35 R ⟨a pair of virginals⟩ *386:34*
R ⟨she home and he to Paul's⟩ *Cf. 390:39–40*
R ⟨for aught he knew⟩
R ⟨to night (stanotte)⟩ *391:6?*
R ⟨Dought, likely man⟩ *391:2?*
40 at nine at night all
R ⟨ten of the clock⟩ *390:22–23*
R ⟨which put him . . but . . now.⟩
R ⟨looked v. ill and in a sick
       dress & stunk mightily⟩ *390:12*
45 R ⟨chamberlover⟩
R ⟨darkish⟩
what do angry men ail to rail?
R ⟨dry flag catch at 1ˢᵗ fire⟩ *390:16*
R ⟨manse⟩ *389:29*   R ⟨Soon as⟩
50 R ⟨he give me⟩
R ⟨the betraying him.⟩ *389:23?*
R ⟨seed to sprout⟩ *390:11*

LEFT COLUMN HORIZONTAL

lever
more harder
55 R ⟨Sir G heard in the leaves cry on high⟩ *381:30?*
As = when
he nighed it so nigh
R ⟨he did do make⟩ *380:24–25*

he is gone

60 repent him,　*R* 〈marvelled them〉 *Cf. 381:31*

me list, me liketh

all to—shivered

he childed or I fathered

R 〈this shield behoveth to him〉 *Cf. 389:16*

65 *R* 〈as much as he might suffice〉 *380:25–26*

R 〈a spear wherewith he was smitten him〉 *380:23–24*

(attacks) I have endured you

R 〈it shall so heavy me〉 *379:29*

she feebled so

70 there should be no man nixt thee

by no mean,　*R* 〈a 2 mile〉 *Cf. 390:10*　all thing

horse shoulder, heart root

thou were

I ?etc be.

75 here is I and my brother (was)

many causes causen me

he alight(ed) he wend(ed)

strong verbs p. part in en

drad,　*R* 〈brake,〉 *387:27*　brast,　*R* 〈halp,〉 *381:18*　stack, strake

80 for then I (should have) rewarded

?he have shame.　　Woe worth.

also = altrettanto　　　　　　　*R* 〈tofore〉 *381:40*

like as = sicut　　　　　　　　　till the table

not for that　　　　　　　　　　to himward

85 say evil by him　　　　　　　　or ever

R 〈for ?becausen〉

R 〈all long upon〉

　　　　　　　　　　　　(. . . . .)

when he drank & he both

90 besweat

every of 2, Very God, much man

R 〈best knight of the world one〉 *382:5*

R 〈our alter liege lord (of us all)〉 *381:27*

G 〈in any danger〉

95 *R* ⟨?thou lapses into yes⟩
doors shut by themself
R ⟨that   1.) which 2.)⟩ after that
R ⟨I marvel what man (that) he is⟩ *381:31*
who that   *B* ⟨gramercy⟩ *383:13*   all when
100 either gave other   refund it   bled
bright(e)   *R* ⟨he nist not⟩ *381:23*
ne . . . not   runagate   ?his
board at foot of bed
Prorsa, Postverta, Nixii,   *R* ⟨Partula,⟩ *417:4–5*   Genita Mana
105 milk fever 3rd day
B ⟨Fallopian tube (hall)⟩ *379:17*
egg: bird 1st stage
R ⟨Womb, 1st dense then spongy, ovum sticks⟩
Y̶o̶l̶k̶   *R* ⟨dear sir,⟩   *R* ⟨wotted,⟩ *389:15*
110 physic, *R* ⟨tipple,⟩ *418:22*   *R* ⟨innocent as babe unborn⟩ *410:8*
R ⟨lions, sword:⟩   *R* ⟨simpering⟩ *399:31*
these words were said
sorry me,
?doubling,   in fate,
115 lavish of his money
R ⟨thither⟩ *377:32*   *R* ⟨: ?at ?a place⟩
R ⟨if peradventure⟩ *383:37*   *R* ⟨?Law?⟩
R ⟨?venturous.⟩   thought good
received of me
120 his original the dunghill
open towards the ?sunrising
any, even any,
R ⟨that then you—withal⟩ *389:4*

RIGHT COLUMN HORIZONTAL

R ⟨throes⟩ *380:6*
125 ?fend guest
unspelling guest

R ⟨rehearsed⟩ *386:23*

R ⟨hold opinion⟩ *401:25?*

fetus 1st independent

130 R ⟨Item⟩ *419:39*

R ⟨childbearing healthy⟩

cheesecoat 6 m—on

R ⟨Voluntary movement, 5th m⟩

meconic, white—bilegreen

135 milk = white blood

R ⟨not look at maimed⟩

R ⟨influence in womb⟩ *383:35?*

R ⟨false appetites⟩

R ⟨twilight sleep⟩ *403:42, 159:16*

140 R ⟨to witwanton⟩ *388:17*

by chance medley

like mummy (dead flesh)

R ⟨most brightest⟩

R ⟨insult over him⟩ *414:30*

145 upon a question

magnity

it is a pity but such

R ⟨prate⟩

adder   R ⟨jump with⟩ *395:14*

150 R ⟨chafe⟩ *403:21*   outwent

maze

lovingkindness

J.B.'s salvation

no other notion than

155 J.B.'s wish to be Judas

" phthisis

R ⟨Q & A⟩

R ⟨have endeavored to have⟩ *389:3*

R ⟨?known⟩

160 R ⟨congee⟩

for why?

R ⟨beck⟩ *397:31, 419:13*

R ⟨excern⟩

antepast

165   *R* ⟨ravish(er)⟩ *393:29*

R ⟨sorites⟩

R ⟨but to return⟩

R ⟨had some guess of⟩ *391:29?*

R ⟨beshrew⟩ *398:27*   *R* ⟨granados⟩ *402:17–18*

170   in order to their condemnation

Mr W .. .. Mr W

R ⟨of Paul's⟩ *391:40?*

R ⟨plasmic memory⟩ *404:25–26*

abundantly to fly

175   *R* ⟨(but secretly)⟩

R ⟨lead him into⟩

R ⟨all prayer⟩

NOTES

My arrangement of phrases in the right column is somewhat arbitrary. Janusko (pp. 199–209) lists two sources for many of the phrases on "Oxen" 2: Defoe's *Col. Jack* and Sir Thomas Malory's *Le Morte d'Arthur*. The following words and phrases on "Oxen" 2 are from Peacock:

"Oxen" 2	Peacock	"Oxen" 2	Peacock
Line 31	Page 88	Line 46	Page 128
32	122	47	115
34	128	48	117
35–36	127	49 "manse"	Cf. 296
37	Cf. 126	50	Cf. 119
38	124	51	116
39	126	52	117
40	123	140–141	80
42–44	123	142	81

Line 22   Repeated at "Oxen" 14:39.

26   *Very uneasy* and *to me* are on succeeding lines and may not be connected.

38   *Stanotte*: Italian for "tonight."

39   One would expect *doughty* here, but the *y* is missing.

42   The ellipses are Joyce's.

43   *V.*: very.

71   *A 2 mile*: cf. "Oxen" 1:1.

82   *Altrettanto*: Italian for "as much."

83   *Sicut*: Latin for "just as."

102   The ellipses are Joyce's.

104   *Postverta* (Postvorta): "properly a surname of Carmenta, describing her as turning backward and looking at the past, which she revealed to poets and other mortals. In like manner the prophetic power with which she looked into the future, is indicated by the surnames Antevorta, Prorsa (i.e. Proversa), and Porrima" (*Dictionary of Greek and Roman Biography and Mythology*, III, 510). See also Gellius's *Attic Nights* xvi.16.4. *Nixii, Partula*, and *Genita Mana* are all deities who preside over childbirth. If these names were related to line 103, the bedboard would be interesting indeed. See also "Oxen" 4:79 and note.

106   *Fallopian tube*: the hall of the hospital. Bloom is the sperm, Nurse Callan, the ovum. See *Letters*, I, 139–140.

116   There is an arrow after *place*.

132–133   *M*: month.

134   *Meconic*: a white crystalline acid obtained from opium.

153, 155, 156   *J.B.*: perhaps James F. Byrne, the model for Cranly in *A Portrait*. *Phthisis*: mentioned in one of Joyce's letters (*Letters*, II, 230).

158–159   This may be *have endeavored to have known*.

166   Repeated at "Oxen" 14:77 and 16:57.

171   The ellipses are Joyce's.

175   *But secretly* may be connected to the phrase above it or to "lavish of his money" in line 115.

"Oxen of the Sun" 3

LEFT MARGIN HORIZONTAL

R ⟨displode⟩ *416:39*
disembowel
R ⟨put in his word⟩ *393:30*
R ⟨Lapland⟩ *418:13*
5   R ⟨Jacob & Esau struggle in womb⟩ *403:29–30?*
R ⟨Joseph's dream⟩ *391:6–9?*
R ⟨loaves & fishes⟩ *397:6*
R ⟨Doctor Diet⟩ *416:4*
R ⟨—   Quiet⟩ *416:5*
10   not to do so by any means
R ⟨did nothing fail⟩ *408:12?*
R ⟨want the effect⟩ *386:1*
R ⟨for that⟩ *381:34, 382:19, 384:29*
R ⟨unneth⟩ *380:7*
15   R ⟨When he was once come about that present time⟩
R ⟨witty,⟩ *382:27, 409:10*   R ⟨dissembling,⟩ *384:6*
R ⟨so as there remained⟩ *384:33*
R ⟨soldiers which⟩
R ⟨a sort of⟩
20   R ⟨other her friends⟩ *Cf. 382:11*
that . . . did anything abound
not so grievous as strange
R ⟨challenge to be⟩ *388:19*
foregoing
25   R ⟨pregnant remark⟩ *384:11–12?*
Yea, nay, ay, yes, no,

R ⟨beastly⟩ *383:42*

R ⟨household word⟩ *399:5–6*

word changed as to pronunciation aright

30 R ⟨longest wanderings⟩ *382:23–24*

shall we through such discovery obtain

at twain, at one

R ⟨he would witness⟩ *383:25?*

R ⟨catch pole⟩ *391:42*

35 R ⟨fall in with⟩

CENTER COLUMN HORIZONTAL

R ⟨Berners, Elyot, More, Latimer⟩   R ⟨:as well as other;⟩   R ⟨of this
   imagination⟩ *382:36*

R ⟨because, they said . . . . and in the beginning, they said . . . where-
   fore they maintained . . . and they said farther . . . ⟩ *382:33–36*

40 R ⟨the mean people⟩ *382:39–40*

nor shall not do till . . . camlet furred with grise . . .   R ⟨to the
   intent to be⟩ *382:8–9*

R ⟨Such as intended to no goodness said how he said truth.⟩ *382:20*

R ⟨affirming how John Ball said truth⟩   a 2 or 3 months,

45 R ⟨had conscience to let him die,⟩ *382:37*   R ⟨right evil governed⟩ *382:39*
       R ⟨Howbeit⟩ *382:39*

a 100, 200, by 20 and 30 entered   R ⟨never durst tarry⟩ *383:28*

a 100 mile off, 60 m, 50 m, 40 m and 20 m off

R ⟨demanded ever for the king,⟩ *382:17?*   R ⟨was in great doubt

50   lest⟩ *382:38?*

R ⟨but the king nor his council did provide no remedy⟩ *382:40–41*

R ⟨desired him to smthg⟩ *381:41?*   R ⟨& so little & little⟩

R ⟨Sir . . . but sir . . . sir, now . . .⟩ *383:10ff.?*   R ⟨Now let us speak
   of⟩ *382:8*

55 3 heads in 1 hood   R ⟨as it was informed me⟩ *384:6*

He saw such as . . . he saw them   R ⟨orgulous,⟩ *383:31–32*   doublet words

R ⟨this was scant done but⟩ *382:41*   R ⟨and when . . whereby they⟩ *383:9*

R ⟨they all cried with one voice⟩ *382:42*   R ⟨let⟩ *383:8?*

174

R ⟨and the best word he could have of him was⟩ *383:18–19*

60   R ⟨then Sir John of K said to Roger Stanforth⟩

R ⟨gested,⟩ *382:16*   R ⟨farther,⟩ *382:34, 415:19*   R ⟨plenitude,⟩ *401:4*
    plenary indulgence

R ⟨I promised to have gone, sith,⟩ *382:19–20*   R ⟨she is trespassed
    out of the world⟩ *382:31–32*

65   R ⟨dishonest a woman,⟩ *383:19–20*   R ⟨a wariness of mind⟩ *384:4*
    R ⟨he would make⟩

translators,   B ⟨1ˢᵗ. Euphuists⟩

R ⟨that is to wit.⟩ *382:10*   these lords so sitting, be.   R ⟨quarrel
    (?pretext)⟩ *383:2?*

70   R ⟨It was never other,⟩ *382:39*   R ⟨the self night next before his
    death⟩ *382:32*

R ⟨Flower for his cognisance,⟩ *386:9*   R ⟨reserved⟩ *382:16*   R ⟨(except)
    they judge,⟩ *382:40?*

R ⟨Had to the prince these words following⟩ *383:10*   R ⟨at least

75   way⟩ *383:4*

R ⟨Showed all the whole affair.⟩ *383:5*   R ⟨as touching⟩ *382:28*

R ⟨An ancient and sad matron⟩ *385:40–41*   R ⟨the merger to do the same⟩

R ⟨eyepleasing,⟩ *389:21*   R ⟨dam,⟩ *383:42*   R ⟨shut up in sorrow,⟩ *384:26*
    his cuisses

80   blaze army   R ⟨without a blemish⟩ *385:29*

R ⟨accompagnable solitariness & civil wildness,⟩   R ⟨: forepassed
    happiness⟩ *384:27*

R ⟨of his enemies embraided⟩ *386:2*   R ⟨parcel of our house⟩ *384:38*

natural of those rivers: supposing to be better guarded

85   R ⟨other some⟩   R ⟨ocean sea,⟩ *392:27*   so over hard,   R ⟨abaft.⟩ *417:19*
    R ⟨by course⟩

R ⟨real parts,⟩ *384:28*   R ⟨accompted him,⟩ *384:28*   R ⟨jealous,⟩ *385:39*   R ⟨barren⟩

neither am I so much a lover of life nor believe so little

R ⟨Chamber delights,⟩ *386:42*   prevent him,   leaves to (be) do (ne)

90   R ⟨the time's haste,⟩ *Cf. 385:4, 386:10*   R ⟨the wind's advertisement⟩

Cast about,   R ⟨sprang their luff,⟩ *394:40*   strowed,   R ⟨in such sort⟩

R ⟨becalmed,⟩ *382:23*   R ⟨past ten of the clock,⟩ *390:22–23*   licensed to—

R ⟨reclaimed him,⟩ *386:2*   used him   R ⟨scholar of my lord of—⟩ *391:3*

R ⟨shorten the honour,⟩ *385:40*   in the mean seasons,   R ⟨as the

95   night increased⟩ *390:21*

    R ⟨This agreeth also with,⟩ never so wounded as that, a-dressing

    R ⟨deliverly escaped,⟩ *384:10* R ⟨countervail the same,⟩ study,

      R ⟨paganry⟩ *388:18*

    R ⟨the ?capt. certain days, who coasting . . . . be . . . . ⟩

100   R ⟨it so fortuned,⟩ *383:20–21* R ⟨wishly,⟩ *392:14* R ⟨blandishments,⟩ *386:3*

      R ⟨intershow⟩ *386:20*

    R ⟨tasted storms,⟩ *388:22–23* R ⟨terror causing roaring⟩

    R ⟨so seldom seen an accident,⟩ *384:8* R ⟨advertised.⟩ *388:34–35*

    G ⟨the one half part,⟩ R ⟨recovered England⟩ *395:2?*

105   R ⟨were these as followeth,⟩ *385:4* R ⟨shrouded their approach,⟩ *414:32?*

    to be wrecked of injuries   R ⟨to pleasure thee,⟩ *381:19–20*

    R ⟨honourablest manner, they feasted him for that time,⟩ *382:24–25*

    R ⟨which now he did begin⟩

    to prove fortune once more

110   R ⟨hearing, he was a marvelous glad man⟩ *384:12–13*

    passion: R ⟨turmoiled with⟩ *385:39?*

    R ⟨now that he was even in that taking it appeared right

      eftsoon.⟩ *384:15*

    G ⟨brought him⟩

115   R ⟨was pricked forward with,⟩ *383:24* R ⟨insomuch as :⟩ *382:24*

    R ⟨malice and envy him⟩ *383:25* R ⟨: presently⟩ *390:5*

    R ⟨bewray,⟩ *383:30* this only surname, R ⟨hurt,⟩ *389:40, 417:33*

    suitor, take the chimney's hearth

    R ⟨to make away,⟩ R ⟨leman,⟩ *383:20*   straight examen,

120   R ⟨about the midst of the night⟩ *Cf. 384:24* R ⟨I vow⟩ *416:13–14*

    R ⟨still basted it very busily⟩ *384:34–35*

    R ⟨clean consumed⟩ *390:13* R ⟨{to work the feat}⟩

    R ⟨straight ways⟩   R ⟨{— — — ?oracle}⟩

    R ⟨delivered of his languor.⟩ *Cf. 383:21*

125   —— at all   obvious to the generality

    to tell the voices

    R ⟨jocundly,⟩ *383:28* R ⟨evil hap⟩ *384:21*   R ⟨a divine⟩

    R ⟨able to do any manner of thing that lay in man to do⟩ *383:26–27*

    I heartily wish the ?brood were at an end

NOTES

All the ellipses on "Oxen" 3 are Joyce's. Janusko (pp. 187–188, 202–204, 211) lists three source books for Joyce's material: *The Prose Works of Jonathan Swift, D.D.*, ed. Temple Scott, vol. XI: *Polite Conversation*, p. 282; *Froissart's Chronicles*, trans. Lord Berners; George Saintsbury, *A History of English Prose Rhythm*. The following words and phrases on "Oxen" 3 are from Peacock:

"Oxen" 3	Peacock	"Oxen" 3	Peacock
Lines 36–37	Page 15	Line 100 "it so"; "wishly"	Page 52
38–39	14	100–101 "blandishments"; "intershow"	53
40–43	15	102 "tasted storms"	45
44–46	16	102 "terror"	52
47–50	17	103 "so seldom"	53
51	18	104	35
68 "that is"; "these lords"	18	105	35
68–69 "quarrel"	19	106 "to be wrecked"	33
70 "It was"	19	106 "to pleasure thee"	34
70–71 "the self night"	20	107	34
72 "Flower"	21	109–110	34
72 "reserved"	24	111	31
74 "Had to the prince"	25	114	31
76 "Showed all the"	25	115	32
89	55	116 "malice"	32
90 "the time's"	55	116 "presently"	33
90 "the wind's"	56	117	33
91 "Cast"	35	118	33
91 "sprang"; "in such sort"	36	119	29
92 "becalmed"; "past"	36	120 "about the"	29
92 "licensed"	42	121	29
93 "reclaimed"	43	122	30
93 "scholar"	Cf. 42	123 "straight ways"	30
94	39	124	30
94–95 "as the night"	Cf. 38	125 "at all"	30
96	37	126	30
97 "deliverly"; "countervail"	46	127 "jocundly"	30
98	48	127 "evil hap"	31
99	49	128	30

Line 4   Repeated at "Oxen" 4:80.

6   *Joseph's dream*: just above are two wavy lines.

36   This is the second Baron *Berners*, John Bourchier (1467–1533), deputy of Calais and translator of Froissart (1523–25). Sir Thomas *Elyot* (1490–1546) was a moral philosopher. Sir Thomas *More* (1478–1535) was the author of *Utopia*. Hugh *Latimer* was a Protestant martyr. See the Table of Contents to Peacock.

81   Note the inherent contradictions.

"Oxen of the Sun" 4

LEFT MARGIN HORIZONTAL

$$\begin{array}{r} 6 \\ 19 \\ \hline 40 \\ 280 \end{array}$$

5
$$\begin{array}{r} 280 \\ ?678 \\ \hline 10 \end{array}$$

R ⟨then came up C⟩
R ⟨ox's goad⟩ *407:16?*
R ⟨question with him⟩ *392:41*
catch a ?slip
R ⟨wherein, O x-⟩ *390:3*
R ⟨grievous rage⟩ *390:5*
R ⟨spill thy soul⟩ *390:5–6*
R ⟨made at him⟩ *389:32*
R ⟨was got to the door⟩
R ⟨quag⟩ *390:12*
gave back
what he had best to do
R ⟨hubbub⟩ *388:35, 389:7*
R ⟨for:⟩
R ⟨first:⟩
durst not so much as mutter
R ⟨at commons⟩ *413:11?*

25 *R* ⟨to brood (breed)⟩ *392:37?*
    R ⟨dyed his desperation⟩ *388:28–29*
    G ⟨in regard he—⟩
    more is but the same brought again
    stranger & new halcyon
30 *R* ⟨catched⟩ *390:26*
    R ⟨to be at⟩ *386:4–5*
    R ⟨sad coloured⟩ *390:11*   *R* ⟨heifer⟩ *390:41*
    to hit
    R ⟨smoking shower⟩ *390:24–25*
35 *R* ⟨wind sitting in the west⟩ *390:20*
    R ⟨for their abuses done by them⟩ *390:6*
    R ⟨chew the cud⟩ *406:4*
    R ⟨a very pretty man⟩ *389:24*
    R ⟨chanced to⟩ *390:35?*

LEFT COLUMN HORIZONTAL

40 pier—bridge *25:32 and elsewhere*
    Sargent *28:15ff.*
    R ⟨foot & mouth disease⟩ *34:7ff.*
    Dixon warns SD
    European conflagration *33:42*
45 *R* ⟨pluterperfect imperturbability⟩ *412:38–39, 34:1–2*
    R ⟨Rinderpest in Habsburgs⟩ *393:3, 34:8*
    R ⟨Bull by the horns⟩ *393:5, 34:12*
    R ⟨thanking you for hospitality⟩ *393:2–3, 34:12–13*
    R ⟨fruitful mothers,⟩   *R* ⟨Austr. doctors,⟩ *34:17–18*
50 *R* ⟨sinned v the light⟩ *34:40, 387:13, 420:35*   : who not?
    R ⟨Bullockbefriending bard⟩ *408:5, 36:40, and elsewhere*
    R ⟨God shout in street.⟩ *388:14–15, 35:30*
    Helen, O'Rourke of Breffni *35:38, 35:41, and elsewhere*
    Field M.P. = hero *36:23*
55 *R* ⟨pelican in her piety⟩ *402:31–32*
    peacock in his pride

R ⟨Damon wants Fr. letters: Poyntz⟩ *398:30*

B ⟨beef to the heel⟩ *390:42, 366:2, 65:38–39*

R ⟨Model farm Kinnereth⟩ *59:12–13*

60 *R* ⟨dead sea barren⟩ *61:4, 407:25*

R ⟨Womb -oomb-tomb⟩ *48:42, 386:15*

Melon dream   SD   *47:42, 556:28*

changeling   *46:16, 593:14*

R ⟨Ineluctable⟩ *38:1 and elsewhere*

65 *R* ⟨Flor. MacCabe.⟩ *38:38 and elsewhere*   *R* ⟨creation from nothing⟩ *38:42*

R ⟨navelcord not by death severed⟩ *38:42–39:2, 385:16–18*

R ⟨omphalos,⟩ *39:3, 396:6*   mystic monks *39:3*

God: couples

R ⟨Kidneys of wheat,⟩ *381:11–12*   *R* ⟨bulls of Bashan⟩ *407:17–18*

70 *R* ⟨fichue position, c'est le pigeon, Joseph⟩ *42:12–13, 509:25–27, 385:25*

R ⟨seeds of brightness, wind⟩ *383:34, 45:10*

R ⟨bulrushes saved from water⟩ *387:41, 46:5 & 26–27*

dwarfs, blubber of turlehide whales *46:10–12*

R ⟨chap frigs in bath: she conceives⟩ *383:38*

75 *R* ⟨knew her:⟩ *389:32*   lay with her

R ⟨I put it to you⟩ *421:5*

R ⟨matriculation⟩ *392:21, 666:33*

B ⟨LB to study medicine⟩

deae virginenses, prema,   *R* ⟨pertunda:⟩ *417:5*   Deus Subigus

80 *R* ⟨Lapland:⟩ *418:13*   no menses or / in anno   *R* ⟨⎰N Pole ⎱⟩

R ⟨. . . . . in anno ?licet ?menstruam⟩   *R* ⟨⎱Brazil ⎰⟩

B ⟨Priests deflower virgins, Madagascar⟩ *386:24–25*

Menses: breath stinks too LB

R ⟨SD's bridal rite⟩ *386:24ff.?*

85 to fray them away   *R* ⟨incubator⟩ *395:18*

R ⟨1st month unnoticed, fear, resigned⟩

honoris causa

B ⟨no reasonable offer refused,⟩ *362:24*

G ⟨wrung ringless hands⟩

90 must cover my neck (SD)

R ⟨which, as we judged, were, with the fury of great floods,
    rooted up⟩

both to be and to be: a rewarder

R ⟨use vivid present⟩

95   the argument fire, the place whence heaven,   the mood

& figure devotion, the conclusion death to be overcome

B ⟨old woman peeps (Hades)⟩ *86:14*

B ⟨coiled coffinband, (Hades)⟩ *111:10*

R ⟨a proper man of person⟩ *396:41*

100   *R* ⟨a very ass⟩

R ⟨became from a clown to be⟩

R ⟨against her lover came⟩ *Cf. 385:38*

composed gait, clothes, gestures, action, all composed

R ⟨being her mind is to do well⟩

105   *R* ⟨there never breathed that person to whom mankind was more

        beholden⟩ *387:6–7*

R ⟨'twas a milkmaid⟩   *R* ⟨teeming earth⟩ *Cf. 379:4*

I use to sell none.   *R* ⟨I sung⟩ *Cf. 386:27*   *R* ⟨tice him⟩ *389:34–35*

prentice,   *B* ⟨cozen⟩ *393:38*   *R* ⟨No question but⟩ *Cf. 401:12*

110   that you ere were there

B ⟨lock hospital⟩ *617:12–13*

R ⟨a matter of 200 yrs ago⟩

R ⟨in pod⟩ *385:34*

R ⟨in family way⟩ *399:35*

115   *R* ⟨passage happened⟩ *397:3?*

R ⟨delights noble⟩ *386:42?*

R ⟨sit upon⟩

R ⟨concluded the deaths⟩ *Cf. 395:41*

RIGHT MARGIN HORIZONTAL

R ⟨labour⟩ *384:18 and elsewhere*   forward to talk

120   *R* ⟨dearest pledges⟩ *395:33*   *R* ⟨outlandish⟩ *404:29*

R ⟨except to smthg⟩   *R* ⟨nought else but notion⟩ *389:33*

R ⟨hortative⟩ *385:42*

R ⟨not to can⟩ *378:20*

R ⟨delivery⟩ *401:19, 404:7*

125   interlace

if he be inward & no other cause

I think it be   R ⟨will strain hard but⟩ *389:31?*

G ⟨serve you?⟩ *409:18?*

R ⟨nor is it not meet they will kill.⟩

130   R ⟨by my troth⟩ *386:39*

R ⟨outstrip⟩ *408:25*

even ?as --- that look to be

B ⟨round with you⟩

R ⟨what have you, good my friend⟩ *395:23–24*

135   R ⟨look you⟩

R ⟨no other thing⟩

R ⟨he plucked one ope⟩ *388:21?*

draff   stung

R ⟨what a devil⟩ *386:4*

140   B ⟨I'll be sworn⟩ *399:23*

every art his due

cause

R ⟨which thy --- erst planted⟩ *394:10?*

soue't gurnet

145   R ⟨to my best remembrance⟩ *386:40–41*

R ⟨inconceivable⟩

R ⟨of mean fortunes⟩ *391:38–39*

R ⟨to ?slumber (act)⟩ *388:34?*

itself

150   he had ?maimed the other

R ⟨to make shift⟩ *386:42*

low in money

B ⟨: ?Jehu⟩ *597:29*   R ⟨hatch⟩ *406:29*   R ⟨so dark is destiny⟩ *384:20*

R ⟨saluted on the by.⟩ *400:13–14*

155   memory of things in youth better than age

R ⟨lying at⟩   ?of kin

R ⟨seek unto him⟩

R ⟨man of art⟩ *384:20*

R ⟨remember him⟩

160   R ⟨shaked this house⟩

R ⟨feel hard to⟩

thus he replied   currish

R ⟨polite & terse⟩   R ⟨put case⟩

R ⟨nice⟩

165   R ⟨slicks his hair⟩ *398:3*

could not tell what to think

R ⟨he was but a word & a blow⟩ *388:25–26*

and said he   he

R ⟨that is it what I ?said⟩

170   crown

R ⟨beat pitifully⟩ *390:18?*

B ⟨this talkative⟩ *396:41*

R ⟨Bous Stephenoumenos⟩ *408:5*

NOTES

My division of phrases between left and right columns is somewhat arbitrary. The following words and phrases on "Oxen" 4 are from Peacock:

"*Oxen*" *4*	*Peacock*	"*Oxen*" *4*	*Peacock*
Line 25	Page 319	Line 107 "teeming earth"	Page 72
93	57	108 "I used to"; "I sung"	73
95	62–63	108 "tice him"	75
96	63	109 "prentice"	75
99–101	66	109 "cozen"; "No question"	76
102–103	67	110	77
104	68	155	62
105–106	71	163–165	67
107 " 'twas a"	73		

Lines 1–7   This looks like a computation not meant for *Ulysses*.

40ff.   Many of the phrases which follow are related to the "Nestor" episode.

53   *O'Rourke*: see "Cyclops" 5:42 and note.

54   William P. *Field, M.P.*: president in 1904 of the Irish Cattle Traders and Stock Owners Association (see Adams, pp. 18–19).

57   *Damon* and *Poyntz*: not identified.

76   Repeated at "Oxen" 14:36.

79   *Prema* and *Pertunda*: Roman goddesses. The former presides over newlyweds and the latter

over the loss of virginity. *Subigus*: protecting god of the wedding night. This is probably from St. Augustine's *City of God* VI.9.3: "Adest enim dea Virginiensis et deus pater Subigus, et dea mater Prema et dea Pertunda, et Venus et Priapus" (ed. J. E. C. Welldon [London, 1924], I, 267). See also "Oxen" 2:104 and note.

80 *Lapland*: repeated at "Oxen" 3:4.

87 See *U* 700:22–23. *Honoris causa*: for the sake of honor. To the right is a sort of pyramid with two perpendicular lines on the left.

111 Repeated at "Circe" 3:89.

144 *Soue't gurnet*: "soused gurnet" is used by Falstaff in *1 Henry IV* IV.ii.10ff.

158 Repeated at "Oxen" 8:80.

165 Repeated at "Oxen" 14:38.

"Oxen of the Sun" 5

LEFT MARGIN HORIZONTAL

live on ?sobs
R ⟨Hugh Hyacinth the MacDermot prince of Coolavin † 8/2/904⟩
R ⟨?WM: motherhood ?immune from joy and pain. If she knew her
    love awkward. If not her ?ignorance & her manifestation
5   of love is indecent⟩
transubstantiality combated by Duns Scotus
In Gaul bread Jesus laid on altar, each took his bit.
Temple—where's the jakes, young man.
Toga girilis
10 the wherewithal.
R ⟨Malachi Mulligan   Fertilizer⟩ *395:18*
R ⟨Les petites femmes des boulevards⟩ *418:26*
An enemy hath done this.
R ⟨Dry nurse (OG for SD)⟩
15 *R* ⟨Learn what heart is & what it suffers.⟩
R ⟨Who called you from Paris?⟩
the present by no means desperate condition
Give commonplace for a pearl.
R ⟨Besmirch the lily virtue of a confiding female⟩ *386:18–19*
20 *B* ⟨MacHugh Buonaparte, Cicero Racine, Jesus Doyle
      Dixon = taking gilt off the gingerbread⟩ *607:2–3*
R ⟨Fire Brigade⟩ *420:29*
R ⟨?Connery stands drink to medicals⟩

185

CENTER COLUMN

R ⟨Jesus Christ save Mary Magdalen, (Mac)⟩   *R* ⟨dolt⟩ *386:4*

25   *R* ⟨For the ?oak! (B. Mulligan)⟩   *R* ⟨bawdyhouse⟩ *420:32*

R ⟨Give us a shake of pepper, young fellow,⟩ *418:24*   *R* ⟨ballad⟩ *420:38*

When the fringes of her drawers were like . . . . . . of . . . . . ,

When the candle on the . . . . was like ?flickerings of pale thin

 ?flame   *R* ⟨"Doc"⟩ *418:13*

30   Children want presents   ?down

How Buckley shot the Russian general

Hat left behind. S.D. shows LB personality of ?eve

R ⟨3 triplets huddled in womb: queen's bounty⟩ *403:35–36*

R ⟨Death depends on cells. Nothing to do with life secretions.⟩

35   *R* ⟨Examine me know the hour of my death. Kismet.⟩

B ⟨Clery 'a pleased bottom' (B.Mull)⟩ *212:33*   *R* ⟨Vicar of Christ

   — " Bray⟩ *384:36–37*

LB & SD I'm experience he youth. What is wrong?

B ⟨Italian verse—ear of cow elephant⟩ *606:28*

40   *R* ⟨?pear of ?buggets⟩

R ⟨many never . . . . . with big ?bells.⟩

"Did you just find out the ?causticity for causivity,:" SD to BM

R ⟨sodbox:⟩   *R* ⟨coalbox.⟩ *749:35*   *R* ⟨childbed⟩ *380:5*

B ⟨I larruped into her.⟩ *498:11*   *R* ⟨Bless us & save us!⟩

45   *R* ⟨ma mère m'a mariée⟩ *417:21*

?Crothers: ?sod.   *R* ⟨B.M. ?proves S.D. unclean poet. Punch Costello

 recalls SD at Clongowes.⟩   *R* ⟨"O our is the ruddy birth."⟩ *418:16*

 R ⟨SD spits.   ?Dixon suave, civil.⟩ *418:16?*

 SD wishes to . . . . him but no. Kelwe's

50   *R* ⟨Laetabuntur in cubilibus suis.⟩ *420:33–34*

on the penultimate   B.M.   jump with delight

With that the shepherd whooped for joy.

B.M.   *B* ⟨?exposed ?cabmen.⟩ *411:33*   put up a 12 of stout.

R ⟨Lightning. SD afraid⟩ *388:14ff.*   Franklin: conductor.

55   SD. paralyse Europe.

186

R ⟨SD. laugh at funerals⟩   LB. sleek chops.   *R* ⟨chick⟩ *391:15*
    or child

R ⟨″ Eternal youth.⟩ *386:22*

Cabinet: where Scotchmen meet Scotchmen

60   *R* ⟨Mead ?100 B.C. in Europe (Ludovisi: Aristocracy)⟩

clapped hat on head

R ⟨noosing cows,⟩ *392:10?*   *R* ⟨quicks (young shoots)⟩ *390:13*   *R* ⟨proud
    possessor⟩ *417:35*

Mute crash of ?froth.

65   *R* ⟨Chap thinks he ?has swallowed fly, deposit of lead in penis⟩ *420:7*

R ⟨omphalos⟩ *396:6 and elsewhere*

exponent of Hamlet   *R* ⟨greylunged citizens⟩ *411:28*

R ⟨spat flat on floor.⟩

R ⟨dust in houses causes adenoids⟩ *411:29–30*   *G* ⟨he ?hatted himself⟩

70   aquacities.

addled absinthe

B ⟨Haines I was polite.⟩ *Cf. 397*   *B* ⟨SiD's a fool's advice re friends⟩ *507:16*
    B ⟨hat's awry: He sleeps in my bed⟩

R ⟨So & not otherwise.⟩ *415:30–31*

75   Church which has the words of eternal life, takes ?times ?easy

R ⟨SD big job keep body clean⟩ *Cf. 17:23–26*

Make dog drunk (LB.)   sick as a dog.

R ⟨SD returns to thoughts of a.m.⟩

Milly delicate, heavy sleeper.   *B* ⟨change if mother. Brings out
80   latent diseases⟩

R ⟨Too full for words⟩ *419:2*

Pat Harding,   *R* ⟨the flower of the flock⟩ *384:23*

R ⟨words to that effect⟩ *387:4*

R ⟨Rock saltpetre⟩

85   ⟨Her father's fault—at least it ought to be⟩ *401:30–31*

R ⟨there's six of them.⟩

R ⟨Br. 8 Beat. Beef, Beer, Battleships, Bills, Business, Bulldogs,
    Buggery & Bishops⟩ *417:21–29*

R ⟨Oxtail university,⟩ *387:5*   Pale ?case . . .

90   Holy office, ...

        SD would this interest a woman . . . .

        B ⟨SD speaks to the unknown, unseen what⟩

        I held out thick lips for beer

        R ⟨throw down, pass (medical)⟩

95   *R* ⟨Go thou & do likewise⟩ *387:3–4*

        Urinal: 4 pissers: oxen in stall, hanging heads, jokes,
           epigraphs.

        R ⟨Those who have 'passed' on⟩ *413:27*

        Eternity cannot be hustled

100   Plenty of time in eternity

NOTES

    This is one of the more illegible of the *Ulysses* notesheets. On some lines Joyce seems to have been writing more rapidly and carelessly than usual.

    Line 2   See "Cyclops" 6:39–40 and note. See also "Cyclops" 7:57 and note.

   6 *Duns Scotus*: looks like *Dung Scotus* as at "Cyclops" 1:26; see also note there.

   8 *Temple*: perhaps Swift's patron, Sir William Temple (1628–99), who is mentioned by Saintsbury. There is, however, a character named Temple in *Ulysses* (31:40, 40:41) and in *A Portrait* (*passim*). An archbishop's son by the name of William Temple was a friend of Oliver St. John Gogarty (Ulick O'Connor, *The Times I've Seen* [London, 1964], p. 69).

   9 *Toga girilis*: the *toga virilis* is the white toga of manhood assumed by boys of ancient Rome at the end of their fourteenth year. Cf. *FW* 112:30 and *Stephen Hero*, p. 182.

   11 *Malachi Mulligan*: Buck Mulligan, as in lines 25, 36, and 46.

   14 OG: Oliver St. John Gogarty, a friend or enemy of Joyce's and the model for Buck Mulligan. *Dry nurse*: repeated at "Oxen" 14:46.

   15 Cf. *A Portrait*, p. 252: "what the heart is and what it feels."

   20–21 Some of these names are repeated at "Cyclops" 2:5–6 and "Circe" 3:40; see note to the former reference. Professor *MacHugh* is not mentioned in these other two instances, but he appears in the "Aeolus" episode (*U* 122–148). *Dixon* is an intern at the hospital (*U* 380ff.).

   23 *Connery*: a Dublin pub (*U* 197:17, 680:27).

   31 *Buckley*: see "Cyclops" 5:65 and note.

   36 *Clery*: Clery's is a Dublin clothing store; also a brand of toilet paper still sold in Dublin.

   46–47 *Cro[t]thers*: mentioned in "Oxen" and "Circe" (*U* 382 and elsewhere). *Punch Costello*: a medical student (*U* 382ff.). *Clongowes* Wood: the Jesuit school Stephen (and Joyce) attended as a boy.

   49 *Kelwe's*: not identified.

50 *Laetabuntur . . . suis*: They will take pleasure in their beds.

54 Benjamin *Franklin*: inventor of the lightning conductor.

60 *Ludovisi*: name of a prominent aristocratic family in seventeenth-century Bologna. Alessandro Ludovisi became Pope Gregory XV (1621–23). The family died out by 1699. See Ellmann, p. 233, on the Ludovisi section of Rome.

72–73 *A fool's advice*: see *A Portrait*, p. 31. The phrase is repeated at "Circe" 3:74. *He . . . bed*: repeated at "Circe" 3:75.

82 *Pat Harding*: not identified.

86 Cf. "Oxen" 6:41.

87 These are the eight British beatitudes. See Ellmann, p. 72.

90 The *Holy Office*: title of a satirical broadside by Joyce.

"Oxen of the Sun" 6

LEFT MARGIN HORIZONTAL

R ⟨bull Br. china shop⟩ *393:9*
R ⟨bully beef⟩ *392:11–12*
R ⟨we too, he said will seek the kip⟩ *420:32–33*
R ⟨Young Man in Cape Horn⟩ *398:35?*
5   *R* ⟨Lusk midwifery⟩ *411:19*
R ⟨egg nogg etc.⟩ *417:41*
R ⟨quick with child⟩ *381:28*
R ⟨learns⟩
to learn her
10   *B* ⟨LB let myself in for this. Well?⟩ *630:41*
R ⟨Woman looks at mind after adieu⟩
B ⟨SD objects to English abroad⟩
B ⟨SD address letters Paris.⟩
R ⟨Caraway seed to carry away⟩ *418:24–25*
15   *R* ⟨corruption of minors⟩ *386:19*
R ⟨Richmond hospital⟩ *420:6*
R ⟨T. W. Hamlet⟩
R ⟨the word x was a⟩
R ⟨languages⟩ *484:29 and elsewhere*
20   *R* ⟨stap my vitals⟩ *400:20*
R ⟨drove her trade⟩ *392:39*
R ⟨more money than⟩
R ⟨forecast⟩ *401:2*
R ⟨lay together⟩ *383:36?*
25   *R* ⟨went for her⟩
R ⟨husband⟩ *413:33 and elsewhere*

R ⟨?gust to it⟩

LEFT COLUMN HORIZONTAL

R ⟨nurse ought to count sponges in peritoneal cavity⟩ *412:8–9*

R ⟨Bull minotaur⟩ *404:33*

30   O.G. knows which side his bread is buttered (LB)

Taormina

neir Elohim: le gerre: phalli:

Lampetie. Phaethusa

R ⟨Ul. goes alone in . . . .   :sleep(?)⟩

35   R ⟨LB alone⟩ *387:23?, 409:20ff.?*

R ⟨Ireland: pontine marsh⟩

B ⟨LB ?laid on ?fire of b. . . .— ?Knough ?rose⟩

R ⟨S. Joseph patron of unhappy marriages⟩ *385:23–24*

He picked up the crumbs that fell from the table

40   R ⟨Glory Allelujerum, oo–oojerum!⟩ *401:33*

R ⟨And so say all of us:⟩   R ⟨there's 11 of them.⟩ *420:21*

R ⟨the 1st said (SD)⟩

R ⟨O.G.—Kinch, have you any children⟩ *Cf. 386:20–21*

R ⟨SD I am the eternal son.⟩ *386:22*

45   B ⟨SD By the way have you the lamp, the w. . . , the k. . . . .⟩

     Cf. 508:9–10

long ?hopeful lord.

R ⟨Keep a watch on the clock (Dixon)⟩ *417:20*

R ⟨?Leeave   it to yr own honour⟩

50   R ⟨Lenehan—Telliagraphic boy⟩ *Cf. 419:7–11, 631:15–16*

Drunkard sings with hat back, funnel mark

R ⟨Elizabeth ?Westbrook ?Nevagh ?Sands⟩   WBC

south & mouth   R ⟨a little moved but very handsomly⟩ *392:42–393:1*

carry her   R ⟨:about her lawful occasions⟩ *401:18*

55   R ⟨old age regressive metamorphosis⟩ *387:36–37*

R ⟨More in room four hostile ?against   ?incomes⟩

R ⟨/ J.C. Foreskin in Calcata, Rome to quicken

     pregnant women. Resurrected with or without?

     ?Kaynalous   S.J. holds he had. ?but   of finer earth.

60   Salmeron S.J. calls it carnal bridal ring for his
      spouse the church. Is it in eucharist? at last supper
      he had it not. No. Risen? yes ∴ yes Rocca,   see of
      H.H., the chief eunuch, deserves 4th degree of latria not
      hyperduly. hair toenails & clothes. after end of world?
65   Constellation?⟩ *688:1–7*
      R ⟨departed to incorruptible eon when god of⟩ *409:23–24*
      R ⟨Karmic law. wished to kill him.⟩ *409:26*
      R ⟨SD = vow of involuntary poverty⟩ *386:16*
      R ⟨Lords of Moon members of orangecoloured shipload from planet A
70   of lunar chain declined to assume the etheric doubles
         which men incarnated by the rosy ones from C.
         incarnated by the golden haired egos from planet B &
         the rosy ones from C.⟩ *409:26–30*
      R ⟨doldrums⟩ *409:32*   *B* ⟨ : oil of ?peserpenae⟩   *B* ⟨: parasangs⟩ *417:18*
75   *R* ⟨LB sets watch right⟩ *417:42–418:1*
      R ⟨survival of fittest, grandparents⟩ *412:34–35*   —Postnatal not
         sent ?on
      R ⟨Male & female zoa?⟩
      R ⟨—   —   ?ora?⟩
80   *R* ⟨Evolution, body residence of germcells (plasm immortal)⟩
         412:28–30
      under all the circs   *R* ⟨Dr. Meldon⟩ *397:17*
      R ⟨for reasons which have not since transpired⟩ *410:3–4?*
      R ⟨Timothy of the battered naggin⟩ *417:7–8*
85   *R* ⟨Cornerboys ?arguing round pub⟩ *Cf. 762:1*
      R ⟨Ulysses projects envy at each chapter⟩
         R ⟨mother gets⟩
      R ⟨Church sacrificing baptism & funeral⟩ *384:9–10*
      R ⟨Mead drinkers⟩ *381:16 and elsewhere*
90   *R* ⟨Molly put inside vest on Rudy dead⟩ *Cf. 763:36ff., 384:22*

RIGHT COLUMN HORIZONTAL

B ⟨son dentist⟩

R ⟨Cuffe's meadow auction⟩ *392:39–40*

R ⟨corking fine⟩ *421:5–6*

R ⟨gospeller⟩ *420:39, 203:41*

95 *R* ⟨Yank to glory⟩ *421:3*

R ⟨which he had eyed in the daytime and found the place where
by laid them⟩ *392:14–15*

R ⟨Egan's Hop bitters⟩ *Cf. 80:35*

R ⟨nauseate the man⟩ *400:35*

100 swear harm

R ⟨took on so⟩

R ⟨impudent mocks⟩ *400:26*

R ⟨vicar of Bray⟩ *384:37*

R ⟨law of probability?⟩ (Weissmann)

105 *R* ⟨ " " anticipation⟩ (Rudy)

NOTES

My arrangement of phrases in the right column is somewhat arbitrary. The following phrases on "Oxen" 6 are repeated on "Circe" 3.

"Oxen" 6	"Circe" 3
Line 12	Line 85; cf. "Eumaeus" 7:75
13	86; cf. "Cyclops" 2:14
36	107 (note)
45	87

Line 1   *Br.*: British.

5   Graham *Lusk*: an American physiologist (1866–1932).

14   Repeated at "Cyclops" 2:21.

16–17   See "Cyclops" 3:2 and note.

31   *Taormina*: Greek for "ox isle." It is located on the coast of Sicily near Mount Etna and is now generally considered to have been near the original isle of the Oxen of the Sun. It is mentioned in Bérard (II, 369–370, 374–375, 391).

32   *Neir Elohim* ("candles of God"): to the left is a crude drawing of a menorah. Lines 31, 32, 33, and 35 are all on one page of *Ulysses* notebook VIII.A.5. at Buffalo (p. 300). (Line 36 is on page 303). *Le gerre* and *phalli* are in the notebook as "le gerre - phalli adored" and are from Bérard (II, 380). See also Gilbert, p. 297, on phallic worship at Naxos.

33   *Lampetie* and *Phaethusa*: daughters of Hyperion and tenders of the Oxen of the Sun. Lampetia is the English spelling.

41   Cf. "Oxen" 5:86.

52   These names are unidentified.

53   *South & mouth*: see *U* 136:35.

57–65   The essence of this passage is repeated at "Ithaca" 12:42–45. *Kaynalous*: unidentified. Alphonsus *Salmerón* (1515–85), a Jesuit Biblical scholar and one of the first companions of Ignatius Loyola, wrote sixteen volumes of spiritual commentaries on the Bible. He taught for many years in Rome, although he was Spanish by birth. A contemporary Italian theologian was Angelo *Rocca* (1545–1620). The source of this passage in *Ulysses* can probably be found in one (or both) of these theologians' works.

67   Related to the "metempsychosis" motif and the problem of the resurrection of the foreskin of Christ in line 57ff. is the Oriental equivalent—the law of karma. Karma is "the force generated by a person's actions that is held in Hinduism and Buddhism to be the motive power for the round of rebirths and deaths endured by him until he has achieved spiritual liberation and freed himself from the effects of such force" (*Webster's 3rd*).

74   *Peserpenae* may be a spelling error. Reserpine is a sedative used in the treatment of hypertension and various mental disorders.

85   See "Cyclops" 2:53 and note.

86   Repeated at "Cyclops" 2:75.

88   See "Cyclops" 1:44 and note.

90   See "Cyclops" 3:19–20 and note.

104   August Weismann: a German biologist and professor of zoology at Freiburg (1834–1914).

105   *Rudy* is, of course, the dead son of Leopold and Molly Bloom.

"Oxen of the Sun" 7

LEFT MARGIN VERTICAL

R ⟨LB pays? compliment⟩   feebled   curious and fearful
R ⟨potent man⟩ *401:38?*   R ⟨bovril⟩ *420:5*
?there be (who knows not that there be)
To him he adheres   dresses us for heaven
5   R ⟨feast him⟩   lodge him
R ⟨brewage⟩ *381:16*
who looks ?they should be?   apprehend it
R ⟨a homer of manna⟩ *416:22*   it rained sadly
R ⟨not without,⟩ unseen
10   R ⟨as was the Roman wont⟩ *408:32–33*

LEFT MARGIN HORIZONTAL

R ⟨uterine brother⟩ *403:30*
R ⟨this meanwhile⟩ *381:26*
R ⟨every each⟩ *381:19*
Well, sd. A-
15   R ⟨-the which⟩
R ⟨Archer up⟩
blue butter
R ⟨white swelling⟩ *399:35*
I owe none homage to him
20   R ⟨but, or it be long too, he'll . . . . ⟩
R ⟨without he do me⟩
Now is there any here, said Arthur

195

R ⟨a knight that hight⟩ *381:33, 382:12*

R ⟨a passing good man of his body⟩ *382:1–2*

25 with a mighty puissance

R ⟨each slew other⟩ *Cf. 380:20–21, 382:28*

R ⟨by cause of . . . but by cause⟩ *Cf. 381:35, 384:16–17*

R ⟨aventried their spears⟩ *Cf. 385:11*

R ⟨sore of limb⟩ *380:35*

30 R ⟨marvellously⟩ fast *380:42*

R ⟨stood full of ladies⟩ *Cf. 384:33*

R ⟨the place as they fought⟩

R ⟨or now⟩ *381:32*

R ⟨to their both's health⟩ *382:1*

35 Sine that   R ⟨on live⟩ *384:20*

R ⟨it happed me⟩ *380:20*

R ⟨that stood fore him⟩ *381:40*

R ⟨he was ware⟩ *381:32*

R ⟨Also⟩ *381:40*   R ⟨on this side the . . . ⟩ *381:33*

40 R ⟨That is truth, said Bloom⟩ *384:11*

R ⟨What by water & what by land⟩ *Cf. 383:2*

R ⟨ran out freshly⟩ *408:20*   R ⟨an I may⟩ *382:9?*

R ⟨him needeth none⟩ *381:40–41*

R ⟨wist I that he . . . ⟩ *383:18*

45 And as they rode, Arthur said,

I have no sword. No force, sd. Merlin

R ⟨sir Leopold,⟩ *381:29*, king   R ⟨I marvel⟩ *381:31*

R ⟨had ado with⟩ *380:20–21*

You shall have no worship to . . . .

50 R ⟨jeopard her person⟩ *384:4*

R ⟨Leave this weeping⟩ *Cf. 381:28*   R ⟨his liefest love⟩

R ⟨her time hied fast⟩ *381:29*

what thou there seest

who would have weened   hard

55 R ⟨as far as he might⟩ *381:42–382:1*   ⌣

R ⟨all they had hoods⟩ *Cf. 384:2–3*   temple

R ⟨this will more comfort than the other will dismay⟩ *384:40–41*

LEFT COLUMN HORIZONTAL

R ⟨for the intention of the sovereign pontiff.⟩ *384:35–36*

old hag in Hollis Street window

60   *R* ⟨Stephens hospital.⟩

Wrinkles of sucking babe

R ⟨Pregnant⟩ *384:11*—Cape of good hope

R ⟨Fire! Fire!⟩ *390:16?*

Betting pubs carmen can't recover debt (guessing act)

65   *B* ⟨Porter carries docket in hat.⟩

R ⟨Behold the mansion reared by dedal Jack

    See the malt stored in many a refluent sack,

    In the proud cirque of Ivan's bivouac.⟩ *388:11–13*

R ⟨?Fliers—periodic & wavelike, rut, birth etc⟩

70   *R* ⟨unfolding of flower & leaf, reaction of seabeasts to tide⟩

      R ⟨climbing sap, blood temperature:23 .28: sex mixed:

        sickness dates. 7 years. worked by stars⟩

R ⟨business proposition (Deity)⟩ *421:4–6*

R ⟨English: orate pro me⟩ *387:8*

75   *R* ⟨Dixon from Eccles Street.⟩ *386:12–13*

R ⟨S.D. forgets to pay.⟩

R ⟨Shrieks of silence⟩ *418:25*

R ⟨Greasy hog and wether wool sales⟩ *392:37–38*

R ⟨Every moment be our next.⟩ *381:39–40, 331:42*

80   *R* ⟨Here's to us.⟩ *418:22*

Commit his ideas to paper

Dairy arse Darius.

R ⟨nefarious designs⟩ *386:17*

R ⟨Places remember events.⟩ *163:17?*   Druggist

85   *R* ⟨risk life to save life⟩ *413:18–19*

G ⟨Boosiness is boosiness⟩

R ⟨Congering in church⟩

R ⟨O.G. patriot of solar system⟩

R ⟨Yank to glory⟩ *421:3*

90   *R* ⟨winefizzling, ginsizzling, booseguzzling existences⟩ *420:41*

R ⟨Come on, you bullnecked, beetlebrowed, hogjowled

peanutbrained weaseleyed fourflushers, false
alarms and excess baggage⟩ *420:42–421:2*

R ⟨milk and money⟩ *387:21*

95 R ⟨And . . . and . . . . . . and⟩

R ⟨contrarious to his list⟩ *380:33*

R ⟨Say them, for to be slain⟩,

R ⟨most fairest damosels,   in hope to have⟩

R ⟨cautelous,⟩ *380:29*   R ⟨they assembled them⟩ *415:20–21?*

100 R ⟨and it is not long gone sithen⟩ *380:20?*

R ⟨Voided it clean, apertly⟩ *381:20–22*

R ⟨fully richly,⟩ *381:42*   R ⟨clept,⟩ *380:19 and elsewhere*

R ⟨And he let pour (mure) all the mountains about⟩ *381:17?*

R ⟨a full fair castle and a strong   that no man

105   could devise a fairer ne stronger⟩ *381:4*   R ⟨thilk⟩

R ⟨to his desport,⟩   R ⟨hardy and noble,⟩

R ⟨moved by craft,⟩ *381:5*   seemed quick

R ⟨I have heard counted⟩ *386:18*

R ⟨unto his own marches environing⟩ *380:35–36*

110 R ⟨and he trowed that they had said sooth⟩ *380:30*

R ⟨against (verso)⟩ *380:18*

R ⟨bring ye,   eat we⟩ *384:37–40*

R ⟨this thy son⟩ *382:22*

R ⟨murdered his goods with whores⟩ *384:30–31*

115 after that   R ⟨pardee⟩ *384:11*

R ⟨that was possible thing. yet natheless⟩ *381:7*

R ⟨thing that was false⟩ *380:31*

R ⟨murmur eke is oft among servants⟩ *383:10–11*

departed him his goods

120 husks of swine

hinds in my father's house be full of loaves

nigh a mile,   R ⟨dureth,⟩ *381:32*   men ?sayen

R ⟨treasure that there is.⟩   R ⟨avis⟩ *380:29*

R ⟨ne of Cristen men nor the⟩

125 R ⟨adread⟩ *379:26*   R ⟨nighen⟩ *380:17?*   R ⟨trowed well⟩ *380:30*

R ⟨they shriven him⟩ *379:33*

R ⟨as him thought⟩

R ⟨and x and y great plenty⟩
R ⟨whiles,⟩ *380:16*   *R* ⟨halp,⟩ *381:18*   *R* ⟨withouten⟩ *381:6*

RIGHT COLUMN HORIZONTAL

130   stiffness of a tower
no other proof doth need with easy compliance no
R ⟨Sight of married man bad⟩
R ⟨bumshow⟩ *421:5*
R ⟨Prussia Street⟩ *392:41*
135   *R* ⟨Gavin Low⟩ *392:40*
R ⟨SD lies.⟩
R ⟨purling ale⟩ *393:8*
burly barboy
take notice
140   *R* ⟨sung full delectably⟩ *381:42*
R ⟨whereof anon⟩ *383:1?*
R ⟨any of the tother⟩ *381:34*
R ⟨vizard⟩   9th long legs
?shoon: *R* ⟨he drank never no⟩ *381:20–21*
145   *R* ⟨repreved⟩
R ⟨fully delectably⟩ *381:42*
this . . this

199

NOTES

In lines 20, 27, 39, 44, 49, 95, and 147, the ellipses are Joyce's. The following phrases on "Oxen" 7 are repeated on other notesheets:

"Oxen" 7	"Cyclops" 7	"Oxen" 7	"Cyclops" 10
Line 73	Line 12	Line 84	Line 12
74	13	85	101
75	15	86	55
76	23	87	61
77	24		"Cyclops" 8
78 & 134–135	32–34	25	Cf. 61
	"Cyclops" 4	88	63 (note) and
79	Cf. 37 and "Oxen" 8:78		"Circe" 6:76
80	109	89	69
81	110	90–93	70–73
82	117	138	1
83	130	139	22

Janusko (pp. 186–187, 193–199, 201) lists three source books for Joyce's notes on "Oxen" 7: Saintsbury, *A History of English Prose Rhythm*; *The Travels of Sir John Mandeville*; and Sir Thomas Malory, *Le Morte d'Arthur*. The following words and phrases on "Oxen" 7 are from Peacock:

"Oxen" 7	Peacock	"Oxen" 7	Peacock
Lines 19–20	Page 8	Line 109	Page 3
21–31	9	110	1
32–36	10	111–112	6
37	11	113–114	7
39	12	115 "after that"	6
40	13	116	3
41	14	119–121	6
42 "ran out"	Cf. 14	140	4
94–99	5	141–142	5
100	4 & 5	144 "he drank never no"	2
101	5	145	2
102–107	4	146	4
108	2		

Line 25 *Puissance*: cf. "puissant" at *U* 385:11.

69–72 Repeated at "Nausicaa" 3:58–63.

127 Janusko says this phrase disappeared in a draft of the "Oxen" episode (Spielberg, item V.A.14 at Buffalo).

136 Cf. "Cyclops" 5:67.

"Oxen of the Sun" 8

LEFT MARGIN HORIZONTAL

R ⟨?Such a pinch of time⟩ *402:6*
?barred clouds
bloom ?surprising day.
signs of rain
5   *R* ⟨prophecy of Malachi⟩ *391:25*
R ⟨no man remembered to be without⟩ *390:14*
R ⟨in ken⟩ *391:8 & 24*
R ⟨birthmark⟩ *404:22?*
flawed skin of face
10   *R* ⟨climacteric⟩
R ⟨miscarriage⟩ *403:36*
R ⟨abortion⟩ *386:7, 412:6, 383:33*
'twas answered
he was sending   *R* ⟨a brace of⟩ *390:23–24*   bullets
15   sumpter   pillion
Mr. Hater & I did put to null the pretence
R ⟨make this return⟩ *386:16–17*
R ⟨project⟩ *395:14 and elsewhere*   : & what & which
R ⟨Horace, a Roman poet⟩ *404:34?*
20   *R* ⟨congratulate with⟩ *397:28–29*
R ⟨with movements⟩ *412:16?*
misses of quality
R ⟨bamboozle⟩ *605:18*
R ⟨incog.⟩ *570:12 & 30*   *R* ⟨brangling disputes⟩ *Cf. 391:2–3*
25   was at home but is not gone out yet
R ⟨as cheap sitting as standing⟩ *395:25*

201

B ⟨was yr father a glazier⟩

B ⟨have it now or wait till etc⟩ *514:9–10*

    poetry

30 *B* ⟨Mumchance hanged for saying nothing⟩

R ⟨tomorrow's a new day⟩ *398:28–29*

B ⟨comes from a hot place⟩ *538:30*

B ⟨tell me news⟩ *549:21*

LEFT COLUMN HORIZONTAL

R ⟨levity⟩ *402:7*

35 Story of Darius

?erin ex lectularius

R ⟨Big Wind, fire,⟩ *390:16–17*

R ⟨Cupric . . . . . .⟩   *R* ⟨nice clean old man⟩ *404:39*

buttockbone of Pentecost

40 *R* ⟨whose breath is ashes⟩ *387:24*

R ⟨the bull of Clontarf, ?sprung horns⟩

    (Gilderslieve)

and when there's no-one looking

cure of ?souls

45 *R* ⟨Venus Pandemos.⟩ *418:26*   *R* ⟨⟨to the woman who seduced him⟩ *418:28–29*

R ⟨blessed Stephen, ever virgin.⟩ *386:22*

R ⟨SD drunk black greeted by arabs⟩ *417:11–13*   *R* ⟨O.G. imparts the

    papal benediction. SD salutes the urchins, himself in

    them.⟩ *417:12–13*

50 SD attacks hellenism, appendicitus of Europe

Lockjaw, tendon between thumb and finger.

R ⟨Mickey O' (sir Michael O'Dwyer) chucking sisters in Mater

    under the chin⟩ *399:27*

R ⟨Wardmaid (Hester)⟩ *399:28–29*

55 *R* ⟨Not a one of me knows⟩ *417:9–10*

Gregory of the golden mouth

Yeats ?remains a dear fellow

a power of young men.

202

Irish winter ending in July, to recommence in August

60   B ⟨who made the world. British bible Society⟩

R ⟨Rose of Castille⟩ *419:3 and elsewhere*

Hamlet: 2/2/9–

R ⟨What you want for ninepence?⟩ *418:29–30*

Shakespeare

65   Roger O'Laughlin (O'Nowlan) too stupid

R ⟨Rom. Church sacrificing mother to child, ?.eans baptism &
    funeral.⟩ *384:9–10*

R ⟨Our impotentia supplex B.V.M. (S. Bernard)⟩ *385:13–14*

LB: bicycle tour

70   R ⟨Never know who's yr son. Instance 20 yrs ago. Wise father
    knows his own child.⟩ *406:27–29*

R ⟨Yeats ?history designing females⟩ *417:23–24*

R ⟨Man as old as his arteries⟩   R ⟨G.P.O.: Metchnikoff inoculated
    anthropoid apes 1904⟩ *510:4–5*   R ⟨⅓ of children born blind⟩

75   Lenehan 8? for a . . . 2 Mrs. ?Moby ?3: Anno Domini
    made the ?Tutu (Camden Street)

R ⟨O.G. go forth & preach the gospel. Lenehan: say ?no ?more⟩

R ⟨would be his next⟩ *381:39–40*

R ⟨Bonsoir la compagnie⟩ *419:33*

80   R ⟨Man of Art (M.D.)⟩ *384:20*

. . . . . one is my ear

R ⟨Birds of a feather laugh together⟩ *402:10–11*

B ⟨Gent: patriot scholar: judge of malt⟩

joke: always make ?remd. to self no ?laughs 1st self

85   to make up for . . . .

. . . . . : . . . .

B ⟨who live by the pen shall . . . ⟩

R ⟨?all . . . same: . . . different (laughs)⟩

R ⟨Hurrah there!⟩ *417:10*

90   R ⟨Agendath Netaim⟩ *407:12–13 and elsewhere*

Fucker obliges God to create

R ⟨Pregnant woman not to step over shaft ∴ umbilical cord might
    strangle⟩ *404:15–17*

R ⟨?Voglie. touch her backside.⟩

203

95   Roast apple in mouth of babe so that not smell

       B ⟨?churching of women⟩

       chicken ?volte puerpere ?wind

       not praise her own milk

       not leave clothing under moon

100   *R* ⟨Cut nails after 1 year else thief with teeth⟩ *391:16?*

       Give bit of all at table

       R ⟨?Good after baptism⟩

       bosom friends become backbites.

       R ⟨nice by name &—by nature⟩ *Cf. 393:7–8*

105   *B* ⟨what did thought do?⟩ *468:18*

       R ⟨if you fall don't wait to— —⟩ *418:7*

RIGHT MARGIN HORIZONTAL

       R ⟨Victory one to Lane, 4 winners yesterday & 4 today.⟩ *408:30–32*

       R ⟨Won in a canter⟩ *408:32*

       R ⟨Towards end in close order⟩ *408:24*

110   *R* ⟨Run home.⟩ *408:24*   *B* ⟨1 length.⟩

       R ⟨Jap ship sunk by Russian war correspondents⟩ *420:19–20*

       Question of magnet & high tension

       ?Bow ?de ?Catesy ?Germany

       R ⟨to forestall⟩

115   *R* ⟨fraction of bread⟩ *384:39*

       R ⟨bold bad girl (Mullingar)⟩ *418:26–27*

       R ⟨infanticide,⟩ *412:7, 403:36*

       B ⟨Mrs Thornton⟩ *66:13 and elsewhere*

       . . . .

120   Antisthenes

       R ⟨LB. other son? (6th week)⟩

       R ⟨soul born: conception⟩

       R ⟨rice dries milk⟩ *391:12*

NOTES

For "Oxen" 8 lines 20–35 and 104–106, see Mackie Jarrell, "Joyce's Use of Swift's *Polite Conversation* in the 'Circe' Episode of *Ulysses*," *PMLA*, LXXII (June 1957), 545–554. All the phrases marked through in blue pencil on "Oxen" 8 (plus a few others) are on "Circe" 3 except for "Mrs Thornton" at line 118. Those repeated are:

"Oxen" 8	"Circe" 3	"Oxen" 8	"Circe" 3
Line 27	Line 84	Line 60	Line 76
28	82	61	91–92
30	83	83	77
32	81 & 148	87	78
33	80	105	79

Janusko (pp. 210–211) lists one source book for lines 19–33, 104–106 on "Oxen" 8: Swift's *Polite Conversation*.

Line 16 Cf. Peacock, p. 128.

27 *Was yr father a glazier*: facetious question meaning "you are opaque," to a person who is obstructing one's view.

30 *Mumchance*: an old dice game. The phrase means to be silent out of caution or stupidity.

36 *?Erin ex*: this almost illegible phrase might be *erin ex*, *crinex*, or *cunex*. The line is repeated at "Cyclops" 4:122.

41–42 *Clontarf*: from *Cluain Tarbh*, "bull's meadows." The bull is a fertility symbol in the "Oxen" episode; hence *sprung horns* might refer to the slaughter of the oxen in the *Odyssey* and in *Ulysses* to the crime against fecundity. In 1014 Brian Boru defeated the Danes at the Battle of Clontarf and in this context *sprung horns* would refer to the horns on the helmets of the Danes. *Gilderslieve* is unidentified. Cf. *FW* 17:9–12.

45 *To the woman . . .*: Joyce appears to have opened a parenthesis before this phrase and failed to close it.

50 Cf. Scholes and Kain, p. 91.

52 *Mickey O' (sir Michael O'Dwyer)*: evidently a local character. See *FW* 116:16, 446:31, and 529:25.

56 *Gregory of the golden mouth*: a reference to Lady Gregory. See "Gas from a Burner" (in *The Portable James Joyce*, ed. Harry Levin [New York, 1947], p. 661): "I printed folklore from North and South / By Gregory of the Golden Mouth."

57–58 These lines are probably connected.

65 See "Cyclops" 1:26 and note.

66 See "Cyclops" 1:44 and note.

68 See also *U* 350:23–26.

70–71 This is a parody of Telemachus in the *Odyssey* (p. 8). See also *U* 87:17–18.

73 *Man as old as his arteries*: cf. "Cyclops" 10:112. *Metchnikoff . . . apes*: repeated at "Circe" 1:50. Elie *Metchnikoff*: a Russian biologist (1845–1916).

76 *Tutu*: the French term for a ballet dancer's short skirt. Cf. *U* 43:10.

78 Cf. "Cyclops" 4:37 and "Oxen" 7:79.

80   *Man of Art*: repeated at "Oxen" 4:158.

94   *Voglie*: Italian for "desires" or "wishes."

97   The phrase is partly illegible, but *puerperium* means "childbirth" in Latin.

120   *Antisthenes*: a Greek philosopher and founder of the Cynic school. The name is repeated at "Circe" 3:155.

"Oxen of the Sun" 9

R ⟨grame crawlers⟩ *379:27?*
R ⟨lovesome⟩ *379:18*
for that
R ⟨cessile air⟩ *416:12*
5 *R* ⟨horrid imprecation⟩ *400:18–19*
wallaby
R ⟨harkee⟩ *386:38*
R ⟨decamp⟩ *600:21, 419:14*
R ⟨prandy⟩ *419:40?*
10 *R* ⟨cot⟩ *419:40*
R ⟨cheese⟩ *419:5*
R ⟨the true fold⟩ *400:20*
R ⟨bilbo⟩ *415:36*
R ⟨up to the present time⟩
15 ?Jawal forms on egg
R ⟨cellular division⟩
R ⟨it = he   she⟩
R ⟨proliferent⟩ *377:18, 378:20*
R ⟨emission of globes⟩ *Cf. 392:21*
20 race heredity acquired
ovulum
sperm
ovul.   1) form. nutrid
sp.   2) segment
25 *R* ⟨ovocita⟩   *R* ⟨hermaphrodite⟩
R ⟨globes = elimination of male = monosexual⟩

207

R ⟨defunctive music⟩ *416:34*
R ⟨trentals⟩ *416:33*
R ⟨repugnance⟩ *403:29*
30 ?greengowned
(?fumble)

RIGHT MARGIN VERTICAL TOP

R ⟨Madden backs Madden⟩ *419:13*
R ⟨shortcomings⟩ *412:12–13*
R ⟨bisons⟩ *416:37*
35 *R* ⟨ladies⟩
wooden legs
      (run in family)
R ⟨?wonder is how⟩
R ⟨comes off so well⟩
40 *R* ⟨serve (fuck)⟩ *416:18?*
R ⟨fam. resembl.⟩
R ⟨schedule time⟩ *420:11*

RIGHT MARGIN VERTICAL BOTTOM

lollop, bumpo
R ⟨I vear⟩ *418:12*
45 here be
distemper
R ⟨ruminating⟩ *406:4*
R ⟨?do his baisemains⟩ *406:19*

CENTER COLUMN HORIZONTAL

R ⟨hoi polloi⟩ *418:12*
50 *R* ⟨To such a pitch had it gone that⟩

Envy possessed certain

R ⟨this splendour of mine.⟩ *Cf. 377:15–16 & 23*

R ⟨Who is he whom . . . ?⟩ *377:21?*

R ⟨lutulent⟩ *377:23*

55 *R* ⟨vinolent⟩

R ⟨that high mind's humility in him I knew⟩ *377:13*

there is no shame in you

R ⟨You are daring excessively⟩ *377:32–33?*

R ⟨No more odious crime is there to me⟩ *377:33–34*

60 *R* ⟨No man's lot bitterer⟩

R ⟨Emolument⟩ *378:16*   Rarely   *R* ⟨Child's murder = Bush⟩ *403:32–34*

R ⟨of evils⟩ *377:19*   *R* ⟨doc.⟩   Crusoe

R ⟨all things being favourable⟩ *377:10–11?*   *R* ⟨blue look out⟩

there is in him   *R* ⟨matres familiarum⟩ *396:33*

65 In memory you are worth much

R ⟨whatsoever things⟩ *377:10*

or certainly to none

R ⟨You wit I hold very little ?blunt about what best is
      to be learnt⟩

70 *R* ⟨in that one case⟩ *378:30*   *B* ⟨?swanee ?river⟩

R ⟨It is not why we shall wonder⟩ *377:39*   *B* ⟨Tom Rochfor. invent⟩ *177:4–5*

R ⟨Who nothing of any kind has learnt⟩ *377:21–22*

R ⟨Many⟩---- and ?those indeed

R ⟨in doctrine erudite, ornamented⟩ *377:12–13*

75 *R* ⟨it behoves⟩ *377:26*

R ⟨that highest in him quality⟩

R ⟨a plan was by them adopted⟩ *378:7–8*

Me a great doubt holds   vitelline membrane

R ⟨I fear lest what was excellently begun you may not so well end.⟩ *377:28–29*

80 the genius he had received from nature

R ⟨He did nothing not suitably commodious⟩ *378:30*   *R* ⟨econ. balance⟩

R ⟨Whatever he did with ----- ?and wisdom⟩ *Cf. 378:30–33*

to which—   he ignored

R ⟨whether . . . . it is not ∧ clear⟩

85 *R* ⟨was provided valiantly⟩ *378:16*

this work not only not—but even   you ?left

R ⟨So distantly removed from . . that⟩ *378:11–12*

whom   they would

R ⟨Nothing is it of gravity⟩ *378:6*

90   that no-one you, that you no-one, can ?use

R ⟨in every public work it is to be considered⟩ *378:5*

R ⟨terrestial orb⟩ *378:36*

R ⟨with sapience endowed⟩ *377:11*

concealed from them were not

95   part of wisdom

R ⟨what pertains to⟩ *378:34?*

that no age be silent about your praises

R ⟨not solely for the copiously moneyed⟩ *378:13–15*

R ⟨scarcely & not even scarcely⟩ *378:15*

100   *R* ⟨not sufficiently⟩ *378:14–15*

R ⟨cogitate the ?country to relax mind⟩ *378:37*

R ⟨tumescent⟩ *378:38*

R ⟨aspect of the most ?diverting spectacles⟩ *378:35*

NOTES

The following phrases on "Oxen" 9 are repeated on "Oxen" 20:

"Oxen" 9	"Oxen" 20
Line 75	Line 87
76	88
77	90
78	93
79	91

Line 32   The first *Madden* is one of the medical students; the second is a jockey (see *U* 126:35).

36–37   These lines may be connected.

38–39   These lines may be connected.

42   Written in pencil.

48   The word *baisemains* is "baisemoins" in the 1946 and 1961 Random House editions of *Ulysses*; this is probably an error.

49   Written in pencil.

53   The ellipses here are Joyce's, as is the question mark.

55   *Vinolent*: the first letter has been struck over with another letter.

71   *Tom Rochfor.*: Tom Rochford. See "Cyclops" 2:11 and note and *U* 228ff. and elsewhere.

84   The ellipses and caret are Joyce's.

87   The ellipses are Joyce's.

103   *Diverting spectacles*: in the text it is "distracting spectacles," but here I read *diverting*.

"Oxen of the Sun" 10

CENTER COLUMN HORIZONTAL

I hate (≃)   I hold (course)
ago = push   remit = l.s.d
   act   ?wind
Itus .   *R* ⟨I think that yes⟩ *419:11–12*
that fool one was obliged to loose
never from him was one able to loose
R ⟨deserves to be praised⟩ *378:26?*
it was not able to be persuaded to ?her that . . .
R ⟨to her nothing already then and thenceforward was
     able to be molestful.⟩ *378:18–19*
R ⟨Among the Romans to those badly their affairs waging it was
     accustomed to be interdicted⟩
R ⟨Trieste was begun to be besieged⟩
R ⟨That she by him suddenly to be ?loved   had been begun she
     felt⟩ *378:27–28*
R ⟨This they felt chiefly except among good friendship not to
     can be⟩ *378:19–20*
R ⟨So I have recd. cleanliness to women, hardship to men,
     to ?befit⟩
R ⟨Hannibal huge desire urged/impelled on of Tarentum to be captured⟩
R ⟨It is of a wise state⟩ . . .
R ⟨I ?so ?loving.⟩   *R* ⟨ :there is need⟩ *378:33–34*
R ⟨O thing not merely in being heard foul but even in being⟩
     378:25–26
R ⟨it is difficult in being said⟩ *378:9*
R ⟨the thing so ?hard itself⟩ *378:22*

R ⟨carrying in a car⟩ *378:23*

R ⟨envy among one another⟩ *378:23*?

R ⟨recd. her into that domicile⟩ *378:24*

30 *R* ⟨Her they saw mother⟩ *378:27*

Pres—Propino hoc tibi

       pauper sum, fateor

R ⟨She receives habitual⟩

R ⟨hist. pres.⟩

35 didici = ho appreso

R ⟨inchoative⟩ *680:5*?

R ⟨si Brutus conservatus erit, vicimus⟩

R ⟨perf. logic. aorist. gnomic⟩

R ⟨use imperfect⟩

40 *R* ⟨?quos—los qui⟩

R ⟨?praesens ?corratus = vendo una coza⟩

R ⟨durvia repente ?mutarerant imperator ?mutatus⟩

R ⟨ventus, veniendus (pass. part of intrans. verbs) it was (to be)
      come⟩

45 *R* ⟨e perituram (adj) Sallust.⟩

R ⟨le cose tenute (things being held)⟩

        R ⟨evolution⟩ *412:15*

        R ⟨gasteropods⟩ *416:25–26*

        R ⟨she shivers⟩

50 *R* ⟨Woman 9 yrs island conceives (Livy)⟩

R ⟨ — look at W.   ″ (Virgil)⟩ *383:35–36*

B ⟨consanguineous—sterile⟩ *404:10*   *R* ⟨to cover⟩ *416:37*

fertility :: no of privations   *R* ⟨ablation⟩ *387:37*

B ⟨spermatozoa—upstream contr. gravity⟩

B ⟨electric discharge kills sperm⟩

55   *R* ⟨brown nipple⟩   *R* ⟨hymen⟩ *386:30*

worms   fertile piss

    You to say this?   *R* ⟨many zoa boys⟩ *411:15–17*

            B ⟨after règles boys (∴ gens girls)⟩

              R ⟨azote diet⟩ *70:41*

60 *R* ⟨Young hopeful⟩ *414:8*   *R* ⟨pothecary,⟩ *382:33*   *R* ⟨spit⟩ *418:16*

    (Loeb ?ch. genesis)

213

R ⟨for sperm no gravity⟩   *R* ⟨10 her teetee (not—claret)⟩ *418:42*
   R ⟨conjugation⟩   *R* ⟨hard to breathe,⟩ *390:12*   full   ⟨Sir A Horne⟩ *Cf. 413:13*
   R ⟨matriculation⟩ *392:21*   1m.   ?dog = ?pill
65   2m. clavicle,   *R* ⟨lower jaw⟩ *384:5*   child
   R ⟨2m. soul⟩ *383:39–40*   *R* ⟨Sacred Penitentiary of ?U.S.⟩
   features, limbs,   *R* ⟨soul⟩   6m. hymen   7m8 live
3m. sex   .4m. feto   5m. move scissors & knife
                         R ⟨tripe⟩ *392:4, 71:1*
70   *R* ⟨cowheel⟩ *71:1*

RIGHT MARGIN HORIZONTAL

R ⟨I start tomorrow⟩
ut potero, explicato
R ⟨quicquid egero continuo ?suis⟩
respiravero, vita ?videto
75   *R* ⟨scriptum sum⟩
epistolary style
R ⟨how far forward?⟩ *377:17*
            R ⟨punch⟩ *416:42, 421:10*
wom. 30—38   breeder
80   M.P. red ?wom ?he grey
?wom. eleph. (Pliny & Voltaire)
                R ⟨cronion⟩ *414:11*
R ⟨flagellary movt. tail.⟩
R ⟨fusion pronuclei⟩
85   *R* ⟨headfold—feto⟩
R ⟨tailfold—annex⟩
R ⟨ ❁   —cronion⟩ *414:11*
R ⟨amnion sack⟩ *404:2?*
B ⟨whiteflowers acid kills sp.⟩ *Cf. 403:12*
90   fucked in ?sleep
drugged
B ⟨syringe fuck (?hypsorp)⟩ *404:4*
R ⟨bog Latin⟩ *394:24*   ?geasa

NOTES

Line 2   *L.s.d.*: may mean "pounds, shillings, pence," but the first letter is not a pound sign.

4   *Itus*: Latin for "a movement, going, departure."

8   The ellipses are Joyce's.

20   Joyce first wrote *urge* and then *impelled* above it.

21   The ellipses are Joyce's.

31–32   *Pres*: present tense. *Propino hoc tibi*: I make this toast to you. *Pauper sum, fateor*: I admit that I am a pauper. These phrases could possibly be connected.

34   *Hist. pres.*: historical present.

35   *Didici = ho appreso*: "I have learned" in Latin and Italian.

37   *Si Brutus conservatus erit, vicimus*: If Brutus shall have been preserved, we have conquered. Joyce was experimenting with the future perfect.

40   *Quos*: a pronoun in the accusative case (*ad quos*). *Los qui*: those who, perhaps, although the particular language is uncertain.

41   The Latin is not clear. *Vendo una coza*: Italian for "I sell a thing."

42   *Durvia . . . mutatus*: as above, the meaning of the Latin is not clear, but it might be something like "they had changed curious things when the emperor changed."

45   *Sallust*: a Roman historian (86–34 B.C.). *E perituram*: this should perhaps be *eperituram*, "will perish utterly," but the initial *e* is separate.

46   The English here is an accurate translation of the Italian.

50   *Livy*: another Roman historian (59 B.C.–17 A.D.).

56   *Worms . . . piss*: repeated at "Oxen" 11:3.

61   Jacques *Loeb*: a German-American biologist (1859–1924), who "did pioneer work on artificial parthenogenesis and also carried out research in comparative physiology and psychology" (*Chambers's*).

64   *1m.*: first month of foetal growth. In the following lines are characteristics of the foetus during the various months mentioned. Cf. Gilbert, p. 309.

72   *Ut potero, explicato*: explained as best I can.

73   *Quicquid egero continuo ?suis*: whatever I shall have done or . . . .

74   *Respiravero*: I shall have taken another breath. *Vita ?videto*: let life be seen to . . . .

75   *Scriptum sum*: I have been written.

93   *Geasa*: Irish for "magical injunctions (tabus)" (Brendan O Hehir, *A Gaelic Lexicon for Finnegans Wake* . . . [Berkeley, 1967], p. 221). The word is repeated at "Circe" 16:67 and appears in *FW* 392:24.

"Oxen of the Sun" 11

LEFT COLUMN HORIZONTAL

R ⟨where you slep las night⟩ *417:7*
jerk
worms fecund piss.   R ⟨amongst⟩ *409:42*
R ⟨beaver & visor⟩ *Cf. 381:19*   R ⟨whilst⟩ *613:1, 646:11*
            its
R ⟨kirtles,⟩ *390:26*   R ⟨born its like Crookback
                  feet 1st & toothed⟩ *400:37–38*
            deep dissimuler,   aglet,   R ⟨dame Venus⟩ *Cf. 391:7,*
                                    399:4
                        R ⟨homily⟩ *396:20*
            steplord
themself   what = ?why
R ⟨entire⟩ *409:33?*   R ⟨wink at it⟩ *392:11?*
                  weet
            R ⟨guise⟩ *386:25*
one of these ---an
      R ⟨fain⟩ *360:21*   R ⟨minim⟩ *386:30*
R ⟨by this hand⟩ *408:34*   R ⟨hereof⟩ *386:18*
R ⟨swashbuckler⟩ *385:34*
                        B ⟨cry you mercy⟩
R ⟨much admirable⟩ *386:29*   R ⟨gotten⟩ *392:3*
      R ⟨passing⟩ *382:1 and elsewhere*   a sequel
R ⟨chanceable⟩ *391:42*   R ⟨concent⟩ *386:33*
                  R ⟨swains⟩ *454:5, 398:21*
                        broil
B ⟨noncorrosive sublimate (?hell)⟩

216

chivalry (cycl. ?rows)

> R ⟨no more but⟩ *Cf. 385:10*
>
> R ⟨stayed for⟩ *390:40*

30   R ⟨Darby & Joan⟩ *416:23–24*

R ⟨of Christian walking⟩ *385:41*   R ⟨puny⟩ *386:5, 400:9*

> R ⟨cide⟩ *386:14*

poor four us   R ⟨chuff⟩ *386:5*

amnios protects fetal urine at end in it

35   B ⟨Menopause—involution of uterus⟩ *404:4–5*

B ⟨OG's aunt going to write to Si. D⟩ *418:18*

R ⟨Mr B. dearest Papli⟩ *65:31, 373:18, and elsewhere*   R ⟨I'm off⟩

> R ⟨fifteen yester. ?Turn⟩ *Cf. 65:32, 66:11*   R ⟨colt⟩ *392:23, 419:18*

B ⟨cloven hoof⟩ *432:29*

40   R ⟨blinking the facts⟩ *411:10*

B ⟨referred marriage of O'Hare⟩ *366:35–36*

R ⟨?purgue dell'umanità   (N. ?Maceh.)⟩

R ⟨foundling,⟩ *301:38*   mistake, didn't intend,

B ⟨another pair of trousers⟩

45   they sticked not to

R ⟨fasciations,⟩ *387:41*   R ⟨bands,⟩ *29:25 and elsewhere*   R ⟨agreeable unto⟩ *387:38*

R ⟨eugenics:⟩   sterilize wastrels

simple pleasures of the poor   *47:33*

R ⟨Tolstoy, Kreutzer Sonata⟩

50   R ⟨thy son shall come from afar.⟩

R ⟨airy fairy⟩ *398:41?*   R ⟨paddy whack⟩   scratch

> R ⟨terra⟩

get his hole,   down wind, soft pitch

          —fools   with rare ?virus

55   clutch   runner up

pass 1st sleep in Persia   abbreviature

R ⟨brake⟩ *387:27, 428:13*   exantlation

                equable

?notes of prebeings   entelechy

60   R ⟨ghost of a rose⟩   to be

Milton—kick up again

R ⟨who   . whither.⟩ *389:34*   R ⟨-s   -eth⟩ *Cf. 387:29–30*

R ⟨embryo philosopher⟩ *413:4*   R ⟨septuagint⟩ *387:26*

                                        R ⟨assuefaction⟩ *387:28*

RIGHT COLUMN HORIZONTAL

65 to quite

    R ⟨North.   pl.⟩   more sounder

    it (red)

    R ⟨incontinent⟩ *386:1*

    ironsides

70 R ⟨blubber⟩ *502:28*

    R ⟨gently grinning⟩ *386:13*

    R ⟨G—self⟩ *388:17–18*

    R ⟨clean contrary⟩ *386:21*   R ⟨mainly⟩ *388:7*

    B ⟨deluthering⟩ *440:4*

75 R ⟨popinjay⟩ *395:21*   R ⟨jolly⟩ *385:34, 394:42*

    dehort us   R ⟨pitch⟩ *388:20*

    imp in love   lapt

    R ⟨curious⟩ *386:23, 405:4*

    R ⟨he plucked down⟩ *388:21*

80 R ⟨lift(¢d)⟩   R ⟨viands⟩ *334:21*

    think -- what require

    R ⟨spermacetic ointment⟩ *393:33*

    R ⟨indenture (appr)⟩ *392:17*

    R ⟨yale⟩ *388:24*   R ⟨angerly⟩ *385:36*

85 R ⟨this day morning⟩

    R ⟨megrim⟩ *385:42*

    I sent thee late

    R ⟨dinged⟩ *385:32*   hidebound

                                   pecunia

90   pygarg

        -divide hoof   R ⟨& chew the cud⟩ *406:4*

    adventure to set her foot

    B ⟨Gordon Bennett⟩ *96:6 and elsewhere*

    R ⟨Childs murder⟩ *403:32, 405:18, and elsewhere*

95   R ⟨wrongfully condemned⟩ *403:34, 448:20*
law of tendency   Messedaglia
food.1.2.3.4.5
men.1.2.4.8.10   colonization
mov.1.2.4.6.8

100   R ⟨bottom of reason⟩ *391:28*

R ⟨moist relentment⟩ *404:2?*

R ⟨conclamation⟩ *388:1*

Origen, mark time

R ⟨Miss O'B. No's headache⟩

105   R ⟨infanticide⟩   WC   *412:7, 403:36*

R ⟨gradient of 1 in 9⟩ *420:18*   R ⟨"rev"⟩ *420:17*

B ⟨-for 5 wickets⟩ *418:23?*   R ⟨nativity⟩ *404:11*

catachresis   diuturnity

acies of the eye

110   R ⟨Moses   his man⟩ *Cf. 383:37–38*

gardens   before gardeners

NOTES

    My arrangement of phrases in the right column is somewhat arbitrary. Janusko (pp. 188–189, 193, 205–206) lists two source books for the material on "Oxen" 11: Saintsbury's *History of English Prose Rhythm* and Sir Thomas Browne, *Religio Medici* (1635).

    Line 3   *Worms . . . piss*: repeated at "Oxen" 10:56.

    26   Repeated on "Circe" 3:70.

    42   *Purgue*: this word is obscure, but it may be the English word "purge" or from the Italian *purgare*, thus "purge of humanity." *N. Maceh.*: perhaps an abbreviation for Niccolò Machiavelli (1469–1527).

    49   *Tolstoy* published his *Kreutzer Sonata* in 1889. The novel was "shocking enough to the prudish to have achieved a popularity quite beyond its deserts. It is a study of love, jealousy, and revenge, all the product of sexual attraction" (Vincent F. Hopper & Bernard D. N. Grebanier, *Essentials of European Literature* [Great Neck, N.Y., 1952], II, 569).

    51   Joyce inserted *whack* above a caret after *paddy*.

    62   The *-s* and *-eth* endings are a stylistic trait of Sir Thomas Browne.

    70   *Blubber*: this may be *blubble* (U 420:14).

    89   *Pecunia*: property, money.

90 *Pygarg*: from the Greek *pygargos*, literally "white rump." It is an obsolete word in English for both "a white-rumped ungulate (as an addax)" and "sea eagle" (*Webster's 3rd*).

93 See "Cyclops" 6:9 and note.

96 Angelo *Messedaglia*: an Italian economist, sociologist, and statistician (1820–1901).

98 In this line *8* and *10* have been superimposed on *6* and *8*.

103 *Origen* (A.D. 185?–254?): the "most learned and original of the early church fathers" (*Chambers's*).

104 Unidentified.

"Oxen of the Sun" 12

LEFT MARGIN HORIZONTAL

ubi ?consistum

CENTER COLUMN HORIZONTAL

R ⟨betook himself⟩ *403:17*
R ⟨peels off⟩ *418:5*
R ⟨caloric⟩ *417:39*
R ⟨duck⟩ *396:39*
R ⟨collar the leather⟩ *418:20*
R ⟨now, alas, a thing of the past⟩ *406:16*
R ⟨l.b.w.⟩ *418:23?*
What tack
R ⟨itinerant vendor⟩ *402:1*
R ⟨breather⟩ *419:27*
R ⟨Aristotle's masterpiece⟩ *404:11–12*
R ⟨declare misery⟩ *417:36*
odd trick, suit,   *R* ⟨guinea to a gooseberry touch⟩ *419:10–11*
revoke.
lead from a tenace (mistake)
R ⟨2nd hand plays low⟩ *419:32*   *R* ⟨spot that fancy⟩ *419:16?*
R ⟨pardner⟩ *419:32–33*
revoke   penny map   *R* ⟨Beat to the ropes⟩ *417:36*
full of the trick
bumble puppy   *R* ⟨any old time⟩
Pass.   rubber.   *R* ⟨cookies⟩ *419:39*

221

(mis) deal, shuffle pocket   *R* ⟨papoose⟩ *418:14*

cut (R) deal (L) eldest hand   *R* ⟨timepiece⟩ *417:42*

25 *R* ⟨LB depressed⟩   *R* ⟨gumboots⟩ *417:8*

R ⟨mutilation⟩ *411:32*   *R* ⟨paranoic bachelors⟩ *411:34*   *R* ⟨Dusty Rhodes⟩

420:3–4

R ⟨nickel⟩ *421:4*

threw up sponge   rubbers

30 *R* ⟨Man & woman instruments of spermatozoon⟩ *383:15–17*   *R* ⟨women

who die pregnant⟩ *382:29–30*

R ⟨LB & servant (Abram & Agar)⟩ *402:36*   cossemolando

Many daughters proof of fecundity   i tappeti bollivano

″   sons   ″   -non-

35 only daughters (rare)

parthenogenesis—sea hedgehog

inhibitory lobes, cerebral cortex

R ⟨2nd m. notocorda, formation of cartilage knobs in membrane⟩

4th m. closure of verteb. col.

40 at 60 yrs. interdiscal gelatinous blobs of corda ?dorsal ? . . .

triple segmentation ‿◡‿ protoverteb & verteb.

2nd m. reduc. no of verteb. tail piece

welding of atlas & epistrophs

R ⟨2nd m. formation of thoracic ribs,⟩ *Cf. 388:32*   other processes

45   only hunchback: *R* ⟨yr. spud:⟩ *418:11*   *R* ⟨Costello, big

head.⟩ *400:34–39*   ?b̸o̸n̸e̸d̸ ?a̸tt

2nd Sternum   fused from 2

6th ossific of stern.

double monsters, if striction of blastoderm lobe only

50   peripheries equal & unequal Siam. twins

If parassite twin connected only with autossite by placenta

may die (feto ?papiracco):   *R* ⟨usually acardiacs.⟩ *403:37*

R ⟨foetus in foetu⟩ *403:37*

teratomi: compl. in part of twin

RIGHT MARGIN VERTICAL

55 heredity
Muscles from vertebrae follow structure evolution
3 arcs
osso ?foide ?ossofrats begin 9 m ends at 50 yrs.
R ⟨agnatia (no chin) = defective reunion of maxillary
60   buttons on medial line
          one (ear) can hear what other says⟩ *403:37–40*

BOTTOM COLUMN VERTICAL

R ⟨blood islands⟩: cordoni
4th m.—all red corpuscles
heart descends fr. brain
65 ?tube, middle swell, curve L.
S (3 wk.)   *R* ⟨2 cavities (fishheart)⟩
R ⟨2 ventric. (reptile heart) 7 wk⟩
5 aortic arch & div. of aortic bulb
        = arteria polmonare
70   (little developed)
R ⟨Getting out they breathe⟩ *416:12?*
veins 2 fused = heart
1st ?calf vitelline circulation
interembryonic veins
75   (double perfect)
liver
        lymph ganglion 4–5 m
R ⟨2nd spleen—fin 9 m⟩
R ⟨3rd wk. 1st ?rud. of limbs⟩
80 *R* ⟨5   arm & hand⟩
6 wk fingers
R ⟨4 m arm & forearm⟩
R ⟨feet a little later⟩
foot & arm divers ways

85 7 wk clavicle 1st posit of ossif

 B ⟨ossificat of thigh 15 d before birth⟩

 brain, 2 lamine ?cefalithes

   unite, capsule, elongation of precordial flexion cause

   pilasters & chambers of brain (2 m)

90 *R* ⟨3 m. ossif.⟩

 1 m. 3 arco, bronchiale eye, nose,

 R ⟨4 & 5 m (ear hammer & anvil)⟩

 R ⟨harelip⟩ bad palatal suture

 pressure of amnios on face ear, jaw, buccal

95 if 1ˢᵗ arco arrest *R* ⟨aprosopia⟩ *403:37*

 1 polygonal

 2 m. lachrym & palate

 second m nasal ?suture

 joined ?internatalia

NOTES

 Line 1 *Ubi consistum*: perhaps means "where consist"; it is incorrect Latin.

 8 *L.b.w.*: probably an abbreviation for "leg before wicket" (*U* 418:23).

 16 *Tenace*: "a combination in one hand (as in bridge) of two high or relatively high cards (as ace and queen) once separated in rank" (*Webster's 7th*). Cf. lines 14, 17, 18, and 22–24.

 26 *Dusty Rhodes*: most likely a fictitious name.

 32 *Abram & Agar*: variant names of Abraham and Hagar, the concubine of Abraham and the mother of Ishmael. See Gen. 16; cf. *FW* 276:9 and 530:34.

 32–33 *Cossemolando i tappeti bollivano*: this Italian phrase is difficult both to read and to translate. Ottocaro Weiss and several other Italians whom I consulted were unable to decipher it. The *tappeti bollivano* seems to mean "boiling carpets."

 34 This line should read: "Many sons—proof of nonfecundity." The following lines refer to foetal development during the various months of pregnancy.

 45 Punch *Costello*: a medical student at the hospital.

 51 Autosite (not *autossite*): "that part of a double fetal monster that nourishes both itself and the parasitic twin" (*Webster's 3rd*).

 52 *Feto papiracco*: although the meaning of this Italian phrase is unclear, it refers to the parasitic twin in the line above.

 53 *Foetus in foetu*: "believed to arise when one member of a pair of conjoined twins, very early

in development, starts to lag behind the other and eventually becomes encased in the body of the more normal twin" (B. M. Patten, *Human Embryology* [Philadelphia, 1946], p. 217).

54 *Teratomi*: mixed tumors sometimes producing monsters (cf. Patten, p. 217).

57 *3 arcs*: there are three arcs of embryonic circulation—intra-embryonic, vitelline (which runs to yolk-sac), and allantoic (runs to chorion). The latter two are extraembryonic. See Patten, p. 137.

58 *Osso*: bone. These words in Italian and those which follow reveal that Joyce was using either an Italian book on embryology or an Italian medical dictionary, or both.

62 *Blood islands*: "*Vitelline vessels* . . . can be traced into prevascular cords of mesodermal cells as yet not hollowed out. In these cellular cords are frequent knotlike enlargements, known as *blood islands*, containing not only cells which are destined to form vascular endothelium but also cells which give rise to blood corpuscles" (Patten, p. 135). *Cordoni*: cords.

69 *Arteria polmonare*: pulmonary artery.

79 This phrase probably can be expanded to read: "Third week first rudiment of limbs."

91 Joyce wrote *arch* first and then changed it to *arco*.

95 Joyce wrote *arceo* first, then changed it to *arco*. *Aprosopia*: literally, "facelessness."

"Oxen of the Sun" 13

LEFT MARGIN VERTICAL

R ⟨mettlesome⟩ *401:13*
R ⟨grandam⟩ *385:16*
goblin   no man in's sober senses
dream children
5 *R* ⟨Relieve pentup⟩ *402:9*
R ⟨having us to⟩
R ⟨?her   ?house⟩
R ⟨I hold with⟩
R ⟨put me in thought of⟩
10 Development of egotism in LB
They do not seek Lavinian shores

LEFT MARGIN HORIZONTAL

R ⟨Haines = dope⟩ *405:25–26*
R ⟨happened along⟩
R ⟨enceinte⟩ *399:40*

LEFT COLUMN HORIZONTAL

15 was wont that he would go on night to sea
B ⟨till that they both to   sea came⟩
B ⟨Then did Cuthbert as his wont was⟩ *384:6*
R ⟨twey seals⟩ *Cf. 384:1, 379:5*
Sithence   worldthing

226

20   *R* ⟨wreak (avenge)⟩ *379:12?*
                      wound
      wintersettle   waxen
                      wellwilling (ness)
                      wean
25   *R* ⟨worthful⟩ *379:15*
                      R ⟨weep⟩ *395:40, 398:26*   wield
                      G ⟨wifehalf⟩
                      R ⟨wight⟩ *381:4*
                      R ⟨upfloor⟩ *381:30*
30   *R* ⟨unseeming⟩
                      R ⟨undeadliness⟩ *379:38*
    de congrus
    S. John Damescene
    R ⟨BVM no pangs of childbirth⟩ *385:29*   but passion
35   "   Wife (not consummated)
    gothroughsomeness
    R ⟨Dublin townhithe⟩ *379:20*
    for that   *B* ⟨eachwhen⟩
    R ⟨Ho!⟩ *389:24*   *B* ⟨such an one⟩
40   *R* ⟨Knock a child out of her⟩ *401:39*
    R ⟨25/3 Lady Day   Easter LB⟩ *391:15*
    R ⟨" 6 S. John   Rudy⟩
        " 9 ?Conc.   John   Purefoy
        " 12 Xmas   ?Birth   ?SD
45   *R* ⟨though I'm stricken in years⟩ *384:21?*
    virgin   Eve   *R* ⟨forbidden tree⟩ *401:16*
    S. Mary

RIGHT COLUMN HORIZONTAL

    R ⟨?how herself is dreading⟩ *379:12?*
    white
50   *R* ⟨link in chain of beings⟩ *400:40*
    R ⟨and self⟩ *401:1–2*

227

R ⟨but he farther adds⟩ *382:34?*

R ⟨now > 30 yrs. ago that⟩ *400:41–42*

devoted deer: law

55 *R* ⟨a most gallant scene⟩ *410:23*

R ⟨Waltham chase⟩

a vast spring

nidification

R ⟨wonderfully unequal faculty⟩ *402:2–3*

60 *R* ⟨what ?cares ?unity from⟩

hot stifled innyard

R ⟨with the readiest precaution⟩ *401:4*

feel stillborn

from the ?press

65 *R* ⟨recovered the ?blo.⟩ *395:2?*

My appointment

made accession

R ⟨such is the . . . that⟩

R ⟨My opinion (Who ought not to)⟩ *401:25*

70 *R* ⟨I was, however, I confess discouraged⟩

R ⟨tolerable, & but tolerable⟩ *401:6*

R ⟨prefer a request to⟩ *401:34–35*

R ⟨accepted of it⟩ *395:26*

R ⟨resiled from⟩ *400:32*

75 *R* ⟨reckon upon a speedy dissolution⟩ *401:19*

R ⟨Gad's bud⟩ *399:25*

R ⟨I must acquaint you⟩ *401:31–32*

R ⟨were not often bloody⟩

R ⟨tumultuary election⟩ *400:30?*

80   perch

R ⟨trice⟩ *396:21*

R ⟨it will burst anon⟩ *401:37*

BOTTOM HORIZONTAL

R ⟨upon what considerations⟩   tirewoman

R ⟨in   ″   place soever⟩ *396:9*   I was

85   R ⟨Most men anywise eminent⟩ *402:7–8*   R ⟨premature⟩ *404:1–2, 410:28*

R ⟨To express any notion of the thing⟩ *401:25*   R ⟨to auspicate⟩ *401:21*

R ⟨charged upon the great⟩ *400:28?*   R ⟨choler rising⟩ *401:3*

R ⟨freshest news⟩ *401:27–28*   R ⟨megrims⟩ *385:42*   R ⟨enjoin themselves⟩ *401:2*

R ⟨beat a retreat⟩ *401:12*   cheapen   R ⟨in their behalf⟩ *400:34*

90   R ⟨a short meagre man⟩   R ⟨outrageous furioso⟩ *400:31?*

B ⟨I like them (spaghetti : Eng)⟩   R ⟨extravagancy⟩ *400:29*

R ⟨to revert to—to conclude⟩ *400:25?*   R ⟨dotard⟩ *401:14*

R ⟨to those . . . . I would say to them⟩ *401:6–8*   R ⟨late ingenious

                         Dr Mould⟩ *400:40–41*

95   R ⟨sharp antidote of disgrace⟩ *401:11*   R ⟨fund⟩ *400:33*   cloth yard

                                       shaft

R ⟨difficulty⟩ *405:1*   R ⟨testiness⟩ *400:31*

R ⟨unaccountable muskin⟩ *395:37*

R ⟨overgrown children⟩ *400:29*

100   R ⟨strong animal spirits,⟩ *400:33–34*   R ⟨?wan ?constitut. & a cold

      genius⟩ *401:26–27*

R ⟨create themselves wits⟩ *401:6–7*   foul craven, did he blench!

R ⟨scrupulously tender if rank⟩ *Cf. 400:32–33*

R ⟨light under a bushel⟩ *395:35–36*   antiquarian (Scott)

105   interest   cake & oranges

R ⟨by intercepting them⟩ *401:3*

R ⟨1000 vicissitudes ?fill⟩ *400:42–401:1*

R ⟨having lost all, we can lose no more⟩ *401:10*

R ⟨they are a little hasty, it is true.⟩   R ⟨trifle with⟩ *356:21–22*

110   B ⟨redoubled the enclamatio of the mournful & appl. ?by Senate⟩

R ⟨— the name - - - & the spirit, of Romans⟩

R ⟨Singular, he again muttered   R ⟨broke her mind⟩ *401:24*

     to himself,⟩ *402:1–2*

B ⟨Did he? No, fair reader⟩ *406:37–38*   R ⟨Joseph—of—⟩

115   *R* ⟨clapping her hand so as to produce a sonorous token of
       satisfaction⟩
     R ⟨Not but what we have⟩ *401:12–13*

NOTES

My arrangement of phrases in the right column is somewhat arbitrary. Janusko lists one source book for material on "Oxen" 13: Saintsbury's quotations from translations of Aelfric in *History of English Prose Rhythm*. The following words and phrases on "Oxen" 13 are from Peacock:

"Oxen" 13		*Peacock*	"Oxen" 13		*Peacock*
Line	1	Page 282	Line	77	Page 242
	2	279		78	Cf. 244
	3 "goblin"	279		79	245
	4	279		80	250
	5	282		81	251
	6	281		82	252
	7	Cf. 279		83 "upon what"	170
	8–9	278		83 "tirewoman"	169
	11	277		84 "in ″ place soever"	169
	49–53	210		86 "To express"	168
	54–56	211		98	241
	57–58	212		102 "foul craven"; "did he blench"	256
	59	215		104 "antiquarian"	Cf. 261
	61	215		112–113 "Singular"	259
	62	218		112 "broke her mind"	Cf. 264
	70	Cf. 240		115–116	265
	76	241			

Line 11   *Lavinian shores*: Lavinium was a town in Latium built by Aeneas and named for his wife Lavinia.

18   The "watchers twey" became "watchers they" in the 1961 Random House edition (385:9–10).

32   *De congrus*: in agreement.

33   St. *John Damascene*: a Greek theologian and hymn writer (A.D. 676?–754?). See also line 42.

41–44   March 25 is Annunciation Day; June 24 is the Day of St. John the Baptist; September 25, 1903, was apparently the day of conception of the *Purefoy* child born in the "Oxen" episode, but according to *U* 414:8–9 his name is Mortimer Edward and not *John*. If Stephen Dedalus were born on Christmas Day, it would strengthen his symbolic role as Christ figure in the novel.

49   Gilbert *White*: English natural historian and writer (1720–1793). Lines 50–62 contain notes from White's essays in Peacock.

68   The ellipses are Joyce's.

93   The ellipses are Joyce's.

"Oxen of the Sun" 14

LEFT COLUMN HORIZONTAL

B ⟨herds of waves⟩ *47:10?*

R ⟨oof⟩ *418:36*

R ⟨skip⟩ *390:26?*

R ⟨Monsieur Moore⟩ *398:33*

5   R ⟨complacent⟩ *398:2–3*

R ⟨bosom⟩ *398:17*

R ⟨I had wrote⟩ *398:5–6*

R ⟨cherish,⟩ *398:5*   trip.

R ⟨My God! Just Heavens!⟩ *397:39–40*

10   dance ⟨a world of⟩ *398:6*   her hereafter

R ⟨whispered Caution⟩ *409:20–21?*

glided

the cause was pleading

R ⟨c'est bien comique . . . c'e.b.c.⟩

15   R ⟨there wanted nothing⟩ *397:38*

Lord!

R ⟨clapping hands⟩ *398:28*

R ⟨cheerily⟩ *397:37*

R ⟨popped⟩ *398:4*

20   R ⟨I declare⟩ *398:13*

Peace be to her

R ⟨was it possible (if it were)⟩

R ⟨that I do most   sadly (want)⟩

R ⟨La Fleur . . . . came in⟩

25   B ⟨he retired à ses terres⟩ *399:17?*

R ⟨Pshaw! said he⟩ *416:25*

231

R ⟨coxcomb⟩ *398:21*

R ⟨desire the landlord to⟩ *Cf. 408:11*

R ⟨wiped his eyes⟩ *398:17–18*

30 R ⟨crust and wallet⟩ *397:40*

R ⟨bless him with 3 sons⟩ *398:15–16*

clue

R ⟨picture in black ribbon⟩ *398:4–5*

R ⟨kneeling down upon the ground⟩ *397:41–42*

35 R ⟨treated him with⟩ *397:36*

R ⟨I put it to you,⟩ *421:5* gentle reader,

B ⟨inconceivable⟩

R ⟨slicked his hair⟩ *398:3*

R ⟨cordial waters⟩ *397:31–32*

40 but of this hereafter

R ⟨beck⟩ *397:31, 419:13*

R ⟨But to return⟩

R ⟨household word⟩ *399:5–6*

R ⟨ennobling profession⟩ *400:1*

45 R ⟨congratulated with⟩ *397:28?*

B ⟨dry nurse⟩

    R ⟨dust⟩ *379:42, 410:40, 411:30*

R ⟨puny child of clay⟩ *400:9–10*

50 R ⟨glorious incentive⟩ *400:6*

R ⟨revile the living⟩ *400:1?*   R ⟨ladylike man⟩ *399:30–31*

born so far from home   R ⟨approached the goblet⟩ *398:2*

R ⟨Bless me!.⟩ *399:32*   R ⟨debauching⟩ *399:18?, 403:7*

R ⟨perpetual anastomosis⟩ *385:17*   R ⟨bonze⟩ *395:35*

55 R ⟨luckless⟩ *398:38, 408:33*   R ⟨royal exercitation⟩ *400:5*

R ⟨I want patience . . . what?⟩ *399:41–42*   R ⟨we are positive when we

                                          say⟩ *400:3*

R ⟨laudable fortitude⟩ *399:40–41*

B ⟨Grand Turk⟩ *324:7*   R ⟨put a period to his life⟩ *399:39*

60   —Cairo   to jot

R ⟨queerity⟩ *391:30* R ⟨gibbosity⟩ *400:36–37* ?sated

R ⟨a cloud of witnesses⟩ *400:4*   R ⟨parish beadle⟩ *392:24*

shrilling cock   yon R ⟨small clothes⟩ *396:25*

What . . . time only can discover   B ⟨Allah⟩ *420:22*

65   R ⟨Not less severe than beautiful⟩ *399:19–20*

R ⟨repaired to⟩ *400:14*   R ⟨Such an one⟩

R ⟨rendezvoused⟩ *399:24*

then ?only . . . when

RIGHT COLUMN HORIZONTAL

R ⟨quit the field⟩ *398:13*   R ⟨sparks⟩ *400:28*

70   seek, seek . . .   R ⟨delivered himself of⟩ *400:13*

R ⟨très volontiers, most w—⟩   R ⟨I owe him for⟩

R ⟨have the obligingness⟩ *397:31*   R ⟨expatiate⟩ *395:26*

R ⟨Would to God⟩ *398:24*   R ⟨May this drink⟩

B ⟨hand her to her coach⟩   R ⟨As I look to be saved,⟩ *399:27–28*

75   R ⟨tut⟩ *398:32*   R ⟨pooh⟩ *398:39*   R ⟨Young blood⟩ *399:30*

B ⟨Mercy on the gouty⟩ *408:33?*   R ⟨pot of ale⟩ *399:34*

R ⟨beshrew⟩ *398:27*   R ⟨sorites⟩   R ⟨suds⟩ *223:6?*

R ⟨heyday,⟩ *398:22*   R ⟨polished⟩ *398:21*   R ⟨seminary⟩ *402:4*

R ⟨swain⟩ *398:21*   R ⟨scouring Brush⟩ *402:34*

80   R ⟨heart begins to bleed⟩   R ⟨low fellow⟩ *399:22*

R ⟨of a sedate look⟩ *385:41*   R ⟨fuddled⟩ *399:23*

R ⟨affecting (ed)⟩ *398:8*

R ⟨conjecture⟩ *399:15*

R ⟨suffice it⟩ *402:6?*

85   B ⟨tante belle cose⟩ *225:35*

B ⟨mille compliments⟩ *397:37*

for his pains

R ⟨(blushing,)⟩ *399:2*   R ⟨justiciary⟩ *392:24*

my brains

90   R ⟨reasons good & cogent⟩ *412:26*

to do the same by

B ⟨fiacre⟩ *390:30*

gone off by damps

R ⟨little fume of a woman⟩ *397:28*

95   R ⟨a capful of wind⟩ *408:9*

233

R ⟨Almighty director of every event⟩

R ⟨artless disorder⟩ *398:10*

G ⟨. . . . .⟩

thillhorse   his story

100   *R* ⟨in good earnest⟩ *398:38*

R ⟨rose up to meet⟩ *414:26*

at the age he was then of

R ⟨full 2 hours⟩

the happiest turn to science, an heathen

105   ?imagined his life to be . . . . & that

R ⟨?Such ?won't . . . ,⟩   *R* ⟨glory of her own sex & astonishm.

     of ours⟩ *Cf. 395:39, 397:21*

                 set the table in a roar

R ⟨I was for returning⟩

110   *R* ⟨I shudder to think⟩ *400:10*

R ⟨abridged in its commence⟩ *Cf. 400:18*

R ⟨without cunning to protect or . . . ⟩

RIGHT MARGIN VERTICAL

R ⟨Babytalk⟩

R ⟨Deborah, my life,⟩

115   *R* ⟨my dear mamma⟩

this, you'll say

     belabour

R ⟨stop gap⟩ *398:41*

R ⟨man in gap⟩ *401:42*

120   accuse him to have wanted

     rarities   smart

R ⟨vulgar mind—,⟩ *401:5*   *R* ⟨the ingenious⟩ *400:40–41*

R ⟨—and all—⟩

R ⟨a power upon the earth⟩

125   gentle gales

R ⟨squabble in womb⟩

~~replete~~

234

R ⟨Supreme Being⟩ *401:23*
if he be any artist
130   B ⟨some poet⟩ *410:35?*

NOTES

Except for those at line 98, all ellipses are Joyce's. Janusko (pp. 189–190, 212–221) lists three source books for the material on "Oxen" 14: Saintsbury's *History of English Prose Rhythm*; Laurence Sterne, *A Sentimental Journey through France and Italy*; and *The Works of Oliver Goldsmith* (*Citizen of the World*, "The Deserted Village," and two essays).

Line 4   George *Moore*: the novelist. Buck Mulligan has just come from Moore's house (*U* 390: 33–34).

10   *Her hereafter*: written in pencil.

36   *I put it to you*: repeated at "Oxen" 4:76.

38   Repeated at "Oxen" 4:165.

39   Repeated at "Oxen" 2:22.

46   Repeated at "Oxen" 5:14.

51   *Ladylike man*: see Ellmann, p. 477, on Joyce's theories about Jewish men and their effeminacy, and "Circe" 16:52, "Ithaca" 10:70, and "Ithaca" 14:20.

60   Cf. Peacock, p. 162.

77   *Sorites*: repeated at "Oxen" 2:166 and "Oxen" 16:57.

85   *Tante belle còse*: "a lot of good things" in the sense of "best wishes" in Italian.

114   Cf. Peacock, p. 268.

"Oxen of the Sun" 15

LEFT MARGIN HORIZONTAL

(which . . . I have seen)
R ⟨Know all men⟩
tootache—rheumatism
Squabble STC & ?TdQ
5   held such language
?to that you can speak
averted signs
Sat mighty ?mists
in extremity of haste
10   sickening lamps
purple granite
opium ≷ wine
R ⟨lancinating⟩ *407:16*
else drooping
15   tootache   (Haines)
not deadly
R ⟨house of (astron.)⟩
coach & ?jig
ship & pinnace
20   1) stains
2) trembled into terraces
3) we ?entire suburbs
70 leagues
R ⟨the secret word⟩

236

LEFT COLUMN HORIZONTAL

25 shined

 R ⟨toast⟩ *386:20?*

 R ⟨extol⟩ *401:38*

 R ⟨overjoyed⟩ *397:3*

 droll

30 *R* ⟨alleviation⟩ *401:20*

 R ⟨ladies' friend⟩

 R ⟨conjugal vexations⟩ *395:30*

 R ⟨jointure⟩ *395:34–35*

 R ⟨to lose their bloom⟩ *395:36*

35 *R* ⟨caressed by many pretty fellows⟩ *395:39–40*

 R ⟨interesting condition⟩ *397:11*

 R ⟨happiness to take place⟩ *397:13*

 R ⟨to advise with⟩ *396:1*

 ashlar

40 *R* ⟨value themselves upon⟩ *396:40*

 R ⟨tautologous⟩

 R ⟨mended their pace⟩ *396:23*

 R ⟨fell a praising her⟩ *401:39*

 R ⟨piebald⟩ *396:25*

45 *R* ⟨touched on⟩ *Cf. 382:28, 403:35*

 R ⟨of it⟩

 senses

 R ⟨this was so happy a conceit that it renewed the storm of⟩ *397:22–23*

 R ⟨led into this thought⟩ *395:27*

50 *R* ⟨rallied upon⟩ *397:15*

 R ⟨the young gentleman, his friend, to bear him out⟩ *397:2–4*

 R ⟨passage which had happened⟩ *397:3–4*

 R ⟨good woman (?sentim)⟩

 R ⟨that exc.—⟩ *397:21?*

55 had like to

 R ⟨inestimable jewel⟩ *395:38–39*

 guessed at

 R ⟨applying herself to⟩ *396:41–42*

banter & brigue
60 *B* ⟨sublunary⟩ *398:24*
R ⟨sackposset⟩ *392:2*
hamated
R ⟨hawking⟩ *420:25?, 753:35?*
R ⟨a covey of⟩ *391:2*
65 *R* ⟨thorn in the flesh⟩ *385:6–8?*
to halse
R ⟨housel bread⟩ *379:33*
R ⟨mazes⟩
dight, scathe
70 *R* ⟨advance a paradox⟩ *397:2?*
as the chemists said   *B* ⟨of this dashing mercury⟩
R ⟨multiply the inlets to happiness⟩ *395:38*
R ⟨encomiums⟩ *397:2*
R ⟨direct to him⟩ *396:9–10*
75 *R* ⟨latent heat⟩ *396:1*
R ⟨I cannot forbear to tell⟩ *397:4*
R ⟨pray, sir (to LB)⟩ *397:7*
R ⟨belly that never bore a bastard⟩ *397:22*
R ⟨hussy, trollop,⟩ *402:34, 397:22*   drab
80 *R* ⟨most violent agitation of delight⟩ *397:24–25*
R ⟨SD coadjutor bishop⟩ *405:3*
R ⟨prolific⟩ *396:17*
R ⟨sylvan ?honours⟩
R ⟨when was it known⟩
85 *R* ⟨wheres X? X!⟩
instituting unnecessary emulation by insidious incitements

RIGHT COLUMNS HORIZONTAL

R ⟨bedside manner.⟩ *399:24–25*
rather   *R* ⟨Some man⟩
nap   man offslew
90 bug   woe worth

holy

hale

beareth

R ⟨couth⟩ *380:20*

95 sought

teem

fere

?bow

R ⟨herd⟩ *385:12*

100 *R* ⟨healer⟩ *385:12, 403:8*

deal

R ⟨vat⟩ *381:5*

R ⟨bet⟩ *417:36, 418:2 & 32*

R ⟨wife⟩

105 *R* ⟨bairn⟩ *379:5, 391:29*

evil

sorrow

burden

R ⟨groom⟩ *386:26*

110 elders

blithe

former

?an Irish Kin

R ⟨twain⟩ *379:8*

115 *R* ⟨minish⟩ *387:37*

the ilk

R ⟨thilk⟩

knave

?Us – – – –

120 1 ½ min, 70 sec ——

sweet moonlight, dreamlight

fluttering, whispering love

R ⟨So agreeable a man⟩ *395:34?*

R ⟨made his court to⟩ *396:29–30*

125 person very much of his care

R ⟨preserving his distance⟩ *397:9*

R ⟨behest⟩ *387:19*

lock

bide

bid

unbind

fang

heave

yield

?gern

R ⟨swink⟩ *380:41*

neat

B ⟨bedesman⟩ *383:7*

might = could

R ⟨masspriests⟩ *379:33*

withseek

dryshod

R ⟨hurricane⟩

naughty

avveruncation

cresset ?spearming

bequeathed by the ?Horn

offence that walks

sad truths, elder truths

God smote Savannah la mar

(& his voice swelled)

B ⟨32 ft. per sec⟩ *71:10–11 and elsewhere*

road sank into silence

R ⟨who, upon his offer,⟩ *397:8*

R ⟨larum⟩ *397:26*   *R* ⟨Ephesian matron⟩ *401:31*

R ⟨as it dwelt upon his memory⟩ *396:31*

130 *R* ⟨in the main of America⟩ *395:2*

R ⟨solicitous for its preservation⟩

B ⟨favour of moonlight⟩ *392:28–29*

R ⟨?at the feet of the table⟩ *391:31*

R ⟨what is the reason = why⟩ *386:13–14*

135 *R* ⟨I here fetched a deep sigh⟩ *397:12*

R ⟨Gladness grew in me⟩ *386:22–23*

R ⟨suitable to the relishes⟩ *Cf. 396:37–38, 395:13*

R ⟨grazing,⟩ *402:36*   *R* ⟨artless⟩ *398:10*

B ⟨a drum of figs⟩ *289:23*

140 *R* ⟨sir fopling⟩ *395:21*

R ⟨cornetcy⟩ *395:12*

R ⟨his name N. N.⟩

B ⟨in ⟨fashion⟩⟩ *390:36*   *R* ⟨clumsy⟩ *398:39*

B ⟨King's evil⟩ *485:12*

145 *R* ⟨Sir⟩

R ⟨Sharpset⟩ *392:16*

NOTES

The following words and phrases on "Oxen" 15 are from Peacock:

"Oxen" 15	Peacock	"Oxen" 15	Peacock
Lines 123–124	Page 146	Lines 130–132	Page 152
125	Cf. 148	134	163
126	149	135–136	165
127–128	150	137–138 "suitable"; "grazing"	166
129	151		

Line 1   The ellipses are Joyce's.

3   *Tootache*: Joyce omitted the first "h" in "toothache" here and at line 15.

4   *STC*: Samuel Taylor Coleridge. *TdQ*: Thomas De Quincey. De Quincey attacked Coleridge at the beginning of the revised edition of *The Confessions of an English Opium-Eater* (1856).

39 *Ashlar*: a square hewn stone.

62 *Hamated*: bent at the end into a hook.

72 *Multiply the inlets to happiness*: Janusko cites the source for this phrase—Oliver Goldsmith's *Citizen of the World*, Letter XI.

109 Joyce misspelled "averruncation."

114 *God smote Savannah la mar*: see Thomas De Quincey, *Collected Writings*, ed. David Masson (Edinburgh, 1889–90), XIII, 359. This is from his *Suspiria de Profundis*, which is quoted in Saintsbury, p. 319.

"Oxen of the Sun" 16

LEFT COLUMN HORIZONTAL

R ⟨let me ask you⟩ *402:12?*

R ⟨Have you ?quite forgotten? or is it?⟩ *402:20–21*

   R ⟨lord paramount⟩ *402:14–15*

R ⟨doubts in the marital breast⟩ *403:4*

5   *R* ⟨Remember⟩

R ⟨arms of faded beauty⟩ *403:6*

R ⟨I will not adduce⟩ *403:5*

R ⟨a deluder⟩ *402:22*

R ⟨dead sea Agendath⟩ *407:12*

10   *B* ⟨Loves Old Sweet Song⟩ *63:24–25 and elsewhere*

R ⟨15/6 Milly b.⟩ *66:11*

R ⟨Bullock harbour⟩ *391:20*

the Irish youth

B ⟨interjacent⟩ *699:23?* ?brown

15   *R* ⟨engross attention⟩ *403:4?*

R ⟨morals⟩ *402:31, 403:8*

R ⟨debauched his wife⟩ *403:7*

R ⟨opprobium⟩ *402:42*

R ⟨consist better with⟩ *403:3*

20   *R* ⟨reprehensible at puberty⟩ *402:41–42*

R ⟨stuff that comes away from you⟩ *403:11–12*

R ⟨restore you to health⟩ *403:2*

R ⟨repository⟩ *403:4–5* *R* ⟨public papers⟩

R ⟨Be it so⟩ *402:28* *R* ⟨it ill becomes him⟩ *402:39–40*

25   *R* ⟨Coition   illusion of strength⟩ *406:42*

R ⟨Wander from the point⟩ *398:23*

R ⟨unfledged profligate⟩ *403:3*   *R* ⟨decorum⟩ *403:5*

R ⟨children cry in Holles Street⟩ *417:10–13?*

before ?thiss nobleman escapes out of ?hit

30   If . . . if . . the duke is guilty

R ⟨respectable lady⟩ *402:25*   *R* ⟨:it imported him⟩ *628:14*

quit infest   *R* ⟨domestic servant⟩ *402:33*

R ⟨LB   Kiss a skivvy, drawn from the lowest strata of
        society,⟩ *402:33–34*

35   *R* ⟨Far be it from⟩ *402:24*

R ⟨the most distant reflection⟩ *402:25–26*

R ⟨tenants at will⟩ *402:19–20*

R ⟨it is indeed highly yr. interest⟩ *402:27*

R ⟨second nature⟩ *402:31?*

40   *R* ⟨the noble colonel⟩ *402:12?*

R ⟨unhappy man⟩ *402:28*   *R* ⟨discharge his piece⟩ *402:18–19*

R ⟨Where is now that . . . ?⟩ *402:15*   *R* ⟨be affected with some
                                    pleasantry⟩ *404:38–39*

R ⟨a gracious prince⟩ *402:13*   *R* ⟨conqueror who had never⟩

45   *R* ⟨eloquent historian of nature⟩

R ⟨accouchement⟩ *413:23*   *R* ⟨lying fallow ploughshare⟩ *402:41*

R ⟨couched in terms⟩ *402:38–39*   *R* ⟨quidnuncs⟩ *395:21*

R ⟨seedfield nearer home⟩ *402:40*   *R* ⟨milksop⟩ *395:21*

R ⟨dupe⟩ *402:23*   *R* ⟨fee simple⟩ *396:3*   Walpole French

50   *R* ⟨bedchamber⟩ *402:24*   *R* ⟨sublime Porte⟩ *403:14*   fond of travelling
                                    severest   engagement (battle)

R ⟨peevish asperity⟩ *402:37*   *R* ⟨ties of nature⟩ *402:32*

B ⟨he . . . . . for him nor⟩   ?Monogebirist

R ⟨four per cents⟩ *402:20*   all at once

55   *R* ⟨stagnant & ineffective⟩ *403:12*   we are arrived at

R ⟨grazing lands⟩ *402:36*   heaven . . . earth . . . secret rivers

R ⟨Junius says ?this who⟩ *404:34?*   *B* ⟨sorites⟩

R ⟨dedale⟩ *415:37*   *R* ⟨time was⟩ *380:10*   end

I durst ?go never   —∪∪ —∪ —

60   *R* ⟨widow's mite⟩ *374:14*

                          Besides

                          I played, I am, I—

243

RIGHT COLUMN HORIZONTAL

   B ⟨sick or whole⟩

   R ⟨pumproom⟩

65   *B* ⟨cut bob⟩ *390:35*

   G ⟨place of worship⟩ *645:29–30, 680:30*

   R ⟨John ?Darcy⟩   *G* ⟨widow's mite (Naus)⟩ *374:14*

   R ⟨deserted village⟩

   pad,   *R* ⟨abigail⟩ *403:23*

70   *R* ⟨Mr Commissioner Smollett⟩

   R ⟨fuddled⟩ *399:23*   rasp

   R ⟨plaguily⟩ *395:32*

   B ⟨gentleman's gentleman⟩ *390:33*

   R ⟨cast of countenance⟩ *607:39–40*

75   *R* ⟨boon⟩ *377:25* *R* ⟨perennial⟩ *407:7*

   B ⟨a footman (virtuous) who⟩ *401:42?*

   R ⟨circumspect⟩ *403:13*

   B ⟨shed a pint of tears⟩ *392:32*

   progress various & doubtful

80   maintained & improved advantage

   R ⟨voice of—was heard⟩

   R ⟨to urge, to restrain, to push⟩ *403:26*

                R ⟨High school⟩

   R ⟨prerogative⟩ *402:29*   *R* ⟨any the least colour⟩

85   *R* ⟨look daggers⟩ *342:21–22* *R* ⟨retrospect⟩ *406:6?*

                R ⟨?Whose are ?not of Elia⟩

   R ⟨quit⟩ *398:13*

   B ⟨SD drunk ?hears rain⟩ *388:29–36*

   R ⟨coxcomb⟩ *398:21*

90   *R* ⟨finicking⟩ *396:28*

   R ⟨eulogy⟩ *396:27*

   severest

   B ⟨oftentimes⟩ *348:8*

   by by by

NOTES

My arrangement of phrases in the right column is somewhat arbitrary. In lines 30, 42, and 56 the ellipses are Joyce's. According to Janusko lines 1–57 (*passim*) are from *The Letters of Junius*.

Line 10   Repeated at "Circe" 3:91.

11   *15/6*: June 15, Milly's birthday.

18   *Opprobium*: Joyce's misspelling.

33   *Skivvy*: see "Cyclops" 2:9 and note.

42–45   These phrases are from Gibbon as quoted in Saintsbury, pp. 282–284.

49–50   Sir Horace *Walpole* (1717–97). *French* and *fond of travelling* also refer to Walpole. Although the significance of *French* is not clear, it might refer to his correspondence with Madame du Deffand, with whom he exchanged 1,600 letters.

57   *Sorites*: repeated at "Oxen" 2:166 and "Oxen" 14:77.

59   This is a dactyl followed by a cretic (opposite p. 1 in Saintsbury, and *passim*). Cf. "Oxen" 19:55–56.

60   *Widow's mite*: repeated at line 67.

67   *John Darcy*: unidentified. *Naus*: Nausicaa.

68   *Deserted village*: "The Deserted Village" is the title of a poem by Goldsmith, one source for phrases on "Oxen" 14.

70   Tobias *Smollett*: English novelist (1721–71).

86   *Elia*: pseudonym of Charles Lamb the essayist (1775–1834).

"Oxen of the Sun" 17

LEFT COLUMN HORIZONTAL

Sea

R ⟨armstrong halloring⟩ *417:6*

R ⟨oily⟩ *381:8*

knife becket

5   betty betty

?block meat

? fanny about

R ⟨Horry war⟩ *419:16*

R ⟨query.⟩ *417:35* R ⟨sneaking regard⟩ *641:5*

10   ?Shreep

       R ⟨for he swore a round hand⟩ *400:19*

       R ⟨impregnated⟩ *404:6, 416:9*

       R ⟨chestnut blossoms⟩ *408:39–40*

         R ⟨yeast⟩

15   R ⟨Meredith the bread⟩ *418:17* R ⟨dead cert⟩ *419:7*

    R ⟨Lewis ?boch⟩ R ⟨I'm about⟩ *419:38–39*

    R ⟨Lloyd George⟩ R ⟨ad lib⟩ *418:34*

    B ⟨contrive to⟩ *614:35, 618:40, 623:27*

    R ⟨acid⟩ *403:12, 413:6* R ⟨alkali⟩ *413:6* R ⟨move a motion⟩ *419:23*

20   R ⟨under ?cow skunk⟩ *419:34?*

    R ⟨cooked bread⟩ *408:42–409:1* R ⟨cuss⟩ *420:6* teached

tickle nipple abort R ⟨precious glad⟩ *421:5?*

R ⟨loins⟩ *407:1*   cock won't fight

              R ⟨all serene⟩ *417:11*

25   R ⟨handed in his checks⟩ *420:13*

     R ⟨madam⟩ *404:24, 416:8* R ⟨skunk⟩ *419:34?*

help me get tea

sorrowful tail   R ⟨going it some⟩ *419:23*

                 R ⟨I reckon⟩ *401:19?*   R ⟨tight⟩ *418:41*

30   R ⟨apostate's creed⟩ *417:19*   R ⟨want it bad⟩ *420:5*

R ⟨chokey⟩ *419:12* R ⟨catched⟩ *390:26* R ⟨bestest⟩ *419:39*

R ⟨cowslips⟩ *419:17* R ⟨scrum⟩ *417:32* R ⟨tootsy⟩ *417:33*

copper's nark   R ⟨come a home⟩

R ⟨a spell ago⟩ *418:35*   R ⟨lou'll⟩ *417:15?*

35   R ⟨where in tunket⟩ *420:3*   R ⟨all same⟩ *417:16*

clam fritters   R ⟨heap good⟩ *417:15–16*

R ⟨abaft⟩ *417:19* R ⟨real fine!⟩

R ⟨1 dime⟩ *421:4?* R ⟨sartin I do⟩ *418:4*

did the donkey work

40   R ⟨a strong order⟩

entered into the picture

bating   R ⟨stripped a credit⟩ *418:5*

R ⟨barring⟩ *416:14*   R ⟨up to you⟩

                R ⟨break⟩ *414:12*

45   R ⟨jubilee mutton⟩ *420:4–5*

      R ⟨?Tarn⟩ *419:38?* R ⟨scabbard⟩ *415:36*

              sheath

R ⟨coito interrotto⟩

mezzo ritiro

50   R ⟨coit. intermet⟩

R ⟨(8 dys before & aft. not)⟩

B ⟨pessario⟩   R ⟨ovuline⟩

R ⟨spugna⟩   R ⟨irrigate⟩

assorbente   B ⟨powder⟩

55   R ⟨Fr letter⟩

capuchon

RIGHT COLUMN HORIZONTAL

R ⟨Seedy & washed out⟩ *420:6, 416:6*

R ⟨afeard⟩ *384:40* R ⟨ax⟩ *418:27*

childer

60 *R* ⟨he've slep⟩ *417:7*

R ⟨of they sailors.⟩

R ⟨naurow⟩   *R* ⟨?his u⟩

R ⟨most wonderfullest⟩ *Cf. 419:39*

R ⟨bricky⟩   *R* ⟨soaker⟩ *400:15*

65 *R* ⟨nine pound⟩ *385:1?*

R ⟨See?⟩   *R* ⟨Crikey⟩ *419:37*

R ⟨stunned like⟩ *418:33*

R ⟨polis⟩ *434:24*

R ⟨got any chink?⟩ *418:34*

70 *R* ⟨a pushing⟩

R ⟨sorrowful tail⟩

B ⟨a ?roaming⟩   *B* ⟨I suppose⟩

storm & strife

? panoe

75 *R* ⟨Poldy bloom⟩ *61:32 and elsewhere*

R ⟨duds⟩ *420:35*

R ⟨Rome boose⟩ *419:31*

down with the dust

R ⟨tell a cram⟩ *419:11*

80 *R* ⟨trumpery insanity⟩ *420:7*

R ⟨Dutch oven⟩ *419:6*

R ⟨my avuncular relative⟩ *417:42*

R ⟨bilker⟩ *418:37?*

R ⟨like old Billio.⟩ *417:8*

85 *R* ⟨bookies⟩ *391:40*   ?square

break from off

R ⟨?brigmella⟩   *R* ⟨buckled⟩ *418:3*

R ⟨brolly⟩ *417:8*

R ⟨this bunch⟩ *417:16*

90 *R* ⟨buster⟩ *417:6*   *R* ⟨nix⟩ *420:11*   *R* ⟨Golly⟩ *420:3*

đ   *R* ⟨Come in door⟩   *R* ⟨our Jenny⟩

R ⟨Tarnally dog gone my shins if this aint the puttiest chance
    yet⟩ *419:38–39*   got on terms with

95

100

105

R ⟨?fancy⟩   R ⟨drew level⟩ *408:25*   took it up

flattered   *"* away   — —?swing

compounded   R ⟨jady⟩ *419:8*   out of the —

R ⟨schedule time⟩ *420:11*   R ⟨told its tale⟩ *416:6*

R ⟨free (touch kicking)⟩ *417:33*   ?faces

    — kick   R ⟨spurt⟩ *417:26*

                            R ⟨hot order⟩ *419:10*

                            R ⟨paddock⟩ *419:9*

                            into his stride

                            in ?the straight

                            R ⟨bare socks⟩ *420:5–6*

                            R ⟨astounding⟩ *416:15*

R ⟨LB & bumblebee⟩ *418:2 and elsewhere* R ⟨Culpepper to —⟩ *411:18–19*

R ⟨Maledicity⟩ *398:24*

NOTES

Line 2   *Armstrong:* a large cannon (see "Penelope" 6:63 and note), which doesn't seem to make much sense in the context of "Oxen."

    4   *Knife becket:* a loop of rope or leather serving as a scabbard.

    8   *Horry:* disgustingly dirty, foul.

   16   This may be a reference (though garbled) to Wyndham *Lewis.*

   17   David *Lloyd George:* the famous Liberal statesman (1863–1945). Much of the American slang in the "Oxen" notesheets was probably supplied by Ezra Pound.

   20   *Under cow skunk:* could be *under low skunk.* All three words are in pencil.

   33   *Copper's nark:* slang (*ca.* 1860) for "a police spy" or "informer" (Partridge).

   34   *Lou'll:* this is not "you'll."

48–56   This birth control terminology is in Italian: *coito interrotto* ("interrupted coition"); *mezzo ritiro* ("withdrawal in the middle" of intercourse); *coit. intermet.* (probably "rhythm"); *pessario* ("pessary," a vaginal suppository); *spugna* ("sponge"); *assorbente* ("absorbent"); *capuchon* (prophylactic). The others seem obvious except *Fr letter,* which refers to the "French letter" (condom) (*U* 364:21, 757:35).

   51   (*8 d[a]ys before & aft[er].* not): this note means that eight days before and after the two or three days when the ovum may be fertilized are danger days for those who practice the rhythm method.

   61   Cf. Peacock, p. 367.

   64   *Bricky:* nineteenth-century slang for either a "bricklayer or his assistant" (hence a low fellow), or perhaps in the sense of "like a brick," or tough (Partridge).

74 *Panoe*: possibly related to "panoistic: producing ova without nutritive cells—used of the ovaries of insects; compare *polytrophic*" (*Webster's 3rd*).

91 *Come in door*: compare with "come a home" in line 33. *Jenny*: a female donkey or an airplane.

106 Probably the famous English physician Nicholas *Culpepper* (1616–54).

"Oxen of the Sun" 18

LEFT MARGIN HORIZONTAL

?odd ?man ?a ?one
B ⟨Glad he didn't ?frig in bath⟩ *362:1*

CENTER COLUMN HORIZONTAL

R ⟨King Jesus⟩ *421:7*
R ⟨shout salvation⟩ *421:7*
5   G ⟨an Ingersoll⟩ *497:12*
R ⟨addicted to⟩ *411:6–7*
R ⟨?candle⟩ *13:36 and elsewhere*
Harvey—magnetic developed by touch of <u>sperm</u>
Fabrizio—?acua seminalis
10   R ⟨womb—suction—she knows⟩ *387:21?*
also fruitful debauch
R ⟨Meetpoint, ovary, tube, womb⟩
R ⟨nemasperm head on⟩ *411:17 & 22*
R ⟨one wins race⟩
15   R ⟨Cone ?rises (attraction, concept. bub)⟩   R ⟨posthumous child⟩ *484:11,*
R ⟨?Sirks = ?disciple⟩   *Cf. 403:30*
R ⟨different appearance of nurse Callan⟩ *416:5–8*
R ⟨male pronucleus & female do fuse)(⟩
R ⟨2 spermatozoa = monster.⟩
20   R ⟨Best time 2nd. half after menstr.⟩
R ⟨when egg not fecundated menstr. angry.⟩
R ⟨regression of follicola, wrinkles, corpo luteo, yellow⟩

R ⟨ 3 & 4 month max. regress leaves scar on ovary⟩

R ⟨Empedocles of Sicily⟩ *411:14*

25 R ⟨Averroes—conception by bath, air, will⟩ *383:37–39*

Redi: omne vivum ex ovo

Easter egg.

R ⟨preformation, male only encourages minute complete embryo⟩ *Cf. 416:16–17*

R ⟨Eve 700 mill germs in ovary (Haller)⟩ *Cf. 385:15–18*

30 ovulists (Eve)—animalculists (Adam)

Epigenesis (Wolff) modern

R ⟨as it transpired subsequently⟩ *410:3*

R ⟨oval⟩ *408:28*

R ⟨acid kills sperm⟩ *Cf. 403:12, 413:6*

35 B ⟨aspermatism⟩

R ⟨a spermatozism⟩

egg. an & veg. pole

R ⟨egg—male & female content (epicene)⟩ *Cf. 717:2*

R ⟨12 days trip from ovary to womb after left follicle⟩

40 R ⟨gravidanza abdominale⟩ *Cf. 412:2* R ⟨embryo 1st· asexual⟩

   — ?ovarica   segmentation (morula)

   — tuberia vera   metaphysics

   — tubo—abdominale R ⟨cavity—blastopore⟩

  — — — uterina   R ⟨ectoderm⟩

45 R ⟨migrazione interna⟩   R ⟨endoderm⟩

R ⟨Hippocrates—r. ovary males⟩ *411:14–17?* R ⟨blastopore⟩

Galen   ″ ″ warmer   R ⟨2 ?rises—3 gaps⟩

R ⟨Henle lie if left to have males⟩   R ⟨intestinal

?choice of sex: difference of age, health   nervous canals⟩

50   sheath of dorsal cord   muscular ?tunics

dorsal—sita di relazione

ventral—intestinal

annessi embrionali (amnios, corios, ombeli., allantoid)

  — uterini placenta

55 chiusura completa 8th. week Suture

amnios 6th m. 1 l. 9th m ½ l. (defend swallowed)

B ⟨LB in bath (amnios)⟩ *Cf. 85:24–30*

1 m. allantoid prolongation   R ⟨deciduously⟩ *418:32*

60

Hunter's membrane,   *R* ⟨deciduas⟩
R ⟨placenta 1 lb, l 20 c, h, 4 c.⟩
R ⟨egg descending clothes itself in decidua⟩

NOTES

Line 1   This almost illegible phrase is written in pencil.

5   Robert Green *Ingersoll*: an American lawyer and Republican orator, famous for his agnosticism (1833–99). The name is repeated at "Circe" 11:17.

8   William *Harvey*: English physician and discoverer of the circulation of the blood (1578–1657).

9   Geronimo *Fabrizio*, or Fabricius ab Aquapendente: Italian surgeon, anatomist, and embryologist (1537–1619).

20   This phrase probably means that the best time for fertilization is the second half of the menstrual period.

22   *Corpo luteo* (*corpus luteum*): "a reddish yellow mass of endocrine tissue that forms from a ruptured Graafian follicle in the mammalian ovary" (*Webster's 7th*).

24   *Empedocles of Sicily*: a philosopher, physician, and soothsayer (died *ca*. 430 B.C.). In the text (*U* 411:14ff.) Joyce attributes to him the theory that males come from the right ovary; in line 46 below it is attributed to Hippocrates.

25   *Averroes* (Averroës): the most famous of Arabian philosophers (1126–98) and the author of "a sort of medical system, which, under the name of *Colliget*, was translated into Latin" (*Chambers's*). The name is repeated at "Circe" 10:76.

26   Francesco *Redi*: Italian physician and poet (1626?–97), the author of a book on animal parasites, and an experimenter who proved that maggots cannot form on meat which has been covered (*Chambers's*).

29   Albrecht von *Haller*: a Swiss anatomist, botanist, physiologist, and poet (1708–77).

30   *Ovulists*: proponents of an "old theory that the egg contains the whole embryo of the future organism and the germs of all subsequent offspring." *Animalculists*: proponents of a "former theory in biology that the spermatozoon contains the whole embryo in miniature" (*Webster's 3rd*).

31   Kaspar Friedrich *Wolff*: a German anatomist and physiologist known as the founder of embryology (1733–94).

35   *Aspermatism*: the inability to produce or ejaculate semen. *Spermatozism*: a meaningless word, perhaps just fanciful word play.

37   *An & veg. pole*: animal and vegetable pole.

40–44   These various terms for abnormal pregnancies probably came from Joyce's Italian handbook on embryology. *Gravidanza*: pregnancy. The following are possible (mis)locations: abdominal, ovario, true tube (as opposed to tubo-abdominal), and uterine.

41   *Morula*: "a globular mass of blastomeres formed by cleavage of the egg of many animals in its early development and distinguished from a typical blastula which may arise from it by the absence of any trace of a central cavity" (*Webster's 3rd*).

43–45   The new *cavity* formed by gastrulation is the enteron; the inner layer of cells is the *endoderm*, and the outer layer the *ectoderm*. The opening from the enteron to the outside at the point of invagination, is called the *blastopore*.

45   *Migrazione interna*: internal migration.

46   *Hippocrates*: the most famous physician of antiquity (460?–?377 B.C.). In the text this theory is attributed to Empedocles.

47   *Galen*: another famous Greek physician and a prolific writer on medical and philosophical subjects (130–201 A.D.). See also J. S. Atherton, *Books at the Wake: A Study of Literary Allusions in James Joyce's* Finnegans Wake (London, 1959), p. 250.

48   Friedrich G. J. *Henle*: a German anatomist (1809–85) who "discovered the tubules in the kidney which are named after him and wrote treatises on systematic anatomy" (*Chambers's*). Although *Henle* would make more sense here, the name looks more like *Henke*. If the latter reading is correct, it might refer to Heinrich Henke, a German theologian (1752–1809).

51   *Sita di relazione*: place of connection.

53   *Annessi embrionali*: everything connected with embryos.

55   *Chiusura*: enclosure. In the eighth week the foetal suture is complete.

56   *Amnios* (Greek form of "amnion"): a sac containing the fluid in which the foetus is immersed. The sac gradually diminishes as the foetus grows.

58   The allantois is "a vascular fetal membrane . . . in placental mammals intimately associated with the chorion in formation of the placenta." *Prolongation*: the allantois stretches between amnion and chorion. Decidua: "the part of the mucous membrane lining the uterus that in higher placental animals undergoes special modifications in preparation for and during pregnancy and is cast off at parturition" (*Webster's 7th*).

59   John *Hunter*: a Scottish surgeon (1728–93), "investigated a large number of subjects from venereal disease and embryology to blood, inflammation and gunshot wounds" (*Chambers's*). *Hunter's membrane*: the medical dictionaries I have consulted list no such membrane.

60   These placental measurements are as follows: weight one pound, length 20 centimeters; and height (width) 4 centimeters. "By the third week the placenta involves about one-fifteenth of the internal surface of the uterus. At the end of the eighth, the placental area has become nearly a third of that of the uterus. Its greatest relative size is reached during the fifth month, when the placental area is roughly half that of the interior of the uterus. In the last months of pregnancy, the relative expansion of placental area is less rapid" (Patten, p. 157).

"Oxen of the Sun" 19

LEFT COLUMN HORIZONTAL

R ⟨combustion of heretics⟩ *387:30?*
R ⟨Who supposes it?⟩ *408:4–5*
R ⟨Reminder of my errors (SD to Lynch)⟩ *Cf. 408:15–16*
R ⟨Mightily⟩ *390:12*
5   R ⟨I wish it may⟩
R ⟨Sosimenes⟩
R ⟨You have spoken of⟩ *408:2*
R ⟨How ?bland art thou and⟩
G ⟨to pry into⟩ *187:4 & 10, 648:42–649:1*
10   R ⟨an apoplexy⟩ *390:9*
R ⟨Do you not think it?⟩ *409:24*
R ⟨greatly more —⟩ *408:9*
R ⟨posies⟩ *409:6*
R ⟨Away! Scamper!⟩ *408:20*
15   good strong cheese
B ⟨Accuse me, rebel. Accuse me traitor⟩ *386:6?*
R ⟨mad romp that she is⟩ *409:6*
?glassmongers   R ⟨rap out oath⟩ *416:2*
R ⟨Painful to be born⟩ *409:21–22*   R ⟨faggot⟩ *390:16*
20   R ⟨Never will she⟩   R ⟨ingot⟩ *416:21*
R ⟨worth ten such⟩ *398:41*   R ⟨quotation⟩ *396:30*
Yes, yes   R ⟨Ha!⟩ *415:41*
R ⟨that moment⟩
say you this
25   I have spoken too much: let me rest. --
in either case

255

R ⟨Pshaw, man!⟩ *416:25*
whither
R ⟨why thinks⟩   I who . . . looked in
30   Men are ready   *R* ⟨I know not⟩
R ⟨obligated⟩ *417:42*
I ---- thanks   *R* ⟨cogent⟩ *412:26*
What then?   *R* ⟨toft,⟩ *390:12*   march
R ⟨propensely⟩ *409:18*   curtilage
35   here's a game   unworn heart, untired feet
R ⟨knight errant⟩ *406:26*   *R* ⟨outset⟩ *411:4*
R ⟨that answer —⟩
and this, being ----, renders
Account to me for ---
40   *R* ⟨O no ?Leontian⟩   at variance with
R ⟨what ?god?⟩
R ⟨boisterous⟩ *408:31*
make light of smthg (Lenehan = burn)
R ⟨That, said master of shop, was once⟩
45   *B* ⟨? why, yes.⟩   *R* ⟨crib⟩ *415:24*
Rudy = Mulvey
R ⟨leave yr mother an orphan⟩ *408:14*
R ⟨In yr. ear!⟩ *409:7*
Wanting that (it) has wanted all
50   *R* ⟨drooping weight of thought⟩ *416:20?*
imagination has a body to it
R ⟨historian of Rome⟩
R ⟨voluptuous⟩ *411:1*
R ⟨medical officer⟩ *403:15*
55   —ᴗ—   — —
—ᴗ—   —ᴗ ᴗ.
R ⟨There There There⟩
R ⟨anker of rum⟩ *418:9*

256

BOTTOM UPSIDE DOWN HORIZONTAL

R ⟨mole on breast⟩ *194:33–34*

60 *R* ⟨What way?⟩

B ⟨6 medicals⟩ *182:20*

quaker

B ⟨female catheter⟩ *182:26*

R ⟨telegram⟩ *183:5, 419:11 and elsewhere*

65 *R* ⟨M. MacLir⟩ *187:16, 499:14 & 20*

R ⟨ovoblastic⟩

superfetation

intussusception

female egg

70 *R* ⟨stamina⟩ *416:26*

R ⟨inkle⟩ *404:21*

B ⟨orchid⟩ *418:17*

R ⟨gestation⟩ *397:16*

R ⟨put a different complexion on the whole transaction⟩ *410:4–5*

75 *R* ⟨ventripotent⟩ *397:15*

R ⟨contempl. statues⟩ *Cf. 174:3ff.*

astrological

R ⟨pollen⟩ *408:41*

R ⟨Blumenbach⟩ *411:19*

80 *R* ⟨night formations⟩

R ⟨albino mule⟩ *416:25*

hot woman no children

R ⟨father sterilize⟩ *395:28?*

RIGHT COLUMN HORIZONTAL

R ⟨Perhaps the greatest, says Teufelsdrock⟩ *400:2?*

85 *R* ⟨chaffering & other racketing⟩ *416:14–15*

R ⟨commodious all-including case (suit)⟩ *416:15*

B ⟨ragman⟩ *429:15*   *R* ⟨besoiled⟩ *Cf. 416:20*

R ⟨& no third⟩ *Cf. 416:13*

R ⟨in thee lay a godcreated⟩ *416:15–16?*

90 R ⟨toil on, labour⟩ *416:18*

R ⟨it is open?⟩   R ⟨tumultuously eddy⟩ *415:42?*

R ⟨impregnated⟩ *404:6, 416:9*   mad witch's hair

R ⟨to partake it.⟩

to make outlive the grave ?those

95 it is rare that I encounter

R ⟨emaciated⟩ *412:39*

R ⟨pretty constant⟩ *410:42?*

R ⟨glances of motherwit⟩ *416:7*

not so — not so

100 R ⟨Mr & Mrs Skene, Mr Wm M-⟩

cronies

R ⟨William Allan R.A.⟩

R ⟨cut & come again⟩ *419:28*

R ⟨of a different description⟩ *409:32?*

105 R ⟨you and I⟩ *413:36–37*   used all men

dauntless

if he joked she smiled

R ⟨reverently⟩ *413:29*

R ⟨a pretty sight it was to see⟩ *413:31*

110 R ⟨before the sacred book⟩ *414:15*

R ⟨harked him on⟩ *415:41*

R ⟨a fond woman⟩ *Cf. 415:13*

R ⟨particularly large & wide ⟨bread⟩⟩

R ⟨work at it, by heaven⟩ *416:18?*

115 R ⟨bandog⟩ *416:18*   R ⟨botch⟩ *416:13*

R ⟨remarkablest⟩ *416:14*

R ⟨life essence celestial⟩ *416:9–10*

R ⟨cleave to⟩ *416:17*

R ⟨on Dublin stone there⟩ *416:10*

120 R ⟨dew moisture⟩ *416:9*

?Percutiam pastorem

R ⟨Barbara was there⟩

the learning of Vossius, the wit of

predial, march, pagus

125   *R* ⟨Amelia, Agnes⟩

        R ⟨brevier⟩ *409:10*

        provender

        R ⟨modicum⟩ *416:17*

        R ⟨-- what not⟩ *392:6*

130   *R* ⟨Neither X nor Y was wanting⟩ *410:18*

        R ⟨female loveliness⟩ *411:1?*

        Siddons—surpassing stage

        R ⟨salted cowhide⟩ *410:33*   *R* ⟨favours⟩ *398:16*

        —∪ —∪

135   opinion about Virgil

        thinks very fine & imitates, or he thinks,

        Well done our side

        ?Whig. Memory, discovering the obvious

        appeal to precedent

140   rule of thumb

NOTES

     Joyce appears to have started at each end of this notesheet and worked toward the middle. Janusko (pp. 191–192, 223) lists two source books for material on "Oxen" 19: Saintsbury's quotations from Carlyle and Macaulay, and Carlyle's *Sartor Resartus*. The following words and phrases on "Oxen" 19 are from Peacock:

"Oxen" 19	Peacock	"Oxen" 19	Peacock
Line 32 "cogent"	Page 294	Line 87 "besoiled"	Page 333
33 "toft"; "march"	296	88–90	333
34 "curtilage"	296	91 "it is open?"	317
35 "unworn heart, untired feet"	299	91 "tumultuously"	331
36 "outset"	300	92 "impregnated"	317
40 "at variance"	302	93	318
49	299	94	320
50	302	95	322
84	Cf. 330	97–98	324
85	331	99	325
86	332	100–102	327
87 "ragman"	Cf. 332	103	328

"Oxen" 19	Peacock	"Oxen" 19	Peacock
Line 105 "you and I"	Page 350	Line 117–118	Page 336
105 "used all men"	354	119	Cf. 337
106	350	120	338
107	351	122	340
108–110	352	123	341
111–112	354	124 "predial"	295
114	Cf. 335	124 "march"; "pagus"	296
115	Cf. 335	125	351
116	Cf. 330;	133 "salted cowhide"	Cf. 294
	335 "venerablest"		

Line 6 *Sosimenes*: unidentified. Eoin O'Mahony says "Zozimus" was the title of a Dublin comic paper by John Fergus O'Hea, a drinking companion of Joyce's father.

29 The ellipses are Joyce's.

40 *Leontian*: unidentified. However, a town on the eastern coast of Sicily is named Leontini.

45 The question mark preceding *why* is Joyce's.

54 *Medical officer* is upside down.

55–56 Cf. "Oxen" 16:59.

61 Repeated at "Circe" 3:93.

63 Repeated at "Circe" 3:94.

65 Mananaan *MacLir*: the legendary founder of the Manx nation. See Gilbert, pp. 190–191.

79 Johann Friedrich *Blumenbach*: an anthropologist (1752–1840).

81 *Albino* and *mule* may not be connected.

84 *Teufelsdrock*: Professor Teufelsdröckh of Carlyle's *Sartor Resartus*.

100 *Skene*: William Forbes Skene (1809–92), a Scottish historian.

102 Sir *William Allan*, R.A.: a Scottish historical painter (1782–1850) elected to the Royal Academy in 1835 and three years later made president of the Royal Scottish Academy.

121 *Percutiam pastorem*: I shall strike the shepherd.

123 *Vossius*: Gerhard Johann Voss, Dutch humanist theologian (1577–1649).

132 Sarah *Siddons* (1755–1831): "English actress. Her tragic question, 'Will it wash?' " (Glasheen). Cf. *FW*, 290:19–20. Janusko suggests that Joyce probably noticed her name in a Macaulay passage in Saintsbury (p. 372).

"Oxen of the Sun" 20

LEFT MARGIN HORIZONTAL

R ⟨catch aholt⟩ *418:24*
R ⟨durnd⟩ *417:31*
R ⟨blob⟩ *371:25*

LEFT COLUMN HORIZONTAL

R ⟨night before performance⟩
5   R ⟨laid in the clay⟩ *390:8*
prize, halted him
R ⟨army parlance⟩ *413:8*
R ⟨say!⟩
R ⟨no 1 on the gun⟩ *417:17*
10   R ⟨old crone⟩ *391:28, 423:1 & 4*
R ⟨Doady⟩ *413:34 & 40, 414:12*
B ⟨wipe (handker)⟩ *398:17?*
R ⟨Sir, to you.⟩
R ⟨this here place⟩
15   R ⟨weary weary while⟩ *413:23–24*
R ⟨done the good deed⟩ *416:13?*
R ⟨Well done, thou good, & faithful servant⟩ *414:19*
R ⟨fought the good fight⟩ *414:18*
R ⟨Universal Husband⟩ *413:33*
20   R ⟨I remembered Who wept⟩ *398:25–26?*
in such case
R ⟨in all the bloom of womanhood⟩ *413:31–32?*

8

R ⟨was the reply⟩
cock his pistol
25   R ⟨?U did⟩
R ⟨God, ?how⟩ *413:42*
R ⟨fruit of their lawful embrace⟩ *413:36*
R ⟨she had manfully helped⟩ *413:25*
G ⟨break all before him⟩
30   R ⟨with the old shake of her curls⟩ *413:41–42*
R ⟨Very, very happy⟩ *413:26–27*
R ⟨O, Jip, it may never be again⟩ *413:40–41*
R ⟨knock the ashes from yʳ· pipe⟩ *414:13*
R ⟨risk of her life to save her life⟩ *413:19*
35   Stipendiary magistrate
convulsions of laughter
R ⟨share her joy⟩ *413:35*
R ⟨when all things are now falling⟩
R ⟨—he is now filled with wine⟩ *414:29*
40   R ⟨cut off from the earth⟩ *414:31?*
R ⟨timbrel & the harp⟩ *414:27*
R ⟨he rises up⟩ *414:26*   abjure
R ⟨falls in with⟩   R ⟨lie under wrath⟩ *414:30–31*
a cultivated mind
45   R ⟨suffered her to come: let her come⟩ *Cf. 414:22–23?*
R ⟨nothing as it seems, there of . . .⟩ *415:21*   R ⟨Mark this.⟩ *415:19*
R ⟨think of it well⟩
gorgeous   R ⟨Go out⟩
seed of the herb
50   R ⟨my lord general⟩   R ⟨put off his hat⟩ *415:35–36?*
R ⟨punctual B—⟩ *415:35*   ?map¢han¢es
R ⟨giving him sharp languages⟩ *416:2*
R ⟨flooding gloomily, ?clamourously out⟩ *415:41–42?*
R ⟨their ulterior goal⟩ *416:1*
55   R ⟨thou art other than⟩ *416:5?*   a good one, I think.
R ⟨All being gone out⟩ *416:7*
R ⟨Yup⟩ *418:4*   R ⟨guy⟩ *420:3*
R ⟨thunderation⟩ *417:31*   R ⟨Stand by⟩

RIGHT COLUMN HORIZONTAL

   R ⟨shiver my timbers⟩ *419:19*
60 *R* ⟨or the 4 square Keep of Grandson⟩
   R ⟨in thunderblue serration⟩ *415:25–27?*
   R ⟨dark with rolling impendence⟩ *415:25–26?*
   R ⟨lulled by flowing of wave⟩
   R ⟨within a minute's race⟩ *415:42*
65 *R* ⟨its gates were angelguarded long ago⟩ *415:23–24*
   R ⟨Godlike & My Father's⟩ *293:26?*
   R ⟨Paraguay tea⟩
   R ⟨all steadily snoring⟩ *Cf. 415:42*
   glitter
70 *R* ⟨sooty hell⟩ *420:34*
   R ⟨noble ever soldier in it⟩ *415:37–38*
   R ⟨?flunkeyhood⟩
   R ⟨wellremembered⟩ *414:42*
   R ⟨habitmakers⟩
75 *R* ⟨perhaps⟩ *415:14 and elsewhere*
   R ⟨Our Lady⟩ *415:7*
   R ⟨yonder⟩ *415:4*
   R ⟨must needs⟩ *415:15*
   R ⟨comely⟩ *415:8*   *R* ⟨You saw⟩
80 *R* ⟨a grove of⟩ *414:42*
   R ⟨uniform, serene, ?aliving⟩
   R ⟨with much real⟩ *415:1–2*
   R ⟨alert⟩ *415:3*
   R ⟨disengage⟩ *414:38*
85 *R* ⟨shaven space⟩ *414:41*
   R ⟨running forward to⟩
   R ⟨it behoves⟩ *377:26*
   R ⟨that highest in him quality⟩
   R ⟨injocund⟩ *383:28?*
90 *R* ⟨a plan was by them adopted⟩ *378:7–8*
   R ⟨I fear lest what was excellently begun you may not so well
    end.⟩ *377:28–30*

R ⟨Me a great doubt holds⟩ *Cf. 378:18*

R ⟨jackanapes⟩ *415:34*   6 hours shift

95   *R* ⟨cockerel⟩ *415:34*   *R* ⟨clever⟩ *12:28 and elsewhere*

R ⟨threnes⟩ *416:33*

R ⟨laudanum for Haines⟩ *405:25*

mighty hard ticket

R ⟨how come you so⟩ *419:2–3*

100   *R* ⟨most anything⟩

rake over the coals

R ⟨?ship long of me⟩

B ⟨by gum⟩ *419:1*

B ⟨P.D. spent good money colouring. Cure for red nose.

105   Drink like—?till it turns adelite⟩ *94:16–17*

NOTES

Janusko (pp. 191–192, 222) lists two source books for material on "Oxen" 20: Saintsbury's quotations from Carlyle and Ruskin and *David Copperfield* by Dickens. The following lines are repeated on "Oxen" 9:

"Oxen" 20	"Oxen" 9		"Oxen" 20	"Oxen" 9
Line 87	Line 75		Line 91	Line 79
88	76		93	78
90	77			

Lines 5–8   *8*: in pencil.

11   *Doady*: see Thornton, p. 346.

32   *Jip*: a dog in *David Copperfield*.

46   The ellipses are Joyce's. A *w* was added above *seems* in pencil.

55   Only part of the sentence was marked through.

60–65   These lines are from Ruskin.

61–63   These lines are probably connected; they appear to have been destined for *U* 415:25–27.

87–93   These lines were marked through with a large *X*.

"Circe" I

LEFT MARGIN VERTICAL

B ⟨gorgeous stuff⟩ *450:25*
B ⟨Old Glory⟩ *496:31*

LEFT MARGIN HORIZONTAL

R ⟨wouldn't do a less thing⟩ *500:18*
salt spilt, diners climb on table to fight
5   *G* ⟨roulette⟩ *496:3*
G ⟨Rien ne va plus faites vos jeux le jeu est fait⟩ *496:3–5*
parsley for corpse (Greek)
B ⟨Hold out hand⟩ *547:7*
SD, long
10   LB, shorter, all fingers equal & round tips
3rd. & 4th. far apart impulsive
1st. & 2nd. self willed
bend back easily ?shy
equal = original
15   triple bracelet, health, wealth, happy
30 yrs each, if sun up ?rise, if not . . . .
purple nails heart
long white cruel
red nails hasty
20   quart hood extravagant
3rd. fingernail ridged
if tender brightred

265

speckled unhealthy
side cushions impulse
25 Mounts of Venus, Jove, Saturn, Apollo, Mercury
love, ambition, conduct, art, industry

LEFT COLUMN HORIZONTAL

B ⟨tennis racket feels heavier & bigger in left hand⟩ *Cf. 445:16–17*

R ⟨Minnie Hauck⟩ *515:15*

B ⟨left hand smaller (si) on unaccustom?⟩ *445:16–17*

30 *B* ⟨fingertips feel without touching⟩ *546:30–31?* *S* ⟨come to bed
hat⟩ *425:3–4*

G ⟨magic lantern⟩ *499:9?* *B* ⟨(Irving Bishop)⟩ *437:12*

B ⟨Juggler⟩ *477:4?*

B ⟨'cushion' between nerve & objects always⟩ *546:15–17?*

35 redhot lava walked on South Sea

plunges bare hand in molten steel (foundry)

G ⟨smoking = to occupy mouth⟩ *469:1*

R ⟨sweet ?bun.⟩ *445:31?*

Close eyes in sun, mist of blood,   *B* ⟨No!⟩

40 see red, bloodvessels of retina

G ⟨SD remembers falsely place not seen⟩ *507:25?*

B ⟨More limelight, Charley⟩ *492:18*

R ⟨only for what happened him⟩ *509:7*

G ⟨Mind the cornflowers⟩ *541:25* *B* ⟨Chummy faithful to trulls⟩ *Cf. 572:19–21*

45 *S* ⟨LB likes to be tempted⟩ *536:28?*

R ⟨Le père d'un satyre, la mère d'un minotaure déroge aux lois
de la nature et au lieu du roi des animaux ne produit
qu'un monstre. C'est faire a la société un tort
considérable (said that very well)⟩

50 *G* ⟨Metchnikoff inoculated anthropoid apes⟩ *510:4–5*

G ⟨whore sneers at other w's big word.⟩ *510:7–9*

B ⟨LB unlaces her boot, learnt to make knots tying parcels for
mail order business.⟩ *517:18–19* *B* ⟨So that? So
that . . . ⟩ *425:15 & 17*

55   *R* ⟨horned man⟩ *551:13, 553:14*

    B ⟨Lambert family pigs⟩ *554:32*

    B ⟨How would it be if I was to bash in your jaw?⟩ *573:22–23*

    snowing & sneezing   money spider

    S ⟨imbecillic⟩ *492:11*

60   *B* ⟨Give a thing & take it back

        Never go to God again

        See a man behind the church

        Washing his face in a bowl of blood⟩ *Cf. 542:8–11*

    does yʳ· father fish for trout?

65   Never brush away a ladybird

    Star on mount of thumb (cautious in love)

    Drop curtsy to new moon & turn silver money

    Put on new on Whitsunday

    B ⟨MB bringing salt to new house⟩ *750:24–25*

70   *B* ⟨Existence of God easily proved by holy writ⟩ *618:21–23*

    R ⟨Wait my love & I'll be with you⟩ *422:12*

    B ⟨Beauty & Beast,⟩ *438:16–17* Comus, *B* ⟨Caliban,⟩ *482:24* Renan,

    B ⟨Lycanthrophy. nabuchodonosor rex,⟩ *Cf. 485:32*

    pockmarked, *B* ⟨blotches⟩ *456:19* *B* ⟨finger short⟩ *549:10*

75   *R* ⟨lunatics,⟩ *S* ⟨mammoth roses⟩ *468:8*

    B ⟨disorderly house⟩ *444:10*

CENTER VERTICAL

    B ⟨maul⟩ *445:20*

    B ⟨LB pros on floor⟩ *519:8ff.*

    B ⟨educated greyhound⟩ *446:22–23*

LOWER RIGHT MARGIN VERTICAL

80   *B* ⟨Ruby⟩ *446:31,*

        523:19,

        527:9

RIGHT COLUMN HORIZONTAL

G ⟨SD drunk remember somethg smby told, not know what reader
   also not⟩ *507:24ff.*

85 SD friends of the ?manner of iniquity

B ⟨son of a whore (Pan)⟩ *509:17–18?*   B ⟨Dunleary⟩

S ⟨all one & same God.⟩ *512:5*

R ⟨God help yʳ· head.⟩ *494:24*

S ⟨L̸B More? and more's mother⟩ *489:31–490:2*

90 R ⟨SD delighted own politeness⟩ *542:26, 543:11*

S ⟨How is yʳ· middle leg?⟩ *443:3*

S ⟨Roman collar b̸a̸c̸k̸ hidden⟩ *508:15*

B ⟨spreadeagle⟩ *492:30*

B ⟨Kick him in the knackers⟩ *576:15*

95 R ⟨I gave it to Nelly to stick in her belly the leg of a
   duck⟩ *423:28–31*   B ⟨?grousing⟩ *538:26?*

B ⟨Jūpītēr īs añimal⟩   King of beasts

lucky number   B ⟨:Noah⟩ *485:24 and elsewhere*   R ⟨″ ″ animals⟩

G ⟨Bohee Bros Livermore minstrels⟩ *436:7*

100 G ⟨MB likes ?sweep:, so dirty.⟩ *436:8?*

G ⟨fawn(ing)⟩ *440:24, 458:22*   S ⟨accost⟩ *466:17*   S ⟨solicit⟩ *435:5, 455:4*

B ⟨cub,⟩   B ⟨have you any tickles⟩ *467:2*

G ⟨sumptuous⟩ *185:23, 345:17*

R ⟨women like sleepy men⟩ *516:14–15*

105 B ⟨vidi acquam⟩ *424:15*   G ⟨mixoldyian⟩ *493:16*

S ⟨Are you out of Maynooth? out of it now⟩   R ⟨Well out of
   it⟩ *508:4ff.*

SD see yʳ· hand on wall

B ⟨Want will be yʳ· master⟩ *579:15–16*

110 R ⟨whore tell of a Mr Dedalus⟩ *Cf. 607:19*

R ⟨(sailor)⟩ *607*   R ⟨(circus rider)⟩ *Cf. 607:30ff.*

B ⟨Give a thing & take it back God'll ask you where is that.
   You'll say you don't know God'll send you down
   below⟩ *542:8–11*

115 Itch palm touch wood

B ⟨My boy's thinking of me⟩ *493:4*

G ⟨Mother slipperslapper⟩ *466:24*

B ⟨devil is in that door (opens self)⟩ *513:23*

end of the world

120   S ⟨Whore to LB—You're not his father? No. I thought on
       account of you both being in black⟩ *466:27–467:2*

NOTES

In the upper left-hand corner is a large *C* in blue pencil. This is a double notesheet, the bottom half ("Circe" 2) being a continuation of "Circe" 1. "Circe" 1 was published by Norman Silverstein and myself in the *James Joyce Quarterly*, II (Spring 1965), 222–226. Some of its notes are duplicated below.

Line 4 *Diners*: cf. a letter of July 1, 1934 (*Letters*, I, 343).

7 *Parsley*: repeated at "Circe" 7:27.

13 *Shy*: might be *sly*.

8–26 These lines deal with palmistry. See the essay on "Circe," pp. 43–48.

28 *Minnie Hauck* (or Hauk): a famous Carmen of the late nineteenth century (1852?–1929). Her name also suggests "hawk," which Joyce associated with Circe. The name is repeated at "Circe" 3:4.

30–31 *Come to bed hat*: cf. "Circe" 2:10.

41 The phenomenon described here is known in psychology as paramnesia.

44 *Chummy*: see "Cyclops" 2:9 and note.

46–49 The speech in French is used in "Circe" notebook V.A.19 at Buffalo, where the passage is also crossed out in red. It does not recur in the fair copy at the Rosenbach Foundation Museum or in subsequent typescripts and proofs.

50 See "Oxen" 8:73–74 and note.

54 The ellipses are Joyce's.

57 Private Carr's threatening of Stephen is used as written here in notebook V.A.19 and altered slightly on *U* 573:22–23.

60 Repeated at line 112.

72 *Comus*: see Litz, pp. 21–22. Joseph Ernest *Renan*: a scholar of Phoenician civilization and professor of Hebrew (1823–92), of interest to Joyce as a source of information on racial parallels. Renan wrote, among other books, the *Histoire générale des langues sémitiques* (1854), *Averroès et l'Averroisme* (1852), and *Vie de Jésus* (1863). See also Ellmann, p. 200, and *Letters, passim*.

73 *Lycanthropy*: a form of insanity supposedly suffered for seven years by King Nebuchadnezzar II (d. 562 B.C.). Samuel Rolles Driver's *Introduction to the Literature of the Old Testament* (London, 1891; p. 469) mentions the king's insanity and his edict respecting it. *Nabuchodonosor*: the Greek form of Nebuchadnezzar.

86 *Dunleary*: see "Cyclops" 4:128 and note. The reference to *Pan* here reveals Joyce's interest in an alternate version of the *Odyssey* in which Penelope sleeps with one or more of the suitors, the

fruit of this union being the god Pan. This was copied from *Ulysses* notebook VIII.A.5 at Buffalo (p. 299) and is originally from Roscher, III, 1909–10.

95 A "Fresh Nellie" is mentioned in Gogarty's poem "The Hay Hotel," which commemorates the destruction of Nighttown in 1924 (Ulick O'Connor, p. 56).

97 The dashes represent scansion.

99 *Bohee Bro[ther]s*: "Tom and Sam, who turn up in Bloom's nightmare ([*U.*] 436) appeared in the Leinster Hall, giving banjo solos, songs, choruses, and dances (*Irish Independent*, August 28, 1894, pp. 4, 5)" (Adams, p. 74).

105 *Acquam*: should be *aquam. Mixoldyian*: should be "mixolydian."

119 Joyce first wrote *earth*, then *end* over it.

"Circe" 2

LEFT MARGIN VERTICAL TOP

cute as a shithouse rat *Cf. 335:6–7*   garlic
B ⟨heart ?torn big grinning claws⟩ *567:3*
B ⟨Moly—circumcis.⟩ *Cf. 532:5 & 11*
B ⟨Circe—pox⟩ *509:20, 541:20*

LEFT MARGIN HORIZONTAL MIDDLE

5   R ⟨Florrie Power, mouldy sweat⟩
     B ⟨briskly⟩ *494:24, 513:34*
     R ⟨square pusher⟩ *425:3*
     R ⟨Maggot O'Reilly⟩ *441:31–442:1*
     B ⟨fetishism⟩   B ⟨picture⟩
10   G ⟨make love to a hat⟩ *425:3–4?*
     R ⟨blow. great guns⟩ *582:23?*
     B ⟨setting to⟩
     R ⟨Tommy Tittlemouse⟩ *489:28*
     B ⟨true lover's knot⟩
15   Let me like a soldier fall
     R ⟨Cat's rambles through the slack⟩ *541:26–27*
     B ⟨whores despise trade⟩
     S ⟨objection to French lozenges⟩ *514:8–9*
     R ⟨don't be all night⟩ *434:23*

271

LEFT MARGIN VERTICAL BOTTOM

20 taken be a friend
   B ⟨Wom. autobiog.⟩
   B ⟨22.14.7.18⟩
   B ⟨drunken engagement⟩
   R ⟨As a matter of fact.⟩
25 B ⟨S.D. ?douces⟩
   B ⟨S.D. no fear of⟩
   B ⟨what can talk ?to⟩
   B ⟨fractious⟩ *446:26*
   cassowary
30 B ⟨lemur⟩ *565:12*

LEFT COLUMN HORIZONTAL

   R ⟨Ul. carries shot stag with ?lugarm & spear⟩
   B ⟨crew lie with muffled heads, they feast.⟩
   B ⟨½ Ul. ½ Euryl.⟩   22 each (mother in law fight)
   B ⟨drew lots in helmet⟩
35 B ⟨Circe sings⟩
   B ⟨Euryloch. comes back⟩
   B ⟨Polites. Ul. favourite⟩
   invent card dealer
   B ⟨lions & wolves⟩
40 B ⟨Circe's web⟩
   R ⟨LB gets roastbeef for S.D.⟩
   R ⟨MB wishes to see brothel⟩ *436:4*
   chairs
   B ⟨cheese, barley, wine ?seed honey⟩
45 R ⟨smitten with wand⟩ *Cf. 492*
   Ul. sword & bow
   R ⟨Eur. beseeches him to abandon others. No.⟩
   B ⟨Circe's oath lest she castrate⟩
   B ⟨Moly hard to dig.⟩   R ⟨Elpenor.⟩

50 *R* ⟨LB women love to be let into little secret⟩
    B ⟨LB beetles, they feel themselves ?upon women⟩
    R ⟨Poodle lion, Circe's pet⟩
    B ⟨Organ do good biz in kips. Soon got soon gone.⟩ *444:18–19*
    Whore after fall, Jesus!   then sings.
55 *B* ⟨bearskin rug⟩ *581:8?*
    B ⟨Leopardstown races. Fox rock⟩ *441:3–7*
    B ⟨Hiccuping whores (O excuse)⟩ *492:15, 493:2*
    B ⟨LB laughs outright.⟩
    B ⟨Someone puts on whore's hat. She whips it ?off⟩ *510:1–2*
60 whore dislikes microscope   *B* ⟨& science⟩ *525:10?*
    B ⟨Fight in street.⟩ *580–586*
    B ⟨Side pockets, broad in beam⟩ *502:16*
    R ⟨Flashing firepins⟩ *561:11–12?*
    B ⟨Drunken sneeze.⟩ *430:8*
65 *S* ⟨Lot of nakedness knocking about.⟩ *501:1–2*
    B ⟨LB like him she knew before⟩ *508:4?*
    B ⟨x Dog if larger, (v other)⟩
    chainsmoking
    B ⟨rooster:⟩ *549:12* *B* ⟨dry rush: sensation⟩ *509:3*
70 *R* ⟨Camel's hump pot still., ferns date juice⟩ *646:37–38*
    R ⟨Unddies pool not to see face, only Mrs?⟩   *R* ⟨stag⟩ *425:6*
    G ⟨object to negro porter⟩ *436:5?*
    B ⟨all that⟩   *B* ⟨the Kildare girl⟩ *Cf. 423:25*
    B ⟨Faithful place⟩ *425:2*
75 *R* ⟨Great unjust God⟩ *495:4*
    B ⟨says the girl (the one)⟩
    G ⟨Ever see me running?⟩ *Cf. 763:17–18*
    B ⟨SD drunk keeps on ?showing⟩
    R ⟨33 is a bitch (log. ?machine)⟩ *434:24?*
80 *R* ⟨colour corresp. to her ama⟩
    B ⟨Danish sailor, drunken animal in kips⟩
    R ⟨why show it me⟩
    B ⟨handsome man, blackguard, women'd like⟩ *647:10–11*
    B ⟨bit of business⟩ *551:14*
85 *S* ⟨LB ?dispraises her dress⟩

B ⟨Dr Swift⟩ *573:14*

B ⟨get connection⟩ *509:2–3*

R ⟨3 children of syph father, couldn't swallow⟩ *509:21–22*

LB hugs SD for wit   *B* ⟨my wife w^d. like you but fears he is not

90   that way built⟩ *647:11*

R ⟨LB wishes SD teach her Italian⟩ *Cf. 643:4–5*

B ⟨whores dance round LB⟩

R ⟨LB & SD walk in street linked⟩ *644:36ff.*

R ⟨twofaced. LB looks at girl's rump⟩ *500–503?*

95   *B* ⟨SD door closed that time, yes⟩ *513:23–26?*

R ⟨Poldy (Saul! Saul!)⟩ *541:23?*

S ⟨commonwoe of Ireland⟩

B ⟨(,) eatondph ⅛ ador dorador douradora⟩ *632:2–3*

?of it

100   *B* ⟨bird that can sing & won't sing.⟩ *507:11*

B ⟨ask & forget question⟩

G ⟨Would you suck a lemon⟩ *500:18–19*

B ⟨Drunk (sober) watches drunk (drunk)⟩ *507:20*

B ⟨Philip v ?sup.⟩

RIGHT COLUMN HORIZONTAL

105   *S* ⟨thank yr. mother for the rabbits.⟩ *513:34–35*

B ⟨πολυφαρμακος⟩

B ⟨SD's unwrinkled face⟩ *640:33*

R ⟨Clap on the back for Charley⟩ *492:25*

B ⟨beauty spot of me behind⟩ *500:14*

110   *B* ⟨Youre that sly, old cocky, I could kiss you, straight⟩ *544:24*

B ⟨Such is life in an outhouse⟩ *320:8*

G ⟨black mass⟩ *583:33ff.*

R ⟨mantrap⟩ *425:5*

S ⟨hell's gates⟩ *442:9*

115   *B* ⟨manhandle⟩ *586:3*

B ⟨SD ?. . room friendly⟩ *575:32?*

B ⟨respect for contemptibles⟩

B ⟨idiot prophet with boiled eyes⟩ *422:15ff.*

B ⟨light from the ?west.⟩ *422:23?*

120 *B* ⟨Give me that money.⟩

B ⟨gunboat⟩ *617:10*

S ⟨bridle up⟩ *442:4*

B ⟨slyboots⟩ *544:24*

R ⟨San Tommaso Mastino⟩ *621:32*

125 *S* ⟨silent means consent⟩ *490:26*

R ⟨Go farther & fare worse⟩ *466:23–24*

B ⟨gridiron hand⟩ *549:5*   *S* ⟨goldstopped mouth⟩ *468:19*

S ⟨swaggerroot⟩ *468:28*   *B* ⟨disguise⟩ *528:12?*

B ⟨those that hides knows where to find⟩ *542:18–19*

130 *B* ⟨neigh⟩ *473:25?*   bray

B ⟨quack⟩ *511:27*

R ⟨working overtime⟩ *466:26*

B ⟨stye in her eye⟩ *492:32*

B ⟨pig it⟩

135 *B* ⟨sow's ear into a silken purse⟩ *542:26–27*

B ⟨higgledy piggledy⟩ *491:35*

G ⟨ugly duckling⟩ *502:5–6*

S ⟨O, you ruck⟩ *436:29*

G ⟨fingers made before forks⟩ *514:6*

140 *S* ⟨after you is good manners⟩ *491:16*

S ⟨Hog's Norton where the pigs play the organs⟩ *489:26*

B ⟨what's mine is my own⟩ *541:28–29*

R ⟨mimic animals⟩ *442:1?*

B ⟨whores put silver paper on teeth. Mycene⟩ *541:30–31*

145 *R* ⟨walking with⟩

R ⟨Fairyhouse⟩ *440:28*

S ⟨LB memory of only spree⟩

B ⟨truffles⟩ *505:6 and elsewhere*

R ⟨Camiknickers⟩ *504:2*

150 *R* ⟨henna of hair⟩ *509:29*

B ⟨ghoststory (Circe)⟩ *526:15*

G ⟨who was it told me her name (SD)⟩ *507:24*

RIGHT MARGIN VERTICAL MIDDLE

B ⟨liontamer:⟩ *446:17* variety

B ⟨Memory hunts for vermin in her clothes.⟩ *505:13?*

155 B ⟨Monster sale⟩ *501:21*

RIGHT MARGIN VERTICAL BOTTOM

horses fuck, learnt that from us?

B ⟨ladies first⟩ *491:18*

horse full

B ⟨Poulaphouca⟩ *535 and elsewhere*

160 B ⟨erotic woman in photo eye on camera⟩

B ⟨vivisection⟩ *460:9*

CENTER TOP VERTICAL

kick over traces

NOTES

There is a large *C* in blue pencil in the upper right-hand corner. This notesheet is the bottom half of "Circe" 1.

Line 3 *Moly*: discussed in "Circe" essay (pp. 40–41); "Circe" 6:105–106 note; Litz, pp. 25–26; Ellmann, p. 511, *Letters*, I, 147–149. The word is repeated at line 49 below, "Circe" 3:110 & 121, 7:110, 10:26–30, 12:32 & 36, and 21:35 & 50.

5 *Florrie Power* (the name was later changed to Florry): one of the prostitutes in "Circe."

10 Cf. "Circe" 1:30–31.

26–27 These lines may be connected. Cf. *U* 574:13–14.

31ff. (*passim*) In the Butcher and Lang translation of the *Odyssey*, the action subsequent to the arrival of Odysseus and his men on the isle of Circe is on pp. 157ff.

33 *Euryl.*: Eurylochus, one of Odysseus's officers.

37 *Polites*: "a leader of men, the dearest to me and the trustiest of all my company" (*Odyssey*, p. 160).

44 Circe gives the men "a mess of cheese and barley-meal and yellow honey with Pramnian wine, and mixed harmful drugs with the food" (*Odyssey*, p. 160).

45–49 After Odysseus's men drink Circe's brew, she touches them with her *wand* and changes them into swine. When Eurylochus brings the news to Odysseus, the latter takes up his *sword &
bow* and sets out to rescue his men. Eurylochus pleads with him not to go, but to no avail. On the way to Circe's house, Odysseus meets Hermes, who gives him *moly* (*hard to dig* up) and tells him it will protect him against Circe's brew. Odysseus is to rush at Circe when she touches him with her wand and make her promise to free his men and play no more tricks on them "lest she make thee a dastard and unmanned, when she hath thee naked" (*Odyssey*, p. 163). *Elpenor*, the youngest of the crew, is killed by falling off the roof of Circe's house. The men later see him in Hades. In *Ulysses* Paddy Dignam is associated with Elpenor.

70 Cf. "Eumaeus" 7:37.

106 This Greek word means "knowing many drugs or charms."

124 *San Tommaso Mastino*: Joyce is having some fun with Saint Thomas Aquinas here. *Mastino* means "mastiff" in Italian. The name is repeated at "Eumaeus" 6:17. See also Thornton, p. 204 (entry 208.9).

"Circe" 3

LEFT MARGIN VERTICAL TOP

B ⟨Eriphyle drove husband Amphiaraos to war. Knew he would fall⟩
Amphi.—asks son to revenge him
Anticlea = Sisiphus bore Ul. on hill in shower
R ⟨Minnie Hauk (Carmen)⟩ *515:15*   S ⟨cuddle⟩ *467:24?*
5 B ⟨Dog in kips.⟩
B ⟨Someone posts in   Too Late Box⟩ *516:22*
S ⟨I'm slightly drunk⟩ *506:34*
R ⟨rosemary⟩ *503:19*
Eannas (SD remembers)
10 B ⟨Woman spits⟩ *424:24, 529:16, and elsewhere*

LEFT MARGIN HORIZONTAL CENTER

S ⟨arabesque⟩ *562:17*
S ⟨?morari⟩
S ⟨anklets⟩ *432:20–21*
B ⟨goatskin⟩ *518:4?*
15 B ⟨gum benjamin⟩ *502:25–26*
B ⟨kohol⟩ *467:26*
S ⟨coin on brow⟩ *432:19*

LEFT MARGIN VERTICAL BOTTOM

S ⟨luscious lips⟩ *468:12–13*   R ⟨Cavan Cootehill and Belturbet⟩ *423:27*
R ⟨china dog with news⟩   R ⟨holster⟩

278

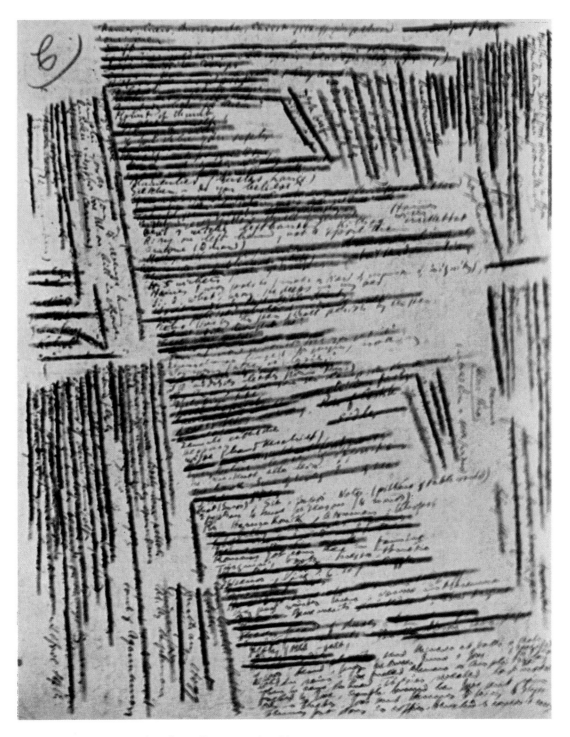

Ulysses notesheet "Circe" 3. (Reproduced by permission of The Society of Authors)

20   S ⟨LB salutes card falls from hat⟩ *447:5–11*   S ⟨mucksweat⟩ *515:21*
     R ⟨Chinese boxes with little wax pellets.   Jonathan Hogg
         Put these in water—they open.   B ⟨fucking ?train⟩
         One a boat, another waterlily   R ⟨guinea pig⟩
         etc.⟩ *612:34–37*   Milly lupanars
25   S ⟨she caught a stray hair deftly and   tomb of Agamemnon
         twisted it to her coil⟩ *468:27*
     B ⟨slyboots⟩ *544:24*
     Proud flesh
     S ⟨Face transformed into landscape⟩ *554:18–20?*
30   B ⟨whore tells his fortune: knobby knuckles⟩ *549:2–3*
     B ⟨Thursday's child has far to go (SD)⟩ *548:17*
     dreams of seeing himself
     B ⟨Artist: make plays of incidents.⟩
     R ⟨Woman's character depends on things they wear⟩ *515:7*
35   B ⟨Left hand, cult of Shakti, Siva's ?spouse black magic⟩ *499:25–26*
     G ⟨Great yoghin of the gods⟩ *499:22*
     G ⟨Pūnarjanam (reincarnation): wildfowl ?Pyth⟩ *499:23–26*
     B ⟨God's handwriting on hand⟩ *548:10*
     B ⟨new taste of chocolate⟩ *515:9*

CENTER COLUMN HORIZONTAL

40   R ⟨Names, Cicero, Buonaparte, Christ   gilt off
         gingerbread⟩ *Cf. 607:2–3*   B ⟨unripe fruit⟩ *532:12?*
     R ⟨'our' men⟩
     B ⟨Swift, 1 man in armour beat 10 in shirts⟩ *573:14–15*
     B ⟨State: 10 soldiers shoot, 1 is bloodguilty (cf. jury)⟩
45   B ⟨Irish missile troops⟩ *580:29–581:1*
     B ⟨Danes & Normans conquered England.⟩
     B ⟨H. M. as fireman or D.M.P.⟩ *72:4*
     B ⟨to have or not to have⟩
     B ⟨noble art of self pretence⟩ *573:25–26*
50   B ⟨Anybody here for there?⟩ *560:12–13*
     Mount of thumb

B ⟨Respect yourself!⟩ *492:14*

G ⟨lily of the alley⟩ *501:33*

R ⟨if you value your safety⟩

55   B ⟨for keeps?⟩ *467:22*

S ⟨that's not for you to say.⟩ *425:4*

B ⟨hooks & tackle: whore's request⟩ *446:25?*

B ⟨wrong one brings ill luck⟩ *518:11*

Blumenlied (Gustav Lange)

60   Gretchen—do you believe?

S ⟨Starve warts, caustic prevents rebirth, wartblood spreads

    blood   snip off ?with horsehair no denned

    neck⟩ *503:27–28*

B ⟨Tansy, pennyroyal spanish fly⟩ *331:7, 504:34*   Haines with cricketbat

65   R ⟨Night insects follow smell of female⟩ *504:10–13*

Devil & witches lefthanded kithog

Ring on left hand, not to spoil them

?chacone (?Durard)   B ⟨limpets⟩ *373:33*

B ⟨Molly will change furniture.⟩ *Cf. 690:14ff.* B ⟨barnacles,⟩ *582:31*

70   B ⟨non corrosive sublimate (hell)⟩   B ⟨tatterdemalion⟩ *492:29–30*

B ⟨that is another pin of trousers⟩ *539:28?*

for 5 wickets

Haines I was polite (make a friend of woman of iniquity,)

    B ⟨fool's advice⟩ *507:16*

75   Si.D. what's wrong. He sleeps in my bed.

B ⟨World made by Brit. Bible Society⟩

B ⟨Gent. patriot scholar & judge of malt.⟩ *576:22–23*

who live by the pen shall perish by the pen.

B ⟨what did thought do?⟩ *468:18*

80   B ⟨Tell me news⟩ *549:21*

B ⟨Came from a hot place⟩ *538:30*

R ⟨Have it now or wait till you get it⟩ *514:9–10*

Mumchance hanged for saying nothing.

Was your father a glazier?

85   B ⟨SD objects to Eng. abroad⟩

SD addresses letter from Paris.

S ⟨By the way have you the lamp, the key the—etc.⟩ *Cf. 508:9–10*

R ⟨Fallopian tube⟩ *424:24–25*

B ⟨Lock hospital⟩ *617:12–13*   *B* ⟨meretricious finery⟩ *501:22*

90   *B* ⟨green rag to a bull⟩ *576:29*

B ⟨Love's old sweet song.⟩ *437:24, 507:6, and elsewhere* *B* ⟨Rose of

Castile⟩ *447:25 and elsewhere*

B ⟨6 medicals⟩ *182:20*   *S* ⟨sidles⟩ *429:19, 549:16*

Female catheter   *182:26*

95   pessary

wipe (handkerchief)

B ⟨Bloom leaves High School (?1884) at 15⟩ *Cf. 687:28*

R ⟨Eurylochus—leader of opposition⟩

Ire. renitente alla leva.

100   *R* ⟨the hawk. Sun of living. Sun of dead⟩

B ⟨Egyptian gipsy⟩

Thot (Enros): Sit: Sapdi. Notos. (pillars of table world)

Egyptian 4 suns for seasons (4 maids)

Ra: Harma Kouiti Atoumou: Khopri

105   *B* ⟨Filling belly with husks of swines⟩ *506:29–30*

B ⟨I will arise and go to my father⟩ *506:30–31*

B ⟨Ireland a pontine marsh⟩

     Romans got corn there in famine.

Tarquin's booty: Suessa Pometia

110   *B* ⟨Homebrew. Moly.⟩   *S* ⟨:truffles⟩ *505:6 and elsewhere*

Elpenor. Virg. 6.107

S ⟨goddess of fauves⟩

B ⟨porcupine⟩ *Cf. 48:20–21*

S ⟨House beyond marsh: woman singing.⟩

115   they pass winter ?there: ?warm in Maremma:

B ⟨Feronia⟩. Bene meriti *B* ⟨servi sedeant, liberi surgant⟩

B ⟨Freeman⟩ *474:24?*

R ⟨Shaven heads of slaves:⟩ *B* ⟨biscuits caps⟩

B ⟨Equine faces⟩ *5:16, 40:40* *R* ⟨snouts⟩ *442:16, 463:25* *B* ⟨Edw. VII.

120   Mason. ?Peka, perfect⟩ *575:10ff.*

Moly (met—salt)   *B* ⟨?peau⟩ *83:35?, 747:17?*

B ⟨Rings candies⟩ *Cf. 199:7*

B ⟨Tiresias, hermaphrodite⟩, saw Minerva at bath . . ?jealousy of gods, ?feud, judge between Juno & Jove   (Helios)

125 Golden rain: Jove fucked Alcmene as Amphitryon for 3 long days
    when he came she knew. Tiresias revealed last mortal
    fucked by Jove. Amph.   burned her   Jove sent rain
    dies in Thebes, Jove send Hermes to bring to Elys.
    Hermes put stones in coffin. Herocleades couldn't carry

RIGHT MARGIN VERTICAL TOP

130 *B* ⟨boa over back of chair catterpillar⟩ *493:6–8*
Malthus in Irel. food decreases arithm
    population incre geometrically
B ⟨Jimmy Pidgeon⟩ *509:21*
B ⟨Shortall⟩ *509:20*

135 *S* ⟨Mrs Mack or Mrs Cohen, 85 Tyrone Street⟩ *713:38*
B ⟨Er kehrt zum Vater wenn er die Erbsünde vermeint.⟩
        R ⟨fag⟩ *500:4, 603:40*
B ⟨whore's silk politics⟩ *515:31–32?* *B* ⟨Sixth of Edward⟩ *572:7*
B ⟨Corporal Punishment⟩ *323:9*   Longshanks

140 *R* ⟨Hai! Hoop!⟩ *557:25*
R ⟨Tommy Tittlemouse⟩ *489:28*
B ⟨maidenhead⟩ *424:20, 434:10*
S ⟨sicksweet weed⟩ *444:32*
B ⟨bogus⟩ *453:15, 501:33*

145 *B* ⟨hoax⟩ *501:32*
B ⟨enema⟩ *538:9*
S ⟨glauber salts⟩ *442:28*
harebrained
G ⟨came from a hot place⟩ *538:30*

150 *B* ⟨what you can't … ?scene⟩
S ⟨birdseye fags⟩ *444:31*
R ⟨knows more than   you've forgotten⟩ *494:24–25*
B ⟨bluecaps⟩ *509:21*   *B* ⟨(D. Fusiliers)⟩ *581:1*
R ⟨bitched ?on funeral⟩ *632:8*

155 *R* ⟨SD tells whore of Antisthenes⟩ *512:1–2*

fresh beef
B ⟨bilgewater⟩ *623:7*
B ⟨Circe's Knot⟩ *517:18–20?*

RIGHT MARGIN VERTICAL LOWER

B ⟨Old sailor after each death, sighs, ay, ay.⟩ *616:8–9*
160   B ⟨East wind bad that comes from England⟩
R ⟨Sinbad the Sailor⟩ *722:8*
Iron ?rare   R ⟨Man with braces down twotailed ape⟩ *491:25–26*
R ⟨Flash woman⟩ *434:23?*   S ⟨Fuck dressed ?beast   in ?furs⟩ *458:8–10?*
B ⟨wet dreams⟩ *444:28*   R ⟨Glory Alice!⟩ *437:4*
165   B ⟨Gadarene swine⟩ *564:11*
         oceanus
      |Helios = Pérse|
(witch) Circe & Aetes (wizard)
S ⟨Stop that & begin worse⟩ *489:28*
170   B ⟨Wait till I tell you⟩
R ⟨You're killing⟩ *437:4?*

NOTES

    "Circe" 3 is one of the most illegible of the notesheets; the colored deletion lines are heavy, and the material is difficult. Some of the material was copied out of *Ulysses* notebook VIII.A.5 at Buffalo. Phrases repeated on "Oxen" 6 are:

"Circe" 3	*"Oxen" 6*		*"Circe" 3*	*"Oxen" 6*
Line 85	Line 12; cf. "Eumaeus" 7:75		Line 87	Line 45
86	13; cf. "Cyclops" 2:14		107	36

Phrases repeated on "Oxen" 8 are:

"Circe" 3	*"Oxen" 8*		*"Circe" 3*	*"Oxen" 8*
Line 76	Line 60		Lines 81 & 148	Line 32
77	83		82	28
78	87		83	30 (note)
79	105		84	27 (note)
80	33		91–92	61

Lines 1–2   Through the treachery of his wife *Eriphyle*, *Amphiaraos* (or Amphiaraus) joined the expedition of the Seven against Thebes and met his death. Joyce's summary here is from notebook VIII.A.5 (p. 310), originally taken from Roscher, I, 1337.

3   *Anticleia* (Anticlea) gave birth to Odysseus on a hill during a shower. By one account the father of Odysseus was *Sisiphus* (Sisyphus), who was also known for his craftiness. Joyce's summary here is from notebook VIII.A.5 (p. 309) and Roscher, I, 374.

4   *Minnie Hauk*: see "Circe" 1:28 and note.

9   *Eannas*: in Irish, *eannaċ* means "tissue, mantle or shirt." This may be related to the time when Stephen rips his coat leaving Bella Cohen's house (*U* 569:2).

21   *Jonathan Hogg*: probably a fictitious name suggesting Circe's transformation of Odysseus's men into swine.

24   *Milly lupanars* (*sic*): in Latin *lupinar* means "she-wolf"; in English it means "brothel." The phrase is repeated at "Eumaeus" 7:74.

25   *Tomb of Agamemnon*: mentioned at the beginning of the final book of the *Odyssey*.

35   The worship of *Shakti* (Sakti) is prevalent in northeast Bengal and Assam. She represents the principal of female energy. *Siva*: "the third god of the Hindu trinity or the third phase of Brahma's energy . . . . He is the god of arts and knowledge as well as of dancing and gaiety. He has four hands and three eyes, one of which has the power to kill . . . he holds various weapons in his hands . . . a trident, a thunderbolt, a bow and arrow, a club, an axe, a sword and a discus" (Herbert S. Robinson and Knox Wilson, *Myths and Legends of All Nations* [1950; rpt. New York, 1961], p. 53).

36   *Yoghin*: one who practices yoga.

37   *?Pyth*: this word is obscure, but it appears that Joyce superimposed the *y* over an *l*.

40   See "Cyclops" 2:5–6 note.

43   See "Cyclops" 2:17 and note.

44   See "Cyclops" 2:23 and note.

45   Repeated at "Cyclops" 2:42.

49   Repeated at "Cyclops" 7:20.

51   *Mount of thumb*: a term in palmistry. See *U* 547:7ff.

59   See "Nausicaa" 1:25 and note.

60   An echo from the "Marthens Garten" scene of Goethe's *Faust*.

61–63   Repeated at "Nausicaa" 3:44–46.

64   *Tansy, pennyroyal*: see "Cyclops" 3:25 and note.

66   *Devil & witches lefthanded*: repeated at "Nausicaa" 3:70.

68   *?Chacone* (*?Durard*): see "Nausicaa" 1:24 and note.

69   *Molly will change furniture*: repeated at "Nausicaa" 2:98; cf. "Nausicaa" 1:7.

70   *Non corrosive . . .* (*hell*): repeated at "Oxen" 11:26.

73–75   See "Oxen" 5:72–73 and note.

89   *Lock hospital*: repeated at "Oxen" 4:111.

90   Repeated at "Oxen" 1:58.

91   *Love's . . . song*: repeated at "Oxen" 16:10.

93   *6 medicals*: repeated at "Oxen" 19:61.

94   Repeated at "Oxen" 19:63.

98   *Eurylochus*: see "Circe" 2:33 and note. The phrase appears in notebook VIII.A.5 (p. 295) and in Bérard, II, 15, 365.

99   *Renitènte alla leva*: Italian for "defaulter"; it seems to refer to Ireland.

100   The essence of lines 100–121 was copied from notebook VIII.A.5 (pp. 302–304) and originally from Bérard. In Bérard, the Circe section bears the title "L'Épervière," literally "sparrowhawk" (II, 261). *Sun of living. Sun of dead*: see Bérard, II, 263. Cf. also "Circe" 7:45 and 11:39.

102   Egyptians believed that heaven rested on four pillars supported by the Earth, viewed as a parallel plane beneath heaven. The wind-gods in this line each dominated one of the four corners of the Earth. In notebook VIII.A.5 (p. 302) Joyce drew a diagram to illustrate this belief, described in Bérard (II, 261–262).

103–104   These lines are from notebook VIII.A.5 (p. 303) and Bérard, II, 263: "Ra symbolisait le soleil au printemps et avant son lever; Harma-Khouiti était le soleil de l'été et du matin; Atoumou, le soleil de l'automne et de l'après midi; Khopri, le soleil de l'hiver et de la nuit."

105–106   This is from the parable of the prodigal son, probably from notebook VIII.A.5 (p. 303) and the Wycliffe version of this parable in Peacock, p. 6.

107–109   From notebook VIII.A.5 (p. 303) and Bérard, II, 274–276. *Suessa Pometia*: a town in Latium subjugated by Lucius Tarquinius Superbus (534–510 B.C.). Gilbert (p. 318) says *Suessa* means "pigtown."

110   *Moly*: Bérard, II, 279, 288. See also "Circe" 2:3 and note.

111   Bérard, II, 279. See also "Circe" 2:45–49 and note.

112   *Goddess of fauves*: Feronia/Circe, the goddess of wild beasts (Bérard, II, 279: "déesse des fauves").

113   *Ibid.*, 284.

114   *Ibid.*, 285.

115   *Ibid.*, 283–284. *Maremma*: a low-lying district in Italy on the Tyrrhenian coast.

116–117   *Ibid.*, 286. *Bene . . . surgant*: *Feronia* liberated slaves by pronouncing this formula (or Circe, wild beasts).

118   *Ibid.*, 287.

119–120   *Ibid.*, 286?. *Equine faces*: from notebook VIII.A.5 (p. 304).

121   *Moly*: see line 110 above, "Circe" 2:3 and note, and notebook VIII.A.5 (p. 304).

122   From notebook VIII.A.5 (p. 305) and Thomas Otway's *The Souldiers Fortune*, V, 592.

123–124   From notebook VIII.A.5 (p. 308) and Roscher, V, 182. *Tiresias* is repeated at "Circe" 4:86 and 10:19. See also *Odyssey*, p. 169; Gilbert, p. 173; Ellmann, pp. 439, 504.

125–129   From notebook VIII.A.5 (p. 309) and Roscher, I, 246–248. *Stones in coffins*: see "Eumaeus" 7:67 and *U* 633:15, where Skin-the-Goat, believing that Parnell is still alive and in hiding somewhere, asserts, "The coffin they brought over was full of stones." See also *U* 111:21–22, 163:8–9, and "Eumaeus" essay, p. 52.

130   *Catterpillar*: Joyce's misspelling.

131   Thomas Robert *Malthus*: the famous English economist (1766–1834), the author of an *Essay on the Principle of Population*, published anonymously.

135   *Mrs Mack*: a notorious Dublin madam, described in Ulick O'Connor (p. 55). In *Ulysses* her address is 82 Tyrone Street.

136   *Er . . . vermeint.*: Joyce's German was not good during this period; this phrase is garbled, but the sense of it is "he turns to his father when he ?supposes the original sin."

155   See "Oxen" 8:120 and note.

167–168   *Helios* (Helius) and *Pérse* (Persa): the parents of *Circe*. *Aetes* (Aeëtes): her brother. The fork under *Helios* = *Pérse* indicates this genealogical relationship.

"Circe" 4

LEFT MARGIN TOP VERTICAL

B ⟨deportment⟩ *560:34*   B ⟨shifting center of gravity⟩ *574:19*

B ⟨?Lung air port for locomot.⟩ *510:7?*   play of muscles and bones

every man anat. except   Atta Troll

    acrobats heart disease   B ⟨fandango saraband⟩ *563:26*

B ⟨cobbler's chest⟩ *455:9*   B ⟨?Ines, dance,⟩   R ⟨dagger in heart⟩ *584:23?*

baker's leg   R ⟨evening hours⟩   B ⟨clown⟩ *565:2*

muscular seldom healthy cf. Greek statues   B ⟨lice dance⟩ *564:21*

B ⟨fragende Frau⟩ *547:10*   B ⟨7 veils⟩ *562:10?*

B ⟨hangende hunger⟩ *547:9*   B ⟨transformation scene⟩ *519:12ff.*

Day & Night   R ⟨forest glade⟩ *492:1?*

Man & Woman   B ⟨Morris:⟩ *491:34*   witches

B ⟨people are queer⟩   R ⟨500 muscles⟩

B ⟨?changes smile⟩   B ⟨fairies dress bull⟩

B ⟨cuckoo⟩ *461:8–10*   B ⟨machines supplant⟩

B ⟨glib p. .ol⟩   B ⟨muscles to free thought⟩

B ⟨it is bad art⟩ *451:9*   B ⟨mouth shut dances⟩ *563:23*

             nose filter

             race downhill

             B ⟨looking forward with eager antici.⟩

             R ⟨impetiginous sores⟩

LEFT MARGIN BOTTOM VERTICAL

R ⟨poetry of motion⟩ *560:32*

?Jig: warlike: relig (jews) esth (Gr)   B ⟨balloon⟩ *496:6*

286

B ⟨limbs escape from reign of brain⟩ *563?*   B ⟨tripundium⟩ *559:28*

B ⟨pressure soil & foot: bowels leap⟩ *563:26–27*   G ⟨who is this?⟩ *565:12*

25   B ⟨?tired ?brats flopping bubbe: races⟩ *564:7ff.*

B ⟨eye spots 1 spot & off jump⟩ *564:20*

rivalry: difficulty overcome

man: then woman going

B ⟨You may touch my, O but lightly⟩ *561:20–25*

30   hands, breast,   B ⟨can't walk⟩ *562:20?*   to place

light, dress, scents

pavement dance,   B ⟨clap⟩ *492:25 and elsewhere*

R ⟨more power⟩

B ⟨think of mother's people⟩ *564:4*

35   B ⟨hear dance you must⟩

B ⟨cock pigeon dance⟩

B ⟨men feather heads⟩

B ⟨m'inchino a lei, signora

signora, a lei m'inchino⟩

40   G ⟨curchycurchy⟩ *562:9–10*

B ⟨dance of death⟩ *564:6*

anthem: arcad. flower dance

?Thersichoir 9th muse

R ⟨light fantastic⟩

45   Soph. 16 nude, oiled, lyre dance pean Apollo's altar

LEFT COLUMN HORIZONTAL

G ⟨lipless⟩ *495:31*

G ⟨no whites of eyes⟩ *495:29?*   B ⟨vivisection⟩ *460:9*

short legs long body

B ⟨Cornwall case,⟩ *630:21–22*   R ⟨on all fours⟩ *519:13*

50   B ⟨foam at mouth⟩ *510:13*

B ⟨incarnation, descent of man to dog⟩ *701:22?*

B ⟨animalism / labour⟩

G ⟨try to remember past greatness⟩

R ⟨His master's voice:⟩ *465:13*   R ⟨gramophone: thinking?⟩ *494–497?*

55   *G* ⟨l'homme qui rit⟩ *496:1*

    B ⟨manufactured monsters: suck⟩

    B ⟨contortionists⟩

    changes juices of glands

    crossbreeding—what use?

60   *B* ⟨Better invent a platewasher⟩ *480:8*

    B ⟨trained animals: parrots⟩ *504:14?*

    alchemists: ?gare ?di bestie

    vaccination: hair of dog that might bite you

    R ⟨animal, night,⟩   winter   *R* ⟨(nightbeasts)⟩

65   Acquired characteristics not transmitted

    B ⟨Melon—meet & love a foreign lady & go abroad⟩ *47:42, 556:28–30*

    B ⟨Air—I flew, there was wind⟩ *557:10*

    B ⟨art of gestures⟩ *425:17?*

    B ⟨Ace of spades⟩ *438:23*

70   Crimson: live old, peaceful death

    B ⟨Ballet—⟩   *R* ⟨rheumatism⟩

    R ⟨shooting a bishop⟩ *508:33*

    B ⟨dream of contrary⟩ *557:2*

    B ⟨dream goes by contraries⟩ *557:2*

75   spades—unhappy in children

    B ⟨Flying escape danger, foes: ambition⟩ *557:10?*

    B ⟨Amor me solo⟩ *239:19*

    B ⟨Earth (moves) round Sun, oblique fall towards Hercules, diurnal

        rotation, oscillation of inclination, annual variation

80   of elipse, displacement of polar axis, (Vega was polar

        star 16000 y^{rs} & will be in 12000 years) ?mutation,

        elipse of equator poles, change of c. of gravity due to

        moon, in front she quickens, behind delays, (monthly)

        action of planets, most Saturn. change of solarterres-

85   tial c. of gravity.⟩

    R ⟨Midnight sun:⟩ *582:31*   *B* ⟨antidote: C and⟩   *R* ⟨?Tiresias⟩

    Roots grow down into earth

    B ⟨Jimmy sittin knittin in her chinashop⟩

    B ⟨Better chance of lighting if match nearer⟩ *546:11–12*

90   *R* ⟨odour of whore's slip⟩ *Cf. 490:30–491:1*   *B* ⟨agorafobia⟩

S ⟨water other in calm light⟩ *Cf. 515:6*

S ⟨lip pomade—swinefat rendered with rosewater⟩ *468:13*

S ⟨sublime to the ridiculous⟩ *503:34*

B ⟨fortunetellers more harm than good⟩ *548:26–27*

95   S ⟨anonymous letter: beware st. roller⟩ *457:11, 646:22*

B ⟨there's not to reason why⟩ *573:9*

G ⟨smooth eyebrows spittle⟩ *500:24–25*   R ⟨:rickets⟩ *Cf. 500:23 and elsewhere*

B ⟨Upright going man = reason⟩ *574:12?*

B ⟨Collapse⟩ *475:20?, 585:21?*

100   R ⟨v hiccup tie a knot on yʳ· shift & stick it back in yʳ·
        breeches⟩ *493:4–5*

G ⟨locomotor ataxy⟩ *510:7*

B ⟨will centre over ?ears back⟩

13 = death : 3 candles.

CENTER RIGHT VERTICAL

105   B ⟨jump lash belly knotted thong⟩ *446:24–25*

B ⟨lions block tackle strangling pully⟩ *446:25–26*

B ⟨redhot crowbars⟩ *446:27*

        B ⟨irons⟩   B ⟨carriage whip⟩ *446:19*

    B ⟨bucking bronchos⟩ *446:23*

110   B ⟨LB bores whore with pessimism⟩ *501:28–29?*

B ⟨Bohee Bros . . . ask⟩ *436:7?*

B ⟨spiked saddles⟩ *446:24*   B ⟨good conduct badges⟩ *447:14?*

B ⟨knockabout men⟩   B ⟨service chevrons,⟩ *447:13–14?*

B ⟨S.P.C.A.⟩ *446:11*

115   B ⟨S.P.C. ?C.⟩

RIGHT COLUMN HORIZONTAL

curvature of spine

none laughs

B ⟨pair not everywhere⟩

aping & shaping

120   R ⟨Dancer Moses⟩ *442:3*

B ⟨oxygenated water gold hair⟩ *502:4–5*

B ⟨whore man's socks⟩ *522:4*

B ⟨Fifi donc⟩

R ⟨Last Day⟩ *494:28*

125   R ⟨End of the World⟩ *496:9–10*

R ⟨It was in the paper⟩ *495:6*

Dead—you hear from living

For anyone to dream they are very handsome

B ⟨rhubarb⟩ *518:2*

130   G ⟨antlered hatrack⟩ *553:14–15*

whore's ring

B ⟨talisman⟩ *517:7–8*

R ⟨stye cure (wheatenmeal honey, nutmeg, salve, smear,
     bath)⟩ *468:13, 503:6–7*

135   R ⟨eagle eye⟩ *514:23–24*

B ⟨mad dog⟩ *445:8?*

foretell weather

B ⟨Serpentine avenue⟩ *557:4–5*

G ⟨Incantation: nonsense⟩ *477:25–27?*

140   Paolini's eyewash

B ⟨evil eye⟩ *429:7*

fennel & bee

R ⟨xrays⟩ *617:40?*

B ⟨black knot⟩ *517:18*

145   G ⟨goldring v stye⟩ *502:34?*

Bitter almonds = amethyst

B ⟨striscio⟩

B ⟨1st step⟩

B ⟨1. 2!⟩

150   passo scacciato

B ⟨LB/SD/?wt = S/T/L⟩

B ⟨palmistry⟩ *547:19*

B ⟨Legget Byrnes⟩ *560:33*

B ⟨tobacco an aphrodisiac⟩ *515:5?*

155   *R* ⟨pinch of t in wine makes drunk⟩ *604:39–40*

    B ⟨chewers deaf⟩

    B ⟨weak eyes⟩ *28:17*

    1600 Urban 8 exc. snuffers

    B ⟨potato came 130 yrs after.⟩ *469:8*

160   rlwys.

    S ⟨weak memory⟩ *483:17?*

    R ⟨ragpicker⟩ *429:15*

    sweat, blood smells alcohol

    B ⟨pianolysts⟩ *Cf. 561–563*

NOTES

Line 4 *Fandango* and *saraband*: Spanish dances.

8 *Fragende Frau*: in pencil.

11 *Morris* (from "moorish"): a vigorous English dance.

21 *Impetiginous sores*: in *FW* (189:32).

38–39 *M'inchino a lei, signora* . . . : I bow to you, madame, madame, to you I bow. This is probably from some Italian song.

43 *Thersichoir*: probably a variation of Terpsichore ("rejoicing in the dance"). Urania, not Terpsichore, is the *9th muse*.

45 *Pean* (or paean): a hymn to Apollo.

46 There is an illegible word written above *lipless*.

62 This phrase may be *gare di bestie*, "contests of animals" in Italian.

86 *Tiresias*: see "Circe" 3:123–124 and note.

90 *Agorafobia* (agoraphobia): fear of squares or of open spaces.

92 Cf. the salve of Circe (*Odyssey*, p. 166).

100 *V*: "versus"—in this case and at line 145 in the sense of "a remedy against."

107–108 *Crowbars* is written directly over *irons*, and *redhot* is at the left centered between the two words.

114 *S.P.C.A.*: The Society for the Prevention of Cruelty to Animals.

115 *S.P.C.C.*: The Society for the Prevention of Cruelty to Children.

147 *Striscio*: "I creep" or "I glide" in Italian.

150 A dance step: *passo*—step; *scacciato*—expelled, thrown out.

155 *T*: tobacco.

158 Clement VIII was pope in *1600*; *Urban* VIII did not reign until 1623. Meaning unclear.

"Circe" 5

B ⟨Purefoy swig out of your whiskey⟩
B ⟨(fleece v cold)⟩ *458:10*
B ⟨mammoth⟩ *468:8*
bear, dog, cat
5   *B* ⟨(carnivora)⟩ *446:24*
B ⟨quadrumani⟩
52   34,   11, 2, $\frac{1}{10}$m.
?12th, 8, 2 $\frac{1}{2}$, $\frac{3}{4}$, $\frac{5}{3600}$
Arab, Red Sea, Aegean
10   ice period
Descent of alpine,
Pyrr. & polar caps
(cosmic cause)
Man with beasts of ?caolrus
15   *G* ⟨Homo Primogenius (dolicocefalic ?propatic)⟩
Homo Sapiens mesaticefalo   cranio largo   triumph of intellect
B ⟨receding⟩ *495:23*
unified races
man in ice period
20   woman race link
B ⟨V. visavis⟩ *561:17, 397:30*
S ⟨Tiroirs, carré⟩ *561:14*
   S ⟨avant deux⟩ *561:14*
   S ⟨?lace ?des mains⟩ *562:25*
25   *S* ⟨balancé⟩ *561:15*
Lignes *S* ⟨saluts⟩ *562:6*

leaves her
  S ⟨chassé croisé⟩ *562:6*
  S ⟨avant huit⟩ *562:6*

30 Moulinet double chain
   <u>S ⟨3 Saluts⟩ *562:6*</u>
   M de cavaliers
1 with 2, 2 with 1
<u>Visites visit 2</u>

35   lady pass before
   double moulinet
   chaine anglaise
<u>Grande Chaine face about</u>
   3 saluts

40   Fox & Geese
   chassé croisé galop
   promenade
   S ⟨avant huit⟩ *562:6*
R ⟨tout le monde en avant reverence, t.l.m. en place⟩ *560:36–37*

45 B ⟨les cavs. avant vos dames⟩
B ⟨donnez le petit bouquet à v. dames remerciez vos dames⟩ *562:29–30*

LEFT COLUMN HORIZONTAL

Mount of Mars ⟨at side⟩ domination
B ⟨″ ″ Moon, imagination⟩ *548:20–22*
Line of Heart, Head, Life

50 If L of L broken on <u>both</u> accident
R ⟨Branches to Jove money marriage⟩ *549:5–6?*
R ⟨If crossed by line from Venus then unhappy love⟩
double L of L luck
L of Heart till under m of Mer forgiving

55 B ⟨Line of Fate influential friends⟩ *548:18*
Girdle of Venus   teagrounds
Triangle B ⟨Sentimental Mulligan⟩ *Cf. 483*
children

twice married

60   *B* ⟨Little finger short henpeck⟩ *549:10*

Will 1st. mount of thumb

B ⟨Face, record of past⟩

B ⟨Head front human, back animal⟩

B ⟨children go by faces⟩

65   *B* ⟨My face is me⟩

head wide over ears anger

Head high veneration

Sanguine (Mars & Jupiter): red: curly hair:

lymphatic (moon & Venus): pale: ash hair: fairness

70   melancholic Saturn: velvety skin: heavy hair:

bilious (sun & Mercury): sallow: lank black hair

face is transparent

B ⟨Wrinkles: 1. Saturn, 2. Jupiter, 3 Mars,⟩

over r. brow sun, over left moon, between

75   brows Venus, Mercury on bridge of nose

B ⟨prudence   volupcy   courage⟩ *Cf. 547:15–16*

Mercury on bridge,   3 wit; 4 deceit

arched foreheads artistic, project eyebrows research

B ⟨No wrinkles, no wit⟩ *547:15*

80   Inter brows wrinkles if short & = anger, not, thought

Knit the brows, far apart openhearted, meeting

        jealous, delicate gentle, lighter than hair weakness

nose length of forehead

—   width length of eye

85   *B* ⟨button nose,⟩   *B* ⟨?snub,⟩ *553:29*   *B* ⟨carnivorous teeth⟩

B ⟨Laughter   A (frank)   E (?enclose)   I (weak)   O (bold)   U (misanthrop.)⟩

B ⟨her risibles, giggle,⟩ *549:27*   *G* ⟨chuckling, chortled⟩ *436:21–22*

B ⟨Loud laugh that speaks the vacant mind.⟩ *553:17–18*

B ⟨odd laughs infectious,⟩   *G* ⟨laundered,⟩ *498:31*   *R* ⟨bedraggled⟩ *47:23*

90   *B* ⟨Handshake⟩ *575:26?*

R ⟨slinking,⟩ *425:13*   glide, slide, prance,   *B* ⟨waddle,⟩ *549:16*   *S* ⟨stumble⟩

graceful carriage, awkwardness (O o U ?Bliz), flare   *558:30, 434:18*

        of skirt up, antics, andrewmartin,   *B* ⟨jerk,⟩ *450:5?*

G ⟨kangaroo hop,⟩ *495:30*   straighthaired rule earth,

95 shapely, long foot diplomacy,   *B* ⟨heartless flirt,⟩ *448:24*
pillar throat long life, short toes & high instep
R ⟨luxury⟩ *468:7*   *S* ⟨hazle eyes⟩ *321:16*
spaewife, shuffle, cut with left, wish a wish, which
Kings, 9 in a row, read cards round Queen
100 Queen his lover, knave his thoughts, read every
7ᵗʰ· from lefthand, top ?dominoes
parasol. handle shoulder = indiff.
"   high = daring
drop to right = lean on you
105 shut = dare all
carried = love
ferule = could beat you
2 hands = well?
beat toes = hate

UPPER RIGHT COLUMN HORIZONTAL

110   Ace of ♢ letter
9   of ♡ wish
Q   of ♢ coquette
G ⟨(fond of what she likes)⟩ *513:35*
7   of ♢ gambler
115   4   of " vexation
Ace of ♠ love, ?rev. death
K   of ♠ ambition, ...
9 of " worst
(deuce)   2 of ♠ coffin
120   Ace of ♣ wealth
K   of ♣ upright
10   " " fortune, friend die
8   " " miser

B ⟨(C.K.)⟩ *588:1ff.*
125 *B* ⟨lacklustre⟩ *590:17*
B ⟨chalked circle⟩ *549:12*

LOWER RIGHT COLUMN HORIZONTAL

umbrellas

over woman, he dripping = courtship

- - -   she   —   = marriage

130   swing umbrella over hand = I am a nuisance

short nails devil to argue

G ⟨fan-flirt quick engaged⟩

R ⟨   "   slow married⟩ *515:26–27*

open & shut wish to speak

135   open wide   wait me

R ⟨place on r. ear = forgot me?⟩ *516:4–5*

twirl in l. hand = we watched   *Cf. 517:13–14*

draw over eyes = sorry

handle on lips = kiss me

NOTES

Much of "Circe" 5 has been discussed in my corrections of Norman Silverstein's article in the *James Joyce Quarterly*, II (Spring 1965), 218–221. See also the essay on "Circe" above, especially on palmistry (pp. 43–48). In the upper left-hand corner is a large *C* in slate pencil.

Line 6   *Quadrumani*: Italian for "quadrumanes," or "primates."

25   Repeated at "Circe" 6:80.

47   The following section concerns palmistry.

50   *L of L*: line of life.

54   *M of Mer*: Mount of Mercury.

74–75   These lines are scratched out in ink.

93   *Andrewmartin*: in *FW* 392:3.

98   *Spaewife*: chiefly Scottish, meaning "witch" or "female fortune-teller."

102–109   Joyce was interested in language as gesture, and these lines give the language of the *parasol*. See also the essay on "Cyclops" above (pp. 19–20) and "Cyclops" 1 for the secret gestures of the "Ribbonmen"; lines 127–130 below for the language of *umbrellas*; lines 132–139 for the language of the *fan*; and "Circe" 8:134–143 for handkerchief language. Cf. *U* 425–426.

110–123   This section deals with fortune-telling by playing cards, which is mentioned in a letter of November 6, 1921, to Budgen (*Letters*, I, 177). Although *Ulysses* was finished, Joyce asked Budgen to send him "any little handbook of fortune-telling by cards."

124–125   *C.K.*: Corny Kelleher. In *U* 590:17 he appears to be dead as he "leers with lacklustre eye."

"Circe" 6

Birth SD Acquarius
(Dublin) Castles in the air
G ⟨Someone in house with Dina⟩ *436:17–20*
B ⟨Rebecca Cohen⟩ *713:38?* (blue, yellow, l.) *477:5?*
5   Maidens (30)   take your due, her garters
B ⟨witch 3 tears only & left eye⟩ *486:17–18*
crooked 6ᵈ· or hole luck
G ⟨the missus is master⟩ *515:31*
hawthorn, ?shaking grass, bad
10   B ⟨4 leaved shamrock⟩ *305:10–11*
B ⟨loves me, loves me not⟩ *490:24*
R ⟨fairies eat daisyroot⟩ *538:3–4?*
R ⟨rosemary strengthens memory⟩ *503:19*
applepeels Hallow eve
15   G ⟨worldly goods I thee and thou.⟩ *434:28*
old new borrowed blue
G ⟨change name & not letter⟩
B ⟨La belle dame sans merci⟩ *426:6*
R ⟨prof. Maghinni⟩ *560–562*
20   B ⟨Jesus, S of Pantherus & parfumeuse⟩ *510:15*
fille d'Israel qui se donna aux porcs
B ⟨castration⟩ *460:9*
antagonistic muscles
B ⟨scratching⟩ *513:7 and elsewhere*
25   G ⟨clean with spittle⟩ *500:24–25?*
R ⟨quel homme ?juste, hien?⟩

297

motor nerve fibres ?endplates

in ?largers of vol. muscle

invol. net of plexuses

30   *R* ⟨lockjaw, ?grip⟩ *431:8*

consciousness secreted by brain

B ⟨left weight call for more effort⟩ *445:17*

deafmutes not sick (Erin's King)

B ⟨speech brain centre left only⟩

35   *B* ⟨kithogue⟩ *422:19*   right   *B* ⟨lefthander⟩ *422:21*

writes muscle left ?ameboid

gesture right speech

B ⟨animals hear extra notes⟩

B ⟨visual loss loss balance⟩ *564:20*

40   incline head L to R causes endolymph

        to press   R hair cells

divide horizontal canal head wags

    -- vertical   *B* ⟨somersaults:⟩ *495:24*   squints

B ⟨SD whirled round (blind)⟩ *564:19–20*

45   *B* ⟨dancing letters midges⟩ *564:21*

B ⟨Stop seen going other way⟩ *564:19–20*   fluid rebound

G ⟨thumb in vest,⟩ *455:13 & 17?*   Indian ?clubs,

wrist up, over, forearm in swing twist

carry square shoulders   Mrs Kane

50   *B* ⟨Cunningham in mirror W.S.⟩ *554:18–19*   *R* ⟨akimbo⟩ *512:30, 516:9*

seguidilla half distances   fandango

tableau, seizes ?Sevile 2 hold same cloth

B ⟨hornpipe,⟩ *564:9*   ropes,   *B* ⟨arms folded⟩ *514:22*

CENTER AND RIGHT COLUMNS HORIZONTAL

                                1st. m like vulva

55   *B* ⟨eleph. bull to knees⟩ *432:30–31?*

                                scrotum other colour

                                Roman wives prefer eunuchs

                                ?guest fat, poppe

R ⟨She is some president⟩

60 grab   table rapping   R ⟨call her up by sunphones⟩ *497:20–21*

B ⟨crystal gazing⟩ *467:25–26*   B ⟨flesh pink⟩

psychometry   R ⟨up to you⟩ *497:8*

R ⟨Something Within⟩ *497:10–11*   R ⟨a God or a clod⟩ *497:6*

R ⟨cosmic forces⟩ *497:9*   R ⟨Just one more word⟩ *497:5*

65 R ⟨harmonial philosophy⟩ *497:19*   R ⟨in this vibration⟩ *497:12*

B ⟨Sex secrets⟩ *508:19*   R ⟨It is immense⟩ *497:16*

Letters vibrate   light & hue   R ⟨joking apart⟩ *497:18*

G ⟨hermetic science⟩

G ⟨petticoat government⟩ *515:31–32*

70 B ⟨mother took the strap to you⟩ *435:5–6*

G ⟨on the job:⟩ ?hug: R ⟨prism (be a):⟩ *497:10*

conscious = phys. resistance   R ⟨Rite poet's rest⟩ *493:13*

?pure sensation impossible, memory   B ⟨whores bad conductors⟩

(sub)liminal consciousness   R ⟨a pig's whisper⟩ *504:10*

75 levels of association   B ⟨mockery of it⟩ *565:15*

S ⟨daggered hair⟩ *562:9*   — patriot of solar system

omne animal triste praeter gallum   R ⟨identify⟩ *448:17?*

B ⟨capillary attraction⟩ *536:25*   S ⟨what can it all mean?⟩

R ⟨embrace all women⟩   B ⟨chain purse⟩ *492:5*

80 R ⟨epil. cry⟩ *519:13*   quadrille: pantalon: S ⟨balancé⟩ *561:15*

R ⟨a year to study religious problem⟩ *503:32*   ch. anglaise dedans

B ⟨Agamemnon du ciel⟩   Été S ⟨traversé⟩ *562:6*   Poule, cav. seul

B ⟨Anthony says creed⟩   B ⟨Changez de dames⟩ *562:29*

homme squelette géant   S ⟨Les Ronds⟩ *562:24*   S ⟨dos à dos⟩ *562:16*

85   — enclume B ⟨nane⟩ *Cf. 558:26*

B ⟨—   caoutchouc⟩ *556:8*

    — electrique

B ⟨femme colone, à barbe⟩

B ⟨chevaux de bois (leap forward to other dame)⟩ *562:24*

90   S ⟨les ponts, escargots, boulangère, corbeille⟩ *562:24 & 16*

B ⟨dansez avec vos dames.⟩ *562:29*   B ⟨cotillion presents⟩

viole mobile parete B ⟨ventaglio, dadi⟩

G ⟨blindman's buff 'who is it'?⟩ *437:12?*   man & man

throw   wipe, B ⟨cuscino⟩ B ⟨fiori, ?pegni, cantoni⟩

95 *B* ⟨specchio, heads same way⟩ *B* ⟨Kinch & Lynch⟩ *543:1*
echoes, *B* ⟨zigzag,⟩ *513:17, 571:8* *B* ⟨aprons,⟩ *462:30, 575:16*
separate, *B* ⟨catch⟩
B ⟨ball, fanfara, minuet cipria,⟩ *560:33–35, 562:2*
B ⟨languid eye, laughing mouth, waspwaist,⟩ *561:9–11, 562:2*
100 *B* ⟨innocent hands, ambitious feet⟩ *561:9*
B ⟨motion weaves net⟩ *562:17–18*
B ⟨lift arms,⟩ *561:12* jeté, highland fling
R ⟨beat thighs⟩ *B* ⟨beat hands⟩ point, pavan
precision of men, grace of women

UPPER RIGHT COLUMN HORIZONTAL

105 allium redyellow flower
allium niger aphros.
no-one, Bloom, has ever
B ⟨are you describing T. ?F.⟩
B ⟨Precisely⟩ *573:28, 618:35*
110 *S* ⟨skiprope⟩ *561:10*
B ⟨marionette (Little Milly)⟩ *440:26*
R ⟨Lynch whinny⟩ *494:21*
B ⟨dislike seen with women⟩ *435:24ff?*
R ⟨whetstones⟩ *493:29–30*
115 *B* ⟨dislike bottle,⟩ *543:30*
G ⟨shut eye to disloyalty⟩ *493:29*
growing pain
R ⟨Conservio lies captured⟩ *512:24*
R ⟨Marcello coeli enarrant gloriam Domini,⟩ *493:14–15*
120 *R* ⟨dumped-⟩ *445:14?*
R ⟨Sultan Napoleon⟩ *514:22ff.?*

NOTES

My division of phrases between columns is rather arbitrary, and some words have been rearranged for clarity.

Line 1   *Acquarius* (Aquarius): one of the signs of the Zodiac.

6   Repeated at "Circe" 17:37.

19   *Maghinni*: changed to "Maginni" in subsequent drafts. See *U* 151:31, 217:22, and elsewhere.

20   By one tradition *Pantherus*, a Roman centurion, was the father of Jesus.

33   *Erin's King*: an excursion boat. The name is repeated at "Eumaeus" 3:141 and "Ithaca" 13:94. See Adams, pp. 86–87.

35   *Kithogue*: i.e., *ciotóg*, a "left-handed person" in Irish.

36–44   These lines refer to the motor reflexes of the brain.

51   *Seguidilla*: a dance of Seville.

58   *Poppe*: Italian for "breasts."

73   In *My Brother's Keeper* (New York, 1958), Stanislaus Joyce says his brother believed *whores* were *bad conductors* of emotion (p. 153). See also Scholes and Kain, p. 97.

76   *Patriot*: repeated at "Cyclops" 8:63 and "Oxen" 7:88.

77   *Omne . . . gallum*: every animal is sad after copulation except the rooster. In Laurence Sterne, *The Life and Opinions of Tristram Shandy* (1760; rpt. New York: Signet ed., 1960), p. 324, this saying is attributed to Aristotle.

80   *Balancé*: repeated at "Circe" 5:25.

84–98   Translations for some of the less obvious French and Italian words are:

squelette: skeleton	*viole*: violet, violas	*dadi*: dice	*cantoni*: corners
enclume: anvil	*mòbile*: furniture	*cuscino*: cushion	*spècchio*: mirror
nane: dwarf	*parete*: wall	*fiori*: flowers	*cipria*: toilet powder
caoutchouc: india rubber	*ventaglio*: fan	*pegni*: pledges	

105–106   "B.[*sic*] Bérard sees in 'moly' the 'atriplex halimus' [appears in *Ulysses* notebook VIII.A.5 at Buffalo (p. 304)], a yellow-flowering shrub. . . . Another view is that garlic is meant" (Gilbert, p. 317n). Joyce "consulted by mail his old friend the Baroness St. Leger, and she suggested that Moly was *allium niger—garlic*, an interpretation homely enough to interest him" (Ellmann, p. 511). See also "Circe" 2:3 note and "Circe" 7:23.

118   Cf. Scholes and Kain, p. 104.

119   *Marcello . . . Domini*: The heavens relate the glory of the lord to Marcellus.

"Circe" 7

LEFT MARGIN HORIZONTAL

B ⟨pelt⟩ *551:21, 571:6*
R ⟨Ben Dollard beats thigh⟩ *511:4*
B ⟨face towards sky⟩ *573:25*
B ⟨face toward earth⟩
5   MB's angle askew ?finds LB   B ⟨Shits   breeches⟩ *428:18*
R ⟨bites his ear⟩ *468:19*
?sinking bed
B ⟨Rawhead & Bloody Bones⟩ *168:35*
Waxworks horrors
10   riding stick broom
B ⟨Kitty ?stands⟩
B ⟨tacher soleil⟩
B ⟨?promiscuous ?pronouns⟩
R ⟨see y$^{r.}$ back view⟩ *501:3*
15   Unisexual dance
     ?leave
Bisexual ?dances
      ?say
B ⟨naked⟩ *480:25 and elsewhere*
20   B ⟨rhododendrons⟩ *537:8*
B ⟨Garrett Deasy, ?shirtsleeves⟩ *558*
B ⟨mutton broth, racer⟩ *559:5*

LEFT COLUMN HORIZONTAL

garlic Mars, red, Saturn
?Diseas 7 + 14 = 28 days

302

25   worms, scurvy, hysteria,   *B* ⟨dropsy⟩ *335:36?*
     Mercury, lavender, valerian, mandrake
     liquorice, fennel, parsley, horehound
     elecampane
     Circe draws Sun from ?herd
30   *B* ⟨makes ?young changes Faunus to Pico.⟩
     Scylla to monster,   *B* ⟨purifies Jason after murder⟩
     aunt of Medea,
     Arete., ?K   Colchis, Telegonus?
     Sphinx
35   Egypt. head feet profile, bust full, ¾ never
     sounding ?Memnon
     bust, head, pathos; legs, joy;
     contract tempo forte
     relax   ″   debole
40   direction of motions melodic line
     ?Demenes, ?Soudaz
     not abdomen & back
     R ⟨3 Legs of Man⟩ *496:23–24*
     R ⟨Heaven becomes a back number⟩ *497:14*
45   *B* ⟨Ra (Phra) sparrowhawk⟩ *141:11*
     B ⟨Pthah—dungbeetle⟩
     Apis—ox   *B* ⟨leapfrog⟩ *432:31*
     Pasht—cat   *B* ⟨shark⟩ *564:11*
     B ⟨Toth—ibis,⟩ *Cf. 191:27*   dogmonkey
50   *B* ⟨Hathor—white cow⟩
     B ⟨a striding bird⟩ *539:3*
     B ⟨camel ?hump⟩ *646:37–38?*
     B ⟨retain his perpendicular⟩ *574:14*
     camel dung for clay walls
55   *B* ⟨rock to and fro⟩ *512:30, 579:31*
     G ⟨dervish (howl, dance, wander)⟩ *496:2*
     B ⟨Old Irel. bag eggs   SD v Carr⟩
     B ⟨LB son. I suppose so.⟩
     B ⟨warm seat—Ware Sitting Bull⟩ *539:4*
60   *B* ⟨SD's mother drag him to hell⟩ *566–567*

B ⟨Don Juan⟩ *458:28*

SD—words of eternal life

B ⟨to all the more influence⟩ *647:37*

B ⟨it is perhaps ?here   retrospect⟩

65   B ⟨turtle⟩ *521:8, 533:10*   hurdles, cycles

B ⟨old gummy granny⟩ *579:24 & 30*

B ⟨Staggering Bob⟩ *537:3*

B ⟨tampered with⟩ *455:30*   B ⟨plop⟩ *551:19*

B ⟨carapace⟩ *465:23*   B ⟨strut⟩ *500:26*

70   vintage dance   B ⟨sidle⟩ *429:19, 549:16*

B ⟨palsy, S. Vitus.⟩ *422:16–12*   B ⟨to ?gore⟩ *439:25*

                                B ⟨bathing⟩ *480:21, 510:23*

CENTER AND RIGHT COLUMNS HORIZONTAL

styx babe   B ⟨fall of man⟩

Persephone soul   B ⟨?orders (Major now)⟩⟩ *581 & 585?*

75   B ⟨head averted⟩ *570:24?*   B ⟨slightly passée⟩ *541:4*

Hermes, S of Maia, babe   B ⟨shot his bolt⟩ *529:10*

1st day robs Apollo's cows, troop   B ⟨?spunk⟩ *541:15*

Ul   ‾‾ back, Iris (Il)   Flies sticky wax of antennae to stick

He (?Od) ?wind   herald

80   Guide, to & from Hereafter

B ⟨wakes souls with caduceus⟩

B ⟨stick 2 serpents,⟩   god of dreams (nightcap) speed

gymn. eloqu sacrif. tongue

B ⟨Trismegistos⟩ *499:22–23*   streets, crossways

85   R ⟨fingerposts⟩ *429:21*   R ⟨⟨?erme⟩⟩   B ⟨travellers⟩

commerce, B ⟨thieves,⟩ ?good   R ⟨?nunnery⟩

shepherd crioforo

Nile swine trample weeds after flood

Kitty Ricketts heart disease

90   B ⟨Corn. Kell. business card sober drivers speciality⟩ *590:31*

B ⟨Sir H. Rumbold⟩ *462–463, 578*

B ⟨jujube of women⟩ *Cf. 575:15*   B ⟨haddock fingermark of God⟩ *548:10–11*

Stork (Purefoy)   silkworm
B ⟨crowd acclaims LB⟩ *476:22?* spider, beetle
95   calling loftily   peacock eyes
B ⟨Handy Andy⟩ *518:8*   B ⟨?sign stripes⟩ *459:20*
B ⟨Leopopold.⟩ *466:9*   tortoise   B ⟨moulting⟩ *511:10*
Mirror with words on it   B ⟨branded sheep⟩ *453:19–20*
B ⟨bellhorses⟩ *564:10*   B ⟨divine origin⟩ *485:2–4?*
100 marionettes adit   B ⟨rostrum⟩ *496:31*
shakes water out of ears?   B ⟨a mare's nest⟩ *449:2*
B ⟨SD begins long sentence & forgets start⟩ *494:2ff.*
B ⟨?car to ground⟩   animals & fools
B ⟨Jackals at Bourse⟩   B ⟨blushingly⟩ *486:17?*
105 B ⟨eternity junction⟩ *497:5*
B ⟨watching brief⟩
B ⟨dragging me along⟩ *554:12*
B ⟨LB fell out of bed⟩ *534:1–2*
B ⟨elicited the information⟩ *457:31*   B ⟨do him in⟩
110 B ⟨stop thief⟩ *458:2*   B ⟨charm = Moly (narrow ?shawl)⟩
impresario to engage criminal
B ⟨dandered⟩ *598:6*   pigeon lofts, fancies
B ⟨to ?pass a stag⟩
B ⟨hypnotism & lies⟩
115 B ⟨black sheep⟩ *453:19–20*
B ⟨Ossian 1 day = 20 years⟩
B ⟨Horn of bull, hoof of horse, smile of Saxon⟩ *24:29*

NOTES

Line 12   *Tacher soleil*: to stain the sun.

23   *Garlic*: see "Circe" 6:105–106 note.

27   *Parsley*: repeated at "Circe" 1:7.

30   *Faunus*: "the Latin Pan, . . . the son of Picus ('woodpecker'), whom Circe turned into a woodpecker for spurning her love" (Graves, I, 193).

31   Glaucus courted *Scylla* and was refused. He then sought a love potion from Circe, but the

latter fell in love with him herself. Circe then prepared a poison for Scylla and poured it into her bath. This changed Scylla into a horrible *monster*.

32–33   These lines probably concern the return of the Argonauts to Greece (see Appllonius Rhodius). They were chased by the Colchians (from *Colchis*, a kingdom on the Black Sea) who visited King Alcinous and Queen *Arete*, demanding on Aeëtes's behalf the surrender of *Medea* (Circe was her *aunt*) and the fleece. *Telegonus*: according to some, the son of Circe by Odysseus. The Colchians also founded Pola, where Joyce went to live in 1904 (Ellmann, p. 192).

36   *Memnon*: the son of Tithonus and Eos and a king of Ethiopia.

38   *Forte*: strong.

39   *Debole*: weak.

41   These names are not identified. The first is not Demeter.

43   *3 Legs of Man*: a reference to the shield of the Isle of Man.

45   *Ra* was represented by a hawk, sacred to him, or by a man with a hawk's head. Joyce also associated the hawk with Circe (see "Circe" 11:39). See also "Circe"3:100–104 and 17:38–39 for more Egyptology. *Sparrowhawk*: repeated at "Circe" 17:38.

46   *Pthah*: known as a master workman. It was Khepera whose symbol was the dungbeetle.

47   *Apis*: the great beast god of Egypt, worshiped at Memphis.

48–50   *Pasht*, *Toth* (Thoth), and *Hathor* are accurately represented here. *Toth* (Thoth) was god of letters and thus the patron of writers.

74   *Persephone*: the queen of Hades.

76–87   *Hermes* is appropriate here since he was thought to be the inventor and source of all magic. Hermes was the son of *Maia* and Zeus. On the day he was born he stole fifty of *Apollo's* cattle, causing them to walk backwards. *Iris* (she appears in *Il*—the *Iliad*), the goddess of the rainbow, was a female messenger of the gods and thus a female counterpart of Hermes. Hermes guides the dead to Hades. His wand is the *caduceus*, which has *2 serpents* wrapped around it. With Morpheus he is the *god of dreams*. He is a patron of physical culture (*gymn.*). To the Egyptians, Hermes *Trismegistos* was Toth. Hermes is honored at *crossways* as the god of roads; he is also the god of *commerce* and of good luck. Hermes spent much of his time with shepherds; *crioforo* (criophore): a statue of a man carrying a ram.

78   Joyce wrote *Ul* in the margin in pencil.

79   *Od*: the *Odyssey*.

91   An article on a British hangman vacationing in Ireland appeared in the *Weekly Freeman* for January 14, 1899. Joyce gave him the name of H. Rumbold because of a grudge against *Sir H[orace] Rumbold*, the British minister to Bern (Adams, p. 228).

93   Mrs *Purefoy* had the baby in the "Oxen" episode.

99   *Bellhorses*: also appears in Connolly, ed., *Scribbledehobble*, p. 119.

104   *Jackals at Bourse*: the Bourse is the Paris Stock Exchange; the inference is probably anti-Semitic. See *U* 35. This phrase might also suggest Anubis, the Egyptian god of the dead, who was represented by a jackal. The phrase is repeated at "Circe" 17:39.

110   *Moly*: see "Circe" 2:3 and note.

112   *Fancies*: may be *fancier*.

"Circe" 8

LEFT MARGIN VERTICAL

B ⟨litter⟩ *484:7*   *B* ⟨steer⟩ *564:7*
boars   *B* ⟨weasel⟩ *501:31*
B ⟨piglings⟩ *564:8*   *B* ⟨polecat⟩ *445:7*   *B* ⟨steer⟩ *564:7*
B ⟨dug on broad of back⟩

LEFT COLUMN HORIZONTAL

5   sturgeon type 1st fish
      cartilage spine, bony plates
      external, tail accretion,
      insects, reptiles,
      Irel. emerges part of America
10   differentiated temperature
      oyster beds
      coral goes to equator
      seppia.   *R* ⟨10 footer crabs⟩
      viviparous reptiles
15   *B* ⟨seaserpent⟩ *495:11*
      crocodile brain = 100 Brontosaurus (20 metres)
      brain smaller than medula
      flying reptiles
      de . . . .
20   (paleozoic formation)
      Monti Caledoniani
      formerly boreal & tropical continents

?Wales middle sea

B ⟨seasons (deduced now from concentric bole of trees) nonexistent⟩

25   ferns   R ⟨Zoe⟩ *466:15 and elsewhere*

diff. angle of earth axis on ecliptic

trilobite—head, chest, belly.

all eyes, roll itself

insects of imperfect metamorphosis

30   6 wings, 6 ?paws

armoured fish

B ⟨ruminants 2 horns⟩ *537:1?*

B ⟨pig⟩ *460:19 and elsewhere*   pachyderm, hipp.   B ⟨rhinoc.⟩ *526:7*   tapir.

perissodachtylic (3)   artiodact (2)

35   solipedi (horse) from perissod. pachyd.

ruminants from artiodact.

B ⟨sheep's trotters,⟩ *427:10*

B ⟨crubeens⟩ *432:18*

Rumin. no incisors in upper jaw.

40   cannot defend ∴ horns

leathery plants = teeth sharp

hoofs to flee

B ⟨sow that eats her young⟩ *579:28–29*   G ⟨corncrake⟩ *496:29*

B ⟨storming petrel⟩ *445:30*

45   feel earthquake, eruptions, epidemics

B ⟨swear by Styx⟩

B ⟨charm said backwards⟩ *584:6*

    signs of rain, bats, fly low

    animals silent when storm nigh

50   spider ceases to weave,   rain

    if good night coming weaves long threads

    In 1st rain if chicks scratch = long

?dogfear   paralyses partridge   snake

B ⟨destroy the charm,⟩   S ⟨break the spell⟩ *540:2?*

55   spider & snake draw prey

R ⟨snake milks female animals⟩ *505:15–16*

R ⟨cow goes to snake's nest⟩ *505:17–23*

B ⟨fascinated boy apes movement of snake⟩ *505:30ff.*

Pythian Apollo of Delphos   B ⟨cochon⟩

60   B ⟨basilisk⟩ *518:21*
      clap your wings and crow
      B ⟨flesh willing, spirit weak⟩ *508:2?*
      B ⟨ce sont des oignons⟩ *573:27* otter
      ?money bubbles *755:9*
65   forget teapotlid = stranger
      bubbles go to side = rain
      B ⟨Mole on throat bad (left breast)⟩ *Cf. 192:15*
            — — — —right thigh good
      B ⟨LB pretend to be jealous⟩ *490:8?*
70   B ⟨LB speak to her seriously⟩
      B ⟨3 acres & cow⟩ *480:6*
      B ⟨Amsterdam . . . .⟩ *446:28–29*

CENTER VERTICAL

      B ⟨beaverlodges⟩
      stockyard

CENTER AND RIGHT COLUMNS HORIZONTAL

75   R ⟨approach⟩ *445:22 and elsewhere*   B ⟨up guard & at them⟩ *581:13*
      R ⟨zigzag⟩ *513:17, 571:8*   B ⟨dog obeys⟩ *460:24*
      G ⟨clog⟩ *436:14*   R ⟨bitch,⟩ *434:24 and elsewhere*   totem
      seldom to back   B ⟨dogs like LB⟩ *445?*
      G ⟨breakdown⟩ *436:14*   B ⟨mad dog in Gloucester Street⟩
80   R ⟨jig⟩ *461:13?*   B ⟨dog bites tail stiff (whore)⟩ *Cf. 465:18*
      B ⟨cavalier⟩ *561:22 & 26*   Knut Hamsun ?Mysterien
      rock   G ⟨promiscuity⟩ *501:1?*
      R ⟨advance⟩ *562:1 and elsewhere*   dozes, horsenod
      figure   R ⟨stubborn as a mule⟩ *425:6*
85   fossil   R ⟨stag that one⟩ *425:6*
      cavity of form   plants can't move

309

?primary   women birds

archaic   R ⟨cocks henpecked⟩ *549:10*

fossil tree (coal)   B ⟨mon loup⟩ *556:20*

90 substitution (veins of leaves fibres in coal) catalepsy

R ⟨primitive man⟩ *496:1–2?* healthy man cheers up

B ⟨whores not persons⟩ *501:32ff.* B ⟨love me, love my dog⟩

G ⟨?Paleologo.⟩   B ⟨lick of dog good—on old

hollow bones   sore⟩ *Cf. 194:35–36, 516:30*

95 bird beaked teeth   doctors live on disease

no groppone   B ⟨hydro⟩

24 verteb in tail   B ⟨??semamitismus⟩

B ⟨marsupials no placenta, short gravidance hold in pouch⟩

emerging archipelago   MB objected Milly sleep with Mrs R *Cf. 723:5*

100 Himalaya   B ⟨scapegoat⟩ *449:3*

earthquake   B ⟨animals healthier⟩

S ⟨man's touch on piano⟩ *466:14* B ⟨cow's lick⟩ *511:15*

glaciers   do ?reins cross

temp. . . . . = 25° (now 11°) B ⟨ducky little⟩ *441:16–17*

105 B ⟨deciduous leaves⟩ *Cf. 540:7* B ⟨S. Anthony⟩

B ⟨flowering plants⟩   G ⟨epilepsy⟩ *483:11*

amber = fossil resin   R ⟨whore whip LB⟩ *Cf. 459 and elsewhere*

human pig dentition   old are young

B ⟨head over heels⟩ *496:23, 537:15* heretic catechism

110 B ⟨RB slept with dog (rheum)⟩ *516:27–30* B ⟨philtre⟩ *510:14*

B ⟨catskin⟩ *516:28* cat & child   filter

R ⟨lap dog⟩ *442:4?*

Jesus born stable h̶o̶r̶s̶e̶ ass and ox

S ⟨Molly ?riding whip,⟩ *458:23* B ⟨?jolts of horse⟩

115 horse knows

R ⟨Give the paw,⟩ *446:6*   R to R sleep R to L wake

R ⟨murderer returns wishes to be killed⟩ *374:42, 634:4–6*

murderer kills self first

R ⟨dog knows death barks⟩

120 B ⟨Walpurgisnacht⟩ *583ff.*

B ⟨deaf & dumb⟩ *582:8–9?*

B ⟨female animals ugly⟩

B ⟨keeper rubs linament leopard⟩ *446:27–28*

B ⟨Bantam game cock⟩

125   puts hounds to flight

R ⟨?volts out of hair⟩

R ⟨sovereign lord of all things⟩ *512:7*

B ⟨Jetez la gourme   que jeunesse se passe⟩ *493:20–21*

ni ?gru ni ?mince

130   emerald v impure

ruby dark at peril

sapphire priests kill spiders

diamond = courage

handk, drop = ?friends

135   both twirl = indiff

over cheek = love

over ?hand = hate

v.r. cheek = yes

″ l. cheek = no

140   twirl l. hand = riddance

     ″   r. hand = love another

fold = wish to speak

in pocket = no more at present

RIGHT MARGIN VERTICAL

ranches

145   inbred

venisons of the forest

NOTES

Line 1   *Steer*: repeated at line 3.

13   *Seppia*: "cuttle-fish" in Italian.

21   *Monti Caledoniani*: "Caledonian mountains," the mountainous region of northwest Ireland. See, for instance, A. R. Orme, *Ireland* (Chicago, 1970), p. 26.

25   *Zoe*: a prostitute in "Circe." See the essay on "Circe," pp. 43–46.

46   "For swearing falsely by Styx a god was punished by being compelled to lie breathless and speechless for a year and by being forbidden to attend the councils of the gods for nine years" (Robinson and Wilson, p. 84).

59   *Pythian Apollo of Delphos*: in Greek mythology Apollo killed a python, a huge serpent, near Delphi.

81   *Knut Hamsun*: pseudonym of Knut Pederson, Norwegian writer and Nobel Prize winner (1859–1952), author of *Mysterier* (Copenhagen, 1892). The reference here may be to a German translation of this novel: *Mysterien* (Cologne and Paris, 1894) since the first English translation was not published until 1927. Joyce owned three books by Hamsun (Ellmann, p. 794).

96   *Groppone*: "back" in Italian.

129   This is a "neither-nor" construction in Gaelic, but the meaning is not clear.

134–143   This section apparently gives the language of the handkerchief, though a fan would seem to work better for some of the gestures. See *James Joyce Quarterly*, II (Spring 1965), 220–221, and "Circe" 5:102–109 and note.

"Circe" 9

LEFT MARGIN HORIZONTAL

Isaac Laquedem
B ⟨I see Keating Clay is vice chairman of the Richmond
    Asylum⟩ *522:11–12*
B ⟨severed head speaks⟩ *511:6*
5   B ⟨don't be greedy⟩ *521:27*
B ⟨Send him to me.⟩
B ⟨3 gallons a day⟩ *528:6*
Can this thing be true
B ⟨Bello belches⟩ *521:2*
10   B ⟨walk on him⟩ *521:25*
B ⟨varsity eight⟩ *524:29–30*
B ⟨he'll be good, Mr. Bello!⟩ *520:10–11*
B ⟨LB wrote in urinal⟩ *525:28–29*
B ⟨to correct you⟩ *520:19*
15   B ⟨I wouldn't hurt yr feelings for the world⟩ *529:6*
B ⟨Shit on LB's letter⟩ *458:36*
B ⟨Satin lined boots⟩ *438:12*
delays to provoke
B ⟨?end bottled stouts⟩
20   Have I given . . . ?
        you have!
B ⟨?coaxingly, now for your short heart to heart talk,
    dear.⟩ *520:15–17*
B ⟨Blazes Kate⟩ *550:28–29*
25   B ⟨hide & uncover⟩ *520:3ff.?*
All ?Dublin

313

LEFT AND CENTER COLUMNS HORIZONTAL

B ⟨Dreck:⟩ *511:13*   gold, Lutetia, amber, musk, embryo, thoughts,

B ⟨?pissed on in death⟩

B ⟨and, rinse them well, mind.⟩ *527:6*

30   B ⟨dirtiest things clean (cf. soot)⟩ *527?*

B ⟨smell trousers and socks v. nose-bleeding⟩

B ⟨Passio ?iliaca⟩   B ⟨LB repeats sentence of BC⟩

B ⟨?Ringpissen v impotence⟩   B ⟨Can I help. Cook⟩ *522:8*

shirt waist   dog!   Exultet.

35   B ⟨black oath⟩ *583–584?*

qualm of conscience

on my sacred honour   B ⟨shall have been saying⟩

victim of intrigue   B ⟨sarcastically⟩ *529:6*

B ⟨will write fully tomorrow⟩ *506:33–34*

40   hounded to death   crow to pluck with you

B ⟨apply his eye⟩ *552:7*   B ⟨nuptual⟩ *525:29*

The Natural   B ⟨fullback (football)⟩ *448:24*

B ⟨where you's teapot⟩ *437:26–31?*   3 bird cries

B ⟨postage stamps on face⟩ *558:36–37*   cordial to support

45   hurl lamp   B ⟨eating grass⟩ *536:27–28*

sweep things off table   short stock (?tothe)

laid on the floor (Pen)   B ⟨sphinx⟩ *546:18*

B ⟨lap up.⟩ *527:6–7*   ?set

B ⟨He spends the day in bed⟩ *525:32*

50   B ⟨With at least 1 woman⟩ *525:22*

B ⟨smothered in blood⟩   Caligula dances

B ⟨dons the cap⟩ *462:17*   B ⟨horse made consul⟩ *473:29–32*

foul play   ape consul

naughty   B ⟨O, cold! (croup)⟩ *460:12?, 528:9 & 22?*

55   B ⟨topping!⟩ *551:23*   move on!

B ⟨jammed⟩ *568:21*   needs round washer

B ⟨Black Church⟩ *525:22–23*   B ⟨Elephantin⟩ *502:24–25*

B ⟨LB worked on the census⟩   B ⟨hidden under sofafringe⟩ *520:3–4*

B ⟨family crest⟩ *700:20*

60   B ⟨Agatha⟩ *539:18*   B ⟨pretend whore is RL⟩

B ⟨I'll hold you down⟩ *521:23*

B ⟨slaps his face⟩ *521:19*

B ⟨God's time is 6:30⟩ *497:3*

B ⟨Lynch him⟩ *482:26*

65 B ⟨Bloodhounds⟩ *571:1*

B ⟨la crevette.⟩

B ⟨duchess⟩ *524:31*

B ⟨the last straw⟩ *540:2*

I am sad you are engaged

70 B ⟨Philip Augustus⟩ *524:26–27*

B ⟨went through a form of marriage⟩ *525:21–22*

B ⟨deploy⟩ *582:23*

B ⟨barbed wire (beads)⟩ *540:18*

B ⟨shrubbery⟩ *531:21*

75 blurred memory

B ⟨Driscoll⟩ *451–455*

B ⟨fog cleared off⟩ *570:21*

B ⟨show! show backside!⟩ *522–523?*

B ⟨black satin shift⟩ *524:17*

80 LB WC dark window open

B ⟨LB peers & sees nothing.⟩   B ⟨hides her face in armpit⟩ *528:26*

B ⟨beastly awful⟩ *451:1*

limbs

B ⟨hawk volant in a field azure⟩ *557:24–25*

85 B ⟨I caught you nicely⟩ *435:21–22*   B ⟨there's no excuse for him⟩ *459:23*

B ⟨LB phones indecently⟩ *525:25*

put you to shame

B ⟨unsolicited testimonials⟩ *533:14–15*

B ⟨pass the evening of his days⟩ *453:27*

90 B ⟨Your wife dressed?⟩ *551:7ff.?*   B ⟨unbuttons her gauntlets⟩ *460:18*

B ⟨Coaxing hand⟩ *520:15?*

B ⟨merry twinkle in his eye⟩ *551:23*

B ⟨not fit to touch the garment of a pure woman⟩ *540:10–11*

B ⟨You ought to feel yourself honoured⟩ *551:19*

95 B ⟨See life⟩ *433:7–8*

B ⟨I have some private business with your wife⟩ *551:14*

has been bled

wandering at night

Molly's ring.

B ⟨Jackdaw of Rheims (P. Beauf.)⟩ *451:6*

might have been   B ⟨poisoned⟩ *429:1?, 454?*

LB   B ⟨& the spinach with hemlock⟩ *454:19*

B ⟨I was indecently treated⟩ *529:18*

B ⟨paroxysm⟩ *459:10*

B ⟨nose to ground⟩ *558:1*

?wo

B ⟨Jimmy Henry with corn⟩ *571:23–24*

?turn round ?&

now ?clockface

loud cough

B ⟨this lot⟩

B ⟨I weakly went astray⟩ *498:6?*

B ⟨squat⟩ *521:23*   *B* ⟨:spittoon⟩ *529:16*   *B* ⟨:pisspot:⟩ *527:4*

B ⟨need mountain air⟩ *570:17*

B ⟨accoutrements⟩ *581:8–9*   forepaws crossed

100   *B* ⟨make the bed⟩ *527:4*   sits on chair

B ⟨don't keep me waiting.⟩ *521:18–19*

B ⟨get my tub ready⟩ *527:4*   animated meat

B ⟨caprice of humour⟩   *B* ⟨chases tail⟩ *508:29*

B ⟨hide & seek, he's not here⟩ *520:3ff.*

105   *B* ⟨flea in her drawers⟩ *530:29*

B ⟨holds in her breath⟩ *523:7*

B ⟨drink me⟩ *527:7*   *B* ⟨peep out hurries back⟩ *520:3?*

B ⟨death rattle⟩ *567:22*   *B* ⟨ma'amsir⟩ *520:13*

B ⟨viveur de pots⟩   *B* ⟨coiled up⟩ *462:30?*

110   *B* ⟨he's after hitting me⟩ *521:21*

B ⟨speak while she pisses⟩   *B* ⟨shit in sawdust corner⟩ *525:14–15*

B ⟨he twists her arms⟩ *521:8*   *B* ⟨looks at ?bird ?notto⟩

RIGHT COLUMN HORIZONTAL

B ⟨LB auctioned⟩ *527*

B ⟨talk of trivial man talk⟩

115   *B* ⟨?shim, ?sher, ?shig⟩

B ⟨women squabble for LB⟩ *543:22, 522:32–33*

enfant martyr

B ⟨Hop!⟩ *527:7*

B ⟨O! O! O!⟩ *522:19*

120   *B* ⟨one pulls off others⟩ *523:2*

B ⟨are you finished?⟩ *523:2*

B ⟨I'm not⟩ *523:7*

B ⟨dowager duchess of K⟩ *524:31*

B ⟨the King v Bloom⟩ *451:29*

125   *B* ⟨extensive property⟩ *456:4*

B ⟨8 men fuck her⟩ *524:29–30?*

B ⟨flew out of room⟩

B ⟨rub shoulders with⟩ *497:11*

B ⟨stunned⟩ *536:2, 585:21*
130 professor Zodiac
B ⟨a man I know named Charles Albert Marsh⟩ *527:17–18*
B ⟨limp ?pissing penis in ?hand⟩ *528:33?*
B ⟨don't be cruel, nurse⟩ *521:10*
B ⟨play horse,⟩ *522:24ff.*
135 B ⟨can't hold this ?lot⟩ *523:5?*
B ⟨Will write fully⟩ *506:33*
B ⟨wide cavalry legs⟩ *522:24?*
B ⟨?she- . . . drawers⟩ *539:28?*
B ⟨I am the daughter of my father what do you call him⟩ *Cf. 509:13*
140 B ⟨LB cuts anus hair⟩ *524:24*
B ⟨kept man⟩ *531:9*
B ⟨jews stand at wailing wall⟩ *532:5–6*
B ⟨sackcloth & ashes⟩ *532:5*
B ⟨lamenting LB's defection⟩ *532:9–10*
145 B ⟨Sheridan the Quadroon⟩ *524:29*
B ⟨Croesus⟩ *524:29*
B ⟨don't ask me⟩
B ⟨they the⟩
at fault
150 B ⟨you can touch & examine⟩ *528:3*
B ⟨wanton⟩ *536:27*
B ⟨handles him⟩ *528:4*
does she
Venus, Juno, Ceres,
155 elite
was in store for you
B ⟨what most revolting obscenity⟩ *526:2–3*
B ⟨LB mumbles⟩ *454:8, 518:18, 589:9*
B ⟨gloating⟩ *525:33*
160 B ⟨the bidding⟩ *527:27ff.*
B ⟨bidder for another⟩ *527:30–31?*
B ⟨pinioned⟩ *522:8*
B ⟨pillory⟩ *486:22, 487:26*
plucks at with nails

165   *B* ⟨elbows his way⟩ *574:8?*

    B ⟨weight of bosom⟩ *502:18*

    B ⟨?take   attitudes⟩

    B ⟨breath good⟩ *527:35*

    what tastes

170   *B* ⟨virgin LB?⟩ *527:35*

    B ⟨powder puff⟩ *538:13*

    B ⟨Hold y^{r.} tongue⟩ *526:21*

    B ⟨dismounted⟩ *523:15?*

    B ⟨lobster⟩ *551:2*

175   *B* ⟨It will hurt you⟩ *521:7*

    B ⟨chemise⟩ *24:17*

    B ⟨No, Leopold Bloom, -⟩ *529:27*

    B ⟨my chest⟩ *533:16?*

    B ⟨infernal⟩ *463:20, 522:15*

180   *B* ⟨don't tear my⟩ *520:23*

    B ⟨this repugnant⟩ *526:13*

    B ⟨?swish⟩ *460:21*

NOTES

Every deleted phrase has been crossed through in blue pencil.

Line 1   *Isaac Laquedem*: a manifestation of the Wandering Jew associated with Brussels (*Encycl. Brit.*, 9th ed.); also the title of a fragmentary novel (1853) by Alexandre Dumas (1802–1870). See Arthur F. Davidson, *Alexandre Dumas, His Life and Works* (Westminster [London], 1902), pp. 242–243.

20   The ellipses are Joyce's.

27   *Dreck*: see *James Joyce Quarterly*, II (Spring 1965), 218. *Lutetia*: Paris; see *Letters*, III, 87.

32   *Passio iliaca*: Latin for "suffering of Troy."

32–33   *LB . . . BC* and *Can I help*: written in green ink.

34   *Exultet*: let him rejoice. The word is repeated at "Circe" 16:52.

46   *Tothe*: perhaps Toth (Thoth) is meant. See "Circe" 7:48–50 and note.

48   *Set*: the principle of evil; his brother Osiris was the principle of good. See also "Circe" 3:102 and note.

51   *Caligula dances* and the two phrases directly below are connected. *Caligula*: the Roman emperor (A.D. 12–41) who made his *horse* a *consul* and a member of the college of priests.

60   *RL*: not identified.

64   *Jackdaw of Rheims*: from the *Ingoldsby Legends* by Richard Harris Barham (pseud. Thomas Ingoldsby). *Beauf[oy]*: supposedly the author of a story which Bloom read in *Titbits* (*U* 68). The British Museum catalog does list a Philip Beaufoy as author of a book for boys published in 1927 (Thornton, pp. 367, 76).

66   *La crevette*: shrimp.

70   *Philip Augustus*: Philip II of France (1165–1223), the son of Louis VII.

138   This line is written in green ink.

145–146   *Sheridan the Quadroon* and *Croesus*: these lines illuminate an error in the text (524:29) which was not corrected in the revised 1961 edition of *Ulysses* (536:27). The text now reads: "Sheridan, the quadroon Croesus." The comma should come after "quadroon" and before "Croesus." *Sheridan*: either Richard B. Sheridan (1751–1816), the Irish playwright, or his grandfather Thomas (1687–1738), the author of *The Art of Punning*. *Croesus*: the last Lydian king (d. 546 B.C.), supposedly the richest man in the world (Glasheen).

"Circe" 10

LEFT MARGIN VERTICAL

B ⟨Know me next time⟩ *541:2*
B ⟨swan⟩ *186:20, 216:5*
R ⟨carefully nurtured⟩ *453:23*
eartips fly across

LEFT COLUMN HORIZONTAL

5   *B* ⟨topknot⟩ *499:5*   *B* ⟨squirm⟩ *459:14*
     B ⟨pigtail⟩ *499:5*   *R* ⟨vindictively⟩ *460:7*
     B ⟨toupee⟩ *499:5*
     little mites drowned in weir
     B ⟨cleaver used by Mrs Pearcy to slay Mogg⟩ *578:16–17*
10   *B* ⟨Hatchet purchased by Koczula to murder his employer⟩ *448:19?*
     B ⟨Voisin dismembered the wife of a compatriot⟩ *578:18*
     B ⟨Hid remains in a cellar⟩ *578:18–19*
     B ⟨phial containing arsenic retrieved from body of Miss Barrow
          sent Seddon to the gallows⟩ *578:20–21*
15   Neil ?Crean, poisoner of 5 young women
     B ⟨drunk cover distance⟩ *444:11*   *B* ⟨scarlet yellow blue green
          & white parrot⟩ *504:14?*
     B ⟨see behind in mirror⟩
     B ⟨Circe's Tiresias, her tipster,⟩ *466:25*
20   carry on back, waiting   lurking fish,
     B ⟨Ostrich monocle   bare legged,⟩ *500:29?* flat head
     B ⟨elephant bagslops⟩ *510:23*   *B* ⟨cabbage ear⟩ *510:21*

B ⟨Seal ?maimed crawl old emperor⟩

B ⟨Camel man under carpet disgruntled hindquarters,⟩ *432:21–24*

25 B ⟨flamingo stilts,⟩ *500:27*

B ⟨Moly—indifference⟩

B ⟨Moly—beauty⟩

B ⟨Moly—laughter⟩

B ⟨Moly—satire⟩

30 B ⟨Moly—pessimism⟩

B ⟨LB no face⟩

B ⟨Monkey picks hat to bits⟩

R ⟨women embrace pugilists⟩ *510:25–28*

B ⟨cockspur,⟩ *458:21*   B ⟨?spawned (?G. ?D.)⟩ *510:13?*

35 Esther Osvalt

B ⟨Alo' ?boyous⟩

B ⟨word known to all men,⟩ *566:3*

R ⟨wild goose⟩ *444:10*   beasts like mirrors

bunny,

40 Bill O'Connell's speech

B ⟨gaitered feet,⟩ *558:30–31*   hackles,

B ⟨honey hair⟩ *558:28?*

B ⟨2 notes (1 torn) 1 sov, 2 crowns, 2s/–⟩ *507:18*

B ⟨If youth but knew⟩ *507:18–19*

45 B ⟨I paid my way⟩ *31:35, 507:22, and elsewhere*

B ⟨Per vias rectas⟩ *32:28, 559:3*

B ⟨rocky road to -⟩ *32:32, 558:31*   backstairs,

B ⟨Duke of Beaufort, Ceylon⟩ *33:12–13, 558:25*   '66 (LB n) *33:13*

B ⟨Even money Fair Rebel⟩ *33:21*   10 to 1 field, *33:21*

50 B ⟨Skeleton horses⟩ *558:23*

proceeded to pound his face to a jelly

B ⟨stick one into Jerry⟩ *576:15*

B ⟨Chinaman J.E. pigtail⟩ *499:5*

B ⟨chalk circle⟩ *549:12*   B ⟨bishop of Down & Connor⟩ *471:9–10, 472:22, 473:2–3*

RIGHT COLUMN HORIZONTAL

55   B ⟨Zoe: I fell.⟩ *498:11*   B ⟨LB red tie⟩ *469:6–7*

       B ⟨I did what I did⟩ *498:6*   J.C. catholic

       B ⟨Kids⟩ *517:29?*   ?practical

                                  R ⟨jellybag⟩

       B ⟨forget how to stand,⟩ *430:1?*

60   peachick

       B ⟨puppy⟩ *460:19?*

       B ⟨lash into fury⟩ *460:5*

       Joachim Abbas

       wolfdog crossed every 4th generation

65   wolf loves dogflesh

       R ⟨wolf's stomach odds & ends⟩ *445:9?*

       B ⟨world without end⟩ *498:17–18, 557:10–11*

       B ⟨Frauenzimmer⟩ *564:12*   B ⟨simper⟩ *399:31, 441:22, 528:26*

       B ⟨Arius⟩ *512:2*

70   B ⟨gutted spears⟩ *581:7*   B ⟨eartips⟩

       B ⟨Cassandra harlot's cry⟩ *582:2?*

       B ⟨prism light on GD's blue eyes⟩ *558:37–559:1*

       B ⟨nightmare history⟩ *135:29–30, 35:19*

       O'Rourke of Breffni

75   amor matris   *29:22–23, 205:5*

       M. Maimonides & Averroes   *671:29, 383:38–39*

       B ⟨to rear up⟩ *393:40, 559:4*

       B ⟨to buck⟩ *446:23, 558:23*

       B ⟨to shy⟩

80   B ⟨caparisoned horse⟩ *471:36*

       B ⟨horserace⟩ *558 and elsewhere*   B ⟨bolts⟩ *558:21*

       B ⟨eaten away nose⟩ *564:27?*

       B ⟨indiarubber woman⟩

       B ⟨swell mobsmen⟩ *598:33*

85   B ⟨playfight of beasts⟩ *Cf. 442:12–14*

       B ⟨waxworks⟩ *620:31*   fire

       B ⟨world's fair⟩ *667:25–26*   ?dam

       B ⟨all follow ?panther⟩   (?BG)

B ⟨he diffuses smell⟩ *523:8ff.?*

90   ?protested   ?punishment

NOTES

Inkblots make it difficult to read lines 1–2, 22–24, 26, and 38–40. The paper appears to be a kind of graph paper. My division of phrases in the right column is sometimes arbitrary.

Line 4   *Eartips*: repeated at line 70.

19   *Tiresias*: see "Circe" 3:123–124 and note.

26–30   See "Circe" 2:3 and note.

35   See *U* 50:11–12.

40   *Bill O'Connell*: Ellmann (pp. 11 & 23) mentions a William O'Connell, who was a brother of Ellen O'Connell Joyce, James Joyce's paternal grandmother.

46   *Per vias rectas*: the Blackwood family motto; Mr. Deasy is supposedly a descendant of this family. See Adams, p. 20.

53   *J.E.*: John Eglinton.

63   *Joachim Abbas*: Joachim of Floris (*abbas*—"abbot" in Greek) (c. 1145–c. 1202); his "mystical interpretation of history, based on historical parallels or 'concordances' between the history of the Jewish people and that of the church, was grouped into three ages, each corresponding to a member of the Trinity, the last, that of the Spirit, which was to usher in perfect liberty to commence in 1260" (*Chambers's*). See *U* 40:37–42; also Ellmann, pp. 151, 353.

68   *Frauenzimmer*: female(s), wench(es).

69   *Arius*: the founder of Arianism (c. 260–336), who maintained that in the Holy Trinity, the Son was not equal with the Father but was the highest of finite beings.

71   *Cassandra*: a prophetess and King Priam's daughter (*Iliad*).

72   *GD*: Garrett Deasy.

74   See "Cyclops" 5:42 and note.

76   *M[oses] Maimonides*: Jewish philosopher (1135–1204) and author of *More Nebukim*. Cf. "Ithaca" 12:68 and 15:69. *Averroes* (Averroës): see "Oxen" 18:25 and note. Both were born in Córdoba, Spain.

"Circe" 11

LEFT MARGIN HORIZONTAL

R ⟨tailormade⟩ *441:2*
B ⟨make it hot for you⟩ *459:17*
R ⟨his carryings on⟩ *452:12*
LB & Virag born same horoscope

5 *B* ⟨when you were . . . . I was⟩
B ⟨antipodes⟩ *614:27*

LEFT COLUMN HORIZONTAL

B ⟨Ireland's sweetheart⟩ *579:31*
B ⟨when in doubt persecute the jew⟩ *455:34*
B ⟨?closes in dumbshow⟩

10 *B* ⟨SD à moi S.D. scream of vulture⟩ *557:15*
sprain
B ⟨zoological biscuits, geographical balls⟩ *667:20–21*
B ⟨geometrical bricks⟩ *667:20?*   *G* ⟨skunk⟩ *526:21*
tyre explodes

15 *B* ⟨LB boasts of successes (1 Waterloo)⟩ *447:31*
B ⟨?slurred⟩
R ⟨A Gautama, A Jesus, An Ingersoll⟩ *497:11–12*
body soul & spirit
I perhaps to build on had some little

20 *B* ⟨?Live cloak⟩   It is a capital
I make question
R ⟨Dark Hidden, Father.⟩ *499:26*   You man
B ⟨As K has said.⟩

324

B ⟨Circe he, LB, she (his or her)⟩ *519:8ff.*

25 Vladimir Pokethankerscheff *Cf. 302:9–10*

B ⟨SD rips coat⟩ *569:2*

B ⟨Rlwy collision⟩ *444:11–14*

B ⟨very much so⟩

B ⟨convex barber mirror elongated ?elargated⟩ *426:34*

30 R ⟨slip twixt cup & lip⟩

B ⟨LB sent verses to woman⟩ *457–458*

R ⟨Jacobs Vobiscuits.⟩ *465:6–7*

R ⟨Circe's luck has turned⟩

B ⟨got up wrong side of bed⟩ *489:15*

35 Gods are in us   R ⟨hussy⟩ *435:6*

B ⟨epilepsy⟩ *483:11*   B ⟨make her smart⟩ *460:7–8*

B ⟨SD smashes lamp⟩ *567:27–28*

Vengeance of Carr

Circe = hawk = fate.

40 B ⟨if so inclined⟩ *436:25–26*

B ⟨Virag points & cries⟩ *508:26?*

don't walk on my train

prophecy = why he know more?

fate of pigmen after

45 B ⟨Goodwin—wig.⟩ *560:5*

B ⟨wear filthy petticoats & things.⟩ *560:6?*

badger full of sandburrs,

I just kept working that bowie knife

B ⟨Hamlet, I thy father's gimlet,⟩ *547:13*

50 B ⟨LB thinks of Cycl & stumbles⟩ *491:10?*

CENTER VERTICAL

?Mr

James Joyce

rue de l'Assomption 5

Passy

55 Paris

RIGHT COLUMN HORIZONTAL

B ⟨hallucination⟩ *454:33?*

B ⟨permeate⟩ *453:27*

B ⟨mirage⟩ *456:10, 432:3, 370:4*

B ⟨clumsy⟩ *436:14*

60   B ⟨bonham⟩ *426:34*

B ⟨dame in pantomime⟩ *431:19*

bloodstock dealer

B ⟨reveal the fact⟩ *501:3*

B ⟨LB goes too far in train⟩ *444:13*

65   B ⟨much in evidence⟩ *501:2*

B ⟨in yr heyday⟩ *441:8*

B ⟨a black ?man⟩ *436:6?*

B ⟨giddy on peak⟩ *537:16?*

B ⟨switchback⟩

70   Sabine women

B ⟨LB button snaps⟩ *539:22*

B ⟨Mary lost the pin⟩ *77:27–30, 539:28–31*

B ⟨LB weeps⟩ *531:31*

coat of fluff

75   B ⟨thistledown refracts⟩ *537:13*

B ⟨SD hates action⟩ *573:26*

B ⟨SD chants⟩ *424:10, 547:7*

B ⟨nightwalker⟩ *764:1, 424:16ff.*

B ⟨flake of mud on cheek⟩ *428:21*

80   B ⟨cycling⟩ *428:1, 429:24*

B ⟨shoelace catch in cog⟩ *428:26*

B ⟨shoeheel catch in track⟩ *428:25*

B ⟨sateen⟩ *539:9*

B ⟨vaccination⟩ *560:20*

85   R ⟨lion of night⟩ *437:15*

B ⟨to retrieve,⟩ *453:20*

R ⟨Rudolph predicts⟩

R ⟨LB non ?eviter⟩

B ⟨Virag tells future in past tense & yawns⟩ *511:11?*

90   *B* ⟨Smbdy hypnotizes⟩
        B ⟨very like a ?wheeler in a pillbox⟩

NOTES

As with "Circe" 10, the paper here is a kind of graph paper.

Line 17   *An Ingersoll*: see "Oxen" 18:5 and note.

32   See "Cyclops" 2:13 and note.

38   See *U* 572ff.

39   See "Circe" 3:100 and note and "Circe" 7:45 note. This may also have suggested Minnie Hauck (*U* 515:15; "Circe" 1:28 and note).

51–55   "The first to give Joyce material assistance was Madame Bloch-Savitsky. She and her husband offered him in mid-July a flat, rent-free, at 5 rue de l'Assomption, in Passy, close to the Bois de Boulogne. . . . the family stayed from July 15 to November 1 [1920]" (Ellmann, p. 501).

70   *Sabine women*: according to legend, Romulus, because of a shortage of women in Rome, "invited the neighboring Sabines to a festival and carried off their women" (*Encycl. Brit.*). Cf. *FW*, 197:21; *Ulysses* notebook VIII.A.5 at Buffalo (p. 303).

76   See "Nausicaa" 1:10–12 and the essay on "Nausicaa," pp. 27–28.

"Circe" 12

LEFT COLUMN HORIZONTAL

       B ⟨cut girl's plaits⟩ *462:2*

       R ⟨beaverdykes⟩

       B ⟨pairing time⟩ *536:24–25*

       B ⟨magpie⟩

5   rogue elephant

       B ⟨company liked by beasts⟩

       flock of soldiers

       B ⟨hennessy's xxx⟩ *498:13–14*

       B ⟨SD frogsplits⟩ *563:22*

10   *R* ⟨business menagerer⟩ *433:2*

       B ⟨—smell of animals⟩ *491:5*

       B ⟨uncertain movements⟩ *445:8*

       B ⟨it's just too sweet⟩

       the latter

15   *B* ⟨soapy sneak⟩ *450:23*   *B* ⟨masquerade⟩ *450:23?*

       B ⟨Virag sloughs skin⟩ *511:10*   ?Lionels

       B ⟨chattering⟩ *495:29, 543:22*

       R ⟨SD Nebrakada⟩ *540:16, 432:27*

       B ⟨LB starts⟩ *540:16*

20   horsework reliable (CK)

       B ⟨somersault⟩ *495:24*

       B ⟨?regains her composure⟩

       took his stand in the dock

       sever the main artery

25   *R* ⟨swing for her⟩ *626:26*

       B ⟨Head R. foot L (O.W.)⟩

LB in topcoat.

B ⟨the latter⟩ *605:38 and elsewhere*   B ⟨bluebottle⟩ *504:30*

hereafter

30　R ⟨ant milks aphis⟩ *505:27*

B ⟨hand to stop traffic⟩ *428:13*

B ⟨Moly = escape from prison⟩

R ⟨pass 5 pm accident 5:5⟩ *428:24?*

B ⟨amnesty⟩ *480:10*

35　R ⟨Kilts⟩ *496:22*

B ⟨Moly = conscience⟩

B ⟨Paleface⟩ *450:13*

B ⟨accessory before the act⟩ *455:29*

B ⟨new-powdered gloves⟩ *527:12*

40　B ⟨trying on wrinkles⟩

B ⟨soft comments exchanged⟩

LEFT COLUMN VERTICAL

Ulysses

II

(continued)

RIGHT COLUMN HORIZONTAL

45　magnetic field　　　　　　　　　B ⟨in a word⟩

B ⟨pack⟩ *455:26, 557:31, and elsewhere* R ⟨lampoon⟩

B ⟨our old friend,⟩ *503:27*

B ⟨?amputate⟩ *503:27*

B ⟨unsophisticated⟩

50　B ⟨Flipperty Jibbert⟩ *508:21*

R ⟨black brute⟩ *436:6*

G ⟨worth whiles⟩　　　　　　　　B ⟨Blum pascha⟩ *447:6*

B ⟨boo⟩ *449:20*

hooter

329

55   *B* ⟨SD & Hamlet reluctant avenger⟩ *579:28*

B ⟨Look facts in face⟩ *411:10*

gauche

B ⟨fine thing & super fine⟩ *542:4*

diamond b. thunderbolt

60   *B* ⟨up to sample or money back⟩ *550:29*

B ⟨stable with these people⟩ *557:22–23*

B ⟨help me save them⟩ *498:2–3*

B ⟨?dad, governor,⟩ *449:22?*

B ⟨?lord⟩

65   *B* ⟨succulent bivalves⟩ *505:5*

B ⟨I am going to talk about⟩ *503:27*

B ⟨this book tells you⟩ *503:24*

B ⟨Oysters are upon us⟩ *505:4–5*

B ⟨LB awkward⟩ *468:25?, 491:10?*

70   *B* ⟨LB & 2/6⟩ *531:2?*

B ⟨whores pat ? . . . . plates⟩

B ⟨SD drunk visit sombdy⟩ *506:31–32*

B ⟨ollav,⟩ *499:13, 182:33*   next king,   21 . . . .

glass, accept reflection only from

75   .lait,   ward sanctuary,

2 hounds, 6 horses

B ⟨Parallax⟩ *478:25, 501:24, and elsewhere*   *B* ⟨high time too⟩

La Stretta

B ⟨ring (keeper)⟩ *515:16*

80   *B* ⟨the world over⟩ *449:14*

B ⟨figures come back⟩ *538:20?*

put a knife through

R ⟨groundbirds⟩ *538:26?*

G ⟨leverett⟩

85   *R* ⟨fall upstairs⟩ *491:12–13*

sledgeharness

deepseafish rise gallbladder

        expand, muscles too flabby,

        distend, burst

90   *B* ⟨all is not well⟩

B ⟨seeing is believing⟩
B ⟨20 button gloves⟩ *Cf. 527:11–12*
B ⟨Gerald, feel laces round bare legs   contrast with tight
   stays⟩ *525:2–4*

NOTES

The paper here is a kind of graph paper.

Line 8   *Hennessy's*: brandy.

26   Joyce may have remembered a picture of Oscar Wilde posing in this stance.

32 & 36   See "Circe" 2:3 and note.

42–44   Joyce employed a tripartite organization in *Ulysses*: Part I was the "Telemachia," containing the first three episodes; Part II was the "Odyssey," the next twelve episodes; and then came the "Nostos," containing the last three. "Circe," being the fifteenth episode, is the last episode in Part II. See *Letters*, I, 113.

50   *Jibbert*: in the text it is "Jippert."

73–75   *21 . . . .lait*: may be one phrase.

75   The first letter in this line is illegible.

78   *La Stretta*: the squeeze, pressure, grip. Since it is capitalized here, it may refer to something more specific.

84   *Leverett* (leveret): a young hare.

"Circe" 13

LEFT MARGIN HORIZONTAL

trilby
S ⟨fawn spats⟩ *440:24*
B ⟨clear my name⟩ *448:10*
B ⟨lingerie⟩ *501:14, 524:1*
5   B ⟨stiffly⟩ *489:14*
R ⟨Dundrearies⟩ *401:34*
B ⟨two detectives⟩ *445:21?*
B ⟨talking to himself⟩ *543:15*
B ⟨keyhole eye⟩ *552:7–8*
10   ?sy / pig / ?plum
Mary Martha
B ⟨Mary lost the string of her⟩ *Cf. 77:33, 539:28*
R ⟨reindeer⟩ *553:14*
goddesses speak through nose
15   R ⟨white slave traffic⟩ *462:16*
manh(e)ater *Cf. 446:27*
B ⟨I hate you⟩

LEFT COLUMN HORIZONTAL

B ⟨as a matter of courtesy⟩ *517:21?*
B ⟨mercury's hats⟩ *21:4*
20   green boots
Haines a soldier
boneless snail

B ⟨heresiarchus⟩ *512:2*

?frognoise,   jelly

25 Harry Gogarty in Mull.

Lycidas

fabled by daughters of memory,

Sargent,   *B* ⟨fox & granny⟩ *545:21, 557:29–30, and elsewhere*

B ⟨epi oinopa ponton⟩ *565:18*   g.p.i *8:14–15*

30 *B* ⟨dogsbody oxy giddy ox⟩ *565:16*

B ⟨Caliban,⟩ *482:24*   *B* ⟨grasshalms⟩ *508:8*

B ⟨offend memory of mother⟩ *565:25, Cf. 10:32*

B ⟨Love's bitter mystery⟩ *565:29*

B ⟨Liliata rubilantium⟩ *564:33*

35 *B* ⟨silk of kine⟩ *580:2–3*

B ⟨Mulligan meets his afflicted aunt⟩ *565:6*

No give in it

B ⟨corset laced vice⟩ *523:28*

B ⟨fascinated by sister's stays⟩ *525:3*

40 *B* ⟨LB at Xmas tree⟩ *438:1*

″ bathing,   Sad thing making ?hunger for your country

B ⟨LB stiff leg⟩ *428:14, 454:18, 517:24*

B ⟨smbdy trails⟩

B ⟨walls fall asunder⟩ *475:19–20*

45 Convers: speak out of turn

arguments don't convince

B ⟨questions not replied to⟩

tread on tail of coat

R ⟨man upholds train⟩ *512:17*

50 *R* ⟨tailwagging⟩ *440:17, 445:5*

?cobblemaiming

B ⟨female impersonator,⟩ *525:1*

B ⟨loitering⟩ *442:11ff.*

intent to commit a felony

55 *R* ⟨life preserver killed⟩ *462:31*

SD wires for cash

B ⟨descriptive particulars⟩ *503:25*

and ruin you? And make me? .. ruin you . . . ,—

RIGHT COLUMN HORIZONTAL

B ⟨superfluous hair⟩ *541:5*

60 pigtail tied to waistband

elbows tight together

R ⟨grizzly⟩

SD ?is but enters

B ⟨bestie sudditanza⟩

65 *B* ⟨bearhead cocked R—L for sugar⟩ *504:16–18?*

B ⟨corsetlover⟩ *525:1*

B ⟨strapped to a bedpost⟩ *435:6*

B ⟨a cod's mouth⟩ *554:8*

B ⟨evensong⟩ *564:14*

70 *B* ⟨LB asks way⟩ *429:9*

R ⟨LB shocked in crowd⟩ *430:1*

B ⟨totters on hams⟩ *430:1*

   B ⟨cranes⟩ *509:12*

head comes round corner & vanishes

75 *B* ⟨reflects, refracts⟩ *57:8 and elsewhere*

B ⟨corpulent,⟩ *412:40*

they strip.

Mrs Europe speaks

B ⟨Tooralooom Tay⟩ *592:8 and elsewhere*

80 *B* ⟨LB talks German⟩ *430:18*

savages   *B* ⟨author⟩ *449:32*

kraal   *B* ⟨savagely⟩ *460:21, 520:25*

stockade

raughty tinker

85 *R* ⟨soldering iron⟩

B ⟨sinking floor⟩

B ⟨Vase appears on table⟩

brought to justice

B ⟨?Corny⟩ *588:1ff. and elsewhere*

90 *B* ⟨tammy toque⟩ *441:17*

run to earth

LB ideas for Zoo

he kicked
R ⟨badgered⟩ 455:25
95 B ⟨pussy four corners⟩ 477:2
B ⟨alanna⟩ 580:1

NOTES

The paper here is a kind of graph paper. In the upper left-hand corner is *0.5*. The meaning is not clear.

Line 1 *Trilby*: a type of hat.

12–13 These lines could be connected.

25 *Harry Gogarty in Mull*[*ingar*]: the brother of Oliver Gogarty, Harry emigrated to South America as a young man. See U 23:16–17, 390:37–38.

26 *Lycidas*: this reference to Milton's poem is probably connected in Stephen's mind with the motif of "death by drowning," and the dead man who was found floating in Dublin Bay.

27 See "Cyclops" 1:8 and note.

28 *Sargent*: see U 28–29.

29 *Epi oinopa ponton*: "on the winedark sea," from the *Odyssey*. Cf. U 48:31, 322:7–8.

31 *Caliban*: see U 8:31–32, where Mulligan shows Stephen his face in the mirror and quotes Oscar Wilde's *Dorian Grey*: "The rage of Caliban at not seeing his face in a mirror."

64 *Bestie sudditanza*: citizenship of animals.

73–74 Joyce first wrote *comes* and then *cranes* above it.

96 *Alanna*: Irish for "child" (O Hehir, p. 351).

"Circe" 14

LEFT MARGIN HORIZONTAL

B ⟨Lion's share⟩
B ⟨witch in vest bare rump⟩ *583?*
B ⟨broomstick⟩ *583:11*
B ⟨?rut end of dance⟩
5   *B* ⟨Mrs Purefoy's belly⟩ *583:25–26*
B ⟨altar of rump⟩ *583:21*
B ⟨black candles⟩ *583:22*
B ⟨frig with crucifix⟩
walk on cross
10   *B* ⟨seed of hanged⟩ *578:27–28*
B ⟨ropes⟩ *578:10ff.*
B ⟨black host⟩ *583:37?*
B ⟨Madame⟩ *581:28 and elsewhere*
B ⟨let him look⟩ *551:28*
15   *B* ⟨Dalila her ?bust was also remarkable⟩
B ⟨dial on arse⟩
B ⟨devil 3 pricks⟩
B ⟨Manx cat⟩ *528:31*
B ⟨tatter clothes off him⟩ *750:4–5*
20   *B* ⟨bub falls in soup⟩ *502:18–20*
B ⟨procurator⟩ *531:23*
Shouts as one man
B ⟨Mr Justice Fitzgibbon⟩ *571:17*
B ⟨turpitude⟩ *556:6*
25   *B* ⟨Brutish empire⟩ *579:16*
B ⟨Rumbold, demon barber,⟩ *578:14*

B ⟨lame gardener⟩ *540:20*

tail through shift

LEFT COLUMN HORIZONTAL

1 2

30 2 1

B ⟨Sweetly hoarsely⟩ *552:29*

B ⟨kiss the whip⟩ *520:26?*

B ⟨Mrs Bloom⟩ *551:7*

B ⟨last articles⟩ *551:10*

35 *B* ⟨ask every 20 minutes⟩ *522:21*

B ⟨administer a regular whipping⟩ *520:16?*

B ⟨(a fact)⟩

B ⟨sodden no hair⟩

B ⟨touches the spot⟩ *529:15*

40 *B* ⟨exhaust him with power⟩ *516:20?*

B ⟨his memory abolished⟩ *483:17?*

B ⟨yoke⟩ *523:17, 559:4*   baptism

B ⟨LB pelted⟩ *571:6ff.*

B ⟨stables of men⟩ *557:22–23?*

45 comes in trousers pocket

B ⟨who docked it?⟩ *528:32–33*

B ⟨Our mutual faith⟩ *526:10*   extreme unction

B ⟨plump for B-⟩ *517:23?*

B ⟨gravel cabbagestumps⟩ *571:6–7*

50 *B* ⟨St. Jacob's oil⟩

B ⟨sold after dark in Paris boulevards⟩ *458:30–31*

let yrself go

B ⟨incredibly small shoe for small foot⟩ *517:30*

B ⟨dark theater unbridles vice⟩ *535:24*

55 in ward politics   *B* ⟨?titter⟩

B ⟨porksteaks⟩ *554:7*

acute trouble   *B* ⟨leprechauns⟩ *335:38*

told the bench

B ⟨whip yrself⟩

60 *B* ⟨the whipping post⟩ *453:26*

B ⟨doorhandle turns⟩ *513:23*

B ⟨WS paralysed speech⟩ *553:13–14*

B ⟨what a lark!⟩ *536:3–4*   *B* ⟨pandemonium⟩ *582:23*

B ⟨flow of animal spirits⟩ *536:29*

65 *B* ⟨Bobs⟩ *524:31*

B ⟨throwing their tongues⟩ *571:4*

B ⟨fresh found,⟩ *571:8*   *B* ⟨?snaps at moth⟩ *505:31?*

B ⟨scrapes at door⟩   *B* ⟨piff paff:⟩ *508:29*

B ⟨blows into   LB's ear⟩ *468:20–23?*   Popo. *508:30*

70 *B* ⟨schooling gallop⟩ *559:1–2*   *B* ⟨⟨he chases his

B ⟨?mare lopes⟩ *559:1*   tail round⟩⟩ *508:29*

B ⟨scent catches⟩ *571:3?*

Most Low   sulpher   *B* ⟨limb of devil⟩

B ⟨LB steals⟩ *531:20–21?*   *B* ⟨Roebuck⟩ *571:30*

75 *B* ⟨LB forgets MB⟩ *473:31–32?*

B ⟨Raoul⟩ *551:20 and elsewhere*   caret

B ⟨Bella avenges other women⟩

B ⟨incest⟩

G ⟨habits form character⟩ *469:7–13?*   last debauch

80 *G* ⟨⟨LB on W.C.⟩⟩ *534:15ff.*

B ⟨Bella   When? How? How often? What time?   Be truthful, for
   once⟩ *526:16*

B ⟨if you have any grace about you⟩ *531:17–18*

B ⟨basted⟩ *521:6*   *B* ⟨prick behind⟩ *584:3*

RIGHT COLUMN HORIZONTAL

85 musk

chive (civet)

mandrake

B ⟨lingam⟩ *508:23*

B ⟨yoni⟩ *508:23*   *B* ⟨relic⟩ *542:6*

90 wash in blood   *B* ⟨exorcism⟩ *514:23*

B ⟨fires spring up⟩ *582:22*

B ⟨?phallos under soutane⟩ *512:15?, 584:22–23?*

B ⟨Sabbath⟩ *50:1 and elsewhere*

B ⟨adonai speaks⟩ *584:7–8, 584:12–13*   B ⟨antidote⟩ *401:11*

95   B ⟨the colonel⟩ *527:15, 571:31*   B ⟨my programme⟩ *469:21*

B ⟨Caesar Borgia walk over living bull's guts⟩

B ⟨Coactus volui⟩ *246:26, 508:26–27*

B ⟨cesspool⟩ *531:25*   B ⟨run to earth⟩

B ⟨suffocated⟩ *531:25*   B ⟨massed bands⟩ *581:20*

100   B ⟨hot pursuit⟩ *571:9*

?sailing kilt   B ⟨OGG poignard hands.⟩ *621:18?*

B ⟨goaded⟩ *522:19*

B ⟨holy abbot⟩ *540:19*

       Leopad

105   B ⟨a saint ∧ couldn't resist⟩ *536:30*

B ⟨you'll drive me mad⟩ *529:24?*

B ⟨LB mad laugh⟩

LB mimic gestures   B ⟨she idolizes him⟩ *Cf. 552:20*

B ⟨Leopoldleben⟩ *431:9*   B ⟨tumble her⟩ *502:1*

110   B ⟨She didn't mean it⟩ *520:10*

B ⟨beats LB for lost race⟩

trapped

B ⟨sign document⟩

B ⟨langue de ?penis⟩

115   B ⟨erection⟩ *578:27 and elsewhere*

hate him for favours

B ⟨Bella false accuser⟩ *530 and elsewhere*

B ⟨deaf Mullins⟩ *625:21?*

B ⟨honey mane⟩ *558:22 & 28?*

120   Theodora pia

make gold

B ⟨Sticks pin through hat viciously⟩

B ⟨I suggest you . . . (JJ O M)⟩ *456:6*

B ⟨brimstone⟩ *582:22*

125   B ⟨spirits sniff round MB & BB⟩

lady Hamilton

B ⟨fruit, flowers⟩ *532:12–13*

NOTES

My division of phrases between columns is arbitrary throughout.

Line 47   Joyce inserted *mutual* above a caret.

73   *Most Low*: a title for Satan.

76   *Raoul*: a character in *Sweets of Sin*. See *U* 232:31 and elsewhere.

97   *Coactus volui*: I have wished it under compulsion.

101   *OGG*: not identified.

120   See "Circe" 15:7 and note.

123   *J. J. O'Molloy*: a solicitor in *Ulysses*.

126   See "Cyclops" 1:29 and note.

"Circe" 15

CENTER COLUMN HORIZONTAL

Did he not from an elevated terrace watch
B ⟨gave examples of an excessive sensuality⟩
not allow such women
B ⟨convulsions.⟩ *509:22*
5 G ⟨?excuses ?me not mentioning him⟩
B ⟨hesitation waltz⟩ *560:4–5*
Theodora empress laments body no 4^(th.) ?altar
B ⟨Adonai—Kill!⟩ *584:7–13?*
muddy boots
10 tore handkerchief with teeth
B ⟨gingerbread.⟩ *525:34–35 and elsewhere*
B ⟨rule against rump⟩
B ⟨in bridal wreath⟩ *564:26*
G ⟨nurse's costume⟩ *484:23?*   B ⟨lingam, the stiff one,⟩ *508:26*
15 B ⟨hate nightdress⟩ *504:6?*
nail in boots
tiny drop of blood
gingerbread
leave you & never come back
20 B ⟨entrails of croppy boy. Rumbold ejaculates⟩ *579:1–3*
B ⟨rob. curtain (?polo)⟩ *458:24?*
B ⟨ride a cockhorse (Lotty)⟩ *536:25, 522:24 & 28*
B ⟨move speech be printed at expense of society⟩ *470:5–6*
B ⟨on the word of a Bloom.⟩ *475:7*
25 B ⟨Mrs Purefoy pregnant⟩ *583:25–26*   R ⟨loquacity lunacy⟩ *480:9*
rising sun

341

of his—of her—Kingdom

B ⟨hyena!⟩ *566:11*

B ⟨tisuepaper hoop⟩ *446:19*

30   B ⟨whodoyoucallhim   T̶h̶a̶t̶strangeface,   Sawyoubefore   Fellowthatslike
    Chapwithawers,   Friend of Lyons   man in the street,
    Footballboots, other man in the street,   Livesin Hardwicke
    place,   rich protestant lady⟩ *571:13ff.*

B ⟨woman allmoist with sweet pudor s̶h̶o̶w̶s̶ ̶t̶o̶ ̶m̶a̶n̶ offers her

35   yoni to man's lingam. almost immediately after man presents
    woman with pieces of meat. Woman shows joy and covers her-
    self with feather skins. Man loves her yoni fiercely with
    h̶i̶s̶ big lingam. Then giddy woman will run about. Strong man
    grasps h̶e̶r̶ woman's wrists. Woman squeels, bites, spucks.

40   Man, now angry, strikes woman's yadgana.⟩ *508:22ff.*

B ⟨word of a Bloom⟩ *475:7*

B ⟨LB's phantom son (Bridie Kelly's)⟩ *406:28ff.*

B ⟨65 C.⟩ *571:9*

forebears

45   B ⟨1ᵈ· one jest got h̶i̶m̶ ?even⟩

naughty,   R ⟨backsliding.⟩ *426:16?*

NOTES

Line 2   Repeated at "Circe" 17:44–45.

7   *Theodora*: Byzantine empress (c. 508–548), consort of Justinian I, "had, according to Procopius, already been actress, dancer and courtesan when she won the heart of the austere and ambitious Justinian, to become in succession his mistress, his wife and the sharer of his throne (527). . . . She lavished her bounty on the poor, especially the unfortunate of her own sex" (*Chambers's*). She is reputed to have lamented the absence of a fourth orifice for sexual intercourse. Her name is repeated at "Circe" 14:120.

11   Repeated at line 18.

24   *Word of a Bloom*: repeated at line 41 and "Circe" 17:35.

29   *Tisuepaper*: Joyce's misspelling.

30   *Whodoyoucallhim*: "whatdoyoucallhim" in the text. Joyce scratched out *That* before *face* and substituted *strange*.

34ff.   The word order has been rearranged for simplicity.

"Circe" 16

LEFT MARGIN HORIZONTAL

R ⟨Glynn at organ⟩ *488:30–31*
R ⟨Bantam Lyons⟩ *485:7 and elsewhere*
S. Michael
R ⟨Crofton⟩ *479:23 and elsewhere*
5   G ⟨amnesty⟩ *480:10*
G ⟨Hornblower⟩ *571:1 and elsewhere*
?fluid invisible hedge
R ⟨the man called Bloom⟩ *472:10?*
G ⟨row in gallery for & against LB⟩ *475?*
10   G ⟨Ecce Homo!⟩ *79:9*
G ⟨Excellency⟩ *238:1 and elsewhere*
G ⟨eagles & palms⟩ *470:35*
G ⟨?laurels⟩ *645:25*
G ⟨phoenix⟩ *458:25, 488:12, and elsewhere*
15   G ⟨crowded wall falls⟩ *475:19–20*
R ⟨bone thrown at LB⟩ *482:27–29*
S Michael archangel
R ⟨Ben Israel⟩ *485:2 & 34?*
G ⟨Hornblower⟩ *571:1 and elsewhere*
20   G ⟨clap clap hands   Poldy come home⟩ *476:28–29*

LEFT AND RIGHT COLUMNS HORIZONTAL

G ⟨Larry⟩ *479:16*

moleskins   witch's wart = devil's teat

343

Spencer   cloven hoof

R ⟨motor jerkin⟩ *483:8*   R ⟨a disgrace to Christian men⟩ *482:17*

25   R ⟨Goggles on brow⟩ *483:8*   G ⟨seamless (J.C.)⟩ *488:11*

R ⟨Messiah⟩ *485:2*   G ⟨babes & sucklings lifted up to see LB⟩ *476:23–24*

G ⟨ . . . A Bloom⟩ *475:7?*   R ⟨caldron of boiling oil⟩ *482:24*

R ⟨municipal morals⟩ *480:4*   R ⟨urine, spittle, saliva, sweat⟩ *483:27 and elsewhere*

G ⟨he scarcely looks 30⟩ *472:7–8*   G ⟨tuber tuberculosis⟩ *480:9*

30   R ⟨stake faggots⟩ *482:23*   R ⟨roots of hell⟩ *482:17*

G ⟨eat roast heretic⟩ *482:26?*   G ⟨you have the advantage of me⟩ *479:21*

R ⟨LB forgets birthday⟩   R ⟨precocious⟩ *482:19*

soutane   *512:15*   G ⟨Stop the War⟩ *480:9*

R ⟨simple & lovable⟩ *483:33–484:1*   G ⟨cattle creep subway⟩ *486:10*

35   R ⟨this stinking goat of Mendes⟩ *482:18–19*

G ⟨rid Dublin of this pest⟩ *462:16–17*   G ⟨JHP chessboard tabard⟩ *471:1–2*

G ⟨Sjambok⟩ *486:21*

R ⟨libertine⟩ *482:18*   G ⟨bishop of Down & Connor⟩ *471:9–10, 473:2–3*

courtesans

40   G ⟨Venus Callipyge Syracusas⟩ *480:25*

G ⟨That man is Leopold Macintosh⟩ *475:26–27*

R ⟨you beast⟩ *481:7*

waters of Salmacis make hermaphrodite

Baubo shows ?bald cunt   Ceres laughs

45   R ⟨embroidered prayerbook,⟩ *488:14?*   G ⟨LB declines honours⟩ *479:21–22?*

G ⟨LB excited social success⟩   G ⟨insults blind beggar⟩ *477:15?*

R ⟨LB walks on net⟩ *485:9*

R ⟨Kept the 10 commandments⟩ *480:4–5*   R ⟨some ghastly joke⟩ *482:33*

G ⟨Man like Ireland wants⟩ *475:4*   R ⟨old offender⟩

50   LB crusader ?gets ?nil   have you been true

G ⟨LB fire raiser⟩ *475:27*

Exultet roll   G ⟨womanly man⟩ *483:33*

R ⟨So may the Creator deal with me⟩ *473:9–10*

R ⟨intrigue very breath of his life⟩ *482:22–23*

55   R ⟨You have said it⟩ *485:4*

I was in bed with Mr X & 2 other gentlemen

R ⟨Sgenl inn ban bata coisde gan capall⟩ *483:4*

G ⟨under canal bridge⟩ *486:13?*   G ⟨LB denounces Citizen⟩ *488:25?*

344

	man pal of mine	?filtre on rumble
60	R ⟨LB going to have a baby⟩ 484:13	
	R ⟨What to do about taxes. Pay them. Thanks.⟩ 478:2–6	
	G ⟨funniest man in world⟩ 481:27–28	
	R ⟨ear covers eye, contacts face⟩ 485:9–13	
	R ⟨LB turns out fools⟩ 475:32ff.?	
65	R ⟨cities of the plain⟩ 482:20	R ⟨O'Madden Burke⟩ 480:14

ass's colt. Gee!

R ⟨love with moon⟩   R ⟨under geasa⟩

Sa père son mère

Aquinas de ?Cabbagitus

70   G ⟨Crab a bushranger⟩ 486:10

G ⟨Bloom 1st Bloom 2nd Sibylline⟩ Cf. 481:25, 482:6

G ⟨Ulster King at Arms   Athlone Poursuivant⟩ 471:2

G ⟨Sirs, take notice   for 6 mths⟩ 478:10–11

G ⟨You're bound over in yʳ· own recognisances in the sum of £5.

75   Where do I draw the £5.⟩ 478:10–16

G ⟨spare my past (weeps)⟩ 486:17–18

G ⟨midsummer madness⟩ 482:33   R ⟨born in bedlock⟩ 483:10–11

R ⟨viper slander⟩ 483:3

G ⟨whores sing litany⟩ 488   G ⟨IHS⟩ 488:11

80   R ⟨LB & little child pokes smile pigmentless eyes hiccup,

           milkcurdles⟩ 476:30–33

R ⟨ ″ distributes medal⟩ 476:2–3

NOTES

    Line 4 *Crofton*: a political appointee who also appears in the *Dubliners* story "Ivy Day in the Committee Room."

   6 *Hornblower*: the porter at Trinity College. His name is repeated at line 19.

   21 *Larry*: written in pencil.

   23 The only *Spencer* in the text is "Spencer Harty" (*U* 655:13).

   33 *Soutane*: cassock.

   35 Catulle *Mendes* (Mendès): French writer born of Jewish parents (1841–1909). See Stanislaus Joyce, pp. 121, 223n.

36   *JHP*: see "Cyclops" 4:61 note; cf. "Circe" 19:6.

37   *Sjambok*: Afrikaans for a heavy leather "whip," often of rhinoceros hide.

41   For the mystery man in the macintosh see *U* 108, 110, 251, 237, and elsewhere. On p. 500 Virag is dressed in a macintosh.

43   Hermaphroditus, the son of Hermes and Aphrodite, bathed in the *waters of Salmacis*. Salmacis, a nymph, fell in love with him and embraced him. When he failed to respond she asked that they be forever united. The gods granted the request, and their bodies merged into one.

44   *Baubo*: an old dry nurse in the household of King Celeus who tried to cheer up Ceres (Demeter) when the latter was in pain (Graves, I, 90).

52   *Exultet*: see "Circe" 9:34 and note. *Womanly man*: see "Oxen" 14:51 and note.

57   *Sgenl . . . capall*: Irish for "a pointless tale (lit. 'tale in the top of a stick') is a horseless coach" (O Hehir, p. 350).

63   *Contacts face*: contracts face is probably meant.

65   *O'Madden Burke*: the newspaper editor (*U* 130ff. and elsewhere). He also appears in the *Dubliners* story "A Mother."

67   *Geasa*: see "Oxen" 10:93 and note.

68   Joyce first wrote *la père, le mère*. The reversal of genders is probably connected with the hermaphrodite theme in line 43.

69   The name is an intentional absurdity.

72   *King at Arms* (King of Arms); *Poursuivant* (Pursuivant): heraldic officers. *Athlone*: the first Earl of Athlone was William III's general, Godert de Ginckell (d. 1703), who captured the town of Athlone (west of Dublin) in 1691.

80–81   Cf. "Nausicaa" 2:85 and 3:18–24.

"Circe" 17

shooting peasants and phartridges. what was that?

G ⟨S. Edw's staff   golden spurs   scep & cross   -with dove
    curtana trainbearer⟩ *471:34–35*

G ⟨Dalton lord mayor   His worship   mayor of Sligo⟩ *471:5*

5   ?Emmet

G ⟨codpiece⟩ *204:23*

pudet. nasonis

nudity—

glass scared

10   G ⟨member standing committees⟩ *476:1*

Caracciolo corpse upright in sea

G ⟨cheered to the echo⟩ *536:5–6*

grumpy

alle Bettpisser

15   James Talbot Power

G ⟨goddesses on car   keeper⟩ *480:23ff.*

G ⟨⟨loincloth⟩⟩ *23:25*

G ⟨tred⟩

G ⟨?Jack   Meyers⟩

20   Jerry Pe. . .

?lady   Doctor

panic

~~pillar~~ pin of collar

G ⟨Gentl. of bedchamber⟩ *471:27*

25   G ⟨Black Rod, Deputy Garter⟩ *471:27*

G ⟨Lord Gt. Chamberlain⟩ *471:28*

347

G ⟨Earl Marshal, High Constable⟩ *471:29*

G ⟨Sword of State, SE's crown⟩ *471:29–30*

G ⟨?oils,   patina⟩

30 G ⟨chalice & bible⟩ *471:30*

G ⟨Goldstick, M of Horse,⟩ *471:28*

G ⟨Gent at arms⟩

CENTER COLUMN HORIZONTAL

G ⟨elephantiasis,⟩ *483:12*   G ⟨fiendish⟩ *482:18*   R ⟨aleph,⟩ *477:25*
   R ⟨Lamech,⟩   R ⟨Lynch him⟩ *482:26*

35 G ⟨pillory,⟩ *486:22, 487:26*   G ⟨word of a Bloom,⟩ *475:7*   G ⟨3 acres
   & a cow,⟩ *480:6*

G ⟨witch 3 tears from left eye⟩ *486:17–18*

ibis sparrowhawk   Hathor a white cow   dungbeetle,   equine face
jackals at Bourse   fanfara

40 G ⟨Bantam Lyons,⟩ *485:7 and elsewhere*   wobbly legs, forelocks shaking,
on horse sidling prances   Adam was tempted,

R ⟨you're a credit to yr. country, sir,⟩ *475:2*   Noah's ark
   R ⟨?exposure⟩ *486, 517:8, and elsewhere*

R ⟨lechery with dissolute grandam, gave example of excessive

45   sensuality,⟩ *482:20*

R ⟨LB visited medically,⟩ *483:5ff.*

G ⟨women pour scent & roseleaves from top window, victor
   Bloom parade,⟩ *471:37–38*

G ⟨LB explains plans,⟩ *469–470*   G ⟨I believe in him, David's

50   house,⟩ *485:2?*

G ⟨Emmanuel,⟩   G ⟨postexilic⟩ *671:27*   hegemony

G ⟨white bull of Apocalypse,⟩ *482:21–22*   G ⟨Belial, Messiah the
   tailor,⟩ *487:17–18*

hid under Jahveh's seat,   G ⟨pseudo Messiah⟩ *487:17*

55 G ⟨ . . . ben Joseph or ben David,⟩ *485:2*   G ⟨Abulafia,⟩ *487:17*   Asher,
Menanem   S. of Judas   Abram,   G ⟨Lammlein ?of Istria,⟩ *487:17*

G ⟨LB pissed against,⟩   R ⟨his prick preserved,⟩ *483:24*

G ⟨fife & drum band,⟩ *470:33*   G ⟨triumphal arch⟩ *471:32*

348

R ⟨escaped from Eustace's private asyl. for lunatic
60   gentlemen,⟩ *483:9–10*

3 × 3, R ⟨LB carries sheep on back, he stinks⟩ R ⟨fetor
        judaicus⟩ *483:30*

G ⟨LB stoned & crucified,⟩ *487:12* all hallow, hallow, hallow

R ⟨I believe in him,⟩ *481:26–27* G ⟨I Bloom tell you so,⟩ *475:6–7*

65   G ⟨Bravo!⟩ *474:29*

G ⟨magnesium photo taken,⟩ *476:22–23* G ⟨LB speaks Hebrew (official
        translation)⟩ *477:25–28*

pregnant, G ⟨don't you believe a word he says,⟩ *475:26* G ⟨throw
        him out,⟩ *Cf. 475:29*

70 G ⟨world's greatest⟩ *472:10*

G ⟨Cead Mile Failte,⟩ *470:24–25* G ⟨Wailing on the Wall,⟩ *532:5–6*

ordeal of witch   G ⟨Music Sculpture Justice Industry Commerce
                  Painting Chemistry Publicity⟩ *480:27–30*

G ⟨600 voices Alleluja chorus, boo⟩ *488:29–30*

75 R ⟨vitrioled lust,⟩ *525:30* G ⟨just like old times⟩ G ⟨rosewater⟩ *468:13*

G ⟨epilepsy⟩ *483:11*   G ⟨ . . . Illustrious Bloom⟩ *474:5* G ⟨dog of a
        christian⟩ *475:29* R ⟨?Dr. Bloom,⟩ *447:5* G ⟨the lady Joan Mulholland,⟩

G ⟨scapegoat with ?sins   sent to Azazel   spirit of wilderness,
        Lilith nighthag⟩ *487:8–9*

80 G ⟨suckeress psychoanalysed,⟩ *Cf. 523:3*

G ⟨LB funny word   Recorder what *is* was that?⟩ *503:4?*   What is the
        man saying?

R ⟨What about mixed marriage?⟩ *480:19* R ⟨Mixed bathing?⟩ *480:21*

G ⟨He is agnostic.⟩ *481:2*   G ⟨Golden City that is to be⟩ *475:8*

85 R ⟨You deserve it,⟩ *474:15* R ⟨lost his reason⟩ *483:17?*

R ⟨virgo intacta⟩ *483:20*   R ⟨Dixon collection for LB⟩ *484:15*

R ⟨American pays,⟩ *484:15* G ⟨that's what you are⟩ *475:2*

R ⟨removes boot to throw at him⟩ *481:7* R ⟨his real name is
        Higgins⟩ *475:27*

90 G ⟨1st citizen thats the famous Bloom now   2nd citizen Is that
        Bloom⟩ *472:7–10*

G ⟨Women touch hem of robe⟩ *476:19–20* G ⟨Little Father,⟩ *476:26*

G ⟨gives Maundy money,⟩ *476:2* G ⟨uncloaks impressively,⟩ *477:24*

R ⟨patellar reflex absent⟩ *483:28* R ⟨LB covers organs⟩ *483:21*

95   Kiss it,

    G ⟨LB swears on testicles⟩ *473:9*   G ⟨Egypt Mizraim,   land of

        Ham,⟩ *487:10–11*

    cuckoos oust other birds, ?hawk   G ⟨bill of health,⟩ *483:32*

    G ⟨ascendants,⟩ *483:13*   ⟨flatty (BC)⟩ *487:29*

100   G ⟨squeak is out, Split (?G)   rattler (NS)⟩ *487:28*

    R ⟨Mother Grogan⟩ *482:27, 14:21ff.*

NOTES

Part of "Circe" 17 was published in Robert M. Adams's *Surface and Symbol* and revised in his paperback edition. Although the word sequence has been maintained in my transcription, the phrases have been rearranged for clarity.

Line 4 *Dalton*: not further identified.

5 *Emmet*: see "Cyclops" 5:12 and note.

7 *Pudet. nasonis*: one who is ashamed of his nose.

11 Prince Francesco *Caracciolo*: at one time the supreme commander of the Neapolitan navy and later, like Emmet, hanged as a traitor (1752–99).

14 *Alle Bettpisser*: literally, "all bedpissers."

15 Sir *James Talbot Power*: the fifth baronet of Talbot-Power (1851–1916) and chairman of John Power & Son, the distilling firm (*Burke's Peerage, 1875*). The name is repeated at "Ithaca" 1:5.

19 *Thom's Directory for 1904* lists several "J. Meyers."

23–24 Joyce first wrote *pillar*, scratched it out, and then wrote *pin* above it.

28 *SE's crown*: Joyce probably meant St. Stephen's crown instead of St. Edward's. See text.

34 *Lamech*: both the slayer of Cain and the first polygamist, according to Jewish tradition.

35 *Word of a Bloom*: repeated at "Circe" 15:24 and 15:41.

37 Repeated at "Circe" 6:6.

38 *Ibis . . . dungbeetle*: these words also appear at "Circe" 7:45ff; see note there and "Circe" 3:100 note. *Equine face*: see "Circe" 3:119 and note.

39 *Jackals at Bourse*: see "Circe" 7:104 and note.

44–45 *Gave . . . sensuality*: repeated at "Circe" 15:2.

55–56 *Lammlein* (Laemlein) and *Abulafia*: "Mastiansky and Citron, accusing Bloom of apostasy, fling at him ([U] 487) the names of two obscure Jewish heretics from the Middle Ages. Laemlein of Istria, the false Messiah, was Ascher Laemlein, an obscure Jewish prophet residing near Pola, who about 1502 proclaimed himself the Messiah; and Abraham Ben Samuel Abulafia was another pseudo-Messiah, born in Saragossa, who lived from 1240 to 1291 (?)" (Adams, pp. 140–141). *Menanem* (Menahem): one of the latest kings of Israel and a usurper.

77 *Lady Joan Mulholland*: Lady Hester Joan Byng, D.B.E., later Joan, Countess of Cavan, the widow of the Honourable Andrew Edward Mulholland, Captain, Irish Guards. Eoin O'Mahony

writes, "Lady Joan Mulholland was in the news as Lady-in-Waiting to Princess Mary from 1918 to 1922. Her name would have appeared regularly in the Court and Personal Columns of the leading English and Irish newspapers *only* during those years."

81   Joyce scratched out *is* and wrote *was* above it.

98   *Cuckoos*: see "Nausicaa" essay (pp. 25–27): cf. "Nausicaa" 3:64 and note.

99–100   *B.C.*: Bella Cohen, the mistress of the brothel. *Flatty*: policeman; *Split*: police informer; *Rattler*: coach (Partridge). Thus in the text "The squeak is out. A split is gone for the flatties. Nip the first rattler." means "The cry has been sounded. An informer has gone for the police. Take the first available coach." *NS*: not identified.

"Circe" 18

LEFT MARGIN HORIZONTAL

B ⟨velvet paws⟩ *490:2–3*
B ⟨Pianola,⟩ *561–563*
B ⟨Father Cowley⟩ *571:24*
B ⟨?Fregoli,⟩

LEFT MARGIN VERTICAL

5   B ⟨Giorgio & D.Sy. & cigarette "No thanks" & takes⟩
B ⟨Flowered man ?pfauen⟩

CENTER COLUMN HORIZONTAL

LB & rlwy separation,   North Wall,
LB follows girl in train   wildgoose, they know their ?holes
International corpse
10   R ⟨vipercatcher's visa⟩
R ⟨should a girl tell?⟩ *360:41*
R ⟨Bridal pair always laughing heartily at each other⟩
Given away
Curtain veil
15   B ⟨trolley maker⟩
G ⟨Moustache comb (H. Flower)⟩ *511:14*
B ⟨LB when I saw artless blush I looked always away⟩ *463:11?*
R ⟨Fringes (Bella)⟩ *523:32*

R ⟨She ofttimes wondered (Naus)⟩ *346:11–12*

20 R ⟨Menstru. hot ?jamrolls⟩ *497:15–16?*

and you let him go ?so. Curtain. No more work

B ⟨Few wellchosen words.⟩ *456:25–26*   B ⟨: at the ready⟩ *558:30*

Cat sleeps on cocaine

LB & MB part after 1 year. B ⟨1st lap⟩ *Cf. 558:33*

25 R ⟨Bareback (I).⟩ *461:21*   R ⟨?pante favourite⟩ *558:28?*

international jamboree   French & ?bear

B ⟨Voulez-vous que je vous embassy⟩ *Cf. 436:26*   B ⟨La Aurora and
        Karini⟩ *533:2–3*

?showring,   lugger   B ⟨I expect that's the (?) drunk⟩ *506:31–34*

30 B ⟨offence complained of⟩ *452:28, 455:3*

B ⟨my name Van- ⟩ *Cf. 178:32*

B ⟨He pleaded he had had some beer⟩ *453:16?*

B ⟨grave predicament⟩ *440:1–2*   B ⟨Eng huge jaws crocodiles⟩

B ⟨in a situation⟩ *452:10*   B ⟨LB my wife jealous of ?others⟩ *490:8–9*

35 B ⟨try to do the right thing⟩ *456:6–7*   B ⟨(?do that at once)⟩

garbage   R ⟨appeal to her (Naus)⟩ *357:40*

B ⟨Bernie, ?Keynan, ?Pull,⟩ ?Benny, Ned,   B ⟨Fido⟩ *445:8*
        B ⟨Towser,⟩ *446:6*   B ⟨Leo,⟩ *466:7–10 and elsewhere*

B ⟨with a request for the use of hairbrush⟩ *527:9–10?*

40 B ⟨down on his luck,⟩   B ⟨let it slide⟩ *445:19*

B ⟨Molly in gent's greatcoat⟩ *435:11–12?*

B ⟨from behind, interfering with her clothes, pinched her⟩ *453:2–5*
                    R ⟨:intimacy took place⟩ *455:2–3*

B ⟨long unintelligible speech⟩ *453:17*

45 B ⟨quite permitted in his native place   (Barbados)⟩ *454:34–455:1*

B ⟨surprised him in the bathroom⟩ *453:2?*

B ⟨You have access to ink & paper⟩

R ⟨deliberate lie (Naus)⟩ *342:21*   nepenthe   B ⟨proprietary
        article⟩ *533:6–7*

50 B ⟨taxed her with⟩ *452:14*   R ⟨weddingbells have ?rg for
        (Naus)⟩ *345:14*

B ⟨girl was in trouble:⟩   ever set eyes on   B ⟨back to back⟩

B ⟨Detained during H.M.'s pleasure⟩ *462:19–20*   B ⟨?bearhug ?pads⟩

R ⟨play a man's part (O. of S.)⟩ *Cf. 402:40–42*

55   *R* ⟨only man in world for her⟩ *358:31–32*

    R ⟨what you might call (Cycl)⟩

    B ⟨head down⟩   *B* ⟨Nelson's Pillar⟩ *482:11, 485:10*   *B* ⟨Don

        Giovanni⟩ *486:23 and elsewhere*

    morphasmos / domest. animals

60   Tango (casto, sornione, languido, sport, amoroso, matematico)

    8 yearly dances (bear) to Artemis / in crocus chlamys

    B ⟨leg up behind⟩ *491:34?*   *B* ⟨feet locked,⟩ *491:34* both bend,

    B ⟨footmarks⟩ *491:33*   clasp head & back   *B* ⟨gunboat⟩ *617:10*

    B ⟨She draws him⟩ *491:20* *B* ⟨plausibly⟩ *447:25, 606:7*

65   He behind her

    danza staccata (r & l in street)

    position woman's hand dancing to hide defect

    Man lives in 4 elements   *B* ⟨evensong⟩ *564:14*

    B ⟨statue holds lapel of coat⟩ *456:17–18*

70   *B* ⟨pocket in underskirt⟩ *431:25–26*

    R ⟨harakiri,⟩ *302:15* *B* ⟨commission peace⟩

NOTES

Line 4 *Fregoli* (*fregola*): "rut," or "violent desire," in Italian.

5 *D.Sy.*: may be Daisy Sykes, whose husband helped Joyce establish the English Players in Zurich.

6 *Pfauen*: "peacocks," the name of a restaurant in Zurich (*Letters*, II, 465n.).

9 This may refer to the drowned man found in Dublin Bay. See Adams, p. 89.

10 Repeated at *FW* 210:27.

25 *Pante*: "muff" in French; it may also mean an easy mark for a pickpocket.

27 This is *embassy*, not *embrasse*.

27–28 *La Aurora and Karini*: supposedly a rather famous musical act, but I have found no trace of them except in *Ulysses*.

29 *Lugger*: a porter, one who carries things.

48 *Nepenthe*: see *Ulysses* notebook VIII.A.5 at Buffalo (p. 295) and *U* 159:16–17, 403:41–42.

59 *Morphasmos* (*morfasmo*): an "old dance of a ridiculous kind," in Italian.

60 This line seems to be related to various movements of the dance, but the meaning is far from clear. *Tango*: a South American dance, but it can also mean "I touch" in Italian. *Casto*: chaste. *Sornione*: sly, sneaking.

61   *8 . . . Artemis*: "The myth of Callisto has been told to account for the two small girls, dressed as she-bears, who appeared in the Attic festival of Brauronian Artemis, and for the traditional connexion between Artemis and the Great Bear" (Graves, I, 86). *Chlamys*: a short mantle or cloak worn by men in ancient Greece.

66   *Danza staccata*: most likely a kind of abrupt dance, such as when someone dodges to the right and left of another pedestrian. Cf. *U* 429:19 and "Circe" 19:104.

"Circe" 19

LEFT MARGIN HORIZONTAL

B ⟨heads all to 1 side⟩   *R* ⟨Burn's second threw in the towel⟩
   313:35–36
B ⟨clasp Hands⟩ *304:33*   Buck M serious   giraffe
   LB hates to read al fresco   believes in
5   *R* ⟨Martha uses knee⟩ *524:2–4?*
B ⟨J.H.P. chessboard costume⟩ *471:1–2, 249:36–37*
?Man not on table
B ⟨Haines ?board   arrow, flee from justice⟩

LEFT COLUMN HORIZONTAL

B ⟨basilicogrammate⟩ *500:25*
10   *B* ⟨plinth⟩ *456:17, 112:38*
Egypt fisheaters
B ⟨flay⟩ *459:12*
Eg. not eat heads
R ⟨bustle (dress)⟩ *431:19*
15   party chest
dream—?Lorenzetto—popgun—voice—rat—
   falls—grows—huge—tailfaced—mush
   boneless—ooze— /Rat, marble eyes—family
   on back—food eaten . . . .
20   America—religion—take off shoes—priest(ess)
?Mrs Barney—fam. song.
LB dislikes books where you must read over twice

356

B ⟨nurtured⟩ *453:23*
B ⟨Yoke of buckets⟩ *559:4*
25   R ⟨painters singers⟩ *367:39*
B ⟨1st. thing in the morning⟩
R ⟨micturate⟩ *687:20?*
R ⟨codicil⟩
B ⟨ball at yr. feet⟩
30   dives   B ⟨cornjuice⟩ *600:26*
B ⟨cow eats yewtree   dies⟩
R ⟨firing squad⟩ *161:25*
B ⟨boy's washing water⟩
R ⟨suffice it to say⟩ *614:17, 645:29*
35   B ⟨quinine⟩
R ⟨concoction⟩ *169:21, 606:35*
knuckle of veal
saddle of mutton
B ⟨ghosts of cats⟩
40   R ⟨speak of weather⟩
R ⟨Natural Le Coultre 55 Boul. Haus⟩
B ⟨LB found purse, don't warrant it held only 9 frs⟩
R ⟨Douglas Hunter, Sicilian House, Southampton Rd. WC 1⟩
R ⟨Tress hat, Norwell Perth N.B. brogues.⟩
45   R ⟨N. ?Dorossa Ramo 2° Barozzi 2153, S.Moisé, Venice⟩
B ⟨cws.   same style of beauty⟩
B ⟨?sleep—all show worst side of self⟩ *533:32–534:1*
R ⟨servant in sheepskin⟩ *458:10*
B ⟨circus mimes in hoop of paper⟩ *Cf. 446:18–19*
50   R ⟨Fels, Bpte. 13, Bd. M. 13 ?g⟩
B ⟨1 way of getting on in world⟩ *157:30–31*   B ⟨⟨?Just⟩⟩
R ⟨policeman's lot is not a happy one⟩ *Cf. 160:9*
R ⟨Martha feels her arms⟩
R ⟨Life of drifting cabmen⟩ *76:9–10*
55   R ⟨Toadbelly wry neck, Coffey (Circe)⟩ *465:2*
R ⟨Vander Pyl, Gay Lussac 13⟩
glands or bumps
R ⟨Pasini, 325 Aleardi⟩

357

R ⟨Steinberg, Battisti, 18,⟩

60   Manna white pearly pea melt in sun on twigs of tamarisk
      tree by bite of ?cacos insect

R ⟨moated grange⟩ *748:12*

¼ Egypt. adults monks

365 monasteries

65   *R* ⟨winelodge⟩ *392:18*

B ⟨looked the part,⟩

R ⟨handicapped⟩ *313:9*   *R* ⟨put it there,⟩   put it mildly

fail to apprehend   *B* ⟨the delinquent⟩ *404:6–7*

G ⟨they will have better manners⟩

70   *R* ⟨Bennett's right eye was almost closed⟩ *313:22–23*

R ⟨brimful of confidence, the bulkier man⟩ *313:21*

R ⟨B—was tricky,   his footwork a treat to watch⟩ *313:29*

R ⟨Referee twice cautioned Bennett for holding⟩ *313:27–28*

R ⟨a hefty battler Myler ?then   got busy⟩ *313:20*

75   *R* ⟨Burns was receiver general of r's & l's,⟩ *313:13–14*

      cub, whelp

CENTER AND RIGHT COLUMNS HORIZONTAL

B ⟨stud fee⟩ *540:28*   *B* ⟨The odds are⟩ *614:29?, 312:36?*

?joists   Haines cleans teeth at ?night

B ⟨?gag⟩ *455:25*   *R* ⟨ragpicker⟩ *429:15–16*

80   *B* ⟨the Pharaoh⟩ *455:1*   *R* ⟨LB false inkstain W. Hely's⟩ *152:34*

B ⟨high jinks⟩ *438:28*   LB want a thing done do it yourself

stand on trevets   *R* ⟨Martha-hag-answer advert.⟩

shaft   *B* ⟨None worse for wear⟩ *637:32–33*

                     B ⟨luring him to doom⟩ *490:28*

85   *B* ⟨coughs of laughter⟩ *37:12*

                     R ⟨make short work of⟩

                     R ⟨Si.D. sings in house he leaves—Shall
                         carry my heart to thee⟩ *513:19–22*

90　R ⟨Rorke's drift⟩ *449:9, 581:13*   Happy Kings whose orders are
　　　　　　　　　　　　　　　　　at once executed (SD)

　　R ⟨Lough Neagh (Naus)⟩ *326:22, 711:19*

　　R ⟨petrified⟩ *209:34 and elsewhere*   R ⟨Girl cyclists free wheel free view⟩ *352:6?*
　　hob of hell　　　　　　　　　　　　fluent (SD)

　　R ⟨faiseuse d'anges⟩　　　　　　　B ⟨girl pianist her bow behind⟩

95　B ⟨on yesterday⟩ *604:4*

　　B ⟨invite to breakfast⟩ *765:4?*

　　small blame to him

　　limitless will = no will

　　LB or MB corns　　　　　　　　　　B ⟨?Sapo ?ait (Cir)⟩

100　R ⟨LB takes off hat⟩ *379:17 and elsewhere*   R ⟨3 garments⟩ *344:32*

　　furniture van

　　B ⟨LB sits on bumwarmed seat⟩

　　　″ meets someone who ?not   salutes

　　R ⟨″ dances right & left of someone (?hot)⟩ *429:19*

105　　　R ⟨:agog:⟩ *440:11*   R ⟨do it now.⟩

　　R ⟨hayfever (O of S)⟩ *416:31*

　　R ⟨slobber (Cir. Gerty)⟩ *435:9*

　　R ⟨fornicating (Cycl)⟩ *308:37*

　　B ⟨sober hearsedrivers (Cir)⟩ *590:31*

110　Lucia finger in mouth

　　hesitates to buy

　　B ⟨woman stand hands crossed there⟩   (+ Dignam photo)

　　Portrait reveals diseases

　　R ⟨povertystricken (Cycl)⟩ *315:37*

115　infested

　　R ⟨Hammam (bath)⟩ *83:38*

　　R ⟨Most of us think⟩

　　G ⟨Without loss of time⟩ *460:22*

　　R ⟨woman ?once   possessed take the starch out of her⟩ *72:40–41*

120　R ⟨marriage has been arranged⟩ *345:13–14*

NOTES

In the British Museum collection this double notesheet here numbered "Circe" 18 through "Circe" 21 was with the "Cyclops" notes. I have placed it with "Circe" because of the content and because "Circe" 20–21 give the *personae* of *Ulysses* through "Circe." It is, however, a transitional notesheet and contains material for various episodes.

Line 1   *Burn's second*: given the name of "Ole Pfotts Wettstein" in the text (313:36). For more on the fight and *Burns* (later renamed *Bennett*), see lines 70–76.

4   *Al fresco*: in the open air.

6   Cf. "Circe" 16:36.

8   *Board arrow*: may be *bow and arrow*.

9   *Basilicogrammate*: "by royal writ," a transliteration of the Greek. Cf. Adams, p. 139.

13   *Eg.*: refers to *Egypt fisheaters* at line 11.

16–19   This is apparently intended to be a free association of ideas (or perhaps a *dream*) similar to examples discussed by Litz (p. 18) and Ellmann (p. 368). It concerns rats in some way, but the meaning is quite obscure. *Lorenzetto*: diminutive of Lorenzo.

21   *Mrs Barney*: Natalie Clifford Barney, a friend of Rémy de Gourmont and Paul Valéry (Ellmann, pp. 500, 502, 569, and elsewhere).

30   *Dives*: may be *diver*.

31   *Yewtree*: a traditional symbol of grief. See Tennyson's *In Memoriam*, for example.

41   *Natural* (not *Naturel*) *Le Coultre*: although LeCoultre is by no means rare as a French personal name, this is not the name of a person. It may be the name of a business firm of some sort. *Boul. Haus*: the boulevard Haussmann in Paris, which runs east and west behind the Opéra and north of the Champs-Elysées.

43   Joyce wrote *Southampton Rd*, but Eoin O'Mahony believes it should be Southampton "Row," which is near Euston Station in London. He says "Sicilian Avenue is an oblique sidewalk on the western side of Southampton Row. . . . It is the headquarters of several private Detective Agencies. . . . Hunter would be a suitable name for a detective, whether real or *assumed*."

44   *Tress*: fashionable London hatters. *Norwell*: perhaps a Scottish shoe factory. *N.B.*: North Britain, not New Brunswick as in Hanley. Joyce was apparently thinking of ordering some clothes.

45   *Dorossa*: not identified. *Ramo 2°*: 2nd branch. *S[an]. Moisé*: a church (and probably a parish district) near the Piazza di San Marco in *Venice*.

50   *Florent Fels*: editor of *L'Action* and author of several books on modern art, who wished to publish a French translation of *A Portrait* in serial form but never accomplished it (*Letters*, I, 120, 142, and elsewhere). (The new vol. I of the *Letters* perpetuates the misreading of "Froment," although it was corrected in the index in vol. III.) There seem to be two addresses here. *Bpte*: the rue Bonaparte. *Bd. M.*: either the boulevard Montmartre or the boulevard Maleherbes.

56   *Vander Pyl*: Fritz Vanderpyl, a Belgian art critic in Paris, whom Joyce visited on July 26, 1920, at the suggestion of Ezra Pound (see Ellmann, p. 504). Vanderpyl presented Joyce with a copy of his book, *Mon chant de guerre*, with the inscription, "Ce chant de 1917 pour James Joyce, irlandais, écrivain, homme, Vanderpyl, Paris 31/7/1920." See also Appendix B, and Connolly, ed., *Scribbledehobble*, pp. 75–76.

58   Ferdinando *Pasini*: a professor of Italian language and literature at the University of Trieste

and author of *L'univers. ital. a Trieste* (Florence, 1910) and *Diario di un sepolto vivo* (Bologna, 1921). In *L'Italia e gli Italiani di Ogg* (Genoa, 1947, p. 545), he is listed as living at "v. dell'Aleardi, 6" in Trieste.

59   Salomon D. *Steinberg*: a Swiss educator, author, and translator who was born in Lucerne in 1889 and was feuilleton-editor of the *Züricher Post* from 1915 to 1923. Since 1925 he has been headmaster of the Maturitäts-Institut Minerva in Zurich (*Who's Who in World Jewry*). See also *Letters*, III, 397.

60–61   *Tamarisk*: a "shrub or small tree of a large genus (Tamarix) of shrubs or small trees that are natives of the eastern Mediterranean region and tropical Asia and have minute scalelike leaves and feathery racemes of small white or pinkish flowers with free stamens and 3 to 4 styles" (*Webster's 3rd*). The manna *insect* or manna scale (*Trabutina mannipara*) bites the leaves of the tamarisk and thereby causes white sap to form on them. The sap is called *manna*.

70–76   Joyce took the information for this fight from the *Freeman's Journal* for April 28, 29, and 30, 1904. In the newspaper account, M. L. Keogh was matched with Garry of the 6th Dragoons. Joyce kept the name Keogh, but for Garry he first substituted *Burns* (lines 1, 75) and then decided on Percy *Bennett*, the name of a Zurich consular official he disliked (Adams, p. 70).

78, 81–83   The phrases on the left side of these lines are thematically connected. *Joists*: "any of the small rectangular-sectioned timbers or rolled iron or steel beams" (*Webster's 3rd*). *Trevets*: trivet, "a . . . three-legged stand (as to hold a kettle near a fire)" (*Webster's 3rd*).

87–88   Cf. *Stephen Hero*, p. 160.

89   *Rorke's drift*: the scene of a famous battle in Zululand during the Boer War.

94   *Faiseuse d'anges*: abortionist.

99   *Sapo*: "soap" in Latin. *Ait*: he says. Cf. *U* 208:11–14. The meaning of this phrase is not clear.

104   Cf. "Circe" 18:66.

110   *Lucia*: Joyce's daughter.

"Circe" 20

1) R ⟨Stephen Dedalus⟩ *5:12*
   B ⟨Buck Mulligan⟩ *5:1*
   B ⟨Stephen's Mother⟩ *7:12*
   R ⟨Simon Dedalus⟩ *58:7*
   B ⟨Haines⟩ *6:12*
   B ⟨Bannon⟩ *23:18*
   B ⟨Clive Kempthorpe⟩ *9:12 & 13*
   B ⟨the Milkwoman⟩ *18:8*
   L. Annegato
   Cranly *9:7*

2) Sargent *28:15ff.*
   B ⟨Garrett Deasy⟩ *28:24*

5) R ⟨Henry Flower⟩ *71:30*
   R ⟨Martha Clifford⟩ *77:6*
   B ⟨C. P. M'Coy⟩ *67:14*
   B ⟨Hoppy Holohan⟩ *72:28–29*
   B ⟨Father Conmee⟩ *79:1*
   B ⟨the Druggist⟩ *83:4ff.*
   B ⟨Hornblower⟩ *85:11*
   B ⟨Bantam Lyons⟩ *73:1*

6) R ⟨Paddy Dignam⟩ *73:9*
   B ⟨Patsy Dignam⟩ *296:39*   B ⟨Corny Kelleher⟩ *70:14–15*
   Brother in law *100:14* Rudy *88:1*
   B ⟨Tom Kernan⟩ *88:41*
   Joe Hynes *89:2*
   B ⟨John Henry Menton⟩ *101:26–27*
   R ⟨Mackintosh⟩ *108, 110*
   R ⟨Father Coffey⟩ *102:15*
   R ⟨John O'Connell⟩ *105:23*
   Bargeman *97:42–98:1*
   B ⟨Ned Lambert⟩ *89:1*
   R ⟨Martin Cunningham⟩ *86:1*
   R ⟨Jack Power⟩ *86:3*

362

3) B ⟨Kevin Egan⟩ *42:15*
B ⟨Patrice Egan⟩ *42:14*
30   Aunt Sally   *39:31, 87:15*
R ⟨Richie Goulding⟩ *40:2*
B ⟨The Gipsies⟩ *48:3ff.?*
B ⟨Anna Kearns⟩ *144:1 & 2*
B ⟨Florence McCabe⟩ *38:38*

35

40

4) R ⟨Leopold Bloom⟩ *55:1*
45   R ⟨Marion Bloom⟩ *61:30*
B ⟨Milly Bloom⟩ *61:36*
B ⟨Blazes Boylan⟩ *62:30*
B ⟨Professor Goodwin⟩ *62:40*
B ⟨Moses Dlugacz⟩ *68:17*
50   B ⟨The Servant⟩ *59:1ff.*
R ⟨Philip Beaufoy⟩ *68:28*
R ⟨Paul de Kock⟩ *64:30*

55

B ⟨Dodd & Son⟩ *93:9*
B ⟨Bootlaces⟩ *92:12*

7) Red Murray   *115:27*
B ⟨Brayden⟩ *116:7*
B ⟨Nannetti⟩ *117:16*
R ⟨Myles Crawford⟩ *124:18*
B ⟨Professor MacHugh⟩ *122:18*
B ⟨Lenehan⟩ *124:10*
B ⟨J J O'Molloy⟩ *123:31*
B ⟨Newsvendors⟩ *127:2*
B ⟨Nelson⟩ *115:3*
B ⟨Moses⟩ *138:8*
B ⟨John F. Taylor⟩ *139:15–16*
B ⟨Tim Healy⟩ *139:23*
B ⟨Gerald Fitzgibbon⟩ *139:16*
Skin the Goat   *134:26*
     B ⟨Seymour Bush⟩ *137:30*
     B ⟨Childs⟩ *137:36*

8) R ⟨Elijah⟩ *149:15*
Parallax   *152:3*
R ⟨Mrs Breen⟩ *154:25*
B ⟨Mr Denis Breen⟩ *157:15*
B ⟨Tisdall Farrell⟩ *157:13–14*
B ⟨J. H. Parnell⟩ *161:28*
B ⟨Davy Byrne⟩ *168:1*
B ⟨Nosey Flynn⟩ *169:6*
B ⟨Paddy Leonard⟩ *175:39*
B ⟨Tom Rochford⟩ *175:39*
L'Aveugle   *178:8ff.*
B ⟨Recorder⟩ *180:13*
Goddesses   *174:3ff.*

363

NOTES

Notesheets 20 and 21 list the dramatis personae. The numbers to the left at the top of each column correspond to the first fifteen episodes of *Ulysses* (there are no characters in section 16). These numbers are in green pencil. Page references here are only to the first appearance of each name in the novel.

9 *Annegato*: "drowned man" in Italian. The name refers to the man who drowned in Dublin Bay. See Adams, p. 89.

33 *Anna Kearns*: in the text it is "Anne."

52 *Paul de Kock*: not a character in *Ulysses*. He was a French novelist (1794–1871) who "produced an endless series of novels, vivacious, piquant, and very readable" (*Chambers's*). A glance at section 8 will show that Joyce included motifs as well as characters in these lists.

53 *L'Aveugle*: the blind man.

"Circe" 21

9) R ⟨Lyster⟩ *197:39, 208:28,*
    498:26

   R ⟨Best⟩ *184:3*

   R ⟨John Eglinton⟩ *182:20*

   R ⟨Geo. Russell⟩ *183:11*

   Geo. Moore *190:19*

   B ⟨Shakespeare⟩ *183:8–9*

   Socrates *188:19–20*

   Ulysses *192:42*

   B ⟨Jesus Christ⟩ *183:13*

---

10) B ⟨Dudley⟩ *219:1*

    B ⟨Sailor⟩ *222:9ff.*

    B ⟨Dilly Dedalus⟩ *223:32*

    Boody Dedalus *222:14*

    Maggie Dedalus *223:5*

    B ⟨Miss Parker⟩

    B ⟨Artifoni⟩ *225:8*

    B ⟨Ben Dollard⟩ *230:35*

    B ⟨Father Cowley⟩ *236:24*

    B ⟨Jimmy Henry⟩ *243:5*

    B ⟨Long John⟩ *240:26*

---

11) B ⟨Miss Douce⟩ *253:27*

    B ⟨Miss Kennedy⟩ *253:27*

    B ⟨Geo. Lidwell⟩ *257:36*

13) R ⟨Gerty MacDowell⟩ *341:40*

    B ⟨Cissy Caffrey⟩ *340:14*

    B ⟨Edy Boardman⟩ *340:14*

    B ⟨The Twins⟩ *340:18*

    B ⟨Father John Hughes S.J.⟩
       347:36–37

    B ⟨Canon O'Hanlon⟩ *352:19–20*

    B ⟨Father Conroy⟩ *352:19*

---

14) R ⟨nurse Callan⟩ *399:16*

    B ⟨Dixon⟩ *380:19*

    R ⟨Punch Costello⟩ *382:15*

    R ⟨Madden⟩ *382:12*

    R ⟨Nurse Quigley⟩ *385:36*

    Mrs Purefoy *391:9*

    B ⟨Theodore Purefoy⟩ *416:12 & 19*

    R ⟨Lynch⟩ *382:11*

    B ⟨Crotthers⟩ *382:13*

---

15) R ⟨Zoe Higgins⟩ *466:15*

    R ⟨Florrie Talbot⟩ *492:29*

    R ⟨Kitty Ricketts⟩ *492:3–4*

25 B ⟨?Bapty⟩ *276:30*

B ⟨James Barton hackney⟩
  275:15

R ⟨Mario⟩ *116, 506:19*

R ⟨Lionel⟩ *270:36*

30 B ⟨Croppy Boy⟩ *278:18*

R ⟨Bella Cohen⟩ *515:12*

B ⟨Private Carr⟩ *423:20*

           (ʼ38)

B ⟨Former Days, Stoer & LB 'Live
  us again'⟩ *535:32–33*

B ⟨scrofulous⟩ *423:13*

B ⟨?syphilitic whore dream⟩

35 B ⟨Moly = absinthe, mercury,⟩ *Cf. 76:18*

B ⟨LB Jim Bludso⟩ *449:27*
 a nigger squats on her safety
 valve,

B ⟨hold her nozzle again the bank⟩
 449:27–28

40 Christ ain't to be too hard on
 a man as died for men.

12) R ⟨I⟩

B ⟨Crawford Crofton⟩ *334:37*

45 B ⟨Alf Bergan⟩ *293:31*

R ⟨Bob Doran⟩ *293:34*

R ⟨Dog⟩ *292:18*

B ⟨Citizen⟩ *290:10*

Moses Herzog *287:19 & 35*

50 Geraghty plumber *287:21–*
   22

B ⟨Beresford⟩ *323:15*

16) Bhang

make his way

B ⟨a 3 yʳ· old⟩

B ⟨Miriam Dandrade⟩ *524:18–19*

Gisella Goldschmidt.

B ⟨LB cheapjack. Won't you
 buy⟩ *444:19*

Moly = chastity

LB in dunce's foolscap.

B ⟨arch conspirator of the
 age⟩ *451:24–25*

55 B ⟨plodge (wade)⟩ *443:6,*
 466:3

B ⟨& don't you forget it,
 old bean,⟩ *531:11–12*

B ⟨the wall of the heart,⟩

60

spirit moved him
B ⟨I am the Virag who⟩ *508:19*
B ⟨Dig deep & win wisely⟩
B ⟨Dublin city & urban
    district.⟩ *453:32–33*

NOTES

Page references here are only to the first appearance of each name in the novel.

Line 16   *Miss Parker*: the name of the girl in the fruitshop (*U* 224), although her name doesn't appear in the text. *Mrs Purefoy*: Joyce first wrote *Beaufoy* and then *Purefoy* over it. Bloom makes a similar mistake (*U* 156).

31   *Stoer*: see "Cyclops" 1:60 and note.

35 & 50   *Moly*: see "Circe" 2:3 and note.

"Eumaeus" I

B ⟨as it is a lifelong slur⟩ *638:9*
B ⟨proved to be in the act of⟩
B ⟨occurance took place as well as if it was yesterday⟩ *613:34*
B ⟨a t . . . . . . ⟩
5   *B* ⟨involving⟩ *638:9*
only man outside of
play lead (CSP.)
should it meet the eye of
B ⟨pretty thick that⟩ *603:12*
10   *B* ⟨bona fides⟩ *610:34*
B ⟨pro rata⟩ *628:26*
sustained a broken neck
came into money
B ⟨grand total⟩ *644:9*
15   fast breaking up   *623:13*
B ⟨qualified man⟩ *619:7*
B ⟨rulings of fate⟩ *610:39?*
B ⟨tuitions⟩ *648:11*
R ⟨a few odd moments⟩ *632:23–24*
20   *B* ⟨how to word it⟩
scar
R ⟨guesswork⟩ *633:1–2*
failed to disclose
B ⟨peruse⟩ *610:22*
25   *B* ⟨repose confidence⟩ *604:32–33*
to good advantages
B ⟨cares of office⟩ *615:17*

LEFT COLUMN HORIZONTAL

B ⟨pale in the face⟩ *597:17*

B ⟨cohabit⟩ *638:17*

30 end of his resources,   B ⟨apparently⟩ *606:13 and elsewhere*

B ⟨made light of it⟩ *598:3*

B ⟨marriage market⟩

B ⟨scheme fell through⟩ *611:1*

B ⟨1ᵈ· to her name⟩

35 B ⟨globetrotters⟩ *612:40*

B ⟨containing the habitual⟩ *638:15–16*

B ⟨in the shape of solid food⟩ *606:8*

B ⟨got into hot water (O'Call)⟩ *630:1–7*

B ⟨slouchy⟩ *603:3*

40 R ⟨make matters worse⟩ *634:41*

B ⟨to benefit his health⟩ *611:6*

B ⟨a new lease of life⟩ *612:7–8*

B ⟨you can safely say⟩ *628:10*

B ⟨then an incident happened (sailor goes out)⟩ *622:25–28*

45 B ⟨on the spur of the moment⟩ *644:23–24*

B ⟨in its most virulent form⟩ *623:19*

B ⟨cured of his partiality⟩ *623:27–28*

B ⟨turning money away⟩

B ⟨he could truthfully state⟩ *617:29–30*

50 B ⟨extraordinary interest was aroused at the time⟩ *634:40–41*

R ⟨affectionate letters passed between them⟩ *634:42*

gathered from the fact

R ⟨an attachment sprung up⟩ *635:2*

B ⟨6–16, tattoo⟩ *615:33*

55 B ⟨Edw. VII House of Lords tattoo all the go then⟩ *630:15–17*

R ⟨Roger Chas Tichborne. SS Bella⟩ *634:18–19*

R ⟨evidence went to show⟩ *634:20*

R ⟨lord Bellew, Indian ink.⟩ *634:21*

B ⟨in a large way of business⟩ *647:34–35*

60 B ⟨financial magnates⟩ *647:34*

R ⟨it pointed a moral⟩ *634:2*

B ⟨proclivities⟩ *600:40*

B ⟨dictates of humanity⟩ *623:16*

B ⟨monetarily & mentally⟩ *648:15*

65   B ⟨Now you mention it⟩ *603:27–28*

B ⟨true to their salt⟩ *625:24?*

B ⟨far from it⟩

B ⟨bow to the inevitable⟩ *609:7*

B ⟨historic⟩ *612:20, 634:40, 638:27–28*

70   B ⟨under all the circs⟩ *599:32*

R ⟨abbreviations⟩ *662:18?*

R ⟨sweet nothings⟩ *635:1*

B ⟨enjoyed the distinction⟩ *638:26*

B ⟨take unto himself⟩ *640:14*

75   B ⟨took it for granted⟩ *645:35*

B ⟨conversazione⟩ *648:4*

B ⟨step in the required direction⟩ *648:14*

B ⟨alongside⟩ *603:24*

B ⟨a wide berth⟩ *623:6*

80   B ⟨sneaking sympathy (Land Act LB)⟩ *641:5?, 641:10?*

R ⟨reverting to⟩ *620:39, 630:34*

R ⟨owed his death⟩ *633:27*   R ⟨it never transpired⟩ *633:27*

B ⟨it became necessary for him to⟩ *622:25–26*

B ⟨I didn't think he had it in him⟩ *638:5*

85   B ⟨clue to his whereabouts⟩ *633:34, 642:16*

B ⟨brought home to him⟩

B ⟨P.C. was the man who⟩ *Cf. 600:30–31*

B ⟨and find him he did⟩ *639:8?*

G ⟨when it suited him⟩ *642:4?*

90   B ⟨forthcoming⟩ *604:18 and elsewhere*

B ⟨with dramatic force⟩ *628:24*

R ⟨idol feet of clay⟩ *634:2*

B ⟨left no loophole⟩ *638:16–17*

B ⟨pin his faith to⟩ *641:8*

95   make for fitness

R ⟨he lay low⟩ *633:10?*

B ⟨intimated⟩ *637:4, 647:4*

R ⟨made the facts public⟩ *634:41*

B ⟨marked difference in their ages⟩ *618:27*

100 *B* ⟨without a care in the world⟩ *646:33–34*

changed hands for £250

B ⟨take by storm⟩ *613:36*

B ⟨had not contributed a copper⟩ *641:7–8*

B ⟨his aim clearly was to clear out⟩ *642:36*

105 *R* ⟨redeeming feature⟩ *634:1*

B ⟨radically altered⟩ *623:1–2, 638:37–38*

hold their own

B ⟨conveyed the impression⟩ *613:27*

stigmatised

110 *B* ⟨prove a success⟩ *611:20 & 27?*

R ⟨as luck wᵈ· have it⟩ *601:35, 631:16*

B ⟨Mr B was the first to rise from his seat⟩ *644:3–4*

B ⟨four times the money⟩ *644:14*

B ⟨would by any chance you⟩ *599:17?, 613:9?*

CENTER COLUMN HORIZONTAL

115 *B* ⟨ejaculated⟩ *603:33, 636:21*

B ⟨ablutions⟩ *597:8*

B ⟨our mutual friend⟩ *619:38*

B ⟨wend his way towards⟩ *642:13* *B* ⟨he concurred⟩ *607:5, 625:13*

B ⟨dumpy⟩ *622:29*   *B* ⟨men in the plural⟩ *639:41*

120 framed in a pleasing fashion

B ⟨imbued with proper spirit⟩

B ⟨greatly improved⟩ *623:2*

had not been able to be found

R ⟨Simon Magus⟩

125 *R* ⟨train over arm⟩

B ⟨that worthy⟩ *615:40*

B ⟨good graces⟩ *647:41*

B ⟨?whether nor its reverse⟩ *621:3?, 641:32?*

B ⟨ask for it! beg!⟩ *522:21*

130   R ⟨this pest!⟩ *462:16–17*
      R ⟨rid Dublin of⟩ *462:16*
      B ⟨object of curiosity⟩ *606:5*
      B ⟨fits & starts⟩ *613:30*
      B ⟨Give points to⟩ *603:2*
135   handsome of him
      B ⟨en route⟩ *598:29*
      B ⟨guardian of law⟩ *599:12*
      R ⟨LB speaks to the Nox⟩
      R ⟨landed in hot water⟩ *630:7*
140   pomp
      R ⟨odalisk⟩ *468:12*
      B ⟨manifested impatience⟩ *643:21*
      R ⟨model household⟩
      B ⟨far reaching effect⟩ *618:19?*
145   temporize
      B ⟨of a doing⟩
      B ⟨never said a word⟩ *601:28–29*
      B ⟨seemingly⟩ *603:21 and elsewhere*
      B ⟨not knowing their own minds⟩ *639:26–27*
150   B ⟨here today & gone tomorrow⟩ *631:5*
      B ⟨LB & whistle⟩ *597:35*
      B ⟨impromptu⟩ *644:26*
      B ⟨vast amt of harm⟩ *642:9*
      B ⟨for the matter of that⟩
155   B ⟨until he chose to⟩ *640:2–3?*

RIGHT COLUMN HORIZONTAL

      B ⟨fictitious⟩ *610:33*
      B ⟨turn of mind⟩
      B ⟨sticking to his original point⟩ *618:28–29*
      B ⟨conflicting versions⟩ *627:40*
160   B ⟨related⟩ *612:34*
      B ⟨pending that⟩ *625:31*

B ⟨tired of wedded life⟩ *640:3*

B ⟨uncommonly able thief⟩ *628:13–14*

B ⟨baffled (beggars) description⟩ *613:26–27*

165 *B* ⟨fond lover's ways⟩ *640:24*

B ⟨for reasons known to self⟩ *630:38?*

B ⟨all about art⟩

B ⟨twitted with being⟩ *641:13?*

B ⟨meted out⟩

170 try to realize

B ⟨dictums⟩ *641:9*

B ⟨prior to then⟩ *605:36*

B ⟨what earthly reason⟩ *605:9–10*

B ⟨pertinent suggestion (change the subject)⟩ *629:26–27*

175 *B* ⟨a rare boon⟩ *647:27–28*

reason to believe

B ⟨loyal to the core⟩

B ⟨a little bit previous⟩

B ⟨hidebound precedent⟩ *642:5–6*

180 *B* ⟨same remark applies to⟩ *618:18–19?*

B ⟨one got of⟩

B ⟨to vary the adage⟩ *598:1*

B ⟨bring common sense to bear on it⟩ *597:36–37*

B ⟨I fail to see⟩ *642:9*

185 *B* ⟨a most glaring piece of⟩ *599:30–31*

B ⟨afford great pleasure if he would let him help⟩ *642:2–3*

B ⟨as distinct from⟩ *617:36*

B ⟨I know my WS⟩ *618:35–36*

B ⟨flutter in the dovecotes⟩ *648:5–6*

190 absent from his wit

R ⟨platonic⟩ *635:1*

B ⟨made no secret⟩

B ⟨gadding about⟩

B ⟨on record⟩ *648:7–8*

195 *B* ⟨mutually useful⟩ *619:7?*

B ⟨he drank⟩ *623:25*

B ⟨hit upon an expedient⟩ *597:8–9*

B ⟨had a vogue⟩ *648:20–21*

B ⟨try to concentrate⟩ *618:1*

200 B ⟨appreciable⟩ *606:15*

G ⟨by all means⟩

B ⟨crux⟩ *641:27*

B ⟨1ˢᵗ· impression⟩ *641:39*

B ⟨for one thing⟩

205 B ⟨approached⟩ *641:42*

B ⟨quixotic⟩ *625:36*

B ⟨best of the bunch⟩ *638:4–5*

B ⟨bibulous⟩ *606:14*

B ⟨made a lot of him⟩

210 R ⟨made the most of⟩ *625:41–42*

B ⟨capital⟩ *648:25 and elsewhere*

B ⟨humourous element⟩ *604:34*

B ⟨in safe hands⟩ *642:8*

B ⟨afford to ignore it⟩ *638:23*

215 B ⟨?all ?no bar⟩

B ⟨on a recent occasion⟩ *604:2*

B ⟨preliminary canter⟩ *640:23*

B ⟨hails from⟩ *608:24*

B ⟨the uttermost farthing⟩ *700:33*

220 R ⟨much to answer for⟩ *628:14*

B ⟨instilled ..... ideas⟩ *639:13?*

transparent heart

B ⟨wise precaution⟩ *644:6*

B ⟨without a moment's hesitation⟩ *644:26–27*

225 B ⟨the why & wherefores⟩ *639:26*

B ⟨chronic impecuniosity⟩ *603:4*

B ⟨outside of the strictly entre nous variety⟩ *613:23*

B ⟨public at large⟩

B ⟨plain sailing⟩ *642:37*

230 B ⟨dunderheads⟩ *611:36*

NOTES

In the upper left-hand corner is *Eumeus* underlined in blue.

Line 7   This line is horizontal.

56   *Roger Chas Tichborne*: "After the death of Sir Alfred Joseph Tichborne (1836–66), eleventh baronet, a butcher from Wagga-Wagga in New South Wales, Thomas Castro, otherwise Arthur Orton of Wapping, came forward to personate an elder brother, Roger Charles Tichborne (1829–54), who had been lost at sea off America. His case collapsed on March 6, 1872, the 103rd day of a trial to assert his claims. The 'Claimant,' committed for perjury on February 28, 1874, the 188th day of his new trial, the cost of which was £55, 315, got fourteen years' hard labour. Released 1884, in 1895 he confessed the imposture, and died April 1, 1898" (*Chambers's*).

58   Lord John Chippendall Montesquieu *Bellew*: author, preacher, and public reader (1823–74). He was involved in the Tichborne case (see above).

87   *P.C.*: Patrick Corley, "Lord John" Corley's grandfather.

96   Repeated at "Cyclops" 3:21 and "Eumaeus" 5:36.

124   *Simon Magus*: a skillful magician mentioned in the Bible (Acts 8:9ff.) and *A Portrait*, p. 159.

138   *Nox* (Nyx): Roman goddess of night.

149   Cf. "Eumaeus" 6:179.

"Eumaeus" 2

LEFT MARGIN HORIZONTAL

R ⟨plaintiff⟩

1ᵈ· piece

B ⟨pry into⟩ *648:42–649:1*

B ⟨. . . . .⟩

5   *B* ⟨passage of arms⟩ *625:27*

B ⟨would you be surprised to learn?⟩ *628:11*

B ⟨in a heated fashion⟩ *627:9*

R ⟨carved his way to fame⟩ *635:36*

R ⟨innuendo⟩ *630:30, 641:16*

10   *B* ⟨mooted⟩ *611:34, 623:38*

B ⟨6 chamber revolver⟩ *642:18*

B ⟨boodle⟩ *600:21*

B ⟨ventilate the matter⟩ *617:32*

B ⟨Xmas festivities⟩ *648:4–5*

15   ?lesser

B ⟨at this stage⟩ *622:25*

R ⟨finale⟩ *625:8*

R ⟨preyed on mind⟩ *633:38–39*

G ⟨swing for it⟩ *626:26*

20   *R* ⟨share her bedroom⟩ *635:11*

R ⟨reminded him forcibly⟩ *629:38–39*

B ⟨ended in blows⟩ *625:28*

B ⟨large size lady⟩ *636:31*

B ⟨despite its⟩ *624:37?*

25   *B* ⟨all very fine⟩

B ⟨transparently⟩ *626:37*

376

30

35

40

45

50

55

B ⟨a much injured person⟩ *627:7–8*

B ⟨command his price⟩ *629:10*

R ⟨carried away wave of folly⟩ *635:28*

R ⟨large size lady⟩ *636:31*

B ⟨the ruse worked⟩ *644:17*

B ⟨sever his connection with⟩ *639:34–35*

B ⟨of no common calibre⟩ *630:42*

embodiment

B ⟨?smooth answer turns away wrath⟩ *627:12–13*

ingress & egress

B ⟨rack their feelings⟩ *642:17*

B ⟨a bit of perfect poetry in its way⟩ *608:35*

R ⟨impetuosity⟩ *621:30, 632:40*

B ⟨in tyro affections⟩ *647:41?*

lifeline   *R* ⟨poles apart⟩ *618:25, 625:42*

B ⟨impetus⟩ *648:30*

B ⟨synopsis⟩ *628:35*

B ⟨honest & aboveboard⟩ *638:12*

R ⟨several 1 / to the bad⟩ *630:40–41*

R ⟨forlorn hope⟩ *633:1*

R ⟨proclaim from housetop⟩ *643:6*

R ⟨marked the termination⟩ *625:8*

B ⟨in private life⟩

. . . . to ?seeing him

B ⟨affection with improper intent⟩ *640:4–5*

R ⟨their eyes conversing⟩ *627:20*

hold its own

quite a clever anthony

LEFT COLUMN HORIZONTAL

B ⟨How — was told⟩   ten

B ⟨erroneously⟩ *602:13, 628:2*   who was known to B

B ⟨paid 15 / VI⟩   *B* ⟨splash page⟩ *638:10*

B ⟨?farms⟩

B ⟨roughly a doz years ago⟩ *641:1*

60 B ⟨SD returned the compliment⟩ *600:10*

R ⟨rural parts⟩ *635:39*   glands fugitive effect

B ⟨90 in the shade⟩ *630:33*

B ⟨wily old cust⟩ *614:16*

R ⟨cooked his goose effectually⟩ *635:42*

65 B ⟨look of settled purpose⟩ *638:39*

B ⟨stake in country⟩ *639:11*

B ⟨debut⟩   B ⟨on the preceding Monday⟩ *647:14*

B ⟨axe to grind⟩ *624:20–21*

R ⟨come within his special province⟩ *631:21*

70 B ⟨gruesome⟩ *598:15*   R ⟨magnificent specimen of manhood⟩ *635:29*

B ⟨distinctly stouter⟩ *638:7–8*

B ⟨barefaced fraud⟩ *Cf. 617:13, 641:16*

B ⟨wooden structure⟩ *605:36*

B ⟨Youthful tyro⟩ *647:41*

75 the tale goes   B ⟨and mixed bathing⟩ *611:17*

means of knowing   B ⟨—a big if—⟩

B ⟨good Samaritan⟩ *597:3*   R ⟨fresh complexion⟩

R ⟨regarded with affection⟩ *635:28*

R ⟨brain v brawn⟩ *629:12–13*

80 B ⟨thought it was something to do with—⟩ *Cf. 602:5–10*

B ⟨remembered dimly⟩ *602:10*

B ⟨erroneously⟩ *602:13, 628:2*

B ⟨under false colours⟩ *610:31–32*

B ⟨not as a habitual practice⟩ *598:34–35*

85 B ⟨demimonde⟩ *599:20*

B ⟨dabbling in politics⟩ *641:1*

he had not been speaking the truth.

B ⟨I remain with much love⟩ *609:7–8*

B ⟨on the quiet⟩ *Cf. 610:32*

90 R ⟨names were coupled⟩ *635:8*

G ⟨seduced⟩ *635:22ff.*

R ⟨saw an act of impropriety between the two⟩ *630:30–31*

B ⟨culminating in⟩ *611:9–11*

B ⟨there followed a lengthy pause⟩ *613:29*

95   *B* ⟨funny, very.⟩ *613:28*
         B ⟨looked in direction of door,⟩ *634:39*
         B ⟨no matter what the cause is from,⟩ *617:16–17*
         B ⟨would answer (suit) very well⟩
         receive a black eye
100   *B* ⟨inadequate means⟩ *630:2*
         begin to get busy with knife
         B ⟨wouldn't hold water⟩ *641:9*
         B ⟨press his attentions on her⟩ *640:4*
         B ⟨professional whistle⟩ *597:34*
105   *B* ⟨youthful tyro,⟩ *647:41*
         B ⟨verged on the tropical⟩ *642:18–19*
         B ⟨painting the town tolerably pink⟩ *623:24*
         B ⟨pass it off as a jest⟩ *639:24–25*
         B ⟨last of Mohicans⟩ *644:11*
110   *B* ⟨Bl. ?dummy⟩
         B ⟨irate⟩ *625:15?, 643:39?*
         B ⟨Standard work on subject⟩ *628:17*
         G ⟨living in hopes⟩ *Cf. 643:9*
         B ⟨genuine forgery⟩ *618:33*
115   *R* ⟨bring off a coup⟩ *632:39*
         B ⟨'blarny'⟩ *642:22*
         B ⟨amused at his expense⟩
         ?lace was the thing then
         in full swing
120   *B* ⟨indulge in recriminations⟩ *625:28*

RIGHT COLUMN HORIZONTAL

         while we mortals
         retracted
         a dog in church
         B ⟨throw a sidelight⟩ *649:6*
125   Deucalion—Crete
         B ⟨or whatever you like to call it⟩

B ⟨legal luminary⟩ *626:34–35*

?there could be seen ?then

B ⟨hilarious moment⟩ *649:4?*

130   playgoers

B ⟨chew with gusto⟩ *642:21?*

R ⟨?sermon of a high order⟩ *635:30*

B ⟨the billing⟩ *643:2*   R ⟨augmented⟩ *635:29*

B ⟨glutton for work⟩ *602:36–37*

135   R ⟨veneer⟩ *630:22*   B ⟨virtuoso⟩ *645:27*

B ⟨detected⟩ *610:30*

evade capture

B ⟨fast women⟩ *599:20*

B ⟨Brummagem⟩ *624:40–41*

140   alive & well

R ⟨bask in her smiles⟩ *635:24*

B ⟨seeing coast clear⟩ *644:17*

B ⟨followed with interest) *625:26–27*

quite all right

145   B ⟨in pursuit of his philosophy⟩ *629:11*

B ⟨surface knowledge of⟩ *645:34*

illfated   *622:12*

G ⟨let yʳ· motto be⟩

R ⟨municipal supernumerary⟩ *645:1*

150   B ⟨initiate against⟩

B ⟨foregone conclusion⟩ *641:24*

B ⟨upshot was⟩ *640:5*

causes its own reward

B ⟨sacred edifice⟩ *645:26–27*

155   B ⟨heaps of love⟩ *648:34?*

B ⟨practitioner⟩ *605:3–4, 649:3*

B ⟨respectably connected⟩ *623:19, 630:2*

B ⟨perambulations⟩ *627:2*

R ⟨candidly⟩ *621:7, 627:40*

160   write me down a fool

B ⟨consult a specialist⟩ *633:29*

B ⟨cold douche⟩ *625:12*

in the wide
B ⟨on a dozen occasions⟩ *614:20*
165   B ⟨Bbbbblllllbbblblobschbg⟩ *537:21*
B ⟨lady who is now my wife⟩ *637:3–4*
B ⟨disparaging⟩ *649:3?*
B ⟨to deprecate you⟩ *649:5*
B ⟨lurid⟩ *610:26, 625:9*
170   playgoers
R ⟨early in life⟩ *630:17*
reading of part

NOTES

Line 23   Repeated at line 30.

35   *?Smooth*: this word is not "soft."

56   *Erroneously*: repeated at line 82.

74   Repeated at line 105.

125   *Deucalion* of *Crete*: the son of Minos, mentioned in the *Odyssey*. The reason for the presence of his name here is unexplained.

139   *Brummagem*: a dialect pronunciation of "Birmingham."

165   The spelling here varies from that in the text.

171–172   These lines are vertical, bottom to top.

"Eumaeus" 3

LEFT MARGIN HORIZONTAL

tender youth
R ⟨addicted to⟩ *635:18*
R ⟨lubric⟩ *635:18*
R ⟨sequel⟩ *635:23*
5   R ⟨upstairs room⟩ *635:15*
local beadle
B ⟨schooling⟩ *618:26*
B ⟨meet needs of the case⟩ *611:38*
R ⟨allembracing⟩ *631:21*
10   R ⟨taken down in⟩
B ⟨the residue⟩
R ⟨writing⟩
B ⟨So it is⟩
B ⟨day of reckoning⟩ *624:35*
15   B ⟨on that subject⟩ *629:26–27, 631:31*
B ⟨with the utmost⟩ *639:8–9*
B ⟨a word of caution⟩ *598:32*
B ⟨to the number of ?days⟩
B ⟨every requisite⟩ *647:39*
20   B ⟨he took particular notice⟩ *610:25*
B ⟨local beadle⟩
B ⟨flusterfied⟩ *616:27*

LEFT COLUMN HORIZONTAL

was not to be beaten

382

B ⟨scarcely intended by nature⟩ *630:23*

25 as far back as

B ⟨improprieties between them⟩ *630:31*

G ⟨not to mix up⟩

B ⟨Did you say to me or I to you?⟩

B ⟨What was I saying? Ah, yes, to be sure⟩ *647:4*

30 *R* ⟨fell a victim to her charms⟩ *635:22–23*

R ⟨leader of men⟩ *633:39*   not practiced per

B ⟨palpably⟩ *616:24 and elsewhere*

B ⟨handicapped by the circumstance⟩ *597:41–42*

R ⟨after his exertions⟩ *624:2*

35 *B* ⟨rough & tumble⟩ *642:20–21*

B ⟨audibly remarked⟩ *628:6*   *B* ⟨our national poet⟩ *618:34, 620:18*

B ⟨button⟩ *597:42–598:1*   *B* ⟨some crowned head⟩ *630:21*

R ⟨pointed question turn a deaf ear⟩ *630:14*

B ⟨fresh fields and pastures new⟩ *614:24–25, 645:3*

40 *B* ⟨never failing.⟩   *B* ⟨tête à tête⟩ *606:34, 649:25*

consideration   *R* ⟨boisterous⟩ *624:11*

was on tenterhooks *Cf. 617:1*   more amenably

maudlin

R ⟨bask in her smiles⟩ *635:24*

45 *B* ⟨blessed with brains⟩ *647:38*

B ⟨transferred attentions⟩ *606:16*

R ⟨congratulate himself on his decision⟩ *633:1*

B ⟨there hanging about⟩

B ⟨nozzle⟩ *622:36*   *B* ⟨harbour master⟩ *614:41*

50 *B* ⟨as warm as toast⟩ *642:8*

R ⟨encompass his downfall⟩ *635:6?*

G ⟨run the normal course⟩ *638:19*

B ⟨described as⟩ *624:23*   *R* ⟨his hand hurt⟩ *633:5*

as a bug in a rug   *R* ⟨by the way⟩ *608:34, 612:25–26, 633:5*

55 *B* ⟨& generally terrorising⟩ *600:17*

B ⟨augmented⟩ *605:14–15, 635:29*

R ⟨acquainted with his movements⟩ *633:33*

B ⟨a brother medico⟩ *599:31*

before many days

60   B ⟨leaving that for the moment⟩ *603:28–29*

         B ⟨euchered⟩ *604:14*

         B ⟨ran the normal courses⟩ *638:19*

         B ⟨consistently refused⟩ *610:39?*   ?fouled

         B ⟨not much palatability about it⟩ *Cf. 598:24*

65   B ⟨once in a ?way⟩   (Trieste)   *Cf. 612:41*

         R ⟨for whom remark emanated⟩ *633:37*

         R ⟨no concern of theirs absolutely⟩ *635:27*

         B ⟨forcible feeble Philippic⟩ *624:21*

         B ⟨?foreclosing⟩

70   B ⟨emolument⟩ *648:10*

         B ⟨from 1 or 2 remarks he let drop⟩ *605:18–19*

         wrapped in red tape   *Cf. 611:35*

         B ⟨strong to the verge of⟩ *635:22*

         R ⟨not singly but in their 1000's⟩ *633:20*

75   R ⟨strong to verge of weakness⟩ *635:22*

         B ⟨LB in court dress⟩

         B ⟨concoction⟩ *606:35*

         B ⟨no small ?share⟩

         R ⟨not up to much⟩

80   R ⟨make the most of both countries⟩ *625:41–42*

         R ⟨petered out in a yawn or so⟩ *633:25?*

         supposition that sexual excesses lead to wisdom

         R ⟨the money question⟩

         B ⟨Squeamish⟩ *617:27*

85   R ⟨can real love exist between married folk? poses.⟩ *635:25–27*

         quartermaster on bridge

         SD shown letter he wrote drunk.

         B ⟨Lord Talbot de Malahide, heredit. Lord Admiral of M⟩ *600:33–34*

                              B ⟨. . . . . ?adorning⟩

90   blow was diverted   B ⟨hang it,⟩ *612:3–4*

RIGHT COLUMN HORIZONTAL

B ⟨pseudo⟩ *626:36*

384

B ⟨ABS drinks from bottle⟩ 622:35–36

R ⟨home ties⟩ 635:23   R ⟨arrived on the scene⟩ 624:17–18

R ⟨for reasons which will occur to you⟩ 630:12

95   R ⟨nothing in common beyond name⟩ 635:20–21

B ⟨to the full⟩   B ⟨put a stop to⟩

puerile assertion

circumvent

from depths of armchair

100   R ⟨show her charms in an open fashion⟩ 636:31–32

B ⟨result being in the negative⟩ 602:3

B ⟨turned up⟩

B ⟨suffering from lassitude generally⟩ 606:27

R ⟨eminently lends itself to⟩ 632:41

105   B ⟨from little I know of you⟩ 629:8

R ⟨commanding figure⟩ 633:40, 638:38

B ⟨as it largely is⟩ 638:22–23   refreshment of the ?lightest

B ⟨on the ?force of it⟩ 630:36?

Mr   James Rourke, Bloomfield, Merrion

110   B ⟨(i.e.) effete fogeydom⟩ 611:36   R ⟨how's the behind?⟩

he'd like ?their to be

chuck it

B ⟨run on teetotal lines⟩   B ⟨rarely, if ever⟩ 605:37

R ⟨put his mind at rest⟩   B ⟨father of a scheme for⟩

115   bright youth

R ⟨noncommital voice⟩ 627:19   B ⟨professional status⟩ 605:5

a masculine voice   B ⟨trouble⟩   worshipped her

flimsy excuse   B ⟨not a bad notion⟩ 611:14

elated   B ⟨remark about backstab⟩ 621:5–6   B ⟨made him

120   smell a rat⟩ 648:39   £sd

B ⟨not one particle of truth⟩ 628:10

B ⟨make arrangements⟩ 611:15–16

B ⟨tempting the fates⟩ 614:29

B ⟨whatever the season⟩ 615:1

125   B ⟨stalwart advocate⟩ 617:30

G ⟨nearer the mark⟩

hemmed & hawed

B ⟨monopolized⟩ *624:36*

egregious error

130   *R* ⟨ere then⟩ *625:40*

B ⟨experienced remarkably rough weather⟩ *615:5–6*

B ⟨her affections centred upon another⟩ *640:5*

B ⟨the harmless necessary cat⟩ *621:11*

R ⟨privilege which he keenly appreciated⟩ *645:38–39*

135   *B* ⟨(LB saw CSP)⟩ *639:1ff.*

B ⟨seaman⟩ *607:23*

B ⟨opinions clothed⟩ *Cf. 638:29*

                         B ⟨touching drink⟩ *599:22?*

ought to go a long way   *B* ⟨epistle to Hebrews⟩ *632:14*

140   short of money

B ⟨LB never forget trip in Erin's King (CSP)⟩ *638:26–27*

B ⟨even supposing⟩ *603:38–39*

B ⟨gave examples of an ex⟩   *R* ⟨proscenium⟩ *386:37*   "set"

rightful owner

145   *B* ⟨wrapped up in . . .⟩ *638:22*

& see a great alteration

NOTES

The chaotic appearance of "Eumaeus" 3 has made necessary some rearrangement of the phrases.
Line 6   Repeated at line 21.

52   Cf. line 62.

73   Cf. line 75.

88   "The Earl of Shrewsbury and Talbot is the premier earl on the Rolls of England and Ireland and hereditary lord high steward of Ireland. The Lords Talbot de Malahide represent a family in Ireland which settled there in 1167" (*Chambers's*).

99–100   These lines may be connected.

109   *James Rourke*: a bakery owner (*U* 598:23). His address, *Bloomfield, Merrion*, near St. Mary's Home for the Blind, may have suggested to Joyce the name of Marion Bloom.

121   Joyce inserted *one* above a caret between *Not* and *particle*.

135   Cf. line 141.

141   Adams dismisses the idea that *Erin's King*, an excursion boat, suggests Charles Stewart Parnell (pp. 86–87). See also "Circe" 6:33 and "Ithaca" 13:94.

145   The ellipses are Joyce's.

"Eumaeus" 4

R ⟨eighty odd⟩ *645:6*
B ⟨be it repeated⟩ *641:19*
B ⟨absorbing⟩ *643:19*
B ⟨Goahead race⟩ *628:20*
5   B ⟨versatile⟩ *604:42*
B ⟨ABS gone out after women⟩
returns you
B ⟨impetus⟩ *648:30*
Eu. lets glass fall
10   B ⟨made a sign while other not looking⟩ *644:7–8*
?sneaky ?gods ?fishy
B ⟨liquid fire⟩ *624:9*
B ⟨where innocence ?is ?bliss⟩ *613:20–21?*
funny story about ?cook
15   B ⟨grandfather⟩ *600:30 and elsewhere*
        (shag?)
?abs   B ⟨kicks chap awake⟩
Pen brother & father advise her
Seat of honour ?memory
20   B ⟨blind moon⟩ *608:30*
B ⟨rainy night⟩ *608:30*
B ⟨bottle in each pocket⟩ *622:33–34*
B ⟨those were the times⟩
love to consult oracle
25   B ⟨in a sober state⟩ *600:25, 629:32*
feck forks

387

Ul. suppliant of Tel   offers him seat
B ⟨average man⟩ *611:39*

LEFT COLUMN HORIZONTAL

R ⟨stifled a yawn⟩ *632:12*   *B* ⟨in the near future⟩ *647:33*

30 *B* ⟨soap to wash at fountains, as⟩

B ⟨not over effusive⟩ *634:26, 641:40*

B ⟨passed some trivial remarks⟩ *644:2*

B ⟨had his say⟩ *622:6*   *B* ⟨annoying fact of it is⟩

B ⟨gravest doubts⟩ *640:16–17*

35 *B* ⟨any idea of the sort⟩ *624:22–23?*

B ⟨upon looking⟩

B ⟨he had a grievance (airing)⟩ *624:21*

B ⟨perpetrators of the outrage⟩ *626:32*

B ⟨thought well to stir it first⟩ *618:42–619:1*

40 *B* ⟨no matter where living⟩

B ⟨truly amazing⟩ *623:18*

B ⟨I might say that⟩

B ⟨remarkable experiences⟩

B ⟨profligate women⟩ *640:12*

45 not a day to be lost

B ⟨well preserved man⟩ *620:8*

B ⟨merely goes to show⟩ *614:34*

R ⟨public property⟩ *635:6*

B ⟨evasively⟩ *603:26*

50 *B* ⟨never more so⟩ *598:31–32*

B ⟨repeated he⟩ *613:10*

B ⟨evil genius⟩ *Cf. 619:26*   *B* ⟨merry old soul⟩ *642:11*

B ⟨wrecked in his affections⟩ *608:39–40*

B ⟨none to come up to her⟩ *645:29*

55 *B* ⟨after mature reflection⟩ *642:31–32*

B ⟨put coin in his way⟩ *642:3–4*

B ⟨talk things over⟩ *642:33*

R ⟨Ulysses S. Grant⟩ *742:7–8*

R ⟨resolved upon it⟩ *635:5*

60 B ⟨none the less⟩ *621:7*

B ⟨on the spot⟩ *611:15*

B ⟨familiarized with⟩ *623:20, 629:35*

B ⟨unlooked-for occasion⟩ *630:39*

B ⟨analogous scenes⟩ *620:29*

65 B ⟨took him one side⟩

B ⟨puff in paper⟩ *611:27–28*

B ⟨Mr D., senior⟩ *604:8*

B ⟨a great field for⟩

who panting and out of breath and whose—

70 B ⟨trying the indomitable Bloom⟩ *644:26?*

B ⟨elite⟩ *644:18*

B ⟨pay through the nose⟩ *624:28*

B ⟨surplus steam⟩ *624:30*

singled out

75 B ⟨sank rather than sat⟩ *624:18*

B ⟨coal in large quantities⟩ *624:25*

B ⟨dame fortune⟩ *Cf. 612:6*

B ⟨?mink coats & mink coats⟩

B ⟨full bloom of womanhood⟩ *636:32*

80 B ⟨liberal display⟩ *636:34*

B ⟨single blessedness⟩ *640:13–14*

B ⟨all star caste⟩ *611:24*

mischance   B ⟨providing⟩ *611:27*

B ⟨temperamental⟩ *626:40*

85 B ⟨by a trick of fate⟩ *610:39*

B ⟨difficulties arose⟩

B ⟨regained his seat⟩ *624:18*

B ⟨religious silence⟩ *613:22–23*

R ⟨his bottom jaw⟩ *632:15*

90 a mitigant

B ⟨chamber of horrors⟩ *613:14*

B ⟨bath in morning⟩

B ⟨poor Pete⟩ *626:17*

B ⟨Convers. became general⟩ *624:30–31*

389

95   *B* ⟨?Breh. . . . .⟩

     G ⟨for her brother⟩

     B ⟨faded to a degree⟩ *648:19*

RIGHT COLUMN HORIZONTAL

     B ⟨picked out by his facial expression⟩ *643:42–644:1*

     Laertes fasts   Tel away

100   Dogs attack Ul not Tel.

     B ⟨parenthesised⟩ *648:12*

     Eum said ship came in

     Ul. don't tell her you saw me

     B ⟨not person he represented himself to be⟩ *610:30–31*

105   *B* ⟨born for the shadow⟩

     going concern

     B ⟨what construction to put⟩ *629:29*

     B ⟨stuck to his guns he remarked for the benefit of them all⟩ *638:28–29, 613:17*

     B ⟨embracing⟩ *611:16*

110   *B* ⟨minor injuries⟩ *639:2*   wanted by police

     was promptly on the scene   looking for him

     R ⟨108 MP's = suitors⟩   *B* ⟨request was complied with⟩ *613:40*

     R ⟨one laughs at ?discomforture of other⟩ *638:41?*   *B* ⟨some little

          time subsequently⟩ *623:7–8*

115   cave   Phorcys   old man of sea

     olive tree naiads   *B* ⟨generous to a fault⟩ *626:40*

     B ⟨two forts at Queenstown⟩ *608:22–23*

     B ⟨sailor £sd in ?bad ?haven⟩

     B ⟨his own case that he himself killed in⟩ *620:13–14*

120   *B* ⟨(a fact)⟩ *624:31?*   *B* ⟨that is quite beyond me⟩

     B ⟨burning interior⟩ *622:34*

     B ⟨considerable stir⟩   ?spunging ?den or bowl with arrow

     B ⟨you're dreaming⟩

     B ⟨perfectly certain⟩ *646:14*

125   *B* ⟨among his other gay doings⟩ *630:3*

     B ⟨he entered holding the object⟩ *609:15?*

B ⟨h̶i̶s̶ n̶o̶⟩   *B* ⟨took umbrage⟩ *627:7*   *B* ⟨. . . . .⟩
on that subject
B ⟨LB a born adventurer⟩ *610:38–39*
130   *B* ⟨as it was⟩   *B* ⟨perfectly simple⟩ *611:26*
B ⟨manoeuvre⟩ *622:38*
about—
R ⟨LB knows . . . . on gate⟩
B ⟨de rigueur⟩ *621:13*
135   *B* ⟨the old party⟩ *643:22*
B ⟨entourage⟩ *634:37*   *R* ⟨staggering blow⟩ *635:4*
B ⟨everything pointed to the fact⟩ *641:37–38*
B ⟨Mr B interested with⟩
kidnapped
140   *B* ⟨touching⟩ *599:22 and elsewhere*
B ⟨floundering about⟩ *614:27*
R ⟨welcome intelligence⟩ *635:4*
B ⟨in no uncertain tone⟩ *624:35*   *B* ⟨a pure invention⟩ *620:28*
B ⟨hole & corner⟩
145   *B* ⟨dissertation⟩ *624:23*
B ⟨all that sort of thing⟩
B ⟨in the same ?strain⟩ *640:42?, 624:30?*
B ⟨ignore⟩ *638:23*
B ⟨weird looking specimen⟩ *620:11–12*
150   *B* ⟨led up to it⟩
B ⟨incredible small shoe for small foot⟩ *517:30*
B ⟨penetrated⟩ *638:31*
B ⟨lodging in stomach⟩ *639:3–4*
B ⟨that's a good knife⟩ *613:10*
155   *B* ⟨loosened many a man's thighs⟩
7 yrs. under him
R ⟨harbour fugitive⟩
R ⟨Pseud. could do jobs⟩ *624:8?*
B ⟨all night long⟩
160   *B* ⟨derelict⟩ *614:22*

391

NOTES

My arrangement of the phrases on this notesheet is often arbitrary.

Line 17   Cf. "Eumaeus" 6:122 and note.

119   Joyce inserted *that* above a caret between *case* and *he*.

122, 127   These lines are nearly illegible. Joyce's penmanship is unusually sloppy here.

"Eumaeus" 5

LEFT MARGIN VERTICAL UPPER (top to bottom)

Circe = Calypso
S ⟨against emigration⟩ *625:4–7*
S ⟨Sailor reads book⟩
600 pigs
5   apocrypha
B ⟨Hengler's Circus⟩ *608:17–18*

LEFT MARGIN VERTICAL UPPER (bottom to top)

sea drowns body   crowd ditto soul
B ⟨obsequies⟩ *631:39*

LEFT MARGIN VERTICAL CENTER

Pen & Freier = Pan (monster) banished
10   Cap. Weldon got Stephens away
B ⟨Best bloody man ever scuttled ship⟩ *609:32–33*
B ⟨circumnavigator⟩ *609:29*
Capt. Costigan swam in dead sea.
what's in middle of the earth.
15   B ⟨auraxi—heavy car⟩
Der Mensch schämt sich des Mund . . . .
B ⟨Lenehan gave wrong account of race⟩ *632:34–35*
B ⟨Peas and sulphate of copper⟩ *619:13–15*

393

B ⟨No-one give what he hasn't⟩ *618:39*

20 *B* ⟨Coffee palace,⟩ *619:2–3*   *B* ⟨speculation, no competition⟩ *619:13*

LEFT MARGIN VERTICAL CENTER (bottom to top)

Catholic cable eaten by 2 seas.

LEFT MARGIN LOWER (bottom to top)

B ⟨mill. years E no coal⟩ *625:36–37*

LEFT MARGIN VERTICAL LOWER (top to bottom)

G ⟨by my way of thinking⟩
B ⟨glum⟩ *644:1*

25 *B* ⟨Chinese boxes of little wax pellets. Put in water they open.
 Flowers boats⟩ *612:34–37*

S ⟨Ascot meeting 1,000 sovs with 3000 in specie added, gold
 cup 2 ½ m. Mr F. Alexander's b.h. Throwaway by   1
 Rightway and Threale, 5 years 9 st. 4 lbs. W. Lane

30 Lord Howard de Walden's ches. Zinfandel   4 years, 9 st.,   2
 (M. Cannon)   Mr W. Bass's b. filly Sceptre 5 yʳˢ· 9 st.
 10 Madden   Also ran J. de Bremond's Maximum II 5 yʳˢ·⟩   3
 632:25–38

S ⟨(G. Stern)⟩   *S* ⟨Winner trained by Braine⟩ *632:33–34*

CENTER COLUMN HORIZONTAL

35 *S* ⟨Col. Everard Cavan grows tobacco⟩ *624:33*

S ⟨lay low⟩ *633:10?*   *B* ⟨to start with⟩ *606:31–32*

B ⟨hails from⟩ *608:24*   *B* ⟨eventually⟩ *604:14 and elsewhere*

S ⟨queen's evidence⟩ *626:16*

Dick Turpin, law.

40 Private property conceded by all ∴.
S ⟨Every man secondo needs or deeds?⟩ *603:35–36*
La legge z'e per tutti (Peter the Painter)
police helmet sweat   B ⟨deteriorated⟩ *648:19*
S ⟨every land govt. it merits⟩ *627:26–27*

45 S ⟨chummies & skivvies⟩ *626:1*   S ⟨R.C. peasants backbone of
empire⟩ *625:19–20*
French urinals
R ⟨why not leave between no 7, no 8 of same street⟩
G ⟨Intellectuals debtors of society⟩

50 Dead govern living.
History daughters of memory. Hume. Edw. II
Heredity secured at cost of all.
1 enslaved by many
Tyrants: elected: G ⟨cut nose to please face⟩

55 S ⟨Dilly's kitchen. Oatmeal water cat devours charred fishheads
& eggshells heaped on brown paper. Shell cocoa in
sootcoated kettle.⟩ *604:22–28*
S ⟨Luck every chap gets his ration⟩ *603:27*   B ⟨poohpooh⟩ *625:30*
S ⟨Lady Hamilton.⟩

60 Judgment of ?God absurd between 2.
Altruism saves race, anarchy individual, half & half
G ⟨Suffering proof of sin⟩
Circumcised coins
S ⟨Anarchy neither achieved nor suppressed by violence⟩ *627:29–30*

65 S ⟨Justice, hard to start principles but room for
improvement⟩ *627:24*
S ⟨jail delivery⟩ *620:10*
felon setting   Cf. *626:14*
S ⟨Skin the Goat⟩ *134:26, 605:39*   S ⟨declaim⟩ *608:34?*

70 John Eglinton, crim. ass. 2 min, 10 years   B ⟨quale
cumque de Parnellio⟩
Freedom of money   nasal passage
State monster fed with our blood. Starve it.   B ⟨slightly
passée⟩ *541:4?*

75   Election = 20 fools elect 1 genius.

R ⟨R.C.C. money on false pretences⟩ *628:18–23*

R ⟨If they didn't believe in heaven work for it here⟩ *628:20–22*

R ⟨History—hokuspokus . . . . on evidence⟩ *183:19–20, 627:39–40*

S ⟨Exports £ 6 mill. pork, 5 & 5 eggs + butter⟩ *624:25–27*

80   *B* ⟨New York = New Jerus. New Dublin⟩ *327:03?*

R ⟨Torquemada banish jews. Cromwell let them in.⟩ *628:11–15*

Hebrew gymn. in Jaffa.

R ⟨Crab & insects get all colour⟩ *628:37*

R ⟨Talismans⟩

85   *B* ⟨D.M.P.   (A, Camden: B, Denzille: C, Cat & Cage: D, Island
        bridge: ?E, ?Har⟩ *Cf. 598:17, 599:9, 600:28–29*

Buckley & Russian general

S ⟨Marcella, midget queen⟩ *620:31*

B ⟨¾ globe is sea⟩ *614:17–19*

90   *S* ⟨Sir Anthony MacDonnell left Euston for chief secretary's
        lodge⟩ *643:17–18*

R ⟨Helen of Troy, Jenkin's ear.⟩

R ⟨Thalassocrats⟩

S ⟨secured verdict by 1 length⟩ *632:35*

95   *S* ⟨where does y�r father live? (I hear he is in Dublin)⟩ *604:6*

B ⟨I went out to seek misfortune⟩ *604:1*

S ⟨King's Proctor showed cause⟩ *638:20*

S ⟨Bennett race⟩ *631:25–26 and elsewhere*   was gratified to learn

S ⟨Decree nisi⟩ *638:20, 318:20*   *B* ⟨evening⟩

100   *S* ⟨X heard tiding undismayed⟩ *625:9*   *B* ⟨evince interest⟩ *603:21–22*

B ⟨X marvelled at huguenot⟩

B ⟨Tartan beard⟩ *643:28*

B ⟨Lottery hell, insurance (other fellow)⟩ *614:36*

S ⟨Irel fight E's wars. why⟩ *626:2–4*

105   *S* ⟨Odys & Pseudo = 2 impostors⟩

S ⟨Circumstantial evidence⟩ *618:24 and elsewhere*

Violence invalidates contracts (violence of birth)

S ⟨Corny Kelleher⟩ *598:40, 631:41, and elsewhere*

S ⟨Bit of sugar for the bird⟩ *646:30?*

110   Ear of world = ear of deaf donkey

why feed maniacs

B ⟨Dunleary⟩

Emmet's grave. Glasnv. S. Michan's. No-one knows.

Epitaph: prophecy: longer the better.

115   Ditto problem of birth. Stable no horse (cf. v. Eng. law.)

B ⟨Derwan's story of bucket of porter⟩ *442:18–19*

B ⟨Mat Kane to make journey by long sea⟩ *689:21–22*

child & smutty ad. all cocottes (?Langetti)

L.B. laid on brim of beaker a knave's move.

120   L.B. son dentist, Bloom SD

B ⟨to do a rere⟩

B ⟨appetite of homing sailors⟩

B ⟨Taphians—pirates⟩

Good, bad shepherd (hireling)

RIGHT MARGIN VERTICAL (top to bottom)

125   B ⟨cabrank⟩ *623:9*

harebrained

S ⟨Earl Cadogan presides at Cabdrivers' Benevolent Association
      dinner⟩ *643:13–14*

B ⟨streetwalker at door⟩ *616:23*

130   B ⟨I like eating liquids⟩ *619:31*

B ⟨box compass⟩ *610:32*

S ⟨LB washes MB's linen⟩ *637:37*

Absinth weakens potency (debility) *Cf. 417:41*

RIGHT MARGIN LOWER (bottom to top)

happy lands—storia

397

NOTES

In the upper left-hand corner is *E* for "Eumaeus" in blue pencil. The following phrases on "Eumaeus" 5 are repeated verbatim or approximately in *Ulysses* notebook VIII.A.5 at Buffalo and on other notesheets:

"Eumaeus" 5	Notebook VIII.A.5		"Eumaeus" 5	"Cyclops"
Line 1	Page 297		Line 60	1:24 (note)
2	297		61	1:34–35
3	Cf. 297		62	1:52
4	298		63	1:58 (note) and "Cyclops" 5:75
9	299		64	1:72
10	305		65–66	1:69–70
11	305		67	1:64
12	305		68	4:58
13	305		69	10:6 (note)
122–124	295–296		70	10:10 (note)
			72	10:32
	"Cyclops"		73	10:36
35	3:3		75	10:41
36	3:21 and "Eumaeus" 1:96		76	10:40; cf. "Cyclops" 1:44 (note)
37	3:23 & 34		77	10:38–39
38	2:24		78	10:72–73
39	2:25 (note)		79	10:70
40	2:27		80	10:89
41	2:29–30		81	5:79 and "Cyclops" 10:104 (note)
42	2:63 (note)		82	8:9 (note)
43	2:48		83	8:18
44	2:72		84	8:5
45–46	2:9–10 (note), "Oxen" 16:33, and "Circe" 1:44		85–86	8:27–33 (note)
47	2:7 (note)		87	5:65 (note), "Cyclops" 8:38, and "Oxen" 5:31
48	1:2		88	8:43
49	1:3		89	8:79 and "Ithaca" 6:9
50	1:4		90–91	6:5–6 (note)
51	1:8 (note); cf. "Circe" 13:27		92	6:31–32 (note)
52	1:16		93	8:46 (note)
53	1:23		94	7:1
54	1:21 and "Nausicaa" 5:90		97	6:7–8
55–57	1:18–20			
58	1:40			
59	1:29 (note) and "Eumaeus" 7:58			

"Eumaeus" 5	"Cyclops"		"Eumaeus" 5	"Cyclops"
Line 98	6:9 (note), "Oxen" 11:93, and "Eumaeus" 6:194		Line 108	4:96 (note), "Cyclops" 8:52 (note), and elsewhere
99	6:7 (note)		110	4:119–120 (note)
100	7:17 and "Cyclops" 10:13		111	4:123 (note)
101	7:24 and notebook VIII.A.5, p. 310		112	4:128 (note) and "Circe" 1:86
102	7:18		113–114	5:12–14 (note)
103	7:26–28		115	5:66 (note)
104	4:80		116	5:70 (note)
105	4:81			
106	4:97			*"Nausicaa"*
107	4:98–101		123	6:103 (note)

Line 7   Cf. Scholes and Kain, p. 95, and *A Portrait*, p. 292.

10   *Cap*[tain]. *Weldon*: may be a prototype of Captain Dalton (*U* 609). James *Stephens*: see "Cyclops" 5:65 and note.

13   *Capt*[ain]. *Costigan*: a character in Thackeray's *Pendennis* (1850). This was probably copied out of notebook VIII.A.5, where Joyce has marked out the following lines in blue pencil: "Cap. Weldon swam Costigan (sailed the dead sea) the best bloody man that ever scuttled ship [*U* 609:33] circumnavigate that poor dear pa drink."

15   *Auraxi*: perhaps related to *auriga*, "one who drives a chariot."

16   *Der Mensch schämt sich des Mund* . . . . : Man is ashamed of his mouth——.

21   Cf. Scholes and Kain, p. 101.

22   *E*: England. Cf. Scholes and Kain, p. 101.

27–34   See *U* 632:25–38 and Richard M. Kain's *Fabulous Voyager* (1947; rev. ed., New York, 1959), p. 59, for clarification.

41   *Secondo*: "according to" in Italian.

70–71   *Quale cumque de Parnellio*: this seems to be a mixture of Latin and Italian—"whatsoever of Parnell."

85   There is an opening parenthesis, but no closing one.

92   Each was the cause of a bloody war. See "Cyclops" 6:31–32 and notes.

95   Cf. "Cyclops" 7:63 and note.

117   Martin Cunningham's character is based on that of *Mat Kane*, a crony of John Joyce who died by drowning.

118   *Langetti*: a dubious reading.

124   *Good, bad shepherd*: Eumaeus and Melanthius in the *Odyssey*.

"Eumaeus" 6

LEFT MARGIN VERTICAL TOP

judge on its merits
might well be   R ⟨iota⟩ *648:33*   B ⟨Dockrell's⟩
                   B ⟨taking stock of our friend⟩   *153:31*,
                        620:6   *453:34*
5   looked transparently   ?oventiles,
                   relieved of   facing bricks,
                   SD & LB both lie
                   B ⟨have the entrée⟩ *647:33*
                   a lady of his acquaintance
10   for all he knew,

LEFT MARGIN VERTICAL LOWER (bottom to top)

bargeman LB I saw you before him.
LB feels sleep of others,
B ⟨my bilgewater⟩ *623:7*

LEFT MARGIN BOTTOM UPPER

their Intensities   B ⟨a close shave⟩ *428:22*
15   B ⟨Swab⟩ *601:4*
                       B ⟨catchy⟩ *648:22*
B ⟨passionate haste of Dante, Leonardo and san Tommaso Mastino
     are the classic examples (SD)   they were certainly

400

wonderfully talented (LB)⟩ *621:26–32*

20   S ⟨Woman: Never Comes back. Enoch Arden⟩ *608:32–37*

S ⟨on the best authority⟩ *618:3*

S ⟨rocked in the cradle of the deep⟩ *609:1–2*

S ⟨simplest thing in the world⟩

sofa in London Freeman

25   S ⟨to the ?fore. With brains, sir.⟩ *630:37*

Eng. Irish: speech & ?ach ?narf ?mister

playing the lead

B ⟨son of a seacook⟩ *624:12*   B ⟨come to stay⟩ *608:40*

R ⟨give him into custody⟩

30   B ⟨cover with revolver⟩ *642:18?*

Stake in the country

displayed wonderful agility

B ⟨come to the fore⟩ *605:1*   B ⟨at her best⟩

make big money

LEFT MARGIN BOTTOM LOWER

35   Melampus

       ——Pseudo

——Neleus

Pero ?Tot, fair, given to man who would rescue kine of N's

     mother, Tyro, from Phylace where Iphiclus kept them.

40   Bias Talaus' son urges broth. Mel. who foreknows

     imprisonment. Arrested two warders man (good) woman

     (bad). Hears earthworms say beam rotten. Carried

     out, man 1st. beam kills woman. King will free M if

     tells why childless. Sacrifice to Z. and all birds—

45   vulture which knows & tells cause. King then begot.

     Mel. gave Pero to brother.

B ⟨Sail: you know Simon Dedalus⟩ *607:19*

B ⟨SD: I have heard of him⟩ *607:20*

B ⟨crocodiles eat bunches of keys⟩ *609:37*

50   hyena devour bones.

S ⟨Much aligator striking⟩ *609:37?*   R ⟨kennel⟩

Longlived beasts

bona fide   glaring absurdity

to occasion

55   mettle of some surprise

B ⟨Got his bearings⟩ *622:31–32*

ostensible reason

B ⟨good allround man⟩ *604:42*

great draw

60   leaf out of his book

Valentine Vousden

LEFT COLUMN HORIZONTAL

B ⟨He ceased: the horse having reached end of his course, halted

        and, before turning, reared proud feathered tail and let

        fall loudly upon the polished floor 4 smoking balls,⟩

65   *649:8–12*

B ⟨up the fundament⟩ *538:10*

B ⟨SD & LB stop in street several times⟩

S ⟨Gradually resolute⟩

S ⟨with a little goodwill⟩ *627:27*

70   S ⟨cabm. shelter image of society⟩

Let him drink out of the saucer but not oblige me

flagellation

to escape druidesses Celts went east /fled to asia & turned jews

in Arabia—woman the evil

75   S ⟨put off the ways at Alexandra basin⟩ *623:31–32*

S ⟨captives⟩

More thieves than handcuffs

12 men's votes, judge 13

judge Monahan

80   S ⟨M.B. as good as new⟩

S ⟨War between Moss street and Skinner's Alley⟩ *627:34–35*

B ⟨Lie like old boots⟩

B ⟨Not get much change out of him⟩ *614:15*

S ⟨swear hole in 10 gallon pot⟩ *599:10*

85 *B* ⟨Jans Pieter Sweelinck studied Venice, then went Amsterdam in
    Shakespeare's time Variations: My youth has here an end
    Johannes Jeep.⟩ *647:17–19*

B ⟨LB—are all those stories true?⟩ *633:22*

B ⟨Put in by monks⟩ *618:33*

90 *B* ⟨Did W.S. write Hamlet (LB to SD)⟩ *618:35*

S ⟨Eumaeus ought to have died (outlived his welcome)⟩ *626:37–38*

B ⟨Sailor stammers slightly liar &/or lefthanded,⟩ *609:18*

Confusion in the brain

B ⟨old sailor got clothes and objects from others⟩

95 *B* ⟨Sailor cute in getting back objects⟩

B ⟨Postcard addressed other name⟩ *610:33–34*

B ⟨we come up⟩

S ⟨Athena disguised⟩

B ⟨ψευδαγγελος slew in Crete Orsilochus, s of Idomeneaus who
    tried to rob him of Troy spoil, ambushed him⟩

100 Pallas never knew ?their

S ⟨Eum. curses Helen⟩

S ⟨wooers eat best meat⟩

S ⟨Eum. boasts of Irish wealth⟩ *624:22–24*

105 Ul. eating all the time

Eum. log. 'worshipful' Ul.

Ul. doublemeaning

Eum. laments Telemachus off to Paris

B ⟨Talk all night⟩

110 *B* ⟨Ul. upbraids Pallas sending off Telem. (didn't want son go
    to sea)⟩ *Cf. 615:12–14*

Eum. built a ?nice house

boars outside: 4 dogs

S ⟨taking off his boot that he bought⟩ *643:40*

115 *S* ⟨Ul. set on by dogs lets staff fall⟩

R ⟨Tel wants to start for Sandycove⟩ *641:35–36*

S ⟨Men. proposes to tour collect pots⟩

Men. Megap. & Helen give gifts, mixing bowl given him by another

Helen gives weddingdress

120 Men sends greetings to Nestor

Bird portent

R ⟨Telem kicks Pisistratus awake⟩

S ⟨Telem doesn't thank Nestor⟩

S ⟨Theoclym, long geneology manslayer⟩

125 *B* ⟨Sailor's tale resembles SD's⟩

B ⟨Ps Ul's tale ″ Ul's⟩

S ⟨Telem harbours Theoclym.⟩

S ⟨(Corley at door of shelter)⟩ *600:27ff.*

S ⟨Changes after a bob. story for you⟩ *602:26ff.*

130 *B* ⟨description of places passed⟩

B ⟨Ps Ul, hates roaming, place as vallet⟩ *615:11–12*

In Amsterdam

Asks for mother & father

Eum. foster son of Laertes, with Ctimene

135 Long nights, midnight sun

Eum. 6 in Syria, no deaths or sick

2 cities (K's & Q's County)

father Ctesius King

Phenicians came. Phen. serv in house *S* ⟨fucked her washing

140 clothes⟩

  d. of Arybas of Sidon

  offer to bring her back

  pretend not to know her

  send messenger with chain to sell,

145 sign: all ready. Stole 3 cups in blouse

  Artemis kills her. Laertes bought him

Tel. sends ship alone

  B ⟨Pay off the crew after⟩

  S ⟨Theo asks if Si D can get job   Tel refers him to Eurym.⟩

150 wooer   *Cf. 601:5ff.*

  birdportent

  S ⟨Sends him to sleep in Pireus' house⟩

Sun in at other carriage window

Ul. ship in harbour not moored

155 Ul. offers chair

  R ⟨Pseudo: Do you submit or are betrayed?⟩

  S ⟨If I were what I was⟩

  B ⟨House of . . . . . heir⟩ *630:16–18?*

  Ul. saved Anti's father

160 Eurym. protests friendliness fateful

  Return of Eurym.

  B ⟨Ul. & Tel. exchange smiles⟩ *Cf. 613:22*

  S ⟨Ul. questions, to work together⟩

  S ⟨Gods will help: Secrecy⟩

165   *B* ⟨T to take away sooty arms which provoke rows⟩

  S ⟨Ul proposes to sound people Tel contrary to this.⟩

CENTER VERTICAL

B ⟨looking forward with eager anticipation⟩ *608:1?*

RIGHT COLUMN HORIZONTAL

S ⟨If she were gone MB! Once the sheets were down & he feared⟩

B ⟨LB to go journey, Stick in the mud⟩ *612:1–3*

170 *B* ⟨took me for a wife⟩ *612:3*

S ⟨sailor with holy medal⟩ *622:10*

S ⟨Achilles' heel⟩ *625:1*

B ⟨Sailor: calm in old age⟩

B ⟨sit looking at sea, tired of each other⟩ *614:22–24*

175 *S* ⟨refusing to go with the constable⟩ *602:33*

B ⟨W^m. Bird, player of virginal in Q E's chapel⟩ *646:7–8*

B ⟨John Bull⟩ *646:9–10 and elsewhere*

B ⟨cheer O⟩ *616:15?*

S ⟨Doesn't know his own mind.⟩ *639:26–27*

180 Go away from language to learn

  (SD & LB = iden)

S ⟨Talk the matter over⟩ *642:33*

B ⟨Hebrew dead language time of Jesus after 20 centuries⟩

405

women pay taxes why not vote

185   End of the world fulfillment

S ⟨ubi bene ubi patria⟩ *628:31–33*

S ⟨LB boasts to SD of his reply to Citizen⟩ *627:8–13*

B ⟨Mercadante wrote Huguenots—⟩ *645:14*

B ⟨Seven Last Words by Meyerbeer⟩ *645:14–15*

190   S ⟨LB & SD to his right walk⟩

Blossoms of tree near house ripen quicker

U near gas lamp (Heat or Light)   *Cf. 651:13–14*

S ⟨MB's hair in photo, her face speaking likeness⟩ *637:8*

S ⟨Gordon Bennett Cup⟩ *631:25–26 and elsewhere*

195   cave—olivetree—bees.

Loom of stone, 2 gates (Men & gods) asleep with gifts   watched

his martial cloak around him

S ⟨Daunt's rock petrified ship.⟩ *622:11–19*

S ⟨Ph cease to convoy⟩

200   B ⟨Ul. loses way in maze⟩

Pallas boasts her help

Ul. denies, upbraids her

She didn't want row with Neptune

S ⟨Ul. wants to try wife first⟩

205   S ⟨Enoch Arden. Face at the Window⟩ *608:32 & 37*

Ul. recognizes Ithaca   Kisses earth, shamrock clod

Pallas & Ul. hide treasure

Suitors 3 years round Pen

S ⟨dim eyes in specs of seagreen goggles⟩ *643:23ff.*

210   Knights of Columbus

S ⟨Eu. & Ul. to die like that?⟩

S ⟨Killed his man⟩

B ⟨Eum treated & was swindled by other ?Etalian who also⟩

    S ⟨saw Ul. in Crete⟩

215   S ⟨Bet he comes back⟩ *633:6–7*

Boar killed with log

Gives Ul. best portion of 7

R ⟨Sail. tells of thunderstorm

    ?and prowess with ice⟩ *615:6?*

220 Mantled with Ul & Ag. shivering. Ul. gets him cloak by trick.
Eum. sleeps in open air
Pallas & Telem.
S ⟨warns against stepmother⟩ *Cf. 640:26*
S ⟨ambush of suitors⟩
225 S ⟨sail by night⟩
ψευδαγγελos—Crete—rich
parents who had legits and concub. Jugurtha
Castor, s. of Hylax father
like firearm, ships
230 went to Troy, came back Egypt, crew outrage Egyptians,
these set on them, he implores king, 7 y$^{rs.}$ there,
Phenician lures Ul. away, 1 year, to sell him in Libya,
shipwreck borne on mast to Thesprotis, Pheidon king
helps, shows him Ul's treasure, Ul gone to Dodana
235 oracle, Ph. sends him to Dulicium grain, crews strip
him swims off
ss. Melampus
Eu. weeps with joy.
Pen hears of T's return
240 Suitors, alarm, recall others
one laughs (Uly ?came back)
Council, plot to kill, Oracle
Medon tells Pen.
Pen weeps
245 S ⟨Pen shillyshally⟩ *Cf. 634:15, 638:40*
Eu to tell her if T back
Maid will tell L.
B ⟨Ath. frowns to Ul to come on⟩
S ⟨U looks young⟩
250 S ⟨T fears him a god⟩
thy father I for whom you   suffer
T doubts
B ⟨ups & downs of life⟩ *609:38*
S ⟨double image (Sail & LB)⟩ *616:1–5?*
255 T & Ul embrace

407

NOTES

Joyce wrote vertically from margin to margin across this notesheet. In the upper left-hand corner is an *E* in blue pencil. The top and bottom halves of "Eumaeus" 6 are torn at the crease and separated, thus giving this double notesheet the appearance of two singles. The following lines on "Eumaeus" 6 are Joyce's notations from the Butcher and Lang translation of the *Odyssey* (London, 1879).

"Eumaeus" 6	Odyssey	"Eumaeus" 6	Odyssey
Lines 35–46	Pages 412–413, n. to p. 247	Line 166	Pages 268–269
98	216	195	210
102–103	224	196–198	210–212
104–105	225	199	213
106	227	200–204	213–218
108	227–228	206–208	218–219
109	228	212–214	234
110–111	220?	215	227, 234
112–115	222–223	216–217	235
117–120	242–245	218–221	236–238
121	245	222–223	240
122	241	224	241
124	249	225	241
127	249	226	228ff.
131	250	228	228
133–134	251	229	229
136–146	253ff.	229–236	229–233
147–150	256	238	259
151–152	257	239–241	269–270
154	257	242	270–271
155	260	243–245	272–273
156–157	262	246	263–264
159	272	247–250	264
159–160	273	251–252	265
162	274	255	266
163	266		
164–165	267–268		

Line 17 *San Tommaso Mastino*: see "Circe" 2:124 and note.

35–46 In the *Odyssey* this is part of the history of Theoclymenus, a descendant of *Melampus*, who had to flee the tyranny of King Neleus, the son of *Tyro* and Poseidon. *Bias*, the brother of Melampus, was deeply in love with *Pero*, the daughter of Neleus. Neleus promised her to the man who could drive off King Phylacus' cattle from *Phylace*. These were tended by his son Iphiclus. Melampus attempted to do this for Bias, but was captured and imprisoned. A sketchy version of the rest of the story is on the notesheet.

61   *Valentine Vousden*: a "music hall entertainer at the turn of the century" (Glasheen). He was about the same age as John S. Joyce and might have been a crony of his. Another Val Vousden, apparently no relation to the above, was about the same age as Joyce and "by the Nineteen-forties he had become an amusing charlatan, with a taste for the bottle" (O'Mahony letter). See *FW* 50:15, 439:17–18.

73   Joyce first wrote *went east* and then wrote *fled to asia* above these words.

79   *Judge Monahan*: Henry J. Monahan, registrar, Consolidated Nisi Prius Court. Eoin O'Mahony writes that Monahan was a "self-made Catholic lawyer who rose by sheer ability to be Lord Chief Justice of the Common Pleas." See also "Cyclops" 7:59.

85–87   *Jan Pieter[szoon] Sweelinck* (1562–1621): "Dutch composer, organist and harpsichordist, born at Deventer or Amsterdam, studied in Venice and composed mainly church music and organ works, and developed the fugue. He founded the distinctive North German school which later included Buxtehude and . . . Johann Sebastian Bach" (*Chambers's*).

92   Joyce wrote the ampersand above *or*.

99   Cf. line 36. Pseudangelos is Odysseus in disguise. See Gilbert, pp. 362–363; Roscher, III, 1906; *Ulysses* notebook VIII.A.5 at Buffalo (p. 298).

108   This line suggests Shakespeare's *Hamlet*.

117–120   *Men.*: Menelaus. *Megap.*: Megapenthes, son of Menelaus.

121   Repeated at line 151.

122   *Pisistratus*: a son of Nestor. Cf. "Eumaeus" 4:17.

131   *Vallet*: Joyce's misspelling of "valet."

136–146   The story of Eumaeus.

158   An inkblot precedes *heir*.

159–160   *Anti.*: Antinous. *Eurym.*: Eurymachus.

167   Repeated at "Eumaeus" 7:9.

179   Cf. "Eumaeus" 1:149.

183   Cf. "Cyclops" 8:8 and "Ithaca" 10:60–61.

188–189   It was Saverio *Mercadante* (1795–1870) who wrote the *Seven Last Words of Christ*, and *Meyerbeer* who wrote *The Huguenots*; Joyce has them turned around here. See Adams, pp. 197–198. *Mercadante*: repeated at "Cyclops" 10:61; see also note there.

194   See "Cyclops" 6:9 and note.

199   *Ph*: Phaeacians.

226   See line 99.

227   *Jugurtha*: king of Numidia (d. 104 B.C.). This was also the name of a vulture owned by Alexandre Dumas (1802–1870). See Davidson, p. 272; *FW* 403.

228   Odysseus claims to be the illegitimate son of *Castor*, son of *Hylax*.

229   Pseudangelos likes *ships* and *firearms*.

237   See line 35.

"Eumaeus" 7

LEFT MARGIN VERTICAL TOP

Mr Bloom deceived him

LEFT MARGIN HORIZONTAL

S ⟨fouilles⟩ *Cf. 642:33–34*
B ⟨borrow yʳ· curlingtongs⟩
information

LEFT MARGIN VERTICAL BOTTOM

5   B ⟨retrospect⟩ *641:3–4*   B ⟨as he anticipated⟩ *597:29*
It is perhaps here   B ⟨attach greatest importance⟩ *629:33–34*
B ⟨to all the more influence⟩ *647:37*
B ⟨haven't met right sort of people⟩   B ⟨I am free to admit⟩ *621:7*
looking forward with eager anticipation
10   B ⟨mind you, I don't say,⟩ *620:28*   B ⟨that is to say⟩
B ⟨leading lady⟩ *611:25*
B ⟨deeply regretted⟩ *631:38–39*
B ⟨retiring for the night⟩ *641:27*
good . . .
15   B ⟨5 miners killed every day⟩
procession 2 deep, 1 yd apart 41 mls long corpse every 70 yds

410

LEFT COLUMN HORIZONTAL

B ⟨s.s. lady Cairns (Swansea) sank with all hands⟩ *622:20–23*

B ⟨Mona, on opposite tacks, no aid given, master feared collision
    bulkhead wᵈ· give way, no water in the hold⟩ *622:20–24*

20   B ⟨Rosslare-Fishguard route coming⟩ *611:33–34*

R ⟨belches handkerchief⟩

B ⟨unfurl a reef⟩ *622:26*

unbeaten certificate

B ⟨yarn⟩ *616:3*

25   B ⟨accompanied with poom! chuk! & grimaces.⟩ *614:1?*

B ⟨Sailor asks do you know him?⟩ *607:19?*

S ⟨M.B. pose for ensemble⟩ *637:11–12*

emergency men

S ⟨Dog if larger belue⟩ *646:34–35*

30   S ⟨X Look suddenly at beast's head.⟩ *646:23–24?*

S ⟨Walk too, best foot hindmost⟩ *646:28*

S ⟨Repellent to hand.⟩

B ⟨spare chaw about you⟩ *609:11–12*

S ⟨two cheats in Opicina train (?game & rogue)⟩

35   R ⟨bunnyhug,⟩   turkeytrot

B ⟨Cornwall case.⟩ *630:21–22*

S ⟨Camel's hump potstill, term. diteguise⟩ *646:37–38*

9 days drowned

turkeytrot,   R ⟨bunnyhug⟩

40   B ⟨sailor has tattooed back⟩ *615:24–25*

S ⟨O Johnny Lever, Johnny Lever, O,⟩ *624:15–16*

S ⟨The biscuits were as hard as brass and the beef as salt as
    Lot's wife's arse⟩ *624:13–14*

B ⟨The sweeper: scythed car⟩ *649:14*

45   B ⟨LB describes how he likes brunettes,⟩ *621:23ff.*

B ⟨hates rumpled stocking⟩ *621:42–622:1*

B ⟨End: they spoke also as they walked ?on ?forward across
    the city⟩

B ⟨Cap. Dalton, sailed Dardenelles.⟩ *609:32*   S ⟨Palgrave Murphy⟩ *623:31*

50   S ⟨Informer⟩

B ⟨Little woman down in Arklow. Knows she's true.⟩ *608:24–26*

B ⟨Perspective at end Whelan from shop door sees 2 figures at end⟩

B ⟨Why are chairs put up. LB answers promptly. to sweep
55   floor⟩ *644:25–28*

S ⟨Danny man⟩ *615:12 & 21*

What do . .eeth mean? SD

Lady Hamilton,   *B* ⟨Eng. home & beauty⟩ *608:26 and elsewhere*

B ⟨prepare to meet yʳ. God⟩ *613:6*

60   *B* ⟨have you such a thing as?⟩ *609:11*

B ⟨Seen Gibraltar? LB to seaman. Altro!⟩ *613:42ff.*

B ⟨any chance of yʳ. washing⟩ *616:35*   *B* ⟨crupper⟩ *649:12*

the camels are coming.

flush the deck

65   *S* ⟨Equality diff. Irish superior or inferior⟩ *627:28?*

S ⟨John Lever of Lever Line struck rock in Galway harb.⟩ *623:36–41*

S ⟨coffin full of stones (C.S.P.)⟩ *633:15*

B ⟨Gospodi pomilouy.⟩ *609:33*

R ⟨Police in rich quarters of city⟩ *599:13–14*

70   *B* ⟨Photograph of murderer in murdered's eye.⟩ *99:3–4, cf. 634:4–6*

S ⟨quiet sendoff,⟩ *631:32* *B* ⟨breakers,⟩ *622:17*

S ⟨I belong there⟩   SD at first repelled then drawn

loss of tooth unfit for . . . ., LB circumcized etc.

could J. Cuffe be R.C. priest.   Milly lupanars

75   bargeman meets old sailor   *B* ⟨SD dislikes Eng. abroad⟩

B ⟨cut off their diddies (savages)⟩ *610:13*

B ⟨It was the schooner Hesperus.⟩ *620:24*

B ⟨. . I pronounces rightly (LB to SD. Ital)⟩ *Cf. 606:18–19*

S ⟨Desperado face, lamp, Money or life⟩ *600:16ff.*

80   *B* ⟨Gives right arm,⟩   riggers, discharge book,
      name, nat, eyes, hair, tattoo, vessel, voyages,
      conduct marks

B ⟨So to speak⟩

clap sacred edifice (MB)

85   murderer at large, boil him

B ⟨minus his coat,⟩

B ⟨let me cross yʳ· bows⟩ *622:27*
in reduced circumstances
?so to Jerusalem, shun it ever

RIGHT COLUMN HORIZONTAL

90 : headstrong stupid
    S ⟨to seek misfortune⟩ *604:1*
    B ⟨distingué⟩ *638:4*
    B ⟨?moonpaved space⟩
    B ⟨driver with humane patience waited while horse discharged
95   (mire)⟩ *649:13*
    B ⟨pastern⟩ *Cf. 517:23, 244:22* . . . of foot,   B ⟨fetlock,⟩
    moon lave face
    B ⟨slenderness of his arm   linked with a strange flesh,
       sinewless, ample & of a whore's approach⟩ *644:39–41*
100 Molly gnashing her teeth broke in sleep
    passionate,   B ⟨Spanish⟩ *636:11–12*
    S ⟨Beware of the steamroller⟩ *646:22*
    Fun without vulgarity
    vanity bag. (mirror of SD's face)
105 B ⟨ABS⟩
    B ⟨invincibles⟩ *613:18*
    S ⟨nighttown⟩ *598:33*
    S ⟨funeral L. Broome⟩ *632:6–11*
    B ⟨Stark ballocknaked⟩ *610:14–15*
110 S ⟨ticket of leave ?man⟩
    S ⟨treadmill⟩ *620:12*
    B ⟨claspknife⟩ *613:1*
    suicide wom. by water
    Ophelia. like to like
115 earthquake
    mouth entrance body
    B ⟨Mullingar 5/6 / 9/9⟩ *611:4–5*
    jollyboat

streak dawn

120 lumbering greens cart

sunrise

?hairy dressing a chancy thing

NOTES

In the upper right-hand corner in blue pencil is *E* for "Eumaeus."

Line 2 *Fouilles*: "excavations," or "diggings," in French.

9 Repeated at "Eumaeus" 6:167.

34 *Opicina*: a suburb of Trieste.

35 Repeated at line 39.

37 Cf. "Circe" 2:70.

58 See "Cyclops" 1:29 and note.

61 *Altro!*: "of course!" in Italian.

66 See Richard M. Kain's note in *James Joyce Quarterly*, VI (Fall 1968), 82–83.

67 See "Circe" 3:125–129 and note for the source of this idea.

68 *Gospodi pomilouy*: Russian for "may the Lord have mercy upon us."

74 *J[oe]. Cuffe*: a local packer who once fired Bloom (*U* 309). The name is repeated at "Ithaca" 11:108. *Milly lupanars*: see "Circe" 3:24 and note.

75 *SD dislikes Eng. abroad*: cf. "Oxen" 6:12 and "Circe" 3:85.

104 Joyce first wrote *cam*, then wrote *vanity* over it.

105 *ABS*: able-bodied seaman.

108 *Broome*: "Boom" in the text.

"Ithaca" 1

ABCD E F GHI J KHLMNOPQRSTUVWXYZ
   YXWVUTSRQPONMLK JIHGFEDCBA

ABC   DEF   GHI   JKL   MNOP   QRST   UVW   XYZ
ZYX   WVU   TSR   QPO   NMLK   JIHG   FED   CBA

LEFT MARGIN HORIZONTAL

5   B ⟨Girl in ?park (Talbot Power) says political allusion—then
       blinks⟩

LEFT COLUMN HORIZONTAL

    B ⟨German names in books struck out⟩
    B ⟨why Milly fair?⟩ *677:22?*
    B ⟨thing broken good luck (hymen)⟩ *718:34ff.*
10   R ⟨LB turns doyley down⟩ *268:30*
    R ⟨If Jesus redeemed inhabitants of other stars⟩ *684:19*
    mercyseat
    B ⟨Nature couples—when unsexed—crepa—when children
       past⟩ *711:6ff.?*
15   B ⟨cry lessens pain⟩ *677:18–19*
    B ⟨dinner of 20 dishes—each harmless⟩   R ⟨20 mixed = deadly poison⟩ *172:29–31*
    B ⟨MB throws gloves on piano⟩ *691:6–7*

B ⟨Parachute—Jones's road⟩ *667:11?*

B ⟨LB sentimental over Alexandra, Maud Branscombe.⟩ *705:20*

20 *B* ⟨Wordblind 3 words ?limit⟩

B ⟨def. much worse in woman⟩

Michael (Pauper ?Dei) & Satan fought for his body

G ⟨the Cat = Argos.⟩

B ⟨pyramid of incense⟩ *692:2–4*

25 *B* ⟨Vere Foster copybook⟩ *705:15*   *B* ⟨steelyard⟩ *699:2*

B ⟨Is the bumblebee bite better?⟩ *695:28*

SD—virtue is sterile

B ⟨LB & flash whore⟩ *707:21–25*

B ⟨life = 2 T shite 2 ettol. blood.⟩

30 *B* ⟨Woman rare who overlooks man's caste⟩ *72:38*

1870—1902—peace

B ⟨SD will win else LB wdn't⟩

Recrudescence of memory (?J & nighttable glasses)

B ⟨SD & LB met 1888. SD shy to give hands⟩ *664:10–11*

35 *G* ⟨Suicide—che ora?⟩ *669:2–3*

R ⟨In ads (cherchez l'argent) we betray⟩ *718:2–3?*

B ⟨LB kisses RB⟩

B ⟨LB & thing to make carpentry⟩ *700:7?*

B ⟨Put Molly in dairy—what to do with our wives⟩ *670:5*

40 *B* ⟨In ?letter explains what he ought to have seen⟩

B ⟨SD invited LB to dine with Si D⟩ *664:15–16*

R ⟨All MB's judgments   wrong if W or R., S. And of LB?⟩ *671:1–3*

B ⟨Milly mercenary—you want etwas?⟩ *677:20?*

SD not in love ∴ trustable

45 *B* ⟨SD LB's vendetta⟩ *712:35–36?*

B ⟨Milly to LB if I only knew 1000th part⟩ *679:19*

B ⟨Toleration⟩ *711:1*

Laertes & Ul.   only kings by marriage, Penelope right

B ⟨SD what LB like to be⟩

50 *B* ⟨MB more given to lilt if LB dumpy⟩ *277:39*

B ⟨chap sold LB razor.⟩ *285:34–35*

B ⟨Geo Plumtree   23 merchant's quay⟩ *668:13*

R ⟨Milly. M. Mill.⟩ *66:10?*

B ⟨MB ?Gone—Well? Most nat. thing in world.⟩ *88:40*

55 *R* ⟨Make hay while sun shines⟩ *59:34–35*

Child drawing ignore cuore. no phallos   dislike arms or legs

B ⟨Papli profile 2 eyes, hair round head, nose more important.
   trunk   not in profile⟩ *705:17–19*

MB's hair in comb, age of return

60 urine = sea,   *B* ⟨girls who longest, boys who highest⟩ *687:26–29, cf. 730:6*

What thoughts? Well—

B ⟨1 level teaspoonful⟩ *660:32*

Tooth & Mouth   Starlings feed on worms dislodged by feet of
   cattle ◯

65 *B* ⟨He liked his cocoa strong.⟩ *660:33?*

B ⟨child's guide for Milly⟩ *693:11*

B ⟨forget street where smthg unpleasant occured
   〃   when bill is not cheque, forget stamp   boring letter, a
   p you dislike⟩

70 People talk about what they haven't & want

RIGHT COLUMN HORIZONTAL

B ⟨bought Blumenlied   finds her playing it when home from
   girl⟩ *274:16–17*

B ⟨star piss designs⟩

LB's ?govern other

75 *R* ⟨Walsingham way⟩ *685:6*

R ⟨watermark⟩ *706:11*

B ⟨crimson morocco⟩ *693:7*

B ⟨goldtooled⟩ *693:7*

B ⟨milky way⟩ *683:9*

80 *B* ⟨LB thinks horror of man who murdered—sleep⟩

B ⟨tablebook⟩

B ⟨no of 6 places⟩ *704:21*

B ⟨Sandglass⟩ *705:29*

B ⟨indoor exercise⟩ *665:25*

85 four in hand

417

R ⟨putting 2 × 2 together⟩

B ⟨Sherlock Holmes⟩ *485:17, 620:7*

Fight disease you produce terrible forms: animal don't

B ⟨LB hates waistcoat⟩ *695:7*

90 Statue like grimy dwarf

rang / ring

B ⟨£sd calculations⟩ *710:1*

B ⟨MB feigns not to know obscene word in company⟩ *732:5–6*

B ⟨cattle park at Liffey junction (banks)⟩ *703:36–40*

95 *B* ⟨LB etwas in cipher⟩ *706:4–5*

R ⟨conveyed heat⟩ *658:2–3*

G ⟨radiant heat⟩ *657:37–658:1*

B ⟨Soap useful⟩ *656:41?*

B ⟨where were you?⟩

100 *B* ⟨ —   are you going?⟩

B ⟨why pay for greens? Grow them⟩ *68:5–6, 700:10?*

NOTES

At the top of this notesheet are *I* in red pencil and *Ithaca* in black ink underlined in blue pencil.

Line 1 Notice the additional *H* after the *K*. This cipher backfired. Cf. *U* 706:3–5, where "WI.UU.OX" is a reversal. This anagram can easily be deciphered by reference to the code in these lines. See also "Ithaca" essay, p. 60.

5 James *Talbot Power*: see "Circe" 17:15 and note.

9 *Thing*: may be *string*.

13 *Crepa*: Italian for "split" or "uncouple."

16 This line is all one sentence.

22 See Jude 1:9: "Yet Michael the archangel, when contending with the devil he disputed about the body of Moses, durst not bring against him a railing accusation, but said, The Lord rebuke thee." The reference to *Pauper Dei* ("pauper of God") is not clear; Michael was known as champion of the Christians against the heathen, but not necessarily as a champion of the poor.

23 *Argos*: the faithful dog of Odysseus; Rudolph Bloom had one named Athos. As Gilbert remarks (p. 134), Leopold Bloom has a daughter and a cat; Odysseus has a son and a dog. The name is repeated at "Ithaca" 11:86.

27 *Virtue is sterile*: Richard Madtes believes this is "virtue is shite."

29 *Ettol[itro].*: Italian for hectoliter (176.077344 pints).

35   *Che ora*: at what time?

48   See "Ithaca" 8:34, where Joyce equates Penelope with Queen Victoria.

54   *Most nat[ural]. thing in world*: repeated at "Cyclops" 10:28.

56   *Cuore*: Italian for "heart." *Arms or legs*: looks suspiciously like *anus on legs*.

60   *Urine = sea*: may possibly be *wine = sea* though the context would seem to support the former reading.

64   After the word *cattle* Joyce drew a circle to indicate the circularity of the idea expressed here.

69   *P*: person.

75   Cf. "Ithaca" 16:25.

81   Repeated at "Ithaca" 13:1.

82   Repeated at "Ithaca" 13:2.

"Ithaca" 2

LEFT MARGIN HORIZONTAL

B ⟨LB conscience probably she has one or two secrets. So there
    you are⟩
B ⟨Milly feared her photo part of self⟩ *677:31–32*
Fire always in wind or rain.
5   Now's our chance
Woman different ∴ flowers in hat

CENTER COLUMNS HORIZONTAL

B ⟨Good morning? Where are you going? I am hastening to purchase
    the only infallible inkeraser Kansell, sold by Messrs
    Hely & Co, Ltd, 23 Dame Street. The Shop for
10   Value.⟩ *152:37–39*
B ⟨in terms of curvilinear⟩ *654:23, 715:11*   oracle = outlive?
R ⟨desire = hidden identity⟩ *674:5*   *B* ⟨LB gave Milly boy doll⟩ *677:21*
B ⟨Return to S. Side. Mrs Riordan in bath chair⟩ *664:22 & 36*
X w^{d.} depopulate, SD starve all,
15   friends of our friends our foes
B ⟨child sano brava madre, malsano papà infame⟩ *Cf. 94:40–41*
B ⟨She moves over in bed⟩
B ⟨LB on 3 Rock Mt⟩ *740:7*   *B* ⟨his soles ache⟩ *696:28*
B ⟨—with a dogvan⟩ *703:27*   *B* ⟨new worlds for old.⟩ *480:5*
20   ″ 's initials inside topcoat   slippers
B ⟨circle of lamp on ceiling⟩ *721:22*   *B* ⟨Milly followed went down one
B ⟨LB tries to recall smbdy's joke⟩   street & up another⟩ *677:33–36*

G ⟨?Ere solids dissolved in water liquids or drinks⟩ *655:41?*

B ⟨MB snoring pillow too high,⟩   G ⟨body throw off white
      dust in sleep,⟩ *766:34?*   B ⟨clothes light⟩

B ⟨MB believed alias was somebody in the scriptures⟩ *670:37*

No weather without moon

B ⟨think things out before⟩

B ⟨hubby learns secret 20 yrs after⟩

LB marked warm bits in book

B ⟨hardy golfers⟩ *703:24?*   God a woman

B ⟨Milly told dream   sleep in direct. of Earth⟩ *721:24–32?*

B ⟨Poetical Works of—⟩ *693:5*

B ⟨LB tells of wonderful friend⟩ *720:17?*

passage of thumb

B ⟨During vast, starspeckled night. Wanderers of the ages.
      Restless⟩ *712:26ff.?*

B ⟨LB in bed   Head E, left side to Earth,⟩ *721:24–27*   ghosts

exhalations, see breath, telegraph wires

B ⟨How hard hydrants are⟩ *656:23–24*

B ⟨Moon our future   no air, no water⟩

B ⟨LB scratches all over without itch⟩ *695:28–30*

B ⟨Scrivenery—add. env. for MB.⟩ *670:12*

?Shows Agendath, land there, absentee

B ⟨SD (Aryan) superstit. (LB) Semite not⟩

Cuore ago (SD.

B ⟨RB drank soup from plate⟩ *709:33–34*

B ⟨Cadby's piano⟩ *691:6*

B ⟨LB's nail same smell as 20 y^{rs.} ago⟩ *696:39ff.*

B ⟨LB met BB at Mesias'⟩ *717:23?*

Horse stops before door.

B ⟨Sleep on side attach button by adhesive to back⟩

B ⟨Still water, moon on wane, dangerous⟩ *656:36–37*

B ⟨verses for the occasion⟩ *661:35–36*

Anything wrong? No

B ⟨Milly pulled plait to remember⟩ *678:26*

B ⟨Women not know luxury of good shave⟩

B ⟨Hist. of LB's bed. Molly conceived there⟩ *715:34ff.*

B ⟨Boylan thinks he's the first⟩ *716:10–11*

60 Woman go up in a corner to do it.

B ⟨LB boasts of confidence rec^d. per ricevere⟩

B ⟨You'll be taking plates from dresser.⟩ *659:5–6*

B ⟨MB has look of old Tweedy⟩ *714:30*

NOTES

Line 16 *Child sano brava madre, malsano papà infame*: perhaps an Italian aphorism of some kind—when the child is healthy, the mother is (or is called) "capable." When the child is unhealthy, the the father is (or is called) "abominable."

45 Note the inconsistent use of parentheses.

46 *Cuore* and *ago*: "heart" and "needle" in Italian. The meaning of the note is obscure. Joyce did not close the parenthesis after *SD*.

61 *Per ricevere*: "in order to receive" or "meet with." The sense is that Bloom boasts of confidence received in order to gain the confidence of a second party.

"Ithaca" 3

LEFT MARGIN HORIZONTAL

B ⟨LB se pese⟩ *652:29ff.*
B ⟨Milly place in pool by spit⟩ *678:21*
B ⟨With relief he leads MB & Milly⟩
B ⟨LB in tree to see entry⟩ *701:31*
5   *B* ⟨Mice in pantry⟩
B ⟨lovers silent⟩
LB no stick
B ⟨Fuck creates love⟩
R ⟨her shift out through buttocks⟩ *91:27?, 741:27–28?*
10   gynecocracy coming
B ⟨Blum Pascha dies & leave LB big fortune⟩ *447:6, 704:20*

LEFT COLUMN HORIZONTAL

B ⟨Lent Haynes 3/– interest?⟩ *Cf. 118:33*
B ⟨Quarter 25/6⟩   *B* ⟨cipher⟩ *706:4*
B ⟨winebins (for distinguished guests)⟩ *698:26–27*
15   *B* ⟨annual income⟩ *702:4?*
B ⟨revol. of wheel⟩ *664:36*
R ⟨integer⟩ *684:11*
B ⟨tithe⟩
repeat; circul. *B* ⟨recurr.⟩
20   terminal   decimal
B ⟨Bought of⟩ *715:20*
B ⟨practice⟩ *718:5?*
Mail leaves Kings. 8:15

B ⟨£5 reward, missing gent aged about 40 height 5,8, full build,
25 dark complexion. May have since grown a beard. Was
dressed when last seen. Above will be paid for his
discovery⟩ *712:13ff.*

B ⟨This question he had often asked himself.⟩ *714:13–17?*

B ⟨Flower & M'Donald. Best Abram coal 21/– 14 D'Olier street⟩ *654:1–2*

30 B ⟨long primer, bourgeois, brevier, minion, pica⟩ *693:39–40*

B ⟨section of public⟩ *655:24*

B ⟨gold tooled⟩ *693:7*   R ⟨:a gross of⟩ *705:28*   B ⟨Modern Society⟩ *706:6*

B ⟨6 in. pipe, South Dublin Guardians, 20,000 gallons at night,
15 galls per day per skull⟩ *655:18ff.*

35 B ⟨Ign. Rice   lawagent of corporation⟩ *655:22–23*

B ⟨to sleep & remember past⟩

B ⟨MB how much is 5/ & 1/3⟩

B ⟨and I said to myself don't go out without it (key)⟩ *652:14–15*

B ⟨?MB tacked clothed list on door⟩

40 LB & frost flowers

B ⟨LB repeats habit of childhood⟩ *704:32*

B ⟨Curlpaper with burnt furrow⟩

B ⟨If too much together all defects⟩ *711:1–2*

B ⟨Hate to see mouth cleaned with paper⟩ *709:35–36*

45 B ⟨Old bazaar ticket⟩ *705:33*

B ⟨Her stockings no smell⟩ *715:7*

R ⟨Honour—selfaid⟩ *719:9?*

B ⟨MB bored at night. (play draughts)⟩ *670:9*

B ⟨Mrs Riordan, colza oil lamp, picture of Immac. Concept.⟩
50 *665:18–19*

B ⟨He feels imprint of BB⟩ *716:6*

B ⟨Jews cannot eat milk & meat⟩ *709:2*

B ⟨Cat meat no mouser⟩ *62:23, 678:23?*

B ⟨Each leaves own smell in room⟩ *716:5?*

55 R ⟨Did you tell me or I you?⟩ *666:37–667:1*

B ⟨Molly takes umbrella if good hat.⟩ *671:22–25*

B ⟨Men stare at poster.⟩ *705:10*

B ⟨LB takes book to remember at once remembers⟩ *694:36–37*

R ⟨Never see dead donkey (R.B.) Shame of death⟩ *109:7*

60   *B* ⟨SD sees face mirrored in LB⟩ *687:15*

    B ⟨Weeps over horns⟩

    B ⟨Somethg behind books⟩ *694:23*

    B ⟨LB tells himself a story⟩ *704:31, 722:15*

    B ⟨His maxims⟩

65   *B* ⟨mare tenebrosum⟩

    B ⟨Cat herb if ill 2 ?miles off⟩ *678:8–11*

    B ⟨to think of new ads⟩ *667:27, 705:9–13*

    To my wife ″ letter Belfast

    B ⟨LB shaves think of smthg cut, plaster, gave himself a

70   nick⟩ *658:29*

    B ⟨Church or stage (SD?)⟩ *674:18*

    B ⟨Osmond Tearle † 1901⟩ *674:20*

    B ⟨cut on generous lines⟩ *715:9*

RIGHT COLUMN HORIZONTAL

    R ⟨what causes that?⟩ *91:24, 713:22?*

75   *R* ⟨they saw same cloud⟩ *651:8–9*

    B ⟨drooping serpents brass bed quoits⟩ *715:35–36*

    B ⟨5—9 what did we do?⟩

    B ⟨kaleidoscope of Milky Way⟩ *667:17*   *B* ⟨parlour tennis⟩ *670:7*

    B ⟨Padney Socks⟩ *677:19*   *B* ⟨eastern limb of sun⟩ *690:1*

80   *B* ⟨RB took drugs⟩ *709:27–28*

    B ⟨counterfoil⟩

    B ⟨bedroom ware⟩ *715:18–25*

    B ⟨trunk with battens⟩ *715:14*

    B ⟨If not love smthg must replace⟩ *716–717?*

85   *R* ⟨under lamp in park⟩

    B ⟨passbook⟩ *707:33, 710:5*

    B ⟨N. Pole climate tisici Dundrum⟩ *697:30–32*

    B ⟨She fucked in his bed⟩ *716:2?*

    R ⟨½ league⟩ *474:19*

90   *R* ⟨LB wrote music Lead Kindly light⟩ *733:31*

    B ⟨He stole her glove (she knew)⟩ *731:5*

NOTES

My division of phrases between right and left columns is often arbitrary.

Line 1   *LB se pese*: LB weighs himself.

10   Listed as item 67 in Connolly's *Personal Library of James Joyce* (p. 13) is a book by Jacques Desroix: *La gynécocratie ou la domination de la femme . . . précédé d'une étude sur le masochisme dans l'histoire et les traditions par Laurent Tailhade* (Paris, 1902). Cf. *U* 763:20.

11   *Pascha*: Joyce's misspelling (repeated at "Ithaca" 14:5); it appears correctly in the text as "Pasha."

23   See "Cyclops" 4:128 note.

29   The firm of *Flower & M'Donald* is still in business, now located on Westmoreland Street.

33–34   Adams (p. 226) says: "the whole latter half of the description of the Dublin waterworks, on p. 655, comes from a letter to the *Irish Independent* written by Ignatius J. Rice, and published in the issue of June 15, 1904."

39   *Clothed*: Joyce's spelling.

53   Cf. line 5 above and "Ithaca" 14:57.

65   *Mare tenebrosum*: "dark sea"—from Stephens, p. 1. See essay on "Penelope," p. 72.

79   *Eastern limb of sun*: may be *extreme limit of sun*. Cf. *U* 712:26.

87   *Tisici*: "consumptives" in Italian.

90   Cf. *Letters*, I, 305: "l'hymne fameux de Newman *Lead, kindly light*! dans lequel le futur cardinal annonce le commencement de sa conversion à l'église catholique."

"Ithaca" 4

LEFT MARGIN HORIZONTAL

    B ⟨LB heard toddling feet⟩

    B ⟨lodge⟩ *702:33?*

    B ⟨LB with cap⟩ *699:23*

    B ⟨to adopt son clown—papa⟩ *681:11*

5   *B* ⟨LB visit Giant's Causeway, Golden Vale, Lough Neagh,
        Mullingar bicycle with umbrella tour ?Killala, caves
        of Moher⟩ *711:18–20*

    B ⟨he felt house empty⟩   (also Lestrygonians)

    R ⟨obverse⟩ *683:24*

10 *B* ⟨reverse⟩ *602:8, 621:3, 641:32, and elsewhere*

    B ⟨net personalty⟩ *707:37*

    B ⟨takes off RB's boots⟩

    B ⟨SD read music?⟩

    B ⟨bolt & staple⟩ *688:18*

15 *B* ⟨letterpress⟩ *693:38*

    B ⟨trains rarely start at 3 p.m.⟩

    B ⟨LB put a marked ½ crown in circ. It never came back⟩ *681:6–14*

LEFT COLUMN HORIZONTAL

    B ⟨LB finds etwas done which he intended ?to⟩ *690:18–19*

    B ⟨LB somewhat bored by men's eyes on MB⟩ *717:1?*

20 *B* ⟨He finds pin⟩ *715:11?*

    B ⟨BB's good points⟩ *717?*

    B ⟨LB's quests⟩

B ⟨waifs & strays⟩ *712:28*

B ⟨cold of space⟩ *689:14*

25 B ⟨LB watering can⟩ *699:24*

Cat rocked on chair to get out

B ⟨Wonder mice don't cry⟩ *55:35*

B ⟨Letter on forehead of cat⟩ *371:29–30*

B ⟨MB leaned on him alighting (Pen)⟩

30 B ⟨LB leaves book open purposely⟩ *671:10–11*

B ⟨LB & waste paper.⟩ *703:7*

B ⟨Tides.⟩ *655:34, 656:31, 703:20*

B ⟨LB repeats jest of Bella⟩

B ⟨didn't get tea or see Leah⟩ *714:26*

35 2 sides < third

B ⟨?Same thing he did in '82⟩ *701:17*?

B ⟨dark suns⟩ *685:23–24*?

R ⟨waggoner's star.⟩ *685:6*

R ⟨white yellow red⟩ *685:4*

40 R ⟨spiral nebulae⟩ *685:8*

R ⟨9 years wander (Cassiopeia)⟩ *685:26, 712:34*

R ⟨cat's shameclosing eye⟩ *55:37*

R ⟨—walks over LB's desk⟩ *55:20–21*

B ⟨Resp girl (RC) wishes to hear of post in fruit or pork

45 shop⟩ *158:10–11*

B ⟨LB understood 2nd. time of reading⟩

B ⟨She keeps bed warm⟩ *713:12*

B ⟨1stly 2ndly⟩ *694:32–34*

R ⟨LB knows end of SD's sentence (mental arith)⟩

50 R ⟨LB memories of Dignam.⟩ *689:24*

B ⟨LB merit and speaks of MB⟩

B ⟨LB trousers under MB—mangling done on premises⟩ *713:18–19*

B ⟨Dolls of provinces, mapball.⟩ *667:21*

B ⟨LB more like dad every day⟩ *692:31–32*

55 B ⟨why did he secretly smile?⟩ *716:9*

B ⟨nobody 1d. the worse⟩

B ⟨Hole in the Wall cold well⟩ *656:15*

B ⟨Days begin to get shorter⟩ *669:38*

B ⟨Body finds out proper foods, vices,⟩ *718:12–13*

60 B ⟨Intermediate superintendant.⟩

B ⟨Cat ate 'em? What? Fish⟩

B ⟨Did not know multiplication table⟩

B ⟨Sealed prophecy of Home Rule⟩ *705:30ff.*

He rinses tumbler

65 B ⟨Sexual sin not the worst⟩ *717:35–718:14*

B ⟨LB finds 1/ in waistcoat⟩ *695:32*

B ⟨LB up when she down & vice versa⟩

B ⟨LB & BB duel, blackmail⟩ *718:23*

B ⟨70 y^rs. birth to death, flash & peal⟩ *704:36–37*

70 B ⟨provided—which—a lie in itself—since—as⟩

B ⟨Room retains story of crime⟩

B ⟨Fuck only time people really sincere⟩

B ⟨Wanted Live man for spirit counter. Cook & general. exc. cuisine.⟩ *158:9–10, cf. 698:21*

75 B ⟨MB in middle of fuck thought of jokes (German emporer)⟩ *725:29*

B ⟨Milly rattling moneybox⟩ *677:20*

35,000 birds killed for ladies' hats

B ⟨LB calculates day of 1878⟩

B ⟨turnscrew, gimlet, awl & tweezers⟩ *700:8–9*

80 B ⟨scutchmills, bleachworks,⟩ *656:29*

Earth knows which side her bread is buttered.

as she (Pen) is

R ⟨SD bath last October⟩ *657:8*

B ⟨beeswaxed margins⟩

RIGHT COLUMN HORIZONTAL

85 B ⟨. . . . .⟩

B ⟨Mount Argus⟩ *716:26*

Kimmage Garden

R ⟨new moon with old in arms.⟩ *685:19*

B ⟨Molly & Milly both turn on LB⟩ *710:26–27?, 721:10–12?*

90 B ⟨LB shaves eves⟩ *658:18ff.*

429

LB hairoil

B ⟨her drawers cigar smell⟩ *715:8–10*

B ⟨fanlight⟩ *653:21–22*

B ⟨renovate old brown boots⟩ *706:20*

95   *B* ⟨3 years suitors.⟩

B ⟨Letter of Citron at ?Xmas a recall⟩

B ⟨magnifying glass⟩ *706:13*

B ⟨wheelbarrow⟩ *699:26*

R ⟨Endymion⟩

100   *B* ⟨newmown hay⟩ *699:27*

B ⟨enclose the Bull⟩ *703:23*

B ⟨harness Poulaphouca⟩ *703:20*

B ⟨double gleams of RB's glasses⟩ *708:17?*

B ⟨LB at dame's school⟩ *666:30*

105   *B* ⟨Maria Theresia⟩ *709:17*

B ⟨Mercalli's projector⟩ *Cf. 337:39, 655:29*

B ⟨at end of life not ½ wishes fulfilled⟩ *704:37–705:2*

NOTES

Line 1   This line is crossed out in ink with vertical lines.

5–7   These are famous tourist attractions in Ireland. By *caves of Moher* Joyce probably meant the cliffs of Moher.

13   *SD read music?*: *Ulysses* takes place on June 16, 1904; on May 16, 1904, Joyce participated in a music festival—the *Feis Ceoil*—but failed to win because he could not or would not sight read music. Cf. Ellmann, pp. 156–157.

21   *BB*: looks like *BG*.

22   *Quests*: may be *guests*.

29   Cf. "Penelope" 1:7.

38   *Waggoner's star*: the constellation Auriga.

41   *Cassiopeia*: a northern constellation between Andromeda and Cepheus. "In 1572 a brilliant new star appeared in this constellation, only to disappear again" (*Shorter O.E.D.*).

61   *Cat ate 'em*: may be *Catch 'em*.

85   This line is smeared with ink.

86–87   *Mount Argus* is a section of Dublin south of the Liffey; to the southwest of Mount Argus lies *Kimmage Garden*.

430

97   Repeated at "Ithaca" 15:7.

99   For *Endymion* Farrell, see Ellmann, p. 375.

102   *Poulaphouca* (or Pollaphuca): a succession of cataracts in County Wicklow. This waterfall was indeed harnessed in 1937 and is now the main power station of the Dublin hydroelectric scheme.

105   *Maria Theresia*: the Empress Maria Theresa's name is spelled correctly in the text.

106   *Mercalli's projector*: this phrase seems to be Joyce's error, but perhaps it was meant for Bloom's repository of false information. Cf. "Mercator's projection" (*U* 655:29) and "Mercalli's scale" (*U* 337:39).

"Ithaca" 5

discard factor
B ⟨Shew that⟩
HCF Algebra
LCM arith
5 Maitland
drug distance
B ⟨It was understood that⟩
every power of $9 = 9$
R ⟨abc $=$ bac $=$ cab⟩
10 one factor 0 all 0
B ⟨?there ?sits ?enthroned in brain⟩
JC $= \sqrt[3]{\text{God}}$
like & unlike
collect terms
15 $a + b - c = b + a - c$
$a + b + (-c) = b - (+c) + a$
$ax^3 = 4$ dimensions
$a^6 + a^4b^2 + b^6$
B ⟨homogeneous⟩ *700:31*
20 R ⟨component parts⟩ *683:35*
B ⟨device⟩ *469:1, 482:4*
B ⟨Step by step⟩
B ⟨Prove that⟩ *701:9*
$x = 10$ A.D. $-3x = 30$ BC
25 $\sqrt{5329}$ $70 = 80$
resolved into algebraic sum of $+ 8 - 12 = -4$

432

LEFT COLUMN HORIZONTAL

B ⟨reduce to lowest terms⟩ *666:3, 705:11, 719:13*

B ⟨idea of idea of Peter⟩

B ⟨he knew that he knew that he knew⟩ *666:8*

30   *R* ⟨Bloom's Cranly — Budgen⟩

R ⟨on same base & between same parallels⟩

B ⟨intercept⟩

R ⟨on same line & same side of it⟩

sides about the angles

35   *B* ⟨will meet if produced⟩ *712:4?, 715:1*

B ⟨superposition,⟩ *717:8?*   side fall on both not acute

R ⟨given in species⟩ *684:18*

B ⟨meet at infinity⟩ *715:1*

B ⟨supplemental⟩

40   *R* ⟨similar to the whole⟩ *684:34*

R ⟨making any angle⟩ *688:24*

undivided

B ⟨concyclic⟩

B ⟨describe a circle⟩ *695:19*

45   *R* ⟨according ?as⟩ *663:28, 684:25*

B ⟨a system of⟩ *655:8*

B ⟨find the locus⟩ *678:23?*

all whose sides pass through a given pt.

same property is true of

50   coplanar

R ⟨dihedral⟩

left hand = Mary of Magdala

make ⟨ x= ⟨ y

polygon

55   *B* ⟨directly inversely⟩

extremes & means meet

whole: greater: :greater: less

R ⟨position magnitude⟩ *685:5–6*

complete rectangles

60   perimeter

433

R ⟨homothetic Δ Δ ⟩ *692:5*

cylinder formed by revolution of rect.

B ⟨cone⟩ *691:30 & 36* ″ ″ ″ Δ

B ⟨sphere⟩ *690:9* ″ ″ ″ ⌂

65 *B* ⟨by trial⟩ *697:31*

infer

B ⟨will lie between⟩

  — fall —

normal perp to coplanar & concurrent lines

70 *R* ⟨which was impossible⟩ *711:10–11*

R ⟨reentrant ∟s polyhedron⟩ *685:14*

B ⟨right prism, oblique prism, pyramid⟩ *698:9*

B ⟨decreases as increases⟩ *717:17*

B ⟨odd even⟩ *652:7*

75 $3^4 = 81$. 4 is log of 81 to base 3

$\log 1 = 0$

$2 = \log 180$ common pnt $\underline{y} = mx$

characteristic — mantissa   4.33013

B ⟨LB taught Milly to read clock⟩ *678:33ff.*

80 *R* ⟨Woman fucked: cries fill space⟩

n things r at a time $= n \cdot n - r$

1 2 3 4 : why $r = 4$ *B* ⟨equidistant⟩ *695:20*

R ⟨farrier 1st mail $\frac{1}{4}^{\text{d}}$., $\frac{1}{2}^{\text{d}}$., 1^{d}.⟩   *B* ⟨cyclic order⟩

rational & real $\sqrt{9}$

85   — & unreal $\sqrt{8}$ $\dfrac{a}{\dfrac{b}{c}}$

ir —   — $\sqrt{-8}$ complex fraction

B ⟨permutation > combination⟩

n, n! factorial n

10 steamers, 90 ways *R* ⟨$x - \frac{1}{x} - \frac{1}{x} - \frac{1}{x}$⟩ *R* ⟨continued fraction⟩ *676:23*

90 *B* ⟨O'Hara, bullfighter, Gibraltar, La Linea,⟩ *711:32–33*

B ⟨Cameron Highlanders⟩ *711:33*

RIGHT COLUMN HORIZONTAL

singly

B ⟨only possible solution⟩

expand R. side

95   R which does not involve x

            R ⟨without actual division⟩ *683:37–38*

            if exp zx–a. R = exp with a for x

$a^{-n} = \frac{1}{a^n}$

index of product distributed over factors not over terms

100     $\sqrt{8} = 8^{\frac{1}{2}}$

R ⟨carry process far enough⟩

$a = \sqrt{a^2} \quad : \quad a^{\frac{1}{3}} = a^{\frac{9}{27}}$

B ⟨in its simplest form⟩ *666:3, 719:13*

an entire surd

105   duplicate ratio.

B ⟨A varies as B   A ∝ B⟩

Interest varies jointly as principal time & %

B ⟨term of series⟩ *716:17*

B ⟨solid angle⟩ *690:10*

110   a + d, a + 2d, l – 2d, l–d, l

B ⟨numerical value⟩ *672:25?*

binary, ternary, quaternary scales

1 2 3 10 11 12 13

10 = 2, 3, 4, 5

115   *R* ⟨again⟩ *678:24*

R ⟨hence⟩ *678:31*   ax = a′x

B ⟨LB broke bank⟩ *702:41*

literal coefficient (?initials)

NOTES

My arrangement of phrases on this notesheet is often arbitrary. At the top is *Ithaca* in ink. For one source of the material here, see the note to line 30.

Line 5   Probably Frederick W. *Maitland*: English historian, barrister, and author of *A History of English Law* and *Domesday Book and Beyond* (1850–1906).

30   *Cranly*: a prominent character in *A Portrait*. Frank *Budgen*: see "Cyclops" 5:5 and note. Budgen probably copied some of the mathematical material present in the "Ithaca" notesheets from Isaac Todhunter's *Algebra for the Use of Colleges and Schools* (London, 1873) and sent it to Joyce. See Budgen, *Myselves When Young* (London, 1970), p. 210. I have not yet been able to establish conclusively that the material came from Todhunter and nowhere else, however. Both Budgen and Cranly were disciples of Joyce in their way, but Stephen believes Cranly betrayed him; thus the allusion to Budgen here could hardly be flattering.

62–64   A *cylinder*, *cone*, and *sphere* are formed by the revolution of a rectangle, a triangle, and a semicircle, respectively.

68   The dashes in the line function as ditto marks.

78   *Mantissa*: cf. *FW* 298:20.

85   $\sqrt{8}$ is actually irrational but real as a mathematical concept.

88   The symbol *!* in mathematics is "used to indicate the product of all the whole numbers up to and including a given preceding number" (*Webster's 7th*).

104   *Surd*: repeated at "Ithaca" 16:11. See also *A Portrait*, p. 104.

110   The *l*'s here appear to be letters, not figure 1's.

"Ithaca" 6

LEFT MARGIN HORIZONTAL

R ⟨pump⟩ *666:23, 667:13*
LB climbed along the branch
bracket = tierod & brace
B ⟨vertical lines not //⟩
5   plumbline
leave out of 9c
R ⟨seesaw⟩

LEFT COLUMN HORIZONTAL

B ⟨get a purchase on⟩ *688:16*
G ⟨land ¼ sea ¾⟩ *655:37*
10   *R* ⟨ ″ ¾ over Eq.⟩ *655:38–39*
old world   *R* ⟨alluvial⟩ *656:3*
new world
R ⟨all point—S—Jutland⟩
N. plain.   S. art
15   Eur. skelet.   W→→→→ E
R ⟨continental⟩ *650:24, 656:6*
R ⟨every particle of surface water with every⟩ *655:31*
R ⟨continental (self contained stream)⟩ *656:6*
to what S of Eq. corresponds Dublin?
20   *R* ⟨gulfstream carries Amer. weeds⟩ *656:8?*
R ⟨ocean rivers⟩ *656:7–8*
G ⟨spring, neap⟩ *655:34*
tide in Bristol chanel 30 ft

437

normal 3 & 4 feet

25 R ⟨sea contains all soluble subst. in solution⟩ *655:41*

R ⟨soundings⟩

4 qts of globe

R ⟨2 m. T. silver in sea⟩ *656:1*

Height of brick wall?

30 rolling < sliding friction

R ⟨exert force⟩ *653:6*   sextant

B ⟨weigh the matter⟩ *686:1*   mass

scalepan balance

acting, acted upon

35 jaws of a vice

magnit. dir. pt of application

pointer cross section

malleable (foil)   ductile (wire)

R ⟨coiled steel spring of bells⟩ *654:23*

40 elastic arches of feet

—— fibres of body

R ⟨break shock⟩ *652:26?*

R ⟨Roundwood Co Wick.⟩ *655:2*

R ⟨2400 m. gall. filter mains⟩ *655:3–4*

45 R ⟨Callowhill, Stillorgan 22m.⟩ *655:7–8*

R ⟨250 ft fall to city boundary at Leeson St.⟩ *655:9–10*

R ⟨drought, canal used 1893⟩ *655:16–18*

R ⟨Bloomfield SCR⟩ *651:20–22*

knock alley behind S.M. & John's

50 R ⟨Simpson's hosp. poor decayed blind & gouty⟩ *710:21–23*

R ⟨Ᵽ floating, graving docks⟩ *656:30*

Stable C of G lowest position

unstable —   — highest   —

neutral

55 leaning tower of Pisa

B ⟨true⟩ *671:5*   sensitive stable B ⟨balance⟩ *671:1*

B ⟨with false bal. weigh true⟩ *671:4–5*

fluid, R ⟨compressible⟩ *685:13?*

R ⟨piston⟩ *717:9*

RIGHT COLUMN HORIZONTAL

60 *B* ⟨allowing for⟩ *674:24, 686:2*
    shortest — between 2   ″   . . . . . —
    L.Bl. in 1914   . . . . . —
    R ⟨Mercator's projection⟩ *655:29*
    B ⟨ordnance map⟩ *711:15*
65 scale
    B ⟨?contours⟩
    B ⟨hachures⟩ *711:16*
    cutting below surface when embankment
    R ⟨torrid zone⟩ *656:5*
70 *R* ⟨between tropics⟩
    R ⟨frigid zone⟩ *656:5*
    R ⟨temperate zone⟩ *656:5*
    R ⟨interstellar⟩ *689:14*
    -w̷¢̷- static
75 dynamic
    R ⟨plastic⟩ *650:24*
    needle show true
    R ⟨ravine⟩
    variation of Cork 26°W
80 lines of no variation
    in log day added or dropt for r. world voyage
    B ⟨Woman's arse honest⟩ *719:21–22?*
    stands to reason
    G ⟨how can her fuck fuck me⟩
85 compass invention 12th. cent. old
    R ⟨navigation coastwise⟩ *703:32–33*
    R ⟨cent per cent⟩ *669:31*
    inclined plane
    3% grade or pitch
90 *R* ⟨arms of lever⟩ *653:6?*
    R ⟨fulcrum⟩ *653:7*
    G ⟨olivepress⟩
    crossbeam

winepress

95   R ⟨millwheel⟩ *656:28*

R ⟨hydraulic⟩ *656:28*

NOTES

Line 9   Cf. "Cyclops" 8:79 and "Eumaeus" 5:89.

23   *Chanel*: Joyce's misspelling.

32   *Mass*: may be *mars*.

45   *Callowhill, Stillorgan*: place names near Roundwood (line 43).

48   *Bloomfield* Avenue runs between South Circular Road (*SCR*) and the Grand Canal in Dublin.

49   There is a second Bloomfield section in Dublin, a very small area south of one of the Martello Towers. On Merrion Road directly to the east and north of Bloomfield are St. John's Home of Rest and St. Mary's Home for the Blind. There are several alleys in the vicinity without official names, and one leads to Bloomfield; perhaps this is *knock alley*.

61   *Shortest* was written over another, now illegible, word. Cf. "Ithaca" 8:37.

61–62   To the right are two illegible words followed by dashes.

"Ithaca" 7

plain
valley
steppes
G ⟨plateau⟩
5   R ⟨inundated⟩ *656:12*
bog
R ⟨isthmus⟩
R ⟨torrent⟩ *656:10*
desert
10 savannahs
pampas
peninsular War
prairie
Gennesareth N.W. ∟ of Galilee
15 Madeira
Lacrima Xi
Volcano wines
R ⟨atoll,⟩ *656:25*   coral reef
R ⟨dam⟩ *656:20*
20 breakwater
R ⟨archipelago⟩ *656:25*
R ⟨submarine⟩ *656:32*
R ⟨promontory⟩ *656:2*
annual rainfall
25 toe   R ⟨of glacier⟩ *656:27*
Jungfrau

441

ness

B ⟨mull⟩ *715:9*

butt   bill

30   oxidized,   ore

we inhale O_3N_7

we exhale CO_2

plants inhale C

       restore O_2

35   B ⟨uniform⟩ *714:36, 715:2*

foul air $=$?ls in $=$?ts

conduction translation

silver spoon (?Tweedy)

as crow flies

40   making 10 knots

iron retires   angular

heat ?iron hand trajectory

flatirons target rifle butts

Sol over not warm the air

45   dark heat, luminous heat

radiate, lampblack

R ⟨rough dark radiates better⟩ *658:5*

R ⟨part absorbed⟩ *658:6*

R ⟨—   transmitted⟩ *658:7*   R ⟨terrestrial⟩ *684:24 and elsewhere*

50   R ⟨—   reflected⟩ *658:6*

R ⟨meridian of long⟩ *721:26*

R ⟨parallel of lat.⟩ *721:25–26*

concavo-convex

a spread of

55   R ⟨condensed milk⟩ *482:29, 683:9*

spoon gets hot

R ⟨siphon⟩ *667:12*

?bung

fuse, melt,   B ⟨liquefy⟩ *705:25* congeal, freeze

60   R ⟨Saturn's ring⟩ *685:7*

LEFT COLUMN HORIZONTAL

B ⟨aberration of light⟩ *705:6*

purge

B ⟨his wife's admirers⟩ *307:37*

Dignam's insurance

65 *R* ⟨acqueduct⟩

R ⟨water seeks level, dam, leak,⟩ *655:28, 656:20*

B ⟨lawnsprinkler⟩ *699:12*

B ⟨free surface of water⟩ *655:31*

G ⟨level water is curved⟩ *656:13*

70 roads   *R* ⟨lagoon⟩ *656:4 & 25*   knot

iceberg ⅑ over water

R ⟨berg⟩   drops boulder

R ⟨icefloe⟩ *656:27*   (saltwater)

B ⟨decimal system⟩

75 *R* ⟨tributary⟩ *656:7*   *R* ⟨estuary⟩ *656:26*

R ⟨confluence⟩ *656:7*

R ⟨tidal river⟩ *656:26*   *R* ⟨cataract⟩ *656:11*

R ⟨sediment⟩ *674:25*   *R* ⟨gut (Gibraltar)⟩ *711:29?*

right bank S.   *R* ⟨tarn⟩ *656:4*   *R* ⟨eddy⟩ *656:10*

80 *R* ⟨waterparting⟩ *656:11*   *R* ⟨minch⟩ *656:26*

R ⟨   -shed⟩ *656:10–11*   kyles

R ⟨gulf⟩ *656:24*   *R* ⟨coast⟩ *644:17?*   electroplated

R ⟨bay⟩ *656:24*   *R* ⟨loch⟩ *656:24*   clockwise

R ⟨bight⟩ *656:25*   *R* ⟨fjord⟩ *656:26*   *G* ⟨counterclockwise⟩

85 *R* ⟨battery of jars⟩ *659:28*   *R* ⟨turbines⟩ *656:28*

G ⟨tap a current⟩ *654:36*

disregarding   small   lesser

chain of magnets   to retain charge

lines of force

90 *B* ⟨couple of forces⟩   *B* ⟨rod connected to E.⟩

R ⟨residual⟩ *674:25*   polarization

R ⟨arclamp,   glowlamp⟩ *650:15–16*

overshoot the mark

impulse

95 ship $\begin{cases} \text{internal force} = \text{crew} \\ \text{ex}-- \quad --- \quad \text{wind} \end{cases}$

 B ⟨amplitude⟩ *719:20*

 precipitated chalk

 nitrate of silver

100 *R* ⟨change of place⟩

 R ⟨deposited⟩ *715:27*

 atom   lead tree

 R ⟨Milly's hoop⟩ *677:30*

 all 3 cases

105 theory of exchange

 globemapballs *Cf. 667:21*

 watch hole in case

 find out you are in Dublin

 uncharted Persia

110 1860 Syrian coast out 4 miles ∴ Jerusalem

 cyclone

 R ⟨S. Laurence O'Toole⟩ *146:7–8, 333:17*

 R ⟨Royal Hosp. Kilmainham⟩ *710:20–21*

 last of hides

115 *R* ⟨head of water⟩

 ?boromen   ?ashot

 R ⟨temperature⟩ *658:7, 8, & 11*   *B* ⟨popgun⟩ *667:16*

 R h is cold   *B* ⟨bladder⟩ *174:18, 478:18*

 L h is hot   strokes

120 R & L h is tepid

 1000 atmosphere = cannon

 receiver

 he gauged her symmetry

 R ⟨abs. zero = –273 C⟩ *689:15*

125 clock loses time in summer

 wind up clock

RIGHT COLUMN HORIZONTAL

B ⟨the table farted⟩ *714:6–8*

444

immediacy
B ⟨LB believes with each different writer⟩
130 *R* ⟨parabola⟩   LB John o' God's
  carpetbeater   nice nurse
  B ⟨ducks & drakes⟩ *623:22–23* Clondalkin
  B ⟨inertia⟩ *713:5* ?tramjolt Finglas
  R ⟨circushoop⟩ *446:18–19* saturated
135 LB's signature   simmer
  G ⟨dewpoint⟩ *656:16?*   boiling water in Quito will
  S ⟨soluble⟩ *655:41, 659:17, 660:33*   not cook potatoes
  G ⟨crystal⟩ *657:9*   distilled
  alum
140 *R* ⟨stress⟩ *715:37*
  R ⟨strain⟩ *715:37*
  R ⟨state of rest⟩ *667:8*
  diamond cryst. carbon
  B ⟨diffusion⟩ *660:35, 689:26 & 36, 691:26* *B* ⟨thermal⟩ *658:9*
145 door stuck   *R* ⟨equilibrium⟩ *718:11, 653:4*
  crackling of wood   water greater
  sieve   . . . . sea
  drop formed   moderature ?C2′
  weld   evaporation
150 *B* ⟨cohesion⟩ *683:31*   chill
  terracity
  R ⟨acquacity⟩ *657:18*
  B ⟨elastic⟩ *667:16, 696:36, 699:24*
  tempering   graphite
155 *R* ⟨miscellaneous effects⟩ *715:5* escape gas
  inspector of gauges   *R* ⟨gain access⟩ *653:7*
  B ⟨clergyman⟩ *707:2*   ballast
  saleswoman   topheavy
  oil the doors
160 E spins W̶ ?towards E
  R ⟨pressure on body = 19 T⟩
  suction   MB crack inflated paperbag, bubbles
  exhaust   *R* ⟨adulterated milk test⟩ *659:23*

445

distended   *B* ⟨belljar⟩ *692:10?*

165 spec. gravity

B ⟨dans cette sale prison depuis 2 mois que je suis dans cette

sale prison ?etc⟩

rails of railroad never touch

B ⟨freezing point⟩ *689:15*   35

170 *R* ⟨boiling point⟩ *658:8*   27

?annuitant

R ⟨a spread of⟩

real & apparent expansion

vessel of liquid expand

175 *R* ⟨pneumatic⟩ *665:3*

NOTES

At the top is the abbreviation *It*, the *I* in red pencil and the *t* in green. The notesheet has a chaotic appearance, and a great deal of information has been crammed onto it. My division between columns is often arbitrary.

Line 12   *Peninsular War*: fought in Spain between England and France (1808–1814). Joyce may have been thinking of Sir William F. P. Napier (1785–1860), *History of the War in the Peninsula and in the South of France from . . . 1807 to . . . 1814*, 6 vols. (London, 1828–1840). This work was reprinted in abridged versions several times, one of which was a cheap Thomas Nelson and Sons edition (London, 1910). Joyce may also have noticed it mentioned in Stephens, p. 7 (see essay on "Penelope," p. 72). "Lord Napier" is mentioned at *U* 757:10. Cf. *FW* 3:6.

14   *Gennesareth*: an alternate name for Galilee. *N.W.* ∟: probably "northwest angle."

15–17   These are wines. *Lacrima Xi*: Lacrima Christi.

18   According to Richard Madtes, "and atolls" was to have followed "lagoons" at *U* 656:4. This omission was not corrected in the 1961 Random House edition.

26   *Jungfrau*: the famous mountain in southwestern Switzerland.

65   *Acqueduct*: one of Joyce's frequent misspellings. He apparently confused the English "aqueduct" with its Italian equivalent, *acquedotto*. See also "acquacity" at line 152 below.

78   *Gut*: in this case means "narrow passage."

81   *Kyle*: Scottish for "channel, sound, strait."

83   *Loch*: may be *lock*.

87   *Lesser*: possibly *losses*.

113   *Kilmainham*: a section of Dublin just south of Phoenix Park.

118–120   The notes on the left refer to water faucets.

130   *John o' God's*: a Dublin mental hospital (*U* 288:18).

132–133   *Clondalkin, Finglas*: Dublin suburban communities.

136–137   *Boiling . . . potatoes*: it is, of course, the high altitude of Quito which causes this phenomenon.

169–170   The numbers to the right are apparently not related to the content of the notesheet.

"Ithaca" 8

LEFT MARGIN VERTICAL (from top to bottom)

R ⟨vertical shaft⟩ *683:11*
obliquity   H.P.
R ⟨latitude⟩ *700:32, 721:26*
thread of screw nut lubricant
5 delivery tube   *B* ⟨axle⟩ *221:28, 420:18, 550:7*
?augur
force   work   resistance
R ⟨propel⟩ *664:34*
B ⟨ignited⟩ *653:8, 654:3, 691:35, 691:36*
10 steady pull
LB's experiment
B ⟨man heats others⟩ *713:16–17*
vice
machine   cannot create work
15 freight efficiency
B ⟨kinetic potential⟩ *669:19–20*
B ⟨frequency⟩ *716:35*
pulse = compress state of air
candle illuminate objects
20 *B* ⟨Throwaway⟩ *660:6 and elsewhere*   *B* ⟨flash⟩ *Cf. 660:20ff.*
   B ⟨He won⟩   *B* ⟨report⟩ *660:20*

LEFT COLUMN HORIZONTAL

B ⟨J.F.X. O'Brien⟩ *701:25*
HCF × LCM = A × B
prove the rule

448

25 *B* ⟨Prince Consort † 1861⟩

   B ⟨play duets with M.B. LB⟩ *670:11?*

   scalene, isoceles, equil.

   oblong   sector   sine

   insist on.

30 *B* ⟨Mrs Thornton = Euryclée⟩

   Pretenders = suitors *Cf. 46:22*

   Ul. evasive answer

   croaking ?raven

   Victoria = Penelope

35 concave convex

   B ⟨curvilinear⟩ *654:23, 715:11*   rectilinear mixed

   shortest way / *2··*

   a compass

   where property is ?formed to ?chose ?St

40 minuto terzo *"*

   B ⟨alternate⟩

   R ⟨internal⟩ *670:29*   inflexible

   R ⟨external⟩ *670:30*

   scale of g

45 $M = PR^n$ M = amt

   $I = P (R^n - 1)$ I = total interest

                                 r = rate of interest of £ in 1 yr

                                 R = amt in 1 yr

                                 P = principal

50   n = years

   100 C *5%* ?in in 100 = ?600

    "   *"*   C.I. —   = 16.390

   Still waters

   gauging mechanically

55 tilt of boat

   B ⟨end of line = .⟩

   solid resist change of shape or division

   liquid little   —   —   —   —   —

   gas   no   —   —   —   —   — — & tend to expand

60 physic. molec. motion

449

B ⟨age we live in⟩ *705:12–13?*

circle = ∞ of isoc. Δs

B ⟨dial,⟩ *679:5*   quadrant   B ⟨?dominos⟩ *670:7*

power of line = ☐ ,

65 R ⟨odd nos, even nos⟩ *Cf. 652:7, 672:25*

1 2 3 4 5 6 7 8 9

$1 = \frac{1}{2} + \frac{1}{4} + \frac{1}{8} + \frac{1}{16} \longrightarrow ∞$

0 1 2 3 4 5 6 7 8 9

1 2 4 8 16 32 64 128 λ 256

70 landsurvey, 2 pts.

B ⟨horse Joseph, ripple⟩ *678:28*

R ⟨J.C. excrescences⟩ *688:7*

R ⟨heaventree & its nightblue fruit⟩ *683:4*   R ⟨flue⟩ *257:27*

B ⟨waterrings⟩ *678:22*   sweep

75 R ⟨lack of ventilation⟩ *657:32*   R ⟨downdraught⟩ *Cf. 657:31–32*

Florence flask   smoke

R ⟨heat & water do work fall from level to level⟩ *656:32*

R ⟨source of energy⟩ *657:37?*

R ⟨fuels,⟩ *657:34*   G ⟨food, rain,⟩ *657*   wind, tides = sun

80 R ⟨coalfire burning forest⟩ *657:33–36*

RIGHT COLUMN HORIZONTAL

adhere

chalk & slate

?glue wetted

of fine bore

85 capillary attraction

lampwick

blotting paper

B ⟨viscous cream⟩ *661:5*

G ⟨floating woods rush together⟩

90 molten butter

pitch liquid   saline

450

wax solid   sugar

B ⟨sufficient time⟩ *660:34–35*

middlemost

95   G ⟨selfevident⟩ *714:13*

B ⟨vertical⟩ *659:6, 683:11, 691:6, 692:3*

pricked line obtuse   B ⟨volatile⟩ *717:14*

B ⟨adjoining⟩ *650:16, 651:14* contiguous   filings   *Cf. 687:19–20*

B ⟨mechanical mixture⟩ *674:25*

100   B ⟨chemical union⟩

pneumatic trough

halved

n yʳˢ· ?purchase

where 2 ?trams meet

105   laboratory

bending of bow

R ⟨compressible⟩ *685:13?*

substance

porous

110   body, matter, property of

nat phen = phys. chem. change

contained in

described in Δ

supposition

115   ?in—

B ⟨incommensurable⟩ *705:6*

R ⟨odd nos, even nos⟩ *652:7?, 672:25?*

sight

Stationary SD

120   R ⟨draft chimney⟩ *657:32*

any no of parts

B ⟨3 Rock Mt.⟩ *337:7, 740:7*

source of error

R ⟨convection of heat⟩ *658:2*

125   R ⟨the vessel A⟩ *657:29, 658:5*

R ⟨known weight⟩ *652:29*

change of vol. temp   R ⟨state⟩ *667:8 and elsewhere*

451

NOTES

Line 2 *H.P.*: horsepower.

6 *Augur*: "auger" would seem to make more sense.

25 *Prince Consort*: Albert, Prince Consort of England (1819–61), who married Victoria in 1840 and was granted the rank of Consort in 1842. See line 34 and note, and "Cyclops" 6:24.

27 *Isoceles*: Joyce's misspelling.

30 *Mrs Thornton*: a midwife who delivered Margaret, Charles, Eileen, and Florence Joyce (Ellmann, p. 760). The line is repeated at "Ithaca" 11:82. *Euryclée* (Euryclea): the nurse of Odysseus and faithful housekeeper of his palace. She assisted at his birth.

34 In equating *Victoria* with *Penelope*, Joyce may have had in mind her fidelity to Prince Albert and the overwhelming sense of grief she felt at his loss. See also line 25 and note, "Cyclops" 1:48, "Ithaca" 1:48, and *U* 101:2–9.

37 A line is the shortest distance between two points. Cf. "Ithaca" 6:61.

40 This is apparently a joke. A *minuto primo* is a "minute," a *minuto secundo* a "second," but there is no measure of time in Italian or English to correspond with *minuto terzo*.

51–52 The first *in* presumably means "interest." *C.I.*: Compound interest.

65 Repeated at line 117.

66 This appears to be a numerical cipher.

67 This looks like one of the classic Greek paradoxes of Zeno of Elea (5th century B.C.). In a race between Achilles and a tortoise, Achilles could never win if he were required to run in measurements of half the distance to the finish line.

76 A *Florence flask* has a pear-shaped body and a long neck; many Italian wines are bottled in such flasks.

106 This may refer to the banquet scene in the *Odyssey*.

111 *Nat . . . change*: a natural phenomenon is caused by a physical or chemical change.

"Ithaca" 9

B ⟨receives ?imbecilic prospectus⟩ *706:26 & 31ff.*

B ⟨ebreata⟩

B ⟨corkscrew⟩ *667:11, 668:7–8*

B ⟨let x be⟩ *707:11–12?*

5   proportional

duplicate

R ⟨state in Euclid⟩

R ⟨prove in algebra⟩ *19:32*

R ⟨ma = mb⟩

10   *B* ⟨convergent⟩ *695:15, 719:13*

ratio x recip = 1

$7^{14}/_{10} < {}^{15}/_{10} \quad {}^{141}/_{100} \; {}^{142}/_{100}$

B ⟨LB juvenis made fun of jews⟩

G ⟨7 = (1 + 1 + 1 + 1 + 1)⟩

15   fall per sec = W

B ⟨mind develops muscle   exercise before glass   stiffness pleasant⟩ *665:29*

R ⟨contract muscles   wet head first   then splash chest &

     head⟩ *657:13–14*

dress undried

20   *B* ⟨Lake of Dreams⟩ *686:22*

B ⟨Sea of Fecundity⟩ *686:22–23*

B ⟨Swamp of Mists⟩

B ⟨Gulf of Dews⟩ *686:22*

B ⟨Sea of Rains⟩ *686:22*

25   B ⟨alps, Pyrennees⟩

B ⟨crater⟩ *692:2*

B ⟨?focus⟩ *691:19?*

B ⟨people at equator travel quicker⟩

B ⟨geyer⟩ *656:11?*

30   R ⟨condensed nebula = sun⟩ *685:8*

G ⟨heat mode of motion⟩ *658:2*

B ⟨comets,⟩ *685:13*   R ⟨meteors, satellites.⟩ *684:18, 685:15 & 17*

B ⟨L. goes W.E.⟩ *721:29–30?*

B ⟨waterless lunar seas⟩

35   violet longest seen after sunset

R ⟨red — — — —   eclipse⟩

R ⟨roygbiv⟩ *369:42, 477:6*

R ⟨shadow of moon flies over earth⟩ *685:38*

B ⟨vortex⟩

40   G ⟨coal fossil trees sunlight⟩ *657:34–37*

B ⟨peninsula delta⟩ *703:23*   R ⟨greater, lesser inequality⟩ *700:30–31*

fire into sky frighten eclipse dragon. hide in perfumed cellar.

      beating cans

B ⟨line of nodes⟩ *695:17*

45   2 eclipses 1 yʳ· not more than 7.

B ⟨transit⟩ *685:38, 699:13, 704:9*

R ⟨bats come out children, birds silent, cold, wind drops, men

      pale, black sea⟩ *685:37–40*

R ⟨operaglass reveals stars of 7ᵗʰ· mag.⟩ *685:5–6?*

50   never see more than 3000

light from polestar 36 years.

B ⟨no fixed stars⟩ *712:27*

B ⟨variable suns⟩ *712:27*

R ⟨Δ in Cassiopeia brighter than Sirius⟩ *712:33–34?*

55   B ⟨reappeared in Scorpion   1914⟩

B ⟨in Northern Crown   1866 new star.⟩ *685:26–29?, 712:32–33?*

B ⟨Collision⟩ *685:23*

R ⟨but took place centuries before seen.⟩ *Cf. 686:9–11*

B ⟨occultation.⟩ *712:11*   i Zingari, *731:14*

60 R ⟨SD & LB a double sun⟩ *685:22–24*

R ⟨Cassiopeia—never sets⟩ *685:25–26*

R ⟨circumpolar⟩ *655:35*   stars turn in 24 hours

B ⟨♈ ♉ ♊ ♋ ♌ ♍ ♎ ♏ ♐ ♑ ♒ ♓⟩ *667:18*

R ⟨magnitude = brightness⟩ *685:5?*

65 B ⟨snakespiral⟩ *715:35*

Moly = hazel,   G ⟨ash, olive⟩

R ⟨jews round table at abend think ?biz talk different⟩

B ⟨travel round earth in front of sun, gain 1 day, steal a
     march on him.⟩ *57:14–15*

70 B ⟨meridian, latitudes,⟩ *721:26*   comet July 1903

R ⟨Aug. 10—S Laurence' ?tears⟩ *685:17–18*

R ⟨insects under stone,   bacteria midge.⟩ *683:27–29*

B ⟨L cemetery,⟩   R ⟨geology embedded storia⟩ *683:26–28*

B ⟨E obliges L to present same face⟩ *686:30–34*

75 R ⟨Galileo & S.M. discover Jupiter together⟩ *685:10*

R ⟨Bode's Law (0 + 4) (3 + 4) (6 + 4) (12 + 4)⟩ *685:11*

?at 57 time l = 1 degree

B ⟨parallax⟩ *683:19*   B ⟨aberration of light⟩ *705:6*

R ⟨Kepler dist^3 = t of revol^2⟩ *685:11–12*

RIGHT COLUMN HORIZONTAL

80 B ⟨SD bootsoles on flags of hollow lane twanged a fourfold chord,
     scale of a jew's mouth harp⟩ *689:10–12*

B ⟨below zero⟩ *689:15*

R ⟨deal logically with the unknown⟩ *682:5 & 12?*

R ⟨working hypothesis⟩ *684:28–29*

85 R ⟨reductio ad absurdum⟩ *666:3–6?*

prod. elim. of some elements of complexity

     1) state of ignorance

     2) respect for as yet unknown

     3) never shirk absurd

90 B ⟨heavy wt. lifting, ringwts.⟩ *665:34*

B ⟨parallel bars (H.S.)⟩ *665:37*
B ⟨Union Jack in 1 bouse⟩ *690:18?*
R ⟨finite differences = curve⟩ *684:34*
R ⟨away with false hypothesis⟩
95   R ⟨non⟨entity⟩⟩ *712:20*
infinity = escape from hypothesis   15.vi. 1904
o produces ∞   15.vi 1889
B ⟨clean sheets⟩ *716:5*   15.ix 1888
B ⟨alternate⟩   . 1870
100   Homer saw same stars
B ⟨her hemispheres⟩ *719:15 & 18*
R ⟨cuckolded by jew?⟩
R ⟨Ul. estranged⟩ *712:35?*
R ⟨E daughter of Sol⟩
105   a fair proportion of public
B ⟨Bloom Flower & Co⟩
B ⟨RB counts money⟩ *710:1*
B ⟨zenith,⟩ *688:10*   B ⟨apogee⟩ *684:33*
B ⟨athens time⟩
110   B ⟨produce both ways⟩ *695:18–19*
4[th.] dimension
veining of wood = growth
strain,   B ⟨wet,⟩   B ⟨drought⟩ *655:11*
tangent,   B ⟨diagram,⟩ *705:16*
115   G ⟨normal⟩ *650:3 and elsewhere*   R ⟨divide externally⟩ *712:4*
roundness   ?good to eat
logic forked sticks in . . .

NOTES

There is a large *I* in red pencil at the center top.

Line 33   *L. goes W.E.*: listener goes from west to east.

42   *Fire . . . dragon*: "At an eclipse the Ojebways used to imagine that the sun was being extinguished. So they shot fire-tipped arrows in the air, hoping thus to rekindle his expiring light.

The Sencis of Peru also shot burning arrows at the sun during an eclipse, but apparently they did this not so much to relight his lamp as to drive away a savage beast with which they supposed him to be struggling" (Sir James George Frazer, *The Golden Bough* [1896; abridged ed., New York, 1963], p. 90).

59   *I Zingari*: Italian for "gypsies."

63   These signs of the zodiac in Joyce's hand vary in some respects from the standard symbols. The twelve signs for the months of the year are as follows: Aries, the Ram; Taurus, the Bull; Gemini, the Twins; Cancer, the Crab; Leo, the Lion; Virgo, the Virgin; Libra, the Balance; Scorpio, the Scorpion; Sagittarius, the Archer; Capricornus, the Goat; Aquarius, the Water Bearer; Pisces, the Fishes.

71   *S Laurence' tears*: may be *S Laurence' feast*.

73   *Storia*: Italian for "history, story, tale."

86   *Prod.*: may be *prov*.

96–99   See *U* 720:27ff. for dates at right.

117   The phrase runs off the page.

"Ithaca" 10

LEFT MARGIN HORIZONTAL

Jews   J. 3771   D. 2200
G ⟨D.B.C.A.—Ailm
        oak birch Coll⟩
oak

5   R ⟨chieftain trees⟩ *321:8*
timber, bark for tanners.
burned ?cane
fish
acorns

10   B ⟨Grand Canal 1765⟩ *655:17?*   B ⟨Royal 1789⟩ *655:17?*
B ⟨drowned dogs⟩ *47:21–25?*
B ⟨Limerick to Lough Neagh⟩
B ⟨?E mls an hour relays⟩
B ⟨molecule of iron in old key and Mendelssohn's brain⟩

15   B ⟨atoms of old man are not old⟩
B ⟨Sky—we are looking at the past. Even if didn't exist we'd
        see it.⟩ *686:8–11*
B ⟨martyrdom 2000 y^rs.⟩

LEFT COLUMN HORIZONTAL

B ⟨LB 'I see her' Amiens Street⟩ *714:28ff.*

20   B ⟨Easter egg ribbon⟩ *706:7*
B ⟨W^d. they ever have same age?⟩ *663?*
B ⟨Neither w^d. SD at any time have LB's age at that time, nor

458

LB SD's age.⟩ *663?*

of 2ⁿᵈ· dimension.

25 bring down x

R ⟨LB & SD see shooting star.⟩ *688:8ff.*

gives x.   *B* ⟨Jews invented everything⟩ *667:7ff.*

B ⟨addenda⟩ *670:30, 698:30*

B ⟨Proof add. Rem. & Subtrah.⟩

30 *B* ⟨southerly aspect⟩ *697:17*

B ⟨geom. biscuits⟩ *667:20–21*

B ⟨LB invents recline⟩ *667:8*

B ⟨ready reckoner⟩ *693:8*

B ⟨quick long ?tots⟩   *?A.J.*

35 *B* ⟨saved £sd.⟩ *696:2?*

B ⟨in words & figures⟩

spider at night money in sight

Musical insect.

she reigns in disorder's house

40 Mithaca

Heavy weather, glass low ∴ little pressure

R ⟨betting ticket⟩ *659:32–33*   folded eves paper

gross = 144   rule of 3

B ⟨antecedent, consequent,⟩ *690:12*

45 greater put down the less

B ⟨pack of 11 for 1 (envelopes)⟩ *696:12, 706:10*

B ⟨computed⟩ *684:5*

B ⟨quire reams, sheet⟩ *684:9*

R ⟨fathom⟩ *655:30 and elsewhere*

50 22 yds = 100 links = 1 chain

B ⟨acres, roods & perches⟩ *697:11*

B ⟨gill, noggin, pint,⟩ *659:22–26*   *R* ⟨quart⟩

B ⟨20 grains 1 scruple, 35 = 1 dram⟩ *708:32*

B ⟨Irish mile⟩ *697:28?*

55 *B* ⟨Joe Toomey Esq ?Dundrum "best place in world"⟩ *694:15–16?*

R ⟨reduce to,⟩ *653:10–11 and elsewhere*   *G* ⟨avoirdupois⟩ *652:30*

as plain as 2 × 2 = 4

B ⟨take care of pence & £ . .⟩ *709:19*

459

G ⟨perch,⟩ *697:11*   R ⟨league, furlong⟩ *655:38, 702:18*

60   B ⟨statute mile⟩ *697:28*   B ⟨Hebrew dead language in Jesus
          time⟩ *672:8?, 672:34–35?*

B ⟨E passes never through same place⟩ *721:32*

R ⟨In a pinhead milliards of milliards⟩ *683:31–32*

B ⟨Nurves transmit pain 28 m per sec⟩ *690:9–13?*

65   R ⟨the nebula we see is now sun.⟩ *685:8*

R ⟨Red stars are spenti⟩ *685:4?*

R ⟨Libyan floods Mars 1882–1888⟩ *685:15*

B ⟨Martian humans older⟩ *684:31*

R ⟨Sundam trench of Pacific deep⟩ *655:29–30*

70   B ⟨LB's sure womanhand showing⟩

B ⟨telescopic planets⟩ *712:28*   B ⟨Ein Marsbewohner . . .⟩ *684:17–20?*

R ⟨cd put comet in thimble⟩ *685:13*

B ⟨comet wandering jew⟩ *712:26–27*

B ⟨Wire Paris 12 hear Brest 11:40 ?chess⟩

75   Dubliners wake & continue (Vesuvians)

RIGHT COLUMN HORIZONTAL

B ⟨Judaism misfortune not religion (?Heine)⟩

B ⟨deforesting for military reasons⟩

B ⟨1765 timber ceased⟩

timber a crop must be cut

80   B ⟨elm of Kildare 38 ft. r.⟩ *711:21–22*

B ⟨We dream 20 yʳˢ· out 70⟩ *704:36–37*

      B ⟨(3 score & ten)⟩ *683:22*

R ⟨new sun every day⟩

B ⟨waterborne goods cheaper⟩ *703:34–35*

85   B ⟨manpower⟩

R ⟨synagogue—Mary's Abbey⟩ *673:7–8*

B ⟨Leonardo invented canal lock⟩ *667:12?*

R ⟨1846. Jew dress act⟩ *673:10*

B ⟨Sabbath⟩ *709:7 and elsewhere*

90   april fool

almanac people swallow bad with true.

B ⟨ounce⟩ *659:17*

B ⟨more dead stars than living⟩

atom in solar syst in neb. spiral

95   every system born of sph & nebulae

B ⟨Sun calls comet back⟩ *712:31*

B ⟨Lost ten tribes⟩ *320:25*

NOTES

2   The old names of the Gaelic letters were tree names: *ailm*—"elm"; *beith*—"birch"; *coll*—"hazel"; *dair*—"oak" (Myles Dillon and Donncha ó Cróinin, *Teach Yourself Irish* [1961; rev. ed., London, 1966], p. 4). See also *Letters*, I, 225–226. There are lines connecting each initial letter with the corresponding tree on the notesheet.

29   *Proof . . . Subtrah.*: in subtraction one may check the answer by adding the remainder to the subtrahend.

55   Listed in *Thom's Directory for 1904* is a J. T. *Toomey*, esq., Rutland Square, Dublin.

58   The ellipses are Joyce's.

60–61   *Hebrew . . . time*: cf. "Cyclops" 8:8 and "Eumaeus" 6:183.

62   *E . . . place*: the earth supposedly does not pass through the same point in space twice.

64   *Nurves*: whether this spelling was intentional or an oversight remains a mystery.

66   *Spenti*: from the Italian *spengere*, meaning "extinguished" or "spent." Cf. "Ithaca" 11:4.

70   See "Oxen" 14:51 and note.

71   The ellipses are Joyce's.

76   There appears to be something erased above this phrase in the top right portion of the notesheet.

"Ithaca" 11

LEFT MARGIN HORIZONTAL

15

$\frac{33}{18}$

B ⟨crimson star dying⟩ *685:4*

5 B ⟨Orion's belt⟩ *683:15*

B ⟨nebula in Orion could contain solar system hundreds of
    times⟩ *683:15–17*

B ⟨1 rook in 1 yr eats 52 lbs⟩

B ⟨sundial⟩ *699:8*

10 overdoor shelf

B ⟨bullnose plane⟩ *700:9*

chamfer

carburetter

clutch fork

15 gudgeons & pins

B ⟨epicentre⟩ *681:32*

deflected needle

2 waves, surface

arc & durcherde

20 chord

B ⟨quadrature of ◯:⟩ *684:4, 703:1*

180 d of long. no time

    far from men

B ⟨proper motion⟩ *721:31*

25 B ⟨DUTC mileage⟩ *704:13*

B ⟨worked = 46⟩

462

B ⟨harbour commissioners⟩ *703:18*
B ⟨Lamp quickens buds—light or heat?⟩
B ⟨her rump = promised land⟩ *719:16–17*
30 B ⟨9th. power of 9th. power of 9⟩ *684:7*
B ⟨33 vols.⟩ *684:8*
B ⟨rhythm of life 23—28⟩
B ⟨lightyear⟩ *683:13*
B ⟨Nova—new star 1901. 1st. mag now 13th.⟩ *683:17–18*

LEFT COLUMN HORIZONTAL

35 blood dripping walls
death misty cloaks
B ⟨LB sits in ashes⟩
B ⟨— — on settle⟩
B ⟨— — — hearthstone⟩ *653:33–34*
40 B ⟨return of crusader⟩ *712:36*
B ⟨Laertes digs round plant in rough gloves⟩
B ⟨Himself ill cared plant⟩
B ⟨Ul. lies to him⟩
B ⟨Laertes doubts he had a son⟩
45 Eperitus,   R ⟨Oudeis⟩
B ⟨Laert. ashes on head⟩
B ⟨ ″   gives little Ul. 63 trees⟩
     ″ faints
Old Dolius
50 B ⟨Laertes boasts He ...⟩
Rumour
Eupeithes—"Ul lest all men now kills here"
Heavenly council
Laer. kills Eupeithes, father of Antinous.
55 bow = long range gun
Tel. forgets to lock armoury door
Melanthius is hanged up alive
Mentor—old friend of Ul.

B ⟨Pall. lifts aegis and maddens them⟩

60 Leiodes wooers' seer begs but is killed

Phemius (bard) & Medon spared

B ⟨12 unchaste virgins swab up and are killed hanged all in row⟩

Melanthius mutilated

R ⟨Feast of Apollo—archergod—morn.⟩

65 *B* ⟨Ul. beggar given inch takes all (iew gets ?on)⟩

many masters rope on door

Swallow tone of bow,   *B* ⟨Ul shoots sitting⟩

B ⟨Antinous never knows who killed him⟩

B ⟨Eurymachus offers damages.⟩

70 *B* ⟨Oxfootbone hurled. Ul. ducks⟩

Wooers mad laugh with their lips, bloody flesh

Theoclymenus, vision of disaster

Ul = W. Tell.

B ⟨Bow of Iphitus, pledge of friendship killed by Hercules⟩

75 *B* ⟨Ul went to recover debt⟩ *710:12–13?*

B ⟨Tel tries bow, greased.⟩

B ⟨Ul. tries common herd & reveals himself⟩

B ⟨Brothels for women save trouble⟩ *670:16*

footbath water spilled.

80 Pall "You have wife & child"

R ⟨offers to wash SD⟩ *657:5ff.*

Eurycleia = Mrs Thornton

B ⟨Ul. child of wrath: scar⟩ *Cf. 549:18 & 695:26*

B ⟨Ul. appeals to & is insulted by women⟩

85 *B* ⟨Ul. lampadites, broken bread.⟩

B ⟨Argos verminous. Ul. kicked.⟩

B ⟨Well of Ithacus⟩

B ⟨Irish Civ. Service Build. Society / incor. 1874⟩ *701:39–40*

B ⟨Prospectus⟩ *701:38 and elsewhere*

90 poundage rate was 10^d.

B ⟨poor rate & deputy cess collector⟩ *710:13–14*

B ⟨Velocity determined by parallactic drift of socalled fixed
    stars⟩ *683:19–20*

B ⟨ ~~LB~~ ⟩   *B* ⟨SD cocoa 'creatura'⟩ *661:11*

RIGHT COLUMN HORIZONTAL

95   *B* ⟨(Anti) nous⟩

   B ⟨Ul. begs from all to test⟩

   B ⟨"Sei bello ma non savio" Antinuo⟩

   R ⟨?gnostafeste⟩   *B* ⟨Mack Intosh⟩ *714:12?*

   know not salt

100   Tel sneezes. Pen laughs

   B ⟨Irus a bounder (Iris)⟩

   R ⟨Ul with sausage uneasy to roast⟩

   B ⟨Ul & Irus prizefight⟩

   B ⟨LB hates apple in glass⟩ *694:21*

105   *B* ⟨place for everything⟩ *694:19–20*

   B ⟨Ul prays signs. Zeus farts⟩

   bakewoman curses wooers.

   Melanthius = Joe Cuffe

   Philoetius = neatherd

110   *B* ⟨scarfpin⟩

   black hunchback

   B ⟨hassock⟩

   R ⟨doss on sofa⟩ *764:9*

   B ⟨send Irus to Echetus⟩

115   *B* ⟨maimer of men⟩

   B ⟨Ul—philosopher⟩ *Cf. 704:38*

NOTES

  Ithaca appears in ink in the upper left-hand corner. The following lines or phrases on "Ithaca" 11 are from the Butcher and Lang translation of the *Odyssey*.

"*Ithaca*" 11	*Odyssey*	"*Ithaca*" 11	*Odyssey*
Line 35	Page 394?	Line 44	Page 397
41	395	45	397
42	396	46	398
43	395	47	398

"Ithaca" 11	*Odyssey*	*"Ithaca"* 11	*Odyssey*
Line 48	Page 399	Line 72	Pages 341–342
49	400	73	344?
50	400	74	344–345
51	401	75	344
52	402	76	348
53	403	77	350–351
54	405	79	325
56	364	80	331
57	365	83	323
58	365–366	84	305–306
59	368	86	284–285
60	369	87	281
61	369–371	96	286
62	373–374	97	289
63	374	99	176
64	352	100	292
65	353?	101	295
66	356	103	298
67	357	106	357
68	359	109	336–337 and elsewhere
69	360	110	317?
70	340	114	299
71	341	115	298, 354

Lines 1–3 This appears to be doodling: 33 − 15 = 18.

4 Cf. "Ithaca" 10:66.

25 *DUTC*: the Dublin United Tramways Company.

45 *Eperitus*: a pseudonym of Odysseus when he tricks his father. *Oudeis*: Greek for "no one" or "none." It is also a pseudonym for Odysseus, who identifies himself to the Cyclops as "noman." Laertes gives Odysseus 43 trees.

49 *Dolius*: a slave of Penelope who embraces Odysseus when the latter reveals himself to Laertes.

50 The ellipses are Joyce's. Laertes boasts that he would have killed his share of the suitors if he had been present in the banquet hall.

59 *Pall.*: Pallas Athena.

60–61 *Leiodes* the soothsayer begs for mercy but is killed, for he was a suitor. *Phemius* and *Medon* the herald also beg for mercy, and Odysseus spares them.

65 *On*: may be *own*.

68–69 *Antinous* and *Eurymachus*: the leaders of the suitors.

72 *Theoclymenus*: a seer in Ithaca.

74 *Iphitus*: an Argonaut and guest-friend of Odysseus who was slain by *Hercules*.

82 See "Ithaca" 8:30 and note.

85 *Lampadites*: from λαμπᾰδίας, a kind of comet resembling a torch.

86   *Argos*: see "Ithaca" 1:23 and note.

94   *Creatura*: Italian for "creature."

95   This suitor's name makes a nice pun in French. As Odysseus's principal opponent Antinous is also *anti nous*, "against us" (the "royal we") since Odysseus is king in Ithaca.

97   "*Sei bello ma non savio*" *Antinuo*: Italian for "you are handsome but not wise, Antinous." Odysseus tells Antinous "Lo, now I see thou hast not wisdom with thy beauty!" (*Odyssey*, p. 289).

101   *Irus a bounder* (*Iris*): perhaps this is meant as a pun. *Iris* is a messenger of the gods in the *Iliad*. *Irus* literally bounds as a lackey for the suitors. The latter name is derived from the former. To Joyce it may also have suggested the relationship of the Irish to the English.

108   *Joe Cuffe*: see "Eumaeus" 7:74 and note.

110   According to Madtes, Rudolph Bloom was to have had a *scarfpin*. After *U* 705:39 "deceased;" was to have come "a cameo scarfpin, property of Rudolph Bloom (born Virag), deceased:". This was somehow omitted from the text.

"Ithaca" 12

LEFT MARGIN HORIZONTAL

B ⟨problem⟩
B ⟨theorem⟩
B ⟨if a = b⟩
B ⟨thing required done.⟩ *704:23*
5 *B* ⟨Join A B⟩

LEFT COLUMN HORIZONTAL

B ⟨Night slept. In ample air the moonglow diffuses.—a milky
luminous. She slept. Within her a multitude was made
flesh, fruit of her womb. She slept, fulfilled and
overcome, mighty, big with seed.⟩ *721:36–37*
10 *B* ⟨Wonderworker, world's greatest remedy for rectal complaints
direct from Wonderworker   Coventry House, Sth. Place,
London E.C. trouble in breaking wind, assists nature in
most formidable way, heals and soothes. while you sleep,
insures instant relief in discharge of gases, keeping
15 parts clean and free for natural action, initial outlay
of 7/6, make a new man of you & make life worth living,
or adjacent parts. Ladies will find it especially useful
a pleasant surprise, Wonderworker, note delightful result,
a cool drink of fresh spring water on a hot summer's day.
20 A soldier who served in S. Africa recently remarked What
a pity the Gov. didn't? What a relief   recommend it to
y^r. lady & gentleman friends, lasts a lifetime   insert

468

long round end   Wonderworker.⟩ *706:26–41*

B ⟨LB sleeps other end of bed⟩ *721:24ff.*   R ⟨cubic capacity⟩ *655:3*

Walk into my parlour   B ⟨cycle⟩ *653:1, 699:16*

B ⟨LB lived on samples⟩ *301:4–5*   B ⟨then A = C⟩

R ⟨No stops.⟩ *705:38?*   any side

B ⟨lunatics work by mathematics⟩

B ⟨LB's favourite dream⟩ *697?*

B ⟨Sexual impulse only root of tree⟩

Virag—Hungarian—Stephen

B ⟨Gelatine lozenges on window⟩ *667:20*

B ⟨Barclay & Cook's candle, guess when it burns out⟩ *668:1–4*

B ⟨Very long time ago I was going to bed ?somewhere and there was
      a squareshaped or was it when I was where was that⟩ *722:15*

B ⟨Mendoza—jew boxer⟩ *672:6*

B ⟨Sons of the Law⟩ *672:3*   B ⟨solution⟩ *655:41 and elsewhere*

B ⟨R.B. tootache⟩   B ⟨demonstration⟩ *683:5–6*

B ⟨drugs⟩ *709:27*   B ⟨inscribed in⟩ *708:1*

                         B ⟨described about⟩ *695:19–20*

                         by construction

B ⟨Foreskin in Calcata. resurrected   + o –   Salmeron S.J.
      carnal bridal ring in eucharist? at last supper had it
      not ∴ no. risen yes ∴ yes. 4ᵗʰ· degree of latria not
      hyperduly with hair toenailpairings.⟩ *688:1–7*

B ⟨After last day, constellation⟩

R ⟨Sandow—Whiteley pulleys,⟩ *706:23*   B ⟨men 15/– athl.
      20/–⟩ *706:23–24*

R ⟨bacon 6ᵈ·   9 protein grammes   7295 calories energy⟩ *657:21–22*

R ⟨salt cod 3 ½d 259—⟩ *657:22*   1105-

R ⟨butter   no protein⟩ *657:21–23*

R ⟨corn meal 1ᵈ· 20, 230 c of en.⟩

B ⟨measurement before & after⟩ *706:21–22*

B ⟨chest 29—32 ½⟩ *706:24*   axis

     B ⟨30—34⟩   B ⟨pure truth⟩ *671:34*

B ⟨biceps 10–13⟩ *706:24*   B ⟨S.E. by E.⟩ *721:25*

B ⟨f. arm 9 ½—12⟩ *706:25*

B ⟨thigh 10 ½—12⟩ *706:25* $1 + \frac{1}{2} + \frac{1}{4} + \frac{1}{8}$ to ∞ = 2

B ⟨calf   11–13⟩ *706:25*

60   *B* ⟨consecutive⟩ *706:23 and elsewhere*

drew a parallel

RIGHT COLUMN HORIZONTAL

B ⟨Notice of change of Name. I, R.V. now reside, formerly of
hereby give notice that I have assumed and intend
henceforth upon all occasions & at all times⟩ *708:6–9*

65   *B* ⟨LB takes off boot. Before ?sole Ah!⟩ *696:32ff.*

B ⟨From Moses to Moses arose none like Moses⟩ *671:28–32*

B ⟨Both make same gesture⟩ *674:4ff.?*

B ⟨More Nebukim⟩ *671:29*

SD objects to teach Molly Friday

70   *B* ⟨heaventree⟩ *683:4, 686:3*

G ⟨pulsetur classicum⟩

B ⟨bringing into play⟩ *665:30*

B ⟨variable⟩ *712:27*

B ⟨coincide⟩

75   touch

B ⟨singular solution⟩ *670:6*

calculus = sacrifice = slaughter of wooers

R ⟨multip ×. prelim   answer merged in final⟩ *700:38–39*

R ⟨fluxions = 17 × 3 (1 & ?carry 2)⟩ *700:39*

80   human   *G* ⟨tangent⟩ *688:26*   thinks itself divine line

R ⟨family of curves (Pen)⟩   = slayer & slain *Cf. 719:20*

R ⟨LB tangent   Pen . . . . . when⟩

R ⟨SD radius vector   LB & SD = 0⟩ *688:26ff.?*

B ⟨visuality limit   3 — 16⟩ *667:29?*

85   cf   cat & kitten   *B* ⟨in like manner⟩

parabola   *B* ⟨trajectory asymptote⟩

fly off at a tangent

v — vi — vii   *B* ⟨lozenge⟩ *667:20, 149:3*   *R* ⟨bisect⟩ *659:20, 680:31*

10 11 12   *B* ⟨intersect⟩ *695:18, 712:3*

90   *B* ⟨side all in common⟩

R ⟨concurrent⟩ *687:30, 697:7*
jew & olives dispersal to shed light
B ⟨enter every house with circumspection also yᵣ. own⟩ *715:34*

NOTES

The top portion is in the form of a draft rather than a notesheet. The division between columns at the bottom is arbitrary, as is that labeled "left margin."

Line 24 *LB . . . bed*: see "Cyclops" 5:57 and note.

31 *Virag—Hungarian—Stephen*: suggests a further relationship between Dedalus and Bloom, since Saint Stephen I (c. 975–1038) was the first king of Hungary and united Magyar territory under one crown for the first time.

33 Repeated at "Cyclops" 3:4–5.

36 *Mendoza*: see "Cyclops" 3:31 and note.

42ff. See "Oxen" 6:57–65 and note.

47 Eugene *Sandow*: German strong man (1867–1925). See Thornton, p. 72. The name is repeated at "Ithaca" 15:12.

52 *C of en.*: calories of energy.

57 *F. arm*: may read *forearm*.

62 *R.V.*: Rudolph Virag.

68 See "Circe" 10:76 and note.

71 *Pulsetur classicum*: let the (military) signal be given.

"Ithaca" 13

tablebook

R ⟨no of 6 places⟩ *704:21*

$x^4 + 4x^3y + 6x^2y^2 + 4xy^3 + y^4$

R ⟨show that—⟩ *701:9?*

5   got 10 marks

overtake

B ⟨prove 2 absurd ∴ 3rd true⟩

R ⟨equidifferent nos⟩ *652:7–8*

R ⟨in sufficient conditions⟩ *684:32–33*

10   G ⟨¼ reciprocal of 4⟩

$a^{-3} = \frac{1}{a^3}$

B ⟨exponent⟩ *674:20*

R ⟨a vessel of water⟩ *657:29*

G ⟨boundary of space⟩ *712:29*

15   R ⟨£ 1000 in 10 years⟩

R ⟨at. c. int = 1700?⟩

groping,   R ⟨listed feet⟩ *653:28*

G ⟨Satisfy equation⟩ *713:2*

G ⟨cannot be proved impossible⟩ *684:29*

20   Sum of 2 roots of quadratics = coefficient of 2nd.

terms give ?changed

prod = ?last term

R ⟨whence⟩ *712:32*

If + and − then + in ?Ans

25   R ⟨by supposition⟩ *712:37*

R ⟨in cipher⟩ *706:4–5*

472

R ⟨rectangular, oval fl. plots⟩ *698:33*

double x ?stout ?or thus artifice

$$x^3 - 3xy \, (x + y) + y^3 = -$$

30 ?springtailed rainbow—

scaly in mildewed wood.

earth shine on paschal moon

R ⟨low power microscope⟩ *706:13?*

LEFT COLUMN HORIZONTAL

R ⟨which is absurd⟩ *711:9*

35 R ⟨article of belief⟩ *686:17*

ropy wine unfit for consecration

R ⟨answer does not bear⟩

old age (no more than sexual excesses) leads not to wisdom,
    past memory

40 R ⟨lessening as future years were added⟩ *663:28–29*

R ⟨and ceaselessly varying event produce only an unvarying
    indifference,⟩

G ⟨repeated to infinity.⟩ *716:15*

B ⟨comforted himself⟩ *682:10*

45 B ⟨LB & SD pissjets (LB palmarius)⟩ *687:19ff.*

a man (name) of weight

R ⟨the minor is proved by fact that⟩ *684:39*

G ⟨men less longlived after flood (damp = death)⟩ *663:34ff.*

R ⟨raise to nth. power⟩ *684:15*

50 R ⟨daybreak in—⟩ *689:26*

B ⟨which was absurd⟩ *711:9*

B ⟨LB dislikes meet Ithacans⟩

G ⟨cent per cent⟩ *669:31*

B ⟨67 Eccles Street, Butt⟩

55 B ⟨Belles of George's,⟩ *688:29*

B ⟨Vartry Roundwood, normally Ap—May water falls below sill
    of overflow weir, shopfronts not washed, Borough
    surveyor.⟩ *655:12ff.*

60

B ⟨semidetached residence situate   dwellinghouse standing in
    6 acres⟩ *697:14–16*

B ⟨fee simple farm.⟩ *697:15–16*

divisional auction rooms opp. 4 courts

B ⟨nurseryman⟩ *698:37–38*

pat ?grown, patting mould,

65

B ⟨rhubarb   scarlet crowns⟩ *698:34?*

B ⟨RB drank soup from plate⟩ *709:34*

B ⟨wipe mouth & arse paper, 1ˢᵗ· dirtier.⟩ *709:34–35?*

In search for money (ads) truth display

B ⟨cosy corner fitment⟩ *698:5*

70

B ⟨tiled kitchen⟩ *697:35–36*

B ⟨sweettoned Japanese Gatebell.⟩ *699:10*

B ⟨outoffice,⟩ *698:25*   *B* ⟨demesne⟩ *697:10*

B ⟨acres, roods and perches⟩ *697:11*

B ⟨bathroom (h & c)⟩ *698:16*   *B* ⟨999 years⟩ *697:33*

75

B ⟨premises held under feefarmgrant   compute⟩ *697:32–34*

B ⟨on a gentle eminence⟩ *697:21–22*

B ⟨thatched,⟩ *697:16*   *B* ⟨gas throughout⟩ *698:28*

B ⟨1 sitting, 3 bed, lounge hall & linen press⟩ *697:35–37*

B ⟨a donkey & trap⟩ *699:17–18*

80

B ⟨pleasant reflections produce sleep⟩ *704:32–34*

R ⟨simple interest at 5% of —⟩ *702:2*

B ⟨rabbitry⟩ *699:7*

B ⟨baronial hall, groaning table⟩ *697:12–13*

MB spasm old clockface

85

G ⟨space reversible time no⟩ *713:2–4*

Eucl. space no total curvature of spine (Milly)

Lobatschewsky   const. tot. curv. neg

Riemann   ″   ″   ″   pos.

Tin variable in fire or electric oven

90

LB & man on rolling platform

showed picture of beauty as wife

B ⟨?hole to see, ?hole to hear⟩

B ⟨LB builds up ?fire⟩ *653:35–37*

B ⟨gulls kept up with E.K. LB threw biscuits into starboard

95   wake, 30 yds astern gull picked up, / ?stamp swooped
over to put over ?topmost⟩ *151:6ff.?*

RIGHT COLUMN HORIZONTAL

B ⟨basement⟩
R ⟨waterworks committee⟩ *655:14*
collective work
100   *B* ⟨?eleventhly⟩
B ⟨a smile goes a long way⟩ with a woman   *Cf. 92:25–26*
Q.E.D.
B ⟨Q.E.F.⟩
B ⟨LB locked out⟩ *652:8ff.*
105   *R* ⟨LB & census 1891⟩ *703:14–15*
R ⟨fishes (numerically) inhabit earth⟩ *656:32–34*
R ⟨disasters⟩ *686:18*
R ⟨influence⟩ *686:18*
B ⟨end of a perfect day⟩ *714:18*
110   *R* ⟨See star by day from bottom of gully⟩ *683:9–12*
B ⟨ruched cosy⟩ *352:34*
3 ply w^d. ?crumbtray
R ⟨?astounding low figure⟩ *374:20?*
R ⟨parsing⟩ *719:2 & 5*
115   *B* ⟨painter = ?man maker⟩
B ⟨strength of school 200⟩ *687:30*
R ⟨LB in tree (jew)⟩ *701:31*

NOTES

Ithaca appears at the top in ink, underlined in blue pencil.
Line 1   Repeated at "Ithaca" 1:81.
2   Repeated at "Ithaca" 1:82.
11–12   There is an arrow from *exponent* to ⁻³.

45   The connection between Bloom's style of urinating and *palmarius* (having to do with palm trees) is undetermined.

54   Probably Isaac *Butt*: famous Irish politician and the first "Home Ruler" (1813–1879).

64   *Pat grown*: may be *pat down*.

87   *Lobatschewsky*: Nikolai Lobachevsky, Russian mathematician (1793–1856), whose ideas were published in *Über die Principien der Geometrie* (1829–30).

88   Georg F. B. *Riemann*: German mathematician (1826–66), who "is best remembered for his development of the conceptions of Bolyai and Lobachevsky which resulted in a fully-fledged non-Euclidian geometry, dealing with 'manifolds' and curvatures on the assumption of poly-dimensional, finite and unbounded space" (*Chambers's*).

94   *E.K.*: *Erin's King*. See "Eumaeus" 3:141 and note.

105   Joyce first wrote *1881* and then *91* over the *81*.

"Ithaca" 14

LEFT MARGIN VERTICAL

B ⟨LB reproaches self re RB⟩ *708:35–37*

B ⟨bankbook⟩ *305:1, 707:33*

B ⟨photo of Ennis⟩ *708:19*

B ⟨Milly's endowment⟩ *707:28*

5   Leopold (Leo), Blum pascha, Virag after Szombathely went to
        Italy

G ⟨?wildreness,⟩ *682:15?, 713:35?*   lower level of obed. to precepts

B ⟨Why earthquakes occur where people are?⟩ *681:32–33*

B ⟨LB holds up Milly's hair⟩ *678:18*

10   B ⟨LB ?lender in books⟩

B ⟨cold pillow⟩ *715:31?*

B ⟨crumbs & potted meat in bed⟩ *716:7*   LB resembles MB

G ⟨wishes to tell story⟩ *676:16?*

RIGHT MARGIN VERTICAL

B ⟨SD drunk lay open weakest⟩   B ⟨Mrs. Bracegirdle⟩ *363:41, 375:26*

15   B ⟨LB in dark bumps side v . . . . . .⟩ *690:9–13*

When things live

paperknife slips

B ⟨Milly 2 more crosses
    to make Celt⟩

CENTER COLUMN HORIZONTAL

20   B ⟨Leopold Paula Bloom⟩ *707:27*   B ⟨⟨throttled voice⟩⟩

B ⟨a place for everything & everyth. in its place⟩ *694:19–20*

B ⟨Kolod balejwaw pnimah Nefesch, jehudi, homijah.⟩ *673:15–16*

Luschuw, l'erez ?abotejnŭ

B ⟨Erbah david chanah.⟩ *673:11*   25

25   38

B ⟨LB—Thora dictated so fast Moses couldn't put in stops.⟩

G ⟨nocturnes—all homegoing⟩   *G* ⟨?germ in ?ouch⟩ *683:29?*

B ⟨LB's beesting⟩ *695:27–28*

B ⟨LB to SD—drink little & well⟩

30   *B* ⟨Sirius 9 lightyears dist and 900 Sol.⟩ *683:12–14*

B ⟨Arcturus 142 lightyears dist⟩ *683:14*

LB gives £sd to Molly

LB praises to SD somebdy different (athlete)

B ⟨LB contemplates wrinkled boots history⟩ *706:20?, 696:33?*

35   *B* ⟨Crumbs in bed.   recooked ?fibres of potted meat⟩ *716:7*

R ⟨Oily paper (.. of olives)⟩ *659:12–13*

R ⟨SD's story. "Queen's Hotel"   LB coincidence⟩ *668:35*

B ⟨Books: Hist of Turko-Russian War.⟩ *693:31, 694:26*

B ⟨astronomy⟩ *693:37*

40   *B* ⟨?nickering gilt ?titles⟩ *693:2?*

bust of Donatello   lights candle & looks

Flotow (jew) Donizetti

B ⟨Her rump, plump melons⟩ *719:27*

R ⟨LB admired all things successfully done⟩ *669:37?*

45   LB found grey hair in basin

B ⟨India mull—MB's drawers⟩ *715:8–9*

B ⟨LB's trousers remember. (SD's mother's funeral)⟩ *680:7–10?*

B ⟨Soll und Haben? Have you read? No!⟩ *693:29*

R ⟨Simon not stylite. (S.D.)⟩ *333:9?*

50   *G* ⟨LB   How will you pay? gives back £sd⟩ *680:15–17*

G ⟨SD & the interest?⟩ *680:15–16*

B ⟨LB took MB to musichall.⟩

B ⟨Tandems—(LB & MB)⟩ *665:3*

B ⟨Woman—make her laugh or cry⟩

55   *B* ⟨   ″   no ?pudor ?but ?verg. . . . . .⟩

R ⟨LB gets SD's signature by ?artifice⟩ *673:29?*

478

B ⟨LB prays death of ?mousers⟩   puff case

B ⟨Rejected—Israel⟩ *672:4*

B ⟨Maynooth ret. 2nd. 2/6 1st w in Aug.⟩

60   B ⟨old—specs in book⟩ *708:17*   B ⟨lipped saucepan⟩ *654:32*
other letter under door.

B ⟨Houses upside down in water⟩ *678:20*

B ⟨ambrosia-cream⟩ *661:5*

B ⟨RB covered up in bed crying⟩ *708:30–31*

65   B ⟨In his grave powdery dung of insects which came even before
     full death⟩   B ⟨model themes which⟩ *669:30–31*

R ⟨?To SD publish Maunsel school essays Si D read out as
     models.⟩ *669:25ff.*

B ⟨LB to SD re menses. What w^d. you suggest⟩ *681:26?*

70   B ⟨LB long time ago.⟩

B ⟨Fear base of life⟩ *681:31*   ?furgrein ?lumberboot

B ⟨Milly soul awake before body⟩
. . . . Poolbeg light.

B ⟨Marks' 1^d. Bazaar 6 ½ shop.⟩ *667:25*

75   B ⟨LB makes mnemotechnic⟩ *694:34 & 37*

B ⟨marble clock⟩ *692:7*

R ⟨LB & MB watched. She put on more happy⟩

B ⟨LB & MB ?tandem.⟩ *665:3?*

B ⟨about hats!⟩ *671:22–25*

80   B ⟨humanity might be different in other systems?⟩ *684:33–34*

NOTES

Line 5   *Blum pascha*: see "Ithaca" 3:11 and note. *Virag*: Bloom's original surname. *Szombathely*: a city in western Hungary. See *U* 708:7 and elsewhere.

20   See "Oxen" 14:51 and note.

22–24   Line 22 is from the first stanza of *Ha-Tikvah* and lines 23–24 are from the second stanza, though they are a somewhat free transliteration of the Hebrew. See Thornton, p. 469; Ellmann, p. 527.

26   See Connolly, ed., *Scribbledehobble*, p. 163.

36 The two dots preceding *of olives* are Joyce's. According to Madtes (p. 73), in the first typescript *Oily* becomes "oleaginous" (from the Latin *olea*, "olives"), and the final text is "black olives in oleaginous paper." This is twice as redundant, reading in effect "black olives in oily olive-ish paper."

40 *Gilt titles*: may be *gilt tooled*.

41 *Donatello*: the greatest of the early Tuscan sculptors (1386?–1466).

42 Friedrich, Freiherr von *Flotow*: German composer of operas, director of the theater at Schwerin (1812–83). Gaetano *Donizetti*: Italian composer, mostly of operas (1797–1848).

55 This confusing mixture of Latin and English is repeated at "Penelope" 1:40. It seems to pose some paradoxical problem related to virginity or chastity: "No shame but . . . ."

57 Cf. "Ithaca" 3:53.

59 *Maynooth . . . Aug.*: Maynooth and return; second class; 2/6 (cost); first week in August.

67 Maunsel & Co., Dublin publishers, was interested in publishing *Dubliners* (see Ellmann, pp. 276–277 and elsewhere). At University College Joyce's essays were read aloud as models (Constantine Curran, *James Joyce Remembered* [New York & London, 1968], p. 6), and it is possible that his father had encouraged him earlier to try to interest Maunsel & Co. in publishing his school essays.

"Ithaca" 15

LEFT MARGIN VERTICAL

R ⟨LB conquered mother by daughter, daught. by mother.⟩ *679:36–37*
LB ?alter will to end of life.
Sturli—too long
R ⟨LB forms a habit⟩ *711:2?*
5 Storm bat flying lust wetterdruck
B ⟨model ?farm⟩ *700:10–13?*
B ⟨magnifying glass.⟩ *706:13*
G ⟨3 hours play re 1 minute's fuck⟩
B ⟨milk sour,⟩ *659:23*
10 R ⟨. . . . . . constellation sets⟩
neither injurious to health nor offensive to nostrils
B ⟨Sandow's⟩ *665:26, 694:3*

RIGHT MARGIN VERTICAL

B ⟨Thames embankment⟩ *600:19*
B ⟨take a g̶t̶ back seat⟩ *645:41*

LEFT COLUMN HORIZONTAL

15 B ⟨weedbeds⟩ *703:35*
B ⟨la morta grottesca⟩
B ⟨frigidity.⟩ *686:16*   B ⟨In darkest Africa (cunt)⟩
B ⟨delirium of love's young dream, stars etc⟩ *686:14*

G ⟨LB not at funeral of SD's mother.⟩ *680:7–10*

20 B ⟨waterways⟩ *703:35*

R ⟨LB exp's to SD ad of girl writing.⟩ *668:23–25*

B ⟨capped corners⟩ *715:14*

slide nozzle locks

B ⟨LB in mask selling ads.⟩

25 B ⟨Slieve Bloom⟩ *337:10*

B ⟨Man lifted out of earth atmosph. bleeds at nose⟩ *684:24–27*

Cats at night, cries of suitors murdered

Valley lay smiling before me

B ⟨Stuffed owl marriage gift⟩ *678:33, 692:11 & 17*

30 B ⟨LB searches 3rd. star⟩ *689:26?*

B ⟨?γλακῶπις⟩

B ⟨SD silent—composing?⟩ *661:25–26*

B ⟨Parallax? he remembers⟩ *683:19*

Gillies (LB & SD) the Bumble Bee

35 B ⟨Planets—they ?wanderers⟩ *712:26–28?*

B ⟨mulch of dung loam,⟩ *68:1–4*   filth

B ⟨LB in bed sees old photo of self (position)⟩ *722:3?*

B ⟨thought of smthg better & ?silent⟩

LB in Dub   SD in Eur.   find in old books (?posts)

40 B ⟨LB lifts reading eyes, feels creeping doubt of dawn⟩ *689:16*

B ⟨E cosa importa?⟩

B ⟨Hist. of Chas. II⟩ *693:9*

B ⟨LB washes under tap⟩ *656:39*

B ⟨Sinbad Sailor, Jinbad Jailer etc⟩ *722:8*

45 SD thinking, thought flies to other (opposite)

LB believes SD wd. of course accept £sd

B ⟨Acrostics. B is for Bloom⟩ *662:18*

B ⟨Wandering jew—moto perpetuo⟩ *215:4, 495:16, 712:26*

where child from? Mine! his!

50 B ⟨Skipping (Milly)⟩ *677:30?*

B ⟨don't go near (box) but face with knee jiujitsu⟩

B ⟨never go near him on ground⟩

B ⟨MB tunes violin⟩

B ⟨Jealousy passion ∴ must contain joy. (LB. True!)⟩ *717:18–19*

55 SD—I give what I get

B ⟨LB—letter from friend of Martha to say she is a cheat.⟩

B ⟨Honest ∴ jealous⟩ *717?*

B ⟨a billsticker!⟩ *716:31*

B ⟨Cat—wash ear over face, back to fire, storm⟩ *67:19, 678:26*

60 B ⟨cat goes luck goes⟩ *678:8?*

If Earth got drunk!

B ⟨LB envies SD literature⟩ *674:2–3?*

B ⟨Stars (like girls) can't see themselves ?planisphere⟩

B ⟨Jupiter Pluvius⟩ *598:6*

65 B ⟨LB not read WS for amusement⟩ *661:29*

B ⟨Man button right over L. Woman L o R⟩ *746:1*

B ⟨why candle grease stains round.⟩

LB and book on astor's quay.

B ⟨Moses Maim. More Nebukim.⟩ *671:28–29*

70 B ⟨Agendath Netaim⟩ *691:33–34, 703:5*   G ⟨: dead faith of devils⟩

B ⟨Stood candle on table⟩ *691:31–32*

B ⟨Virag—Szesfehervar—Photoatelier⟩ *708:15–16*

B ⟨—LB whore liked him—girl too—time yet.⟩ *707:21–25?*

RIGHT COLUMN HORIZONTAL

ecliptic inclination of moon

75 R ⟨deluge⟩ *672:36, 656:12*

B ⟨some ?races never saw⟩

B ⟨adipose⟩ *719:17*

Molly & I & the baby

R ⟨90% of body water⟩ *656:34–35*

80 B ⟨Milly crybaby good prevent congestion⟩ *677:18–19*

⋀ a 7 ?E   G ⟨arc⟩ *650:12 & 15*   G ⟨to each add⟩   R ⟨corollary⟩ *680:5*

B ⟨again, by hypothesis⟩ *714:34?*

B ⟨outsize drawers⟩ *715:8*

G ⟨equestrian⟩ *700:3*

85 B ⟨horns of kettlesmoke⟩ *658:13–14*

B ⟨MB girl ?bore . . . . too⟩

B ⟨?feet also not lecherous⟩ *730:10–12?*

B ⟨reciprocal proportion⟩ *718:11*

B ⟨locality⟩ *697:30, 711:13*   *G* ⟨quantity⟩ *659:25 & 26 and elsewhere*

90   *R* ⟨given length⟩

B ⟨MB wrote Greek.⟩ *670:26*   *B* ⟨constant⟩ *657:31 and elsewhere*

B ⟨LB's grandfather⟩ *709:17*   *G* ⟨odd   even⟩

B ⟨(Newman on Newton)⟩

B ⟨he read J.H.N. for solution of difficulty. disappointed.⟩ *661:28–30*

95   *B* ⟨Woman rights hat at window (good ad)⟩ *365:29?*

B ⟨friendships not of family not renewable⟩

B ⟨Citron like ?rlwy ticket (SD)⟩

logarithm

LB when elderly son & old mother fight looked at sky

100   *B* ⟨SD forgets hank. LB—key⟩ *51:28, 652:10–15*

NOTES

Line 3   *Sturli*: not identified.

5   *Lust*: may be the English word or the German word, meaning "desire." *Wetterdruck*: not standard German; *der Luftdruck* means atmospheric pressure, which Joyce apparently believed to have some sort of effect on bats.

7   Repeated at "Ithaca" 4:97.

11   *Offensive to nostrils*: may be *offensive to morals*.

12   See "Ithaca" 12:47 and note.

16   *La morta grottesca*: Italian for "the grotesque death."

31   A glaucope is anyone with fair hair and blue eyes. An adjectival form in Greek means "gleaming-eyed," a standard epithet for such goddesses as Athena and Minerva.

35   There is an inkblot over *wanderers*.

41   *E còsa importa?*: "And what does it matter?" in Italian.

48   *Moto perpetuo*: Italian for "perpetual movement."

64   The equation of *Jupiter* and *Pluvius* can be found in Virgil and in Albius Tibullus. It is interesting that Joyce gives it a trite quality in context.

69   See "Circe" 10:76 and note.

72   *Szesfehervar*: apparently this should be Szekesfehervar, a city in western Hungary.

94   *J.H.N.*: John Henry (Cardinal) Newman.

97   *Rlwy ticket*: may be *study ticket*.

99   This is a very interesting phrase. Bloom probably sees the symbolic significance of such a fight and expects a solar eclipse.

"Ithaca" 16

LEFT MARGIN HORIZONTAL

B ⟨mixed quantity⟩
R ⟨equivalent⟩ *684:32*
R ⟨integral part⟩ *681:22*
whole no
5 *R* ⟨sum⟩ *660:22 and elsewhere*
index
ex. 3
prime no
R ⟨in(ev)olution⟩ *683:7 & 24*
10 $\sqrt{x} = \pm$
surd
B ⟨irrational quantity⟩ *710:9–10*
R ⟨operation⟩ *692:1*
$a^{1/2} = \sqrt{a}$
15 *B* ⟨complete □⟩
  □ of middle =
4 1 × 3
R ⟨square ○⟩ *684:4, 703:1*
pure & adfected quadratics
20 *R* ⟨function of⟩ *681:24*
roots of □ ?equiv = & opposite
R ⟨degree of accuracy⟩ *684:5–6*
decimal system
R ⟨$\frac{0}{0}$ = indeterminate⟩ *686:30–31*

LEFT COLUMN HORIZONTAL

25   *R* ⟨milky way points to our lady of Walsingham, holy land,⟩ *685:6?*

R ⟨topiary cutting (hedges)⟩ *697:27*

B ⟨verify by substitutes⟩ *681:37*

G ⟨corollary⟩ *680:5*

B ⟨pass equator change sign⟩

30   transpose, collect

answer

R ⟨Given x = 4⟩

R ⟨thing sought⟩ *704:17?*

rule of 3

35   price of mixture of teas

Now since ---.

R ⟨inlet faucet, outlet vent⟩

B ⟨2 sips to his one⟩ *661:22–23*

B ⟨5⁵⁄₁₁ after 1 clock hands together⟩ *679:8*

40   can do a piece of work

navvy

papering a trench

it wanted 3′ ?of.

B ⟨has a start of⟩ *661:20*

45   that w^d· be no if —

B ⟨that man's father⟩ *692:28*

B ⟨proportion⟩ *663:27 & 29*

R ⟨in ratio of⟩ *663:27*

R ⟨solid & hollow ▢⟩ *690:9–10*

50   laid out (spese)

digits of no.

R ⟨mental arithm.⟩

over the fence leaps sunny Jim etc

B ⟨LB & boys pissed high⟩ *687:29–30*

55   *B* ⟨pendule of clock⟩ *679:2*

B ⟨find by inspection⟩ *661:25*

  ″ value of

simplify: mult. tables

in 2.2's: R ⟨?11/– in £⟩

60 bracketed

R ⟨bankrupt assets⟩ *710:14–15*　　　　R ⟨K. 11.⟩ *667:34*

R ⟨Q. Prove it. A—⟩　　R ⟨trespassers will be prosecuted⟩ *698:40?, 701:2*

R ⟨Sign denotes⟩ *687:9–10*

R ⟨comp. interest⟩ *702:34*

65 forgive us our tresspasses

R ⟨worth less than 0.⟩ *710:30–31*

resolve

R ⟨solution of problem⟩ *684:28, 703:1*

B ⟨statement of a/c⟩ *707:34–35*

70 R ⟨obtained the result⟩ *684:7–8*

both sides of equation = if cubed, ☐d, Xd or ÷ ?on same no

+d or –d they are =

B ⟨simultaneous equations⟩

B ⟨　1/ eliminate 1 term,⟩

75 　　　2/ equating values

B ⟨　3/ substitute—⟩ *681:37?*

R ⟨assumed no (& name LB exile)⟩ *712:21?*

B ⟨arbitrary multipliers⟩ *663:28?*

R ⟨units, tens, hundreds,⟩ *684:11*

80 six figures.

B ⟨16 yrs before elder man was 16 years older than the younger

　　　man, 16 yrs later the younger wd be the added elder's age

　　　while latter wd. be twice his age win 10 yrs⟩ *663:23–24*

B ⟨figures centripetal 1. 12. 123. 1234.⟩ *688:13 & 27*

85 G ⟨proceeds divided⟩ *717:30*

B ⟨reduce to simplest form⟩ *666:3, 705:11, 719:13*

S O N D O B A N (Japanese arith)

R ⟨incalculable⟩ *683:30, 712:34*

R ⟨of 1st. magnitude⟩ *685:21*

90 minuend, subtrahend, remainder, 7 from 10 leaves

Subtract (alter sign lower line), as found above,

subtract a pos = add a neg. (photo)

halves

P.C. 47

95   R ⟨—outside brackets ?queers all⟩
        R ⟨2 wrongs make a right⟩ *718:22*
        B ⟨brackets removed⟩
        conversely

RIGHT COLUMN HORIZONTAL

        : clear of fractions
100   R ⟨denominator⟩
        R ⟨LCM, HCF,⟩
        product of extremes = prod of means
        R ⟨like x like = +⟩
        R ⟨unlike x⟩ = − *650:22?*
105   cancels out
        quotient $a^0 = 1$
        divident
        R ⟨arranged according to powers of . .⟩ *700:17*
        R ⟨common letter, descending⟩ *693:1*
110   R ⟨powers⟩ *684:16, 700:17*
        2nd. division ?clerk
        R ⟨even no⟩
           —money
        $a^2 x^2$ is < ax if a, x proper fractions.
115   R ⟨decimate⟩ *681:30*
        R ⟨highest power in land⟩ *700:34–35*
          A) Man = (1) X
        R ⟨Q—(im)properly arranged express⟩ *692:35–693:1*
          A   —   —
120   R ⟨last divisor ÷ last remainder⟩ *683:37*
        R ⟨till 0 is reached⟩ *683:38–39*
        R ⟨reduce $\frac{SD}{LB}$⟩ *710:7?*
        R ⟨LCM included all⟩
        R ⟨HCF nucleus⟩ *684:13*
125   R ⟨Quoties? How oft?⟩
        R ⟨universal arithmetic⟩ *712:19*

R ⟨abc known quantities⟩

R ⟨xyz un—   —   term⟩

radical sign

130   R ⟨binomial⟩ *712:19*

coefficient shows how oft. ?takes

?bcd ?bcd ?bcd   degree

R ⟨literally, numerically⟩ *656:33*

R ⟨power, cube n^{th} raised⟩ *684:15*

135   brackets: vinculum

suppose a = 4

compute value

R ⟨fraction⟩ *676:23, 679:18, 690:11*

R ⟨cross xation = nought⟩ *710:7–10*

140   Diff + sum = 2 > quant.

B ⟨conceive that to be⟩ *663:30*

R ⟨erratic⟩ *657:18*

4 apples, 1 apple > ?20

NOTES

Line 7   *Ex.*: exponent?

11   See "Ithaca" 5:104 and note.

25   Cf. "Ithaca" 1:75.

42   *Papering a trench*: for an analysis of this phrase, see Hayman's review of Scholes and Kain's *Workshop of Daedalus* in *James Joyce Quarterly*, III (Fall 1965), 88. Cf. also Scholes and Kain, p. 103.

50   *Spese*: Italian for "laid out" in the sense of "money spent" or "sick in bed."

65   *Tresspasses*: note that Joyce correctly spells "trespassers" on line 62.

87   *Sondoban*: not a Japanese word; a *soroban* is an abacus.

94   *P.C. 47*: not identified.

"Penelope" 1

LEFT MARGIN VERTICAL

G ⟨Stamps⟩ *726:29, 744:26, 748:2*
G ⟨Cohen's auction⟩ *754:11?, 765:12?, 757:8?*
R ⟨?Griffith ?hooks Dublin by his trousers⟩ *733:37?*
R ⟨1ᵈ· piece⟩

LEFT MARGIN HORIZONTAL

5   B ⟨stallion⟩ *727:12*
     new woman surgeon
     leaned on LB alighting
     B ⟨knock it off⟩ *757:34?*
     B ⟨put you in budget⟩ *739:14*
10   B ⟨MB ?Ld⟩
     B ⟨vicious glint in's eye⟩ *727:14*
     B ⟨openly kiss man friends⟩ *Cf. 762:11*
     adam's apple (?Cowl)   *261:4*
     B ⟨feel LB's eyes at nape⟩ *731:20*
15   or over croups
     B ⟨holds face towel before bubs⟩ *739:8–9*
     B ⟨MB & ?R.W no nerves ?good⟩
     B ⟨Mr Martins—wallflowers⟩ *727:39?*
     B ⟨that Mrs Galbraith⟩ *736:18*
20   B ⟨LB sucked her after Rudy⟩
     B ⟨sag swollen teat in coffee⟩ *739:13?*
     R ⟨?Mrs short shift⟩ *748:38*

490

CENTER VERTICAL

R ⟨Skirt opening up the side⟩ *745:36–37*

RIGHT MARGIN VERTICAL

R ⟨I knocked him off that little habit⟩ *757:34*

CENTER COLUMNS

25   B ⟨he held wire down for her⟩ *740:27*

B ⟨She wondered why she had only 2 (bubs)⟩ *738:9*

B ⟨no of dugs no of possible children (cats—10)⟩ *738:9*

    B ⟨& ?then: ?man upright⟩

R ⟨Woman lovely closets in heaven⟩

30   G ⟨1st. passion loves lover   after loves love⟩   R ⟨gold turds⟩ *755:30*

B ⟨childbearing healthy. She wants?⟩ *727:28–30*

B ⟨princess slip.⟩   no science words

B ⟨sunray pleats⟩ *731:30*   B ⟨made love to her⟩ *732:11*

R ⟨old love is new⟩ *759:18*   learn to blow nose

35   B ⟨Love's old sweet song⟩ *747:27*   R ⟨Penrose⟩ *739:7*

    sleep to look fetching

B ⟨Silkette⟩ *735:20*

G ⟨Bl. Boyl. centre of ?levity.⟩   B ⟨deathscreen in hospital⟩ *96:18*

B ⟨made her laugh, or cry⟩ *766:14*   R ⟨LB Buddha⟩ *756:36–41*

40   B ⟨No ?pudor but ?verges . . .⟩

R ⟨smell in dreams?⟩   B ⟨banana in cunt⟩ *745:27*

R ⟨She sees LB in bed tucked up embryo⟩ *757:39*

B ⟨women afraid, can't run or swim for clothes⟩ *740:29–31*

flat needlepoint and rosepoint

45   B ⟨delightful figure line obviating unsightly broad appearance

    across the lower back⟩ *735:27–28*

LB after hat. wind.

I came to see Jenny ?go.   B ⟨Crib Inchicore⟩ *737:1*

B ⟨think of someone else at fuck.⟩ *725:29?*   B ⟨reveille⟩ *742:11*

50   B ⟨MB liked drunken men ?fine,⟩   B ⟨posted letter to self⟩ *742:28*

B ⟨MB she saw him in street⟩ *731:12–14?*

B ⟨elastic gore on hips, kidfitting corsets,⟩ *735:24–26*   knickers

B ⟨not go to mass⟩ *744:14*

R ⟨LB & burgler on stairs with poker.⟩ *751:7–8*   B ⟨bored her

55   stiff⟩ *729:20–21*

B ⟨beauty sleep⟩ *740:4*   R ⟨blackberrying⟩

B ⟨hair down to her waist⟩ *736:20*   G ⟨S.D. a boy⟩ *759:40–42*

B ⟨Chaste—fear of kids.⟩ *745:24–25*   B ⟨MB buying butter.⟩ *730:29*

B ⟨priest not dangerous⟩ *726:16*   ?carpets laid at feet

60   R ⟨that's from his side of house⟩ *751:30*

B ⟨Belladonna & good breast of milk⟩ *739:10–11*

B ⟨Rabelais—not real: not a marrying man⟩ *734:25–26?*

B ⟨lovers' row⟩ *729:8*   tabs

R ⟨Milly mumps⟩ *752:24*   white favours   B ⟨footlights⟩ *747:28–29*

65   B ⟨Some dean or bishop was there & he tired me out with guns⟩

725:23–26

B ⟨Interest in prince of Wales,⟩ *736:24 & 30*   B ⟨future not like past⟩

B ⟨Wish to change hat (man)⟩   B ⟨Smthg cheap advertised⟩ *735:25*

B ⟨near some allotments,⟩   B ⟨kicked from behind. Where? On the

70   leg. Was it high up? Yes, more or less. Was it where

you sit down? Yes.⟩ *726:2–4*

B ⟨MB & day in City Arms⟩ *723:2–3?*

B ⟨She knew he was coming.⟩

G ⟨Labourers leave LB & MB alone in coupé⟩ *733:18–19*

75   B ⟨LB & boiling soup⟩ *733:4*   I "foresee" (dandy word of LB)

R ⟨LB on horseback⟩ *749:39–40*   B ⟨LB cold feet⟩ *748:21*   Better for

Penelope stay at home

R ⟨MB asks needless questions⟩

MB does not kiss. LB

80   B ⟨MB wants to say. 'Fuck',⟩ *739:25–26*   B ⟨Say I'm out,⟩   B ⟨Big one

he has⟩ *727:3*

queen cakes   B ⟨Her kiss gives new life⟩   B ⟨lets herself go⟩ *739:21*

MB hid in trunk   B ⟨LB's sick voice⟩ *723:4*

B ⟨Bloom was on the sly⟩ *724:11*   B ⟨messtins⟩ *742:13*

85   *R* ⟨MB have to put up with house⟩ *750:24–25*   *B* ⟨ironmould⟩ *753:38*

     R ⟨MB wrote white ink black paper⟩ *752:28*   *R* ⟨red ink
        virginity⟩ *754:33*

     B ⟨Give him onion before go out⟩ *728:14*

     She feels somdy else passing   *B* ⟨MB tries to tell story⟩

90   *B* ⟨She likes person comes always same hour⟩ *732:17*

     B ⟨Gibr. ape went to Clapham⟩ *745:4*   *B* ⟨Kenilworth Sq.⟩ *731:2*

     B ⟨B.B.   knows how to treat a woman⟩ *Cf. 732:10–12*   *B* ⟨liar
        (servant)⟩ *725:3*

     R ⟨LB pale with jealousy⟩ *728:8?*

95   Cup of tea?   No but a timetable   *B* ⟨MB—confession⟩ *725:42ff.*

     B ⟨LB and she buying hat⟩ *737:29–32*

     B ⟨Gibr. gun 5 a.m. Lines (Sp & Eng)⟩ *742:5?*

     B ⟨MB wants to find out⟩ *724:22*

     B ⟨stagedoor johnny⟩ *726:26–27*

100   LB under bed

     B ⟨His trousers⟩ *731:34, 757:30, 761:29, and elsewhere*

     B ⟨what she went through no-one w^d. believe⟩ *727:20–21*

     B ⟨was I in it (dream)⟩ *726:22*

     MB in hammock

105   *B* ⟨Fatten me for him⟩ *738:8*

NOTES

     At top left is *Penelope* in ink underlined in blue.

     Line 7   Cf. "Ithaca" 4:29.

     13   *Cowl*: Father Cowley is not mentioned in the "Penelope" episode.

     17   *R.W*: unidentified.

     36   Cf. line 56.

     40   See "Ithaca" 14:55 and note.

     54   Cf. "Penelope" 3:16, where Joyce spells "burglar" correctly.

"Penelope" 2

B ⟨Pen wishes to excite them but with her two maids.⟩
B ⟨N.B & Mrs Santos⟩
B ⟨quarrel & you're always in good humour.⟩ *729:1*
B ⟨Pen ?repose nitegown before face⟩
5   B ⟨Pen wheedles present⟩
B ⟨Pen upbraids impure servant⟩ *Cf. 724:30ff.*
B ⟨they always talk like that before LB⟩ *728:33–36*
B ⟨he began it not me.⟩ *727:40*

LEFT COLUMN HORIZONTAL

B ⟨her cunt, darkest Africa⟩
10   B ⟨as always empty⟩
B ⟨hate people who bring bad news⟩ *743:17–18*
R ⟨likes little boy on stage (Rudy)⟩ *759:42*
B ⟨like to be a man⟩ *761:39–40*
R ⟨to see petite ?murile⟩
15   B ⟨to give LB bit of her drawers⟩ *731:1*
B ⟨What c^d. you make of a man like that?⟩ *729:22*
B ⟨MB finish it herself⟩ *725:33*
B ⟨ ″ believes in loveletter spite of all⟩ *743:29*
B ⟨He wanted that.⟩
20   B ⟨MB had hero. LB tried to be like him.⟩ *728:37–38*
B ⟨His body hers, jealous,⟩
Mutual fault, poverty, links,

494

B ⟨LB's past. Know but not be told.⟩

B ⟨LB feigned life crossed by great passion⟩ *728:21–23*

25   To find loveletters of real lady. Rage and—flattered, adorned
          with crest

B ⟨MB mocked Bartell d'Arcy⟩ *730:29–30*

MB marriage ?day

B ⟨MB pretends to come⟩ *725:32–33*

30   *B* ⟨MB etwas coming into fashion again⟩ *737:22*

B ⟨MB proud of LB⟩ *728:37–38?*

B ⟨LB kissed her hand⟩ *731:2–3?*

B ⟨LB loth to say he loved her⟩ *728:22–24*

B ⟨she'd love to kiss him wildly.⟩ *725:38*

35   LB late threw watch in pool.

B ⟨MB likes to go away for the coming back⟩ *733:21*

B ⟨MB never find other like me⟩ *729:23–24*

B ⟨MB promised Mulvey a fuck if he came back & found her
          married⟩ *746:6–7*

40   *B* ⟨MB stretches at the thought⟩ *739:20*

R ⟨LB left her nose full of lampsmut⟩ *748:29*

B ⟨Pen asleep during slaughter⟩

B ⟨She thinks god did it.⟩

R ⟨Won't accept travelstained Ul.⟩

45   Music & dance

G ⟨Ul. wash & brush up⟩ *Cf. 615:11*

B ⟨ ″ threats to sleep alone⟩

Lampus & Phaethon dawnstars stayed in E, not in W.

B ⟨Pen, reasons for chastity he might b––⟩

50   *B* ⟨Calypso never won his heart⟩

Ul. tale—Nausikaa

Pen remote. Big Four escape in dark

R ⟨2ⁿᵈ. nekia,⟩   Cyllen. Hermes goldrod.

B ⟨Don't mention Troy (Pen)⟩

55   MB detested LB

Not ?smile like him so much after Lord Melb.

RIGHT COLUMN

Speech of Achilles
funeral of Ach at sea, his Thetis
18 dys mourning, games
60   high tomb on peaks
Ach & Ag. speaks of 1894 ?as 1904
    ″   ″   came to Ith. & stayed with Amphimedon
B ⟨1 month's job to persuade Ul. to go.⟩
?batsouls: her web
65   "if I" . . . '—' "
she weaves a deathshroud for   R⟨Laertes which is Ul. coronation
    robe⟩
B ⟨Pen proud she is not Mrs Maybrick⟩ *729:26*
B ⟨All day hairpins falling   BB⟩ *728:42*
70   Dream of 20 geese & eagle
horn & ivory
Pen proposes 12 axe trial.
B ⟨Pen wakes, prays⟩ *Cf. 726:32–36*
B ⟨Rather die than marry another⟩ *729:22–23*
75   B ⟨way he takes it⟩ *739:27*
B ⟨Dreams BB in her bed⟩ *739:22?*
R ⟨bring salt to new house⟩ *750:24–26*
B ⟨hair—sex⟩
roses—menses
80   ribbon
B ⟨gorgeous⟩
R ⟨weeps over relic⟩
gobble

NOTES

The following list shows the lines and phrases on "Penelope" 2 which Joyce derived from the Butcher and Lang translation of the *Odyssey*:

"Penelope" 2	*Odyssey*	*"Penelope" 2*	*Odyssey*
Line 1	Pages 301–302	Line 53	Page 388
4	302	57	388–389
5	304	58	389–391
6	313	59	390
42	356 & 376	60	390
43	376	62	391
44	379	63	391–392
45	380	64	392
46	381	66–67	392
47	381	70	327
48	384	71	328
49	383	72	346
50	386	82	346
52	387		

Line 2 *N.B.*: probably Nora Barnacle. *Mrs Santos*: wife of Nicolas Santos, a fruit-store owner and friend of Joyce in Trieste and Zurich. Clement Semmler (*For the Uncanny Man* [Melbourne, 1963], p. 115) says Nicolas Santos "used to walk around the lake with [Joyce] reciting bits of the *Odyssey*." According to Ellmann (p. 386), Signora Santos, one of the models for Molly Bloom, "stayed indoors all day to preserve her complexion, for which she mixed her own creams."

6 Cf. "Penelope" 7:47 and Ellmann, p. 48.

15 Ellmann, p. 452.

33 *Ibid.*, p. 182.

51 The tale Odysseus tells Penelope of his adventures is similar to the one he told Nausicaa and her father King Alcinous in Book 7.

52 *Big Four*: Joyce's term for Odysseus and his three companions Telemachus, Eumaeus, and Philoetius.

53 *Nekia* (or *nekuiá*): a magical rite by which ghosts were called up from Hades and questioned about the future. The first *nekia* occurs in Book 11; the second in Book 24. See Gilbert, pp. 166ff., 173.

56 *Lord Melb.*: this reference to Lord Melbourne may spring from the fact that his wife "attained some celebrity as a novel-writer under the title of Lady Caroline Lamb, besides notoriety from her nine months' devotion (1812–13) to Lord Byron" (*Chambers's*, p. 874). Molly (*U* 728:38) tells us that Bloom tried to look like Byron; perhaps Joyce meant this reference as an ironic comment on Bloom.

66–67 On Penelope as weaver, see R. M. Adams, *James Joyce: Common Sense and Beyond* (New York, 1966), p. 168.

81 *Gorgeous*: vertical on the notesheet.

"Penelope" 3

LEFT MARGIN HORIZONTAL

device
?corns
romance ?post remorse
B ⟨tell him some day not now⟩ *730:37*
5   MB jealous of men   R ⟨hates women⟩ *764:6–7*
B ⟨LB thinks he knows everything⟩ *737:27ff.?, 749:38–40?*
B ⟨by inspection⟩ *661:25*
B ⟨$x^4 - x^5y + x^{?2}\,y^{?2}$ etc.⟩
B ⟨cleared of fractions. (abbrev)⟩
10   B ⟨lineal descendant⟩
B ⟨invert—⟩
B ⟨rule exception⟩ *341:6?*
$987^2 = 10^2-$
he   B ⟨proves by algebra⟩

CENTER COLUMNS HORIZONTAL

15   R ⟨Milly away⟩ *751:12*
R ⟨LB & burglar⟩ *751:7*
B ⟨read Wilkie Collins⟩ *741:16*   B ⟨vanity in grief⟩ *758:35ff.?*
B ⟨Breathing exercise⟩ *735:35*   B ⟨Emily Lyons ?emigrant⟩
R ⟨Si.D. flirty⟩ *759:20*
20   B ⟨If girls go for LB win him back⟩ *728:18ff.?*
B ⟨Such a softy his age⟩ *724:17–18*   B ⟨what is ?hers alone⟩
B ⟨BB 4th. time⟩ *739:32–33?*

498

R ⟨Professor SD⟩ *760:23–24*   *B* ⟨her lover's ?died⟩ *734:7–10*

B ⟨Know all about the inside⟩ *728:3–4*   Antonio?

B ⟨MB dislikes erotic book with "Molly"⟩ *741:21*   her roses

B ⟨MB fight with her nails⟩ *742:29*   visual

B ⟨New woman⟩ *735:40?*   tactual

B ⟨MB tie knot on thread with one hand⟩ *741:3*   *B* ⟨currant cake⟩ *740:22?*

  ″ sew bone button.   pepper tree plane   *B* ⟨white poplar⟩ *747:1*

B ⟨ ″ settle her back hair.⟩ *741:1–2*

?crim. spider—idiot   *B* ⟨rainwater in tanks⟩ *740:10*

  oldest insect   *B* ⟨Sp. money till 1898⟩ *744:40?*

fly = 6 legs. spider = 8

B ⟨meet in day ruin effect night⟩ *754:39–40?*

B ⟨MB mistakes her age⟩ *736:16–17*

gynomorphic

B ⟨feels vaguely forgotten cares⟩

B ⟨Kind to her as she was then⟩ *740:13?*

B ⟨sea = distance. distinction of personality & ?dents⟩

B ⟨kept room for days (Pen)⟩

B ⟨1 day to finish a row⟩

Lucia knits dowry

BOTTOM HORIZONTAL

B ⟨MB urges LB to enter hospital if ill⟩ *723:22*   *B* ⟨brave to
    travel alone⟩

B ⟨MB write—if she could only remember.⟩ *739:14–16*

B ⟨MB go back & change in shop⟩ *735:21–23*

B ⟨Prefer child of his by other woman (not risk her womb)⟩
    727:29–31

B ⟨Fatigued by LB   likes BB⟩

R ⟨LB couldn't adulter   go gets BB to do it⟩ *758:16–17*

B ⟨MB laughs at his fall yet propped him⟩

B ⟨MB peneloped before marriage⟩ *746:2–8?*   *R* ⟨Ul. overcirces her⟩

B ⟨MB loved Mrs Galbraith's blouse⟩ *736:18?*

B ⟨MB look of naval officer made her seasick⟩ *741:36–37*

NOTES

In the center of "Penelope" 3 is a map of Gibraltar drawn in Joyce's hand similar to the following one; it was probably copied from a book other than Field's *Gibraltar*.

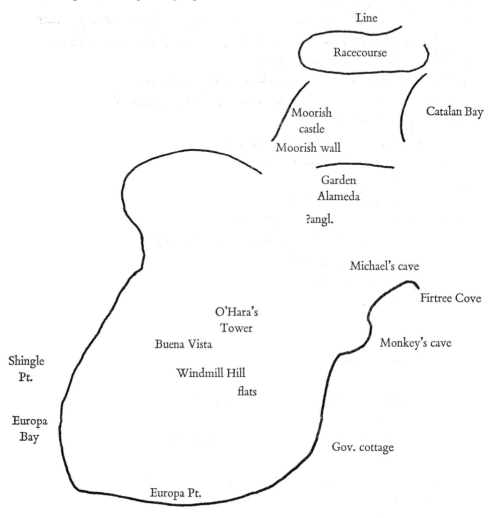

Much of "Penelope" 3 (and "Penelope" 7) originated in Joyce's notes for *Exiles*, as the following list shows:

"*Penelope*" *3*	*Exiles*	"*Penelope*" *3*	*Exiles*
Line 3	Page 122	Line 26 (right)	Page 122
17 (right)	122	27 (right)	122
18 (right)	121	28 (right)	122

"Penelope" 3	Exiles	"Penelope" 3	Exiles
Line 37	Page 122	Line 47	Page 124
38	122	49	124
39	122 & 123	50	125
43 (right)	122		

Lines 7–14   These are notes for the "Ithaca" episode.

8   The superscripts here are obscure.

16   Cf. "Penelope" 1:54.

18   *Emily Lyons*: apparently a friend of Nora Barnacle's (*Exiles*, pp. 121–122). At "Penelope" 7:27 Joyce wrote "Her name?", probably as a reminder that he wished to change it to "Hester." see *U* 740:42, 767:30. Lady Hamilton, the mistress of Lord Nelson, was born Emma Lyon and later called herself Emily Hart (see "Cyclops" 1:29 and note). See also lines 43–44 below and "Penelope" 7:26.

21   *Softy*: repeated at "Penelope" 4:103. *Hers*: seems to have been imposed over *his*.

29   *Pepper tree plane*: Joyce failed to delete this, but he did use it (*U* 747:1).

31   *Crim.*: probably an abbreviation of "crimson."

37   Repeated at "Penelope" 7:29.

43–44   *Brave to travel alone*: cf. "Penelope" 7:26.

47   Cf. "Penelope" 7:31.

50   Cf. "Penelope" 7:34.

"Penelope" 4

LEFT MARGIN HORIZONTAL

R ⟨LB kneel to piss   she never heard!⟩ *756:32*

B ⟨frown meet B.B.⟩

B ⟨LB feigns cold⟩ *723:3–4*

B ⟨Read same book twice⟩ *736:38–39*

5   B ⟨Incipit—Because⟩ *723:1*

B ⟨He told her J.C. was a Socialist carpenter⟩ *727:39–728:1*

B ⟨quietly insolent shopgirl (LB?)⟩ *737:34ff.*

B ⟨She pulled green twigs & threw away⟩ *747:1–2?*

R ⟨LB wouldn't eat.⟩ *758:8–9*

10   R ⟨MB needless locking⟩ *751:1–3?*

B ⟨MB had row with LB re politics (?hat) because he had pity
     for wallflower girl⟩ *727:39*

B ⟨MB sets out for Clery's, goes to Arnott's⟩

B ⟨take newness out of it⟩ *745:20*

15   B ⟨MB watches no 2, no 8⟩

R ⟨LB slept naked on floor⟩ *758:7*

B ⟨LB to MB, Ah . . . who did I meet?⟩ *724:2–3*

B ⟨took off my things⟩ *727:5*

LB disliked to go to theatre with MB

20   R ⟨Her new novel⟩ *750:12*

G ⟨woman cat out of window⟩

B ⟨MB knew he was after that one.⟩ *724:34*

B ⟨Dog smelt her fur⟩ *723:17*

B ⟨excite, Belfast new⟩ *734:17–20?*

25   B ⟨MB decants LB⟩

odyss of Pen

LEFT COLUMN HORIZONTAL

B ⟨LB have I offended you? MB silent⟩ *732:2*

B ⟨MB got LB promoted⟩ *737:18*

G ⟨why? and why?⟩

30 *B* ⟨For any excuse to touch her (Mulvey)⟩ *731:24–25*

R ⟨Innocent boy (SD) now?⟩ *759:40*

B ⟨what did he mean?⟩ *759:31?*

B ⟨LB took off her stockings⟩ *730:20*

B ⟨LB thanked her for frig⟩

35 *R* ⟨LB made her cry⟩ *727:41*   *B* ⟨?might be was someone else⟩

B ⟨a kiss in eye of glove & in openwork sleeve⟩ *731:23–24*

B ⟨How did my foot excite him?⟩ *730:12*

B ⟨Is he thinking of me?⟩ *726:22*

B ⟨Leave him smthg to make him⟩

40 *G* ⟨MB pass outside urinal⟩ *738:25*

B ⟨LB's obscene letters to MB⟩ *756:6ff.*

B ⟨Days seem like years⟩ *742:27*

B ⟨Where? she tells when. When? she tells where.⟩

R ⟨MB to put ?him in BB,⟩ *765:31?*   *B* ⟨mad about her crazy⟩ *756:6*

45 ?Lisped as a girl. Him!

ashes good for carpet

R ⟨darling little boy (SD) children like MB.⟩ *759:41–760:1*

B ⟨he smelt of drink⟩ *726:23–24*

B ⟨pyromania|menses⟩

50 tutor L.B.

B ⟨MB not recognize her face⟩ *741:12*

B ⟨MB breathing—her belly⟩ *735:29 & 35*

B ⟨MB impressed by LB's knowledge⟩ *728:3–4*

R ⟨LB as boy long curly hair⟩ *759:41?*

55 *B* ⟨Sip coloured water⟩ *726:25–26*

R ⟨MB embraced Milly in public,   she doesn't like it,   take

   yʳ· foot away⟩ *752:21–22*

B ⟨changed her mind⟩ *737:23–24*

B ⟨MB likes that Breen liked LB⟩

60 *B* ⟨nice to be in love⟩ *743:25?, 762:31?*

B ⟨shoplifter,⟩ *741:23*   at football match

B ⟨Beauty ?in expression. Mirror dead⟩ *734:28–29*

R ⟨1ˢᵗ· dislike to see man's prick then—no⟩

B ⟨She found everything out.⟩ *728:14ff.?*

65   B ⟨female spider devours male after⟩

R ⟨Milly won't let MB sit down⟩ *751:18?*

B ⟨LB opened rwy door with penknife⟩ *733:11–12*

B ⟨MB no respect for drunken admirer because he'd give it the
    same to the next⟩ *742:25*

70   B ⟨MB letter twice a year⟩ *743:5–6?*

B ⟨Pen—stupid⟩

B ⟨Pen—genitophilia⟩

MB hate shaving suds

B ⟨LB writes her letters⟩ *756:6*

75   G ⟨Church of Three Patrons, Rathgar⟩ *666:24–25*

B ⟨Company manners⟩ *731:42–732:1*

B ⟨MB dressed to please LB⟩ *737:27ff.?*

RIGHT COLUMN HORIZONTAL

1ˢᵗ· pubic hair

B ⟨Silk socks BB⟩ *734:36*

80   G ⟨BB MB LB fish supper⟩ *763:3*

MB at boxing match

R ⟨—wore apron 3 dys⟩ *766:28?*

In that case I'll take a cup of tea

R ⟨dust of bedroom grows in sleep⟩ *766:34*

85   B ⟨MB like Chartreuse colour⟩ *726:25–26*

houselights (theatre)

B ⟨shore leave⟩ *741:36*

Gracepark rd

R ⟨Lost obj. turns up at last⟩ *753:23–24*

90   R ⟨clean⟩ *723:22 and elsewhere*

B ⟨MB couldn't touch him if she thought —⟩ *725:2–3*

G ⟨incestuous MB⟩

B ⟨feeding cup⟩ *765:20?*   *R* ⟨LB sleeps hand on nose⟩ *756:36*

L̶B̶

95 *G* ⟨MB heard toddling feet overhead⟩

B ⟨?oh⟩

B ⟨way he made love.⟩ *732:11*

B ⟨LB got drenched⟩ *731:28*

B ⟨long jobber candle in bed⟩ *Cf. 745:26–30*

100 touch line   song liked by many

B ⟨lead in her sleeves⟩

old gods slumber in her brain

B ⟨Kimono⟩ *734:18*   *B* ⟨LB softy⟩ *724:17*

B ⟨like a devil (?U go)⟩ *734:38–39*

105 *G* ⟨MB chooses chair to fall on⟩

B ⟨atlas (Gibr.)⟩ *747:11*

B ⟨MB 'forgot' her gloves⟩ *730:6*

B ⟨Concone's⟩ *740:18*

B ⟨otherwise amusing things⟩ *740:19–20*

110 *G* ⟨weed in tea⟩ *753:11*

R ⟨my uncle John has a thing long⟩ *761:42*

Isaac Varian's sweeping brush

B ⟨she said she liked & didn't⟩ *725:32–33*

R ⟨MB & beggar⟩ *750:38*

115 *B* ⟨MB hates dispute at night⟩ *724:9–10*

B ⟨She asked LB question & forgets answer⟩ *730:25*

NOTES

Since the arrangement of phrases on this notesheet is more chaotic than usual, my division of phrases into columns is often arbitrary.

Line 4   Repeated at "Penelope" 7:2.

5 Joyce apparently contemplated beginning the "Penelope" episode with the word *Because*; he probably settled on "Yes because" to emphasize structural circularity.

13   *Clery's* and *Arnott's*: two of the largest department stores in Dublin.

17   The ellipses are Joyce's.

18   See Connolly, ed., *Scribbledehobble*, p. 166.

39   An arrow points from the second *him* to the line above, thus indicating the phrase to mean "something to make him think of me."

41   Cf. the obscene letters of 1909 from Joyce to Nora in the *Letters*. Some letters of this period, now at Cornell University, were excluded from the *Letters* because of their obscenity.

67   *Rwy*: railway.

93–94   Under *LB sleeps*, Joyce wrote and then scratched out *LB*.

103   *Softy*: repeated at "Penelope" 3:21.

112   The I. S. *Varian* Company ("manufacturers of all types of brushes") is still in business at 91 Talbot Street in Dublin.

"Penelope" 5

LEFT MARGIN HORIZONTAL

B ⟨way it takes him⟩ *734:35*
B ⟨drink was talking⟩ *742:24–25*
B ⟨a great compliment to be noticed⟩ *735:13–14*
B ⟨Some brandnew idea⟩ *730:5?*
5   B ⟨disease or smthg⟩ *754:1*
R ⟨MB & criminals⟩ *750:40ff.?*
B ⟨let ?— finish it, God⟩ *727:18?*
B ⟨really & truly Mrs Bloom⟩ *737:20*
B ⟨I squeezed back⟩ *725:8–10*
10   B ⟨nothing kills me altogether only⟩ *737:26–27*
B ⟨Yours aff'ly⟩ *743:29–30?*
B ⟨once & for all⟩   got to
B ⟨1ˢᵗ· class do it in train.⟩ *733:13–15*
R ⟨O Jesus wait yes that thing has come on me damn it wouldn't
15   that pester the soul out of a body when it came on me at
          the Empire⟩ *754:6ff.*
R ⟨all the poking & rooting he had up in me men like
          menses⟩ *754:7ff.*
B ⟨is he he doesn't look it⟩ *733:37*
20   R ⟨Milly imitating me whistling⟩ *751:36*
B ⟨MB regrets chicken not picked at Glencree⟩ *735:6*
B ⟨looking for last year's paper⟩ *740:1–2*
R ⟨MB flushes her bottom⟩ *755:36*
B ⟨I'm   he will⟩
25   R ⟨tramp at door⟩ *750:39*
B ⟨MB ?kisses in ?tunnel⟩

507

B ⟨Cunt what we go into & came out of⟩ *745:30–31*

B ⟨thing⟩ *755:17?, 754:6?*

CENTER COLUMN HORIZONTAL

B ⟨bell it round the town⟩ *734:22–23*

30 R ⟨my 'ass'⟩ *736:34–35?*

B ⟨not one way everybody goes mad⟩ *729:14–15*

B ⟨bring me that and don't forget it⟩ *735:40–41*

B ⟨dirty old pantry was open⟩ *732:19*

B ⟨shaking like a jelly all over⟩ *731:37*

35 G ⟨Knew Rudy ?wᵈ. ?1ˢᵗ. ?cry⟩   B ⟨enough for me⟩

B ⟨I wonder was he satisfied⟩ *726:18*

G ⟨SD was on the cards⟩ *760:2*

R ⟨my drawers hanging out on exhibition⟩ *753:37–38*

R ⟨Mrs Fleming⟩ *749:29, 753:20?*

40 R ⟨Glorious⟩   B ⟨set of teeth make you hungry to look at them⟩ *731:28–29*

R ⟨I told him that⟩

B ⟨1 thing I didn't like the way he slapped me behind going away
    I'm not a horse or an ass am I I suppose he was thinking
    of his father's⟩ *726:19–21*

45 B ⟨what kind of pricks do old men have⟩

B ⟨his trousers⟩ *757:30, 761:29, and elsewhere*   B ⟨like Kitty O'Shea⟩ *736:21*

B ⟨LB cook⟩ *737:28*

B ⟨where he'd get regular money⟩ *737:10–11*

B ⟨if they knew him as well as I do⟩ *724:11–12*

50 B ⟨mightn't be all like Poldy⟩ *739:28*

B ⟨hair on her ....⟩   B ⟨Ontario terr⟩ *724:24, 757:13*

B ⟨See her combing it she loved it⟩ *736:22*

B ⟨fart have him down slobbering me over again⟩ *748:18*

R ⟨LB looks at whores when daughter there⟩ *758:22*

55 B ⟨MB hear Kinderschrei⟩ *727:27?*

R ⟨Knew 1 day before we moved⟩

B ⟨magnificent⟩ *736:20*

B ⟨men weak in sickness⟩ *723:27*

508

B ⟨swell of ship⟩ *741:35–36*   ?Luna

60   *B* ⟨making us with a big hole like that in us⟩ *727:11–12*   Benady

R ⟨talks to Milly all the time.⟩ *751:28–30*   *G* ⟨Hugh⟩ *743:30*

R ⟨suppose he thinks I'm finished well I'm not⟩ *751:33–34*

B ⟨her Christian name⟩ *746:37–38?*

Easter duty Milly

65   *R* ⟨I winked at him re Milly⟩ *758:23*

R ⟨wdn't that sicken you⟩ *754:12?*

R ⟨tatter them down off him⟩ *750:4–5*

B ⟨weltering in the heat⟩ *741:26–27*

R ⟨MB gets angry,⟩   *R* ⟨likes student⟩ *760:20?*

70   *R* ⟨afraid of her life   crush her skirt⟩ *752:12*

R ⟨Si.D. hole in his sock⟩ *753:30*

G ⟨I want to show you⟩

B ⟨never came back⟩ *734:7–9?*

R ⟨like to smather it all over his face⟩ *755:31*

75   *R* ⟨plans picnic⟩ *749:27*

R ⟨Start giving us his orders⟩ *749:8*

R ⟨weight of boat all on my side⟩ *749:41*

R ⟨Milly learns to men's cycle   night Nelson street⟩ *751:38–39*

R ⟨crookeding about regatta⟩ *749:41*

80   *B* ⟨his tattarattat⟩ *732:28*

R ⟨LB spoke biz to her⟩

R ⟨MB propose to LB⟩ *767:18–19*

NOTES

In the upper left-hand corner is a large *P* in red pencil.

Line 11   *Aff'ly*: affectionately.

15–16   *Came on me at the Empire*: separated from the preceding part of the sentence by the line following (*all the poking . . .*). Joyce drew a line to connect the two separated parts of the sentence.

29   Chapter Four of Field's *Gibraltar* is entitled "Round the Town."

46   *Kitty O'Shea*: the mistress /wife of Charles S. Parnell.

60   See *U* 746:18 for *Benady*, a Gibraltar merchant family listed in *Kelly's Directory of Merchants* (1938), II, and the *Gibraltar Directory for 1902*.

509

"Penelope" 6

LEFT MARGIN HORIZONTAL

    G ⟨he's so cold,⟩ *762:20*
    R ⟨powder Milly⟩ *752:41*
    G ⟨MB Thibet⟩
    MB leaves G—plans
5   *G* ⟨In love with picture⟩ *750:33?, 759:31?*
    R ⟨Bill Bailey⟩ *759:8*
    G ⟨universe⟩ *767:13*
    B ⟨BB not ?pound⟩
    G ⟨gave her a rosary⟩ *764:14–15*
10   *R* ⟨flirted with MT before LB⟩ *759:20?*
    Russian gun spiked
    alameda
    ceiling cracked
    red & blue (artillery)
15   fife & drum company
    squad of buglers parading
    answers

CENTER COLUMN HORIZONTAL

    R ⟨Mr & Mrs ?Santery melt!⟩
    R ⟨Byron too beautiful for a man⟩ *728:38–39*
20   Holy Week in G.
    G ⟨MB asks question & doesn't listen to answer⟩
    MB girl's dream

510

G ⟨MB & governor (Louis XV)⟩ *735:3*

G ⟨MB confesses fault to herself⟩ *726:8–9?*

25   Siege eating dandelions

G ⟨calf's pluck⟩ *749:27*

red sands (Alameda)   R ⟨Knitting in Jew's Temple,⟩ *725:24*

her birthday S. Maria

R ⟨domineering⟩ *744:10*

30   G ⟨Black Watch &⟩ the Staffordshire *734:13–14*

R ⟨relief of Khartoum   1886 Gordon⟩ *742:18–19*

B ⟨march past⟩ *734:13*   R ⟨a ?kiss is best⟩

B ⟨levanter black clouds⟩ *740:5*

G ⟨soldier's funeral reversed arms⟩ *758:26–27*

35   soldier homeless defend home

sir Arth. Hardinge gov now 1881

U.S. consul's son & 1886   G ⟨ch. . . . . cup⟩

major gen. Walker empty sleeve

Old Elliot,   R ⟨Dear Madam⟩ *743:7*

40   lord Gifford

R ⟨gun take down china, mirrors open window⟩ *742:6–7*

riding parties in Sp.

R ⟨band by Alameda⟩ *741:7*

R ⟨Sp. sent. sullen⟩   R ⟨Union Jack flying⟩ *744:12*

45   G. ?cheats,   R ⟨caval. S.Roque⟩ *734:10*

B ⟨carabineros⟩ *744:12*

arms   castle & key

Zebehr Pasha, arab prison in Gov's cottage

G ⟨Margate on N.E. side⟩ *760:40–41*

50   MB ?dome under ?paper

B ⟨drapery photo show no age⟩ *759:31–33*

stagestruck: R ⟨lock up in WC.⟩

hates falling f. . . . . .

G ⟨wash cobbles off himself.⟩ *767:10*

55   donkey carry lady up.

Supply vessel unlade New Mole

R ⟨red geranium⟩ *768:10?* white clematis

vine, fig, almond, myrtle,

511

Pillars of Hercules, Abyla   rockgun top
60   officer in signal station,
     G ⟨the Malta boat⟩ *745:17*   Line Wall
     B ⟨Straits shine,⟩ *747:10*   R ⟨boom of gun⟩ *742:5*
     1000 ft cliff G   2000 T gun Armstrong
     confess in Sp.   guns guns guns
65   milit. secretary order to see galleries
     G ⟨Q's birthday guns. ?Her⟩ *742:6*
     political refugees
     church on Sunday
     G ⟨longbearded jews⟩ *742:14*
70   R ⟨rock scorpions (natives)⟩ *745:6*
     levantine & Maltese   G ⟨not a God's notion⟩ *764:40*

NOTES

The following list gives the lines and phrases on "Penelope" 6 which Joyce derived from Field's *Gibraltar*. See "Penelope" essay (pp. 71–72) and *Ulysses* notebook V.A.2 at Buffalo. James V. D. Card first discovered that Joyce had made notes from Field.

"Penelope" 6	*Field*	*"Penelope"* 6	*Field*
Line 11	Page 27	Line 36	Page 53
12	27	37 (left)	7?, 54–55?
13	28	38	60
14	30	39 (left)	56
15	31	40	58 and elsewhere
16	31	41	61
18	5 & 6 ?	42	61
20	10	43	62
25	77	44	113
26	82	45 (right)	70
27 (left)	92	46	115
30	37	47	120
31	36 & 37	48	134–135
33	46	55	12
34	46	56	12
35	47	57 (right)	13

512

"Penelope" 6	*Field*	*"Penelope" 6*	*Field*
Line 58	Page 13	Line 65	Page 24
59	13	66	26
60	14	67	33
61 (left)	16	68	32
61 (right)	19	69	33
62 (right)	17	70	34
63 (left)	18	71 (left)	34
63 (right)	22		

Line 10   *M.T.*: Marion Tweedy, Molly's maiden name.

28   Molly's birth date was September 8, 1870, the day traditionally held to be the Virgin's birthday (Card, p. 48).

31   General Charles G. *Gordon* (1833–85) commanded the South Staffordshire regiment in an attempt to relieve Egyptian garrisons situated in rebellious territory. Besieged for ten months by troops of the Mahdi, Gordon was finally captured and murdered when *Khartoum* fell.

36   *Sir Arth*[ur]. Edward *Hardinge* (1828–92): governor of Gilbraltar from November 1, 1886, until September 25, 1890.

38   *Major gen.* Charles *Walker* (1817–94) lost an arm at the battle of Sebastopol (Field, pp. 57, 60).

39   *Old Elliot*: General George Augustus Eliott, later the first Baron Heathfield (1717–90), whose "heroic defense [of Gibraltar], from June 1779 to February 1783, ranks as one of the most memorable achievements of British arms" (*Chambers's*).

40   *Lord Gifford*: a "hero of the Ashantee War," (1873–74) and winner of the Victoria Cross. Henry Field met him in Gibraltar in 1887 (Field, pp. 58, 60).

48   *Zebehr Pasha*: an Arab sheik influential in the Sudan. The British feared his power and imprisoned him in the Governor's Cottage in Gibraltar from 1885 to 1887. In the *Gibraltar Directory* his name is correctly spelled "Zobehr Pasha."

56   *New Mole*: the main pier on Gibraltar.

59   *Pillars of Hercules*: the name given Gibraltar and *Abyla*, "the Mount of God," on the African side, by ancient navigators, who believed they represented the limits of the habitable world. Cf. Field, p. 13.

63   *2000 T gun Armstrong*: a huge gun named after its inventor, William G. Armstrong (1810–1900). Field says it is a "hundred-ton gun [which] would throw a ball weighing 2,000 pounds over eight miles!" (p. 22). Cf. "Oxen" 17:2.

"Penelope" 7

LEFT MARGIN HORIZONTAL

B ⟨MB hears train whistle⟩ *739:34*
B ⟨MB reads same book twice without knowing⟩ *736:38–39*
R ⟨let out the smell⟩ *748:21?*
R ⟨cut his teeth,⟩
5   *R* ⟨around BC 4000⟩
R ⟨bite off thread of button⟩ *751:42–752:1*
B ⟨looks at corner of room to look at man first⟩
B ⟨2ⁿᵈ· time he looked he changed⟩ *737:37–38*
B ⟨my dearest Doggerina⟩ *740:13*
10   *B* ⟨had a jolly hot bath, enjoyed it,⟩ *740:15–16*
B ⟨am⟩ *740:15?*
B ⟨I am a very clean dog⟩ *740:15–16*
B ⟨cᵈ· wᵈ·⟩ *740:16*
I suppose you've heard nothing
15   she cdn't play ?as she cdn't start it ?on ?ground
B ⟨one for my own wogger⟩ *740:16 & 26?, 741:33?*
candles
B ⟨newphews⟩ *743:24*
B ⟨B. Marché⟩ *740:12, 747:9*
20   *B* ⟨what a shame!⟩ *740:12*
B ⟨I wish I⟩
R ⟨my precious one⟩ *756:6–7*

CENTER COLUMN HORIZONTAL

B ⟨what is hers—not hers & his⟩

514

R ⟨she will be old⟩ *729:5–8?, 736:18?*

25   Jesus no wife ?or sister or mistress

B ⟨Emily Lyons goes: she cries⟩ *741:39–40?*   brave to go alone

B ⟨Her name?⟩

present of buttoned boots

B ⟨feels vaguely forgotten cares⟩

30   *B* ⟨her girlself is more⟩

B ⟨prefer child of Boylan by other woman⟩ *727:31*

fuck—secrets of flesh

her mind ?on   *B* ⟨earth mist objects loom⟩ *740:40*

B ⟨Cdn't he go & fuck Mrs Breen?⟩ *758:15–16?*

35   Her 24 hours

B ⟨shopmen⟩

B ⟨overcoats making place stifling⟩ *740:2–3*

B ⟨no fool like old fool⟩ *724:20*

B ⟨woman, woman, woman⟩

40   *B* ⟨LB sent her to plead⟩ *737:17*

G ⟨MB = spinning Earth⟩

R ⟨MB visits museum⟩ *756:37*

B ⟨MB early ?son⟩   Milly hiccup

B ⟨LB   Shackleton⟩

45   *B* ⟨MB avarice⟩ *734:25–26?*

R ⟨two mummies sleep⟩ *763:17*

B ⟨upbraids impure slavey⟩ *724:30ff.*

MB sent LB to MD with penis

B ⟨MB notices contrast⟩ *739:29–30*

50   *B* ⟨MB makes up to LB⟩ *758:9–11?*

B ⟨Marie Celeste derelict Gibraltar⟩

B ⟨BB's return⟩ *732:16*

B ⟨that thing came on me in the café⟩ *754:12ff.*

B ⟨MB objects to bandage LB's toe⟩ *723:36–37*

55   *B* ⟨MB nice with LB in café to show off v. ?SJ & FS.⟩

B ⟨MB wants to steal spoon⟩ *735:9–10*

B ⟨Indignant at Ciolkowska flirting with girl⟩ *724:4–6?*

R ⟨MB moved by play 2 days after⟩

B ⟨kiss the heart⟩ *732:13*

60   *B* ⟨MB embrace tight after fuck⟩ *739:25–26*
        B ⟨Can't hide thing from lover⟩ *732:42*
        LB & SD smaller ?saved ?quake
        B ⟨MB felt like nothing on earth⟩ *732:14–15*
        G ⟨think of first no, double it ?treble,⟩

65   *B* ⟨take your 1st. thoughts away from it.⟩
        saddle bags
        B ⟨rummage sale⟩ *737:25*
        B ⟨if it's a thing that⟩
        B ⟨give us our tea,⟩ *749:8–9*   *R* ⟨rattle of china⟩ *749:13*

70   *B* ⟨sun faded my blouse⟩ *740:10–11*
        B ⟨turned her back on him in café⟩ *724:5–6*
        B ⟨he's mad.⟩ *731:6*
        B ⟨Mrs Galbraith told her how he did it⟩ *736:18?*
        B ⟨bought fashion journal⟩

75   *R* ⟨loved him, full of him⟩ *727:10?*
        B ⟨can't help herself⟩ *725:39*
        B ⟨Yes, yes, yes, yes, yes.⟩ *768:18*
        R ⟨brisk grocery man⟩
        B ⟨like asking ?fine policeman⟩

80   *R* ⟨young all suit you⟩ *752:9*
        Milly carries LB's hat
        B ⟨when he grew a beard   hairy face of Man⟩ *723:35*
        R ⟨deathwatch⟩

NOTES

A number of items on "Penelope" 7 originated in Joyce's notes for *Exiles* (see also "Penelope" 3):

"Penelope" 7	*Exiles*	"Penelope" 7	*Exiles*
Line 25	Page 120	Line 30	Page 122
26	121 & 122	31	124
27	121	32	124
28	121 & 122	33	125
29	122	34	125

Line 2   Repeated at "Penelope" 4:4.

9   *Doggerina*: Joyce may have made up this word from "dogger," used in Field's *Gibraltar* (p. 81) to refer to a Dutch fishing boat.

18   *Newphews*: Joyce scratched out the first *w*. See Joseph Prescott, *Exploring James Joyce* (Carbondale, Ill., 1964), p. 92.

25   Cf. Ellmann, p. 449.

26–27   See "Penelope" 3:18 and note.

29   Repeated at "Penelope" 3:37.

31   Cf. "Penelope" 3:47.

34   Cf. "Penelope" 3:50.

40   Interestingly enough, Joyce asked Nora to intercede for him with his publisher on a trip to Dublin (Ellmann, pp. 333–334).

41   See *Letters*, I, 170.

44   *Shackleton*: perhaps Sir Ernest Henry Shackleton (1874–1922), Irish-born explorer of Antarctica.

47   Cf. "Penelope" 2:6 and note.

51   *Marie Celeste*: a 100-foot brigantine of 282 tons which was found *derelict* in December 1872. Captain Benjamin Briggs, his wife, their daughter, and a crew of eight "had disappeared from an untouched ship in what is now a classic sea mystery" (Allen Andrews, *Proud Fortress* [1958; rpt. New York, 1959], p. 152).

55   *SJ & FS.*: perhaps Stanislaus Joyce and Frantisek Schaurek.

57   Mme. Muriel *Ciolkowska*: a literary critic and journalist whose acquaintance with Joyce dated from 1915 or earlier. See *Letters*, I, 194–195; Scholes, ed., *Cornell Joyce Collection*, items 447, 448, 1303, etc.

77   See Ellmann, p. 531.

Appendixes

Bibliography

Appendix A

Errata for Hanley's *Word Index to James Joyce's* Ulysses

ONE of the most valuable tools for any scholar working with the *Ulysses* manuscripts is Miles L. Hanley's *Word Index* (1937), based on the 1934 Random House edition of *Ulysses*. I have made constant use of the *Word Index* in editing the British Museum notesheets and have kept a record of errata. Since my use of it was to a great extent confined to the last seven episodes there are probably many errors I failed to catch. Hence this list is really more of a *caveat lector* than a complete list of errata. Perhaps an error-free machine concordance will be made when a definitive edition of *Ulysses* is finally published.

The most lengthy omission in Hanley is on page 470 of *Ulysses* where all but the last four lines—a total of some 263 words—were left out. With a couple of exceptions, I have not incorporated this page into the list which follows but wish rather to call especial attention to it here.

annoyed—720:2 (omit), 728:2 (add)

aristocrat—349:20

avis—380:29

Bantam—references begin on 73:1

bat—547:25 (omit)

bath—367:1 (omit), 362:1 (add)

Bishop—437:12

Bode—685:11 (cap.)

burning—448:13 (omit)

button—543:5 (omit)

Buzz—82:21

Corpus—79:31 (cap. in appendix)

Dearer—358:10

Devils—760:37 (cap.)

De Wet—160:40, 633:16

dovecotes—648:5–6

drawn (for draw)—342:22

dressed—344:10 (omit)

Elijah—223:41 (omit), 223:39 (add)

flanelette—374:19

fool—(not in alphabetical order; one entry follows "folly")

gegee—187:7 (omit)

geegee—351:7 (add)

goddesses—444:5 (omit)

Gold—659:36 (cap.)

Ham—169:12 (cap.)

Harrington—470:3

healthier—163:39 (omit), 163:29 (add)

image—197:37 (omit), 197:38 (add)

introibo—5:5

Jacobs—465:6

kisses—740:25 (omit)

K.M.R.I.A.—(not "Member of Royal Irish Academy") See 145:15

lover—387:2 (omit)

M. (for Marion or Molly)—746:32

Mario—(not "Marie," after "mariner's")

M'Coy–265:14 (omit), 165:14 (add)

Moran—623:30 (omit), 571:30 (add)

More—671:29

N.B.—(North Britain, not "New Brunswick")

Nebukim—671:29

nerve—723:6 (omit), 733:6 (add)

pandybat—547:25

perragordas—744:40

pesetas—744:40

Pillar—485:10 (cap.)

Prince's—136:1

printed—470:5

prolongation—403:12 (omit), 403:42 (add)

settled (instead of "settle")—746:24

Sherlock—470:1, 470:10

simplest—omit one 719:13

sticking—618:28–29

Sue—496:34 (cap.)

wandering—197:37 (omit), 197:38 (add)

Watch—109:1 (omit)

Whit—755:18 (cap.)

xxxxx—740:25

6½—667:25

14—308:36 (omit)

14A—308:36 (add)

32—447:6 (omit)

Appendix B

Dating the Notesheets

As we have seen, the notesheets represent the second stage in the creative process of *Ulysses*, the first being either the rough notes or primitive drafts. One must, however, keep in mind the distinction between dates of compilation for the individual notes (many originated in Joyce's notes for *Exiles*, the *Ulysses* notebook VIII.A.5 at Buffalo, and other earlier manuscripts), the notesheets themselves, and the various stages of implementation for each item in the creative evolution of *Ulysses*. The problem is a complex one, since particular ideas moved continually upstream like salmon, briefly stopping off at way stations only to rest. Some died en route; others continued on to their destination and became fertile passages in the final draft of the novel. Still others lay dormant until resurrected for inclusion in *Finnegans Wake*.

Paradoxically enough, the earliest notes I know anything about were originally for *Exiles* (see below) and appear on two notesheets for the final episode of *Ulysses*: "Penelope" 3 and "Penelope" 7. Litz (p. 18) mentions the similarity between the notes for *Exiles* and the *Ulysses* notesheets, but he did not notice that Joyce had borrowed from the earlier manuscript. Here is a sample page from the notes for *Exiles*, page 122, with the words and phrases which appear on the "Penelope" notesheets in italics:

A persistent and delicate sensuality	"Penelope"
(*visual*: pictures, adorned with holly and	3:26
ivy; gustatious: *currant cake*, . . . *tactual*:	3:27–28
. . . A persistent and delicate *vanity* also,	3:17
even in her *grief*; her pinafore and *buttoned*	7:28
boots. . . . she *feels vaguely* the *forgotten*	7:29, 3:37
cares . . . She thinks of them kindly, not	
because they were *kind to her* but because	3:38
they were kind to *her girlself* which is now	7:30

gone . . . over the dark *sea* which is   3:39
distance, the extinction[1] of interest and
and death. . . . the friend is older,
stronger, can *travel alone, braver,* . . .   3:43–44, 7:26

The entire passage is prompted by a string of associated images, a favorite memory device of Joyce,[2] which evokes the reactions of a young girl (who could only have been Nora Barnacle) to the emigration of her friend Emily Lyons.[3] These few pages of *Exiles* (pp. 120–125) are especially intriguing because they point backwards and forwards in Joyce's work and ultimately tell us more about Joycean heroines in general than they do about Bertha Rowan of *Exiles.* One could perhaps find a parallel as early as the *Dubliners* story "Eveline," where a young girl stands frozen with fear as her fiancé attempts to persuade her to board the departing ship with him. But the notes of November 1913 (*Exiles*, p. 117) were intended to round out the characterization of Bertha, though they survived as material for "Penelope." Most of the borrowed *Exiles* notes were in the end omitted from *Ulysses*, but several significant ones were used. In "Penelope," Emily Lyons of Galway becomes Hester of Gibraltar (*U* 740, 767). Here the identities are functionally split: Joyce suggests that a lesbian attraction existed between Bertha and Emily, and thus infuses their separation with the sorrow of parting lovers (*Exiles*, p. 122). There is scarcely a hint of this relationship in *Ulysses* (cf. *U* 741), the main force of such amorous alienation in Molly's memory having been shifted to the departure of her first lover Lieutenant Mulvey (like Odysseus) from Gibraltar and the death of her first son Rudy (cf. "Oxen" 19:46: "Rudy=Mulvey").

In addition, Molly envisions a child by Boylan (*U* 727), one for whose birth she dares not risk her own womb. The notesheets make it clear that she wishes to perform the interesting gynecological feat of having a child by Boylan and another woman.[4] She blames her husband for her adultery: he did not have the nerve to share another man's wife, so he got Boylan to do it.[5] Both of these ideas originated in the

---

[1] On "Penelope" 3:39 "distinction of personality" appears; perhaps Joyce meant to write "extinction of personality."

[2] Cf. "Circe" 19:16–19 and Ellmann, p. 368.

[3] See "Penelope" 3:18 and "Penelope" 7:26. Curiously enough, Emma Lyon was the maiden name of Lady Hamilton (mentioned at "Cyclops" 1:29), the mistress of Lord Nelson. At one time she called herself "Emily Hart."

[4] *Exiles*, p. 124; "Penelope" 3:47, 7:31; *U* 727.

[5] *Exiles*, p. 125; "Penelope" 3:50; cf. "Penelope" 7:34 and *U* 758.

notes for *Exiles*. The most fascinating thing is not the actual borrowing, however; it is the persistence with which Joyce exploited the character and background of Nora Barnacle in his modeling of Bertha, Molly, and even Anna Livia Plurabelle, and the extent to which each of them is really only one turn in his kaleidoscopic portrayal of the archetypal Woman.

If the *Exiles* notes prove the early date of some of the ideas in the *Ulysses* notesheets, *James Joyce's Scribbledehobble: The Ur-Notebook for* Finnegans Wake illustrates that the collection was not abandoned when *Ulysses* was published in 1922. A thorough search would probably uncover notesheet residue in other *Finnegans Wake* notebooks as well. *Scribbledehobble*, according to its editor, Thomas E. Connolly, was mostly compiled in 1922–23; it is divided into forty-seven parts corresponding to each of Joyce's works from *Chamber Music* through each of the eighteen episodes of *Ulysses*. Only *Pomes Penyeach*, published in 1927, is absent. Connolly emphasizes that *Finnegans Wake* is an extension not merely of *Ulysses*, as Ellmann suggests, but of all that Joyce had written.

Joyce apparently reexamined all of his work for the purpose of salvaging material of potential value for *Finnegans Wake*. He probably reread each of his published works, the notesheets, and any rough notes he had and added new material suggested by the style and content of each particular work. Joyce's method here was much the same as in *Ulysses*: the material he found useful was crossed through in red, blue, green, and orange and was transferred to a subsequent draft.

Evidence that material from the British Museum notesheets went into *Scribbledehobble* can be seen in the following:

Scribbledehobble		Notesheets
Page 86	γλαυκῶπις	Cf. "Ithaca" 15:31
113	little sufferers	"Nausicaa" 7:15
119	bellhorses	"Circe" 7:99
159	pettifogging	Cf. "Cyclops" 2:50
163	Thora dictated so fast Moses couldn't put in stops.	"Ithaca" 14:26
163	piss violets	Cf. "Nausicaa" 5:38
166	take off your things	Cf. "Penelope" 4:18

Three examples from a "Penelope" sheet (p. 6) in notebook V.A.2 at Buffalo, a notebook Joyce used for the typescripts and proofsheets of *Ulysses*, should be enough to establish that he consulted this manuscript in the early stages of *Finnegans*

Wake. These phrases appear on three consecutive lines: "Tarik, . . . Café Universal, Sp-Eng. dude, waiters smoke[,] racecourse & polo." On page 163 of Connolly's edition of *Scribbledehobble*, lines two through four contain "Spanish waiters smoke: . . . racecourse and polo ground: Calpe Tarik (1 eye):."

As I indicate in Appendix C, the British Museum notesheets were used sparingly in the augmentation of the 1920 *Little Review* versions of "Cyclops," "Nausicaa," and "Oxen of the Sun," Joyce having already mined the collection assiduously prior to the Rosenbach Manuscript draft. We would probably not be far wrong in dating the compilation of each episode of the notesheets as several weeks or months earlier than the following periods of composition already established by Ellmann and others for each of the last seven episodes of the novel:

Ulysses Episode	Approximate Dates of Composition	Place
"Cyclops"	June–September 3, 1919	Zurich
"Nausicaa"	September–early February 1920	Zurich–Trieste
"Oxen"	February–May 1920	Trieste
"Circe"	June–December 1920	Trieste–Paris
"Eumaeus"	January–February 1921	Paris
"Ithaca"	February–October 1921	Paris
"Penelope"	January or February–October 1921 (before "Ithaca")	Paris

There is some internal evidence by which we can date individual notesheets, but little that points to dates of compilation for either the entire collection or any particular episode. On "Nausicaa" 3:2–13 is a list of Slovene words which points to the Triestine ambiance, as does the even stronger evidence provided by the information on matters of birth control, pregnancy, and embryology in Italian on three "Oxen" notesheets (12, 17, and 18).[6]

The two notesheets that can be dated with the greatest certainty are for "Circe." They were compiled shortly after Joyce and his family arrived in Paris (July 8, 1920) from Trieste. This was a difficult transitional period for them because adequate lodging was nearly impossible to find and royalties Joyce had expected to be waiting for him had not arrived by July 15. Ezra Pound was especially energetic during these depressing days, helping the Joyces with loans and introductions to influential friends. One such friend was the Belgian writer and critic Fritz Vanderpyl, whom

---

[6] See *Letters*, I, 139: "Am working hard at 'Oxen of the Sun,' the idea being the crime committed against fecundity by sterilizing the act of coition."

Joyce visited on July 26.[7] At "Circe" 19:56 his name and address are listed.[8] An acquaintance of Vanderpyl, Joyce, and Pound is mentioned at line 50: Florent Fels, editor of the fast-fading *L'Action*, who had hoped to publish a French translation of *The Portrait*.[9]

On the same notesheet (line 21) Joyce listed another new acquaintance from the late summer of 1920: Mrs. Natalie Clifford Barney, an American writer and friend of Rémy de Gourmont and Paul Valéry.[10] His letter of September 6, 1920, suggests that he has known her for several weeks.[11]

Still another item on "Circe" 19 (line 44) points to the difficulties of that summer. This time the subject is clothes: "Tress hat, Norwell Perth N.B. brogues." In a letter of June 5, 1920, to Pound, Joyce complains that he was wearing his son Giorgio's castoff suit and shoes.[12] He finds the price of clothing in Trieste prohibitively high and, with typical Joycean logic, contemplates a shopping trip to Dublin. Having given up this plan after his arrival in Paris, he probably intended to order a Tress hat from London and brogues from Scotland (N.B.=North Britain).

The second notesheet, "Circe" 11, can be dated quite simply. At lines 51–55 is "?Mr James Joyce, rue de l'Assomption 5, Passy, Paris" (commas mine), which was his address from July 15 until November 1, 1920.[13] These are the only notesheets that lend themselves easily to the process of dating by internal evidence.

[7] *Letters*, III, 12 and elsewhere; Ellmann, p. 504.
[8] Cf. *Letters*, III, 31.
[9] *Letters*, II, 450 n. 4; III, 12.
[10] Ellmann, p. 500 and elsewhere.
[11] *Letters*, III, 18.
[12] *Letters*, II, 467–468.
[13] Ellmann, p. 501.

Appendix C

The Coloring Pencils

SOME understanding of Joyce's use of coloring pencils can aid in dating the British Museum notesheets within the creative evolution of *Ulysses*. The scope of Walton Litz's *The Art of James Joyce* did not permit the sort of thorough investigation of this subject found in the doctoral dissertations on specific episodes, and he is not sufficiently precise when he says that the "material of the note-sheets was used in an advanced stage of composition, either to augment an episode already in print or to expand a manuscript draft" (p. 10).[1] By far the greater part of the material was used for the latter purpose—expanding a draft—and only a very small amount for augmenting episodes in print. In 1920 the *Little Review*, having already published the preceding episodes, printed versions of "Cyclops," "Nausicaa," and "Oxen of the Sun" (through *U* 388) which Joyce later revised. No subsequent episode appeared in the *Little Review*. The periodical versions, Litz claims (p. 130), are "substantially the same" as those in the Autograph Manuscript now in the A.S.W. Rosenbach Foundation in Philadelphia. I have not checked this, but assuming he is right, then the bulk of the notesheet material for the three episodes in question entered the manuscript at some stage prior to the Rosenbach /*Little Review* drafts and thus is earlier than 1920. After this date Joyce apparently drew more heavily on notebook V.A.2 at Buffalo.

The following list, admittedly based on just one collation of the notesheets and *Little Review* episodes, illustrates that Joyce's mining of the notesheets for "Cyclops,"

---

[1] Robert M. Adams (pp. 144–145) is completely in error in doubting Litz's assessment of the nature of these notes when he says "a good many of them represent primitive acts of creation, written down at high speed, without any attempt to express ideas fully or to indicate emphasis, subordination, or relation between them." He leaves us with a picture of an intellectually constipated Joyce, who, when his mind became sufficiently crammed with information, would sit down before a blank sheet of paper and rapidly disgorge. The notesheets are in fact the documents of a meticulous and pedantic mind, not a chaotic one.

"Nausicaa," and "Oxen" was about spent before this publication of the episodes. It also demonstrates the exceptions one must account for if he is to unravel the entire color scheme. Almost always in these three episodes a deletion in blue indicates a post-*Little Review* addition or an item transferred to another episode, but some red ones fall into those categories ("Cyclops" 10:1–2, "Nausicaa" 5:68–69), and a few blue deletions appear in the *Little Review* versions ("Nausicaa" 6:10, 6:65, and 8:79).

Additions to Little Review Episodes of Ulysses

"Cyclops"

1:63	R ⟨royal Stuarts⟩	*324:19*
2:20	B ⟨Nannetti: the mimber⟩	*309:21*
2:25	B ⟨. . . Dick Turpin . . .⟩	*292:10*[2]
3:25	B ⟨tansy pills,⟩	*331:7*
4:41	B ⟨wafted (wafty)⟩	*289:3*
4:56	B ⟨impeach a nation⟩	*319:17*
4:57	B ⟨a bill of attainder⟩	*319:17*
4:68	B ⟨a mitred abbot⟩	*332:35*
5:47	B ⟨Finn McCool.⟩	*311:34*
5:49	R ⟨Art: Colleen Bawn⟩	*292:10*
5:51	B ⟨Cycl. Cusack bespatten.⟩	*325.37ff*
5:69	R ⟨L.B. lives on samples⟩	*301:1–5*
6:17	R ⟨her bloomers (M.B.)⟩	*318:34*
8:36	B ⟨Leprechaun,⟩	*335:38*
8:62	B ⟨couch spear.⟩	*292:17*
9:4	B ⟨red Jim MacDermot⟩	*291:35*
10:1	R ⟨Peter the packer⟩	*292:6*
10:2	R ⟨taxation swindle,⟩	*329:41–42*
10:2	R ⟨Irish consuls,⟩	*329:42*
10:22	B ⟨paraphernalia⟩	*328:11*
10:29	B ⟨. . . roaring mares,⟩	*289:35*
10:29–30	B ⟨sheep dip scab,⟩	*309:30*

"Nausicaa"

1:8	B ⟨golden syrup.⟩	*340:38*
1:18	R ⟨photographs⟩	*359:39*
2:4	B ⟨perfectly appointed⟩	*346:13?*
2:20	B ⟨Yester eve⟩	*361:13*

[2] Ellipses in this list represent irrelevant words deleted.

2:42	*B*⟨Pavement artist (Nausikaa)⟩ *351:14*
2:43	*R*⟨λευκόλενος⟩ *Cf. 349:20–22*
2:90	*B*⟨quick as lightning (? how)⟩ *356:16*
3:33	*B*⟨optical illusion⟩ *370:4*
4:68	*B*⟨she knew it was him⟩ *351:42*
5:93	*B*⟨scents hide in ?places⟩ *368:25–27?*
5:95–100	*R*⟨black 6⟩ *Cf. 370:1*
	R⟨blue 5⟩
	R⟨green 4⟩
	R⟨red 3⟩
	R⟨yellow 2⟩
	R⟨white 1⟩
6:74	*B*⟨Moustache & beards carry germs⟩ *348:27?*
7:44	*R*⟨smiled wanly⟩ *361:17*
7:78	*B*⟨pinny,⟩ *346:36*
8:2	*B*⟨radiant reflection mirror gave back to her⟩ *344:17–18*
8:4	*B*⟨smile that verged on tears⟩ *361:17–18*
8:19	*B*⟨Strained look in her face⟩ *345:5*
8:34	*B*⟨sparkling waves⟩ *340:13*
8:133	*B*⟨perfectly served lunch⟩ *346:24*
8:138	*B*⟨Mrs Reggy Wylie (not Mrs W —)⟩ *345:14–16*
"Oxen"	
2:99	*B*⟨gramercy⟩ *383:13*
7:115	*R*⟨pardee⟩ *384:11*
7:141	*R*⟨whereof anon⟩ *383:1?*
13:17	*B*⟨. . . as his wont was⟩ *384:6*
15:102	*B*⟨bedesman⟩ *383:7*

As Richard Madtes and James Card have found in their studies of "Ithaca" and "Penelope," the pattern becomes even more blurred in the episodes which follow "Oxen of the Sun." They were able to agree, however, that in the British Museum notesheets "notes [for "Ithaca" canceled] in blue formed the heart of the Rosenbach Manuscript; entries cancelled in red were inserted on the typescript." In "Penelope," Card continues, "entries deleted in blue . . . can be found in the first half of the Rosenbach Manuscript . . . cancellations in red formed the second half."[3] Shown below is the pattern of deletions on the "Ithaca" notesheets as charted by Madtes.[4]

[3] Pp. 29–30.
[4] P. 34.

Deletions on the "Ithaca" Notesheets

	Blue		Red		Green	
	No.	*%*	*No.*	*%*	*No.*	*%*
Basic manuscript	345	87	46	12	4	1
Additions to manuscript	27	48	28	50	1	2
First & second typescript	26	10	212	85	13	5
First galley proof	49	66	2	5	21	29
Second galley proof	13	36	22	61	1	3
Page proof	6	35	3	18	8	47

The patterns found by Card in the deletions from the "Penelope" notesheets are given below.[5] Only the color green showed no definite pattern. The "Basic manuscript" referred to by Madtes above is here more precisely called the "Rosenbach MS."

Deletions on the "Penelope" Notesheets

Notes cancelled in blue	*Number*	*Corresponding text pages*
Rosenbach MS	113	723–46
Additions to Rosenbach	24	723–48
Typescript	2	726, 745
All entries on ["Penelope" 6] on fifth galley		

Notes cancelled in red	*Number*	*Corresponding text pages*
Rosenbach MS	38	748–60
Additions to Rosenbach	8	748–60
Eighth sentence	1	761
Typescript	1	745
Fifth proof	2	727, 766
Every entry on ["Penelope" 6] on typescript except *red geranium* on fifth galley		

There are, of course, the inevitable exceptions to these patterns. Nevertheless, the three of us are of one mind that the British Museum notesheets supplied the basis for the Rosenbach Manuscript and notebook V.A.2 at Buffalo for later additions.

[5] P. 30.

Appendix D

Conversion Table for Three Editions of *Ulysses*
Compiled by Patrick A. McCarthy

ML 1934—New York: Random House (Modern Library ed.), 1934
ML 1961—New York: Random House (Modern Library ed.), 1961
BH 1960—London: The Bodley Head, 1960

ML 1934	ML 1961	BH 1960	ML 1934	ML 1961	BH 1960
5:1	3:1	1:1	65:1	65:12	78:29
7:1	5:5	3:28	67:1	67:11	81:20
9:1	7:8	6:20	69:1	69:14	84:12
11:1	9:11	9:10	71:1	72:1	87:8
13:1	11:13	12:1	73:1	74:2	89:31
15:1	13:13	14:22	75:1	76:5	92:22
17:1	15:15	17:16	77:1	78:5	95:12
19:1	17:18	20:7	79:1	80:4	98:4
21:1	19:18	22:31	81:1	82:7	100:34
23:1	21:23	25:21	83:1	84:11	103:28
25:1	24:1	28:9	85:1	86:13	106:24
27:1	26:1	30:31	87:1	88:3	109:8
29:1	28:3	33:23	89:1	90:3	111:33
31:1	30:5	36:15	91:1	92:6	114:22
33:1	32:5	39:8	93:1	94:7	117:13
35:1	34:4	41:30	95:1	96:11	120:5
37:1	36:4	44:17	97:1	98:10	122:31
39:1	38:1	46:20	99:1	100:10	125:28
41:1	40:1	49:12	101:1	102:12	128:20
43:1	42:3	52:2	103:1	104:13	131:14
45:1	44:3	54:27	105:1	106:14	134:6
47:1	46:6	57:23	107:1	108:18	136:30
49:1	48:9	60:16	109:1	110:20	139:24
51:1	50:11	63:10	111:1	112:20	142:16
55:1	55:1	65:1	113:1	114:20	145:9
57:1	57:3	67:26	115:1	116:1	147:13
59:1	59:4	70:20	117:1	118:1	149:27
61:1	61:7	73:12	119:1	120:1	152:15
63:1	63:7	76:2	121:1	122:2	155:1

ML 1934	ML 1961	BH 1960	ML 1934	ML 1961	BH 1960
123:1	124:2	157:18	219:1	222:4	284:20
125:1	126:1	160:3	221:1	224:7	287:10
127:1	128:5	162:27	223:1	226:6	289:29
129:1	130:9	165:15	225:1	228:6	292:17
131:1	132:12	168:1	227:1	230:7	295:5
133:1	134:16	170:16	229:1	232:12	297:28
135:1	136:26	172:33	231:1	234:14	300:21
137:1	138:23	175:16	233:1	236:18	303:10
139:1	140:26	178:4	235:1	238:18	305:32
141:1	142:30	180:24	237:1	240:19	308:26
143:1	144:32	183:13	239:1	242:23	311:18
145:1	146:31	186:1	241:1	244:23	314:9
147:1	148:26	188:8	243:1	246:26	317:5
149:1	151:1	190:1	245:1	248:22	319:23
151:1	153:3	192:23	247:1	250:23	322:15
153:1	155:5	195:20	249:1	252:27	325:14
155:1	157:8	198:14	251:1	254:30	328:8
157:1	159:12	201:6	253:1	257:1	330:9
159:1	161:13	203:32	255:1	259:1	332:29
161:1	163:14	206:26	257:1	261:4	335:22
163:1	165:15	209:21	259:1	263:6	338:18
165:1	167:17	212:14	261:1	265:9	341:10
167:1	169:19	215:10	263:1	267:10	343:34
169:1	171:20	217:34	265:1	269:13	346:25
171:1	173:20	220:19	267:1	271:11	349:13
173:1	175:21	223:11	269:1	273:12	352:6
175:1	177:23	226:6	271:1	275:14	354:32
177:1	179:25	228:34	273:1	277:16	357:23
179:1	181:27	231:28	275:1	279:19	360:17
181:1	183:28	234:20	277:1	281:21	363:6
183:1	185:1	236:13	279:1	283:23	365:30
185:1	187:4	239:4	281:1	285:25	368:20
187:1	189:6	241:29	283:1	287:29	371:15
189:1	191:9	244:19	285:1	289:31	374:6
191:1	193:11	247:13	287:1	292:1	376:10
193:1	195:15	250:6	289:1	294:2	379:5
195:1	197:16	252:31	291:1	296:3	381:33
197:1	199:18	255:19	293:1	298:5	384:24
199:1	201:19	258:7	295:1	300:7	387:17
201:1	203:18	260:30	297:1	302:9	390:10
203:1	205:19	263:25	299:1	304:9	393:1
205:1	207:22	266:14	301:1	306:11	395:32
207:1	209:20	268:29	303:1	308:15	398:27
209:1	211:25	271:14	305:1	310:15	401:21
211:1	213:28	274:8	307:1	312:16	404:15
213:1	215:30	276:30	309:1	314:18	407:9
215:1	217:32	279:21	311:1	316:21	410:1
217:1	220:2	281:26	313:1	318:23	412:28

ML 1934	ML 1961	BH 1960		ML 1934	ML 1961	BH 1960
315:1	320:23	415:18		411:1	418:6	547:13
317:1	322:28	418:12		413:1	420:8	550:6
319:1	324:29	421:1		415:1	422:10	552:32
321:1	326:31	423:27		417:1	424:13	555:27
323:1	328:34	426:20		419:1	426:15	558:21
325:1	330:37	429:13		421:1	428:17	561:14
327:1	332:38	432:7		423:1	430:1	562:22
329:1	335:1	434:32		425:1	432:1	564:15
331:1	337:3	437:23		427:1	434:6	566:7
333:1	339:7	440:16		429:1	436:5	567:27
335:1	341:8	443:8		431:1	438:4	569:18
337:1	343:8	445:28		433:1	440:7	571:4
339:1	345:9	448:21		435:1	442:11	572:20
341:1	347:2	450:29		437:1	444:13	574:8
343:1	349:6	453:21		439:1	446:19	575:30
345:1	351:8	456:15		441:1	448:20	577:9
347:1	353:9	459:7		443:1	450:23	578:29
349:1	355:8	461:30		445:1	452:31	580:18
351:1	357:9	464:21		447:1	455:1	582:10
353:1	359:12	467:15		449:1	457:7	583:31
355:1	361:14	470:5		451:1	459:10	585:25
357:1	363:15	472:31		453:1	461:8	587:7
359:1	365:15	475:20		455:1	463:14	589:7
361:1	367:17	478:12		457:1	465:13	591:8
363:1	369:18	481:6		459:1	467:18	593:14
365:1	371:20	483:33		461:1	469:16	594:32
367:1	373:20	486:25		463:1	471:20	596:22
369:1	375:23	489:19		465:1	473:22	597:33
371:1	377:24	492:12		467:1	475:26	599:20
373:1	379:27	495:5		469:1	478:3	600:33
375:1	381:29	497:32		471:1	480:10	602:30
377:1	383:1	499:24		473:1	482:10	604:26
379:1	385:5	502:23		475:1	484:15	606:17
381:1	387:9	505:15		477:1	486:19	608:14
383:1	389:10	508:7		479:1	488:18	610:3
385:1	391:14	510:34		481:1	490:22	611:15
387:1	393:16	513:27		483:1	492:30	613:2
389:1	395:19	516:20		485:1	495:1	615:5
391:1	397:22	519:13		487:1	497:4	616:28
393:1	399:22	522:5		489:1	499:10	618:22
395:1	401:24	524:32		491:1	501:14	620:6
397:1	403:26	527:23		493:1	503:18	621:33
399:1	405:28	530:16		495:1	505:17	623:14
401:1	407:33	533:11		497:1	507:25	625:2
403:1	409:36	536:4		499:1	509:23	626:32
405:1	411:38	538:31		501:1	511:31	628:27
407:1	413:42	541:25		503:1	514:3	630:21
409:1	416:3	544:19		505:1	516:5	632:23

ML 1934	ML 1961	BH 1960	ML 1934	ML 1961	BH 1960
507:1	518:6	634:28	605:1	620:42	714:31
509:1	520:9	636:15	607:1	622:40	717:19
511:1	522:9	637:29	609:1	624:37	720:3
513:1	524:18	639:14	611:1	626:35	722:27
515:1	526:20	641:11	613:1	628:35	725:20
517:1	528:25	642:31	615:1	630:34	728:10
519:1	530:24	644:10	617:1	632:32	731:1
521:1	532:27	645:25	619:1	634:36	733:25
523:1	534:30	647:8	621:1	636:37	736:16
525:1	536:33	648:34	623:1	638:36	739:10
527:1	539:4	650:27	625:1	640:35	742:1
529:1	541:7	652:22	627:1	642:36	744:28
531:1	543:12	654:13	629:1	644:35	747:22
533:1	545:13	655:34	631:1	646:36	750:13
535:1	547:17	657:18	633:1	648:36	753:4
537:1	549:25	659:12	635:1	650:37	755:32
539:1	552:3	660:33	637:1	652:38	758:26
541:1	554:8	662:30	639:1	654:37	761:17
543:1	556:14	664:10	641:1	656:37	764:9
545:1	558:19	665:25	643:1	658:38	767:1
547:1	560:20	667:3	645:1	660:37	769:26
549:1	562:21	668:13	647:1	662:37	772:18
551:1	565:1	669:23	649:1	664:40	775:6
553:1	567:6	671:3	651:1	667:1	777:22
555:1	569:13	672:22	653:1	668:37	780:7
557:1	571:16	674:8	655:1	671:1	782:27
559:1	573:28	676:1	657:1	673:1	785:20
561:1	575:34	677:25	659:1	674:38	788:6
563:1	577:27	679:13	661:1	677:1	790:27
565:1	580:4	681:8	663:1	678:40	793:17
567:1	582:4	682:22	665:1	680:37	796:6
569:1	584:6	683:31	667:1	682:36	798:26
571:1	586:9	685:13	669:1	684:33	801:14
573:1	588:5	687:9	671:1	686:34	804:3
575:1	590:6	688:24	673:1	688:30	806:24
577:1	592:10	690:12	675:1	690:19	809:5
579:1	594:14	692:3	677:1	692:21	811:11
581:1	596:15	693:18	679:1	694:21	814:1
583:1	598:22	695:1	681:1	696:21	816:19
585:1	600:21	696:27	683:1	698:15	819:2
587:1	602:23	698:2	685:1	700:16	821:24
589:1	604:27	699:11	687:1	702:17	824:15
591:1	607:3	700:25	689:1	704:15	827:4
593:1	609:6	702:15	691:1	706:16	829:24
597:1	613:1	704:1	693:1	708:13	832:8
599:1	614:43	706:29	695:1	710:12	834:26
601:1	616:43	709:18	697:1	712:10	837:17
603:1	618:43	712:9	699:1	714:10	840:10

ML 1934	ML 1961	BH 1960		ML 1934	ML 1961	BH 1960
701:1	716:13	843:1		735:1	750:3	887:29
703:1	718:12	845:25		737:1	752:3	890:19
705:1	720:10	848:13		739:1	754:3	893:10
707:1	722:12	851:6		741:1	756:3	896:1
709:1	724:11	853:22		743:1	758:2	898:26
711:1	726:10	856:8		745:1	760:1	901:16
713:1	728:11	858:28		747:1	762:1	904:7
715:1	730:10	861:15		749:1	763:42	906:30
717:1	732:9	864:4		751:1	765:41	909:20
719:1	734:11	866:26		753:1	767:41	912:11
721:1	736:12	869:15		755:1	769:40	914:34
723:1	738:1	871:14		757:1	771:41	917:25
725:1	740:1	874:8		759:1	773:40	920:15
727:1	742:1	876:33		761:1	775:39	923:6
729:1	744:2	879:23		763:1	777:38	925:31
731:1	746:2	882:13		765:1	779:38	928:21
733:1	748:2	885:4		767:1	781:39	931:11

Bibliography
Works Cited and Consulted

Adams, Robert M. *James Joyce: Common Sense and Beyond*. New York: Random House, 1966.

——. *Surface and Symbol: The Consistency of James Joyce's* Ulysses. New York: Oxford University Press, 1962; rev. paperback ed., New York: Oxford University Press, 1967.

Andrews, Allen. *Proud Fortress*. 1958; rpt. New York: E. P. Dutton & Co., 1959.

Atherton, J. S. *The Books at the Wake: A Study of Literary Allusions in James Joyce's* Finnegans Wake. London: Faber & Faber, 1959.

——. "The Peacock in the Oxen." *A Wake Newslitter*, VII (Oct. 1970), 77–78.

Augustine, Saint. *De Civitate Dei Contra Paganos*. Ed. J. E. C. Welldon. 2 vols. London: Society for Promoting Christian Knowledge, 1924.

Autenrieth, Georg. *A Homeric Dictionary*. 1876; rev. ed., Norman, Okla.: University of Oklahoma Press, 1958.

Barnard, Francis P. *Strongbow's Conquest of Ireland*. 1888; 2d ed., London: David Nutt; New York: G. P. Putnam's Sons, 1910.

Baugh, Albert C., *et al. A Literary History of England*. New York: Appleton-Century-Crofts, 1948.

Beach, Silvia. *Shakespeare and Company*. New York: Harcourt, Brace & World, 1956.

Benco, Silvio. "James Joyce in Trieste." *The Bookman*, LXXII (Dec. 1930), 375–380.

Bérard, Victor. *Les Phéniciens et l'Odyssée*. 2 vols. Paris: Librairie Armand Colin, 1902.

Blamires, Harry. *The Bloomsday Book: A Guide through Joyce's* Ulysses. London: Methuen & Co., 1966.

Boldereff, Frances. *Reading* Finnegans Wake. Woodward, Pa.: Classic Nonfiction Library, 1959.

Budge, E. A. W. *The Gods of the Egyptians.* 1903; rpt., 2 vols., London: Methuen & Co., 1904.

Budgen, Frank. *James Joyce and the Making of* Ulysses. 1934; rpt., with new appendix, Bloomington, Ind.: Indiana University Press, 1960.

——. *Myselves When Young.* London: Oxford University Press, 1970.

Bulfinch, Thomas. *Bulfinch's Mythology.* New York: Random House, n.d.

Bury, J. B. *A History of Greece to the Death of Alexander the Great.* 1900; 2d ed., New York: Random House, 1913.

Butler, Samuel. *The Authoress of the* Odyssey. 1897; rpt. Chicago: University of Chicago Press, 1967.

Campbell, Joseph, and Henry Morton Robinson. *A Skeleton Key to* Finnegans Wake. 1944; rpt. New York: Viking Press, 1961.

Card, James V. D. "A Gibraltar Sourcebook for 'Penelope.'" *James Joyce Quarterly,* VIII (Winter 1971), 163–175.

——. "A Textual and Critical Study of the 'Penelope' Episode of James Joyce's *Ulysses.*" Ph.D. dissertation, Columbia University, 1964.

Chambers's Biographical Dictionary. 1897; new ed., New York: St. Martin's Press, 1962.

Cicero, Marcus Tullius. "On the Nature of the Gods," in *The Treatises of M. T. Cicero.* Trans. C. D. Yonge. London: G. Bell, 1892.

Cirlot, J. E. *A Dictionary of Symbols.* 1958; Eng. tr., New York: Philosophical Library, 1962.

Colum, Mary, and Padraic Colum. *Our Friend James Joyce.* Garden City, N.Y.: Doubleday & Co., 1958.

Colum, Padraic. *The Adventures of Odysseus and the Tale of Troy.* New York: Macmillan Co., 1918.

Connolly, Thomas E. *The Personal Library of James Joyce: A Descriptive Bibliography.* University of Buffalo Studies, XXII, no. 1. Buffalo: University of Buffalo Press, 1955.

——, ed. *James Joyce's Scribbledehobble: The Ur-Workbook for* Finnegans Wake. Evanston, Ill.: Northwestern University Press, 1961.

Curran, Constantine. *James Joyce Remembered*. New York and London: Oxford University Press, 1968.

Curtis, Edmund. *A History of Ireland*. 1936; 6th ed., 1950; rpt. London: Methuen & Co., 1961.

Davidson, Arthur F. *Alexandre Dumas, His Life and Works*. Westminster (London): Archibald Constable & Co., 1902.

Deming, Robert H. *A Bibliography of James Joyce Studies*. University of Kansas Publications, Library Series, no. 18. Lawrence, Kans., 1964.

De Quincey, Thomas. *Collected Writings*. Ed. David Masson. 14 vols. Edinburgh: Adam and Charles Black, 1889–90.

Desbarrolles, Adolphe. *Les Mystères de la main*. Paris: Garnier Frères, 1880.

Dictionary of Greek and Roman Biography and Mythology. Ed. William Smith. 3 vols. London: Walton & Murray, 1849.

Dillon, Myles, and Donncha ó Cróinin. *Teach Yourself Irish*. 1961; rev. ed., London: English Universities Press, 1966.

Doyle, Sir Arthur Conan. *The Great Boer War*. London: Smith, Elder & Co., 1900.

Drinkwater, John. *A History of the Siege of Gibraltar, 1779–1783*. 1785; later ed., London: John Murray, 1844.

Driver, Samuel Rolles. *An Introduction to the Literature of the Old Testament*. London: International Theological Library, 1891.

Ellmann, Richard. *Eminent Domain*. New York: Oxford University Press, 1967.

——. *James Joyce*. New York: Oxford University Press, 1959.

——. *Yeats: The Man and the Masks*. New York: E. P. Dutton & Co., 1948.

Field, Henry M. *Gibraltar*. New York: Charles Scribner's Sons, 1888.

Frazer, Sir James George. *The Golden Bough*. 1896; greatly expanded, 1912; abridged ed., New York: Macmillan Co., 1963.

Frith, Henry. *The Language of the Hand*. New York: G. Routledge and Sons, 1899?

Gellius, Aulus. *Attic Nights*. Trans. John C. Rolfe. 3 vols. 1927; rpt. London: W. Heinemann; Cambridge, Mass.: Harvard University Press, 1946.

Gheerbrant, Bernard. *James Joyce: Sa vie, son œuvre, son rayonnement*. Paris: La Hune, 1949.

Gibraltar and Its Sieges. London: T. Nelson & Sons, 1879.

The Gibraltar Directory and Guidebook. Gibraltar: Garrison Library Printing Establishment, 1873—.

Gilbert, Stuart. *James Joyce's* Ulysses. 1930; 2d ed. rev., 1952; rpt. New York: Random House, Vintage Books, 1960.

Glasheen, Adaline. *A Second Census of* Finnegans Wake. Evanston, Ill.: Northwestern University Press, 1963.

Goldberg, S. L. *The Classical Temper: A Study of James Joyce's* Ulysses. 1961; rpt. London: Chatto & Windus, 1963.

Gorman, Herbert. *James Joyce.* 1940; rev. ed., New York: Rinehart & Co., 1948.

Graham, Philip G. "Note." *A Wake Newslitter,* III (Oct. 1966), 117.

Graves, Robert. *The Greek Myths.* 2 vols. Baltimore: Penguin Books, 1955.

Greene, David H., and Edward M. Stephens. *J. M. Synge: 1871–1909.* 1959; rpt. New York: Macmillan Co., Collier Books, 1961.

[Hamon, Louis] *Cheiro's Language of the Hand.* 1894; 7th ed., New York: F. T. Neely, 1897.

Hamsun, Knut. *Mysterier.* Copenhagen: P. G. Philipsen, 1892. *Mysterien* (German trans. by M. von Borch), Cologne and Paris: A. Langen, 1894.

Hanford, James Holly, ed. *A Milton Handbook.* 1926; 4th ed., rpt. New York: Appleton-Century-Crofts, 1961.

Hanley, Miles L. *Word Index to James Joyce's* Ulysses. 1937; rpt. Madison, Wis.: University of Wisconsin Press, 1951.

Hart, Clive. *A Concordance to* Finnegans Wake. Minneapolis: University of Minnesota Press, 1963.

——. *James Joyce's* Ulysses. Sydney: Sydney University Press, 1968.

——. *Structure and Motif in* Finnegans Wake. Evanston, Ill.: Northwestern University Press, 1962.

Hayman, David, ed. *A First-Draft Version of* Finnegans Wake. Austin, Tex.: University of Texas Press, 1963.

Herodotus. *Herodotus.* Trans. A. D. Godley. 4 vols. London: W. Heinemann; New York: G. P. Putnam's Sons, 1921.

Herring, Phillip F. "The Bedsteadfastness of Molly Bloom." *Modern Fiction Studies,* XV (Spring 1969), 49–61.

——. "Joyce's Politics." In Fritz Senn, ed., *Spotlight on Joyce: The Dublin Symposium*. Bloomington, Ind.: Indiana University Press, 1972.

——. "More Peacock in the Oxen." *A Wake Newslitter*, VIII (August 1971), 51–53.

——, ed. "*Ulysses* Notebook VIII.A.5 at Buffalo." *Studies in Bibliography*, XXII (1969), 287–310.

—— and Norman Silverstein. "Some Corrections and Additions to Norman Silverstein's 'Magic on the Notesheets of the *Circe* Episode.' " *James Joyce Quarterly*, II (Spring 1965), 217–226.

Hodgart, Matthew, and Mabel Worthington. *Song in the Works of James Joyce*. New York: Columbia University Press, 1959.

Hoffmann, Bernhard. *Kunst und Vogelgesang*. Leipzig: Quelle & Meyer, 1908.

Homer. *The Odyssey*. Trans. S. H. Butcher and Andrew Lang. London: Macmillan & Company, 1879 and subsequent printings.

Hopper, Vincent F., and Bernard D. N. Grebanier. *Essentials of European Literature*. 2 vols. Great Neck, N.Y.: Barron's Educational Series, 1952.

Horace. *Works*. Trans. E. C. Wickham. 2 vols. Oxford: Clarendon Press, 1891.

Hurley, Robert E. "The 'Proteus' Episode of James Joyce's *Ulysses*." Ph.D. dissertation, Columbia University, 1963.

Ireland Guide. Dublin: Bord Fáilte Éireann, n.d.

Janusko, Robert. "The Sources and Structure of the 'Oxen of the Sun' Episode . . ." Ph.D. dissertation, Kent State University, 1967.

Jarrell, Mackie. "Joyce's Use of Swift's *Polite Conversation* in the 'Circe' Episode of Ulysses." *PMLA*, LXXII (June 1957), 545–554.

Joyce, James. *The Critical Writings of James Joyce*. Ed. Ellsworth Mason and Richard Ellmann. New York: Viking Press, 1959.

——. *Dubliners*. 1914; corrected ed., New York: Viking Press, 1967.

——. *Exiles*. 1918; rpt. New York: Viking Press, 1961.

——. *Finnegans Wake*. New York: Viking Press, 1939.

——. *Giacomo Joyce*. Ed. Richard Ellmann. New York: Viking Press, 1968.

——. *The Letters of James Joyce*. Ed. Stuart Gilbert (vol. I) and Richard Ellmann (vols. II and III). New York: Viking Press, 1957–66.

——. *The Portable James Joyce*. Ed. Harry Levin. New York: New Directions, 1947.

——. *A Portrait of the Artist as a Young Man.* 1916; corrected ed., New York: Viking Press, 1964; Viking Critical Edition, ed. Chester G. Anderson, New York, 1968.

——. *Stephen Hero.* 1944; rev. ed., New York: New Directions, 1963.

——. *Ulysses.* 1922; corrected eds., New York: Random House, Modern Library, 1934 and 1961.

——. *Ulysses.* London: Bodley Head, 1960.

——. *Ulysses.* Harmondsworth, Eng.: Penguin Books, 1968.

Joyce, P. W. *The Origin and History of Irish Names of Places.* 1869; rev. ed., Dublin and Cork: Educational Co. of Ireland, 1913.

——. *A Short History of Gaelic Ireland.* 1893; rpt. Dublin and Cork: Educational Co. of Ireland, 1924.

Joyce, Stanislaus. *My Brother's Keeper.* New York: Viking Press, 1958.

Kain, Richard. *Fabulous Voyager: A Study of James Joyce's* Ulysses. 1947; rev. ed., New York: Viking Press, 1959.

Keating, Geoffrey. *The History of Ireland.* Trans. D. Comyn. Dublin: Irish Texts Society, 1913.

Kelly's Directory of Merchants, Manufacturers and Shippers of the World. London: Kelly's Directories, 1877—.

Kenner, Hugh. *Dublin's Joyce.* 1956; rpt. Boston: Beacon Press, 1962.

Kittredge, G. L. "Ballads and Songs." *Journal of American Folklore,* XXX (1917), 283–369.

Klein, A. M. "The Oxen of the Sun." *Here and Now,* I (Jan. 1949), 28–48.

Köhler, Erich. "Nausicaa, Danae und Gerty MacDowell: Zur Literaturgeschichte des Feuerwerks." In *Lebende Antike: Symposion für Rudolf Sühnel,* ed. Horst Meller and Hans-Joachim Zimmermann, pp. 451–472. Berlin: E. Schmidt, 1967.

Larbaud, Valerie. "The *Ulysses* of James Joyce." *Criterion,* I (Oct. 1922), 94–103.

Levin, Harry. *James Joyce: A Critical Introduction.* 1941; rev. ed., New York: New Directions, 1960.

Litz, A. Walton. *The Art of James Joyce: Method and Design in* Ulysses *and* Finnegans Wake. London: Oxford University Press, 1961.

——. "Evolution of James Joyce's Style and Technique from 1918–1932." Ph.D. dissertation, Oxford University, 1954.

——. "Joyce's Notes for the Last Episodes of *Ulysses*." *Modern Fiction Studies*, IV (Spring 1958), 3–20.

MacManus, Seumas. *The Story of the Irish Race*. 1921; rev. ed., New York: Devin-Adair, 1944.

McMillan, Dougald. "The Influence of Gerhardt [*sic*] Hauptmann in Joyce's *Ulysses*." *James Joyce Quarterly*, IV (Winter 1967), 107–119.

Madtes, Richard E. "Joyce and the Building of 'Ithaca.' " *ELH*, XXXI (Dec. 1964), 443–459.

——. "A Textual and Critical Study of the 'Ithaca' Episode of James Joyce's *Ulysses*." Ph.D. dissertation, Columbia University, 1961.

Magalaner, Marvin, and Richard M. Kain. *Joyce: The Man, the Work, the Reputation*. 1956; rpt. New York: Macmillan Co., Collier Books, 1962.

Marcus, Philip L. "Three Irish Allusions in *Ulysses*." *James Joyce Quarterly*, VI (Summer 1969), 299–301.

Mason, Ellsworth. "The 'Oxen of the Sun.' " *The Analyst*, no. 10 (March 1956), pp. 10–18.

Muirhead, L. Russell, ed. *Ireland*. The Blue Guides. 1932; rev. ed., London: Ernest Benn, 1952.

O'Brien, Darcy. *The Conscience of James Joyce*. Princeton, N.J.: Princeton University Press, 1968.

O'Connor, Sir James. *History of Ireland, 1798–1924*. 2 vols. London: E. Arnold & Co., 1925. New York: George H. Doran Co., 1926.

O'Connor, Ulick. *The Times I've Seen: Oliver St. John Gogarty, A Biography*. London: Jonathan Cape, 1964.

O Hehir, Brendan. *A Gaelic Lexicon for* Finnegans Wake *and Glossary for Joyce's Other Works*. Berkeley: University of California Press, 1967.

Orme, A. R. *Ireland*. Chicago: Aldine, 1970.

O'Shea, Henry G. *Guide to Spain and Portugal*. 1865; rev. ed., Edinburgh and London: Adam and Charles Black, 1869.

Otway, Thomas. *Works*. Ed. J. C. Ghosh. Oxford: Clarendon Press, 1932.

Ovid. *Metamorphoses*. Trans. Rolfe Humphries. Bloomington, Ind.: Indiana University Press, 1955.

Partridge, Eric. *A Dictionary of Slang and Unconventional English*. 1937; rev. and enlarged ed., New York: Macmillan Co., 1961.

Patten, Bradley M. *Human Embryology*. Philadelphia: Blakiston, 1946.

Pausanias. *Description of Greece*. Trans. W. H. S. Jones. 6 vols. London: W. Heinemann; New York: G. P. Putnam's Sons, 1918.

Pavitt, William Thomas, and Kate Pavitt. *The Book of Talismans, Amulets and Zodiacal Gems*. London: W. Rider & Son, 1914.

Peacock, William. *English Prose from Mandeville to Ruskin*. World's Classics series. London: Oxford University Press, 1903.

Pinguentini, Gianni. *James Joyce in Italia*. Florence: Libreria Commissionaria Sansoni, 1963.

Prescott, Joseph. *Exploring James Joyce*. Carbondale, Ill.: Southern Illinois University Press, 1964.

———. "James Joyce's *Ulysses* as a Work in Progress." Ph.D. dissertation, Harvard University, 1944.

Robinson, Herbert S., and Knox Wilson. *Myths and Legends of All Nations*. 1950; rpt. New York: Grosset & Dunlap, Bantam Books, 1961.

Roscher, Wilhelm Heinrich. *Ausführliches Lexikon der griechischen und römischen Mythologie*. 6 vols. and 2 supp. vols. Leipzig: B. G. Teubner, 1884–1937.

Ruff's Guide to the Turf. London: Office of Ruff's Guide, 1923.

Saintsbury, George. *A History of English Prose Rhythm*. London: Macmillan & Co., 1912.

Schneider, Ulrich. "Freemasonic Signs and Passwords in the *Circe* Episode." *James Joyce Quarterly*, V (Summer 1968), 303–311.

Scholes, Robert E., ed. *The Cornell Joyce Collection: A Catalogue*. Ithaca, N.Y.: Cornell University Press, 1961.

——— and Richard M. Kain. *The Workshop of Daedalus: James Joyce and the Raw Materials for* A Portrait of the Artist as a Young Man. Evanston, Ill.: Northwestern University Press, 1965.

Semmler, Clement. *For the Uncanny Man: Essays, Mainly Literary*. Melbourne: F. W. Cheshire; London: Angus & Robertson, 1963.

Seyffert, Oskar. *Dictionary of Classical Antiquities*. 1882; rev. ed., New York: World Publishing Co., Meridian Books, 1956.

Silverstein, Norman. "Joyce's 'Circe' Episode: Approaches to *Ulysses* through a Textual and Interpretative Study of Joyce's Fifteenth Chapter." Ph.D. dissertation, Columbia University, 1960.

——. "Magic on the Notesheets of the *Circe* Episode." *James Joyce Quarterly*, I (Summer 1964), 19–26.

Slocum, John J., and Herbert Cahoon. *A Bibliography of James Joyce*. London: Rupert Hart-Davis, 1953.

Spielberg, Peter. *James Joyce's Manuscripts and Letters at the University of Buffalo: A Catalogue*. Buffalo: University of Buffalo Press, 1962.

Stanford, W. B. *The Ulysses Theme*. 1954; rev. ed., Oxford: Basil Blackwell, 1963.

Staples, Hugh. " 'Ribbonmen' Signs and Passwords in *Ulysses*." *Notes and Queries*, XIII (March 1966), 95–96.

Stephens, Frederic G. *A History of Gibraltar and Its Sieges*. (With photographic illustrations by J. H. Mann.) 1870; 2d ed., London: Provost & Co., 1873.

Sterne, Laurence. *The Life and Opinions of Tristram Shandy*. 1760; rpt., New York: New American Library of World Literature, Signet Editions, 1960.

Sullivan, Alexander M. *New Ireland: Political Sketches*. Glasgow: Cameron & Ferguson, 1877.

Sultan, Stanley. *The Argument of Ulysses*. Columbus, Ohio: Ohio State University Press, 1964.

Swift, Jonathan. *Gulliver's Travels*. Ed. Louis A. Landa. Boston: Houghton Mifflin Co., Riverside Editions, 1960.

——. *Prose Works*. Ed. Temple Scott. 12 vols. London: H. G. Bohn, 1903.

Thom's Official Directory of the United Kingdom of Great Britain and Ireland for the Year 1904 . . . Dublin: Alex Thom & Co., 1904.

Thornton, Weldon. *Allusions in* Ulysses: *An Annotated List*. Chapel Hill, N.C.: University of North Carolina Press, 1968.

Todhunter, Isaac. *Algebra for the Use of Colleges and Schools*. London: Macmillan & Co., 1873.

Vico, Giambattista. *The New Science*. Trans. T. G. Bergin and M. H. Fisch. Ithaca, N.Y.: Cornell University Press, 1948.

Witt, Carl. *Myths of Hellas; or, Greek Tales*. London: Longmans, Green & Co., 1883.

DATE DUE

261-2500

Printed in USA